THE RURAL REVOLT THAT FAILED

Farm Workers' Trade Unions in Wales, 1889–1950

John Owen Jones ('ap Ffarmwr').

(Source: Eryl Wyn Rowlands Collection, Gwynedd Archives Service, Anglesey Area Record Office.)

THE RURAL REVOLT THAT FAILED

Farm Workers' Trade Unions in Wales 1889–1950

DAVID A. PRETTY

CARDIFF
UNIVERSITY OF WALES PRESS
1989

British Library Cataloguing in Publication Data
Pretty, David A., 1942
The rural revolt that failed: farm workers' trade unions in Wales, 1889–1950
1. Great Britain. Agricultural industries. Trade unions
I. Title
331.88′13′0941

ISBN 0-7083-1024-9

Typeset by Megaron
Printed in Great Britain by The Alden Press, Oxford

I

Lynwen,

Eurliw a Cerian

'O werin Cymru y codais i, ac ni bu ynof awydd erioed i berthyn i ddosbarth arall. Ohoni hi y cefais i bopeth a gyfoethogodd fy mywyd, ac iddi hi y rhoddais fy amser a hynny o dalent a oedd gennyf . . .'

T.E. Nicholas.

CONTENTS

ILLUSTRATIONS

PREFACE

This book has its origins in the incident at Aberffraw in 1890 when dinary rural labourers stood in the local school board election to fend their rights. From then on my interest just grew. The course of e farm workers' movement was extended from my native county of nglesey to cover the whole of Wales, and not merely in the 1890s but iring the period of the Great War and beyond. If a week is a long ne in politics, a decade of historical research could often seem an ernity. Moreover, it became increasingly tinged with regret that any of those who had close personal connections with the subject, id who helped me on the way, were unable to see the final result. My ppe is that I did not fail them.

Over the years many debts have accumulated, the majority dating ick to the main period of research in the years 1977–81. Apart from e names cited in the end-notes and list of interviews, I must single it J.T. Hughes, Elizabeth V. James, Tom Jones, Owen Parry, Owen oberts, W.G. Roberts, John Saer, Iestyn Thomas, John P. Thomas id W. Llewelyn Williams for special thanks. When I began writing, avid Smith, now Professor in the School of History and Archae-logy, University of Wales College of Cardiff, very kindly agreed to ad each individual chapter as it appeared. I am deeply grateful for is comments and suggestions, but more especially for paving the way their publication as a book. For any faults that remain I alone am sponsible.

In a brief preface one cannot adequately acknowledge the valuable ssistance given by the staff of the various libraries that I visited. Vithout their help the process of research would have been a far less leasurable pursuit and I take this opportunity to thank them all most ncerely. A word of appreciation is also due to Ceinwen Jones of the Jniversity of Wales Press for adding the final touches when editing ne manuscript. Above all there is the personal debt to my wife and aughters for their acceptance of the idea that I should sometimes egard a library as my second home.

onteg, Mid Glamorgan. David A. Pretty.

ABBREVIATIONS

ASRS	Amalgamated Society of Railway Servants
ILP	Independent Labour Party
NALRWU	National Agricultural Labourers' and Rural Workers' Union
Subsequently	
NUAW	National Union of Agricultural Workers
Subsequently	
NUAAW	National Union of Agricultural and Allied Workers
NALU	National Amalgamated Labourers' Union
NFDWU	National Farm and Dairy Workers' Union
NFU	National Farmers' Union
NUGW	National Union of General Workers
NUGMW	National Union of General and Municipal Workers
NUR	National Union of Railwaymen
NUT	National Union of Teachers
NWMA	North Wales Miners' Association
NWQU	North Wales Quarrymen's Union
SWMF	South Wales Miners' Federation
TGWU	Transport and General Workers' Union
TUC	Trades Union Congress
WEA	Workers' Educational Association
WLA	Women's Land Army

INTRODUCTION

In the historiography of rural Wales the Rebecca Riots, the Tithe War and the Land Question have been elevated to a place of honour. The struggle against injustices in the countryside during the nineteenth century has become an integral part of the Nonconformist radical tradition; popular figures like William Rees ('Gwilym Hiraethog'), Samuel Roberts ('S.R.'), Thomas Gee and T.E. Ellis who provided the leadership have almost achieved beatification. But although acting ostensibly in the name of the *gwerin*, the common people of Wales, in truth they only represented the interests of one section of the rural community: those of the middle-class farmers. Moreover, this obsession with Nonconformist radicalism, however compelling, has tended to obscure even greater injustices suffered by those immediately below them. As the direct descendants of the feudal peasantry the agricultural labourers belonged to a quite separate caste, one that often took on the character of a social underclass. Individually, they were for the most part poor, backward, inarticulate and raw. Indeed, with his reputation for docility and deference the agricultural labourer could be virtually ignored by employer and historian alike: in K.O. Morgan's phrase he became 'the forgotten man of Welsh agrarian debate.'[1] It was the celebrated grievances and battles of the tenant farmer that usually captured attention. The ordinary farm hand seemed hardly deserving of notice; he knew his place at the base of the rural hierarchy. From the inception of feudalism until the close of the nineteenth century the voice of the downtrodden rural labourer was seldom heard. Yet, throughout history, there has never been a more potent symbol of working-class subjugation.

Exploitation by industrial capitalists is a familiar theme in Welsh labour history, and the struggle of the politically conscious proletariat in the mining valleys is well documented. But what the infamous coal and slate barons practised on a grand scale in the Rhondda or Penrhyn quarries was repeated in microcosm on the land. Existence on the darker side of the rural world often verged on slavery and those agricultural labourers who migrated to the south Wales coalfield in their thousands were merely exchanging the tyranny of the farmer for the tyranny of the coal-owner.

The tyranny of the countryside was real enough. To secure employment in agriculture a labourer had initially to face the indignity of the hiring fair, where he would stand alongside fellow workers in the street to sell his labour. Having agreed on a contract he remained virtually tied to his employer for six months or a year; during that time he was expected to work all hours for a pitifully meagre wage. At the end of a hard day he either retired to an insanitary stable loft or rejoined his family in a disease-ridden hovel. Rural poverty might be less conspicuous than the concentrated urban variety but it was just as brutal. With its time-honoured traditions, customs and values, life in the Welsh countryside for the labouring poor went on unchanged and unchallenged.

Any outbreak of rural discontent was invariably led by the small farmers and usually directed against the landlords. Among the Welsh tenant class there developed a strong identity of interests based on economic, religious and political issues. Consequently, other tensions within the agrarian community were largely overshadowed in a welter of platform and press rhetoric. In the same way, radical Nonconformist propaganda conveniently fostered the idea of a relatively unified structure beneath the ranks of the anglicized and Anglican landowners. More often than not, tenants and labourers found unity in the face of adversity, or shared a common sectarian allegiance, but this was not always so. However thin the social or economic barrier between the farmer and his men, that barrier nevertheless existed, and it cannot be easily discounted. In addition to this fundamental economic distinction, the exploitation of the rural work-force by the farmer-employer marked one class off from the other. Conflict was often endemic in the nature of farm work.[2] At times, situations were to arise when this division of interest could not be ignored. The small farmer certainly did not have the monopoly on suffering and injustice; class conflicts within rural society took on different forms. And once the farm workers began overtly to propagate *their* own cause, in the pursuit of shorter hours or higher wages, the dividing line between both classes became much sharper, a trend which the farmers instinctively viewed with alarm.

Just as tenant unrest led to a revolt against landlordism in Wales, the seeds of another rural revolt were being sown: the revolt of the farm workers. After generations of sullen quiescence agricultural labourers became more independent-minded and self-assertive by the end of the nineteenth century. As the high point of this independence came the events of 1917–20. Men revolted against the system in an effort to secure a fair wage, a reduction in working hours, better housing and improved living standards. Even joining a trade union became an act of protest and defiance. Ironically, at the precise moment the farmers witnessed the final throes of the old order as represented by the landowning class, they themselves became the target of the last rural revolt. It is equally ironic that this is an unwritten story.

The primary aim of this study, therefore, will be to reclaim a lost historical heritage for the agricultural workers by tracing the vicissitudes of rural trade unionism up to 1950. Unfortunately, a great deal is submerged in the often inaccessible world of the customarily silent rural work-force. Nevertheless, certain strands can be closely followed, in particular the leadership provided by both prominent and long-forgotten local figures who braved every kind of hostility to espouse what inevitably turned out to be a dispiritingly futile and ill-rewarding cause. From Joseph Arch, the father of agricultural trade unionism in England, to Cesar Chavez, who fought to establish the United Farm Workers' Union in California in the 1960s,[3] the crucial importance of personalities in the farm workers' struggle is recognized. In the absence of a much-needed dictionary of Welsh labour biography it is hoped that this account will also be seen as an anthem to the neglected pioneers of the rural labour movement. To call them rebels in an unjust society might seem an exaggeration, but they were most certainly representative of the *gwerin* in the true meaning of the term. Interwoven with this main theme is the general development of trade union organization in rural Wales, the rise of the Labour Party in the agricultural constituencies, the response of the religious bodies to the cry of the labouring poor, and the progress of social improvement for the disadvantaged inhabitants of the countryside.

The counties of Wales (to 1973).

From *Rebirth of a Nation: Wales, 1880–1980* by Kenneth O. Morgan (Oxford University Press, 1981).

CHAPTER I

A CLASS APART

RURAL unrest was an inherent feature of Welsh agricultural society throughout most of the nineteenth century. Hostility and discontent arose from a variety of social, economic and political injustices, and flared up at intervals with varying degrees of intensity in different parts of the country. More often than not, it was the desperate response of a particular social group to grievances it could tolerate no longer. Each protest contained an element of spontaneity, each developed its own special character, a level of violence and consequent measure of seriousness. All the disturbances, however, reflected the underlying tensions of a rural society where various forms of exploitation and oppression intermingled to exacerbate social conditions of often appalling misery and deprivation. Possessing few rights, and with limited means of expression, particularly in the earlier decades, those who were trapped in such adverse circumstances had little alternative but to resort to direct action in order to gain relief or redress. Aggression was not only an expression of despair but also the principal weapon at their disposal. Those who had most at stake reacted the most strongly, by taking the initiative and giving body to their aspirations through word and deed. Periodic eruptions of this nature were a clear reminder of the fragile harmony that sometimes existed in rural areas. Violence and brutality were not necessarily confined to the cradles of capitalist production in the industrialized towns and mining valleys of Wales.

Economic depression, poverty, enclosures, rents, rates and tithes were the virulent precipitants that shattered the peace of the countryside, causing rural rioting in which the small tenant farmer assumed a prominent role. Acting in concert to safeguard their own material interests, tenant farmers were prepared to utilize violent protest as a mode of expression. During the course of the nineteenth century they engaged in a number of historic struggles that gave direct impetus to a middle-class consciousness increasingly fortified by common allegiance to Nonconformity. Sectional self-interest nurtured a separate identity and produced situations which distinguished the farmer from his hired labourer. Though the boundary line between the small farmer and wage labourer was frequently indistinct because of the communal nature of farming, a division of interest certainly existed, however close-knit the social relationship. There remained always the basic economic difference between the classes: the farmer held possession of the property and control of capital, the farm worker sold his labour-power in return for wages. Moreover, this difference of interests could at any time develop into a conflict of interests, especially when setting wages and the length of the working day. The hired farm labourer traditionally occupied a subordinate status at the very base of the rural class hierarchy. And within the wage structure the master-servant nexus was divisive and exploitative by nature; indeed the designation *gwas ffarm* (farm servant) was in itself synonymous with subservience. Property and its obligations placed the farmer a grade above, however slight, in social rank, and this was sufficient reason for him to act independently. By any test, the great mass of farm workers remained what they had always been since feudal times: an inferior, impotent and cheap labour force at the call of their masters.

Though the pattern of their lives was very much interlocked, each day for both farmer and labourer being a ritual of work and rest, the farmer, as employer, always strove to maintain a distinctive distance between himself and his workers.[1] His group status endowed him with occupational prestige and whatever the margin of economic difference he clearly cherished a measure of independence and superior social standing within the local community. Living at subsistence level with the merest of creature comforts, the wage labourer, in contrast, remained the underdog in that he could be exploited economically by all those above him. He was generally hired by the year, receiving wages partly in cash and partly in kind, living in or living out in a rented cottage; the very nature of his employment made him psychologically and physically dependent on his master.[2] From time immemorial the labourer's hours of work were long and excessive: 5 or 6 a.m. to 6 or 7 p.m. in summer, with extra hours for harvest operations, and dawn to dusk in winter, those who slept on the farm having no fixed hours whatsoever. The tradition in south-west Wales for seasonal migration to the English border counties or the Vale of Glamorgan in search of harvest work enabled the labourer to supplement his meagre wage. Many other landless labourers, particularly in periods of unemployment, saw emigration overseas as their only hope. Otherwise, there were few opportunities in the first half of the nineteenth century to improve their material welfare. For the great majority, therefore, this necessarily meant a passive submission to conditions of unremitting hardship and human suffering. By far the most numerous social group in rural society, the agricultural labouring class were, by definition, a class apart.

Distress in the wake of the recession that followed the Napoleonic Wars accounted for the turbulence of the small farmer in the opening decades of the nineteenth century. Nevertheless, as D.J.V. Jones has shown, the labourers were not drawn into this general outburst of discontent, except on a very limited scale.[3] Whereas the south and west of England experienced a serious labourers' revolt in 1830–1, with machine-breaking and rick-burning, the farm labourers of Wales never took to such extremes although the border counties caught a whiff of incendiarism. With farm workers suffering great adversity, threats to threshing machines (which deprived them of their livelihood) were reported in Monmouthshire and hay ricks were set on fire in Glamorgan.[4] Far more significant was the unilateral attempt made by Vale of Glamorgan labourers to articulate their demand for higher wages. The chief squirearchy, in correspondence with their agents, were intrigued by the news that men were banding together to push their own claims. Lord Bute's agent, for instance, referred to a meeting of workers at Boverton in December 1830.[5] It seems that the current air of excitement and disturbance had inspired at least some of the hard-pressed agricultural labourers to emerge from the shadows in an unprecedented, yet apparently forlorn, display of nascent class consciousness.

As the high point of agrarian protest in the first half of the century, the Rebecca Riots brought the attention of the government to the plight of the tenant farmers. The feeling of outrage in south-west Wales that manifested itself mainly in the destruction of toll-gates in 1839 and 1842–4 was the product of a long-standing range of complaints. Of course, the farm labourers remained free from the burdens of rates, tithes and tolls, and though they had a collaborative hand in the actual attacks, the riots, naturally enough, 'were entirely an affair of the small farmers'.[6] Yet, there is enough evidence to suggest that the prevailing atmosphere of unrest once more incited the beginnings of an alternative movement. The cry for justice was easily imitated, and by August 1843 the farm workers were taking advantage of the situation to stage separate meetings to plead their case for improved wages and allowances.[7] The ominous prospect of a revolt from below, with its attendant danger of rick-burning (as happened in Carmarthenshire) was a risk the farmers were not prepared to take. Even the presence of troops seemed more palatable than a recalcitrant labour force.[8] In this way, what can be interpreted as the rudiments of independent-minded working-class struggle were effectively nipped in the bud. The Rebecca Riots may have concluded in a 'substantial victory'[9] for the farmers, but narrow class interests would not tolerate a rival movement striving to legitimize its own grievances.

Again during the early 1840s, at a time of severe economic hardship in farming, there is evidence of unrest among the labourers of Glamorgan.[10] Disturbances in Denbighshire saw the familiar weapon of arson — farm property and hay ricks were set alight — being used as an expression of rural discontent.[11] Such occurrences, however, were usually uncoordinated affairs, more the unconsidered reaction of a peasant people who had suffered enough wrong. Whatever the impression given by contemporaries, anxious to present Wales as a law-abiding nation in answer to the slanders of the infamous Education Report of 1847, there still persisted a strong undercurrent of rural crime. The prevalence of poaching, theft, arson and attacks on property offered proof that not all was well in the Welsh countryside.

All the same, the years following the repeal of the Corn Laws in 1846 provided sufficient prosperity to restore the semblance of rural calm. Now the emphasis shifted to the emergent growth of Nonconformist political radicalism. As a gradual development, closely allied to awakening middle-class consciousness, it placed the removal of civil and religious disabilities as its central considerations. Although both urban and rural strands of Liberalism shared the same broad political aspirations, each also had its particular axe to grind. Familiar rural resentment of tithes, rates and rents was compounded by anger at the rough-shod treatment of the tenantry by landlords and their stewards; all of which was skilfully manipulated by Nonconformist propagandists. Foremost among the influential leaders of popular opinion in this crucial formative period were William Rees ('Gwilym Hiraethog') and Samuel Roberts ('S.R.'). Both were prominent Independent ministers and social reformers who recognized the power of the press. Through the medium of their writings the two men played a decisive role in the polarization of Welsh society along class and sectarian lines, whereby the Welsh-speaking dissenting tenantry stood up to the established authority of the anglicized and Anglican landowning gentry.[12]

In the columns of *Yr Amserau*, Gwilym Hiraethog hit on a perfect medium to reach the embittered tenantry when he created 'Llythyrau 'Rhen Ffarmwr' in December 1846. Attacks on the tithe payment and other injustices were given greater force when couched in a homely, rustic dialect. Characteristically, these letters betray the atmosphere of the farmhouse rather than the labourer's cottage,[13] for his sole aim was to focus attention on the predicament of the tenant farmers. It was precisely this concern that moved him time and again in the late 1840s and 1850s to advocate some form of association for the farmers so that in unity they might find the necessary confidence and strength to face their landlords. On the other hand, no political advantage was to be gained by stirring the agricultural workers; they counted for nothing and could be virtually disregarded. Once, in response to a correspondent, he waxed righteously on the importance of a regular weekly wage, although it is clear that he was far more mindful of the losses a farmer might incur from having a disgruntled employee.[14] When one recalls that Gwilym Hiraethog had toiled as a labourer in his early years, and struggled to raise a family on a subsistence wage, it is all the more surprising that his sympathies now lay exclusively with the farmers. Prominence and respectability had transformed him into a spokesman for the rights of the middle class.[15]

For S.R., likewise, injustice only befell the industrious small farmer. Much in the same manner as Gwilym Hiraethog he had been brought up on a poor upland farm, and it was this image of penury and struggle that impressed itself on his mind and later coloured his political views. Pamphlets like *Farmer Careful of Cilhaul Uchaf* (1850) and *A History of Diosg Farm* (1854) depict the separation of society into an exploiting and exploited class in terms of the sway of the landlord over tenant. It resulted, he opined, in an enslavement worse than that suffered by Russian serfs.[16] In his continual drawing of attention to the tenants' rights, the hapless farm workers, unwittingly perhaps, were mentioned only in passing. He assumed that the long-sought-after improvement in the condition of the tenant farmer would in turn secure an abundance of profitable employment for willing labourers. As things stood, excessive burdens prevented the farmers from paying decent wages; consequently the drift to the towns left many areas short of farm-hands.[17]

As an ultimate aim, it was intended that the farmers should break out of their inhibiting mould and display an independent political will. And with their highly tendentious use of the press and pulpit, Liberal leaders began a gradual process which first found expression in the elections of 1859, 1865 and 1868. The eviction of those who had voted against the wishes of their Tory landlords intensified the political struggle and endowed the economic sufferings of the tenant farmer with the additional halo of martyrdom. But in facing the landlords they turned their backs on the labourers. In their public utterances, Nonconformist radicals stopped short of advocating justice and equal rights for those below them in society.[18] Neither did the farmers share sufficient affinity with the labourers to forge a united front to fight a common tyranny; on every count they preferred to maintain the labourer's status of cliency. In this strongly partisan atmosphere no one displayed enough compassion, or mustered enough courage, to speak out on behalf of the forgotten majority class. And the more farmers preoccupied themselves with their own side of the rural question the more blatant the contrast became. As a general statement it would be difficult to say who suffered the greatest oppression: the tenant farmer at the whim of the gentry class or the wage labourers at the hands of the farmers.

All this was in keeping with a Liberal Party keen to foster its essentially middle-class values and a Nonconformist philosophy that gave a salient place to independent action. Insofar as the Nonconformist conception of religious and political liberty and equality exalted individualism, it was hardly likely to harbour socialism or collectivist ideas. But in denying economic equality it then appeared to accept the social order with all its wrongs. Because the Nonconformist hierarchy also showed initial hostility to trade unionism and the labour movement, it followed that the proletariat would be encaged in perpetual degradation with only the uncertain prospect of salvation to give solace. Moreover, the contradiction implicit in this view meant that the future alienation of the working class was predictable. Even within Nonconformity itself the gulf between the classes became manifest. As K.O. Morgan has pointed out, the degree of democracy in Nonconformity is frequently overstated: 'deacons more often than not were chosen from farmers rather than from their labourers.'[19] Over the years, the process of *embourgeoisement* was accomplished as decisively within the denominational leadership as within the local political structure and society in general. This put a greater distance between the leaders of Liberal Nonconformity and the labouring poor. Rarely did they find a reason or an advantage in improving the economic condition of the agricultural labourers, and as the great army of labourers seemed to accept the inevitability of their lot it was more convenient that they be kept in their place.

It was quite exceptional for the labourers to be singled out for special notice, even more surprising to hear a landlord plead their case. Though the landlord in question was a Herefordshire man, he had some plain words to say about the 'sadly neglected' agricultural workers of Radnorshire, and Wales in general. Speaking at the annual meeting of the Knighton Farmers' Club in 1854, W.T. Kevill Davies of Croft Castle delivered a stinging indictment of his fellow landlords and farmers in that they held ultimate responsibility for their workers' condition. 'We treat them more like slaves than fellow men', he averred, 'and seldom do much for them.'[20] Poor wages, wretched cottages, lack of schooling, the indifference of clergy, landlord and farmer alike made the labourer ignorant, poverty-stricken and immoral. And at the root of all these evils was the scandalously low wage he received. It compelled the labourer's wife to neglect her family and home in order to supplement his meagre wage; it forced his children to waive their schooling at a young age thus making them more susceptible to harmful social influences. Worse still, poverty and starvation could lead a labourer to crime. Then when he reached the limit of his physical usefulness he was expected to end his days, ignominiously, on parish relief.

To Kevill Davies's mind, the blame as much as the remedy rested solely with the farmers.[21] Alleviation of the labourers' condition would only come as a result of higher wages. This was the key to a stable family life. Just how many agreed with his progressive views, let alone acted upon them, is not too difficult to guess. Humanitarian farmers were as few on the ground as enlightened landowners; even fewer were radical Nonconformist agitators willing to identify with the labourer or promote his class viewpoint. No William Cobbett emerged in Wales to publicize the social conditions of the farm workers. As Cobbett had observed in his famous *Rural Rides* (1830), whereas landlords and farmers were able to defend themselves, 'nobody tells the tale of the labourer'.[22]

Nor did the agricultural labourer merit a place in the popular Welsh literature of the period. In this sense, the publication in 1860 of the novel, *Huw Huws neu y Llafurwr Cymreig* by Lewis William Lewis ('Llew Llwyfo'), constitutes a rather notable exception.[23] As the author intended, it is in many ways an accurate mirror of the prevalent attitudes and relationships existing between masters and men. True, its chief character is idealized as an essentially noble, upstanding figure who, unlike the majority of workers, finds fulfilment in his work, regarding it as a duty rather than an endless, back-breaking toil. But when he takes his place alongside other farm workers at the annual hiring fair all sentiment is thrust aside. With his description of the boisterous and unsavoury nature of tavern life in which they freely indulged, Llew Llwyfo uncovers some of the unacceptable aspects of a labourer's life. Having no specific creed to impart, the motivating ideal, however, was purely ethical, with its typical Victorian emphasis on self-help and self-improvement. It offered no hint of rebellion.

With very little opportunity to raise their social status it seemed axiomatic that wage labourers should accept their place in the community. As few above them had any reason or inclination to instigate any change the very structure of society militated against improvement or, alternatively, the possibility of organized protest. Handicapped by the absence of indigenous leadership or any form of pre-existing collective organization, they remained passive and vulnerable, social outcasts in the hypocritical Nonconformist world of great theological disputes and Missionary Society endeavour. Another serious impediment to change was the absence of a medium of self-expression; largely uneducated, the agricultural labourers were conditioned to accept injustice rather than encouraged to question it. Thus, as forces within society either ignored or held down the worker, the opportunity for change remained severely restricted. It was rare for farm labourers to demand a better deal from their masters, and even then the numbers involved could only have been an insignificant fraction. Unlike the factory, mine or workshop, where strength in numbers and a close comradeship heightened the worker's perception of class and his resolve to oppose the employer, the farm with its small work-force was more likely to instil conformity based on a bond of mutual dependence.

About the only time the labourers gathered together in force was on the day of the hiring fair, held once or twice a year in the principal market towns, usually in May and November. By tradition, farm hands (and servant girls) stood in the open street to sell their labour to the highest bidder. Often condemned as a relic of the days of slavery, the custom nevertheless survived as an affront to human dignity until the beginning of the twentieth century.[24] To the humane observer it embodied the ultimate degradation: 'It was a disgrace to a Christian country to see a parcel of men and women in a row on each side of the road and farmers, etc., surveying and engaging them as he would buy cattle.'[25] Here again, it was the individualistic aspect which predominated. The service agreement, which tied a man for periods of six, or most commonly twelve, months rested on an individual wage bargain sealed by a handshake and the acceptance of earnest money. It was every man for himself and each went his own way. This deeply humiliating system underlined both the labourer's basic insecurity and his bondage to the farmer; moreover, the presence of a large labour pool could be twisted to the employer's advantage in that it kept wages down. Any sense of collective feeling was restricted to the much-maligned social life of the tavern on the night of the fair. All the labourers' frustrations were then given release, invariably ending in the sort of drunkenness, immorality and fist-fighting that gave the temperance cause a good name.

It has been argued that when the labourers were in shorter supply at the close of the nineteenth century the economic role of the hiring fair could be reversed. In some counties it reportedly fulfilled the function of a surrogate trade union in that it increased the bargaining strength of the workers, allowing them to lever up wage rates.[26] Broadly speaking, however, it is highly improbable that they were sufficiently mature in labour matters to act in any form of tactical unison which allowed them to exploit this situation to any great degree.

Why resentment and disaffection failed to burst into open revolt is therefore easy to see. The lack of leadership and means of unifying a scattered, isolated work-force meant that the two preliminary preconditions were wanting at the outset. Neither should we ignore the basic character of an ill-educated country labourer: his ingrained conservative outlook, deferential nature and general indifference minimized the risk of widespread discontent. But these factors are not a sufficient explanation in themselves. More important to the individual farm worker was the fact that real wages had almost doubled in the period 1845–70[27] due to the expansion of the railway system in mid-century, and the alternative employment it offered. Railways drew large areas of the countryside into closer proximity with industry and so provided the competition which increased the average weekly wage to twelve shillings. Easier access to the coal-pits and ironworks of Glamorgan and Monmouth meant that the rates of wages in some Welsh counties could reach fifteen shillings or even as much as eighteen shillings by 1870. At the same time, the railways offered an avenue of escape for the discontented in that they facilitated the internal migration from rural to industrial Wales that characterized the latter decades of the century.

Although agricultural labourers still composed the majority class, this period saw a massive fall in their number; between 1851 and 1891 they decreased from 73,300 to 44,900.[28] In other words over a third of the rural work-force, for a variety of reasons, abandoned the land to seek a better life elsewhere. Many flocked to the manufacturing centres of England, or emigrated to America or the colonies, but the greatest exodus, as we have noted, was to the Glamorgan coalfield where the unskilled but hardened labourer could cope with the rigours of mining. At a time of severe agricultural depression in the last quarter of the century, the attraction of higher wages in the coalfield was a major stimulus. So that he might earn a few more shillings, the agricultural labourer willingly substituted his sickle for the pick. Moreover, this unprecedented outflow acted as the safety-valve which gradually eased off much of the tension endemic in Welsh rural society and so made a large-scale labourers' revolt all the more unlikely.

A continuing feature of Welsh agricultural society was the fine margin distinguishing employer and employee. Unlike the counties of southern England, with their substantial farms and high ratio of outdoor servants that fostered a strong caste distinction,[29] Wales was predominantly a land of small farms (generally averaging under fifty acres) and smallholdings. This often meant that the tenant farmer stood only a shade higher in the social scale, many having climbed from the position of agricultural labourer. With such a large number of small farms this step was within the reach of many an ambitious, hard-working labourer.[30] Again, small farms which employed one or two male workers formed a close, paternalistic unit, labourers who received board and lodging being generally regarded as part of the family. In some cases the role could be interchangeable, with the tenant farmer doubling as a labourer when the need arose. All this created a comradely social relationship and made the hired servant more sympathetic to the small farmer's problems and hardships. Since social divisions were blurred in this way, it was difficult for the labourer to regard his employer as a class opponent.

On top of this there was no organization to bind the workers together, no opportunity to lay the foundations of class solidarity, nothing that would enable them to challenge the farmers. Various localized trade unions that appeared in some English counties in the 1860s and early 1870s were short-lived;[31] but with the formation of the National Agricultural Labourers' Union in 1872, led by Joseph Arch, the 'Revolt of the Field' took shape.[32] Yet, whilst Joseph Arch's union marked a decisive step in the formal organization of the farm labourers on a wide scale, the concept of rural trade unionism was foreign to their counterparts in Wales. Without the means of mass communication the mainly Welsh-speaking labourers were effectively immunized from contemporary developments and this method of social protest. Needless to say, the Welsh farm labourer was better known for his sullen acquiescence than for his tendency to revolt. Apart from the actual achievement of unionizing a hitherto largely unorganized work-force, the initial success of the revolt in England also underlined the importance of personality and the asset which the dignified leadership of Joseph Arch gave to the movement. As with all labour movements, the presence of an articulate and gifted leader was the one basic element which pulled men together.

If the outlets for protest were strictly limited, the sources of injustice remained real enough to the work-worn farm labourer. Very often a tied cottage, let annually, kept him in thrall to his employer, and securely at the bottom of the social hierarchy; so that when a man was dismissed from his employment he faced a double blow in that he lost his house as well. Overall, the standard of housing in most rural districts was extremely defective as a government report in 1870 testified.[33] All the Commissioners agreed that the majority of cottages for farm workers were in a wretched condition, often totally unfit for human habitation. Particularly bad in this respect were the small, damp, ill-ventilated, insanitary, overcrowded mud cottages in south-west Wales. As a rule, it meant that a whole family had to live and sleep in a one-roomed house with all the hazards to health this presented. So deplorable were the hovels of Cardiganshire that they were said to be a 'great blot' on the county. Although the contrast between wealth and poverty was not as general or perhaps as evident as in a crowded industrial town, the false green image of the countryside could hide a far worse squalor.

Then there were always those labourers who received wages that fell way below the average (which varied considerably from district to district), wages that were scarcely sufficient to provide them and their families with clothes, food and shelter. Maintaining a large family on a low rate of wages was enough in itself to sustain a smouldering discontent. As a consequence, many parents — labourers and small farmers alike — were forced to send their children off to find occasional work in the fields at an early age; earning an extra wage was considered far more important than schooling. As one labourer put it succinctly: 'Education is a good thing, but bread for a poor man is better.'[34] Evidence of children of agricultural workers being unable to read or write was quite common and, even in the era of compulsory attendance towards the end of the nineteenth century, absenteeism in country areas remained an insuperable problem. Parents could neither afford to pay the school fees nor provide adequate clothing. In the wake of Forster's 1870 Education Act it was the shrewd-minded farmers who dominated most rural school boards. Whilst they kept an eagle eye on the level of rate expenditure they turned an equally effective blind eye to absenteeism; indeed, well-to-do farmers, who could afford to give their own children private tuition, often employed many of the offenders.[35] Education, the key to social advancement, could therefore be turned by unscrupulous farmers into an instrument of social control. Naturally, it satisfied their needs to keep the unprivileged children of the poorer class chained to the 'stupidity of rural life'. It guaranteed yet another generation of docile workers and cheap labour.

All these factors together proved an effective deterrent to the emergence of the agricultural labourers as a self-conscious segment of the working class. Allowing for the generalizations implicit in a background survey, it is nonetheless clear that the small farmers and agricultural labourers held much in common. Throughout most of the century they shared the same degree of poverty, injustice and lack of opportunity. Similarly, they displayed the same unyielding conservatism and air of political indifference. As a result there was little sense of alienation, or anything approaching the class antagonism that characterized the farmer-servant relationship in England. Yet, as the farmers gradually matured in attitude and became even more conscious of their social status there appeared an ever-growing cleavage within the lower ranks of rural society. In pursuit of particular political aims, and in defence of property and economic interests, the farmers were more likely to emerge as an organized body. By pushing aside the labourers they laid bare the division and inequalities that confirmed their separateness as a class.

Thus, the process of self-realization developed among labourers at the very time when the farmers volubly proclaimed their aspirations and banded together for their own ends. The heightened class-consciousness of the farmers produced a situation in which the labourers were subsequently encouraged, in direct imitation, to act as a group and assert their own demands. What was good for the master became good for the servant. In this way a 'riot' or 'war' conducted by the small farmer became the occasion for the revolt of the labourer. What they had to say, of course, clearly distinguished both groups. Notwithstanding the close social ties or the nebulous line dividing the classes, it was at a time like this that people began to perceive their existence as a distinct class. The pursuit of specific objectives became the impulse which drew members of the same class closer together, to the exclusion of others. In the same way that the demand for fair rent, greater security of tenure and compensation for improvements placed the tenant farmer in opposition to his landlord, a call from the labourers for an amelioration in working conditions ran directly counter to the vested interests of the farmers and so put them at loggerheads with each other.

Well to the fore as a specific grievance was the number of hours the labourers worked. Because the majority of servants in Wales were single men lodged on farm premises — often quartered in an unhealthy loft above the stable or outhouse — there were no regular hours or indeed any restriction on the time they spent in the fields or with the animals.[36] Whatever resentment they felt on the matter of wages,[37] housing or education, the grievance of long hours was the single issue that could bring together a disparate work-force. If solidarity among the agricultural labourers was to be forged, and consequently mobilized in a coherent movement, this would be the main focus of unity. Given the circumstances, a popular leader with an effective agency at his command could well succeed, but first it needed a protest movement among the farmers to prepare the way.

After a comparative lull in mid-century, the 'Tithe War' of 1886–9 was, on the face of things, a further indication of widespread discontent among tenant farmers. The disturbances that broke out in the Vale of Clwyd, and which eventually spread to other parts of rural Wales, emanated from the refusal of the Nonconformist tenantry to pay the church tithe in a period of acute agricultural depression and fall in prices.[38] Farmers, it was claimed, were often worse off than their labourers. Unlike previous agitations this conflict was largely fomented and exploited by Liberal activists for overtly political reasons. Steered by Thomas Gee of Denbigh, owner-editor of the premier radical newspaper, *Baner ac Amserau Cymru*, a carefully staged bid was made to link the anti-tithe campaign with an ambitious political programme that called for a Land Bill as well as the disestablishment and disendowment of the Church of England.[39] Refusal to pay the hated tithe, meanwhile, resulted in attempts by Ecclesiastical Commissioners to sequester goods, and this, in turn, led to considerable disorder and violence when farms were distrained. As with the Rebecca Riots, some of the farm hands proved to be the natural allies of the tenant farmers, and willingly joined in the physical confrontations.[40] When thirty-one rioters from Llangwm, Denbighshire, faced prosecution in July 1887 there were a number of labourers among the so-called 'martyrs'.[41]

Thomas Gee's technique of organization involved drawing the farmers together into an effective alliance that could arouse public opinion and so exert maximum political influence. For some time the Welsh radical press had deprecated the conservatism of the farming fraternity and their disappointingly apolitical nature. Now, by 1885–6, various local leagues and associations were springing up and no bones made of their intention to safeguard the direct interests of the tenant farmers. Welcoming such moves, Gee at the same time regretted their exclusivist nature: complaints had reached him that farm labourers were being debarred from membership and no mention made of their rights or conditions of work in official meetings.[42] A broad platform to include not only farmers but workers, craftsmen and merchants was, he believed, the means to gain general sympathy and support. It may be no coincidence that a rival land reformer, the Revd E. Pan Jones of Mostyn, editor of *Y Celt*, had already (since 1881) advocated the rights of workers and their inclusion in a proposed Land League which Gee at first backed in Autumn 1885.[43] In Pan Jones's view the treatment given to labourers was proof that farmers meant to keep them in their grip. Both landowner and farmer were oppressing the workers, so what advantage might the latter gain from a measure which merely incorporated the 'three Fs' (fair rents, fixed tenancies and free sale of leases) and favoured the tenant farmers? The logical alternative, he thought, would be a separate organization for the labourers.[44]

The fundamental difference in ideological approach soon emerged when Pan Jones and his ally, the Revd Michael D. Jones, invited Michael Davitt, founder of the militant Irish Land League, to lecture in north Wales early in 1886. Gee would have no truck with any extremist theories of land nationalization and, with the farmers also banded against Pan Jones,[45] he was given fair weather to form his own abortive Welsh Land League, out of which emerged the Anti-Tithe League in September. Justice for the farmer, it was argued, would secure better employment prospects for the labourers and so stem the volume of rural emigration. Gee was keen to see a government measure — a view aired prior to the July 1886 election and redolent of Jesse Collings's call for 'three acres and a cow' — that would enable the agricultural labourers to buy or rent an acre or two of their own.[46]

Nothing illustrates better the enormous gulf between Gee and Pan Jones than the proceedings of the Denbigh conference held in October 1886. Under the chairmanship of Thomas Gee, an array of MPs and almost all the influential farmers of the Vale of Clwyd met to consider clauses of a proposed Land Bill for Wales. Modelled on the Irish Land Act of 1881 it fixed attention on the rights of tenant farmers to such a degree that when Pan Jones proposed an amendment calling for the nationalization of land and measures for safeguarding the interests of working men, he failed to find a seconder.[47] Michael D. Jones had already been ordered off the platform by Gee on the grounds that he was peddling doctrines harmful to Welsh farmers.[48] Balked in this fashion, Pan Jones never ceased to attack Gee's narrow concept of land reform or the selfish concern of farmers bent on their own salvation.[49] From this point on he parted company with mainstream Liberalism to pursue what was essentially a one-man crusade for land reform based on the aims of the Land Nationalization Society.[50] From the start, Pan Jones had consistently advocated, on platform and in print, the claims of the labouring class. Unfortunately, these were but part of the wider socialist vision which saw state ownership of land as the panacea to poverty, pauperism and other social ills. In the context of late nineteenth-century rural Wales this was a vision way ahead of its time.

To talk of *gwaedu gwerin*[51] in the context of the 'Tithe War', therefore, is to yoke two classes together at the expense of the underlying differences between them. It was fought by the small tenant farmers in their own self-interest, urged on by Nonconformist ministers and political radicals. But the conditions which helped fashion a succession of none-too-successful leagues to promote the farmers' case did not take long to stir a more general interest in the plight of the agricultural labourer. Whilst expressing sympathy for the tenant farmer in his distress, a correspondent in *Baner ac Amserau Cymru* in November 1886 called attention to the relative silence on matters pertaining to the worker.[52] In answer, Gee maintained that frequent attempts to rouse the labourers had come to nought; nevertheless he agreed to open a special column ('Colofn y Gweithwyr') in his newspaper dedicated to workers of every grade, including the agricultural labourer.[53] Although this gesture drew little reply, Hugh Roberts, a self-educated quarryman from Abergynolwyn, Merioneth, took the opportunity to air his views.[54] Such matters as the Tithe War, disestablishment and intermediate education were of secondary importance to the workers compared with their wages and conditions. And he challenged the paper, which had fought so hard for the rights of the farmer over the years, to take up the cause of the labourer. Otherwise, he predicted, it would not be long before a Moses would arise to lead the workers from their bondage.

Gee's cold response was particularly revealing.[55] Though he was gratified to see the workers stirring at last, he made it clear that they would have to take the matter in their own hands and fight their own battle in the way the farmers were conducting the Tithe War. In other words, the labourers had to fend for themselves.[56] Those vain attempts to amalgamate both farmers and labourers into a common alliance were now revealed to be the product of a limited vision. In the pursuit of his religious and political aims, Thomas Gee paid no more than lip-service to the ideal of an alignment of classes and the rights of the farm worker. At no time did he attempt to raise basic labour questions such as hours of work and rates of wages, let alone preach the principles of trade unionism, which in the nature of combination he practised with his assortment of leagues for tenant farmers. In the final reckoning, Thomas Gee, the respectable newspaper proprietor and Calvinistic Methodist minister, stood, like Gwilym Hiraethog and S.R., as the champion of the farming class.[57] Adding the legend

'Farmers' Journal' to the masthead of *Baner ac Amserau Cymru* in October 1887 merely confirmed this truth.

To an up-and-coming Liberal radical like David Lloyd George, on the other hand, the presentation of the Land Question as the prerogative of the farmers was a fundamental tactical error. Mindful that a good number of agricultural workers had been enfranchised in 1884–5, he considered it electorally expedient that the Liberals pitch their appeal much wider. Political wisdom as well as social justice demanded the inclusion of the labourers in a proposed new Land League.[58] 'Here is a class more numerous', he wrote in November 1887, 'and far more fearless than our cautious Welsh farmers.'[59] In an attempt to capture the full potential of the rural vote all the victims of agrarian injustice had to be properly harnessed into the Liberal Party. Accordingly, the first editorial of *Udgorn Rhyddid*, the newspaper started by Lloyd George in 1888, promised to foster the interests of both farmers and agricultural labourers.[60] But its avowed 'socialist' aim was merely the nascent collectivism of radical Liberalism; it did not mean going the whole hog and upholding workers' trade unionism. Lloyd George knew that this held little electoral appeal in a rural county like Caernarfonshire where Nonconformist farmers reigned supreme.

His proposition appears to have evoked very little enthusiasm within Welsh Liberal circles. As the major figure, T.E. Ellis MP, himself the son of a Merioneth tenant farmer, remained mesmerized by his hatred of landlords. And during a brief political career he made it his main business to uphold the rights of the Nonconformist tenantry in the Commons.[61] Thus each Liberal manifesto and utterance equated 'Neglected Wales' with the adversity of the unhappy farmer. In his bitter tirade against Anglican-Tory landlordism, written at the request of the South Wales Liberal Federation, T.J. Hughes ('Adfyfr'), in like vein, graphically exposed its evil grip on all aspects of Welsh life.[62] Even the indigence of the farm labourers could be attributable to this affliction; landlordism made it impossible for tenant farmers to pay a fair wage or employ more workers.[63] There was nothing to be gained from broadcasting the peculiar claims of the labourers.

Lloyd George's advice did not go entirely unheeded. When it suited him, Gee showed once again that he was willing to court the agricultural labourer, this time with the launching of the grandiosely titled Welsh Land, Commercial and Labour League in December

1887.[64] He strove to gain the co-operation of the labouring classes by holding out the possibility of more jobs, and the familiar promise of a bill that would guarantee the labourer a small plot of land. To a cynical Pan Jones this turn-about was a vindication of his long-held view that workers should also benefit from the current agitation.[65] But by now it was rather late in the day to hope for a successful combination of classes. Both sides appeared to be going their separate way and the class feeling which had been gaining force over the last few years was leading to entirely new developments. Having seen the farmers detach themselves from the concept of a common front in all but name, it was only a matter of time before the labourers would be tempted to strike out on their own. Significantly, the Llannefydd branch of Thomas Gee's latest league was to hold a discussion on the 'Rights of the Workers'.[66] Already, letters in *Baner ac Amserau Cymru* were drawing attention to the gap between farmers and their employees in Pembrokeshire.[67] They condemned the long hours (sometimes twelve to thirteen hours a day), the low wages and the abiding poverty as unjust, oppressive and enslaving, adding that not many farmers in the county could escape this serious indictment.

For far too long the movement for land reform and the removal of agrarian grievances in Wales had been equated with the farmers as a class. Even Joseph Arch, who visited Swansea in February 1888 to give a lecture on the Land Question under the auspices of the Trades Council, concentrated on the rights of the tenantry and on the tithe.[68] No reference was made to agricultural labourers' trade unionism and no attempt made to instigate an interest in the subject. But times were changing. The traditional farmer-servant relationship based on feelings of goodwill was coming under severe strain as workers became aware that they were not receiving a fair deal. Many saw through the façade: farmers who professed to be Liberal in politics, and true to the principles of justice, freedom and equality had shown little conscience or done hardly anything that would substantially improve the lot of the labourer. Unpaid tithe money rested securely in their pockets; not even the local Nonconformist minister or chapel, it was said, benefited from the payments they withheld over the years.[69] All the farmers were concerned about was their own basic interests, and it was in the pursuit of these explicitly self-serving aims that they gave the clearest expression of class division. Thus when Thomas Gee made a pious attempt to reconstruct his Welsh Land League to incorporate the farm labourers, quarrymen and even the colliers, the sceptic could well ask if the lower classes amounted to anything more than a convenient addendum calculated to swell its numbers and gain more votes for the preponderantly middle-class Liberal Party at parliamentary and local elections.[70]

As soon as the labourers felt they would reap little benefit from such an alliance it became more and more difficult to hide the fact that the growing estrangement between both groups was based on a conflict of class interest. The politically aware recognized how their particular complaints were directed against their immediate employer, and that a reduction in hours or an improvement in wages would only come if they organized to confront the farmers and did not let themselves be diverted by propaganda attacks on landlordism, or be enticed by vague promises of a share of the spoils. But bold letters to the press in defence of their material interests were a far cry from the reality of positive action.

Yet a point could be reached when men had to stand together. Labourers in the small village of Cellan, near Lampeter, held a number of meetings in May 1889 to voice strong opposition to their fifteen-hour working day.[71] Interestingly enough, this was only a few weeks after the opening of the tithe campaign in south Cardiganshire. Nevertheless, such raw pockets of resistance were rare, and in this particular case it was confined to the locality and quickly extinguished. At no time did the protest reveal the makings of a cohesive movement; indeed the lack of unity among the men of Cellan accounted for its failure.[72] Even so, the long hours of labour which agricultural workers had to endure was a sufficiently sensitive cause of complaint to sharpen class-consciousness and provoke a revolt in any part of Wales given the right conditions. By the end of the year the cause which had merited only the cursory blessing of Thomas Gee and *Baner ac Amserau Cymru* was taken up in earnest by another journalist with immediate results. Assertive leadership combined with the influence of the press provided the essential ingredients. As it turned out, the silence of slavish acquiescence was broken in more than one quarter as the authentic voice of the agricultural labouring class struggled to be heard.

CHAPTER II

'NEW UNIONISM', 'AP FFARMWR' AND THE FIRST REVOLT, 1889–1893

THAT the years 1889–91 saw a fundamental change in the course of labour history became at once apparent with the flowering of general unions for the unskilled worker and a dramatic growth in trade union membership. Beginning with the National Labour Federation on Tyneside in 1886, the development of so-called 'new unionism' gave both the National Union of Gasworkers and General Labourers and the Dock, Wharf, Riverside and General Labourers' Union the opportunity to widen their scope. In no time, industrial south Wales proved a highly promising field for the expansion of 'new unionism'.[1] Even before the gasworkers and dockers became active in the area, another regional union, the National Amalgamated Labourers' Union, had been formed at Cardiff in June 1889. Such was the success of trade unionism in the coastal towns that organizers were being given a timely reminder in the press of the infinitely greater grievances of rural farm workers. What the urban proletariat had to suffer was nothing in comparison with the low wages and long hours of this 'class of white slaves'.[2] Very often, self-interest demanded their attention. From the inexhaustible reservoir of the countryside, compliant rural workmen were being used to undercut industrial wages or break strikes.[3] The National Labour Federation already encompassed farm workers among its diverse membership, whilst the secretary of the National Amalgamated Labourers' Union announced his desire to 'organize even the agricultural districts'.[4] Efforts by the Dockers' Union to unionize farm labourers in some English counties,[5] however, had to be abandoned because of the cost involved. As with the main railway unions, there is no evidence of any fraternal efforts by the 'new unions' to recruit Welsh farm workers at this stage.

Even before the advent of 'new unionism' there had been a remarkably high incidence of agricultural trade unionism in England during the 1870s. At a county level there were unions, for instance, in Huntingdonshire, Cambridge, Kent, Lincolnshire, Suffolk and

Gloucestershire.[6] One of the most successful independent regional unions, the Kent and Sussex Labourers' Union (1872–95), had 16,000 members at its peak.[7] Founded by Alfred Simmons, a Maidstone journalist, it utilized a local newspaper, the *Kent Messenger*, to publicize its cause. Arch's union, the National Agricultural Labourers' Union, had gone into early decline like most other local unions, but this period of general union activism in the early 1890s led to a brief revival in its fortunes, with independent organizations once more appearing in counties such as Berkshire, Dorset, Norfolk, Hereford, Wiltshire and Warwickshire. Although such unions often operated across county boundaries, none of them extended their reach into Wales.

At its annual conference in Liverpool in September 1890, the Trades Union Congress underlined the importance of propagating the principles of combination among agricultural workers, and it resolved to urge all the trades councils located in rural areas to assist.[8] But such pre-conditions can hardly be said to have existed in Wales; it was not until 1891–3 that trades councils appeared in the major industrial towns of south Wales. As the official delegate of the National Agricultural Labourers' Union, Joseph Arch must have been heartened by the sentiments uttered. No doubt they also gave added inspiration to a young journalist attending the TUC conference as an observer.[9] Combining the compassionate intensity of a social reformer and the vision of a committed activist, John Owen Jones ('ap Ffarmwr') had already made a unique reputation for himself as the tribune of the farm workers of his native county of Anglesey. Moreover, he did this virtually single-handedly in an area devoid of any tradition of working-class organization. As he noted, in contrast with south Wales, there were no labour representatives from north Wales at the TUC conference, not even from the North Wales Quarrymen's Union. Yet, it is within the context of the climacteric years of labour struggle in 1889–91 that he took up their cause, and strove to form a local agricultural labourers' trade union. As with Joseph Arch in England, the name of ap Ffarmwr became synonymous with the 'Revolt of the Field' in nineteenth-century Wales.

Born in 1861 at Trefdraeth, Anglesey, the son of a small farmer, J.O. Jones had combined periods of formal schooling with intensive self-education during which time he studied the works of Ruskin and Carlyle.[10] After studying in Aberystwyth College and then Owen's College, Manchester, he became London correspondent of the Welsh

National Newspaper Company, publishers of influential Liberal papers like *Y Genedl Gymreig* and *The North Wales Observer and Express*. But after only a short stint in London, J.O. Jones returned to his rural roots to set up a private grammar school at Dwyran. His return coincided with unquestionably hard times in Anglesey. The depression which first hit Welsh agriculture in 1879 had intensified in its severity to such a degree that the Land Question now emerged as a major social and political issue. Tenant farmers were loudly demanding a reduction in rents, rates and tithes. At this stage, J.O. Jones took up a well-recognized Liberal position and sided with the farmers. As he joined the swelling chorus of protest his articles on the Land Question in *Y Genedl Gymreig* in 1886 echoed a theme popularized by S.R.[11] He defended the rights of tenant farmers in the face of oppressive landlordism and looked forward to the day when a leader like Parnell would appear in Wales to remove its tyranny. Indeed, it was this sympathetic interest in the plight of the farmers that inspired him to adopt the appropriate journalistic pseudonym of 'ap Ffarmwr' ('son of a farmer').

Why ap Ffarmwr went further and took up the cause of the agricultural labourers is not immediately clear. For a man who had absorbed the ideas of Ruskin and Carlyle he was perhaps bound to harbour a natural empathy for the downtrodden, a feeling no doubt emotionally reinforced as his eyes were opened to the miserable conditions of the ordinary farm worker in Anglesey. From time to time letters appeared in *Y Genedl Gymreig* spotlighting the case of the labourers.[12] Only a few months prior to his articles, 'Gwas Cyflog' and 'Gweithiwr' were drawing attention to the fifteen-hour day of Caernarfonshire workers and the merciless attitude of some farmers.[13] At a time of increasingly vociferous complaint among the farmers, ap Ffarmwr could only have been aware, as a journalist, of those suffering an even greater hardship.

Whatever the exact reason, the publication of a series of articles on 'Agricultural Labourers' in *The North Wales Observer and Express* in 1889 under the pen-name 'A Son of the Soil' presented a trenchant piece of social criticism.[14] Here was a class at the bottom of the social scale characterized by poverty, starvation, ignorance and apathy, working apallingly long hours for low wages and with very little hope of self-improvement. 'The land question is ever on people's lips, but the tiller of the land is left out in the cold.' Neglected by society in general, and by politicians, ministers of religion and newspapers in particular, they remained totally vulnerable to the 'cruel greed' of their employers. Unlike other sections of the working class they had no trade union to protect them. Even education offered little salvation. Because farmers were able to manipulate the board schools, compulsory education had become a sham ensuring that Hodge (a countryman) remained a 'dull, unspeakably stupid creature'. As employers, farmers could only be described as the 'meanest, stingiest, most cowardly being(s) under the sun'.

Such a fierce, uncompromising indictment reflected considerable courage. Yet it led to nothing because *The North Wales Observer and Express* was an English-language newspaper with a modest circulation among the middle class. Nevertheless, the ideal medium lay close at hand. In order to capture the working-class potential *Y Werin* had been introduced in 1885 as a halfpenny Welsh-language weekly specifically designed to reflect the voice of the ordinary labourer. It soon achieved a circulation of 10,000 in Anglesey and Caernarfonshire, concentrating in particular on the activities of the North Wales Quarrymen's Union. When a letter appeared in November 1889 calling for a reduction in the number of hours for agricultural labourers, the editor was prompted to open his columns to a debate on the matter.[15] By the end of the same month the first Welsh version of J.O. Jones's seminal articles appeared under the familiar pseudonym of ap Ffarmwr.[16]

Once more he elaborated in detail on the condition of the farm labourers in language suffused with passionate rage. Again he pointed to the miners and quarrymen who were successfully arguing their case through trade unions and parliamentary representatives; only a few weeks before the London dock strike had ended in a spectacular victory for the men. No one in Wales had even dreamt of forming a trade union to speak on behalf of the farm workers. Utilizing his considerable literary talent, ap Ffarmwr succeeded, in a unique way, in identifying himself with their class. Though he attacked the excesses of capitalism and hinted at the public ownership of property there was little, as yet, overt socialist ideology in his writings; he spoke in the conventional tradition of radical dissent and humanitarian reform. What emerged as his central tenet was the Victorian creed of self-help and self-reliance as the means of attaining social amelioration. For this reason, ap Ffarmwr was particularly scathing of the educational system as it stood. Although he did not issue any specific manifesto, his formidable social critique soon aroused the collective consciousness of the agricultural workers and provided a starting point for an unprecedented labour movement in rural Wales.

Over the next few weeks the strength of the reaction could be measured in the number of letters which reached *Y Werin*. From all parts of north Wales came indications of widespread approval for ap Ffarmwr's views. Among the very first letters was the suggestion that a trade union be immediately formed and turned into an effective weapon to elevate their status.[17] As they could not expect much help from the traditional leaders of society, ap Ffarmwr agreed it would be an excellent idea to have a trade union for the whole of north Wales, beginning in Anglesey.[18] He then proposed that labourers came together in their localities to choose representatives to meet at Llangefni, the county town, where they could elect an executive committee. Thus, from almost the outset, ap Ffarmwr regarded the formation of an independent trade union for the farm labourers as the principal objective. Its first priority would be to secure a reduction in working hours and an improved wage; only then could the union proceed to political matters.

Social circumstances in Anglesey were propitious and the will to revolt perhaps stronger among its 2,500 farm workers. Agricultural depression or not, there were many prosperous farmers on the island; by all accounts more 'small fortunes' had been made on the land here than in any other part of Wales.[19] Moreover, the great number of farms over 100 acres meant that farmers formed a distinct middle class and were separated, both economically and socially, from their labourers by a very clear line of demarcation. As a result there was little mutual understanding or fellow-feeling between the classes. Labourers were becoming more independent-minded, a tendency strengthened through direct working contact with the slate quarrymen of Caernarfonshire. Scores of Anglesey farm labourers became migrant workers in the quarries, where they had experience of shorter hours.[20] From the numerous letters in *Y Werin* it was clear that the consensus of opinion among the labourers favoured a reduction of the working day to twelve hours, from 6 a.m. to 6 p.m.[21] (at a time when the trade union movement was agitating for an eight-hour day).

Despite the anger and prejudice directed against ap Ffarmwr personally, once the movement gathered momentum there was little the farmers could do to balk it. Letters in *Y Werin* testified to the effectiveness of his articles and the excitement engendered among the agricultural labourers in Anglesey, south Caernarfonshire and even the Vale of Clwyd.[22] They had become the main topic of conversation. Following the first formal public meeting held at Llanfair-yng-Nghornwy, Anglesey, on 28 February 1890,[23] labourers began to assemble in local schoolrooms and smithies to ventilate their grievances. All this proved heartening to ap Ffarmwr and he reiterated his call for a conference at Llangefni, which Thomas Lewis MP and other luminaries of the local Liberal establishment were welcome to attend.[24] In order that a firm declaration on the formation of a trade union could be made he urged local meetings to give the matter full consideration. Discounting any political motive on his part, ap Ffarmwr professed a purely humanitarian concern of the kind ministers of religion had palpably failed to show.

Activity at grass-roots level, meanwhile, created an unprecedented display of class solidarity. By the day of the Llangefni conference on 7 April, *Y Werin* had recorded meetings at fifteen different localities. It also provided an opportunity for local leadership to emerge. In spite of their poverty and lack of schooling some were to display extraordinary personal qualities, particularly John Hughes, George Jones ('ap Dafydd'), and Hugh Williams. Under such guidance meeting after meeting intimated a determination not only to win a twelve-hour day but also a Saturday half-holiday. By all accounts, far less interest was evinced in the idea of a trade union.

With good reason, many farmers felt uneasy at the turn of events. Accustomed to unquestioning obedience they strongly condemned the 'revolutionary' tone of the articles whose author's name was now anathema in some quarters.[25] Though there were calls for the formation of a Farmers' Defence Society to meet the challenge, others thought it wiser to attend the labourers' meetings in order to contain any extremism. Ap Ffarmwr, too, wished to allay their fears and it was for this reason that public figures like Captain Owen Thomas, Brynddu, and the Revd David Rees, Capel Mawr, were specially invited to the meeting at Llangefni. Showing the kind of well-meaning yet carefully qualified support for the aspirations of the working class that characterized his later political career, Captain Owen Thomas spoke at labourers' meetings but expressed equal sympathy for the farmers in their predicament.[26] Similar views were also conveyed by the Revd David Rees, doyen of the Anglesey Independents and Liberal activist.[27]

The historic conference held at Llangefni on Easter Monday, 7 April 1890,[28] to discuss the claims of the agricultural labourers of Anglesey was without parallel, and it represented a singular achievement for a 29-year-old journalist. Representatives from the various parishes, a number of farmers, two ministers of religion and ap Ffarmwr were present. In a conciliatory opening speech the chairman, William Thomas, the local postmaster, announced that the ultimate aim was to elevate the social, religious and moral status of the agricultural labourers. The resolution in favour of a reduction in working hours was successfully moved by John Hughes, but although the conference called for a twelve-hour day inclusive of three meals, a further motion in favour of a 4 p.m. Saturday stop had little support. Ap Ffarmwr then raised the trade union question, which was backed by John Hughes (who drew on his experience of a six-month strike when working as a coal-miner) and a member of the North Wales Quarrymen's Union. Another speaker, William Edwards, Hologwyn, favoured a union, particularly if it bonded both farmers and labourers. However it soon became clear that they were arguing against the grain of the conference. Most were anxious to avoid an open collision; it was felt that employers should first have an opportunity to meet their demand for a shorter day. A proposal deferring the decision on the formation of a trade union for six months thus found approval. The question of wages was not raised.

In tribute to their hero a reported crowd of several thousand escorted ap Ffarmwr through the streets of Llangefni. This triumphant expression of collective unity among a normally undemonstrative mass of workers was without its like in the whole of Wales. Informed opinion welcomed the spirit of co-operation rather than confrontation.[29] Ap Ffarmwr, on the other hand, regretted the decision to defer the establishment of a trade union because he saw the benefits it could have secured for workers.[30] Throughout his espousal of the farm labourers' cause he continued to press the ideal of a trade union, and it remained throughout as the centre-piece of his strategy. If the sixteen-man committee appointed at Llangefni to meet the farmers failed to extract a satisfactory concession, the men would have to reconsider their position. Their comrades in Llŷn, Caernarfonshire, had sent representatives to the Llangefni conference as observers; it was now up to the farm labourers of Anglesey to show the way.

Over in south Caernarfonshire the appearance of ap Ffarmwr's articles had excited great interest among the workers, many of whom had a similar connection with slate quarrymen. Letters from Llŷn and Eifionydd appeared in *Y Werin* and in no time meetings were arranged in the district of Dyffryn Madog to demand a shortening in the hours of labour.[31] During March and April further local meetings were held,[32] but there was apparently little co-ordination and no single leader of status emerged to give unity to the mass of labourers. With no obvious social gap separating the labourer from his master many a sympathetic farmer actually sided with his men and assisted in organizing meetings.[33] Knowledge that Anglesey workers were busy organizing a conference at Llangefni on Easter Monday led to a call for Llŷn labourers to convene at Pwllheli on the same day. Those at Eifionydd hoped to invite David Lloyd George and ap Ffarmwr to a gathering at Porthmadog,[34] but nothing came of either suggestion. That Lloyd George, then in the throes of the Caernarfonshire Boroughs by-election, should exchange mutual letters of support with ap Ffarmwr at this time indicates a common strain of radicalism.[35]

The agitation for shorter hours of labour also spread to neighbouring Merioneth. March 1890 saw a small brush fire of revolt break out in the village of Bryn-crug near Towyn. Here again, the direct inspiration was ap Ffarmwr and the events in Anglesey and Caernarfonshire, only this time a local union with some fifty members came into being.[36] Two open-air meetings, attended largely by young farm-hands, led to its formation and the appointment of officers. Demands were made for better sleeping accommodation, improved wages and a twelve-hour working day. Outside the fleetingly deceptive unity of crowded meetings the movement was demonstrably bereft of eloquent speakers and mature leaders to put their case to the farmers. All the same, a further meeting was planned for the eve of the May hiring fair at Towyn with the aim of arranging a conference with the employers. But as only a few labourers turned up on the day it had to be abandoned and the whole enterprise fell through without producing any results, leaving the union stillborn.[37] Compared with the outcome in Anglesey (widely reported in Merioneth papers) the isolated attempt by Bryn-crug labourers to combine together to negotiate improvements turned out to be a disastrously short-lived affair that caused ill-feeling and recrimination among the workers themselves. Otherwise, in the remainder of the county there was little animosity between farmers and labourers; wages had improved and farmers tended to show a genuine interest in the condition of their labourers.

As it happened, ap Ffarmwr's articles also drew a response in Denbighshire. Initial enthusiasm was expressed in the form of letters from the Vale of Clwyd, an area, like Anglesey, riven by the worst kind of class division. The farmers who danced so avidly to Thomas Gee's tunes constituted an almost 'semi-aristocratic' class that often treated its servants with unconcealed contempt.[38] To one of their number the agricultural labourers were the 'refuse of society'.[39] Still, the undercurrent of class hatred flowing in the Vale was not sufficiently strong to form a combination to challenge the employers, despite the yearning for better wages and shorter hours of work. Far removed from the direct influence of ap Ffarmwr and *Y Werin*, no one was prepared to come out into the open to initiate an organized protest.

Whereas Denbighshire farm labourers failed to convert aspiration into action, the agitation in Anglesey in the mean time had forced the farmers to respond favourably. At a special meeting in Llangefni they agreed to reduce the hours of labour to twelve.[40] Labourers were still expected to put in additional hours every hay and corn harvest and only two (instead of three) meals were allowed during working hours. Despite its shortcomings, the settlement was hailed as a major triumph by *Y Werin*.[41]

The flame of revolt still flickered in south Caernarfonshire with the labourers demanding a reduction in working hours plus an early Saturday stop. A series of further meetings at Clynnog, Llangybi, Llanaelhaearn and other places produced a local leadership that took heart from the example of Anglesey workers.[42] At a gathering of Eifionydd labourers in Cricieth one of the organizers read a letter of encouragement from Anglesey,[43] yet not once did Caernarfonshire men raise the possibility of establishing a trade union. By the day of the Pwllheli hiring fair in May a united front of several hundred workers resolved only to work from 6 a.m. to 7 p.m.[44] The farmers had little option but to fall in line. While it did not match the twelve-hour day won at Llangefni, south Caernarfonshire labourers were content to have scored their own modest victory spurred on by *Y Werin*. There was no grain of truth in the rumour that David Lloyd George had a hand in the movement.[45]

Ap Ffarmwr seemed well pleased with the outcome at Llangefni.[46] But only as the first step. Once labourers realized the potential power of the vote they could contest school board elections and even stand for the county council. Not all the workers, however, accepted the terms of settlement with the farmers.[47] Aberffraw emerged as the main hotbed of working-class dissent, with men determined to stand by the original decision reached at their conference. A Llangefni court heard how one labourer left his employment rather than risk the wrath of the farm workers at Aberffraw who threatened to throw him into the river if he dared work extra hours during harvest-time.[48] Ap Ffarmwr interpreted this growing opposition as a sign in favour of setting up a trade union.[49] Indeed, it was reported that he had disrupted a farmers' meeting at Brynsiencyn with a gang of some fifty labourers to deliver a tirade on the benefits of unionism.[50]

When the workers' committee, under its chairman John Hughes, met to consider their next step there was a strong determination to stand fast by the twelve-hour day and claim overtime for any extra harvest work.[51] A further indication of the remarkable confidence within their ranks was the declaration that Aberffraw labourers would enter candidates in the forthcoming school board election. Addressing a local meeting at Llannerch-y-medd, Richard Williams, an ordinary farm-hand, waxed boldly on the advantages of forming a trade union: it could provide sickness benefits, foster emigration, sponsor candidates on to the county council, even (he asserted prophetically) enable workers to return their own member of parliament.[52] In a further series of articles ap Ffarmwr, too, envisaged a trade union with precise social and political aims.[53] Attractions such as a retirement pension, savings scheme and financial assistance to emigrate were similar to those offered by agricultural labourers' unions in England. Once labourers utilized their voting strength at local and parliamentary elections they would be in a position to draw up a political programme under the direction of their union, thus forcing the Liberal Nonconformist establishment to take notice.

For all these reasons the men who attended the committee meeting on 13 June 1890 unanimously agreed that a trade union be formed.[54] Entitled the Anglesey Agricultural Labourers' Union, its declared aim was to secure basic rights for the farm workers and promote their interests generally. Members would pay an entrance fee of one shilling and a weekly contribution of one penny. Each locality was to have its own branch with elected officers and representatives on the general committee. William Thomas agreed to become treasurer and ap Ffarmwr indicated his willingness to serve as temporary secretary. In recognition of past support, it was hoped that Captain Owen

Thomas would become the first president. At long last, therefore, the basis for an independent trade union existed in name. But, as ap Ffarmwr recognized all too well, there could be little substance to the union if the labourers themselves failed to take advantage of this opportunity by setting up local branches.

It did not take long for the sad truth to dawn. Only three local meetings materialized. George Jones presided over an enthusiastic meeting at Llandrygarn; a branch was formed at Brynsiencyn with the Revd Owen Parry as its president, whilst at Carreg-lefn local officials were appointed and thirty-six members enrolled.[55] Otherwise, much to the dismay of ap Ffarmwr,[56] the farm labourers had retreated into their customary shell of indifference. Although the men at Llanfair-yng-Nghornwy and Llanfechell were belatedly stirred into action,[57] Brynsiencyn branch was soon struggling to survive.[58] A brooding, disconsolate ap Ffarmwr could find some comfort in the widespread publicity given to his movement. Under the title 'A Welsh Agricultural Labourers' Union', the *South Wales Daily News* gave prominence to the 'startling' innovation in Anglesey.[59] After his own unsuccessful efforts on behalf of the agricultural working class, Pan Jones in *Y Celt* could well rejoice in the 'valiant spirit' of Anglesey labourers.[60] Even the normally staid denominational periodicals indulged in some uneasy heart-searching. The Anglican *Y Llan* boasted that the Bishop of St Asaph had already called attention to the primitive social conditions endured by farm labourers.[61] *Y Goleuad*, the Methodist weekly, criticized the unchristian attitude of 'respectable' families who neglected their servants.[62] Whilst the religious bodies could not be expected to advocate radical remedies, ap Ffarmwr (never a great chapel-goer) found his faith restored elsewhere. A visit to the Trades Union Congress in September — where he could have heard Joseph Arch speak — and the realization that a general working-class resurgence was in the making, deepened his commitment.[63] Further ideological enlightenment came through a new-found acquaintance with Fabian literature; he confessed that he found *Fabian Essays in Socialism* particularly stimulating in this respect.[64]

On a more practical level there came the encouraging news of working-class intervention in the school board election in Aberffraw.[65] Often enough ap Ffarmwr had criticized a system which underpaid teachers, endured low standards and tolerated high levels of absenteeism. This effort to break the middle-class stranglehold on the school boards was a phenomenon unique not only in Anglesey, but also throughout the rest of Wales. Even the union-minded quarrymen of Caernarfonshire had not successfully challenged their social betters. Once the proud seat of the princes of Gwynedd, the village of Aberffraw had since decayed into an isolated rural backwater that formed part of the extensive fief of the Meyrick family of Bodorgan. Here, the feudal structure was neatly preserved: an all-powerful landowning family, a subservient farming tenantry who dominated village life, and a downtrodden labour force living hand to mouth. In making the school board election the focus of their discontent, the farm labourers created a wave of excitement in the village.

Five working-class candidates were nominated and a number of well-attended meetings were held in October, usually chaired by the Revd John Thomas, the local Methodist minister.[66] Such was the esteem for their mentor and adviser that ap Ffarmwr was carried shoulder-high through the streets of Aberffraw to the Prince Llewelyn Hotel after addressing a crowd of several hundred.[67] Though a similar accolade was accorded to the two labourers who won seats on the board, the overall result came as a bitter blow.[68] It turned out that almost two-thirds of the votes had been cast for the farmers and their allies; on the day of the contest many workers were unable to break the deferential habits of a lifetime.[69]

Again on the positive side, the current agitation had forced the Calvinistic Methodist hierarchy in Anglesey and Llŷn to take notice of the condition of farm labourers. Resolutions calling for the establishment of reading rooms for workers in connection with the chapels were passed.[70] But such gestures did nothing to hide the reluctance of local ministers to involve themselves in the class struggle of the farm labourers and apart from 'one or two honourable exceptions'[71] they turned their backs on this particular crusade. Greater care and compassion were being shown for the beneficiaries of Missionary Society largesse in Asia and Africa than in the starving rural inhabitants of Gwynedd. Ironically, the only Methodist minister actively to support ap Ffarmwr's movement on the island was the Revd John Thomas, Aberffraw, a former missionary to India. Perhaps his experience in that field had nurtured a real sympathy for the underdog. The leading Methodist minister of his day, the Revd James Donne, Llangefni, wished the movement every success,[72] but nothing more. Insofar as the farmer-deacons were the mainstay of the local chapel, important material considerations blinkered the attitude of the ministers to the point of moral failure. The deacons, typically, were the ones who held out longest against the concession on working hours.[73]

All this meant that ap Ffarmwr remained an outsider. Spurned by the interlocking leadership of Nonconformity and Liberalism he had to steer his own course in the face of all the anger and prejudice directed against him.[74] Unintimidated, and despite his mother's tearful plea,[75] he made a calculated bid to resuscitate the trade union movement in March 1891.[76] The previous year's agitation had achieved little because on the majority of farms the reduction in working hours was nullified by changes in mealtimes. This second attempt soon found a ready response in the correspondence columns of *Y Werin*.[77] Demands were put forward for better wages, improved sleeping accommodation and a 4 p.m. Saturday stop. Slowly the idea gained currency of holding a May Day rally at Llangefni, similar to those celebrated by the labour movement in English towns. At the same time a string of local meetings was held, giving familiar activists an opportunity to reassert their influence, in particular the leaders of what was termed the '23rd Regiment' (after the 23rd Royal Welch Fusiliers) at Aberffraw. But while the men seemed more united in favour of a trade union there was also evidence of counteraction. The blacksmith at Rhos-meirch dared not let the labourers meet at his smithy because of the attitude of the farmers.[78] At Pentraeth a crowd of about a hundred labourers was refused permission to use the local board school and had to make do with an open-air meeting.[79]

As in 1890, ap Ffarmwr was the pivotal figure in a movement characterized by its humble working-class character. Hardly a word of encouragement came from the Nonconformist denominations, the Anglesey Liberal Association or Captain Owen Thomas, their erstwhile champion. When pressed, Samuel Hughes, a leading public figure, welcomed the formation of a trade union restricted to promoting literacy, thrift and improved sleeping accommodation.[80] As long as political Liberalism remained in the control of a middle-class leadership that jealously guarded its own economic interests, there would always be limitations to any sectional movement that promoted the welfare of the workers. A Methodist farmer and Liberal county councillor like Samuel Hughes could hardly be expected to sanction an organized labour movement pursuing a programme of demands more commonly associated with the industrialized areas.

Delegates from the local meetings who came to Llangefni on 2 May once more displayed belief in themselves and their cause.[81] Moved by Richard Williams, the first proposal calling for the formation of a trade union was carried unanimously. Hugh Williams became president, William Thomas, treasurer, and, as ap Ffarmwr declined the post, R.H. Thomas, a Pentraeth tailor, was named secretary. A meeting of the executive committee on 4 June would see the union officially under way. The conference then proceeded to formulate a demand for a working day of twelve hours inclusive of three meals; the idea of a 4 p.m. Saturday stop failed to win sufficient support. Future headway depended on the labourers' response. Again, ap Ffarmwr's fears proved well justified in that just five local meetings were subsequently held. On this poor showing there was little prospect for the union. Pressure of work meant that ap Ffarmwr was unable to attend the meeting on 4 June.[82] Heavy rain on the day restricted attendance to less than half a dozen including the president, while the secretary remained confined to bed with a cold.[83] No further meeting was arranged. Weeks of effort and expectancy came to grief as a second union died in embryo.

Greater inertia seemed to afflict the labourers of Llŷn and Eifionydd. Every so often letters appeared in the press exhorting them to throw off their yoke and follow the example of Anglesey in seeking a trade union.[84] At one moment there seemed a chance that the gathering at Pwllheli May Fair would be repeated and used as a forum to wring further gains,[85] but it was not to be. Many labourers were even accepting a cut in wages.[86] Against this failure could be set the prospect of a successful awakening at Gwyddelwern, Merioneth.[87] Drawing strength from events in Anglesey, a meeting of sixty labourers in mid-April enthusiastically resolved to seek a twelve-hour day. But no definite steps could be taken until other labourers in Edeyrnion showed solidarity. Subsequent silence can only have meant a quick ending for this movement too.

Whatever the depth of discontent among agricultural workers, it was extremely difficult to direct into a coherent movement. The concept of trade unionism was completely foreign to all but a handful. Men were only interested in immediate gains like a reduction in hours; most seemed to have accepted that few farmers were able to afford any increase in wages. Though relations between employers and employed had deteriorated in other parts of Wales it was a case of conform or quit. Labourers in Monmouthshire inveighed against farmers who offered starvation wages or dismissal.[88] Here, long hours and ill-repaired cottages meant an 'absolutely joyless' existence for a typical worker. What appears to have precluded a revolt was the lack of social cohesion, the good wages paid to the employees of estates and large farms, and the alternative work available in the mining industry in the western end of the county. Over in the Vale of Glamorgan 'open hostility'[89] existed between masters and men but no attempt had been made to form a trade union because the flow of labour into the coal-mining valleys created a scarcity which enabled skilled workers to command relatively high wages. Moreover, most districts had seen a shortening of the working day. On the other hand, relations in Breconshire and Radnor, like Montgomeryshire,[90] were reported to be more cordial, although farm servants in some areas of Brecon appeared to be growing more restless and independent. A chronic shortage of labour in mid-Wales kept wages high and afforded the best protection against exploitation. If they still remained dissatisfied, migration to the southern coalfield provided a ready answer.

Only in one other locality did anyone come close to imitating the role of ap Ffarmwr. In south Pembrokeshire, an outside union, the National Labour Federation, became the vehicle for an organized rural labour movement that paralleled the tithe disturbances elsewhere in the county.[91] Socialist in inspiration, the National Labour Federation aimed to draw hitherto unorganized workers into one vast general union and from its home base on Tyneside it spread as far as Southampton and Milford Haven; even Oxfordshire farm labourers were recruited.[92] Once an enclave had been established in Pembrokeshire, the Federation rapidly extended its influence under the able and ambitious leadership of Robert Hazell,[93] the district secretary. With branches formed in Pembroke Dock and Hook Colliery, a colleague, C.S. Caird, pointed to the subsequent advance in the wages of both dockyard labourers and colliers as proof of the benefits of trade unionism.[94] Hazell's long-term aim was to open branches of the Federation in all parts of south Wales, uniting all classes of skilled and unskilled workers, including the agricultural labourers.

Operating in the traditionally English portion of Pembrokeshire presented no linguistic problems, so Hazell and Caird were able to appeal directly to the workers both at public meetings and in the press. Like ap Ffarmwr, Hazell emphasized not merely the industrial rewards of better wages and fewer hours, but also possible political gains like representation on the county council and school boards.[95] With learned eloquence redolent of ap Ffarmwr, he too emphasized the inherent value of trade unionism, in the same way that he deftly answered those detractors who marked him out as a 'paid agitator' stirring up class hatred.[96] As organizer, Hazell undertook a profoundly difficult and strenuous task which meant extensive travel, usually on foot, to out-of-the-way places to address a limited audience late in the evening, often with the hostility of farmers to contend with. Sometimes he would return home at 2 or 3 a.m., exhausted both mentally and physically. Moreover, the process had to be repeated three or four times before a single small branch was properly established.

Such, then, was the resolve with which Hazell addressed open-air gatherings of farm labourers at St Ishmael's, Marloes, Hodgeston, Saundersfoot and other places in south Pembrokeshire between May and July 1891.[97] After he had addressed a meeting of a hundred labourers at St Ishmael's, a strong branch was formed with the local postmaster as secretary.[98] A considerable number of farm workers, mechanics and fishermen were said to have joined the Marloes branch, whilst at Thorn, near St Twynnell's, the audience, though small, was enthusiastic.[99] With migration to the Glamorgan coalfield producing a serious dearth of labour, farm workers, stirred by the gospel of trade unionism, had their hand strengthened in any pay bargaining. And it was reported that Hazell also succeeded in getting men to pay union dues three months in advance of the Michaelmas hiring fair, so that they might have benefit from the union if they struck for more wages.[100] Consequently, when the workers demanded a rise of two shillings a week the farmers were forced to compromise by meeting their claim halfway: thus wages in some areas of south Pembrokeshire rose from twelve to thirteen shillings.[101] This small triumph occurred in comparative isolation and its example was not apparently taken up elsewhere. Hazell made no attempt to incite the labourers of Angle, for instance, because the men were much better paid. The ingrained habits of obedience and respect for authority still prevalent in south Pembrokeshire deprived workers of the stomach for a continuing fight. In many cases a hired labourer in regular employment was better off than a small farmer who paid a high rent. The union did not penetrate the more isolated Welsh-speaking part of north Pembrokeshire and, although Hazell became involved in other industrial disputes within the county later in the year,[102] nothing more was heard of him subsequently. A disastrous slide in the membership of the National Labour Federation in 1892 led to its eventual dissolution two years later.[103]

If nothing else, the outcome in south Pembrokeshire proved the efficacy of collective action, however brief. Not unconnected, perhaps, with the agitation was the appearance of a Mutual Improvement Society at St Ishmael's and the opening of a reading room for the working men of the neighbourhood.[104] Next door in Cardiganshire the long hours of labour had produced tensions, but disgruntled workers at this point seemed to lack leadership in defence of their interests. Recalling the example of the men of Cellan two years before, one writer believed that only a trade union could guarantee reform.[105]

With few exceptions, rural workers in Wales had failed to act as a group. Involvement was sporadic, gains were modest in character and confined to the area of agitation. Even in Anglesey, the centre of the revolt, there seemed to be a basic weakness in the men's attitude. It may be that links with the slate quarrymen primed their interest at the start, but in the event the agricultural workers displayed the same timidity that exasperated a Dinorwig Quarry trade unionist in February 1890 when he excoriated them for 'being too cowardly, not enough manhood in them to demand their rights'.[106] This lack of self-reliance destroyed the Anglesey Agricultural Labourers' Union in the same way as it had broken a string of local benefit societies.[107]

If there was little substantial achievement, at least their spirit had not been entirely extinguished. As D. Lleufer Thomas found, when making enquiries into the condition of the agricultural labourer for the Royal Commission on Labour in 1892,[108] the indoor servants, mainly single men, were becoming much more independent. In some parts of Wales he was able to hold successful public meetings for the labourers as a separate group. At St Ishmael's, the men had even arranged a preliminary meeting of their own to prepare evidence, although the trade union branch founded by Hazell no longer existed.[109] They accepted that farmers were unable to pay higher wages, but asked for shorter hours of labour, especially on Saturdays. In general, the agitation of 1890–1 had left a legacy of ill-feeling, and the unresolved question of poor food and unsatisfactory sleeping accommodation remained a continuing source of discontent even in areas untouched by the troubles.[110]

Positive steps were again taken in Anglesey in 1892. In June, Owen Hughes, a farm bailiff, published a letter on behalf of his fellow workers in the Llanfechell district urging attendance at a public meeting where Captain Owen Thomas would be invited to contest the parliamentary seat as candidate representing both the workers and farmers of the county.[111] It was not forgotten that Thomas Lewis, the sitting member — a colourless and old-fashioned Gladstonian Liberal — had ignored requests that he put in an appearance at Llangefni on Easter Monday, 1890. Over a hundred workers attended the meeting at Llanfechell.[112] Warm tribute was paid to Captain Owen Thomas's interest in the welfare of the agricultural labourers and his role in the reduction of their working hours. Upon receiving a delegation, Thomas asked for time to consider the matter. Subsequent reaction in *Y Werin*[113] and *Y Genedl Gymreig*[114] showed that his intervention would be most unwelcome inasmuch as it threatened to divide the Liberal Party and let in the Tories. Such opposition was enough to deter his candidature.

When it became known that D. Lleufer Thomas would be visiting the island on behalf of the Royal Commission on Labour, interest rose swiftly. An opportunity for ventilating and publicizing the workers' grievances could not be missed, and an appeal was made to Hugh Williams to present their case.[115] Meanwhile, Lleufer Thomas had received a personal letter from 'an Anglesey working man' which he regarded as testimony of the interest shown by ordinary labourers.[116] In it the writer complained of sleeping places unfit for pigs and vindictive employers who 'visited [them] with every form of revenge that they are capable of'.[117] Hugh Williams agreed to speak on behalf of the men and Captain Owen Thomas convened a preliminary meeting of labourers on the day of the Llanfechell hiring fair.[118] So that when Lleufer Thomas duly held five separate meetings to hear the evidence of the agricultural labourers they were not only present in large numbers but well represented by official delegates.

Throughout the year ap Ffarmwr had remained, in the context of the farm labourers, uncharacteristically silent. Apart from personal disappointment, his elevation to sub-editor allowed neither time nor opportunity to pursue the idea of a trade union. Even so, he made use of the press to advocate the nationalization of land with a couple of articles in *Y Geninen*.[119] The Welsh Land Bill introduced by T.E. Ellis in March 1892 did not, he declared, meet the needs of the nation at large. As always, the Land Question was seen from the narrow standpoint of the tenant farmer and it completely ignored the farm labourer. Ap Ffarmwr aimed to introduce the views of Henry George (whom he had heard speak in London),[120] A.R. Wallace, founder of the Land Nationalization Society, and the Fabian Society in the hope that they might inspire others to view the abolition of private ownership as the best answer to rural ills.[121] But in the mean time the pressure of work which had aged him perceptibly finally broke his health, and the illness which brought him to death's door incapacitated him for at least five months.[122]

Just at this time the Anglesey Farmers' Society, with Samuel Hughes as president and William Edwards as secretary, had been formed to seek rent reductions.[123] Rather than pursue sectional grievances, landlords and farm labourers were invited to a conference in January 1893 which led to the formation of the Anglesey Agricultural Union.[124] This time, two labourers (including Hugh Williams) had a place on the committee. A body which fostered the impression that the interests of all classes were conjoined was by definition self-limiting and there was a danger that the peculiar problems of the farm labourers would be conveniently subsumed. Be that as it may, Hugh Williams initiated a move in February to present ap Ffarmwr with a testimonial in appreciation of all he had done on behalf of the agricultural labourers.[125] Together with fellow officials of the erstwhile Anglesey Agricultural Labourers' Union, William Thomas and R.H. Thomas, he set about the organizational work. Scores of local meetings were held and collectors appointed to accept contributions.[126] Amidst the excitement the prospect of forming a trade union was raised again. The news that it had already become a topic for discussion at places like Aberffraw met with the eager approval of Hugh Williams and R.H. Thomas, who favoured a single union for the labourers. Both agreed it would be timely to launch a trade union on the day of the presentation; they knew it was bound to give greater satisfaction to ap Ffarmwr than the testimonial itself.

The mood of the farm labourers reflected a new surge of confidence and this was enough to reactivate the crusading passion of ap Ffarmwr.[127] He believed that Anglesey workers were now more mature. The conference preceding the presentation meeting on 11 May would be the ideal occasion to discuss the possibility of forming a trade union. In addition, he urged them to consider seeking representation on the new parish and district councils. Thus, for the third time the agricultural labourers were to assemble at Llangefni in their hundreds, with ap Ffarmwr at the centre of the proceedings.[128] The preliminary conference, chaired by Hugh Williams, heard how nine localities had declared in favour of a union. In a conciliatory gesture to the farmers it was decided not to press for a 4 p.m. Saturday half-holiday. At the public meeting which followed, the main dignitaries included Captain Owen Thomas, W.J. Parry, Revd John Williams and Ellis Jones Griffith — a letter of apology having been received from David Lloyd George. Before turning to the main business, a resolution proposing that the Anglesey Agricultural Labourers' Union be formed received unanimous support. Captain Owen Thomas, the first speaker to be called, seemed taken aback by the resolution and did not venture an opinion on the matter. As expected, W.J. Parry, the 'Quarrymen's Champion', voiced support though he recoiled from any strike action against the farmers. Next came the presentation of a gold watch and testimonial of £47.14*s*. to ap Ffarmwr.[129] The only other practical suggestion came from the Revd John Williams, who wished to see some form of workers' eisteddfod.

Taking the Llangefni meeting as a sign of awakened labour consciousness, ap Ffarmwr outlined a course the movement towards a trade union might take.[130] The first essential was the appointment of an organizer (journalistic commitments made it impossible for him to undertake the task). Following district meetings, R.H. Thomas, the acting secretary, would summon a conference at Llangefni where the constitution of the union would be drafted. Once again, the onus lay on the rank and file, and almost inevitably, the worst happened. With the solitary exception of Aberffraw[131] there was complete silence. Some localities had expected the committee which organized the testimonial meeting to take the lead.[132] In turning his attention to the workers' eisteddfod, ap Ffarmwr was admitting defeat.[133] After three attempts he had finally lost all hope of establishing an independent trade union for the farm labourers of Anglesey.

One other positive step taken at the Llangefni meeting was the appointment of spokesmen to give evidence before the Royal Commission on Land in Wales. Appointed by Gladstone in 1893 it gave the tenant farmers of Wales an opportunity to ventilate their grievances. Because of the separate inquiry undertaken by the Royal Commission on Labour it was not directly concerned with the condition of the agricultural workers. When the latter published its report, D. Lleufer Thomas listed a series of mainly voluntary social reforms that could be effected without recourse to legislative action.[134] Of these, improved sleeping accommodation supervised by the local Medical Officer of Health was the most important. This point was further emphasized by the Royal Commission on Land, which now employed Lleufer Thomas as its secretary. Being 'wholly dissatisfied' with the sanitary condition of many of the labourers' cottages, it called for urgent remedial action enforced by the local authorities.[135] Also in its findings the commission noted that, in the absence of official trade union bodies, the hiring fair was being used to secure higher wages at times of labour shortage.[136]

Of the 1,086 witnesses called before the Royal Commission on Land, only 21 were agricultural workers, 4 of whom had been selected at organized public meetings. Predictably, 3 came from Anglesey; the exception being David Jones, Llwyngwyn, who spoke for the workmen of Llanfairorllwyn, near Llandysul, Cardiganshire,[137] an area noted for its rural radicalism. As a cousin to the Revd Pan Jones, David Jones reflected many of his qualities. Already he had served as secretary of the local Fabian Society branch set up in March 1892,[138] and was a frequent advocate of workers' rights in the columns of *Cwrs y Byd*.[139] Antagonism towards the farmers surfaced prominently in the area between 1892 and 1894, and the labouring class in Llandysul were sufficiently confident to strike out independently, putting up contestants for both the county council and Board of Guardians.[140] There was even a call for Pan Jones to stand as a Labour candidate in his native county.[141]

Hugh Williams, John Hughes and Richard Rowlands were the three witnesses who represented Anglesey farm workers.[142] In their evidence to the Commission all four labourers' representatives called for the creation of smallholdings, better sleeping quarters and improved educational opportunities. In the haunting words of John Hughes, young children upon leaving school 'go to the farmers and they are put to sleep and live with the cattle, and they lose all that they have learnt in the school, and become of the same nature as beasts'.[143] Self-tuition had moulded John Hughes into a cultured and forceful member of his class. A nine-shilling-a-week farm labourer, he was conscious that his social position did not allow him to tread the parlour of his employer.[144] Such attitudes had accounted for much of the labour unrest in Aberffraw, providing men like him with the motivation for political action. How much social criticism actually coloured his winning essay on 'A Servant's Duties' in the Anglesey Workers' Eisteddfod remains unknown. As it turned out, the Eisteddfod, held on Ascension Thursday 1894, was to be the first and last of its kind.[145] Despite ap Ffarmwr's efforts as organizing secretary, and the backing of the Revd John Williams and John Morris-Jones, it did not have the whole-hearted support of the labourers themselves or for that matter the religious leaders of the county, even though the interests of the farmers were not endangered in any way. Still, it gave an opportunity for other self-educated workers to shine. Among the prize-winners were George Jones ('ap Dafydd'), Thomas Rowlands and Daniel Rowlands — all future activists in the next farm workers' movement.

The Workers' Eisteddfod was to be ap Ffarmwr's final contact with the farm labourers of Anglesey. As fate would have it, even this unpretentious venture had proved a failure. But as he knew from bitter experience it was no easy task to engage the interests of the rural workers in a new undertaking. This final observation by ap Ffarmwr in *Y Werin* in May 1894 epitomized the frustrations of his ill-fated personal efforts over the previous years.[146] Within a few months he became editor of the *Merthyr Times*, moving to Nottingham three years later where he died in March 1899. His final journey brought him back to Anglesey to be buried at Dwyran.

The rapid decline of 'new unionism' in the industrial areas in 1892–3 had meant a serious setback for the unskilled workers. At the same time it became clear that agricultural labourers' trade unionism was also on the wane in England. Membership of Joseph Arch's National Agricultural Labourers' Union had slumped badly and the union was dissolved in 1896. The same fate befell George Edwards's Norfolk and Norwich Amalgamated Labour League, the Kent and Sussex Labourers' Union and a number of small county associations. Rural trade unionism had reached its lowest point since the 'Revolt of the Field' in 1872.[147] The first labourers' revolt in Wales was confined mainly to the years 1890–1, and its ephemerality was borne out by its sudden demise. The reservoir of discontent that existed in many parts of the country had only been successfully canalized in Anglesey, south Caernarfonshire and south Pembrokeshire to enable workers to win any gains. Once improvements were secured, both the indigenous and imported form of trade unionism collapsed. No point emerged more strongly before the Royal Commission on Land than the 'inequitable' nature of the farmer-labourer relationship; so much so that D. Lleufer Thomas made it known that he believed the men should have the power of bargaining with their employers.[148] But, trapped in poverty and isolation, the vast majority were obliged to accept their lot with meek resignation. Collective action was a completely new experience for the intractably backward farm labourer and in this sense ap Ffarmwr, like Pan Jones, suffered the difficulties of promulgating new ideas.

A young man of rare character, ap Ffarmwr became almost a legend during his own short lifetime. Yet, he did not possess a dominating personality, he was no orator, neither could he be described as a profoundly religious man (indeed, as 'A Scribe' he savaged the Welsh pulpit).[149] Ap Ffarmwr's genius flowed through his pen. And in many ways his 'passion for humanity'[150] and style of attack reflected the Carlyle and Ruskin school of capitalist critique. He certainly shared Carlyle's enthusiasm for the role of the 'hero' as much as Ruskin's hatred of social injustice and exploitation. But in the changing times he soon leaned towards a socialist remedy. Unlike Lloyd George, who had flirted with Pan Jones's Land Nationalization Movement in the mid-1880s before parliamentary ambitions got the better of him, ap Ffarmwr seemed uninhibited by political considerations. He stuck to his progressive principles regardless of the cost, and those principles embodied an increasingly ideological commitment to socialism. Contrary to previous opinion,[151] there is every indication that ap Ffarmwr was one of the earliest socialist pioneers in Gwynedd. These were, it should be remembered, the formative years of the labour movement, the founding conference of the Independent Labour Party having been held in January 1893. Perhaps journalistic curiosity first brought him to the Trades Union Congress and Fabian tracts, but in a highly personal way he endeavoured to acquaint a hidebound, parochial rural society with a taste of the ferment that the parallel rise of 'new unionism' and political socialism engendered in the early 1890s. This intellectual attraction to new ideas was more than matched by a growing disillusionment with the self-righteous hypocrisy underlying middle-class Nonconformist Liberalism. Time and again ap Ffarmwr advocated working-class representation on public bodies ranging from the school boards to the county councils because they held the key to social improvement. Unlike Joseph Arch or George Edwards he never envisaged a trade union as an instrument for drawing the newly-enfranchised labourers' vote into the Liberal Party. Ap Ffarmwr remained an outsider who presented a class challenge to the existing political order. Again in contrast with Arch,[152] his advocacy of land nationalization marked an unambiguous progression towards political socialism although he would not go as far as Henry George in seeking nationalization without compensation. He looked forward to the day when a political party would finally restore the land to the people.[153] Thus ap Ffarmwr had more in common with the Revd Pan Jones than is realized, even though he did not acknowledge his writings;[154] neither apparently did he seek membership of the Fabian Society or ILP.

Ap Ffarmwr's call to the agricultural labourers of Gwynedd to form their own trade union had brought a revolutionary dimension to Welsh rural life. Yet, for all his efforts he failed with the first step. He championed a class least expected to respond and concentrated on a county totally devoid of any tradition of organized labour. In Anglesey not even the dockers, railwaymen or quarrymen had been unionized. In such unpromising circumstances it was hardly likely that any industrial or political aim would be realized.

But his work had not been entirely in vain. As a socialist pioneer he provided the vision that would inspire others. For the very first time the hopes of the farm labourer were openly articulated in the press, strengthening his sense of separate identity and creating a spirit of uncharacteristic self-assertiveness. The yoke of deference in rural Wales was beginning to break. Particularly in Anglesey the desire for independent labour representation at parliamentary and local level found immediate expression, unparalleled in any other rural county. Upon the resignation of Thomas Lewis MP another bid was made in 1894 to field Captain Owen Thomas as parliamentary candidate in the name of the agricultural workers.[155] At the first parish council elections in the same year there were calls for workers to contest seats at Aberffraw and Llangaffo, and Edward Pritchard ('Iorwerth') was named as a workers' candidate at Gwalchmai.[156] In a fight with the farmers the labourers only narrowly lost control at Llanfachreth; at Gaerwen no less than eight 'labour' candidates proved successful.[157] At the county council elections in 1895 John Hughes stood in 'labour' colours at Aberffraw but received only a derisory vote.[158] Again, three years later, labourers put up an abortive challenge at Aberffraw whilst at Gaerwen a workers' committee supported the candidature of an enlightened merchant-farmer.[159] In the same year a workers' candidate won a seat on the Gaerwen school board;[160] however a similar attempt by three 'labour' men (including David Lloyd) at Aberffraw in 1899 ended in failure.[161]

If nothing else, ap Ffarmwr had inspired a psychological emancipation. He brought about a recognizable change in the attitude of many farm labourers by encouraging a working-class awareness. This was his principal legacy. The name of ap Ffarmwr became synonymous with their struggle and the movement to organize rural trade unionism. In later years he often acquired the idealistic reputation of a peasant hero. His name certainly stirred strong emotions in those individual activists who defiantly espoused his ideals and who ultimately fulfilled his hopes with the establishment of Undeb Gweithwyr Môn in 1909. Equally significant, David Thomas, the leading figure in the socialist movement in early twentieth-century Gwynedd who similarly pledged himself to organize the farm labourers, also found inspiration in ap Ffarmwr's unique crusade and his strongly influential writings in *Y Werin*.[162]

CHAPTER III

THE RISE OF THE LABOUR MOVEMENT IN RURAL WALES, 1900–1917, AND THE IMPACT OF WAR

THE emergence of the labour movement as a political power in Wales during the early years of the twentieth century was a gradual, uneven process until the Great War provided the vital catalyst. Deeply-rooted religious loyalties took precedence over class feelings and marked out party boundaries in a climate which pioneer socialists found severely disabling. Even the invigorating challenge of the Independent Labour Party failed in its expectations. Some 100 branches were claimed in south Wales by 1912,[1] with a mere 14 in the north;[2] an attempt to form a Welsh division of the ILP the previous year came to nothing. At the general elections of 1910 Labour MPs captured only 5 of the 36 seats and it was not until 1922 that the Labour Party finally succeeded in changing the complexion of Welsh parliamentary representation. To a large measure this underlined the durability of the Liberal ascendancy which dated back to 1868. Buttressed by an able leadership thoroughly committed to a rhetoric of Nonconformist ideals, the Liberal Party could well claim to be the repository of Welsh national aspirations in that it concentrated on the issues of disestablishment, home rule and land reform.[3] Implicitly and often specifically middle-class in its ethos, Liberalism nevertheless drew overwhelming support from all sections of the population. As a result, the Welsh working class were subsumed in a party that relegated industrial and labour issues to a low position in its political programme. The appeal of the Labour Party as a radical alternative could only make headway in a society in which Liberal ideals appeared increasingly outmoded. And as the success of the socialist ideology was closely wedded to the progress of trade unionism, the intrinsic differences between the industrial and rural parts of Wales became more clearly defined.

At least up to 1914 the working-class struggle centred on the trade unions. As it happened, the two principal sectional unions, the North Wales Quarrymen's Union (NWQU) and the South Wales Miners' Federation (SWMF), epitomized, in microcosm, the ideological conflict between orthodox Liberalism and emergent socialism. Based in a largely Welsh-speaking Nonconformist community the NWQU was resolutely opposed to the idea of affiliation to the Labour Party.[4] In the same way it was some time before the old Liberal guard came under challenge from a younger generation of militant political socialists in the mining valleys.[5] Fresh hope for the labour movement came with the recovery of those general unions which catered for the unskilled workers. Once more, it was on the waterfront and in the industrialized towns that the initial push took place, stimulated by a series of labour disputes between 1911 and 1914. The south Wales region soon became a stronghold of the Dock, Wharf, Riverside and General Labourers' Union with 13,000 members by 1911.[6] Another unskilled union to figure prominently in the area was the National Union of Gasworkers and General Labourers. Though the Workers' Union (founded 1898) arrived late in the day it too established itself in the industrial belt. Within eight years of Matt Giles being appointed full-time organizer in 1906, membership had shot up from 100 to 12,000.[7] Though farm labourers were among the first to be recruited, the Workers' Union concentrated mainly on the semi-skilled and unskilled industrial workers so that a separate agricultural section did not emerge as a viable proposition until after 1912.[8] When Evan James assumed organizational charge of a district stretching from Dowlais to Pembroke Dock in 1916 his knowledge of Welsh was considered to be invaluable in the drive to win support in the more rural areas.[9]

Progress in north Wales, as expected, was extremely slow by comparison and confined at first to the industrialized north-east alongside the North Wales Miners' Association (NWMA). Early toeholds by the Gasworkers' Union had scarcely expanded as just six branches were listed in 1913. The Dockers' Union, with fourteen branches in Flintshire by 1914,[10] had attempted a recruiting drive in the previous year in Gwynedd, spearheaded by Tom Robinson, but only two branches materialized, those at the ports of Holyhead and Porthmadog. The Workers' Union hardly fared better. A handful of branches in the Flint-Wrexham area yielded a total membership of some 450 in 1914.[11]

By virtue of geography, organization and industrial experience, the Amalgamated Society of Railway Servants (ASRS) was uniquely placed to bridge the gulf between town and countryside. Long established in south Wales, it had a chain of branches stretching from the Severn Tunnel across the main industrial belt to Neyland and Goodwick in Pembrokeshire.[12] Following the appointment of A.J. Williams as organizing secretary of the south Wales district, the newly-formed National Union of Railwaymen (NUR) had 82 branches and over 17,000 members in 1914.[13] Along the north Wales coast its influence was similarly extended from Wrexham to Llandudno Junction and Holyhead, with John Phipps of Ormskirk prominent as district organizer. Branches at Bala and Blaenau Ffestiniog marked its incursion into Merioneth; by 1914 a remarkable awakening amongst the railwaymen was reported with 3,000 swelling the ranks of the NUR in north Wales.[14] Early progress in mid-Wales saw similar results: the Machynlleth branch, in particular, grew substantially when John Blayney became secretary in 1911.[15] As the harbingers of trade unionism in the darker corners of rural Wales, the railwaymen were often the solitary contacts for organized labour.

As a further demonstration of increased labour unity the banding together of trade union branches into trades councils proceeded at a swift pace between 1900 and 1914. By 1914 at least 33 new councils came into existence, 23 of which were in Glamorgan and Monmouth.[16] As promoters of working-class interests trades councils played a significant local role, giving activist elements within the trade union movement an influential forum through which they could exert a collectivist voice on matters beyond their immediate workplace. Greater involvement in economic and social questions led ultimately to an organized bid for independent labour representation in local government. Another essential function which trades councils sought to undertake was the promotion of unionism amid the unskilled workers. Among the new councils founded outside south-east Wales during the pre-war period were Llanelli (1900), Wrexham (1902), Bangor (1912), Pembroke Dock (1912), North Cardiganshire (1912), Caernarfonshire (1912), Holyhead (1913) and Colwyn Bay (1914).

Drawing heavily on the personnel and organization of the trade unions and trades councils the Labour Party prepared to garner the working-class vote in the industrial areas. But progress was slow. Traditional attitudes and an enduring loyalty to Liberalism proved to be the major obstacles.[17] Despite a legacy of industrial militancy not a single local Labour representative was returned at Cardiff prior to 1914[18] and no Labour parliamentary candidate was fielded. In both general elections of 1910 the Labour Party only contested constituencies within the counties of Glamorgan, Monmouth and Carmarthen. But if the industrial turmoil and economic goals of the working class were not yet translated into a positive vote for socialism, the trade union power base became increasingly secure. Claiming an overall membership of 250,600 in south Wales by November 1914,[19] the trade unions possessed a formidable potential for both the labour movement and Labour Party which would be fully realized when society began to experience the impact of total war.

Developing working-class consciousness in the industrial areas, and its tempestuous corollary of protest and strikes, remained a world away from the apparent calm of the Welsh countryside. Farmers, fearful of any disruption to the pattern of agricultural life, and labourers, cocooned in isolation and ignorance, together maintained the traditional rural equilibrium. Any sign of discontent could be quickly contained: a recalcitrant farm labourer was easily dismissed. However unjust or unbearable the conditions, the 'tyranny of the countryside'[20] remained unchecked. As yet untouched by the general unions there seemed little chance that their grievances might be solved by united action. Rare indeed was the stand taken by the farm servants at Trapp, near Llandeilo, in 1912, when they threatened to down tools if their demand for shorter hours and better conditions was not granted.[21] In general, resentments and tensions were well hidden with few signs of open defiance.

But at the turn of the century a renewed sense of solidarity among the agricultural labourers in south-east England signalled a change that eventually transformed even the seemingly passive Welsh rural worker. After a lull of ten years, George Edwards successfully revived rural trade unionism in Norfolk in 1906 with the foundation of the Eastern Counties' Agricultural Labourers' and Smallholders' Union.[22] Though a strike at St Faiths, Norfolk, during 1910–11 ended in failure, the union leadership passed into the hands of dedicated socialists. This, along with affiliation to the TUC and the appointment of W.R. Smith as president, drew the union closer into the mainstream of the organized labour movement.[23] Changing its name to the National Agricultural Labourers' and Rural Workers' Union (NALRWU) in 1912, it registered as an Approved Society under the National Insurance Act and took on R.B. Walker as assistant secretary to cater for the influx of members. Whilst maintaining its headquarters at Fakenham, Norfolk, union organizers had already embarked on a number of recruiting campaigns even as far afield as Lancashire. As the union reached the threshold of rapid expansion a grant of £500 from the TUC in 1913 enabled it to employ two new full-time organizers. By the end of the year NALRWU claimed over 230 branches and a membership of almost 12,000 spread throughout 26 counties,[24] thus giving every indication of living up to its ambitious title.

With a national union taking shape in England, the only parallel in Wales could be found, once again, among the agricultural labourers of Anglesey. The starting point this time was the suggestion in October 1900 that workers should subscribe to a monument for ap Ffarmwr.[25] Due largely to the efforts of George Jones ('ap Dafydd') sufficient funds were raised to erect a monument on the grave at Dwyran. At the ceremony in 1902 ap Dafydd, as a representative of the working class, unveiled the marble bust of the man he likened to Moses, Wilberforce and Joseph Arch.[26] Amidst the emotional rhetoric of the occasion came an appeal for a further meeting of labourers so that they might consider the idea of a trade union.[27] The following year saw the publication of *Y Wyntyll*, as official organ of the Anglesey Liberal Association, and soon a stream of letters took up the theme of trade unionism.[28] Nothing more was heard until the aftermath of the 1906 general election. Thomas Rowlands, chairman of the Gwalchmai Liberal Society, criticized the negative attitude of the county council towards the working class, in particular its failure to implement the Small Holdings Act of 1892.[29] Then, in an unflinching editorial, Hugh Pritchard, editor of *Y Wyntyll* and secretary of the Anglesey Liberal Association, stressed how the miserable condition of the agricultural labourer had remained unaffected by the recent growth of the labour movement.[30] His words redolent of ap Ffarmwr, Pritchard claimed that their salvation lay in the formation of a trade union which would attract all the labourers of north Wales. Moreover, his sentiments evoked a similar response. Over the next few weeks *Y Wyntyll*, like *Y Werin* in the early nineties, opened its columns so that farm workers and their sympathizers could discuss what form the union should take. Leading the debate were Thomas Rowlands ('Gweithiwr o Fôn'), George Jones ('ap Dafydd') and Edward Pritchard ('Iorwerth'), three men who provided the initial leadership that gave Anglesey such a unique continuity in the organization of farm workers.

What they envisaged was a local union restricted to Anglesey workers, of whom the 3,200-strong agricultural labour force formed the largest group. As a veteran of the first campaign, George Jones hoped to see ap Ffarmwr's industrial programme realized in full: that is, a twelve-hour day inclusive of three meals, a 4 p.m. Saturday stop and improved wage levels.[31] The failure of ap Ffarmwr's campaign had convincingly demonstrated the need for middle-class support and this necessarily meant the backing of the Liberal Party as happened in the formation of both the miners' and the quarrymen's unions.[32] By September 1907 Thomas Rowlands reported that the movement was under way, but almost a year passed before the proposed aims and rules of Undeb Gweithwyr Môn were published.[33] Though George Jones looked to the 'respectable gentlemen' for guidance,[34] Edward Pritchard, on the other hand, favoured not only a genuine workers' union but also the formation of a local Labour Party in Anglesey.[35]

At a conference in Llangefni on 20 March 1909 Undeb Gweithwyr Môn was formally launched.[36] The presence of Ellis W. Roberts, Hugh Pritchard and Cyril O. Jones, who had succeeded Pritchard as secretary of the Anglesey Liberal Association, underlined its dependence on a middle-class leadership. William Edwards, another veteran of the ap Ffarmwr era and a prominent Liberal, became chairman, with Thomas Rowlands as secretary and Hugh Pritchard as treasurer. Though R.T. Jones, secretary of the NWQU, spoke from a labour standpoint, only in a small minority had similar ideas taken root. Tradition ascribes founder membership of the ILP in Anglesey to Lewis Thomas, a Llangristiolus postman.[37] Although the possibility of forming an ILP branch was raised, it was prudently acknowledged that the proposed union would have little chance of success unless the labourers made common cause with members of the Liberal Association eager to champion the working class. Those who harboured incipient socialist feelings, however, were convinced of the dangers inherent in this kind of class alliance.[38] Advocating 'Anglesey for Socialism' a writer in the *Labour Leader* ascribed the deplorable condition of the common people of the island to 'serfdom' imposed by their masters.[39] They had been ignored by their Liberal MP, and the only political diet orthodox Liberalism had to offer was the 'dry bones of disestablishment'. When refuting these charges, Hugh Pritchard enquired whether an agricultural labourers' union existed elsewhere.[40] Although he was informed of George Edwards' union, no further steps were apparently taken; however the debate aroused the interest of a small band of socialist pioneers eager to propagate the gospel of the ILP. As a result of the publicity in the *Labour Leader* David Thomas and William Williams, two eminent ILP scouts from Caernarfonshire, addressed the first socialist public meeting in Anglesey at Llangefni on 25 September 1909.[41]

Appropriately, the campaign to establish local branches of Undeb Gweithwyr Môn began at Aberffraw, with John Hughes as chairman of both the public meeting and the branch that was subsequently formed.[42] Gwalchmai became the second branch.[43] Despite the efforts of William Edwards, Thomas Rowlands, Edward Pritchard and George Jones the workers were slow to respond and only six branches had been set up by January 1910.[44] Further activities were postponed over the period of the general election so that officials could devote their energies to the return of Ellis Jones Griffith. Next came the crucial decision to register Undeb Gweithwyr Môn under the Trade Union Acts of 1871 and 1876, and the day of registration, 17 August 1911, came to mark the official beginning of the union. As its main objectives, Undeb Gweithwyr Môn set out to improve the social conditions of the membership and help those out of work during disputes, strikes, lock-outs and ill health.[45] The government of the union lay in the hands of a general council constituted of branch delegates and an executive committee of nine. Membership was open to a range of workers who paid an entrance fee of one shilling and weekly contributions of one penny, the union fund to be earmarked for trade union purposes; all the officials undertook their duties voluntarily.

From the outset the viability of such a small localized union was questioned. Then came the debate over its future course: should Undeb Gweithwyr Môn become a friendly society or an organization dedicated to winning better industrial conditions?[46] With the introduction of the National Insurance Act of 1911 some officials foresaw the long-term advantages that would accrue from its registration as an Approved Society.[47] Led by Hugh Pritchard and Cyril O. Jones, a campaign was mounted to sell the benefits of insurance. Some forty meetings[48] were held and new members, including women, were enrolled in the face of intense competition from established insurance companies and others in the field. This gave the union an immediate lease of life and on 17 August 1912 the Undeb Gweithwyr Môn Approved Society was registered. New members flooded in and it soon became necessary to appoint a paid full-time secretary. By the time J. Fred Jones began work at the end of the year the insurance section of the union had 900 members.[49] Not everyone welcomed the direction the union was taking. With so many prominent Liberals in administrative control, Undeb Gweithwyr Môn appeared to have become the handmaiden of the Liberal Party.[50] As a reaction to this trend, Edward Pritchard announced his conversion to Labour, and appealed to his fellow workers to press for a reduction in working hours on the lines of ap Ffarmwr's campaign.[51] However, he was unwilling to support the move for a possible affiliation to the increasingly powerful NALRWU because their fees were much too high to suit the paltry wages of Anglesey labourers.[52] Like George Jones he put his faith in the ability of Undeb Gweithwyr Môn to utilize its newly-found strength to tackle industrial grievances.[53] This became possible when the fissure within Undeb Gweithwyr Môn was given official recognition in the form of a new constitution that created two completely separate sections, labour and insurance.[54] Edward Pritchard and Thomas Rowlands threw their weight directly behind the struggling labour section. Though unconnected with any particular party, come the day it declared its political allegiance then, according to Edward Pritchard, it would be on the side of Labour.[55]

In May 1913 at the first annual meeting of Undeb Gweithwyr Môn held under the new regime, it was recognized that the National Insurance Act had marked a decisive turning-point in the fortunes of the union.[56] From a weak, struggling body it grew in a few months to be over a thousand strong. The insurance section, with its separate fund, now boasted 922 members (777 men and 145 women). In its shadow, but keeping alive the tradition of ap Ffarmwr, was the minority labour section with its 97 members.[57] For Thomas Rowlands the extraordinary success of the insurance side threatened to undermine the objectives which gave birth to the union. So when the future of the labour section came under discussion its original aim of improving the working conditions of the agricultural labourers was strongly emphasized. Lewis Thomas then moved that they should claim higher wages, a reduction in hours, a 4 p.m. Saturday stop, and that a committeee be appointed to parley with the employers on the day of the hiring fair. Cyril O. Jones opposed such moves. Echoing the Liberal line he felt that Lloyd George was right in concentrating on the Land Question as a whole; only after setting up land courts empowered to fix fair rents for farmers would it be possible to introduce a minimum wage for agricultural labourers. And it was this argument which won the day. With a moderate Liberal element in firm control of the overall leadership the manifestly weak status of the labour section gave it little hope of fulfilling its industrial aims independently. Consequently, during the following year attempts were made to bring it into contact not only with NALRWU once more, but also with the Dockers' Union. More significantly, it received the renewed attention of the man destined to mould the structure of the labour and trade union movement in north Wales at the beginning of the century: David Thomas.

Raised in Llanfechain, Montgomeryshire, the son of a stonemason and smallholder, David Thomas came from the heartland of rural Wales. After various teaching posts, including one outside London, he moved to become a schoolteacher in the slate-quarrying district of Tal-y-sarn, Caernarfonshire, in 1905. A lust for knowledge had already led him to the writings of Robert Blatchford, and it was *Merrie England* and the *Clarion* which first kindled his conversion to socialism.[58] It lit a burning passion for social reform. Socialism became the ideal that guided his life and on which he trained his mind and energy. Following the success of the Labour Party in the 1906 election he joined both the Fabian Society and ILP and so began a period of extraordinary pioneering work in Gwynedd, when all his spare time became devoted to conducting political work on behalf of the labour movement. There were very few men in whom vision, energy and organizing ability were united to such a unique degree as in the personality of David Thomas, Tal-y-sarn.

Embarking on the propagandist mission that earned him the title 'Honorary Organizer for north Wales',[59] David Thomas arranged the first socialist meetings in both Caernarfonshire and Anglesey in the years 1908–9. During the following years he addressed scores of meetings and helped to set up branches of the Fabian Society and ILP. In this way he secured the acquaintance and friendship of a wide circle of like-minded individuals, each of whom was to play a key role within his own locality. A handbook of ILP supporters he kept over the years 1910–13 reads almost like a future Labour 'Who's Who'.[60] Among the names to become well known were those of William Williams, R.G. Roberts, J.E. Thomas, John Foulkes ('Eithinfab'), John Blayney and E.J. Williams, not to mention Lewis Thomas, Edward Pritchard and David Lloyd of Undeb Gweithwyr Môn.

Indeed, it would be no exaggeration to say that David Thomas became the hub around whom all labour activity in north Wales revolved. Although rightly acknowledged as the 'wizard of the north'[61] he also built up over the years a close contact with many of the south Wales labour leaders, aiming at uniting the movement on a national basis.

Whilst teaching in England he had become acutely aware of the social condition of the working class, and upon returning to Wales he produced a masterly exposition of socialism in the Welsh language which was published in 1910 under the title *Y Werin a'i Theyrnas*. As a statement of faith the book received a warm welcome from those of a similar persuasion. The Revd Pan Jones, by now the forgotten visionary of a previous generation, greeted the emergence of a new prophet in Wales.[62] It also brought him in touch with the Revd T.E. Nicholas ('Niclas y Glais') and both men were prominent at the ILP conference at Carmarthen in 1911 when an ill-fated attempt was made to form a Welsh Independent Labour Party.[63] Although his interest lay primarily in the political side of the labour movement, David Thomas recognized from the outset that the trade unions would constitute its main backbone. As early as 1909 he became active in this sphere and by 1912–13 he was vigorously supporting the Dockers' Union, the NUR and the Workers' Union in their recruiting drives.[64] But there was one class of workers in which he showed a special interest — the agricultural labourers.[65] Childhood memories of rural life and a subsequent knowledge of ap Ffarmwr's campaign made David Thomas an equally undying champion of the farm worker. Interest in this and land nationalization first surfaced in 1906 when he competed in the Corwen Eisteddfod on the topic of 'the best manner of elevating life in the country districts'.[66] Then, when he began formulating his aims for the ILP he listed the return of a Labour MP for one of the Caernarfonshire seats and an intention to 'awaken the agricultural districts'.[67] Though he admitted that this would be a 'very great task' it was one he never lost sight of. At the Carmarthen conference in 1911 delegates attached great importance to the best methods of disseminating propaganda in the rural areas.

It proved a propitious moment. Once the National Insurance Act of 1911 came into operation the rural labourer received greater attention. Among the Approved Societies empowered to administer the compulsory state scheme were insurance companies, friendly societies and trade unions, each body competing for members. The financial contribution which both employers and employees had to pay certainly embittered local pay bargaining at the hiring fairs.[68] At Caernarfon, Pwllheli and Harlech the farmers offered lower rates for the same reason that servants demanded higher wages. Following the example of the Scottish Rural Workers' Society, the same humanitarian and paternalistic design spurred the Glamorgan Chamber of Agriculture to set up the Welsh Rural Workers' Friendly Society in July 1912.[69] Though it aspired to become a national body[70] nothing is known of its strength.[71] All the evidence points to considerable difficulties. Even at an early stage, Illtyd Thomas, the secretary, complained that the element of competition was frustrating his efforts.[72] Smaller societies were able to corner the local market. For instance, the Lleyn Insurance Approved Society, founded about the same time, catered for the farm servants of south Caernarfonshire.[73] While each society was free from any political or industrial motive, recognition of their special interest can only have made farm workers more aware of themselves as a separate group.

Far greater interest in the agricultural labourer attended the evidence of the Land Enquiry Committee in 1913. Always the tactical politician, Lloyd George had deliberately revived the Land Question so as to give a sharper edge to the government's social programme.[74] Under the auspices of the Liberal Party the Committee undertook a comprehensive investigation of the rural areas and the evidence collated by the Welsh Sub-committee offered a grim insight into the life of the farm labourer.[75] Upon publication of the report, Lloyd George inaugurated a great campaign for land reform complemented by a call for a labourers' charter and the enactment of a statutory minimum wage. Immediate legislation seemed the only answer in the absence of a powerful trade union. Indeed, the Welsh Sub-committee reported that no such body existed in Wales, neither did it hold any prospect of combination in the future.[76] As it happened, other political priorities were to rule out the possibility of legislation. Yet, the Land Enquiry Committee, like other events in 1913, aroused further public interest in the state of the agricultural labourers.

With the launching of *Y Dinesydd Cymreig* in 1912, the labour and trade union movement in Gwynedd had acquired an effective mouthpiece through which David Thomas could publicize their cause. Lloyd George's advocacy of a minimum wage for agricultural workers, the TUC grant to NALRWU and a series of articles describing agricultural working conditions appeared in its first year, along with a call to Welsh labourers to join the union.[77] By the same token, Undeb Gweithwyr Môn was evoked as an example to neighbouring counties.[78] When the ILP held its annual conference at Merthyr in May, David Thomas was present to hear William Holmes of NALRWU deliver an address which received full coverage in the paper.[79] Again, in 1913, *Y Dinesydd Cymreig* printed an article by George Edwards,[80] details of a successful farm workers' strike in Lancashire,[81] and a full account of the two NALRWU branches opened in Denbighshire. All this was not without effect. An article on the labourers in September 1913 prompted Morris Nanney Jones, secretary of the Lleyn Insurance Approved Society, to canvass David Thomas with the suggestion that the 750 members of the society were sufficiently mature to form their own trade union if only they had someone to help them at the start.[82]

In the meantime, David Thomas's organizational flair had found expression with the formation of the Caernarfonshire Labour Council.[83] Its aim was to unite the various classes of workers in the county so as to consolidate the political potential of organized labour. Efforts were focused on unionizing those unskilled workers in agriculture and building and, due no doubt to the influence of David Thomas, the secretary, priority was accorded to farm labourers.[84] In May 1913 he was authorized to write for a copy of the rules of NALRWU.[85] No reply came from George Edwards, but by August he had established contact with R.B. Walker.[86] As it transpired, the awakening among English rural workers, now surpassing the peak of the Joseph Arch period, proved so overwhelming that the NALRWU head office in Norfolk could hardly cope. Requests such as an appeal for the union to extend its activity into Flintshire in the summer of 1912 had to be turned down.[87] But once the union took root in north Wales, Walker promised that an organizer would be sent. Moves were afoot to set up a branch in the Wrexham district, and it was felt that Anglesey farm workers should also throw in their lot with his union.

The Wrexham branch provided a perfect example of the kind of aid a strong trades council could give to workers outside the mainstream of organized labour. It appears that when Walker addressed the Wrexham branch of the ILP in February 1913 a plea was made for assistance in the unionization of agricultural workers.[88] Present at the meeting were Tom Pughe, chairman of the Wrexham Trades and Labour Council, and E.J. Williams, a prominent member of the

North Wales Miners' Association. Over the next few months the NALRWU inaugurated a campaign in south-west Lancashire and when a demand for increased wages met with blank refusal its 2,000 members took strike action.[89] In the ensuing struggle the labourers received the help of a militant NUR branch at Ormskirk, the home base of John Phipps, the district organizing secretary, and after an acrimonious strike lasting two weeks the men achieved almost total victory. Against this confident background the Wrexham Trades and Labour Council called a meeting of local farm workers.[90] Tom Pughe gave an address on wages and a NALRWU branch came formally into existence. Although it did not last for long, E.J. Williams was to associate himself with a more successful campaign a few years later.

In Anglesey, 1913 saw trade unionism make great strides in the port of Holyhead. After an unpromising start, both the National Sailors' and Firemen's Union and the Dockers' Union established branches aided by the NUR and Cyril O. Jones.[91] Much as he remained a Liberal, Cyril O. Jones could not ignore the poverty around him, but the more he spoke out against class tyranny and injustice the more he was accused of being an agitator.[92] Nevertheless, trade unionism became a powerful force with 2,500 members in the various local branches, culminating in the formation of the Holyhead Trades and Labour Council in September.[93] Such was the confidence of one labour organizer that he foresaw the day when Anglesey workers would be strong enough to put up a parliamentary candidate.[94] In this spirit, trade unionists at Holyhead were equally keen to organize Anglesey farm workers.[95] It had been known for some time that the labour section of Undeb Gweithwyr Môn remained 'quite lifeless'[96] and the question of linking the union to a stronger body persisted throughout 1914. At a meeting in Gwalchmai, Tom Robinson, district secretary of the Dockers' Union, put forward his claims.[97] A merger with the dockers was again advocated by Cyril O. Jones at the annual meeting of Undeb Gweithwyr Môn in May, although David Thomas, on the other hand, maintained his commitment to NALRWU.[98]

Thomas's initial contact with the farm workers' union apparently came by way of his secretaryship of the Caernarfonshire Labour Council, although it was as much a response to a letter he had received a month earlier, in April 1913.[99] The Revd W.B. Jones, Ruabon, had been asked to address a meeting of agricultural labourers in the village of Henllan, Denbighshire, but, knowing little of the work of NALRWU he passed on the request to David Thomas. The inspiration behind this spontaneous local movement was John Foulkes ('Eithinfab'), a Llannefydd stonemason who doubled as farm labourer at harvest time.[100] His father had been one of the heroes of the Tithe War in the parish in 1888, but subsequently changed from Liberal to become a staunch Labour supporter.[101] As early as 1911 Eithinfab had written to David Thomas asking for a copy of *Y Werin a'i Theyrnas*; his own conversion to socialism having been inspired by the Revd Pan Jones's articles in *Cwrs y Byd.*[102] Turning principles into practice Eithinfab had arranged a meeting at nearby Henllan with the object of forming a trade union branch for farm workers, most of whom worked from 6 a.m. to 8 p.m. for a wage of only ten shillings.[103] The problems of introducing the unfamiliar concept of trade unionism into such an isolated rural area were compounded by an inability to get in touch with labour leaders in the towns. About the only support he could count on locally was that of the Revd Pierce Roberts, an incomparable Baptist minister who throughout his life never relinquished his work as a farm labourer.[104]

If David Thomas's request for NALRWU literature and rule book failed to interest George Edwards, R.B. Walker's reply in August 1913 made suitable amends. And it was on the back of this letter that David Thomas drafted the main points of the address delivered at two gatherings of agricultural workers at Henllan and Llannefydd.[105] Both places jointly resolved to establish a NALRWU branch, officers were appointed, and it was confidently expected that neighbouring parishes would follow this lead. By September, Henllan branch had twenty-nine members.[106] Eithinfab recognized the importance of drawing up an attractive programme to sustain interest in union affairs and both David Thomas and the Revd T.E. Nicholas were asked to provide socialist literature in the Welsh language.[107] The branch's early promise, however, was not fulfilled. After only a matter of months Eithinfab had the sorry task of informing David Thomas of its failure; only a half-dozen were paying their contributions and this broke the heart of the secretary.[108] Undeterred, Eithinfab predicted the rebirth of a stronger union within another five years.

With the future of Undeb Gweithwyr Môn still unresolved, and its labour section down to three branches and some ninety-nine members,[109] David Thomas began prodding R.B. Walker into taking an interest. Still busy, Walker nevertheless showed that NALRWU was sensitive to freelance recruiting by other unions.[110]

He knew that the secretary of the Colwyn Bay Trades and Labour Council had been busy organizing farm labourers in the Abergele area into the local branch of the Gasworkers' Union.[111] In October Tom Robinson once again addressed a special meeting of Undeb Gweithwyr Môn aimed at persuading them to amalgamate with the Dockers' Union.[112] While poaching by rival unions was an unavoidable feature of the general scramble for membership amongst unskilled workers, the relationship between NALRWU and the Dockers' Union had remained harmonious in this respect. Anxious to maintain friendly relations Walker immediately contacted Ben Tillett, who consented to step aside on the understanding that NALRWU took up the matter immediately.[113] Consequently W.R. Smith, the union president, and Walker travelled to north Wales to meet David Thomas and J. Fred Jones with the aim of taking over Undeb Gweithwyr Môn's total membership of 1,100.[114] On the basis of these talks, NALRWU decided to press on with the amalgamation and the organization of north Wales in general.[115]

Taken as a whole, the progress of trade unionism by 1915 contained all the makings of a united labour movement in north Wales. Membership of the Caernarfonshire Labour Council had reached 7,000 as seamen, dockers, quarrymen and railwaymen enrolled in their respective unions. Claims that Holyhead was now one of the best organized towns in the country led to renewed talk of fielding a Labour parliamentary candidate.[116] Much to David Thomas's delight this widespread awakening had at last touched the rural workers. Not only was he anxious to unionize farm labourers in other counties, but also federate all the labour bodies in north Wales into one powerful organization. A conference of trade unions and trades councils in north Wales was planned for September 1914 with the recruitment of farm workers at the top of the agenda.[117]

Although this conference had to be postponed for a few months because of the outbreak of war, David Thomas remained optimistic. Arrangements were soon made to revive the project and in the first copy of *The Labourer*, the journal of NALRWU, in February 1915, he mapped out the strategic conception of his grand design in Wales.[118] The starting point for organizing the Welsh agricultural labourer was to be Anglesey, with Undeb Gweithwyr Môn forming the nucleus for a larger body. Next would come south Caernarfonshire and west Denbighshire where the workers already showed signs of awakening. They could then take in the remainder of north Wales before carrying the campaign into Cardigan and Carmarthenshire. He expected other unions to offer assistance following a lead given by the projected North Wales Labour Conference. To this end R.B. Walker was invited to address the conference at Colwyn Bay in April 1915 attended by 80 delegates representing 29 labour organizations and 40,000 workers.[119] Upon the formation of a North Wales Trades and Labour Council came the proposal that organized industrial workers support every effort to unionize the agricultural labourers. In moving the resolution, Walker attacked the use of schoolboy labour on farms and vouched that those farm hands whom they replaced would never be content to return under the old wages and conditions.

Even upon birth the North Wales Trades and Labour Council found itself in limbo. As the tragic upheaval of world war tore into the life of both town and countryside the labour movement was neutralized by events outside its control. Enthusiasm at a recruiting meeting in Holyhead,[120] for instance, epitomized the war spirit that united all classes at a time of crisis. A series of public meetings planned by the Caernarfonshire Labour Council had to be shelved because workers volunteered for the forces.[121] A second North Wales Labour Conference scheduled for Bangor in November 1915 was similarly postponed. Those actively involved in trade union affairs had to succumb to the passions and politics of patriotism.

The extent of the disruption was reflected in the experiences of Undeb Gweithwyr Môn. Following Walker's renewed interest in the union, David Thomas was asked to arrange a meeting so that the transfer could be finalized. At a meeting in February 1915, chaired by Thomas Rowlands, Thomas succeeded in persuading the membership to join NALRWU.[122] Yet his achievement received but perfunctory treatment as Walker was still overwhelmed by union-led movements for wage rises in no less than eight different English counties.[123] For this reason, perhaps, NALRWU considered the possibility of employing an organizer to take charge of things in north Wales.[124] Anyhow, Walker's visit to the first North Wales Labour Conference enabled him to sum up the position in Anglesey at first hand. Members of Undeb Gweithwyr Môn were invited to throw in their lot, funds included, on the understanding that NALRWU would provide immediate benefits.[125] Unfortunately J. Fred Jones found it difficult to summon the main officials.[126] Wartime emergencies had certainly taken its toll of the union; with so many members on active service they could neither collect contributions nor hold meetings.[127] It proved impossible to obtain the signature of the treasurer and two trustees because they were in the army. Moved to exasperation by the inaction and subsequent silence of its officials, R.B. Walker concluded that Undeb Gweithwyr Môn was defunct.[128]

Coming on top of failure at Wrexham and Henllan, this forced NALRWU to suspend any immediate scheme for organizing the farm workers of north Wales.[129] Already it had been decided not to send a delegate to the proposed second North Wales Labour Conference.[130] It simply did not seem worthwhile to divert the desperately slender resources of the union into a seemingly unproductive region. David Thomas's disappointment could not be concealed and Walker was obliged to assure him that should circumstances change then the union would meet the challenge. It also appears that a piqued David Thomas had threatened to undertake this task independent of NALRWU. Walker could only remind him of the difficulties, dangers and pitfalls awaiting such an enterprise. He fully appreciated the considerable contribution made by Thomas, but the salvation of the rural worker could only come through a large national union.

South Wales was also barren territory. Yet the implementation of the National Insurance Act and the work of the Land Enquiry Committee had provided the agricultural labourers with attention not previously imagined. Privy to Liberal Party 'leaking', the *South Wales Daily News* utilized Land Enquiry findings to press for government legislation that would raise the wages of the labourers to a reasonable minimum.[131] Editorials sympathetic to their cause became more compelling in the wake of the triumphant Lancashire strike, for their two-shilling wage rise and a Saturday half-holiday placed the Welsh farm labourer in an even darker shadow. Conditions in some counties were said to be 'exceptionally bad'.[132] But employers would only respond to the sort of collective pressure trade unionists in Herefordshire had exerted. Once the importance of a labourers' union was realized, improvements might also be secured for the workers in Dyfed. The 'seeds of discontent' were reported to have been already sown in Pembrokeshire,[133] but as yet no inspired individual or labour organization had come forward to give guidance or practical assistance. Even though the NALRWU had received a strong appeal to commence an organizing campaign in south Wales,[134] the conditions were not favourable. Branches listed at

Talybont-on-Usk, Knighton and Newport (Monmouthshire) in 1914 quickly perished, and an application to set up a branch at Llanelli in the same year was left in the air.[135]

If history taught anything it proved that no form of class struggle from within the ranks of the agricultural labourers was possible without positive leadership. An impressive demonstration of this could be found in the person of Sidney Box, the leader of the rural workers' revolt in Herefordshire. The son of a farm hand, Box spent some time as a miner in south Wales before returning to work on the land among men in whose interests he fought so hard for the greater part of his life. In the autumn of 1912 Box became area organizer for the agricultural section of the Workers' Union.[136] A gritty, irascible agitator, he soon became a thorn in the farmers' flesh. Within two years 52 branches had been set up in Herefordshire and soon this success was translated into action.[137] In the summer of 1914 Box arranged for 1,500 men to give in their notice in a bold move to force farmers into granting higher pay and a Saturday half-holiday.[138] Success in Herefordshire, meanwhile, encouraged Box to make a foray into mid-Wales and in July 1914 he held an open-air meeting at Knighton to preach the 'gospel of discontent'.[139] Christianity had done nothing about the poor, so it was up to them to combine together to safeguard their own interests and seek class justice. Enough names were collected to form a branch, enabling Box to hand over responsibility to two local secretaries. This was to be only the start. Box intended to extend the scope of his activities into the remainder of Radnorshire as well as neighbouring counties. But it proved a vain hope. The outbreak of war in August not only disrupted his organizing campaign but left the entire union structure in Herefordshire severely weakened.[140] Box, however, struggled on despite the odds. An attempt to plant the union banner at Abergavenny ended in disappointment,[141] whilst further incursions into mid-Wales in 1915–16 only led to the formation of two small branches composed largely of quarrymen.[142]

Times made it equally difficult for the North Wales Trades and Labour Council to function effectively, and the situation was complicated even further by David Thomas's enforced exile. As a conscientious objector he had claimed exemption from military service. This was subsequently granted subject to him entering non-combatant service as a farm worker.[143] So, from 12 December 1916 until the day of his release on 25 April 1919 David Thomas experienced the life of an agricultural labourer at Higher Berse farm outside Wrexham. At first he was paid eight shillings a week with bed and lodging; when he learnt to plough it rose to twelve shillings. Although the hard physical work and long hours left him with little energy or time David Thomas continued his political work on behalf of the socialist movement. Least of all did the isolation deter him from pursuing the cause of the farm workers, whose transformation was as sharp and dramatic as his own during these years of upheaval.

Inevitably, the strains of total war brought elemental changes in the general character of British society.[144] Those political, economic and social forces which had been at work before 1914 were now given a tremendous impetus. It was the leaven of war which accelerated the process of collectivism. Alongside growing state control of essential industries, the threat of starvation induced government intervention in agriculture. National survival became dependent upon increased production in all spheres of industry and, with the economy geared to this end, war elevated the importance of the working class. As Chancellor of the Exchequer, and then premier, Lloyd George tried to secure the co-operation of the Labour Party and trade unions, and this enhanced political status, coupled with wage advances in key industries, gave trade union membership an unprecedented boost. Yet, working-class participation in national unity was being seriously impaired by growing class antagonisms. Social divisions not only persisted but were exacerbated by blatant injustices. War enabled small sections of the community to profiteer and prosper at the expense of the majority. People tilted away from accepted conventions as society came to embrace new values. Especially for the agricultural labourer, war produced a set of circumstances which profoundly changed his traditional attitude and this happened on such a scale as to dislocate the calm of rural society with its apparently ordered class relations.

Although still the predominant industry in the majority of counties, agriculture in Wales on the eve of the war remained backward and underdeveloped.[145] Since the 'Great Depression' of 1873–96 there had been a steady conversion of arable into pasture so that by 1914 little more than a sixth of the land was tilled.[146] Only in Anglesey and the corn-producing areas of Monmouthshire, the Vale of Glamorgan and south Pembrokeshire did arable cultivation represent an appreciable proportion of total acreage; indeed, the whole of the arable land in Wales only just exceeded that of the single English county of Norfolk. Again in contrast with England, the farms were very much smaller, almost 70 per cent of the Welsh holdings being under 50 acres. Consequently, the pastoral nature of agriculture and the small scale of the farms coupled with gradual mechanization meant a reduced need for labour. Between 1891 and 1901 the number of male agricultural labourers fell from 44,900 to 37,800.[147] Recovery from the depression accounted for the slight upturn by 1911, but even then the total of 39,500 was only some 3,000 more than the figure for Norfolk.[148] Family farms, if not self-supporting, made do with relatives or a single hired worker, usually a young lad. And the general tendency was to stick to those farming methods which yielded sufficient to provide them with a living.

Also distinct from England was the custom for workers to lodge in farm outbuildings. English labourers, in the main, resided in a separate cottage and displayed a more independent frame of mind. The 'living-in' system that characterized Welsh farming proved far more conducive to a friendly understanding between masters and men, with both sharing the same table at mealtimes. Various social and religious functions held within the close-knit Welsh-speaking community offered further opportunity for fraternization. What had been emphasized in the reports of the Royal Commission on Labour, the Royal Commission on Land in Wales and the Land Enquiry Committee again proved largely true of Welsh rural society in 1917–18.[149] With significant exceptions, class relations appeared remarkably cordial on the surface. And this continuing close relationship with the farmers remained one of the principal reasons why the organized labour movement prior to 1917 failed to stir the ordinary agricultural worker.

Yet, this mutual bond was now being seriously tested. The feeling of restlessness always present beneath the surface became increasingly discernible as attitudes changed. In a number of counties the writing was on the wall. Even the custom of yearly hirings came to be regarded as a means of holding labourers in bondage.[150] Accommodation in an unhealthy loft over a stable or cow-house, which had been a long-standing source of grievance to some[151] (but an enjoyable source of moral liberty to others), now attracted increasing criticism as modern health standards proved more stringent. Among the married labourers there developed a growing demand for its abolition because the provision of sleeping quarters necessarily meant lower cash wages.[152] More detestable was the system of tied cottages which bound the majority of married labourers to the service of an employer. Found mainly in the anglicized areas of Glamorgan, Monmouth and south Pembrokeshire they were let cheaply by farmers, the tenancy being determinable at a week's notice. As men put more value on their freedom and independence, calls for the abolition of the tied cottage system intensified.[153] Nowhere was the character of rural housing more deplorable than in south Wales, with at least a third of the cottages deserving permanent closure.[154] In Cardigan the worst type featured a thatched roof, clay walls and a floor of beaten earth; in Pembroke labourers' cottages were described as 'two rooms and a hole'.[155] At a time of growing agricultural prosperity the incidence of tuberculosis in both counties was a scandal. Cardiganshire was considered one of the worst areas in Britain: between 1916 and 1918 the annual figure had doubled from 152 to 300.[156] But with farmers dominating most rural district councils the working class could not look to the local authority to redress the defects.[157]

As always the long hours of labour and the low rate of payment provided the most durable constituents of discontent. It was recognized that workers who lived on the farms fared worse because they were continually at the beck and call of their employer. In north Wales the hours varied from thirteen to sixteen (including mealtimes) with only a few having a half-day holiday on Saturday. Past agitation had succeeded in curtailing the working day in Anglesey and Caernarfonshire; otherwise there was little movement in the direction of shorter hours since the report of the Royal Commission on Land in 1896.[158] In mid-Wales the hours were longer in the outlying rural areas; labourers in Montgomeryshire worked up to thirteen or fourteen hours a day. Of course, at haytime and harvest men were required to work indefinite hours. Taken in the round, the number of hours worked continued to be one of the principal unresolved grievances.[159]

Workers in the immediate proximity of the coalfield and industrial belt again fared better when it came to wages. Wage rates were fixed by word-of-mouth agreements reached on the day of the hiring fair. Depending on such local factors as provision of lodgings, perquisites and payments in kind, these showed considerable variations even between one locality and another within the same county. If labour was in good supply rates tended to fall. In the more inaccessible parts of Anglesey in 1912 they were said to have dropped to the Irish level of 10*s*. a week.[160] Nevertheless wages generally showed an upward tendency: by 1914 the average earnings were put at 19*s*. 4*d*., ranging from 18*s*. in Cardiganshire to 20*s*. 9*d*. in Glamorgan.[161] But with a greater rise in the price of food it was clear that wages had actually diminished in real terms, so that the labourers were even worse off.[162] Migration to the colliery districts continued to be an attractive alternative; miners drawing strike pay could take home more than what a labourer earned on a farm.[163]

The effect of war on agriculture was immediately felt as thousands volunteered to join the armed forces. An exodus of farm labourers led to a serious depletion of manpower with south Wales particularly hard hit. Concern was voiced in every quarter, ranging from the hiring fair to farmers' union meetings and county chambers of agriculture. By March 1915 enlistment had caused a shortage of 5–600 men in the rural districts around St Clears, Whitland and Newcastle Emlyn.[164] When labour was at a premium, especially at harvest-time, the workers were in a position to demand higher wages. Harvesters engaged at Pwllheli hiring fair in June 1916 made the most of their good fortune;[165] at Denbigh labourers received as much as seven shillings a day.[166] No accurate figure of the actual reduction in the labour force is available; besides, the position quickly improved with the introduction of cheap replacement labour.

Bending to pressure from a powerful agricultural lobby the government agreed that children of school age be excused from attendance at harvest and sowing time.[167] By 1916 local education authorities in every Welsh county save Caernarfon and Denbigh had sanctioned the premature release of pupils so that they might work on the farms. As the demands of war coincided with the self-interest of farmers, what proved so prevalent during the school board era now intensified with official approval. In May 1916, 562 children between the ages of 12 and 14, and even 33 under the age of 12, were reported to be in full-time employment in Wales.[168] With as many as 148 in Anglesey alone, Undeb Gweithwyr Môn had every reason to condemn the county education authority for depriving children of the right of education.[169] Farmers found it cheaper to exploit child labour than pay an adult worker a fair day's wage and despite many protestations this practice continued throughout the war. Only Denbighshire stood firm against exempting children of school age. As many as 1,100 schoolboys were freed to work on Monmouthshire farms during the harvest of 1917.[170] At a meeting of the Carmarthenshire War Agricultural Committee food production was declared to be more important in wartime than the education of children.[171] But what people strongly resented was the blatant use of young children to line the pockets of farmers.

The employment of female labour, including the Women's Land Army, to fill the increasing shortage caused by military requirements does not seem to have aroused opposition. What rankled with the labourers of Glamorgan and Monmouth to a high degree was the influx of soldiers and prisoners of war.[172] It caused more ill feeling than anything else, and accentuated the mood of discontent that had existed prior to the war. Allegedly, the drafting of 530 soldiers into the agricultural districts of Glamorgan enabled employers to coerce their men at will.[173] Requests for a wage increase were quickly stifled and if a labourer threatened to leave he was shown the road with the words: 'All right, I will get a soldier — you can go and join up.' Similar resentment was felt in Monmouthshire where soldiers and interned prisoners in the districts of Chepstow and Raglan were receiving payment on a par with full-time labourers although their working hours might be shorter.[174] Far from being a timorous flock of men, the agricultural labourers of both counties came to be regarded as a restless, volatile work-force ripe for trade union propaganda.

Aside from these issues, the sharp rise in the price of foodstuffs and other necessaries hit the low-paid farm worker hard. As it turned out, the economic position of the labourers was often worse than in pre-war days, thus compounding their hostility to the farmers. The custom of giving various allowances in kind became increasingly unpopular with the men, leading to demands that they be commuted for cash.[175] In March 1915 a groundswell of ill feeling among the farm workers at St Ishmael's moved the local Liberal county councillor to intercede on their behalf.[176] Several labourers had complained that wages were not keeping up with the increased cost of living and following a public meeting he succeeded in persuading the farmers to grant a rise of two shillings. This gesture reportedly initiated similar movements elsewhere in the county but no further details were supplied.[177]

Because agricultural workers generally engaged for the year at a fixed wage rate they soon felt the full brunt of the soaring cost of living. By July 1916 the price of food had risen 60 per cent since July

1914, whilst the general price index was between 45 and 50 per cent higher.[178] Two years later the figures almost doubled. More specifically, in certain north Wales villages butter had risen 77.7 per cent, beef 107.5 per cent, bacon 153.5 per cent and sugar 200 per cent.[179] As in former times of adversity, demonstrations against the increased prices of foodstuffs became a familiar feature. The North Cardiganshire Trades Union and Labour Council protested that the 'abnormal increase' in food prices intensified the poverty of the poor.[180] A mass meeting of trade unionists at Holyhead made their voice heard in similar fashion.[181] In some cases, labour protest took a more positive form: workers at Penmaen-mawr organized a successful strike of milk consumers.[182] Llangwm women refused to buy butter at the Haverfordwest market until the price was reduced.[183]

The high price for butter demanded by farmers' wives at Haverfordwest was but one symptom of life within an agricultural eldorado. Farm prices reached their topmost peaks and brought unprecedented prosperity to the primary producer. By all accounts 1916 marked the golden year of British farming[184] and, although price controls introduced a restraining element from November 1916, farmers continued to do well over the remainder of the war. Indeed, prices spiralled to the 'dizzy heights' reached in 1920.[185] On a farm of 300 acres the total annual income was reported to have trebled between 1914 and 1918, the average profit per acre being 21*s.* 6*d.*[186] Naturally enough, such riches invited considerable comment. At a meeting of Caernarfonshire Independents one minister remarked how farmers were 'reaping their harvest of gold'.[187] On the same note, the continuance of the war in 1917 was ascribed to the prayers of the 'godly' farmers of Cardiganshire.[188]

For a variety of reasons the farmers had become the *bêtes noires* of the rural community. All other classes shared a common feeling of resentment that often vented itself in a torrent of scorn. At best farmers met condemnation, at worst they were depicted as rapacious, selfish and hypocritical. In their evidence to the Commission of Inquiry into Industrial Unrest in 1917, one labour organization after another singled out profiteering as the principal contributory factor in the rise of social discontent.[189] Public opinion in every Welsh county reflected the general belief that farmers were taking advantage of the war to charge the highest prices for their produce. Branded as 'food thieves' and 'bloodsuckers' their attitude towards the families of fighting men was said to be no better than the cruelty of the

Germans towards the Belgians.[190] Agricultural labourers were not only immediate witnesses to this prosperity, but they also had a direct hand in its making. What they certainly did not have was a share of the large profits. Nothing attested better to the prevailing lust for money than the conduct of Cardiganshire farmers. Living up to their reputation as a 'mean, ungenerous lot of employers' they poured their gains into War Savings Certificates.[191] Over a period of sixteen months (ending 31 March 1918) the Cardiganshire War Savings Committee took in a staggering £288,958 — the overwhelming proportion invested by farmers. So rich had Pembrokeshire farmers become that deposits in the Haverfordwest banks increased by a quarter of a million pounds since the start of the war.[192]

Long-standing, deep-rooted antagonism over low wages, long hours and poor accommodation now received the additional thrust of those factors directly associated with the war. The gulf that had been opening for some years became an abyss. Social attitudes changed completely as farmers appeared in more than one bad light. Apart from profiteering, their dominance on the local military tribunal[193] was turned to advantage. Farmers safeguarded their own sons at the expense of the defenceless labourers. The Llandysul tribunal heard how six servants in the Rhydlewis district had been sacked to make room for farmers' sons.[194] The majority of exemptions granted at Pembroke in October 1916 were to sons of farmers, including members of the tribunal.[195] Equally unprincipled was the threat of military service to coerce men into accepting lower wages. A Solva farm labourer suffered a three-shilling reduction in his weekly wage because his employer secured his remission from the army, and this practice was said to be rife in the neighbourhood.[196]

By the time of the Great War the wheel of oppression in rural Wales had turned full circle. During the nineteenth century it was the tyranny of the Anglican Tory landlord which underscored the Land Question. It gave rise to a middle-class revolt that expressed itself through Nonconformist radicalism. Spearheaded by the tenant farmers, it fuelled the Tithe War, the campaign for land reform and disestablishment. Victories at parliamentary and local elections paved the way for a Liberal political ascendancy that ultimately replaced the rule of the gentry. Before long the Anglican squirearchy would be selling off their great estates to tenants all too eager to buy. The process begun in 1910 continued through the war, reaching its apogee in the years 1918–22.[197]

In the struggle for power the tenant farmers and farm labourers are usually presented as being yoked together in a common cause, and this idealized picture of social solidarity is accepted almost without question. Over the years much has been made of the relatively classless nature of Welsh rural society and the absence of class distinctions.[198] What is less appreciated is the depth of hostility among rural labourers; the points of conflict between the classes have not been sufficiently explored. The revolt led by ap Ffarmwr in Anglesey appears as an isolated and temporary aberration without regard to just how widespread the mood of discontent had become. What ap Ffarmwr did was give expression to the real feelings of many farm workers. Failure came partly because he expected too much of the inexperienced labourers; in effect they were being asked to build their own organization. A closer view of the discontent of the 1890s has shown how it presaged later developments. The militancy of the agricultural labourers in the years of the Great War did not spring from nowhere; on the contrary it had very deep roots; particularly so when the farmers came to exercise their newly-found power within the local rural community, for it then became the turn of the working class to feel the sharper edge of oppression. By now, the political obsessions of the Nonconformist middle class seemed almost irrelevant; disestablishment held little interest for a labourer on the verge of existence. What he desired was a just wage, his own cottage and a few acres of land to cultivate. Yet where farmers dominated the county councils every obstacle was put in the way of the Small Holdings Act of 1908. Brecon and Radnor councils were the most hostile,[199] whereas Cardiganshire council appeared totally indifferent to its responsibilities.[200] Again, little attempt had been made to improve the standard of rural housing in areas where the district council came under the lordly sway of the farmers.[201]

Hardly anything had been done by employers to improve life for the ordinary rural worker: a Merioneth labourer, for instance, would have seen very little change in half a century.[202] Nor could much be expected of the Nonconformist hierarchy. As a body, Nonconformist ministers were extremely reluctant to condemn the tyranny of the countryside. Nevertheless, new attitudes slowly began to emerge. At its third annual session in 1913 the Welsh School of Social Service discussed the condition of the agricultural labourer.[203] Under the inspired guidance of the Revd Gwilym Davies the school had been set up two years earlier to tackle the delicate question of church leadership in social work. Symptomatic of this awakened humanitarian consciousness was the appearance of *Cristionogaeth a Chymdeithas* in 1914, one of the first books to emphasize the social aspect of the gospel message in the Welsh language, although few ministers shared the strong socialist philosophy of the author, the Revd J.H. Howard. In truth, there was little chance that organized religion would inspire radical change. Even within the chapels ministers were aware of the widening gap between the 'new aristocracy' of farmers and the labourers.[204] Religion no longer gripped the working class; nor was this surprising given the hypocrisy of those profiteering farmers who as deacons professed to be followers of Christ.[205] When the Revd John Williams stood up at the Corwen Association meeting in 1913 to remind his fellow Methodists that the Christian ministry was paying too little attention to the social evils of the day,[206] his charge that Welsh farmers were 'oppressing' their labourers angered a well-known Pembrokeshire agriculturist and divine. A minimum wage, retorted the Revd W.M. Lewis, would produce a 'minimum labourer', more lazy and worthless than ever.[207] Religious leaders did little of practical value. Only in a few places were efforts made to provide a reading room for those whom the Revd Lewis accused of spending their money on drink once the working day was over.[208] All the more remarkable, therefore, is the way that individual labourers overcame their numerous social disadvantages to display a natural genius for scriptural knowledge, Welsh literature, poetry and music.[209]

With so many points of tension and antagonism between farmer and labourer during the war years a major reaction could not be averted. Where class divisions were discernible, as in Anglesey and Denbighshire,[210] some of the workers had already begun to organize. Anglesey men were reported to have become 'more independent' and 'difficult to deal with', and Undeb Gweithwyr Môn, however frail a body, remained at hand. Until now, NALRWU had been unable to offer much help because of insufficient resources. To make matters worse an internal dispute following the Lancashire strike forced John Phipps, the local organizer, to form a breakaway union by taking the majority of Lancashire members. Set up in May 1914,[211] with a head office in Liverpool, the National Farm and Dairy Workers' Union went on to organize the rural labourers of neighbouring Cheshire before turning its sights on north Wales. Despite this reversal the number of NALRWU branches rose to 350 in 1914, and its membership to over 15,000 by the following year.[212] The union was inundated by an unprecedented number of requests for organizers to set up branches, and the opportunity to expand further could not be missed. An appeal by the Parliamentary Committee of the TUC in July 1917 aimed to raise at least £1,000 towards assisting the union in its organizing work and affiliated unions and trades councils located in rural districts were asked to give support.[213]

Outside agriculture, trade unionism was making a phenomenal advance. During the war years total membership increased by 57.6 per cent, from 4.1 million (1914) to 6.5 million (1918).[214] Once again, discontent proved to be the germ of progress. In south Wales a series of disputes enabled most unions to build upon the pre-war growth in membership. By 1917, the NUR had 123 branches and 28,628 members in Wales, mainly concentrated in the south.[215] By far the most successful general union, the Workers' Union, boasted 15,000 members in south Wales; the Dockers' Union had over 8,000 and the National Union of General Workers (NUGW), which now incorporated the Gasworkers' Union, 5,000.[216] One of the significant features of this success was their penetration into the rural areas. The National Amalgamated Labourers' Union began enrolling workers along the south Wales coast as far as Fishguard.[217] The NUGW saw its 'North Wales Group' expand to 15 branches when it recruited miners in the Conwy Valley and council workers in Llŷn.[218] In the middle Teifi valley — centred on Henllan, Dre-fach and Felindre — there had been a long tradition of trade unionism and industrial militancy among the weavers in the woollen industry. After months of negotiations the local union opted to affiliate with the Dockers' Union in 1915;[219] two years later its 'Tinplate District' had 400 members in the flannel weavers' branch.[220] Another local grievance involved the River Teifi itself. The coracle net-fishermen of Cilgerran and Cenarth who had enjoyed the right to catch salmon from time immemorial were fighting the encroachment of riparian ownership. A long-running campaign against exploitation drew in prominent socialists such as the Revd D.D. Walters ('Gwallter Ddu'), Urias Richards, John Davies, J. Gwendraeth James and G.B. Thomas, and led to the birth of the Teifi District Labourers' and Fishermen's Union in September 1916.[221] Within a month it was taken over by the Workers' Union.

Evan James's value as a Welsh-speaking organizer had been put to good use in his native Cardiganshire. An address at Llechryd marked the inauguration of the Teifi branch of the Workers' Union.[222] Further meetings at Aber-cuch and Cilgerran allowed the workers an ample opportunity to register their discontent. Fishermen, quarry-men, timber workers and agricultural labourers found a powerful ally in the Revd D.D. Walters, who railed against the evils of capitalism at meetings organized by both the Workers' and Dockers' Unions. The declaration by the chairman of the North Pembrokeshire Farmers' Union that 1916 would be remembered as a 'prosperous year'[223] only aggravated the hostility felt towards farmers. Mounting criticism of their profits, of their general ill-treatment of the labourers, and of their usurpation of local tribunals culminated in the taunting remark of E. Lima Jones that farmers were the 'locusts of the country'.[224]

Although an exclusively sectional union, the NUR also took a growing interest in the fate of the agricultural workers. The railway companies had always welcomed recruits from a rural background because 'the docile countryman made an ideal employee'.[225] Even an unskilled railway worker or porter earned more than a farm labourer, and the rates the farm labourers received tended to drag down the wages paid to the lowest grade on the railway. To an increasingly militant union like the NUR the menace posed by a large pool of unorganized farm labourers, especially during industrial disputes, could not be ignored. From an element of self-interest, therefore, it was the NUR which provided farm workers' unions with most help. Sidney Box praised his 'good friends' the railwaymen who acted as branch secretaries when fear of the employer restricted the freedom of the farm hand.[226] Joint NALRWU–NUR meetings in English counties were a common event. The success of the NALRWU organizing campaign in Norfolk, Lincoln and Essex in the years 1915–17 was ascribed to the loyal support of NUR members who freely gave their services as speakers and temporary branch secretaries.[227]

In a rural context the railway unions were uniquely placed to proffer aid and advice. Increasingly, railwaymen now took the role reserved earlier for middle-class Liberal sympathizers. This happened at Bala with the formation of the Trades and Labour Council in 1917. Before W.T. Bason and his colleagues called a meeting to effect what was described as a 'revolution' in the mecca of Methodism, only an NUR branch existed in the district.[228] During the latter years of the war trades councils also sprang up in Milford Haven (1916), Gowerton (1917), Rogerstone (1917) and Fishguard (1917). It was a sign of things to come that three agricultural labourers were included on the executive committee of the Fishguard and Goodwick Trades and Labour Council.[229] A desire to raise the standard of the agricultural worker had already been an important consideration in the formation of the Labour Party in Pembrokeshire in the summer of 1916.[230] All in all, those trades councils close to a rural hinterland were in a strategic position to give valuable fraternal assistance in the organization of farm labourers when the need arose.

Towering above all was the South Wales Miners' Federation with 150,000 members in 1913. By now it also appeared as the most politicized; the struggle for a minimum wage had enhanced the reputation of the miners as the shock troops of working-class militancy. Amongst the miners of Glamorgan and Monmouth the creed of socialism and class warfare was propagated with passion. Especially did this prove true of SWMF officials. Checkweighmen and miners' agents were key figures in the 'Fed' as well as in the smaller North Wales Miners' Association. Indeed, the miners' agent emerged as the 'professional trade unionist *par excellence*',[231] very often wielding considerable political influence. Given this heady industrial environment it was little wonder that many an individual farm labourer-turned-collier returned to the countryside imbued with a clear understanding of the strength of organized labour and a willingness to lead the fight against injustice. It had been a long-established fashion for labourers in Pembroke and Carmarthen to buy a smallholding once their savings at the colliery yielded sufficient capital.[232]

Since 1914 trade unions in south Wales had come together under the title of the South Wales Federation of Labour on the lines of the North Wales Trades and Labour Council.[233] David Thomas's counterpart in this context was to be William Harris, Pontllanffraith, a self-educated miner active in the trade union movement since the formation of the SWMF in 1898. Rising from checkweigher at Abertillery colliery he became a member of the SWMF executive and one of its full-time political organizers (with special responsibility for the Monmouthshire section) in 1910. At the request of the North and West Monmouthshire Labour Party he arranged a conference at Cardiff in December 1916 when the constitution of a new political Federation was drawn up.[234] From the outset, Harris strove to unify trade union and Labour Party organizations in Wales and this goal, clinched when he became secretary of the South Wales

Labour Federation, brought him into close touch with David Thomas.[235]

Like Thomas, William Harris's eloquence as platform speaker was utilized to defend the oppressed. At a meeting in Rogerstone early in 1917 he thundered against the exploitation of unorganized workers and the rising profits of the farmers.[236] Already, there had been calls in the local press for someone to take up the cause of the overworked farm labourer.[237] It was well understood that only a trade union could improve their conditions. A further spate of letters denounced the way in which 'chicken-hearted farmers' sons' evaded military service to live in comfort at the expense of others.[238] These were the considerations that doubtless came up in discussion when the organization of agricultural workers became the concern of the South Monmouthshire Labour Party a few months later.[239] In its name, William Harris (who also acted as Labour Party organizer to three divisional sections in the county) issued an appeal to trade unions and other labour organizations for financial assistance in setting up branches of NALRWU.[240] His organizations were willing to pay the initial expenses[241] and he had the co-operation of the NUR. Once established, the branches would then be handed over to the parent body. Signed on 23 June 1917, William Harris's appeal actually pre-dated the circular of the Parliamentary Committee of the TUC. It re-emphasized the familiar argument that unorganized rural labourers were a continuing source of danger to the industrial workers and drew attention to the Corn Production Bill being currently debated in Parliament.

By 1917, the German U-boats were destroying mercantile ships at an alarming rate and with devastating effect upon Britain's food supplies. Only a drastic agricultural policy aimed at increasing home production could avert disaster. Accordingly, Lloyd George's Corn Production Bill, presented to the Commons on 5 April 1917, contained far-reaching proposals: compulsory government powers to ensure maximum cultivation (300,000 acres in Wales were to be converted from grass to arable) and guaranteed prices for farmers balanced by a minimum wage of twenty-five shillings a week for labourers.[242] When G.J. Wardle, a railwayman's MP, tried unsuccessfully to move an amendment that they be paid thirty shillings, he attracted the support of only three Welsh members.[243] Provision was also made for the establishment of an Agricultural Wages Board[244] with powers to control the statutory wage, and of district wages committees to undertake responsibility for fixing minimum rates in the various parts of the country. As both sides of industry were accorded equal representation on the committees it gave the workers a unique opportunity for participation in the wage bargaining process. The urgency of organizing the farm labourers of Wales became greater than ever, as William Harris, David Thomas and all those trade union activists concerned for their interests realized.

The passing of the Corn Production Act on 21 August 1917 proved to be the final trigger for a concerted recruiting campaign. Age-old complaints about hours and pay and even a set of additional grievances thrown up by wartime conditions could not on their own sustain a prolonged rural labour movement; they had to be set against the quality of leadership and degree of organization. What the war did was boost trade union militancy which spilled over from the industrialized centres into the rural districts to give an artificial infusion to labour agitation. It was noticed how this contact 'tainted' the rural workers with the same bitter feelings of class hatred that characterized the miners, railwaymen and dockers.[245] Alienation was particularly discernible in Glamorgan and Monmouth, but the very fact that trade unionism erupted spontaneously on a localized basis in other Welsh counties proved how the attitude of farm labourers had changed utterly. Even in Carmarthen and Brecon, where relations between employers and employed were traditionally friendly, a restive work-force was showing great interest in a farm labourers' union.[246] All around, the peculiar circumstances of Welsh rural life that made it so closely identified with Welsh traditions in the nineteenth century had broken down. The rise of trade unionism in the countryside was yet another example of the merging of Welsh and British trends during the course of the war,[247] thus ending the isolation of the farm labourer. Rural protest had crossed a significant threshold; henceforward it would express itself in the form of an overt class revolt.

CHAPTER IV

A TIME TO STAND: THE BEGINNINGS OF THE SECOND REVOLT, 1917–1918

DURING the years 1917–18 class relations at the lower reaches of rural society underwent a momentous transformation. A change in the character of the ordinary farm labourer caused a revolutionary break in the traditional pattern of life as passive subordination turned to stubborn independence. Never before had the agricultural work-force been made more aware of its position as a separate social group. Poverty and misery created widespread disaffection and during the war years the countryside was rife with developing tensions. Good times for the farmer highlighted the impoverished status of the labourers in the system of economic production. Whilst employers enjoyed the maximum return on capital, the rewards for their men had become infinitely more unequal and unjust, and it was the raw reaction to this form of exploitation that gave the revolt the element of a class struggle. A confrontation proved inevitable. State intervention in the form of the Corn Production Act meant that even the government was at last obliged to recognize the value of the agricultural labourers. In terms of outreach and influence the impact of trade unionism in rural Wales had no previous parallel, and the organizing power it embodied gave the underdog a chance to assert himself.

Such was the nature and extent of the unrest among agricultural labourers that they responded enthusiastically when the opportunity arose. The scattered revolts which broke out during the latter months of 1917 were quite independent of each other, inspired either by zealous individuals or an arm of the labour movement. As yet, the NALRWU was in no position to garner the harvest of discontent on a national basis in Wales. However, the dramatic expansion of opportunities could not be overlooked. R.B. Walker attended the first annual conference of the South Wales Labour Federation in Cardiff in September 1917 in order to emphasize the importance of organizing farm workers.[1] As a result, each affiliated organization promised to assist the NALRWU in its efforts to secure the full benefits that would result from the setting up of district wages committees. All the signs were promising. Very soon also the union realized that its interests would be best served if an organizer was appointed to take charge of Wales.[2] It hoped to secure a Welsh-speaking officer among the six additional organizers to be appointed at the end of 1917 and so the post was duly advertised in the *Merthyr Pioneer*.[3] But already some very positive results had been achieved without any direct participation by the union. In no less than nine of the thirteen Welsh counties the stage was set.

The open-air meeting held in a field adjoining Magor railway station on the evening of Sunday 24 June 1917 marked not only the start in Monmouthshire but also the first shot in the revolt of the Welsh agricultural labourer.[4] Two things determined the course of events: William Harris's firm ambition to organize the labourers and the support given by the local NUR branch. Yet it was not until a similar meeting at Five Lanes, Caer-went, on 29 July, again under the auspices of the Magor branch of the NUR, that the pioneer branch of the NALRWU in south Wales was firmly established.[5] With Arthur Howells, a Llanfaches shepherd as chairman, a committee was formed and by the time the Caer-went branch held its first meeting some eighty members had been enrolled.[6] Over the following months further help in south Monmouthshire came from A.W. Pittman, William Arnold and T.H. Edwards of the railwaymen's union. The co-operation of NUR officials in arranging public meetings, providing experienced speakers and giving assistance in the routine of branch business proved invaluable in the agricultural district alongside the Great Western Railway. But it was William Harris who provided the main leadership that translated task into action. Following his circular of 23 June he took full advantage of his position within the organized labour movement in Monmouthshire to press for practical support.[7] In reply to his appeal for funds, donations were received from the South and West Monmouthshire Labour Parties, the Western Valley Miners' Association and the trades councils at Newport and Abertillery.[8] This money (amounting to over £22) helped to pay the cost of printing posters and pamphlets, the hire of rooms and other expenses with such results as to justify the observation that William Harris had 'great influence amongst labourers'.[9]

From the beginnings at Caer-went the movement began its confident march into neighbouring villages to spread the gospel of revolt and stir up the farm labourers. At meeting after meeting there was a declared intention of freeing labourers from the shackles of poverty and exploitation. As principal speaker, William Harris could hold an audience with an hour's address in which he explained the provisions and significance of the Corn Production Act.[10] A trade union would safeguard the men's interests, allow them to fight the injustices of the military tribunals and be the means to secure better housing. Other speakers like A.W. Pittman advanced a headier brew of national ownership and control.[11] Many of the railwaymen had been formerly employed on the farms and knew by experience what conditions were like and why the men were afraid to join a union. But as protégés of the NUR and SWMF their confidence visibly increased.[12] Moreover, leading officials of the Newport Trades and Labour Council and the Municipal Employees' Association appeared on the platform alongside Harris.[13] Between them they held a run of meetings prior to the formation of another seven branches: at Shirenewton, Magor, St Arvans, Castleton, Marshfield, St Bride's Wentlloog and Catsash. Thus, by the end of the year a solid foundation was laid for the NALRWU in Monmouthshire. To what extent Harris and his comrades had successfully trained their charges became immediately clear. Union membership emboldened farm workers to render 'articulate demands which (had) long been felt but (had) hitherto not been openly expressed'.[14] At a mass meeting in Caer-went in December they drew up a programme that comprised demands for a minimum wage of 35*s.* with an overtime rate of 9*d.* per hour, to be raised to 1*s.* for Sunday and night work. Also, for the very first time the men had a representative on Newport Trades and Labour Council and a delegate at a county Labour conference held in the town in December.[15]

An awakening of labour in the midst of so much social discontent gave Pembrokeshire farmers some unpalatable food for thought. One farming official warned that a labourers' union 'might possibly eat them up'.[16] In most industrial centres of the county, trades councils and various trade union branches had already appeared, and once the Labour Party had achieved a firm footing, a movement to awaken the agricultural labourers took little time to get going. The guiding spirit here was E.P. Harries, a Pembroke Dock shipwright and general secretary of the county Labour Party. Via the South Wales Labour Federation a personal contact with William Harris gave him foreknowledge of the campaign to unionize Monmouthshire farm workers. It was therefore no coincidence that members of the Associated Society of Shipwrights should raise the matter at the first annual conference of the Pembrokeshire Labour Party in August 1917.[17] At its behest a series of meetings were held in the rural extremities of south Pembrokeshire at the beginning of September under the direction of E.P. Harries and Miles Clarke, chairman of the Pembroke Dock Trades Council.[18] Harries shared William Harris's desire to uplift the working class; he was, as he put it, intent on interfering with everything that affected the 'poorly paid, crushed' farm servants.[19] This meant not only fighting for a minimum wage but also the abolition of slum housing and direct representation for the workers on public bodies. Meetings at Merrion, Cosheston, Angle and Wallaston gave the movement an encouraging start with a considerable number of workers reportedly joining the NALRWU.[20]

Harries's equivalent in the north of the county was Evan Anthony, headmaster of Goodwick Council School. Fearless and outspoken as parish councillor he had criticized the Haverfordwest military tribunal on the way it safeguarded the interests of materialistic farmers.[21] His ties with the National Union of Teachers drew him into the committee of the county Labour Party and he became first president of the Fishguard Trades and Labour Council in August 1917.[22] When the council was being first mooted, Anthony identified himself with the plight of the labourers, recognizing that only a powerful organization would enable them to improve their position.[23] He saw it as a struggle to achieve self-improvement by means of a full education, something which had been denied to the labourers in the past. As headmaster he knew how the children of workers lacked medical care because their parents were unable to pay. In addition, he urged working-class representation on parish, district and county councils as a way of removing the scandal of insanitary housing.

As soon as the trades council was in operation, Evan Anthony took the lead. An open-air meeting on Fishguard square on the afternoon of the Michaelmas Fair set off the campaign in north Pembrokeshire.[24] On the initiative of the county Labour Party, W. Holmes of the NALRWU executive was billed to speak, and £5 voted towards his expenses.[25] But when Holmes was unable to attend at the last minute, Anthony filled his place. Further meetings were arranged and in October Holmes arrived for a week's tour of the county. After meeting Harries and Anthony, and seeing the trades councils at

Pembroke Dock and Goodwick at work, he was full of praise for the 'fine body of trade unionists' now busily engaged in the campaign of organizing rural workers.[26] At Mathry he had his first experience of a Welsh agricultural audience on the day of the fair, and it was on this occasion that another schoolteacher, D.T. Lewis, came forward to give support.[27] Other meetings at Croesgoch, Pembroke and Letterston confirmed his optimism. All around he saw evidence of 'a great future for the union in wild Wales'.

Branches were soon set up, some being fortunate enough to attract that one essential component, a local activist. Indeed, all three Lloyd brothers — John, Thomas and William — were prominent at Mathry, and when a branch was formed, D.T. Lewis agreed to serve as chairman. Like Evan Anthony he had been cut to the quick by the poverty of rural school children. The living conditions of the working class converted him from a staunch Conservative into an uncompromising socialist.[28] At Solva, W.H. John, proprietor of a printing business, presided over the meeting which launched the local branch aided by two Nonconformist ministers.[29] Altogether, the union made remarkable progress in the space of a few months. In south Pembrokeshire, branches were firmly established at Bosherston, Merrion, Castlemartin and Cresswell, in the north at Mathry, Solva, Croes-goch, Pen-caer, St Davids and St Nicholas.[30] The revolt touched the farmers on all points and made them distinctly sensitive. Complaints about 'agitators' and 'outsiders' who caused 'friction and unpleasantness' began to be uttered aloud.[31]

Equally promising steps had been taken by the trade union movement in south Cardiganshire, where both the Workers' and the Dockers' Unions were endeavouring to strengthen their hold. A cluster of local socialists provided leadership and oratorical fire, none more forcefully than the Revds D.D. Walters and J.H. Jenkins, the vicar of Cilrhedyn. At first, issues concerning the fishermen and flannel weavers of the Teifi Valley occupied their minds, but gradually the suffering of the agricultural labourers came to the fore.[32] Efforts were thus made to recruit farm workers into both unions. Following E. Lima Jones's celebrated outburst in July 1917 a stream of letters appeared in the *Welsh Gazette* condemning the farmers as the 'locusts' of Cardiganshire.[33] In its wake, one correspondent asked for the workers to be considered,[34] a plea soon taken up by the Revd T.E. Nicholas. He implored the men to organize themselves; the workers of Cardiganshire, he declared, 'had nothing to lose but their chains'.[35] As the most prominent Welsh-language exponent of Marxism he provided, with these familiar words from the Communist Manifesto, an appropriate rallying cry.

Best known as 'Niclas y Glais', the Revd T.E. Nicholas became a unique figure in the Welsh labour movement. Raised on a smallholding on the Presely mountains in Pembrokeshire he knew what it was to suffer poverty.[36] Whilst serving as an Independent minister at Glais in the industrialized Swansea Valley, his Liberal Nonconformist radicalism matured into an intensely socialist credo that deeply coloured both his writing and poetry. He became one of the early leaders of the ILP in Glamorgan and Welsh editor of the left-wing *Merthyr Pioneer*. Although he left Glais to take charge of the pastorate of Llangybi in the heart of Cardiganshire in 1914, his Christian-socialist vision remained undimmed. In spite of the work of S.R., Gwilym Hiraethog and the Revd Pan Jones,[37] T.E. Nicholas saw for himself that nothing had changed for the ordinary rural labourer. His condemnation of private ownership was already known,[38] and these socialist convictions, enriched by a dozen years of experience with the trade union movement in Glamorgan, he now offered to the Welsh-speaking rural worker. Over the following months Niclas y Glais became to Cardiganshire and the uplands of Pembroke what William Harris was to Monmouthshire and David Thomas to north Wales.

His promise to speak in any locality was soon taken up and in the first week of November the farm workers of Llanilar flocked to hear his address.[39] It marked the inaugural meeting of the NALRWU in Cardiganshire and the formation of its first branch. Among those who joined that night was R. Llewelyn Jones, a young farm worker. He was to remain a member of the same branch for the next fifty-seven years of his life, often struggling to keep the movement alive in times of adversity. No other branch was established in the county in 1917 because T.E. Nicholas transferred his interest, temporarily, to the lead miners centred on Ysbyty Ystwyth in the north of the county, thus opening the door to the National Amalgamated Labourers' Union.[40]

Signs of disaffection had surfaced on a smaller scale in Breconshire. The mutual nexus that helped to preserve stability within agricultural society began to slacken. Even the generous wages and allowances which the labourers of the county had enjoyed hitherto were not enough to offset the rising cost of living.[41] And very soon the catalyst needed to transform social discontent into revolt was at work. A recently established branch of the NUR at Hay held a propaganda meeting in the Liberal Club in October with the intention of forming an agricultural branch of the Workers' Union in the district.[42] It brought together A.J. Williams, the organizing secretary of the NUR, and Sidney Box, who had the previous year renewed his organizational activity in Herefordshire on a voluntary basis.[43] By contrast, the farm labourers found a most unlikely champion in T.J. Stokoe, who chaired the meeting. A prominent young Liberal and chairman of Hay Urban District Council, with substantial business interests in the town,[44] Stokoe gave the notorious 'agitator' Box a warm welcome and full backing. Each speaker identified the problems facing the labourers and emphasized the merits of combination. A few weeks later labour forces within the county were organizing on political lines.[45] Amongst its first priorities the Breconshire Labour Party put the unionization of farm workers, although it chose to communicate with the NALRWU and not the Workers' Union.[46]

As in the south, developments in a number of north Wales counties also promised well in 1917. The attitude of the farmers had created a lot of bad feeling, and social disjunction between them and their men became the occasion for action. In no time, the various labour bodies began to tackle the problem of organizing farm workers in earnest. On a formal level the North Wales Trades and Labour Council continued to maintain its interest. At the third annual conference at Llandudno on the 11 August David Thomas led the discussion in the absence of Dr G.B. Clark, president of the Scottish Farm Servants' Union, who had been invited to address the delegates.[47] The Corn Production Act and the forthcoming district wages committees brought home the need for unity. Speaking as fraternal delegate from the South Wales Labour Federation, William Harris was able to relate how his organizations had responded to the challenge. While the disruption caused by the war had seriously hampered the work of the North Wales Trades and Labour Council, David Thomas remained surprisingly active. He still maintained a close link with his labour confederates and, as his correspondence so richly shows, he was giving regular advice to a host of local activists. What is more, his involuntary sojourn at Higher Berse enabled him to practise what he had so steadfastly preached. By August, the organizer *par excellence* could boast the successful establishment of a NALRWU branch at Wrexham.[48]

Directions from the TUC regarding the organization of agricultural labourers were being noted. The question came up for discussion at the Wrexham Trades and Labour Council in September when it reported that 'action was being taken on lines suggested by David Thomas'.[49] A month later the Caernarfonshire Labour Council broached the matter.[50] It resolved to devote itself to the task of uniting the farm workers of the county and to write to R.B. Walker for advice. Although these proceedings offered assurance of official support, it was only on the initiative of inspired individuals that the first practical moves were taken within each county. Once more, the conspicuous part played by local activists was the common denominator which gave a singular character to events. One way or another there might have been greater co-ordination than meets the eye. But to all appearances, the spontaneous response at community level underlines the considerable latent potential for revolt which allowed the movements successfully to take off independently of each other.

Nowhere is this point better illustrated than in Anglesey. Of course, the tradition of ap Ffarmwr had found its heirs in the small group of men behind Undeb Gweithwyr Môn. But the war cost the union dear. A quarter of its membership had joined the army.[51] Down to three branches and 99 names on its books, the separate labour section was in complete disarray.[52] Trustees and committee members were either away on active service or unwilling to act; by the same token it proved difficult to hold the usual meetings and collect members' contributions. Yet officials put on a brave face, pointing to the need for a strong union to defend the workers once the war was over.[53]

It was precisely this concern over the future of the labour movement that brought W.J. Jones ('Brynfab') to the forefront. Under the title 'Yfory Llafur' he wrote a series of highly perceptive articles in *Y Clorianydd* which analysed the social changes spurred by war, the awakening confidence of the working class and the answers which socialism provided.[54] It was the opportunity he had been seeking for some time. Born on a smallholding outside Brynsiencyn, he had experience of farm labouring before crossing the Menai Straits to work at the Dinorwig Quarry.[55] Here he became a conscious disciple of socialism, so much so that around 1907 he penned a letter to Robert Blatchford, editor of the *Clarion*, to order some socialist literature. Brynfab's convictions burnt so fiercely that he yearned to serve the socialist cause in some way. 'I shall be glad', he wrote, 'to be its missionary in this part of the island.'[56] About the same time he returned to Anglesey to take charge of the 'Half Moon' stores at Brynsiencyn. Contact with agricultural labourers and their wives who were his chief customers gave him an insight into their daily lives and sufferings. In the event, Brynfab's business became a mere sideline to his political interests, and among the many socialist works in his library was F.E. Green's study, *The Tyranny of the Countryside*. Elected to Llanidan parish council in 1913, he emerged as a public figure, renowned for his platform oratory.

Living in the next village to Dwyran, Brynfab was certain to know of the work of ap Ffarmwr. How much he consciously felt his influence or deliberately adopted his model is hard to say. But it was in the style of ap Ffarmwr that he shrewdly exploited the potential of the press with his polemical articles aimed especially at the agricultural labourers. In 'Yfory Llafur' Brynfab recognized that war gave the working class a deserved opportunity for improvement and he urged the leaders of Undeb Gweithwyr Môn to seek full representation on the district wages committee. The workers could not expect their MP to show sympathy. In the twenty-two years he had represented Anglesey in Parliament, not once did Ellis Jones Griffith speak up for the workers; he even failed to support the recent amendment proposing a minimum wage of thirty shillings for agricultural labourers. Like ap Ffarmwr, Brynfab advocated trade unionism and land nationalization, but in his case there was no hiding his political aspirations, nor his full-blooded commitment to the union becoming a vehicle for the realization of explicitly socialist aims. The one specific trait which distinguished the two men was Brynfab's outstanding talent as a public speaker. As it turned out, he possessed the one essential quality needed to win over a work-force ripe for revolt and to put new life into the ailing labour section of Undeb Gweithwyr Môn.

Anglesey workers were already showing that they were alive to their chance. A large crowd of farm labourers met at Llangristiolus on 8 October to select representatives for the district wages committee.[57] Now the name of W.J. Jones was added alongside the more familiar ones of Thomas Rowlands, William Edwards and Hugh Pritchard. Days later Thomas Rowlands and J. Fred Jones were explaining the provisions of the Corn Production Act to the labour section of Undeb Gweithwyr Môn.[58] At Penmynydd, a meeting overflowing with workers heard a similar enunciation by Daniel

Rowlands, a humble road labourer from the village,[59] while over in the parish of Llanidan events took the same course. A decision to band together was taken and Brynfab instructed to send for a copy of the rules of Undeb Gweithwyr Môn.[60] There was no mistaking the new mood among agricultural labourers, with *Y Wyntyll* at hand to give free expression to their opinions. Some would have no truck with the patronizing middle-class leadership of Undeb Gweithwyr Môn;[61] it had to be a trade union for Anglesey workers led by Anglesey workers. As a veteran who had spent most of his life attempting to awake the farm labourers, 'Iorwerth' sounded a note of caution before inviting interested parties to Llangefni in the name of Undeb Gweithwyr Môn.[62]

History again repeated itself as representatives from the various localities made their way to Llangefni on 8 November. With well-known figures like Thomas Rowlands, Iorwerth and David Lloyd speaking in favour, the meeting resolved to reactivate the labour section of Undeb Gweithwyr Môn by holding meetings and establishing local branches.[63] To give the campaign new effectiveness Brynfab was made organizer aided by an impressive list of speakers. Morale and purpose restored, many of the old warriors of Undeb Gweithwyr Môn began to shed the spirit of ap Ffarmwr upon the present generation of workers. One veteran hero, John Hughes, soon demonstrated his characteristic vigour with a fiery speech at Aberffraw.[64] At the same time, Cyril O. Jones urged the Holyhead Trades and Labour Council to render farm labourers every assistance.[65] Before long southern Anglesey was in ferment. From one village to the next a coterie of speakers carried the message of unity. Many branches were founded, and as the movement spread to the centre of the island its originator could well sense the breaking of a new dawn.[66]

Over in Caernarfonshire the localized nature of events became equally apparent with an awakening in Llŷn quite separate from that in the north and centre of the county. In fact, so strong were the insular feelings that its protagonists thought initially in terms of a Llŷn agricultural labourers' union. Wartime inequities were etched deep in the minds of the labourers and unrest came to a head on 8 October when the men met at Sarn Bach Chapel, near Abersoch, intent on forming a union.[67] Behind this move was John W. Thomas, the district relieving officer, a man with strong Labour views. In the course of his duties he had come across examples of wretched poverty amongst the families of farm labourers.[68] Unable to tolerate such misery he took it upon himself to show the way. His efforts met with considerable success: all but three of the forty-four labourers in the parish of Llanengan were said to have attended the meeting. That the district wages committee was soon to be established underlined the urgency of organization, and subsequent gatherings at Abersoch, Llannor, Boduan and Llanbedrog attested to the unusual fervour among labourers. At Boduan the local schoolmaster had called the meeting and acted as secretary; at Llannor the vicar took the chair.[69] While some farmers declared sympathy others were reported to be angry at 'outsiders' who interfered in their business. By the end of October branches had been formed in seven parishes and more meetings planned.[70] Progress was rapid. Within a matter of some six weeks the Lleyn Agricultural Labourers' Union claimed over 700 members.[71]

When the men gathered for a conference at Pwllheli in November to plan the next step, John W. Thomas announced that meetings had been held in thirteen different parishes with membership now approaching 800.[72] As he pointed out, the need for a trade union was real enough; farmers were manipulating the young men into accepting low wages at the hiring fairs with the promise of an escape from military service. Accompanying him on the platform were Richard Griffith, a drover at Madryn Castle Farm School, and O. Ellis Jones, one-time president of the NWQU who worked as a journalist at Pwllheli.[73] An ILP sympathizer yet Liberal Party member, O. Ellis Jones drew attention to the terms offered by the NALRWU. And his rosy picture of its strength and successes was sufficient to persuade the audience to decide unanimously in favour of linking up with the national union.

Friction between farmers and workers along the Conwy Valley, at the opposite end of the county, had triggered the labour instincts of Hugh J. Thomas ('Huw Tudur').[74] A lead miner at Trefriw by trade — he later served as branch secretary of the National Union of Gasworkers and General Labourers — Huw Tudur raised the possibility of farm hands from Conwy to Ysbyty Ifan coming together to form a trade union. The farmers had a membership of 500 in their own Vale of Conway Farmers' Union. Apparently a letter containing his proposal was circularized and in response one correspondent called for a conference at Llanrwst, where workers could decide whether to form their own independent union or join one of the 'English' combinations.[75] As it happened, Huw Tudur had already addressed agricultural workers at Henryd and a NALRWU branch had been formed with 30 members. Owen Chambers, a local farm labourer who presided over the meeting, became extremely unpopular with the farmers as a result.[76] Very soon, this effort was matched by activists in the district around Llandudno Junction.[77] Under the patronage of the local branch of the NUR a mass meeting of agricultural labourers in the public hall heard the rudiments of trade unionism explained by the Revd W. Washington Owen, a Baptist minister-cum-railwayman.[78] A branch of the NALRWU was then established with W. Washington Owen as secretary.

All this successful activity in Anglesey and the rural areas of Caernarfonshire put extra pressure on labour leaders connected with the town of Caernarfon.[79] With tens, if not hundreds, of agricultural labourers in the district completely untouched, they were under a strong obligation to extend the scope of trade unionism. Caernarfonshire Labour Council had always been full of good intentions but when the NALRWU approached the NWQU for assistance, their application was merely left on the table.[80] All the same, officials from both bodies at last took the initiative and arranged a meeting at Caernarfon on 8 December.[81] Convened by William Williams on behalf of the Labour Council, the meeting heard addresses by J.E. Thomas and R.T. Jones of the NWQU. A close friend of David Thomas, J.E. Thomas, a schoolteacher, along with R.G. Roberts, a quarryman, had pioneered the labour movement in Dyffryn Nantlle. Drawing upon their experience, each speaker declared that the hour of the agricultural labourer had come. The men of Anglesey and Llŷn provided an inspiration and, citing his own union as an example, R.T. Jones made known his preference for an independent Welsh organization. But instead of following this course the meeting decided that the newly established branch should become an annexe of Anglesey by affiliating with Undeb Gweithwyr Môn!

Again, almost unnoticed outside its borders, similar developments took place in Merioneth, with the Bala Trades and Labour Council acting as recruiting station for the farm workers. The two leading participants in the struggles of 1917–18, W.T. Bason and D.R. ('Rolly') Williams, were highly respected public figures and lay preachers with a gift for oratory — Bason in English, Williams in Welsh. Experiences of hardship and poverty in his early days left an indelible mark on Bason[82] and, as a railway signal lineman, he fought for the underprivileged by being active in union work. Sharing similar views and equally outspoken, Rolly Williams,[83] a GWR engine-driver, had fought strongly along with Bason to improve the working conditions of fellow railwaymen through their respective unions, the NUR and ASLEF. As out-and-out socialists both men were eager to strengthen labour interests in the town as well as organize the low-paid workers in the outlying agricultural districts. Within a month of its formation the Trades and Labour Council set out to get them to join their own particular union.[84] Taking the lead in this respect, Bason wrote off to the NALRWU head office for details of how best to form a branch.[85] Agricultural labourers were then specifically invited to a meeting of the council so that the aims of the union could be explained.[86] When a local branch came into existence in November, twenty-five farm-hands immediately joined up and a local shopkeeper, Humphrey Ellis, acted as secretary.[87] Shortly after, Rolly Williams addressed a successful meeting at Llanuwchllyn which led to the formation of a sister branch, this time with T. Llew Williams, a farm labourer, as secretary.[88] With thirty-five members in Bala and forty in Llanuwchllyn by the end of the year, the Trades and Labour Council had made good use of its opportunities.[89]

Railwaymen also laid the foundations in mid-Wales. Along the railway network in Montgomeryshire, NUR organization had flourished; the Machynlleth branch numbered 400 members. On his tour of the area in October 1917, A.J. Williams, the organizing secretary, addressed a series of meetings attended by both railwaymen and agricultural labourers.[90] It had been pointed out to him by the secretary of NALRWU how badly organized the farm workers were in reality.[91] By explaining the advantages of trade unionism and the significance of the Corn Production Act he hoped to arouse their interest. Labourers were certainly embittered, the chief cause of complaint being the long hours of work — thirteen or fourteen hours per day on average — and low wage levels.[92] Of all the unions catering for agricultural workers it was the Liverpool-based National Farm and Dairy Workers' Union which first established a bridgehead in the county. Even more surprising it opened its first branch (on 13 October) at Sarn, a small isolated village near Newtown.[93] Little detail was given in the press.[94] But when steps were taken to form a second branch at Montgomery in December, John Blayney of the Machynlleth NUR branch presided over the meeting and introduced John Phipps, the secretary of the union (who still maintained his membership of the NUR).[95] Additional meetings at Bryn-crug, Towyn and Llanegryn in south-west Merioneth reflected a clear ambition to extend its scope. It was not altogether unexpected that Blayney and Phipps would incur the displeasure of the farmers[96] nor that a conservative local newspaper might describe their demand for a forty-two shilling minimum wage as a 'mad proposal'.[97] In the mean time, it was fitting that the Workers' Union, through its Midlands organizers, should begin to make its presence felt in the urban centres of Montgomeryshire with an inaugural branch at Newtown, the birthplace of Robert Owen.[98]

With good reason, therefore, the year 1917 proved to be the major turning-point in the history of the agricultural labourers. The Corn Production Act had awarded them the cachet of recognition and status. Under the act, an Agricultural Wages Board composed of 39 members was constituted; farmers and labourers each had 16 representatives with another 7 independent members. One Welshman sat on the workers' side, Robert Richards, a lecturer in economics at the University College of North Wales, Bangor. This body would then determine the statutory minimum wage. Adopting the same principle of equal representation balanced by 'neutrals', district wages committees were set up to fix the rates of remuneration (with differentials for the various special classes of skilled men),[99] hours of labour and overtime at local level. Although the district committees could propose more than the minimum rate they only had the right of recommendation; the final decision lay with the central board. Of the thirty-nine district wages committees in operation by May 1918, six were in Wales. Administrative counties were coupled together as a single unit, the exception being the three counties which form present-day Dyfed.[100] For the very first time, agricultural labourers were an integral part of the wage-negotiating machinery and for a work-force that had been hitherto ignored or taken for granted the significance was enormous.

Equal rights, however, meant matching the employers' power of organization. The farmers were already furthering their own interests as a class by enrolling in the National Farmers' Union (founded 1908) or similar bodies that were eventually affiliated to the NFU. For instance, the short-lived Welsh Farmers' Union had, by February 1918, 40 branches and 7,000 members in north Wales.[101] Very often such facts were of great propaganda value to trade union promoters in that it served as an added inducement to the labourers themselves.

Full advantage had to be taken of this golden opportunity and all in all the onus of organization lay as much with union leadership as with the workers themselves. Appeals for the services of organizers arrived thick and fast at the NALRWU head office. Soon the union found itself in the sphere of industrial relations involved in collective wage bargaining at every level. A new monthly journal called *The Land Worker* was planned and this, together with the transfer of the union's head office from Norfolk to London in May 1918, signalled an end to the parochial phase of the union. As a truly national body it had to be better placed to cope with the astounding growth encountered in 1917–18. From 249 branches in 1916, the number increased to 402 in 1917 and 1,537 by 1918. Converts came in by the hundred. No accurate membership figures are available (some are grossly exaggerated) but Michael Madden has calculated a membership of 3,676 in 1916, doubling to 7,738 in 1917 and rising to an extraordinary 40,855 in 1918.[102]

The Workers' Union also responded to the challenge in similar fashion. Starting from almost nothing in 1917, it claimed 400 branches and a membership (again inflated) of 30,000 in its agricultural section by May 1918.[103] In order to avert the friction and recrimination which inter-union rivalry might induce, both organizations were brought together by the TUC to discuss the overlapping of organizing work.[104] It transpired that the NALRWU had a tacit understanding with the Dockers' Union and the National Union of Gasworkers and General Labourers (who had also taken in agricultural labourers), but not with the Workers' Union. Neither side appeared willing to give ground, so no agreed compromise was reached at this stage. The organization of the remaining farm labourers would still be on a free-for-all basis.

Additional officers were engaged to deal with the extra load and in 1918 NALRWU had thirty regional organizers at work. It was against this background that the union executive decided to engage a Welsh-speaking organizer in December 1917. Although the number of appeals from Wales was by no means exceptional, the position was deemed promising enough to warrant his appointment. Territorially, the union listed 19 branches spread over six counties,[105] but the movement needed direction and cohesion and there was always the desire to win new ground. When interviews were held in December, only one name cropped up in the Welsh context, that of David Rees, Aberafan. But no man was better qualified than he was to school the agricultural labourers in the fundamentals of trade unionism. Labour politics dominated his life; since 1903 he had been a member of Aberafan Town Council. He was employed as a crane-driver at Port Talbot, and there his name became equally synonymous with trade union activity. In 1913, the year he became Mayor of Aberafan, he was appointed the Welsh representative of the General Federation of Trade Unions Approved Society, and at that time his ILP links brought him into touch with David Thomas. His experience and connections made him an ideal candidate. Though he failed to turn up for the December interview, David Rees was officially appointed 'Organizer for Wales', with a salary of £3 a week plus expenses, on 5 January 1918.[106] Given the geographical area and the purely physical problems alone, David Rees must have felt he was facing a continent rather than a country.

As his first priority Rees decided to concentrate on building up an organization in Glamorgan.[107] Still completely untouched, the county appeared to be the appropriate starting-point, and during January he was said to be busy organizing farm labourers in the Vale of Glamorgan between Bridgend and Barry.[108] On 23 January Rees spoke to a large crowd of workers at the White Lion Hotel, Llantwit Major, and on the proposal of James Kennett, a local labourer, the first branch was founded.[109] Because the farm workers' capacity for organization was as limited as his own, Rees could only operate effectively in conjunction with established labour unions. Here, as in Monmouthshire, the SWMF and NUR soon came forward with support. When another public meeting was arranged at Cowbridge a local NUR man presided and T.I. Mardy Jones, the SWMF parliamentary agent in east Glamorgan and one of its top officials, delivered a rousing speech.[110] He wished to see the farm labourers link up with the miners and railwaymen to take an active part in public affairs. To ensure that the importance of the Corn Production Act was brought home, Mardy Jones addressed several gatherings in the Vale as well as the annual meeting of the Llantrisant and Cowbridge Trades Council.[111]

Not all went smoothly. The staunchness of the men who joined the branches at Llantwit Major and Cowbridge was in marked contrast to the attitude shown by workers in the neighbourhood of Bridgend.[112] Whereas farm labourers near this town were expected to have profited from a closer contact with the industrial unions, they proved in fact to be far less responsive than their fellow workers in the remoter farming areas. Though David Jenkins of Boverton, a prominent farmer and leading NFU official, had claimed that farmers did not in any way disapprove of the men's organization, this was far from the truth. During his enquiries Edgar Chappell found that the labourers' union had aroused considerable alarm and hostility amongst the farmers of the district.[113] Moreover, what Jenkins uttered in public he manifestly failed to practise in his own backyard. One of his employees was none other than James Kennett, now secretary of the Llantwit Major branch and chief spokesman for the labourers. And the unvarnished evidence he supplied on behalf of the men for the 1918 inquiry[114] gave the farmers so much offence that Jenkins dismissed him with a week's notice to quit his tied cottage.[115]

William Harris's continuing progress in neighbouring Monmouthshire allowed Rees to bypass the county and move on to less promising territory. With seven branches at work in south Monmouthshire, Harris took steps to form a district council made up of delegates from each branch.[116] Unionizing efforts continued so that within a month Harris could notch up four more branches.[117] By the time of the first meeting of the Monmouthshire District Council in June, the labourers had an organization to match the NFU. David Rees took advantage of the occasion to acknowledge his debt to William Harris, A.W. Pittman and the other railwaymen, and to thank the SWMF and NUR for providing financial assistance.[118]

Previous groundwork in Pembrokeshire enabled the union to function with the same air of self-reliance. There was no need for David Rees to do much more than pay an occasional visit to drum up extra support. Political objectives guaranteed the continuing patronage of the county Labour Party, while local activists helped to keep branches on their feet. By March, the Solva and Croes-goch branches had close on 200 members between them.[119] Of the 70 labourers in St Nicholas only 7 were not in the branch.[120] Working-class political aspirations, in turn, made the farmers fearful of the farm labourers challenging their supremacy on local bodies. Outside agitators propagating socialism 'made in Germany' were particularly unwelcome.[121] Independence of mind was something the farmers could not tolerate and their rage often knew no caution as Thomas Francis, the secretary of St Davids branch, found to his cost. Farmers who dominated the rural tribunal at Haverfordwest decided, at a private hearing, to cancel his exemption certificate when all the other agricultural labourers were granted a renewal.[122] Regarded as an example of glaring victimization, his case was raised in the Commons by William Adamson, chairman of the parliamentary Labour Party.[123] Meanwhile at Mathry, John Lloyd found it impossible to get employment locally, whilst his brother William was forced to leave for the Glamorgan coalfield.[124]

Although C.H. Ralph, the secretary of Pembroke branch, showed great interest in agriculture,[125] the Workers' Union had yielded primacy to NALRWU in Pembrokeshire. Neither did it find much support in Cardiganshire outside Aberystwyth and Lampeter despite the element of open competition between the various unions. In the lead-mining districts, the National Amalgamated Labourers' Union drew in a number of agricultural labourers among its 344 members.[126] Likewise, the Dockers' Union successfully attracted farm workers when enlarging the boundary of its rural operations.[127] District organizers and experienced orators, including Ben Tillett, gave the Dockers' Union campaign a professional touch, but the omission of agricultural workers as branch officials enabled David James ('Dafydd Iago'), Glynarthen, to promote NALRWU as the labourers' 'own union'.[128] Already, the Revd T.E. Nicholas had become an emissary on its behalf. Using his bicycle to travel from village to village he covered south Cardiganshire as well as north Pembrokeshire. In March he teamed up with David Rees at Llanfyrnach.[129] Perseverance paid off. By the end of the month he could announce that the 'farm labourers' union is coming A1. They come in in scores.'[130] As the district wages committees were about to be set up, Nicholas was equally keen to familiarize himself with the Corn Production Act so that he might represent the workers, regardless of the danger signs. 'The Farmers' Union', he wrote, 'are opposing the minimum wage with all their usual bitterness.'[131]

Trade union propaganda taught the individual worker to understand the market value of his labour much to the consternation of Cardiganshire farmers. To them, the union spelt 'danger',[132] and their wrath was specifically directed at those 'schoolmasters and retired sea captains' who knew nothing about agriculture. They might also have added ministers of religion. For the labourers of Cardiganshire and north Pembrokeshire were fortunate in having a circle of friends to speak out in their interest. On several occasions, on the platform of both the Dockers' Union and NALRWU, schoolmasters, mariners and ministers voiced support. Names that crop up regularly include those of J. Rees, Tegryn, J. Davies, Hermon,

J. Gwendraeth James, Blaenporth (all schoolmasters) and Captain David Davies, Aberporth, an ex-master mariner. Whenever the Revds D.D. Walters ('Gwallter Ddu'), J.H. Jenkins and E.J. Davies, Bangor Teifi, were billed to speak, the audience could expect 'some sweet socialistic music'.[133] The main theme of Gwallter Ddu's popular lecture, 'O Gaethiwed i Ryddid', emphasized universal brotherhood and the abolition of class distinctions; he put his faith in the class struggle and internationalism.[134] But the farmers' chief enemy was the Revd T.E. Nicholas. His persuasive speeches, often lasting two hours and into which he weaved the Sermon on the Mount,[135] were regarded as the worst form of intrusive extremism.

Because of its remoteness the vast agricultural portion of west Carmarthenshire, in contrast, was virgin land with no tradition of trade union activism. When David Rees opened his campaign in Laugharne town hall in February it was seen as a 'fresh movement'.[136] But as the miners' organization in the east of the county and the local NUR remained aloof, he had his work cut out. Rees's only real support came from John Sharp, a former collier who had returned from Glamorgan to his native county to become a smallholder.[137] A stirring speech on the advantages of trade unionism led to the creation of a branch at Laugharne with Sharp as temporary secretary.[138] Sharp also accompanied Rees to Pendine and St Clears when two other branches came into being.[139] By July, however, the initial burst of enthusiasm seemed to be in danger of running out. When David Rees came back to address the St Clears branch he found that he had no audience![140]

At this point the agricultural section of the Workers' Union in south Wales was confined to a frail presence in the border counties. A rural outpost in Catbrook, Monmouthshire, relied mainly on local woodcutters.[141] On Christmas night 1917, T.J. Stokoe had taken advantage of a social function at Glasbury to plug the Workers' Union.[142] By May, Sidney Box was again on the warpath, leading a recruiting drive among the landworkers of Hay and Glasbury.[143] The meeting at Glasbury was considered to be one of the most successful held in the village.[144] David Rees, meantime, had secured the official backing of the Breconshire Labour Party. One of its members promised as much at the meeting of the county council in January.[145] While his remarks were greeted with laughter, the party held true to its word. Having invited Rees to address their meeting in February a sub-committee was formed to aid him.[146] As a political organization it aimed to unionize all the working men in the county prior to winning parliamentary representation. By May, Rees was reported to be busy preparing for the task,[147] but little progress had been made before the summer, when he received the assistance of local NUR officials.

As far as one can make out, David Rees managed to fit in at least two visits to north Wales in the first half of 1918. On his first journey in February he addressed the Vale of Clwyd branch at Denbigh.[148] The meeting attracted a fair attendance and was regarded as the start of a local drive to win more converts.[149] By May another branch had been established at Rhuthun.[150] The following month, two Labour Party stalwarts from Colwyn Bay, the Revd J.H. Howard and D. Price Evans, a railway clerk, succeeded in reactivating interest at Llannefydd.[151] Prior to a second tour in April, Rees had contacted the Wrexham Trades and Labour Council inviting their assistance.[152] This time it appears he concentrated more on north Caernarfonshire where NALRWU enjoyed greater support. At Llandudno Junction he spoke at a well-attended public meeting together with the Revd T. Washington Owen, now designated district organizer.[153]

David Rees's missions to north Wales could only have made him more keenly aware of the magnitude of his task. Denbighshire and Flint proved unproductive because his union arrived too late in the day; it had already been outdistanced by the National Farm and Dairy Workers' Union. Firmly established across the border in Lancashire and Cheshire, Phipps's organization was neatly poised to win over the north-east corner under the articulate command of D.W. Jones ('ap Rhydwen') of Whitford. A timber-feller by trade, ap Rhydwen became aware of the day-to-day problems confronting the illiterate farm worker.[154] His column 'Telegrams' in *Baner ac Amserau Cymru* had shown him to be a perceptive humanitarian increasingly in sympathy with the labour movement.[155] Turning from Liberal to socialist during the war years he undertook organizing responsibility for the NFDWU in January 1918. Moreover, he utilized *Baner ac Amserau Cymru* — officially a 'Farmers' Journal' — to propound his views. The case then before Denbighshire Quarter Sessions of a farm labourer charged with sheep stealing added substance to his rallying call. Paid but twelve shillings a week, the defendant had been driven to crime because of sheer poverty. As ap Rhydwen emphasized, it behoved every farm worker to join a union so that he might be guaranteed of receiving the statutory minimum wage.[156] The fact that the NFDWU was an English union based in Liverpool should not deter them; members were free to conduct every aspect of branch business through the medium of the Welsh language.[157]

His first steps were made in the Whitford district. And as 'Welsh organizing secretary' ap Rhydwen became ever more involved with the spread and popularization of trade unionism in Clwyd. Within a matter of weeks the response exceeded all expectations.[158] The union's ambitious programme gave workers a goal to strive for: a ten-hour day with a minimum wage of forty-two shillings per week. Union members at Hawarden soon put in their claim for higher wages.[159] Although Holywell workers made similar noises they agreed, in the event, to await the decision of the district wages committee.[160] By May, the union had at least six branches in Flintshire and a membership of 500.[161] Then, in an apparent attempt to link up with the NFDWU enclave around Towyn, established the previous December, ap Rhydwen led a push into north Merioneth. But, apart from a public meeting at Gwyddelwern,[162] he made little headway. Central Merioneth, in any case, was being consolidated into the ranks of NALRWU. Agricultural labourers made a spontaneous effort to form a branch at Talsarnau in January;[163] in the same month Bason and Rolly Williams were able to set up a branch at Llandrillo.[164] Subsequent meetings at Cynwyd and Llandderfel strengthened the union's hold on the Bala district. However Bason and Humphrey Ellis failed to get things going at Trawsfynydd.[165]

For a time Denbighshire remained untouched and it was not until May that ap Rhydwen began following on the heels of NALRWU. Meanwhile, the National Union of General Workers (formerly the Gasworkers' and General Labourers' Union) had taken advantage of its strength in the Abergele area. Farm labourers came from a long distance to hear W.G. Parry, secretary of the Colwyn Bay branch, give an address at Llaneilian-yn-Rhos in January, whereupon a branch was formed.[166]

The reception given to the NFDWU in Montgomeryshire proved impressive by any reckoning. Splendidly supported by the NUR, Phipps made hay while the sun of discontent blazed on the farmers. When a Berriew farm-hand enquired how a workman and his family could exist on their 'starvation wage'[167] he doubtlessly spoke for all those who came to hear Blayney and Phipps.[168] Another vigorous speech by Phipps to a large congregation at Montgomery went down well with all but the employers.[169] Indeed, the way Phipps burst on the scene advocating a ten-hour day and 42-shilling weekly wage provoked the local press to slate the 'wild programme' of the labourers' union.[170] Nothing, however, could dampen the warmth of the welcome given to trade unionism. On professing sympathy with the men's cause, the Revd Gwilym Rees, rector of Llanbryn-mair, presided over a number of enthusiastic meetings in the village.[171] Times had surely changed. Sixty years before it was S.R., the Independent minister and favourite son of Llanbryn-mair, who had led the struggle against oppression in the parish. The current minister of 'Yr Hen Gapel', ironically enough also named Samuel Roberts, was found wanting. It was left to G.H. Peate, a deacon at the chapel and a great friend of the rector, to ensure that the radical Nonconformist tradition lived on. A carpenter by trade, he felt strongly about the low wages and long hours suffered by farm workers and agreed to act as branch secretary.[172]

Fearless leadership at Llanbryn-mair gave the labourers' organization sufficient confidence to present the Farmers' Union with a demand for a reduction in working hours.[173] At the same time, workers in the county continued to join by the dozen. An inspired address by John Blayney launched the Aberhosan branch with twenty-four members.[174] This meant that a considerable rural area around his home base of Machynlleth was brought firmly under the control of the NFDWU. When Phipps and ap Rhydwen came to address a joint meeting of four neighbouring Merioneth branches at Towyn, 174 members were claimed,[175] and a schoolroom filled to capacity heard both men offer trade unionism as the panacea for rural poverty.

When localized movements took off there existed, as in Anglesey and Llŷn, an almost self-protective tendency towards independence. At a second conference of south Caernarfonshire labourers in January the men went back on an earlier decision to join NALRWU.[176] Instead, there was a declaration in favour of the original idea of an independent farm workers' union.[177] On the assumption that Welsh labourers had their own special needs and traditions they opted for autonomy, and invited branches of other workers' unions to join them. Once a strong Welsh union was formed they could then discuss linking up with NALRWU or the TUC. As a prelude, meetings were to be organized in all parts of Llŷn and Eifionydd. Led by the officers of the Lleyn Agricultural Labourers' Union, including John W. Thomas who remained as secretary, it hoped to see the farm workers themselves take more part in the running of the projected union. In the event, this challenge proved too much and plans for a Welsh agricultural labourers' union progressed no further.

Paradoxically, the kind of independence sought at Llŷn was being exemplified in full over in Anglesey where a deep-rooted historical tradition predisposed its agricultural labourers to the ideals of Undeb Gweithwyr Môn. Under Brynfab's direction a band of talented publicists carried the union's message to all corners of the island, a task made considerably easier in that Brynfab was one of the fortunate few to own a Ford Model T car. Almost in the spirit of a religious revival, Brynfab, Thomas Rowlands, J. Fred Jones, the Revds Richard Morris and E.B. Jones went from village to village where they were 'always received with open arms'.[178] Embracing both a moral dimension as well as biblical conviction, the Revd E.B. Jones likened the presence of the union to the 'Good Samaritan'.[179] Reports of their public meetings filled the local press. By February, Undeb Gweithwyr Môn had over 20 branches and some 1,000 members.[180] No other county produced such fruitful results in so short a time; in Anglesey the movement became one of the most dramatic developments of the age. Its effectiveness at local level derived in no small measure from the help given by committed sympathizers. Brynfab could count on a phalanx of schoolmasters, ministers, clergymen (even the Catholic priest of Beaumaris), craftsmen and officers of other unions to act as chairmen, speakers or branch officials. Although they endeavoured to co-ordinate all sections of the working class, both skilled and unskilled, within Undeb Gweithwyr Môn,[181] the farm labourers still formed the great majority. As a mark of confidence branch meetings began discussing a variety of topics. Apart from industrial matters they called for better housing and for working-class representation on public bodies, including the county council.

Labour Day celebrations at Llangefni in May provided a striking demonstration of the strength of Undeb Gweithwyr Môn.[182] On Whit Monday some 1,000 workers marched through the streets of the town on the pattern of the *Gŵyl Lafur* staged by the north Wales quarrymen. The number of branches in the labour section had risen to 33 within five months whilst membership exceeded 2,000. As their president Thomas Rowlands remarked, they could feel a sense of growing power. They elected officers and a twenty-strong executive committee. The pay and working conditions of the farm labourers came up for discussion. But unquestionably more far-reaching were the decisions to contest the county council elections and nomin ate a Labour parliamentary candidate jointly with the Holyhead Trades and Labour Council (representing a further 2,000 workers). The 'feeble cheers'[183] that greeted the unexpected appearance of Ellis Jones Griffith MP became a portent of the political direction the union was taking. In every aspect Undeb Gweithwyr Môn was becoming a worthy monument to the name of ap Ffarmwr.

Along these broad lines of development the map of revolt unfolded. NALRWU prevailed in south Wales with pockets in some northern counties, while from its north-east base NFDWU made inroads into mid-Wales, leaving Anglesey proudly independent. By any standard, it was an extraordinary 'rural awakening'.[184] Agricultural workers had begun a process of gradual emancipation and the North Wales Trades and Labour Council, at its fourth annual conference at Wrexham in May, could well rejoice.[185] A resolution urging local labour organizations to render the movement every assistance was moved by Brynfab, the Undeb Gweithwyr Môn delegate. Trade union propagandists had effectively presented their case. At no other time did so many farm workers hear such truths or enjoy the sheer freedom to register their discontent. A network of branches covered all thirteen Welsh counties, often reflecting their diverse traditions. NALRWU branches in Monmouthshire would meet in the local tavern on a Sunday afternoon; in Nonconformist Anglesey the Welsh-speaking executive committee of Undeb Gweithwyr Môn always started proceedings with a prayer. With both national and localized organizations attracting so many new members from amongst the rural work-force there was now urgent need to ease the heavy load put on the respective organizers.

The NALRWU's failings in this respect soon emerged. When J.E. Thomas began unionizing labourers in the Caernarfon district in early March,[186] he also tried, unsuccessfully, to convince R.B. Walker of the importance of sending his Welsh organizer along.[187] Later both he and William Williams were reported to be tired of waiting for David Rees to arrive.[188] In order to maintain the interest of the men they hit on a plan whereby R.G. Roberts would give up his work at the quarry[189] for a month to go around the countryside organizing farm workers. If NALRWU was unwilling to support him financially, then the Caernarfonshire Labour Council agreed to pay his wages. Thence followed a concentrated campaign which yielded promising results at Llandwrog, Brynaerau and Clynnog.[190] Though R.G. Roberts was referred to as the 'prospective organizer' of NALRWU, his work had to be financed locally, again prompting J.E. Thomas to bewail Walker's lack of concern. By chance, there were equally hopeful signs in the south of the county. Following early setbacks to the Lleyn Agricultural Labourers' Union, Caradog Jones, a young schoolteacher at Rhiw, took over its remnants and began revitalizing the movement,[191] starting at Four Crosses. At the end of 1917 he had come into contact with R.G. Roberts and other union-minded quarrymen who had left the slate districts to work at the manganese quarry at Rhiw.[192] Inspired by the quarrymen and the idealism of the ILP, he began to practise the socialism of service that later made his name a byword in Llŷn. Travelling on his bicycle to hold meetings, he had succeeded by the summer in opening branches at Four Crosses, Aberdaron, Mynytho and Nefyn.[193]

Once R.B. Walker grasped the full significance of the situation in Caernarfonshire, R.G. Roberts was invited to meet W.R. Smith, the union president, for an interview. Strongly backed by R.T. Jones's recommendation,[194] Roberts was formally appointed organizer for north Wales on 6 July at a salary of £2.10*s*. a week plus expenses.[195] As a pioneer of the ILP, founder member of the Caernarfonshire Labour Council and one-time president of the NWQU he seemed to hold all the necessary qualities. Against many odds, and showing great personal courage,[196] R.G. Roberts had never retreated from the fight to improve the condition of the working class. In this characteristic spirit he gave his best on behalf of the farm labourer. His immediate plan was to unite all the farm workers in Caernarfonshire within NALRWU.[197] Acting in partnership with Caradog Jones he addressed the surviving branches of the Lleyn Agricultural Labourers' Union in preparation for their eventual merger with the national union.

A month after R.G. Roberts's appointment the union invested in the services of John Davies, Llangeitho, as organizer in west Wales.[198] Almost a mirror image of R.G. Roberts in his socialist pedigree, he proved to be an equally suitable choice. With his roots in rural Cardiganshire, Davies's early years were spent in the Rhondda, where his father was killed in a mine explosion.[199] Apprenticed to the drapery trade, he developed a keen interest in the trade union movement during the coal strike of 1898, becoming one of the first members of the ILP in south Wales. Joining the staff of *Llais Llafur*, he gave further expression to his religio-socialist convictions through voluntary work with the YMCA during the war. This combination of ideology, organizing experience and knowledge of rural Wales enabled John Davies to build on the positive achievements of his predecessors in Cardigan, Pembroke and Carmarthen. In appointing a trio of able organizers NALRWU heralded its strong commitment to extending the union's holdings in Wales, and to facilitate their work it sanctioned the translation of propaganda leaflets into the Welsh language.[200]

As organizer in north Wales, R.G. Roberts's main role in 1918 was to give structural unity to NALRWU branches in Caernarfonshire, Merioneth and Denbigh. Three branches founded in the detached part of Flintshire at this time probably tied in with a campaign undertaken by James Lunnon, the organizer for the adjoining English counties.[201] By arranging meetings on fair days and regularly visiting existing branches R.G. Roberts further improved the position in Caernarfonshire, so that by September almost all the agricultural labourers were said to have joined the union.[202] Of the men who helped him none showed more loyalty than Richard Griffith and Henry Davies, a farm-hand at Henryd in the Conwy Valley. Upon visiting branches in Merioneth and Denbigh in August, Roberts followed the same pattern of consolidation. Even though he received a good reception in Merioneth his endeavours only succeeded in starting one new branch, at Corwen.[203] A tour of the Vale of Clwyd strengthened his base in Denbighshire and gave John Foulkes ('Eithinfab') an opportunity to rekindle his involvement in agricultural labourers' trade unionism at Llannefydd.[204] An official round-up of the position at the end of the year showed that there were seventeen branches in Caernarfonshire and six apiece in Merioneth and Denbigh.[205] Both Llandudno Junction[206] and Nefyn branches[207] claimed 200 members, while Bala had 100.[208]

When John Davies took over in Dyfed, David Rees's charge was considerably eased. But as it turned out, Davies made little impact in Carmarthenshire, where the county branch of the NFU, curiously enough, became the first in the kingdom to admit labourers.[209] He fared much better in Pembroke and Cardigan. On assuming his duties in Pembroke there were fifteen branches in the county; by December they numbered twenty-five. Now 2,000 strong, NALRWU membership outstripped that of the NFU.[210] Apart from Labour Party officials he found an able ally in south Pembrokeshire in the person of John Picton, a Carew quarryman. That the fortunes of the union stood so high in Cardiganshire testified to the dedication of T.E. Nicholas. In the capacity of unpaid organizer, Nicholas had, by the end of October, held at least twenty-two meetings in the villages and remote hamlets of both north Pembroke and Cardiganshire.[211] But his emphasis on the social message of the gospel soon made him the most abused man in Cardiganshire. For those who preferred scriptural doctrines to be pulpit-bound, the actions of ministers like Nicholas and J.H. Jenkins verged on blasphemy; indeed the latter was fast becoming a twentieth-century version of the turbulent priest. On many occasions John Davies acknowledged his debt to T.E. Nicholas's pioneering work.[212] In accompanying Nicholas, and hearing socialist rhetoric delivered with such poetic eloquence, he had served an inspired apprenticeship. At the end of 1918 west Wales had nearly fifty branches and close on 3,000 members.[213]

Left with only the south-east counties, David Rees pushed on with his mission. In the summer he shared a platform at Brecon with T.J. Stokoe and C.T. Cramp, president of the NUR, who pledged the continued support of railwaymen.[214] Arranged by the Brecon branch of the NUR the meeting attracted a very large attendance. Success in Monmouthshire had advanced to a stage whereby he could count on the district council to speak for the county's fifteen branches.[215] Later in the year, Rees concentrated on opening up west Glamorgan and the Gower. A fine reception at Reynoldston in October[216] was followed by a similar meeting at Sketty.[217] Although the Gowerton Trades and Labour Council had expressed a keen interest in his enterprise at the beginning of the year[218] there is no evidence of subsequent support. It was rather a matter of relying on a local personality, in this case Alderman Thomas James, a boilermaker and NUR-sponsored Labour councillor.

For NALRWU the year 1918 had been one of solid triumphs in terms of branches and membership. The number of Welsh branches listed in its annual report shot from 19 to 99.[219] Unfortunately, because no official membership figures were kept there are no reliable totals to provide a statistical guide in real terms; all we have are the local claims. Given another four months, John Davies for one hoped to unionize at least fifty per cent of the rural workers in his area.[220] The results thus far seemed to justify the presence of three full-time organizers. Yet, the phenomenal success of NALRWU had not come without its quota of problems, difficulties, set-backs and personal sacrifice. Perhaps the greatest difficulty was to get the farm labourers themselves involved in the running of their branch. At Llannefydd, for instance, the local committee included a plasterer, postman and roadman much to the dismay of a farm labourer who demanded a 'real agricultural union'.[221] For David Rees, having the whole of Wales as his diocese meant being frequently away from home; even with additional organizers his family usually came second.[222] Unlike Brynfab he did not own a car, neither did he learn to drive. Travelling about meant train journeys and lodgings. As he later recalled, campaigning in the outlying and often inaccessible rural districts could be hard and rough; he knew what it was to address meetings 'under hedges on the road, in barns and cottages'.[223] For a man more used to industrial struggles in an urban environment the organization of the rural worker must have seemed a huge challenge. 'We are progressing in the south,' he confided to David Thomas in November 1918,[224] 'but not so fast as I would like.' Yet his faith in the future of the union was undiminished. 'I suppose we must exercise patience,' he added; 'good causes were not built in a day.'

Its main rival, the Workers' Union, meanwhile, had made a fresh spurt in rural Wales when it took over the NFDWU.[225] Financially insecure, the NFDWU threw in its lot with the agricultural section of the Workers' Union in May following negotiations and a ballot of members. Phipps retained responsibility for Lancashire and Cheshire, and ap Rhydwen was kept on as organizer in north-east Wales. Of the seventy branches (sixty of which agreed to amalgamation), some fifteen were found in Flintshire, Merioneth and Montgomery. Having stolen a march on NALRWU in Flintshire and Montgomery, ap Rhydwen crossed into Denbighshire in May to establish at least another ten branches by the end of the year.[226] He even had a local schoolmaster, O.E. Jones, acting as district organizer in the Pentrefoelas district.[227] (Later, complaints of his controversial extra-curricular activities were brought to the notice of the Denbighshire Education Committee.)[228] Not everything went his way. In August he expressed regret at the lack of interest shown by farm workers in the Holywell area.[229] Co-operation with the existing Workers' Union structure in Montgomery meant that a greater wedge was driven into mid-Wales. By October there were 25 branches in the county and a following of 4,000; Newtown and Welshpool had 800 and 700 members on their books.[230] Farm labourers, roadmen and town workers had come together in a way undreamed of twelve months earlier.

For its comparative size, Undeb Gweithwyr Môn continued to make great strides in splendid isolation. At the beginning of 1918 it had 10 branches and 255 members. By July there were 40 branches and a membership of between 2,500 and 3,000,[231] almost twice that of both Farmers' Unions in the county.[232] Llannerch-y-medd, the largest branch, had over 200 members. Female members were being admitted and Brynsiencyn and Llanfairpwll, at least, formed a separate women's section. To cope with the sudden influx of members, J. Fred Jones was appointed full-time county organizer. From October, members were able to wear their own union badge (inscribed 'Undeb Gweithwyr Môn, 1911') with defiant pride. Trade union activity had monopolized the columns of *Y Wyntyll* to such an extent that it finally dropped the sub-title 'Newyddiadur Rhyddfrydwyr Môn' from the mast-head to become almost the Anglesey version of *Llais Llafur*. Support continued to come from every quarter, and unlike ap Ffarmwr's crusade the movement attracted a growing band of Nonconformist ministers. At Tŷ Mawr, the Revd William Morris, a young Methodist minister with strong socialist sympathies, not only presided over a meeting to establish a branch but also tried, in the face of 'slanderous' retorts, to persuade his farmer-deacons to give their servants a fair deal.[233] As labourers became more involved in the fight to secure better working conditions and political recognition, the situation in Anglesey, as in the rest of Wales, was charged with deep hostility.

Norfolk became the first county to issue a minimum wage order in May, and its rate of 30*s*. a week was accepted by the Agricultural Wages Board as the legal minimum for adult male workers. Any advance on this would depend on the case presented by the workers' representatives during formal wage negotiations. In Wales, wage orders set by the district wages committees were to range from 30*s*. to 36*s*.6*d*. in Glamorgan and Monmouth.[234] Similarly, most committees followed Norfolk in applying a 54-hour week in summer and 48-hour week in winter. For the great majority of employers it was an altogether cheerless experience and most would have probably concurred with the speaker at a meeting of west Wales farmers who described the workers' organization as a 'power for evil'.[235] The conflict of interest was often irreconcilable. Labourers thought the farmers swam in money and pushed for the highest wage. Farmers always refuted such notions, setting their face against any wage rise or attempt to fix definite working hours. Consequently, whenever both parties met to discuss working conditions it became a matter of gaining the best bargain at the expense of the other side.[236]

Led by David Rees, the workers' representatives in Glamorgan and Monmouth had secured an exceptional bargain. But at once there was an outcry from farmers' organizations in both counties. Monmouthshire farmers pointed to the unfair anomaly in the Wye Valley where labourers on the Welsh side of the river were paid 36*s*.6*d*. compared with 31*s*. on the other — yet they did not receive higher prices for their farm produce.[237] Both the chairman, D. Lleufer Thomas, and the neutral members of the district wages committee were accused of bias against the employers, an attack roundly condemned in the press as being 'peevish and unfair'.[238] The substantial award to skilled workers in Flintshire could also be ascribed to trade union pressure. From early April the NFDWU had demanded a 35*s*. wage accompanied by the threat of a strike.[239] When it came to the vote, the workers' case was backed by the independent members on the committee.[240] Such awards could then be used to bolster the arguments put forward by David Rees for greater organizational strength within other counties.[241]

Representatives of both NALRWU and the Workers' Union were bracketed together on the employees' side of the district wages committees. They included many well-known figures: Thomas Rowlands, William Williams, John Picton, R.L. Jones, also David Thomas and John Foulkes, who sat together on the Denbigh and Flint committee. Although a number of farm workers can be identified, to the farmers' chagrin they were invariably outnumbered by non-labourers. Of all the surrogate members, employers took a particular dislike to railwaymen and professional trade unionists. A Farmers' Union official in Cardiganshire complained that the west Wales wages committee was led by a docker, a Dockers' Union organizer and a schoolmaster.[242] At Brecon and Radnor a spokesman for the farmers enquired if there was one bona fide labourer on the committee; the workers seemed to be represented by railwaymen and what did they know of farming?[243] Tough opposition meant that employers would find it difficult to impose their own terms. J. Gwendraeth James (the schoolmaster referred to above) knew from experience how farmers could be 'bigger Kaisers than the Kaiser himself'.[244]

Ill-educated and unacquainted with the finer points of wage bargaining, the agricultural labourers appreciated the protective mantle of the stronger unions. In turn, it became more difficult for the farmers to manipulate the men. In their anger, many resorted to threats, insults, intimidation and dismissal of workers directly involved in trade union activity. One labourer who joined the Letterston branch on a Saturday night received his marching orders the following Monday.[245] After receiving the sack James Kennett became a free-lance hay cutter in the Vale of Glamorgan.[246] But his interest in trade unionism never waned and the opportunity for revenge came the following year when he led the farm labourers' strike. Another activist to suffer victimization was R.L. Jones, Llanilar. When the time came to settle the year's wages his employer asked him 'sarcastically' if he wished to stay for another year or work for T.E. Nicholas, adding that there was no room for any 'union man' on his farm.[247] At the next hiring fair at Aberystwyth he found himself on the blacklist. Unable to find employment on a farm again, R.L. Jones became a council roadworker. However it did not prevent him from helping to run the Llanilar NALRWU branch or serving the union on the district wages committee and even its national executive. In submitting the grievances of the agricultural labourers to the notice of the Wrexham Trades and Labour Council, Francis Thomas invited retaliation. As the men's spokesman he had reported on working conditions and wage rates and this led the executive committee of the Trades Council to recommend a joint meeting with the Farmers' Union.[248] Not only did the farmers refuse to meet the men, but Francis Thomas was dismissed from his employment.[249] Despite the inaction of R.B. Walker and R.G. Roberts the Trades Council fought hard to win his immediate reinstatement.[250] But by the time the north Wales organizer finally arrived on the scene to lead a deputation it was too late; Francis Thomas had already secured alternative employment at a local mill.[251] A blatant case of victimization had been compounded by NALRWU incompetence.

In contrast with those labourers who suffered at the hands of the farmers, there were others fortunate enough to escape their wrath because of the particular nature of their employment. Two Caernarfonshire activists who successfully pursued union work with comparative immunity were Richard Griffith and Robert Thomas. As an employee of Madryn Castle Farm School, Richard Griffith was able to evade the 'terrible hostility' of Llŷn farmers and remain an outspoken trade unionist for many years.[252] Enjoying a similar status at the University College of North Wales Farm at Aber, Robert Thomas represented NALRWU on the district wages committee and was well known as a local labour activist.[253]

Even when wage rates and working hours had been set, the farmers employed every unscrupulous stratagem to make the act inoperative. Complaints that they flagrantly breached the compulsory minimum became a frequent *cri de coeur*. According to the south Wales organizer of the NUGW many labourers in Radnorshire were only receiving 23*s*. a week.[254] Cases of alleged underpayment brought to the notice of the Glamorgan and Monmouth district wages committee were promised immediate investigation with a view to legal proceedings.[255] Agreements, observed R.G. Roberts, were but 'a scrap of paper' to Caernarfonshire farmers; one in ten had completely disregarded their side of the bargain.[256] He found it hard to accept that farmers would stoop so low in their unchristian behaviour towards fellow chapel members. John Davies attacked those west Wales farmers who tried to circumvent the act by pressurizing their employees to accept a lower rate.[257] Reports of the threat of military service and other 'mean and contemptible' methods came to his notice from all quarters. Some farmers even employed women and young children under the misapprehension that they were exempt from statutory working hours.[258] At a conference of agricultural labourers, John Picton cited instances of men working a 70-hour week for 30*s*.[259] Failure to pay the legal minimum and resentment at having to work longer hours provoked the Pembrokeshire men to issue threats of industrial action.[260] Certain dishonourable farmers in Merioneth had dismissed their servants in order to employ German prisoners of war from the Frongoch camp at only 10*s*. a week.[261] With more workers under threat at Bala, Llanuwchllyn and Llandrillo, W.T. Bason contemplated asking his fellow railwaymen to give their support to a farm workers' strike.

On the men's side there could be similar opposition to the decisions of the district wages committee. NALRWU representatives in Cardiganshire met the Farmers' Union at a conference in Aberystwyth but failed to raise the official wage levels.[262] Dissatisfaction with the long working hours in Anglesey led the Llannerch-y-medd branch of Undeb Gweithwyr Môn to embark on a militant course. Independent of the other branches, it instructed its members not to work after 1 p.m. on Saturdays in pursuit of a campaign to win a Saturday half-holiday (noswyl un) and threatened to deal with any farmer who reacted by holding back wages.[263] Although a half-day holiday was the accepted practice in some English counties, the Agricultural Wages Board was unwilling to sanction its universal adoption in view of the wartime food shortage.[264] Nevertheless, a Saturday half-holiday had been a long-standing goal in Anglesey since ap Ffarmwr's day and the men at Llannerch-y-medd were determined to press ahead with its implementation. When George Jones ('ap Dafydd') questioned the legal and moral implications of their decision[265] he was unceremoniously expelled. That a follower of ap Ffarmwr and one of the founder members of Undeb Gweithwyr Môn should be treated this way was an index of their aggressive mood. As soon as the men's stand received the endorsement of the union's executive committee other branches began to work 'union hours'.[266] At the same time, some were instructing their members not to work with non-unionists (ap Dafydd, meanwhile, had been allowed to join another branch). Subsequent meetings with the Farmers' Union failed to resolve the dispute,[267] and only those labourers brave enough to stick to their guns worked 'union hours'.[268]

Because of the procedure laid down in the Corn Production Act, the Agricultural Wages Board found it impracticable to fix special rates in time for the 1918 harvest. Consequently, it was open to employers to make their own arrangements with the men regarding extra payment. In Conwy a deputation from the local NALRWU branch met the Farmers' Union to discuss harvest wages.[269] A local agreement at Llanasa and Newmarket was hammered out by both sides in a 'friendly spirit'.[270] But this independent initiative met with the disapproval of the executive committee of the Farmers' Union in Flintshire and separate harvest agreements at Caerwys and Whitford were scuttled.[271] Later in the year, however, the Workers' Union and the various farmers' unions came to an understanding on the retrospective payment of the minimum wage.[272] If friction was largely avoided in Flint these issues only added to the tension in Monmouthshire. There, the district council of the union asked for an extra harvest payment of 2*s*. an hour plus a retrospective payment backdated to 1 April.[273] At a meeting with the Farmers' Union, David Rees admitted the men did not have a legal right to the payments but asked for a sympathetic hearing on moral grounds.[274] Although the union was 'very strong' in the county he wished it to be seen as a request rather than a demand. Whichever way it was presented, the employers would have nothing to do with the proposal. Some of the men in the Magor and Newport district were, they claimed, already paid as much as 45*s*. The issue left unsettled, it appears once again that union leaders were sharpening their own skills as negotiators and challenging employers in order to test their resolve.

At the heart of the social programme propounded by trade union leaders came the assumption that agricultural workers would secure improved living standards through representation on local public bodies. Time and again, labour propagandists presented this wider political outlook in the interests of the working class. In many districts they fought successfully for a voice on the food control committees. Then again, claims were laid to an active part in any post-war scheme of reconstruction. Most pressing of all was the need for adequate rural housing, the provision of smallholdings and improved education. In the past farmers and landowners had enjoyed full control of all bodies operating the relevant acts to the obvious detriment of the labourers. Insanitary housing and the lack of smallholdings remained a scandal; discussion in education committees was often bogged down in arid sectarian disputes. To change the system organized labour had to win seats on parish, district and county councils, whilst beyond these lay the ultimate goal of parliamentary representation.

As it happened, labour interests in most rural constituencies had little time to build up an organization before the General Election of December 1918 was called. For this reason the Labour Party found itself unable to contest Flint, Merioneth, Carmarthen or Montgomery, although officers of the Newtown branch of the Workers' Union had considered political organization in Montgomery that summer.[275] Indeed, it was not until late in the following year that divisional Labour parties took shape in Flint and Merioneth; in the case of Carmarthen and Montgomery this had to wait until 1922 and 1923 respectively. Early optimism soon faded in other counties. Even though it claimed 4,000 members,[276] the Brecon and Radnor Labour Party decided not to fight, but to concentrate instead on perfecting its organization in preparation for the local elections.[277] As another sign of premature confidence NALRWU members in the Monmouth division had called upon William Harris to convene a conference of all organized workers with a view to nominating Tom Higdon, hero of the Burston School strike and the union's treasurer, as candidate.[278] When this fell through, the Shirenewton branch advised its members to vote for H. Martineau, a farmer, the Liberal candidate.[279] On the other hand, when R.H. Wynne of the Henryd branch suggested that the labourers' union make common cause with the Welsh Farmers' Union in selecting a parliamentary candidate[280] he fell into hot water. At a meeting at Llandudno Junction his indiscreet action was condemned on the grounds it might prejudice the labour cause; members were reminded of NALRWU's affiliation to the Labour Party and the TUC.[281]

The North Cardiganshire Trades Union and Labour Council seemed set to form a Labour Party for Cardiganshire in June,[282] and Second Lt. I. Aronfa Griffiths (then on active service in France) was provisionally nominated to contest the seat.[283] Delay in its actual formation prompted the two NALRWU organizers, T.E. Nicholas and John Davies, to write a joint open letter urging all labour sympathizers and trade unionists to get together to set up a provisional committee.[284] Further delay only lessened their chances, but the final blow came with the news that Griffiths had been severely wounded and forced to withdraw. Unable to field another contender, John Davies could only advise members to support a radical candidate with sympathy for the rural workers.[285] A move within the Cardiganshire Liberal Association to adopt a truly radical posture on questions of social reform had few takers.[286] Indeed, when one delegate ventured to say that the 'poor devils of farm workers were being exploited by Liberal farmers' he met with a chilling silence. However in the same month that the Liberal Coalitionist was returned unopposed, representatives of the various labour organizations in the county, including branches of NALRWU, met at Aberystwyth to lay permanent foundations for the Cardiganshire Labour Party.[287]

Followers of Lloyd George's Coalition were to capture 25 of the 36 Welsh seats. Although the Labour Party doubled its representation to 10 and took over 30 per cent of the popular vote, many of the Labour candidates suffered a heavy defeat.[288] After spending twelve months as unpaid NALRWU organizer in west Wales, T.E. Nicholas saw his electoral ambitions buried at Aberdare. Another rural agitator who shared the same fate was Sidney Box in south Herefordshire. Lacking firm historic roots, Labour candidates in the agricultural constituencies found it hard going; but in an attempt to galvanize the rural vote they did all they could to exploit their affinity with the developing political aspirations of the agricultural workers.

Labour's original choice in west Denbighshire had been the Revd J.H. Howard, an ardent socialist and champion of the rural underdog.[289] Following his political conversion from Liberalism it was E.T. John who came forward, and farm labourers were reminded of his parliamentary support for a 30*s*. minimum wage.[290] Hugh Hughes, a miner's agent and Labour's candidate in the neighbouring Wrexham division, had also done his best to organize and enlighten the farm workers. In return, he received the support of David Thomas, and at one meeting farm labourers promised that if the NWMA should fail to meet his electoral costs they would willingly contribute 4*s*. each.[291] As a tribute to E.P. Harries some NALRWU members in Pembrokeshire felt that he should receive the party's nomination,[292] but in the event Ivor H. Gwynne of Swansea stood as the first Labour candidate in the county. (Also standing as 'Practical Christian Socialist' candidate was G.B. Thomas, Cilgerran, another trade union propagandist and friend of the farm labourer.) Supported by John Davies, W.H. John and Evan Anthony, Ivor Gwynne carried the message of land nationalization into the rural areas and everywhere agricultural labourers flocked to hear the leaders of the Labour Party.[293] Although the Nefyn branch had discussed the possibility of running a NALRWU parliamentary candidate[294] for the county, it was at the tripartite request of quarrymen, railwayworkers and agricultural labourers that R.T. Jones stood as 'Independent labour' candidate in Caernarfonshire.[295] NALRWU members were therefore able to repay their debt to one of the outstanding leaders of the trade union movement in Gwynedd. Though he polled well his defeat was just as predictable as that suffered by candidates in the other agricultural constituencies. Even in Pembrokeshire, 'under organization' was cited as the principal cause of the Labour defeat.[296]

Outside its industrial base in Glamorgan and Monmouth, Labour's single rural success in 1918 was the capture of Anglesey, where Brigadier-General Sir Owen Thomas unexpectedly defeated the Liberal Coalitionist, Sir Ellis Jones Griffith, by 140 votes. What had been prophesied, and hoped for, in the days of ap Ffarmwr came to pass. This time, Brynfab provided the inspiring vision. And the immediate beginnings can be traced to the socialist alternative which he had outlined in 'Yfory Llafur'.[297] Equally significant, the need for labour parliamentary representation had been first mooted at a meeting of the Brynsiencyn branch of Undeb Gweithwyr Môn in the previous February.[298] In due course the executive committee of the union drew up a political programme in tandem with the Holyhead Trades and Labour Council. Trade unionists at Holyhead were already in contact with Arthur Henderson, who, in turn, urged the formation of a divisional Labour Party for Anglesey.[299] By the time Undeb Gweithwyr Môn held its Labour Day, all thirty-three branches of the union had decided in favour of running a Labour candidate, and a joint election committee linking rural workers and their urban counterparts in Holyhead was immediately set up.[300] With the resignation of Hugh Pritchard from the Liberal Party and his defection to Labour, the joint election committee also acquired a well-qualified registration agent. To all appearances, the Anglesey Labour Party came into being. The workers were now promoting their own political party with its district programme, a move greeted by Brynfab as the biggest 'revolution' in the history of the county.[301] In the struggle for the salvation of the ordinary labourer his name was now spoken of in the same breath as ap Ffarmwr.[302]

Next came the task of nominating a Labour candidate. Various contenders, among them Cyril O. Jones and Brynfab, were mentioned, but then like a bolt from the blue it was announced that Sir Owen Thomas had accepted the invitation of the joint election committee.[303] Lacking a political fund, their main concern was the payment of the £150 deposit which Sir Owen Thomas agreed to pay. As a personality he could not be surpassed. His connections with the farm labourers dated back to the first stirrings of ap Ffarmwr's crusade; in 1892 and 1894, it will be recalled, he was being asked to stand as a parliamentary candidate in the name of both workers and farmers. Knighted for his service in recruiting Welsh troops during the war, Sir Owen Thomas was already a much respected figure with a long record of public service in Anglesey. Equally prominent in the political sphere, he had been president of the Anglesey Liberal Association and an unsuccessful Liberal candidate at Oswestry in 1895. All in all, Sir Owen Thomas brought a stately aura to the Labour challenge but mixed with a curious duality. In agreeing to stand, he not only pledged his support for Lloyd George and the

Coalitionist programme but also demanded parliamentary freedom of action.[304] At one point in the campaign he even declared he would not sign the Labour ticket or consort with men like Ramsay MacDonald.[305] Ideologically, the principles of socialism and land nationalization propounded by Brynfab placed the two men poles apart. As expected, agriculture figured prominently during the campaign, but here again Sir Owen Thomas was to follow the middle course he took in the early 1890s. In seeking the support of all three agricultural classes — landowner, tenant farmer and labourer[306] — he fostered the idea of a harmonious agricultural 'one nation' that was patently false. Both the Farmers' Union and the Conservative Association (there was no Tory candidate) urged their supporters to vote for Ellis Jones Griffith. While his admirers often evoked his personal links with ap Ffarmwr, in reality he had done nothing of practical value.[307] What is more, Sir Owen Thomas made it plain that he did not intend to oppose the farmers: he would have similarly responded to an invitation from the Farmers' Union.[308]

Duality of a kind even existed within Undeb Gweithwyr Môn itself as traditional political loyalties cut across allegiance to the trade union. While Hugh Pritchard, Cyril O. Jones and Thomas Rowlands abandoned former allegiances, the Revd E.B. Jones and William Edwards remained in the Liberal camp. Yet, with the Revd Richard Morris as election agent, assisted by thirty-seven local sub-agents (more than half of whom can be identified as union activists), Undeb Gweithwyr Môn offered a decisive organizational advantage over a torpid Liberal Association.[309] It was, however, Sir Owen Thomas's tremendous personal popularity that helped carry the day. People admired him as a soldier and patriotic Welshman who had suffered the loss of three sons in the Great War. Given that Anglesey electors voted more for the man than any political programme, it was the labour unions, nevertheless, which *guaranteed* his victory. Whereas the main towns remained loyal to Liberalism (Holyhead electors were said to have plumped for Ellis Jones Griffith on a 3:1 ratio), Sir Owen Thomas's main support came from the Undeb Gweithwyr Môn strongholds in rural villages.[310] Moreover it was a debt which he graciously acknowledged with his donation of £50 to union funds. Nothing comparable had happened in any other Welsh agricultural constituency; even in Norfolk, with its strong tradition of rural radicalism, neither George Edwards nor R.B. Walker had been returned.[311] Nowhere else did the agricultural labourers lay claim to be a political power. For the *gwerin* of Anglesey the return of a Labour MP to Westminster in their name was to be the crowning glory to an eventful year.

Seen in retrospect, the years 1917–18 stand out as a climacteric. The image of the docile, obsequious rustic labourer had become a thing of the past in as dramatic a fashion as the idea of rural social cohesiveness. A very different breed of worker strode the countryside, one with a backbone and an independent mind, a man willing to take a stand on matters which affected his well-being. The Corn Production Act had become the starting-point of a period of extraordinary activity in rural Wales. It contributed to the rapid spread of self-confidence and confirmed the presence of an identifiable working class set apart from their employers. Trade unions such as the NUR, SWMF, and NWQU had been an invaluable constant in the various campaigns to unionize agricultural labourers in the same way as the trades councils and divisional Labour parties. They provided the individual men of character who did so much to bring the rural workers into the mainstream of trade unionism and so enable NALRWU, NFDWU and the Workers' Union to build up an organization in Wales from virtually nothing. Together with Undeb Gweithwyr Môn in Anglesey a formal union structure spanned all thirteen counties. United in this way, rural workers were thus able to stand up to their employers with a programme of demands for which they could bargain collectively. The district wages committees gave them the opportunity to press home claims for substantial improvements in wages and working hours that would have been almost unthinkable before 1917. And as they became versed in the ways of the industrial workers they gained, too, a capacity for political involvement. Ultimately, their aspirations and actions gave a new meaning to rural discontent. The questions now remaining were: what would be the limits of this revolt, and how long could it last?

CHAPTER V

THE WILL TO FIGHT: THE ZENITH OF REVOLT, 1919–1920

Now that the farm workers were drawn into the ranks of organized labour, their perception of social status and industrial rights changed dramatically. What had been achieved thus far was but a prelude to the next phase, more active and assertive in character. In practical terms the years immediately after the war provided the opportunity for further expansion. Total trade union membership in Britain more than doubled in the years 1913–20 to reach a peak of 8.3 million and this strength in numbers underlined the industrial power of organized labour. Stoppages involving coal-miners, dockers and railwaymen in 1919 reactivated much of the militancy of 1911–14. As workers went on the offensive, usually in pursuit of higher wages, an average of some 100,000 men were on strike each day, turning 1919 into a 'critical year'.[1] Industrial disputes became the most tangible expression of unrest. Even men from a rural background were found to be less amenable to social discipline. Naturally, those organizations specifically concerned with the agricultural work-force benefited directly from the current boom in trade unionism. Both NALRWU and the Workers' Union fed on their own dynamic. Area organizers followed their earlier success by winning new recruits. NALRWU fortunes reached a high point in 1920 when the number of branches rose from 1,537 to 2,735. It claimed a membership of 181,000 (levelled down to 92,700 by Madden)[2] and adopted the title National Union of Agricultural Workers (NUAW). Likewise, the Workers' Union announced that the 120,000 farm labourers on its books in mid-1919 constituted a quarter of the total membership.[3] Whilst both claims exaggerate the actual number it was generally accepted that NUAW had the greater following.

For NUAW David Rees kept up his missionary zeal in south-east Wales. In the first issue of *The Land Worker* he announced that in the opening months of 1919 he would concentrate on Brecon and Radnor.[4] Union organization in both counties was backward, with the minimum wage well below those of neighbouring counties.

Successful meetings were held at Llandrindod Wells, Bugeildy, Newbridge-on-Wye, Builth Wells and Presteigne. To the unabated anger of the farmers he continued to work closely with local railwaymen,[5] and by May the number of branches in Radnorshire rose to sixteen.[6] Rees could be equally satisfied with the position in Glamorgan and Monmouth where the eighteen NUAW branches and their membership far exceeded those of the Farmers' Union.[7] In Glamorgan it became a matter of consolidating the union's hold on the Vale and Gower peninsula. Branches at Whitchurch and Pyle marked an extension in the scope of activity; the appearance of a solitary outpost in the industrial Aberdare valley was short-lived. In Monmouth, as in Brecon and Radnor, Rees had to contend with competition from the Workers' Union although in this case the recruitment boundary was more clearly demarcated. NUAW retained control over the southern portion, leaving Sidney Box to campaign on behalf of the Workers' Union in the north of the county.

West Wales by the summer of 1919 reported a future full of promise. Where not a single branch had existed eighteen months earlier, the counties of Pembroke, Cardigan and Carmarthen now chalked up seventy.[8] John Davies had paid his way. By the time of his appointment as organizing secretary of the Workers' Educational Association in south Wales in October the number had increased to eighty and the district was regarded as the best organized in the Principality.[9] Pembrokeshire became a show-piece. With the formation of district councils for Fishguard, Solva and Pembroke there was a measure of effective decentralization.[10] Pembrokeshire easily topped the Welsh counties in sales of *The Land Worker* — though Carmarthen and Denbigh were close behind.[11] That there were 29 branches and over 2,000 members in Pembrokeshire alone by January 1920 was largely attributable to Davies's efforts.[12] Several branches requested that a full-time organizer be appointed for the county.[13] To succeed Davies in west Wales the union selected D.S. Jones of Penllwyn, near Capel Bangor, Cardiganshire. Following a stint as lead-miner and then as collier in the Rhondda, D.S. Jones took up a job in agriculture upon returning to his native locality. T.E. Nicholas had addressed the farm workers of Penllwyn in October 1918 and from the time of its inception D.S. Jones acted as secretary of the NUAW branch there.[14] This experience gave him an insight into rural problems as they affected the labourers. Soon he was hard at work in Cardigan and Pembroke. On a tour of Pembrokeshire in

March 1920 he addressed gatherings of workers in meeting-places as different as a cowshed and a village school.[15] Further progress became more and more difficult in that he was reaching the limits of what could be done within his constituency; subsequently to manage such a large district became a formidable challenge in itself.

The advance in north Wales was on a smaller scale. R.G. Roberts's persuasive tongue won many new converts but also created a lot of bad blood. Most employers resented the interference of the 'man from Penygroes' and did all they could to bar him from their property.[16] Geographically, the area was proving too much for one man to handle; from his home base it spread as far as Wrexham in the east and Dolgellau to the south. Although head office sanctioned the purchase of a new Raleigh bicycle, the nature of the terrain took its toll in time and energy. Some 15 new branches were to be founded in Caernarfonshire, Denbigh and Flint during 1919; none in Merioneth. An attempt by R.G. Roberts to start a branch at Dolgellau the following year proved only a limited success.[17] Nevertheless, he could report considerable progress in Caernarfonshire where 20 branches boasted individual membership ranging from 50 to 300.[18] Like Pembroke, the movement in the county was becoming self-organized with three district councils. Nine local branches in Llŷn had their own executive presided over by Richard Griffith. Members were then encouraged to take a more direct part in running their own affairs, and from the range of matters discussed by the Llŷn council there emerged a clear determination to defend the workers' interests.[19]

Generally, however, it was felt in London that the union had failed to get the best results from the Principality. In terms of income from entrance fees and contributions, the financial position had remained stationary and this gave cause for concern. Consequently Rees, Davies and Roberts were summoned to head office in October 1919 to meet the executive committee of the NUAW.[20] At this interview the position in Wales was carefully reviewed and, having accepted the explanation that 'exceptionally difficult' circumstances were to blame, the committee concluded that the union was, after all, 'well served' by the three. To encourage future growth the executive committee agreed to appoint an additional organizer and arrange the translation of more union literature into Welsh.[21] As it happened, the NUAW organizing secretary, James Lunnon, had already instructed R.G. Roberts to write to David Thomas inviting him to consider the post of organizer in Denbigh, Flint and Montgomery.[22] Thomas failed to oblige, but, to ease R.G. Roberts's burden, E.J. Williams of Wrexham, a checkweigher and active member of NWMA, was duly engaged to take command of the north-east corner.

The Workers' Union's success also continued: from 91,000 in 1913 membership had soared to 495,000 by 1919. Claiming a record of expansion unequalled in the history of trade unionism, it penetrated villages hitherto neglected to enrol thousands of farm workers. And whereas NUAW organizers struggled manfully on Raleigh bicycles the Workers' Union evolved a scheme for supplying its organizers with motor cycles. Since amalgamation with the NFDWU, the agricultural section of the union had made further headway in the Wrexham area and in Montgomeryshire.[23] However, it failed to gain the support of the Wrexham Trades and Labour Council because of a prior commitment to the NUAW.[24] Even in the remote rural outback of Montgomeryshire more branches were founded, lifting the total to 20.[25] Most farm labourers in the three parishes of Llanerfyl, Llangadfan and Garthbeibio, for instance, had rallied to the cause.[26] At this point the movement attracted the support of the Revd T.D. James ('Iago Erfyl'), the rector of Llanerfyl. Formerly an active supporter of the Conservative Party, Iago Erfyl changed his political views during the war to become a socialist. Utilizing his gift of eloquence — his lectures on socialism and Robert Owen kept audiences spellbound for upwards of two hours — he maintained a close link with the working class of the county. But apart from Iago Erfyl and the Revd Gwilym Rees of Llanbryn-mair, support from the Christian ministry was rare.[27]

It was this success in mid-Wales which provided the opening for David Thomas to return to active service on behalf of the labour movement. Upon his release from non-combatant duties at Higher Berse he was determined to devote his organizational talent to the realization of the political ideals and trade union work which had been ruptured by the war. As he told Arthur Henderson in the summer of 1918, he had 'a thousand plans brewing in (his) mind for building up the Labour Party in north Wales'.[28] Because teaching would not allow him sufficient time to carry out these plans he hoped to secure a post as full-time political organizer. But there was no prospect of this, or even a chance of becoming political organizer for Caernarfonshire alone.[29] Most likely, a subsequent interview for the post of organizing secretary for the Workers' Educational Association (which went to John Davies) compelled him to turn down R.G.

Roberts's offer of a job with NUAW. But the opportunity David Thomas sought so badly did not take long to materialize. Through William Williams he learnt in August 1920 that the Workers' Union urgently needed a bilingual organizer in mid-Wales.[30] Everything was well run but the Shrewsbury-based officer who had oversight of Montgomery was a monoglot Englishman, and responsibility for Denbigh, Flint and Merioneth had proved too much for ap Rhydwen. By coupling Montgomery and Merioneth it would therefore be possible to carve out a separate district. Added to this was the possibility of nursing either constituency in the run-up to a parliamentary election. It was a challenge David Thomas could not refuse. On 20 October he began his duties as district organizer for Montgomery and Merioneth on £5 a week, and, true to character, he planned his duties meticulously. A notebook lists 25 Workers' Union branches put in his charge (with another 4 in Brecon and Radnor), 9 of which were designated agricultural workers' branches.[31] Even the large urban branches like Newtown and Llanidloes had their share of farm workers, but as in the case of Llanidloes they were in the minority with 'plenty' still unaffected. A circular to branch secretaries intimated his desire to follow any lead that might result in the opening of new branches.[32] In sanguine mood, he headed his first pamphlet with the announcement: 'Farm workers, there is hope for you.'

Under ap Rhydwen the Workers' Union consolidated its presence in Denbigh and Flint. Not many new branches were set up but in 1920, for the first time in the history of the area, a Labour Day was held at Cerrigydrudion when members from six district branches marched with banners.[33] E.T. Roberts, a local miller, who acted as branch secretary and Labour Day organizer, represented one of the many hard-working silent members who ensured success at grass-roots level. Sidney Box, on the other hand, was anything but silent. Unceasingly vocal in his denunciations of injustice he pursued his mission in Brecon, Radnor and north Monmouthshire. As organized labour asserted itself in Abergavenny — around the 500-strong NUR branch — Box spoke up for the rural underdog.[34] But not everyone appreciated the harsh language and propagandist tone in which he couched his message. When addressing an open-air meeting at Grosmont in the summer of 1920 he was heckled by women in the audience and accused of 'preaching class hatred to a law-abiding and contented people'.[35]

Two fresh appointments by the Workers' Union in 1918 had signalled the advancement into territory previously monopolized by the NUAW. That their new district organizer in Pembrokeshire, H.N. Hunt, should first write to David Thomas in north Wales seeking the names of contacts in the county was a further tribute to the latter's influence.[36] Following an aggressive unionizing campaign, Hunt attracted great support among industrial and general workers in the south of the county; indeed Pembroke branch soon became one of the largest in Wales.[37] In the wake of the NUAW Hunt also attempted to win over the farm labourers by holding public meetings at Haverfordwest and St Davids.[38] At Haverfordwest the gathering was chaired by C.H. Lawrence (hitherto a pioneer trade union propagandist on behalf of the NUAW), who alluded to the 'deep hostile feelings' that the organization of farm labourers engendered. At St Davids, Hunt urged all those outside the NUAW ranks to become members of his union.[39]

Only a year or so before he roped in David Thomas, William Williams had started as full-time district organizer for the Workers' Union in north-west Wales. One of the first ILP scouts and founder member of the Caernarfonshire Labour Council, he was already a well-known figure within the labour movement. A cluster of branches in rural Caernarfonshire and adjacent parts of Denbigh marked some modest gains,[40] but his greatest prize came when he successfully persuaded Undeb Gweithwyr Môn to cast in its lot with the Workers' Union.

The take-over of Undeb Gweithwyr Môn proved to be a significant coup, but one that was only achieved at the cost of internal dissension. By August 1919 the union had 42 branches and a membership of 2,613 still chiefly employed in agriculture.[41] Hoping to emulate the political success of the 1918 general election, it made an assault on the county council in March. But to great dismay only three of the union's nominees were returned. All the same, Undeb Gweithwyr Môn continued to make its presence felt. It successfully negotiated wage increases for council workmen at Holyhead and Amlwch, two of its representatives met the Farmers' Union to discuss harvest payment and a half-day holiday, and it initiated a movement to set up co-operative stores in the county. Beneath the surface, however, there was a desire within many branches that they should link up with a stronger organization. No doubt many realized that a small poverty-stricken union lacked the resources to go on alone.[42] It had failed to embrace other workers (notably craftsmen) in sufficient numbers, it could not offer adequate benefits, neither could it hope to wield sufficient power in the unsentimental sphere of industrial bargaining. And these were the advantages which William Williams emphasized when he requested an opportunity to state the Workers' Union case before the general committee of Undeb Gweithwyr Môn.

Bit by bit, facts emerged which suggest that Undeb Gweithwyr Môn was indeed inveigled into selling out to the Workers' Union.[43] Key members of the union's executive committee having been won over beforehand, the matter came before the branches as a *fait accompli*. There was no hint of controversy when the union combined the annual general meeting with a Labour Day rally at Llangefni on 9 June 1919, the presence of Sir Owen Thomas MP adding kudos to the occasion.[44] After a persuasive speech by William Williams a resolution was passed in the AGM advocating affiliation with a 'stronger' union so long as its separate identity could be retained. Accordingly, the new president, W.J. Pretty, and secretary, the Revd Richard Morris, began to sound opinion in the branches on the propriety of uniting with the Workers' Union. No other body was invited to present its case. Communications between Undeb Gweithwyr Môn and NUAW were merely empty overtures.[45] Yet the procedure did not have the backing of Brynfab, now vice-president of the union. As the person who had shaped and moulded the union since its revival in 1917, he became understandably aggrieved at the one-sided way things were done.[46] Resigning his post, Brynfab then embarked on a war of words with the Revd Richard Morris. Pushing aside the terms of the NUAW, Morris presented his tour of the branches as the necessary mandate for uniting with the Workers' Union even though it was questionable if the majority understood the full implications. In the event, the majority of delegates attending the general committee on 2 August voted that Undeb Gweithwyr Môn be joined to the Workers' Union on 1 September. Application forms were then distributed to all branches, and the fact that over 2,500 members opted for transfer in this way was taken to be equivalent to an affirmative card vote.[47] No one, it seems, contemplated a ballot of the entire membership as happened prior to NFDWU's merger with the Workers' Union.

When it transpired that the executive committee had utilized £126.18*s*. from union funds to pay the entrance fees of the members, Brynfab exploited the error.[48] In correspondence with the Registrar of Friendly Societies he also found that amalgamation could only follow the legal dissolution of Undeb Gweithwyr Môn, a procedure requiring the consent of five-sixths of all individual members. As most farm workers in Caernarfonshire belonged to NUAW it made more sense to present a united front on the district wages committee and so he invited R.G. Roberts to Llangefni to speak his piece. When Roberts was debarred from addressing the executive committee, relations between Brynfab and the Revd Richard Morris took a turn for the worse. But however justified in his suspicion and concern, Brynfab found few allies. More and more members favoured amalgamation[49] and altogether forty-six branches of Undeb Gweithwyr Môn were absorbed *en bloc* into the Workers' Union.[50] The former executive committee now operated as the district committee of the Anglesey Workers' Union (as it became known), with the Revd Richard Morris relinquishing his pastoral charge to act as organizing secretary. Although there was an initial drop in membership the union soon reasserted itself to reach an all-time high of 3,246 by March 1920.[51] William Williams's initiative had paid off; the Anglesey union's inclusion gave a significant boost to the Workers' Union in north Wales.

A unique tradition had ended. While retaining a measure of autonomy the sense of county identity inevitably suffered. But in view of Undeb Gweithwyr Môn's size and limited potential the decision to link up with a larger union seemed totally justified in that it enhanced its capacity to exercise effective influence. Transfer to the Workers' Union meant automatic affiliation with the Labour Party and TUC. In a way, this was the final realization of a socialist vision first projected by ap Ffarmwr in the 1890s. Yet, the decision still rankled with Brynfab and once again he attacked the actions of those who had allowed Undeb Gweithwyr Môn to be 'swallowed body and soul'.[52] At a further meeting of the union's executive committee all the personal asperities resurfaced.[53] While the union had been annulled technically rather than legally, it was too late to reverse the decision. In spite of Brynfab's plea that Undeb Gweithwyr Môn be revived as a 'political organization', the Registrar of Friendly Societies quashed any such idea, preferring to let the 'mud remain undisturbed'.[54] Because the separate insurance section continued to function independently as the Undeb Gweithwyr Môn Approved Society the name did not fall into immediate disuse. Neither did Brynfab sever his association with the Brynsiencyn branch of the newly termed

Anglesey Workers' Union.[55] Indeed, at a workers' eisteddfod in the village in April 1920 members presented a testimonial to their favourite son in recognition of his past contribution to Undeb Gweithwyr Môn.[56]

Overall progress in Wales had followed the pattern already set. Lists of branches offer proof of how trade unionism reached the most secluded rural byways. Union outposts could be found on the westernmost seaboard at Aberdaron in Llŷn and St Davids in Pembrokeshire as well as the tiny hamlets which clung to the foothills of the Hiraethog, Berwyn, Pumlumon, Epynt and Presely ranges, establishing contact with scores of agricultural labourers for the very first time. Some 60 additional NUAW branches in 1919 raised the union's total in Wales (allowing for the few that lapsed) from 99 to 158, a level subsequently maintained at 160 in 1920. Anglesey and Montgomeryshire remained untouched; they were the only Welsh counties where *The Land Worker* did not circulate.[57] Though E.J. Williams opened five branches in the 'much neglected' county of Montgomeryshire by January 1921,[58] they failed to take root. To all intents, both counties remained under the sway of the Workers' Union. By 1919–20 there were around 116 Workers' Union branches covering the agricultural areas of Wales,[59] although they are not designated as such in the annual reports. David Thomas claimed that the number of Workers' Union branches in north Wales had grown from 7 in 1917 to 96 by June 1920, the membership in the great majority being entirely agricultural.[60] A survey listing 41 branches in 1921 (at the onset of decline) put the agricultural membership of the union in Wales at 936, excluding that of Anglesey.[61] Actual membership figures, however, are still tantalizingly hard to come by. But a cumulative minimum total of 10,000 for both unions combined would seem a realistic estimate.[62] Taking the number of male agricultural labourers to be near 33,400,[63] the proportion of those unionized in Wales may then be calculated at around 30 per cent. Of course, adjustment has to be made for those recruited from the ranks of gardeners, foresters and the large pool of 'casual workers' engaged on agricultural holdings. Yet, it is equally fair to assume that perhaps only the regular farm worker would display a genuine interest and commitment to trade unionism. In any case, so large a number, arrived at from next to nothing in so short a time, gave this subsequent phase of trade unionism the makings of a significant mass movement at the base level of rural society.

From a position of strength the labourers began to impose their presence on every aspect of industrial relations. As the men became more articulate, more confident and better organized so they had to be heard. Both sides recognized the need for a continuing dialogue in addition to the district wages committees. To this end, county and sometimes district conferences were arranged to discuss mutual problems, something not known of before 1919. As invitations emanated from the two sides it seemed that both parties were predisposed to create a better understanding. Often, this would lead to the establishment of an *ad hoc* conciliation committee made up of employers and employees. When issuing their invitation, leaders of the Pembrokeshire Farmers' Union were anxious that the men should be represented by agricultural workers.[64] Again, five genuine farm labourers had to be found at Brecon and Radnor because of the farmers' long-standing resentment against railwaymen.[65] By offering an olive branch, and insisting upon the presence of farm-hands on conciliation committees, some employers hoped, as did the chairman of the Pembrokeshire Farmers' Union, to separate the men from the 'labour agitators' who supposedly 'knew nothing about agricultural interests'.[66] However this sounded more like convenient fiction. Elsewhere, it was being frankly acknowledged that the workers' representatives on the district wages committees were clear-headed negotiators armed with facts and figures.[67] Every now and then, the presence of professional trade union officials allowed the gut feeling of farmers to get the better of them. When a district organizer of the Workers' Union wrote to the executive committee of the Montgomeryshire Farmers' Union asking them to receive a deputation of labour representatives his overtures were consistently dismissed on the grounds that the men would only be 'agitators' and 'Bolshevists'.[68]

From the employers' viewpoint it made good sense to meet on an official basis if only to defuse any hostile situation that might arise. As in the case of Merioneth farmers it allowed them an opportunity to investigate and settle local disputes amicably without the intervention of the Agricultural Wages Board.[69] Following a joint conference in Pembrokeshire, two conciliation committees were set up for the 'Welsh' and 'English' areas respectively with a brief to monitor the implementation of the minimum wage and investigate charges of underpayment.[70] Infringement of the Corn Production Act was endemic throughout England and Wales, and several district wages committees reported cases of employers threatening their workers with dismissal when being asked to pay the statutory rate.[71] John Davies testified that complaints of underpayment reached him in ever-increasing numbers.[72] Although the watchdog committees were to settle many such cases in Pembrokeshire, the problem remained a serious one throughout south-west Wales. As justice would have it, the first prosecution under the act in Wales had been in Cardiganshire in April 1919, the guilty party being none other than the secretary of the local Farmers' Union![73]

Once round the negotiating table, the farmers made formidable opponents, adept at stonewalling and saying no. A good bargain was hard to come by. To find them at their worst one need look no further than the talks regarding the implementation of a half-day holiday. Only after long discussions and much argument did Brynfab and his colleagues squeeze out some form of agreement on a Saturday half-holiday in Anglesey.[74] At first, only the Welsh Farmers' Union would enter into discussions; the NFU refused one request after another.[75] When an understanding on a 1 p.m. Saturday stop (noswyl un) was eventually reached, it merely benefited the ordinary worker; those on dairy farms were excluded because of the nature of their duties. Much depended on the goodwill of the employer and in many a locality farmers went out of their way to evade the settlement. As one of the men's representatives, William Jones, Cemlyn, a farm worker, had to pay the price of being a 'rebel'; he found himself blacklisted even by farmers who were his fellow deacons in Siloam Chapel.[76] Though not a total victory, the attaining of the workers' right to finish a week's work at 1 p.m. on Saturday was regarded by Thomas Rowlands as 'one of the great concessions won by organization and possibly the most valued of all'.[77]

A strong demand for a Saturday half-holiday by Caernarfonshire men was never satisfactorily resolved.[78] Only after a series of meetings did employers in Merioneth finally concede a 3 p.m. Saturday stop.[79] Any real concession had to be fought for and David Rees was left in no doubt that only union power could budge the farmers.[80] With the backing of their union more and more farm-hands gathered sufficient courage to bring cases of injustice to court. Caernarfonshire was probably the most productive in this respect. Evan Hughes of Morfa Nefyn, a prominent NUAW official, successfully pursued his claim for an accommodation allowance.[81] Upon consulting R.G. Roberts, farm labourers at Nantlle and Rhydyclafdy were able to secure sums due to them.[82] But what sort of justice the workers could expect before the courts became open to question. In rural areas, where farmers dominated local government and the bench, there was considerable unease at the obvious partiality of some judgements. Two cases in Carmarthenshire, in particular, resulted in dubious rulings. When a Llandovery farmer appeared before the local sessions on a minimum wage prosecution he was to plead total ignorance of the Corn Production Act.[83] By a majority decision, the bench accepted his explanation and dismissed the case, refusing to make any order that the arrears of over £68 be paid. An earlier case of underpayment at Laugharne resulted in a derisory fine of 5*s*. W.R. Smith MP, president of NUAW, then raised the matter in Parliament and suggested the act be amended so that more adequate penalties could be imposed.[84] In fact these already existed, he learnt in answer, but the amount of the fine rested in the discretion of the magistrates.

Right through this period considerable anger was also registered at the insidious way farmers harassed and victimized trade unionists. In his column in *Y Dinesydd Cymreig*, R.G. Roberts frequently levelled charges of oppression against employers.[85] Some farmers, he alleged, refused to hire union men simply because they wished to avoid paying the minimum wage. Before a bargain could be struck at the hiring fair labourers were often asked if they belonged to a union, yet the same farmers might also be members or officials of the NFU. Ap Rhydwen attacked the way farmers utilized their high social standing within the chapel and community to intimidate the uneducated labourers.[86] As a branch official, Ifan Gruffydd of Llangristiolus recollected how he was cold-shouldered when going from farm to farm collecting members' subscriptions.[87]

On the vexed question of extra payment for harvest work considerable resentment was provoked, especially in those areas where latent tensions had smouldered beneath the surface for some time. Because of its very nature, harvest-time was a particularly busy period in the farming calendar. During the hay and corn harvest the work was hard and the hours much longer, in some instances as late as 10.00–10.30 p.m. Traditionally, this extra work had meant bonus cash payments or food allowances in most Welsh counties; in Glamorgan it amounted to an extra shilling a day.[88] Against this background, harvest money came high on the agenda of conciliation and district wages committee meetings, more so when the Agricultural Wages Board decided not to fix any special rates for the hay harvest in either 1918 or 1919. After protracted negotiations some district wages committees agreed to an overtime rate of 1*s*.2*d*.; in other areas the employers and their men worked out mutual agreements on a voluntary basis.[89]

As the trade union movement gathered strength the rank and file became more ambitious in their demands. And, if need be, they were ready to exert economic pressure on employers by withdrawing their labour. The effectiveness of a strike as a potentially powerful weapon against the farmers was well recognized. Ap Ffarmwr had written how 'they would very soon yield to the irresistible onset of a united and well-timed strike'.[90] At no period would they be more vulnerable than at the beginning or middle of the harvest season. While agriculture always ranked amongst those industries with a low incidence of strike action,[91] there had been several stoppages in the eastern counties of England in 1872–4 in Joseph Arch's heyday, and again in 1891–2. Traditional rural tranquillity was soon broken after the formation of NALRWU with the 'great strike' at St Faiths, Norfolk. When pre-war industrial militancy reached its peak, agricultural labourers had been involved in countless numbers of minor disputes.[92] The victorious strike of 2,000 farm workers in Lancashire in 1913 was described as 'one of the strongest conflicts in modern industrial warfare'.[93] Immediately after the war the number of industrial stoppages in Britain rose again at an alarming rate. While the 1,352 strikes in 1919 had not passed the 1913 total, the number involved (2.5 million) was far greater. In the year of the ill-fated Triple Alliance, when agricultural labourers downed tools in Norfolk, Suffolk, Cheshire and Shropshire, a 'very serious strike' also took place in Glamorgan.[94]

On the very day that 50,000 Welsh miners were reported to be out on official strike it was announced that farmers' profits had jumped from 9*s*.6*d*. to 33*s*.2*d*. per acre over the period of the war.[95] Agricultural labourers could justifiably feel that there were material as well as moral grounds for raising their standard of living. In poignant terms, Richard Griffith described how some of their wives knew what it was to stay up through the night converting flour bags into shirts for their children.[96] In a lecture on insanitary housing in rural Wales, Edgar Chappell maintained that conditions in

Pembrokeshire, south Cardiganshire and parts of Anglesey were considerably worse than those which labourers in England and Scotland had to suffer.[97] Yet, if the workers refused to 'grin and bear it', they were branded 'agitators' and 'Bolshevists'.[98] Basic injustices drove men into action and to employ the ultimate weapon at their disposal. In common with the majority of strikes,[99] most Welsh disputes were over wages; moreover they were chiefly spontaneous outbreaks and localized in extent. That strikes occurred at all in rural Wales was a sign of the times.

Agricultural labourers were rarely a militant class, but in 1919 they displayed the will to fight. At the annual meeting of Undeb Gweithwyr Môn it was noted that £7.10*s*. had been expended on strike pay.[100] Early in July, farm labourers at Glan Conwy passed a resolution demanding wages of £3 per week with board for all workers over eighteen during the hay and corn harvest.[101] The Llandudno Junction branch of the NUAW, which extended as far as Colwyn Bay and Eglwysbach, had over 200 members, and in pursuit of their claim all the labourers in the district came out on unofficial strike leaving the hay lying in the fields.[102] Not even the union officials were consulted. At a mass meeting the following day, W. Washington Owen rebuked the men for taking industrial action without the prior consent of their union. When R.G. Roberts attended a subsequent meeting he urged them to return to work, but the farmers refused to re-employ the strikers. By now, the men's claim had been toned down to £2.10*s*. per week plus a guarantee of reinstatement. Though it took some time for the enmity to die down, a local agreement was hammered out at a joint meeting: workers under 21 were to receive £1.17*s*.6*d*. with food, those over 21 would have £2.5*s*.[103] Further evidence of rank-and-file militancy in the area came in August when, at an open-air gathering organized by the National Union of General Workers in Colwyn Bay, there was a call for an increase in farm labourers' wages coupled with the threat of a stoppage.[104]

A major dispute in the Vale of Glamorgan fed on a legacy of poor industrial relations. Farmers and labourers had been at loggerheads for some time and the four-week strike by 300 men during June and July represented the culmination of a period of unrest. Indeed, as far back as the 1830s and again the 1890s, a strong undercurrent of discontent and even open hostility had surfaced in the Vale. Relationships at a personal level were further soured over the period of war. Bad social conditions, tied cottages, profiteering and the threat of the khaki provided the essential boost to trade unionism. In the agricultural area of the Vale the NUAW built up formidable strength, enabling a large number of otherwise socially isolated workers to feel a strong element of group cohesion. The mining valleys to the north had long been a battlefield between capital and labour, with the coal industry notorious for its strike-proneness. In the circumstances it was hardly surprising that the farm labourers should become more class-minded, or that a mass grievance should lead to industrial action. The tyrannical behaviour of hard-faced employers fuelled their resentments. Badly victimized, James Kennett, for one, was a man with a particular grievance. Dismissal, however, did not prevent him from undertaking union duties as district secretary and he relished the opportunity to assert positive leadership when the clash came over harvest wages.

Resolutions passed by several NUAW branches in the Llantwit Major district of the Vale in January 1919 were as bold as they were extravagant. Instead of the current rate of 33*s*.6*d*. they claimed 50*s*. for a 45-hour week, with double time over the harvest period (21 June to 21 September). The farmers could hardly believe their ears. Before the claim was formally submitted to the Glamorgan and Monmouth District Wages Committee[105] the men's leaders were strongly criticized. At the annual meeting of the Glamorgan Chamber of Agriculture, Alderman Illtyd Thomas considered the demand to be 'Bolshevik in its conception' and merely a 'cloak to secure control of the land in the interests of one class of the community'.[106] Another speaker concluded that they were either 'imbued with Bolshevik ideas' or else completely ignorant of the economics of agriculture. To back this point, a prominent Glamorgan farmer published the costs of labour on his 440-acre farm.[107] A wage bill of £700 in 1918 had already risen to £1,200 and, if the trend continued, he foresaw himself being ruined within two years. The men's demand became the talk of NFU branch meetings.[108] To the sound of laughter, one employer at Newport thought 'they had better have the farms'.[109]

Vale of Glamorgan labourers were soon joined in their claim by NUAW branches at St Arvans and Catsash, Monmouthshire.[110] When the district wages committee convened in March they advised an early meeting of both sides of industry in the two counties to discuss the matter.[111] Six farmers and six representatives of labour duly met at Newport on 9 April, but no settlement was reached.[112]

Even though the workers scaled down their demand to a minimum wage of 45*s*., the employers refused to promise anything; neither would they accept the proposed harvest rate of £3 per week with time and a half overtime. Negotiations were adjourned until the matter was further considered by the employers' organization. But with workers in both counties already receiving 5*s*. a week more than the going rate in other counties, the farmers were in no mood to compromise.[113] Unfortunately for them, official confirmation that farmers' profits were more than three times higher than pre-war figures made the workers equally inflexible. Events also coincided with the annual conference of the NUAW, where it became official union policy to press for a national minimum wage of 50*s*. for a 44-hour week.[114] As Welsh delegate, James Kennett spoke of farmers in the Vale of Glamorgan retiring from business able to buy villas while there were men of seventy, who had toiled on the land all their life, still trudging to work with the aid of a walking-stick.

A supportive editorial in the *South Wales News* urged the NFU to educate the farmer 'out of the habit of chronic grumbler' and adopt a more generous attitude towards the men.[115] Farmers themselves were in the mean time protesting against milk prices and talking of a 'silent strike'.[116] However, only after considerable bickering did their representatives on the district wages committee adopt the new minimum rate of 41*s*.6*d*. for a 54-hour week as proposed by the Agricultural Wages Board.[117] At the same time it was decided by a majority that overtime during the corn harvest would be fixed at the same rate as normal overtime work (that is, a time and a quarter) with no special rate for the hay harvest.[118] Despite protestations the farmers flatly refused to consider the workers' claim or refer it to arbitration. This deadlock left the men seething with unrest. At a meeting of farm labourers in the Llantwit Major town hall on 3 June, David Rees urged them not to take strike action pending a further appeal to the farmers.[119] It was decided that the matter be left in the hands of the organizer and union executive. In an apparent attempt to exert extra pressure on employers, James Kennett, as district secretary, handed in notices of a mass withdrawal of labour on Saturday 21 June.[120] When another meeting between representatives of the NUAW and the NFU failed to arrive at an agreement, the decision to act on the notices was taken at a second gathering of labourers on the Saturday night.[121]

With over 90 per cent of farm workers in the Vale belonging to the NUAW, harvest operations were almost at a standstill the following Monday.[122] A last-minute meeting failed to resolve the dispute and as a result 300 men in the Llantwit Major district came out on strike. Some farmers agreed to pay the £3, others pinned their hopes on using non-union labour to get the harvest in, whilst the more unyielding were inclined to 'let the men stay out until they come to their senses'. According to the secretary of the Glamorgan NFU, the strike remained localized because agricultural workers in other areas had refused to come out. But by the end of the week, labourers from Cowbridge, St Athan and St Nicholas trooped into Llantwit Major to attend two mass rallies.[123] Over 250 were present to hear David Rees condemn the 'unbending attitude' of the Farmers' Union. On the several occasions he presented their case he had met blank refusal; they declined to make any advance beyond the statutory minimum. What Rees had tried hard to avoid had come to pass, but he was now determined to stand by the men until they gained victory. In turn, the labourers closed ranks behind their leaders.

In retrospect, it appears that Rees became inextricably involved in a localized dispute initiated by militant grass-roots feeling. And at their separate meetings both the NFU and the workers' strike committee considerably hardened their attitudes.[124] The farmers even refused to partake in further negotiations. By the end of June the strike had spread to Newton and Porthcawl, thus covering the whole of the Vale. After the men had been idle almost a week, David Rees denied employers' claims that some workers were returning to work. But with no official strike pay the strain was bound to show. To meet this, hardship collections had been organized and it was said that labourers with large families were being partly cared for. Though the men had timed their strike to exploit the tactical advantage which the harvest season offered, they could not possibly hold out without help from other groups of industrial workers in the region. During the first week of July, David Rees reported how a meeting of miners at Pontypridd had decided to ask the SWMF executive to grant financial aid.[125] The miners' local agent, T.I. Mardy Jones, appealed to the Pontypridd Trades and Labour Council on their behalf and, as a result, a representative of the labourers was invited to attend a public meeting in the town, when a collection of 10*s*.2*d*. was made.[126] The following week they received the fraternal support of the Barry branch of the NUR.[127] Members of the NUR district committee visited Llantwit Major with the promise of financial assistance from Barry railwaymen.

In the stalemate that existed, the farmers probably hoped to wear out the strikers. Even intervention by the Board of Agriculture failed to get the parties together.[128] Reports came in of workers being lured back with a promise of £3 plus 2*s*. beer money.[129] Then again, there were reports of victimization and blacklegging. It was alleged that one of the strikers had been given notice to quit his tied cottage. Farmers in the vicinity of St Nicholas were accused of importing German prisoners as strike-breakers, while certain Nonconformist and Anglican ministers (specifically the vicar of St Donat's) were lambasted for giving farmers a helping hand to harvest their crops.

As the dispute entered its third week with no solution in sight, David Rees called upon R.B. Walker to assist.[130] At this point the executive committee of NUAW declared the strike official. Moreover, there was a call to extend the strike into Monmouthshire and farm workers in that county were asked to prepare for action. Entrusted with the future conduct of the strike, R.B. Walker travelled to Llantwit Major to deal with the situation on the spot. In his view, dissension in the Vale had been deliberately kindled by the farmers. NFU delegates visiting the Royal Agricultural Society Show at Cardiff at the end of June hatched the idea of turning Glamorgan into a 'cockpit' for wholly mercenary reasons.[131] If employers stood firm on wage demands in the highest-paying county, farmers everywhere would be able to stave off claims in their own patch. If this be true — and David Rees claimed he had proof — one can only add that a strike of waiters in Cardiff hotels at the time of the Royal Show[132] must have put delegates in a suitably anti-union mood.

Then suddenly and unexpectedly the farmers had a change of heart. At a meeting of the Glamorgan NFU executive a special subcommittee was appointed to meet the workers' leaders with plenary powers to settle the dispute.[133] Why this happened is unclear. By all accounts, farmers were experiencing little difficulty in getting in the hay crop.[134] And there could be little substance in the NUAW threat to call out colliers, railwaymen and dockers in sympathy. Perhaps the agricultural situation was more critical than the farmers cared to admit. There was also a real possibility of trouble spilling over into Monmouthsire and complicating matters still further.[135] At a meeting in the county workers were making similar noises, threatening to down tools unless a joint conference was arranged.[136]

So, on 17 July, at the Royal Hotel, Cardiff, the bargaining began with Walker, Rees and Kennett in the workers' negotiating team. After four hours of hard talking they arrived at a formula to end the strike.[137] Under its terms, the men would be paid a minimum cash wage of 1*s*. an hour for the harvest operations. The guaranteed 54*s*. weekly total thus marked a rise of 30 per cent over the normal minimum wage.[138] All other work was to be paid at the rate set by the Agricultural Wages Board. With minimum wages in other Welsh counties set at 36–7*s*., this settlement represented a substantial victory for the farm workers of Glamorgan.

It had proved a bitter struggle with strikers enduring great hardship in the process. Nevertheless, an almost unbroken solidarity had been achieved, although this had to be sometimes maintained by strong-armed picketing. Two of the official pickets mounted by the union were later hauled before the court for showing excessive zeal at Groes-faen.[139] William Coles, a recipient of a military medal in the war, was fined 10*s*. for assaulting another farm labourer who refused to stop working. A subsequent attempt to evict both him and his brother from their tied cottage failed on a legal technicality.[140] Meanwhile, the union was obliged to take unprecedented steps to deal with four cases arising from the Vale strike. Dispute pay had to be augmented by a grant of 8*s*. from the NUAW benevolent fund for an extra month, especially as one worker had a family of nine children to maintain.[141] Whatever the deprivation and the strain, the spirit of the men had remained high throughout. Proudly they were to pose wearing union badges for a commemorative group photograph outside the New White Hart Inn, Llantwit Major. In the front row stood James Kennett and the youngest of the strikers, his own son, who had just turned sixteen.

Success in Glamorgan was bound to have a bearing on developments in Monmouth, where there had been considerable disaffection for some time. Although the settlement remained confined to farm workers in the Vale, delegates from the Monmouthshire branches of the NUAW (but not the NFU) attended the Cardiff talks.[142] In no time, A.W. Pittman, the railway signalman secretary of the Portskewett NUAW branch, was writing to the Monmouthshire NFU demanding a minimum wage of £3 a week with overtime at time and a half for the harvest period.[143] If this was not conceded within seven days the men were prepared to go on strike. In reply, the farmers said they would only deal with a union official mandated to speak for the whole county. Having called his bluff the employers had no need to summon the special committee which they had set up to deal with labour emergencies. A threat by another union official in the Rhiwderin district of the county in October fizzled out in similar fashion.[144] After so much strife in the Vale, neither side had the stomach to engage in another quarrel and so David Rees was able to bargain for satisfactory terms for men employed in threshing later that year.[145]

In many ways the Vale of Glamorgan strike symbolized the tremendous advance made by farm workers during the previous two years. One could say that rural trade unionism had finally come of age. As the new NUAW structure of county and district committees became operational by December 1920,[146] union organization in Wales was given its final touch-up. Buoyed up by their strength and success, the men faced the future in high spirit. By order of the Agricultural Wages Board a Saturday half-holiday and systematic overtime was granted, wages continued to rise, complemented by a greater standardization and reduction in the number of hours worked. By April 1920 the minimum wage was 42*s*., rising to a new peak of 46*s*. by the summer. Weekly hours were now 50 in summer, 48 in winter. Hailed as 'one of the most progressive and influential in the kingdom',[147] the Glamorgan and Monmouth District Wages Committee maintained its high-paying tradition when it awarded a basic wage of 50*s*. in August 1920.[148] Since the introduction of statutory wage regulation the rate paid to ordinary farm labourers throughout Wales had continued to climb; by 1921 the average weekly wage of 44*s*.2*d*. was 145 per cent above the pre-war level of 18*s*.[149]

What proved to be the high-water mark in the fortunes of both the NUAW and the Workers' Union was reached in 1920. The NUAW knew it could not hope to keep up its 'phenomenal growth' because there was very little new ground left to cover.[150] For the Workers' Union success seemed like a 'fairy tale'; it had 'broken all records in the history of trade unionism'.[151] By solidifying union organization and maintaining membership and funds there seemed to be every prospect of preserving this position. One way was to impose the principle of a closed shop. Not only could it lead to a further strengthening of solidarity but it would also enable the union to boost the workers' bargaining position. Typical of this new awareness was the decision of some Undeb Gweithwyr Môn branches not to work with non-members.[152] Because the matter caused so much unrest in south Caernarfonshire, an NUAW conference at Pwllheli in October 1919 adopted a system of boycotting non-union labour.[153] At other times, the men appealed directly to the farmers to support them in their campaign. The Brecon and Radnor NFU considered a resolution from the Brecon NUAW branch urging them not to employ non-unionists, but no decision was taken.[154] Pressure was greater in Pembrokeshire where the farm labourers had built up formidable strength. NUAW branches at Mathry, St Nicholas and Croes-goch made it conditional that no member would work on any farm during harvest and threshing if non-unionists were engaged.[155] Whereas the Fishgard branch of the Farmers' Union came to a local understanding with the St Nicholas men (who reciprocated by pledging not to work with non-union farmers), any idea of compulsion was turned down by the county executive.[156] In the drive for 100-per-cent trade unionism expectations were only rarely fulfilled.

Harvest time, once again, gave the men an opportunity to make their presence felt. Here was a potential rallying point for organized strength. Workers' Union members around Abergavenny put in a claim for £3 a week over the harvest period, with the usual overtime on top.[157] But there was little chance of the farmers conceding. Rarely sympathetic and certainly never charitable, they felt the time had come to put a firm stop to any further wage increase, regardless of the fact that county council roadmen were earning £3.10*s*.6*d*. More in hope than expectation, the men went on to discuss the possibility of taking collective action.[158] NUAW representatives on the Pembrokeshire conciliation committee presented a similar demand for a special harvest bonus as was the custom of the county.[159] On the employers' side all were opposed to the idea and they refused to ratify any such payment. Signs of rebellion soon appeared. Union members tried to force the issue by publishing a public notice demanding an immediate 5*s*. weekly bonus above the ordinary rate.[160] Subsequent silence can only mean that they failed.

Inevitably, perhaps, farmers and labourers in Glamorgan found themselves squaring up to another confrontation. A motion to raise the basic minimum wage to £3 for a 48-hour week had already been submitted before the district wages committee.[161] Although R.B. Walker, at a labour rally in Llantwit Major,[162] insisted that he and David Rees did not believe in strikes, the omens were bad. By holding a milk strike in February, south Wales farmers showed they could be no more immune from militancy than their men, or less concerned about personal interests.[163] The Monmouthshire NFU even declined to hold a conference to discuss harvest wages as requested by the farm workers' union.[164] If a strike was threatened, some argued, it would be better to make a strong stand and let matters come to a head once and for all. Shortly after, the district wages committee agreed to a basic minimum of £2.5*s*.6*d*.[165] Glamorgan workers then put in a demand for a special harvest rate of £3 a week.[166] In answer, the farmers pledged only to pay statutory overtime; harvest work they regarded as an integral part of farm duties. Both sides seemed anxious to avoid a repeat of the previous year, but at the joint conference held at the Grand Hotel, Cardiff, in April,[167] James Kennett made no attempt to tone down his truculent rhetoric. Employers, he asserted, were charging high rents for 'hovels' and doing everything besides paying their men a living wage.[168] After a long discussion it was agreed, however, to lay the matter before the Agricultural Wages Board. Much to the dismay of the farmers, the Board proposed a minimum of 50*s*. with 1*s*.6*d*. overtime for the duration of the harvest.[169] Monmouthshire farmers deemed this 'vexatious and inequitable' and a deputation was appointed to lobby the Board.[170] The Agricultural Wages Board itself, meantime, came under considerable pressure from both the NUAW and the Workers' Union to award a statutory minimum of 50*s*., the latter union having already authorized strike action in Cheshire and Essex. In Glamorgan, the men's representatives gave an assurance that everything would be done to prevent a disruption to both harvests. On the understanding that 'peace and goodwill' prevailed, the independent members on the district wages committee gave their support to the workers and, with the employers' representatives abstaining, the schedule came into force.[171] Farm workers had registered a second victory. Wages in Glamorgan and Monmouth were up to the level of the best English counties and some 4*s*. above most parts of Wales.[172] Although it secured peace for a time, by the end of the year employers were being presented with a renewed claim for £3 a week.[173]

Elsewhere there was evidence of other local stoppages. As a result of a strike involving farm labourers in the Sealand district of Flintshire, the Hawarden Board of Guardians were asked to provide shelter at the local workhouse for a farm labourer, his wife and five children who had been evicted from their tied cottage.[174] After giving a week's notice the farmer had dumped all the furniture outside, a course of action, according to one of the guardians, which took them back to the 'old days of feudalism'. Elsewhere, the men's unions were drawn into disputes involving other workers outside agriculture. In Anglesey, Workers' Union branches imposed a levy to support roadmen on strike in the former Undeb Gweithwyr Môn bastion of Llannerch-y-medd, as well as striking quarrymen at Penmon.[175] Four NUAW members were numbered among the 150 Cardiganshire county council roadmen (belonging mainly to the Dockers' Union) who held out for eighteen weeks in 1920.[176] In this case, the predominance of farmers — both members and officials of the Farmers' Union — on the council could not be overlooked.[177] There was a danger, warned a Dockers' Union official, that members of the class who faced political persecution following the 1868 election in the county might turn out to be the tyrants in 1920.[178] Politics, trade unionism, and even a sense of history, were patently indivisible.

If the Labour Party was to mount a successful challenge for political power in the agricultural constituencies it needed to involve the rural workers. In concert with the agricultural labourers' union Labour had polled well in the eastern counties of England in the general election of 1918.[179] Although W.R. Smith, the NUAW president, sat for the urban constituency of Wellingborough (Northampton), it was not until George Edwards's victory in the south Norfolk by-election in July 1920 that farm labourers found a natural successor to Joseph Arch in the Commons. Prospects in Norfolk and East Anglia, with their high concentration of unionized rural workers, seemed increasingly bright. Yet, whilst the Labour Party remained intent on sweeping the countryside in order to gain a parliamentary majority, it readily admitted the enormity of the challenge.[180] In those constituencies where Labour organization might be raw or unrealized it could not be anything other than a herculean task. Consequently, the trade unions had to become the forcing ground for political growth, and in most cases, as McKibbin concludes, 'local party organization was utterly dependent on the unions as institutions and upon their officers and members as individuals'.[181]

An ideal opportunity to ally the agricultural and industrial constituencies on a national basis in Wales was lost in 1911, when the Labour Party executive rejected the proposal to set up a Welsh Independent Labour Party as suggested by Welsh socialist and labour leaders at a conference in Carmarthen.[182] Although the South

Wales Labour Federation had been set up in December 1916 as a counterpart to the North Wales Trades and Labour Council, the rural areas still remained in relative isolation. Moreover, Welsh claims for organizational autonomy were continually frustrated until the establishment of a separate Welsh region in 1920.[183]

A less than sagacious political commentator in *Welsh Outlook* had meanwhile pronounced Welsh Liberalism to be a 'mere corpse'.[184] Not only were the industrial areas turning to the Labour Party, but the movement was also making 'enormous strides' among the agricultural labourers as attested by the election of Sir Owen Thomas in Anglesey. True enough, there had been a concerted effort to get the farm workers to think and act politically. Highly motivated activists connected with NUAW, the Workers' Union and Undeb Gweithwyr Môn stood among the firmest enunciators of socialist ideology. By the same token, they accorded a prominent place to the building of a power base for the Labour Party within the agricultural constituencies. In this respect, thanks mainly to David Thomas, the basic framework already existed in rural north Wales. At the beginning of 1919 there were 16 trades and labour councils representing well over 14,000 workers.[185] What was essentially an industrial structure had now to be fashioned into separate political components for each county.

High expectations in Anglesey were marked by a bid to secure working-class representation on every council and public committee. Joining forces once more, Undeb Gweithwyr Môn and the Holyhead Trades and Labour Council saw the county council elections of March 1919 as the ideal opportunity for winning political power and implementing social reforms at local level.[186] Twenty-two candidates were nominated,[187] and with prominent labour leaders pitted against the farmers the contest was seen as the pure milk of class conflict.[188] The unopposed return of two labour nominees raised their hopes but in the end it proved to be an inglorious defeat. Thomas Rowlands and Edward Pritchard ('Iorwerth'), two Undeb Gweithwyr Môn veterans, as well as W.J. Pretty, chairman of Sir Owen Thomas's election committee, and the Revd Richard Morris, his election agent, all lost on the day. Only Lewis Thomas, the precursor of the ILP in Anglesey, won a seat for Labour when he defeated a farmer at Llangristiolus. But with another fifteen farmers elected, their class still dominated the county council.[189] Undeb Gweithwyr Môn, in particular, had taken a 'severe beating', to quote Brynfab's honest verdict.[190] The challenge to the farming establishment ended in a total rout, adding further proof that Anglesey voters had plumped for the man and not the party when they elected Sir Owen Thomas only a few months earlier. Some consolation came in the district elections held later; this time at least 17 Labour candidates were returned including Brynfab, Thomas Rowlands and J. Fred Jones.[191] At joint talks between the two labour organizations the following year, the formation of a county Labour Party was discussed and the post of full-time agent and organizer duly advertised in May.[192]

As individuals, R.G. Roberts and W. Washington Owen were ideal working-class candidates in Caernarfonshire. However, R.G. Roberts failed to dislodge the sitting member in the county council election at Penygroes and W. Washington Owen lost out on the Conwy RDC election. On the other hand, David Thomas celebrated his release by coming top of the poll in the Tal-y-sarn ward of Gwyrfai RDC.[193] Then, in November, with William Williams in the chair, the Caernarfonshire Labour Council, NWQU and the various trade unions came together to form the basis of the Caernarfonshire Labour Party.[194] About the same time, agricultural workers were among the twelve trade unions represented at the Chester conference which launched the Flintshire Labour Party.[195] In Flintshire, unlike in Anglesey, Labour had polled well in the county council elections, winning eight seats.[196] The Revd D. Gwynfryn Jones, a consistent advocate of rural trade unionism, unseated a Conservative to win at Llanasa. No less than five members of the Workers' Union at Abergele in neighbouring Denbighshire won seats on the urban district council,[197] while at Wrexham E.J. Williams was elected to both the municipal and county council.[198] At Bala, Rolly Williams gained a seat on the urban council, but W.T. Bason failed.[199] Along with ap Rhydwen both men were subsequently engaged in preparing the groundwork for the foundation of the Merioneth Labour Party. Indeed, leaders of the NWQU, NUAW and Workers' Union worked hand in hand at local and county level,[200] and when the Labour Party came into being in January 1920 its first secretary was Hugh Williams ('ap Idris'), secretary of the Towyn Workers' Union branch.[201] So intimately linked were the ties between the NUAW and the Labour Party that W.T. Bason addressed trade union and political gatherings on the same night at Llanuwchllyn.[202]

Organized labour, principally in the form of the Workers' Union, forced eight county council seats to be contested in Montgomeryshire in 1919.[203] Personalities again dominated. The Revd T.D. James ('Iago Erfyl'), ex-Primrose Leaguer turned anti-capitalist, was returned for Llanerfyl. At Llanbryn-mair it became a trial of strength between the NFU and the Workers' Union.[204] The Revd Gwilym Rees's slender victory over a local farmer encouraged the local branch to make an all-out bid to capture the parish council. Once again, a contest between the two rival unions gave the workers (including the Revd Gwilym Rees) a majority of one on the new council.[205] Similar excitement surrounded the straight fight between the NFU and Workers' Union at Berriew. This time, the Workers' Union almost swept the board, capturing 11 of the 15 seats.[206] Given the advanced degree of trade union organization it was little wonder that Labour Party propaganda meetings were held in conjunction with the Workers' Union.[207] Already the county council had had its first 'glimpse of the red flag' when the Revd T.D. James demanded a living wage for roadmen.[208] And despite the opposition of a prominent landlord and NFU county secretary in unholy alliance, a 5*s*. rise was secured.

Elsewhere in mid-Wales farm labourers' leaders projected a political profile. Box and Stokoe, the twin pillars of the Workers' Union in Breconshire, were behind the move to form a branch of the Labour Party in Hay.[209] In the urban council elections at Builth Wells the union and Labour Party again appeared in tandem.[210] Labour politics, however, did not have much relevance that year in the Cardiganshire county council elections. Captain David Davies, a supporter of rural trade unionism, was the only Labour Party candidate and he lost at Blaenporth.[211] Also among the defeated stood the outspoken E. Lima Jones. When the Cardiganshire Labour Party was formally inaugurated at Aberystwyth in April, the bond between politics and trade unionism remained strong: D.S. Jones served as secretary, with John Davies and J. Gwendraeth James on the executive committee.[212] At a meeting of the county committee of the NUAW in November 1920, R.L. Jones presiding, it was resolved to support the Labour Party by means of a levy of 1*s*. per member.[213]

The close liaison between the NUAW and the Labour Party in Pembrokeshire was similar to the situation in Anglesey, only here the union was fathered by the party. With three NUAW members on the executive committee of the county Labour Party[214] a united front was presented in the county council elections, especially as the council hitherto had not a single representative from the working class. Well did they realize that parliamentary acts relating to smallholdings, housing and education usually lost their meaning when administered by men of different backgrounds or opposing interests.[215] In the event, Labour candidates won four seats, including Urias Richards at Cilgerran and W.H. John who defeated two gentlemen farmers at Solva.[216] John Picton came within a whisker of ousting Col. Lort Phillips at Carew, whilst William Harries, an NUAW nominee, lost the Mathry division to a farmer by forty-nine votes.[217] Because of their overall showing in the elections Labour had the opportunity of elevating E.P. Harries to alderman. In the parish elections that followed there were substantial gains for Labour on both Mathry and Goodwick Parish Councils, with Evan Anthony and Henry Evans, a farm labourer, being elected at Goodwick.[218] Further recognition came with the appointment of Evans, John, Picton and Richards as magistrates.[219] Probably this was the first time in Wales that two ordinary agricultural workers — Henry Evans and John Picton — had been honoured in this way. By October 1920, twenty-four NUAW branches in Pembrokeshire were officially affiliated to the Labour Party.[220] Along with the trades councils and district Labour parties, the prospect for Labour was such that D.T. Lewis invited E.T. John to consider standing as parliamentary candidate at the next election.[221]

Concern with social issues became the spur to political action in Monmouthshire. NUAW branch meetings at Shirenewton, for instance, discussed housing, transport and the water supply when considering fielding candidates at the forthcoming local elections.[222] Labour's sweeping gains in the county council elections were ascribed to William Harris's generalship, and in the rural wards two NUR-sponsored candidates, A.W. Pittman at Caer-went and the Revd W.H. Williams at Magor, both defeated farmers. However, in the Chepstow RDC elections, Ellis Jones, a schoolteacher, who stood at Shirenewton at the request of the NUAW branch, and Edward Thomas, a GWR inspector, who had been selected by the Caer-went NUAW branch, failed to win seats.[223] In the months that followed, William Harris, often accompanied by Pittman, was instrumental in forming Labour Party branches in parishes where rural trade unionism was already well established.[224] His reward came in December 1919 with the formation of a Labour Party within the Monmouth division.[225] When the Revd Gordon Lang, their prospective candidate, toured the county with Box and A.J. Williams in

1920, he immediately placed himself in opposition to the class that 'suffered the least' in the Great War.[226] In Glamorgan, David Rees capped his personal political career by winning a county council seat at Aberafan. His right-hand man in the Vale was not so lucky. With characteristic grit, James Kennett came out against Col. H.R. Homfray of Penllyn Castle (Conservative) in the Cowbridge division.[227] But because his proposers and seconders signed the nomination form incorrectly, the deputy returning officer upheld an objection from the opposing side and disqualified his candidature. Undashed, Kennett then made a little history by appearing as the first Labour candidate in the district council election at Llantwit Major, only to lose to two farmers by almost 250 votes.[228]

Each electoral challenge marked a path-breaking advance into political territory virtually untouched, but the few victories Labour enjoyed hardly presented a serious threat to the established order in rural Wales. Neither the major parties nor the middle-class ascendancy, of which the farmers remained an integral part, had cause to fear. The Labour Party's successes in 1919–20 were mainly concentrated in the urban and industrialized areas. Political hopes within the agricultural constituencies had only been fleetingly realized, and to cast a deeper shadow over the many disappointments there followed the resignation of Sir Owen Thomas from the Labour Party.

Respectful of the working-class vote which sent him to the Commons, Sir Owen Thomas had allied himself to the Labour Party and voted consistently in the Labour interest.[229] Yet, in his person he epitomized the two conflicting forces of Liberalism and Labour. As a life-long Liberal, company director and major shareholder he could hardly have felt at home on the Labour benches amongst the extreme left-wingers. When the Clydesider Neil Maclean created a stir by refusing to rise for the national anthem in the Commons in July 1919 Sir Owen seemed determined to resign from the party.[230] Upon receiving the approval of both Undeb Gweithwyr Môn and Holyhead Trades and Labour Council, his position became even more ambiguous. He continued to attend trade union conferences in Anglesey and to support Labour in Parliament, but only on his own terms.[231] Another threat to resign his seat in October 1920 compounded an agonizing situation even further.[232] What Brynfab viewed as the 'greatest let down'[233] in the history of the labour movement divided their ranks. Whereas the Holyhead Trades and Labour Council sanctioned Sir Owen Thomas's status as an Independent MP, officials of the Anglesey Workers' Union were bound to accept his resignation because of their affiliation to the Labour Party.[234]

That political power never materialized on a larger scale was understandable given the poorly developed organization within most rural districts. It was also too much to expect uneducated and inarticulate farm workers to take a front-line public role after centuries of acquiescence. Barely literate, most rural labourers lacked the necessary confidence to express themselves openly and were therefore reluctant to act on committees.[235] Imparting education thus became a priority, with farm workers being encouraged to take advantage of the tutorial classes organized by the Workers' Educational Association. As NUAW organizer and subsequently organizing secretary of the WEA, John Davies was instrumental in establishing economics classes in Cardiganshire.[236] Industrial history and economic theory were the subjects taught in a tutorial class at Brongest, an NUAW stronghold.[237] D.T. Lewis acted as secretary to the economics class at Mathry, another union bastion.[238] In the annual report for 1919–20, WEA tutors spoke enthusiastically of the 'keenness and quality' of the work done by agricultural labourers in Cardiganshire.[239] J. Morgan Rees of the University College, Aberystwyth, a prominent Labour Party activist, addressed a public meeting at Ponterwyd on the subject of adult education under the auspices of the NUAW.[240] Again, at certain classes in north Wales, where economic history and political science were studied, the majority of students were reported to be agricultural workers.[241] For their part, the trade unions themselves undertook the task of instilling a more overt political education. At the Four Crosses NUAW branch a lecture on socialism emphasized its aim of destroying poverty and unemployment.[242] Labourers at the Newport (Pembrokeshire) branch were given an address on the nationalization of mines and railways.[243] At Llanuwchllyn, union members heard W.T. Bason outline Labour's plans for nationalization and land reform.[244] Equally important to the enlightenment of the rural labourer was the role of prominent speakers at special conferences. Labour demonstrations in Cardiganshire organized by the Dockers' Union and NUAW attracted 'star' names like Ben Tillett, James Wignall and W.R. Smith. Following the strike in the Vale of Glamorgan, and the initiation of farm labourers in industrial warfare, Labour Party rallies became a regular event at Llantwit Major.[245]

All this activity would, it was hoped, also nurture a local leadership. In most cases, however, farm workers' union branches still depended heavily on the assistance given by the NUR or one of the other major unions. Officers of the Magor NUAW branch were leading NUR officials.[246] The N.U.R. and Dockers' Union provided chairmen for the Clarbeston Road and Vale of Towi branches.[247] In north Pembrokeshire it seemed that NUAW branches were being run by the 'scholastic profession'.[248] In addition to Evan Anthony, D.T. Lewis and others, there was also D.J. Williams, later to become one of the founder members of Plaid Cymru. As a Workers' Union official at Llangurig stressed, what the country districts needed badly were leaders.[249]

The rise of farm workers' trade unionism in Wales was quite unprecedented. By 1920 NUAW employed four full-time organizers, whereas the Workers' Union had six to cover the wider spectrum of occupations within its membership. In their charge was a total of some 300 branches composed mainly of workers employed in agriculture and numbering at least 10,000. In the process, they had transformed industrial relations. Labourers demanded respect and consideration, they expected to be treated as equals in negotiations, through their unions they were able to submit claims and secure agreements, on occasion even score victories over their employers. In partnership with the Labour Party the farm workers' struggle also took on a political character, allowing them a further opportunity to press for improvements in social conditions. The men themselves were well aware of the dramatic change in their status and conscious of what had been achieved. In language evocative of freedom from bondage, one local leader optimistically declared how they had, within two years, 'turned their backs on Egypt, and were now facing Canaan'.[250]

Reverses were not uncommon, even at this high point in trade union fortunes. The obstacles in the way of successful organization were many and formidable. Physical difficulties had to be overcome: distances, poor communications and inadequate transport. The mountains of Wales inhibited the mobility of organizers. It was said that the lack of railway and motor services made the country region of north Pembrokeshire 'almost ungetatable' (*sic*).[251] To overcome the problems in his district David Rees attempted unsuccessfully to obtain official endorsement to an ambitious scheme, involving a prize draw, which would eventually raise enough money to enable him to purchase a motor car.[252] For R.G. Roberts the rugged terrain in north Wales made bicycle travel slow and arduous and was eventually to undermine his health. Then there were the psychological barriers. Notwithstanding the startling achievements, organizers still encountered apathy and indifference not only amongst farm labourers in general, but also amongst the branch members they had recruited. Time and again, ap Rhydwen inveighed against their lack of interest, a condition which often drove him to despair.[253] Neither should it be forgotten that in numerical terms rural trade unionism remained a minority movement amongst the agricultural work-force.

At least there were a few signs that the religious bodies in Wales had begun, somewhat late in the day, to take an interest in the plight of the rural workers. A wide cleavage existed between Nonconformity and organized labour. John Davies, for one, admitted he found more spiritual inspiration inside the labour movement than inside the churches.[254] Perhaps it was guilt which shook the Nonconformist hierarchy from its complacency. Not that they would trade their loyalty in any way; in terms of government and finance Nonconformity had become synonymous with the middle class.[255] However, in December 1919 David Thomas was invited to address the annual conference of the Welsh National Free Church Council during a discussion on the church's attitude to the labour movement.[256] Another speaker, the Revd Gwilym Davies, complained that the church was too often a 'mere spectator' in the working-class struggle for social justice. One man who began to give practical meaning to the Christian spirit was George M.Ll. Davies, a leading figure in the Fellowship of Reconciliation. Because of his pacifist stand during the war he undertook alternative service as an 8*s*.-a-week labourer in Llŷn prior to a period of imprisonment at Wormwood Scrubs and Dartmoor.[257] And he knew what it was to endure poverty and physical hardship. Upon his discharge in June 1919 he embarked on a personal mission of reconciliation. He addressed several Workers' Union branches as well as the Methodist monthly meeting in Anglesey. Not only that, George M. Ll. Davies threw himself into the industrial fray. He met trade unionists and farmers in Anglesey and then Llŷn to offer his services as mediator and foster a better understanding between both parties.[258]

But time was fast running out for the agricultural labourers. The following year the Corn Production Act would be repealed and the Agricultural Wages Board scrapped, along with all the district wages committees. In the same way that one parliamentary act had provided the basis for rural trade unionism, another act bringing agricultural decontrol would help to destroy it. Holding on to the gains in wages and working hours was to prove extraordinarily difficult. Agricultural labourers had displayed the will to fight, now they would have to show equal determination to survive as an organized work-force. With trade unionism exposed to attacks from every quarter, and with the removal of the statutory sanction that gave it a rural base, the spirit of goodwill and reconciliation preached by George M. Ll. Davies took on a special significance as farmers and labourers seemed destined to return to the old conditions.

CHAPTER VI

A CAUSE DEFEATED: DECLINE AND RETREAT, 1921–1929

Changing economic tides brought misfortune to every section of industry and society when the post-war boom ended in 1921. Overseas trade fell by almost a half, pulling down prices and wage rates and doubling the number out of work. By the summer of 1921 over 2 million workers were unemployed. Despite a short recovery Britain was to enter a period of prolonged recession and throughout the 1920s unemployment never dropped below a million. Unemployment overshadowed all else, with only the dole, the Poor Law and later the 'Means Test' to lessen its impact. The National Insurance Act of 1911 had been extended in 1920 to cover more workers but farm labourers were amongst those left outside the scheme. They had to wait until the Unemployment Insurance (Agriculture) Act of 1936 to be included in a state insurance system. Under the strain of poverty their capacity for survival was to be tested to the extreme. For Wales, these were the 'Locust Years'.[1] The country consistently suffered the highest percentage of British unemployment: 19.3 per cent of the insured workers were without a job in 1929.[2] In the mining communities of south Wales the scale of adversity had seldom been equalled; here, a whole generation bore the scars of what seemed to be an economic wasteland. But wherever they lived, few families were spared the suffering. Far-reaching in its social consequences, thick in its pall of despair, the economic slump of the inter-war years became synonymous with decline and defeat.

For trade unionism it spelled disaster on a spectacular scale. Union membership which had stood at 8.3 million in 1920 fell to 5.4 million within three years; by 1929 it had sunk to 4.8 million.[3] Mass unemployment caused havoc amongst the general unions that had enjoyed rapid wartime expansion. Most of the ground gained by the Workers' Union, the NUGW and the NUR was now lost just as quickly. Another union to suffer badly was the SWMF, whose membership shrank from 197,668 in 1921 to 62,089 a decade later. Losses in membership meant a severe weakening of bargaining strength and placed organized labour on the defensive. One result was the acceleration in the process of amalgamation. Ernest Bevin personally welded fourteen separate unions, including the Dockers' Union, into the Transport and General Workers' Union (TGWU) by 1922. Two years later saw the formation of the National Union of General and Municipal Workers (NUGMW) which incorporated both NUGW and NALU. Because of the close correlation between the level of trade union membership and the nature of the economy, any hope of recovery in strength and influence rested upon the prospect of industrial renewal.

The deteriorating economic situation also forced the Coalition Government to reverse its policy on agriculture. Although the Agriculture Act of 1920 promised a continuation of the Corn Production Act with its guaranteed minimum prices, it had to be repealed within six months. As world grain prices tumbled the State was in no position to cover the heavy subsidies involved and so they were abruptly withdrawn. Under the Corn Production Acts (Repeal) Act, introduced in July 1921, the Agricultural Wages Board was to be scrapped along with the guaranteed prices and minimum wage. In place of the district wages committees it proposed conciliation committees of employers and workmen to fix wage rates on a voluntary basis. All of which meant a complete return to the uncontrolled conditions that existed before the wartime emergency. To the farmers it was a 'great betrayal', but at least the freedom of contract regarding wages and hours of employment offered a degree of compensation.[4] On the other hand, as W.R. Smith pointed out during the second reading of the Bill, the abandonment of the Wages Board left the agricultural workers entirely unprotected.[5] Prior to the debate, MPs from rural constituencies were extensively lobbied by union leaders.[6] One such deputation consisted of the main NUAW activists in Cardiganshire, D.S. Jones, R.L. Jones and David James.[7] Whilst Welsh members remained silent on the fate of the farm labourers, a deputation of trade union officials from north and west Wales were at least able to applaud George Edwards when he reminded the House that the measure was also a betrayal of their class interests.[8] The only Liberal Coalitionist from Wales to record his opposition along with the band of Welsh Labour MPs was Sir R.J. Thomas, who had earlier spoken on behalf of the farmers. Wherever Sir Owen Thomas's sympathies really lay, he too filed through the same lobby as W.R. Smith and George Edwards to vote against the Bill.

Agricultural decontrol became effective from 1 October 1921. By the end of the year the prices of agricultural produce declined almost to 1916 values, incurring unprecedented cash losses.[9] Allegations of non-payment of the minimum wage had been commonplace in the last months of statutory control; in Carmarthenshire it was stated to be a 'serious problem'.[10] With the removal of government subsidies farmers had to become self-sufficient in order to survive, and one way was to cut down on labour costs. Unburdened by legal restrictions, the employers quickly took advantage of the free market situation to trim the wages of their work-force, much to the relief of farmers in Glamorgan and Monmouth.[11] In its last order before dissolution the Agricultural Wages Board had reduced the minimum wage to 42*s*. Naturally enough, the worsening situation preoccupied trade union officials and members alike. Though NUAW and the Workers' Union each claimed a strong membership of rural workers, they were hardly in a position to respond to a rank-and-file call for a general strike.[12] Unemployment was rising fast and there were reports of hundreds of farm-hands failing to secure work at the hiring fairs. Business came almost to a standstill at Harlech and Pwllheli Fairs because agreements could not be reached.[13] At the farewell luncheon of the Glamorgan and Monmouth District Wages Committee, David Rees expressed concern that advantage might be taken of the labourers to force them back to old conditions.[14] He had every reason to fear the worst.

Just how shattering a blow the economic slump and the abolition of the Wages Board would prove to be to the farm workers' unions became clear immediately. Even for the mighty Workers' Union, 1921 seemed like a 'nightmare'.[15] During the course of the year membership was almost exactly halved from 495,160 to 247,140, dropping another 43 per cent to 140,000 by 1922.[16] The reduction in membership suffered by the NUAW also revealed the measure of devastation. Within three years it plummeted from 80,000 (1921) to 22,000 (1924), and for most of the inter-war period the figure remained below 25,000.[17] Local branches could not possibly survive this depletion of members and the weakest were the first to disappear. More often than not these proved to be the more isolated branches with which union organizers found difficulty in keeping in constant touch. Between 1921 and 1926 the number of Workers' Union branches fell from 2,600 to 1,800. In similar fashion the NUAW branches crumbled away so that the total of 2,637 which had existed in 1921 was cut to less than half (1,216) by 1924. Further closures left the union with 985 branches in 1929.

A crash of such proportions had a profoundly damaging effect on both organizations. It took the heart out of their strategy and capability. When trade unionism no longer commanded sufficient support amongst the work-force a widespread sense of defeat filled the air, extinguishing unity and hope. Failure to sustain life at local branch level, in turn, put the organizers' own position in jeopardy. As branches became enervated by continual defections, the organizers had to issue frequent appeals to the men to stand firm. After the removal of the Agricultural Wages Board it was only the unions which offered the men security and defence; as their representatives, the organizers needed all the support they could get in order to present a strong case on the voluntary conciliation committees.

This sudden transformation from a position of relative power to one of ominous decline placed the NUAW, as the weakest of the farm workers' unions, in desperate straits. Losses in membership and the consequent reduction in income soon impaired its administrative and organizational base. In an attempt to curtail expenditure, the executive committee was forced to carry out economies and, in the context of its dealings with Wales, the writing was on the wall. Wales had already figured among the areas reporting a considerable fall-off in contributions.[18] Consequently, doubt arose as to the wisdom of printing more union rules in the Welsh language in view of the 'small membership' involved.[19] In the end the executive committee decided to go ahead and print 5,000 copies. More drastic was the decision to rationalize the union's basic structure in terms of staffing, both at head office and out in the field. Organizers became the prime targets for scrutiny. R.G. Roberts was obliged to relinquish his post as union representative on the Caernarfonshire Labour Council in January 1921 on account of the expense it involved.[20] Because NUAW only had a few members in the area it was felt that their interests could be left in the care of the Workers' Union or Dockers' Union. At the same time, D.S. Jones's request to contest a seat on the Cardiganshire County Council had to be refused in view of the deteriorating position in his district.[21] Anticipating the worst, E.J. Williams resigned as organizer in north-east Wales.[22] It came as something of a surprise that he had never given up his post as checkweigher, but after taking legal advice head office decided not to pursue the matter.[23] No one was appointed in his place. Instead, his district came under the control of the Staffordshire organizer and in no time the situation in Denbigh and Flint grew more lethargic.[24]

David Rees, the NUAW's senior organizer in Wales, was already under a cloud because of the insolent nature of his reports to James Lunnon, the organizing secretary.[25] Summoned to London to present his case in person, Rees argued that the difficulties he faced were not fully understood or appreciated by head office.[26] But once he had mastered the art of riding a motor cycle and was able to get around his district more quickly he hoped the situation would improve. Upon considering his explanation, the executive committee granted him three months' grace. By the end of the year his progress was reviewed again, this time as part of a general appraisal of the union's position in Wales.[27]

In its first issue for 1921, *The Land Worker* had reported how union organizers were 'hard at work in Wales'.[28] The unionization of farm workers was proceeding steadily with district and county committees apparently in full working order. Subsequent reports were crammed with a catalogue of activity as organizers kept up the pace, addressing various meetings and obtaining arrears of back-pay for members.[29] When the TUC gathered at Cardiff in September 1921, R.B. Walker took advantage of the occasion to thank his local organizers.[30] It was said that NUAW had grown at a 'phenomenal rate' in the rural districts of Wales, and David Rees, D.S.Jones, R.L. Jones and John Davies were there to join in the celebrations. Yet, beneath this veneer of official optimism all was not well. Before his resignation E.J. Williams had spoken of the great amount of work still to be done.[31] By July, R.G. Roberts was admitting that the position of the union in Caernarfonshire and Merioneth was 'not so prosperous as it ought to be'.[32] Apathy, non-union labour and the hostile attitude of employers were continuing to tie his hands more firmly behind his back. Apart from these endemic difficulties and constraints, the threat posed by unemployment and decontrol of agriculture provided an even gloomier backcloth against which to operate.

No one felt this more than David Rees. Developments in Glamorgan in 1921 gave him first-hand experience of the turn-about which was to diminish the effectiveness of his union. At the beginning of the year the men were claiming a minimum wage of £3; but with the farmers in a high state of nervousness regarding their economic prospects there was little chance of this demand succeeding.[33] When the Glamorgan NFU began to discuss the possibility of exempting labourers over the age of 65 from the minimum wage, James Kennett suggested that they ask for a 'permit to shoot them' rather than starve them to death.[34] At harvest-time another potential flashpoint loomed. As expected, the men's demand for a special harvest payment of £3 was rejected outright.[35] Any danger that it might lead to open rebellion as in the summer of 1919 was quickly defused when the Agricultural Wages Board decided to enforce the 1920 wage rate.[36] An abundance of harvest labour, supplemented by the presence of unemployed miners, meant that the farm workers were in no position to challenge this.[37] The proposed scrapping of the Wages Board then became the signal for the employers to push counter-proposals, and the final meeting of the district wages committee heartily endorsed the proposal to reduce the basic minimum by 6*s.* — to 42*s.*[38] Upon the formation of the conciliation committee for Glamorgan the farmers' representatives pressed for a further cut of 2*s.*, thus increasing the pressure on David Rees as chief negotiator.

By then, Rees's fate was tied to changes at a higher level. The NUAW's financial position had become so bad that drastic measures had to be implemented. To meet the projected deficit forecast for 1922 the union dispensed with the services of fifteen organizers and imposed a ten per cent salary reduction on the remainder.[39] On 1 February 1922 David Rees received a month's notice. If not entirely unexpected, it was nevertheless a shattering personal blow.[40] To fill his place, D.S. Jones assumed charge of the whole of south Wales, with the exception of five branches in the Knighton area of Radnor which were handed over to the organizer for neighbouring Shropshire.[41] At a conference in Newport in March, D.S. Jones was introduced to branch delegates from Glamorgan and Monmouth and in the opinion of James Lunnon the handover had proved successful. Next in line was R.G. Roberts. In order to cut back even further on expenditure, a special meeting of the finance committee in July recommended that he too be dismissed.[42] Following his discharge D.S. Jones would take over the whole of Wales.[43] When R.G. Roberts volunteered his services on a temporary basis the executive committee relented; he was then re-engaged as a part-time organizer in north Wales on half salary.[44] No one could deny that he deserved a second chance.

Within the existing limitations, R.G. Roberts had earnestly tried to promote the name of NUAW in a difficult area. One instance of his success was the recovery of some £300 in 1920 for those members in Caernarfonshire who had been underpaid by their employers.[45] During this time he also endured and witnessed much personal suffering. To disrupt the social balance and to challenge traditional conventions was enough to earn him the reputation of 'extremist', let alone the kind of unforgiving hatred that often manifested itself. As a loyal chapel-goer he found the vengeful behaviour of Caernarfonshire farmers most unchristian, but at least he could understand why the young men were losing interest in religion.[46] One particularly uncharitable act concerned the case of an agricultural labourer from Chwilog who sought relief before the Pwllheli Board of Guardians. The Guardians were mainly farmers, and some took exception to the labourer's record of trade union activism; an attempt was made not only to besmirch his character but also to 'show his class who was the boss'.[47] Despite a plea from the Relieving Officer, the majority voted to allow him and his family of five only £1 a week for two weeks. Instead of administering relief fairly and impartially, the Board had acted more like a 'Papal Inquisition'.[48] An official protest from R.G. Roberts in the name of the union was ignored.[49]

An ideal opportunity to reassert authority over the farm labourers came with the setting up of the voluntary conciliation committees. When the farmers secured an immediate wage cut of 5*s*. the labourers' future looked bleak.[50] More tangibly, it also presented R.G. Roberts with a last-ditch opportunity to rally support for the union. Feeling among the workers ran high as employers contemplated another reduction of 12*s*. a week. In conjunction with the Workers' Union, meetings were arranged in south Caernarfonshire to activate resistance to such unreasonable demands.[51] One speaker asserted that it would be better to accept parish relief than starvation wages. Tied to this was the men's determination to hold on to their Saturday half-holiday. At the request of NUAW, A. Rogers, a Ministry of Agriculture official, attended the conciliation committee to help break the stalemate, and this aspect of the dispute was duly settled.[52] Ordinary labourers would be allowed to finish work at 1 p.m. on Saturday, but cowmen were expected to remain on the farm to tend to the animals until 4 p.m. Relations remained finely balanced for a while amid deep distrust; when the agreement expired in May 1922 it led to a new bout of hostilities.

By this time the Saturday half-holiday was almost universally granted to industrial workers in the towns. Farm labourers had no reason to consider themselves different. With the opening of a new round of negotiations the Caernarfonshire men were adamant that the principle of a 1 p.m. stop should continue unchanged; the farmers would only agree to 4 p.m.[53] At the annual hiring fair at Pwllheli in May, attended by 2,000 farmers and labourers, there was complete deadlock.[54] To make matters worse the employers refused to negotiate. Conjointly with William Williams of the Workers' Union, R.G. Roberts then addressed a mass meeting of the men. Real economic hardship and belief in the justice of their case combined to push the men on; over the past twelve months they had already suffered a reduction of 22*s*. in the weekly wage. For the first time in their history, farm workers in south Caernarfonshire resolved to down tools. Hundreds responded to the strike call and in no time the stoppage was said to be causing great inconvenience to farmers in Llŷn.[55] Further discussions between both parties on the conciliation committee succeeded in working out a tentative agreement. Union leaders conceded that with the exception of those who had already been granted a 1 p.m. stop, the men should work on until 4 p.m. each Saturday afternoon. If engaged unconditionally they were to follow the pattern prevailing in the district.

First reactions showed how the mood of the rank and file had been seriously misjudged. To the majority it was tantamount to a surrender. Farm labourers at Sarn and Aberdaron expressed indignation at the action of their own spokesmen; they wanted uniform terms for all workers.[56] No sooner was the agreement signed than union organizers were being dragged along by a groundswell of militant opinion. Those who still adhered to the original demand refused to honour the conciliation committee decision. Envoys were sent around the farms to compel other workers to leave at 1 p.m., thus intensifying the dispute. Indeed, a force of sixty men was reported to be roaming the district seeking out blacklegs.[57] In an attempt to heal the breach, A. Rogers of the Ministry of Agriculture again tried his hand at arbitration, but to no avail.[58] A meeting at Pwllheli in June broke up after six hours' deliberation without coming to an understanding. Meanwhile, a large number of striking farm-hands attended Cricieth hiring fair to find harvest work — at wage rates 50 per cent down on the previous year.[59] The dispute at Llŷn was left to run its course without an official settlement. Apparently, those who stood firm eventually secured a 1 p.m. stop,[60] with strikers from the Nefyn branch, at least, being recompensed from union funds.[61] On the advice of William Williams and R.G. Roberts they were encouraged to show flexibility by undertaking farm work after 1 p.m. if the need arose.[62] Apart from Caernarfonshire, only in the counties of Glamorgan, Pembroke and Carmarthen did NUAW members in Wales enjoy the privilege of a 1 p.m. Saturday half-holiday.[63]

Best interpreted as a hollow victory, this dispute foreshadowed the imminent demise of rural trade unionism as a force in the county. Significantly, the minute books of the Llŷn branches provide a record of the drift towards defeat.[64] Amongst other things, the farmers were deliberately refusing to hire trade unionists in an attempt to destroy them. Had defeat not been immediately recognizable in 1922, it became an accepted fact the following year when the NUAW branches in Caernarfonshire experienced an almost total collapse. In this context, the strike was the men's final gesture of defiance. It was also the end of R.G. Roberts's career in trade unionism. In yet another purge forced by financial stringency, head office parted with more staff.[65] Along with nine other organizers R.G. Roberts received his notice to quit in January, and this time there was no reprieve. As D.S. Jones shared the same inglorious fate, it meant that the NUAW was sounding retreat in Wales and abandoning what it strategically regarded as its weakest ground. From the end of 1923 Wales was run as a unit from the London head office, with only an occasional visit by a member of the executive committee.[66] On his tour of Pembrokeshire that summer, James Lunnon had personal experience of the difficulties of organizing 'out in the wilds'.[67] Though he successfully restarted the St Ishmael branch he was forced to admit that the men were 'not so eager for organization' as in previous years.

Simultaneously, the same elements also forced the Workers' Union into a defensive posture and, prior to implementing a matching policy of rationalization, its organizers were to experience a similar period of travail. Everywhere, but especially in its erstwhile rural strongholds, there was an air of dejection. In a matter of weeks apathy and indifference could often undo all the hard work put in by an organizer over a period of years. Recurrent in ap Rhydwen's writings was his exasperation with the farm labourers' 'self-neglect'.[68] Considering that the Workers' Union had secured over £1,350 in back-pay for agricultural labourers in north Wales[69] he might well have been soured by a sense of betrayal. Yet, from his experience of fighting on their behalf, ap Rhydwen believed it was a condition to be pitied rather than condemned. Shortly before severing his connection with the Workers' Union in October 1922 he came to the sad verdict that the men were the unwitting victims of a 'hereditary disease'.[70]

By a cruel stroke of irony, David Thomas was to preside over the disintegration of the Workers' Union in mid-Wales. From his first association with the labour movement he had made the farm workers' cause a personal crusade. Within months of accepting the post of district organizer for Merioneth and Montgomery, he began to see everything collapse before his eyes.

Immediately he undertook the job, David Thomas had to shake up a number of sluggish branches. Members at Llangurig, Llanfair Caereinion, Pennal, Llangadfan and Abermiwl were told in plain terms to take more interest in their branch.[71] By holding meetings, issuing circulars (laced with such catchy slogans as 'the union workhouse or the union of workers') and making personal visits, he showed that he meant business. As an indication of what good organization could achieve he pointed to the recovery of nearly £150 in arrears of wages within ten months.[72] But before David Thomas had even a chance of putting the union on an even keel he faced the twin storms of agricultural decontrol and economic depression. Never the best of employers, Montgomeryshire farmers began to trim their sails to advantage. One farmer boasted how the labour glut enabled him to hire workers at almost any rate he cared to offer.[73] Once the conciliation committee came into being there was nothing to stop the farmers' proposals from carrying the day. By the end of 1921 wages for ordinary labourers had been reduced from 42*s*. to 35*s*. a week.[74] Because many workers had already been hired for less than the minimum there was very little David Thomas could do.[75] It was either starvation wages or unemployment. Still, Thomas endeavoured to consolidate his forces by issuing fervent appeals. But as the recession hit the towns he had his work cut out even to hold the main branches at Welshpool, Newtown, Llanidloes and Machynlleth.

As the membership deserted in droves his appeals seemed even more futile. Few turned up for branch meetings and a great many fell behind with their contributions. Members of the Towyn and Bryncrug branches were in arrears because there was no one to receive their money.[76] It was, Thomas admitted, 'a depressing and discouraging time for all'.[77] As part of his last stand he embarked on a policy of uniting some of the ailing branches — such as Llangurig with Llanidloes — and reviving former strongholds. Once the premier branch in Montgomeryshire, Llanbryn-mair was now on the verge of extinction. Although members voted to fight on in October 1921, the end seemed near despite a special plea to those young men without family commitments to shoulder some of the burden.[78] By evoking the spirit of the siege of Ladysmith David Thomas hoped to hold the fort until better times.[79] But where there had once been a force a hundred strong he now failed to muster twenty members to join the Revd Gwilym Rees in ensuring the survival of the branch. Time was running out. At this juncture the Workers' Union was forced to prune its staff. No longer could it afford to maintain a large band of rural organizers and for this reason even a loyal and able officer in the field like David Thomas had to go in March 1922.[80] His successor, P. Grudgings, who operated from the union's Cardiff office, hardly fared better. Some three months later, in a reply to an enquiry from David Thomas, he sized up the position in a single word: 'rotten.'[81]

Before leaving, Thomas had wound up those branches he considered to be beyond salvation.[82] Others still owed the union sums of money. As part of the organizational reshuffle that followed, Sidney Box was obliged to relinquish control over seven branches in Monmouth, Brecon and Radnor.[83] All these branches were within reach of his home base at Hereford and, much to his annoyance, they suffered neglect and went into rapid decline.

The high point of agricultural workers' trade unionism in Wales had passed. A different set of circumstances was rapidly undermining the very basis of unionism making decline inevitable. As each county experienced this catastrophic decrease in membership the number of branches rapidly diminished. In some areas even branches that once counted their members in hundreds were wiped out. By 1922 the number of NUAW branches had plunged from 140 to 82; within another year the union was left with a rump of 37. In view of the fact that a peak of 160 branches had been reached only three years earlier, it made sombre reading. Counties where the NUAW had enjoyed its greatest successes were now the ones to experience a brutally rapid contraction. Over a two-year period (1921–2), Glamorgan lost 10 branches, Caernarfon 12, Cardigan 13 and Pembroke as many as 17. As the union became virtually defunct in the three counties of west Wales the TGWU aired ambitions of stepping in and taking over the organization of farm workers.[84] The fate which befell the NUAW had also proved equally disastrous for the Workers' Union. Around 56 Workers' Union branches in rural Wales disappeared from the annual list by 1923, whilst a further 22 branches were recorded as officially 'closed'. Included among them were those at Montgomery, Machynlleth, Bryn-crug, Towyn, Holywell, Tremeirchion and Whitford — all of which dated back to the pioneering days of the NFDWU in 1917–18. In terms of overall membership both the NUAW and the Workers' Union ceased to be a credible force in rural Wales.

The nature of their weakness was well illustrated in the course of the unrestricted collective bargaining by conciliation committees which followed the termination of the Agricultural Wages Board and the removal of protection to farm labourers. With no statutory minimum wage, the voluntary aspect placed workmen at the mercy of employers, who, in general, set the standard of payment. Workers' representatives on the committees (ten were set up in Wales)[85] made forlorn attempts to secure satisfactory wage settlements, but as trade union strength waned they could do little to prevent a return to pre-war conditions. As soon as the legal minimum wage expired on 30 September 1921, trouble began. The machinery of conciliation often broke down because the wage cuts proposed by the farmers were too drastic and impossible to accept. Whereas this resulted in deadlock in many English counties, the agreement reached at Norfolk fixed the going rate at 36*s*. for a fifty-hour week and this remained the norm until the end of the year.

Set against this figure, the rejection of £2 for a fifty-hour week by Glamorgan workers was deemed unreasonable. Farmers saw a sharp drop in prices after the harvest and were unwilling to grant more. Deadlock ensued.[86] David Rees tried desperately to hold out for more,[87] but, given the surplus in the labour market, there was little prospect of the men taking successful strike action[88] and in the end they had to bow down. Rees was forced to reopen negotiations in November, whereupon the original offer of £2 was accepted.[89] At Monmouth, and especially Montgomery, the farmers were extremely reluctant even to accept the concept of conciliation. They preferred the liberty to make individual arrangements, in other words, to dictate their own terms. Obduracy in the Montgomeryshire NFU came as no surprise and for a time they refused to have anything to do with the new order.[90] As usual, members of the Brecon and Radnor

NFU were wary of having men imported into the district to sit on the workers' side.[91] Mutual distrust eroded much of the middle ground and a breakdown of negotiations became commonplace. Apart from Glamorgan, there was also deadlock at Caernarfon, Cardigan, Pembroke, Montgomery and Anglesey.[92] By adopting a 'take it or leave it' style the employers were rapidly turning conciliation into a farce.[93]

Wage rates for ordinary labourers in Wales in December 1921 varied from £2 in Glamorgan to 35*s*. in Caernarfonshire, Brecon and Radnor. By the end of January 1922 the average wage fell appreciably in a number of counties, coincident with the downward tendency in prices. In January David Rees declared that his members would rather receive unemployment pay than accept the current offer of 35*s*.;[94] by December they had to make do with 33*s*. After several abortive conferences there was further deadlock in Monmouthshire, when the government was asked to intervene.[95] Almost inevitably, the men had to accept the employers' offer of 30*s*. even though one farmer was honest enough to admit that they would be 'better off as paupers'.[96] Separate settlements led to a wide variation between wages in one county and another. By December 1922 the minimum cash wage in the majority of Welsh counties was between 30*s*. and 32*s*., with the rate in Denbigh and Flint as low as 27*s*.[97] Complaints of non-observance of agreements were so frequent that in many cases workers received less than the minimum.

Early in 1923 Norfolk became a testing ground for both sides. Reputed to be not only one of the most prosperous farming counties in Britain, but in terms of trade unionism also the most militant, developments here were watched with interest. Having imposed a wage of 25*s*. early in 1923, the farmers soon gave notice of a further cut, thus provoking a strike. Their offer of 22*s*. 6*d*. was considerably less than the sum paid in the poorest farming district in Wales. Described as the labourers' 'biggest battle' since the lockout of 1873, it lasted four weeks.[98] A settlement based on a rate of 25*s*. for fifty hours did much to stem the decline in wages. All the same, local disagreements continued to produce deadlocks so that by 1923–4 many of the conciliation committees ceased to function. In this situation workers were bound by agreements put in operation in 1922, or else masters and men had to settle between themselves. Cynical employers were thus able to milk every advantage, especially if the men proved leaderless. The Cardiganshire conciliation committee could do nothing in January 1924 because no labour representatives appeared![99] One way or another, the bad old days seemed to have returned. At a labour rally, William Williams spoke of men working 56–65 hours a week for a mere £1.[100]

Acceptance of starvation wages was nothing new; the agricultural labourers had been well schooled to a life of privation. After a brief interlude of fair reward they once more faced hardship with customary resignation. The case of the farm labourer before Ffestiniog Poor Law Guardians, struggling to keep his wife and seven children on a wage (24*s.*) below the scale of outdoor relief, was said to represent the hidden face of rural poverty 'suffered in silence'.[101] Often it was a stark choice between low wages and unemployment, with migration as a possible alternative — if not migration to the industrial towns, then many were lured by the prospect of a better life overseas.[102] The guarantee of work to experienced farm labourers in Canada in 1924, for instance, accounted for the dearth of harvesters at the south Caernarfonshire hiring fair at Cricieth.[103] Unfortunately, emigration to the colonies or coal-mines of south Wales also robbed the labour cause of many of its local leaders.[104]

In times of economic hardship the poor usually looked to the churches for succour. It was expected that religious bodies would be more conscious of their Christian duty and that a compassionate concern might be accompanied by practical help. Whilst poverty stalked the countryside it stamped the farm labourers as the 'have-nots' of rural society and became an undeniable feature which no person could ignore. Perhaps no better test existed than the way churches, chapels and individual ministers responded to the voice of the needy; it most certainly highlighted their attitude to social issues of the day. In truth, however, it was a test which few attempted to pass. Although well-meaning declarations were issued in the post-war years, the churches' failure to involve themselves in the everyday life of the underprivileged serves as a serious indictment of organized religion. The Calvinistic Methodist Association in north Wales broke new ground when its 'Reconstruction Commission' produced a report on social questions in 1921.[105] In the introduction to its findings on rural conditions, reference was made to the excessive hours and hard toil which drove many a labourer to a premature grave. Nevertheless, when one of the lay squirearchy took exception to the passage it was duly modified.[106] Action of this kind reinforced the impression of a denomination dominated by middle-class values.

Despite the apparent concern it was either unprepared or unable to provide real answers. The Anglesey monthly meeting had nothing to say on the matter and took no action.[107] It appeared to be as conservative on social issues as its leading divine, the Revd John Williams, now blissfully insulated by 'worldly comforts' in his old age.[108] Similar platitudinous gestures by the Union of Welsh Independents failed to rouse a practical response from supposedly the most radical of Nonconformist bodies.[109]

By way of example, the Llanelli Trades and Labour Council, in April 1923, considered various ways of rendering financial assistance to agricultural workers, including circularizing the ministers of local churches and chapels.[110] Because its plan for a house-to-house collection was turned down by the police superintendent, it decided to launch a flag-day appeal instead. A discussion on class war at a meeting of the Goodwick Labour Party drew a comparison between the attitude of Labour and that of the religious denominations.[111] Not a single church or chapel in the district had devoted one night to the problem of unemployment and poverty. This was all the more surprising considering that individual ministers like the Revd J.A. Davies of Fishguard were openly sympathetic to the working class. The living conditions of the rural labourers, he maintained, could almost excuse them becoming 'revolutionists'.[112] But as we have seen, from the first days of revolt only a few ministers were prepared to side publicly with the workers in their struggle for survival. A farm worker like Richard Griffith had every right therefore to accuse Nonconformist chapels of catering for the middle class;[113] the impassive attitude of the south Caernarfonshire Calvinistic Methodist leadership was to provide a case in point.

In the aftermath of the farm labourers' strike, the Llŷn and Eifionydd Methodist monthly meeting was asked by the Workers' Union in October 1922 to intercede on behalf of the men,[114] then desperately seeking fair play at the hands of the conciliation committee. It became the task of a special committee, headed by O. Robyns Owen, a solicitor and one of the best-known Methodist laymen, to smooth things out. In many ways the committee's irresolute stand on the question was again totally representative of the Nonconformist establishment. Whilst advocating that negotiations between ministers and men be conducted in accordance with the principles of the Christian gospel, it considered it unwise to express an opinion on such issues as wages, hours of labour and profit margins.[115] The few that dissented thought the church was being too cowardly to face the social problems of the day, but the two ministers[116] who spoke out were hardly likely to sway majority opinion. In the end all that was done was to extend an invitation to George M.Ll. Davies to address the monthly meeting on the topic of Christian Brotherhood. His message of reconciliation based on personal experiences in Llŷn, although well received, led to some angry exchanges. One speaker asserted that agricultural labourers were abandoning the church because farmers had become more 'tyrannical' than the old landlords — a remark greeted with cries of 'No, No' and the stamping of feet.[117] Those holding prominent positions in the NFU protested furiously. Although a joint conference of the farmers and labourers' unions in the south Caernarfonshire area was set up to nurture a spirit of mutual understanding,[118] the feeling of betrayal and alienation amongst ordinary labourers could not be talked away.[119] They knew the extent of the oppression and were reminded that the answer lay with their own trade union not the monthly meeting.[120] But with trade unionism set in rapid reverse it was only a pious hope.

Ironically, this major reversal came at a time when the role of farm workers' unions was being celebrated in the form of a political drama, a medium relatively new to Welsh culture. As a playwright pioneering in this field, J.O. Francis wrote *Cross Currents* to dramatize the 'conflict of forces' in rural society.[121] Although in many ways a contrived set piece, Francis succeeded in communicating the vitality of the socialist challenge as it came into collision with Liberalism and incipient Welsh nationalism. In Gomer Davies, a farm labourer's son who returns to his native environment in the role of a trade union organizer, he portrays a character that might be a personification of David Rees, John Davies or David Thomas. And the aspirations he articulates capture their sense of mission, replete with the working-class rhetoric associated with a 'professional agitator'. After political preparation in a working men's college and time spent in industrial Glamorgan, Gomer Davies is intent on freeing what he terms 'the last of the slaves' by 'class warfare'.

Set in July 1921, *Cross Currents* depicted the rural labour movement in the days of its greatest strength. In building his plot around a parliamentary by-election, Francis tried to demonstrate how the labour movement could mount a political challenge to the farming order once represented by Thomas Gee and T.E. Ellis. This was a theme that carried some substance. In the heyday of their revolt the labourers had shown they were no longer the willing clients of their employers. Socialism became the faith of a good number of farm workers as a result of their trade union links; and by acting collectively they had played a part in some singular electoral triumphs. Further success for the Labour Party in rural Wales, particularly at parliamentary level, depended largely on the movement's ability to organize on a broad-based front. To this end, the Pembrokeshire Labour Party had distributed over 50,000 leaflets and handbooks mainly in the agricultural districts.[122] D.T. Lewis, its secretary, considered it worthwhile to cover great distances in the northern part of the county to spread the gospel.[123] He found it gratifying the way tradesmen, schoolmasters and the like joined district Labour parties. As a significant element in such an alliance it was equally essential that farm workers displayed the kind of mettle shown by men at Llanglydwen, Carmarthenshire. In a rural district council by-election in March 1921, Edwin Davies, a farm labourer, stood against Capt. D.G. Protheroe, chairman of the NFU branch.[124] Fighting as a nominee of the NUAW, Davies, with his followers, canvassed the parish extensively only to lose by a wide margin. The following year Edwin Davies was branch delegate to the conference at Carmarthen which established a divisional Labour Party in the county.[125]

However, by the time *Cross Currents* was published in 1923 — Lloyd George attended one of its early performances and seemed deeply interested in the play[126] — everything had changed. The new force within the agricultural constituencies did not have time to gather strength and the political challenge that seemed to offer promise in 1919 never really materialized. While the Labour Party in Wales increased its representation at Westminster from ten to eighteen seats at the 1922 general election, thus finally supplanting the Liberals as the major party, all the gains, save one, were in the industrial constituencies. Perhaps the new political consciousness among farm labourers had contributed to R.T. Jones's victory at Caernarfon, and even Robert Richards's success in Wrexham,[127] but Caernarfon was lost the following year when Labour's total reached twenty seats. Moreover, Labour failed to hold Anglesey at the critical by-election which followed Sir Owen Thomas's death earlier in 1923. Parallel to the decline in trade union membership was the equally telling blow to political morale and organization. The elections of

1922–4, at local and parliamentary level, exposed the political limitations of the rural labour movement.

Where county council elections were concerned, the difference in the state of the rural labour movement in 1922 compared with 1919 could not be more apparent. Gone was the spirit of combativeness. Thoroughly demoralized, it had neither the will nor the means to involve itself in community action. The contrast in Anglesey was striking; there seemed to be little desire for a repeat of the 1919 challenge under the banner of either the Workers' Union or the Labour Party. Two Labour members were returned, but upon the death of Lewis Thomas, the Labour candidate was beaten. This left Brynfab, returned as an 'Independent Labour' in Llanidan, to look after the interests of the agricultural labourers.[128] Indeed, wherever a farm workers' leader or spokesman was elected in Wales he succeeded virtually on the strength of his own personality and reputation alone. It was true in the case of W.H. John at Solva, Urias Richards at Cilgerran, T.J. Stokoe at Hay, the Revd T.D. James at Llanerfyl and the Revd Gwilym Rees at Llanbryn-mair. At Llanbryn-mair, where Labour candidates were said to be 'anathema to the agricultural mind',[129] Rees held off a challenge from the NFU candidate to retain his seat by two votes. A.W. Pittman was not so lucky; at Caer-went he met defeat at the hands of another NFU nominee.[130] A lifetime of service in the cause of labour had its just reward, on the other hand, when R.G. Roberts, at his third attempt, captured the seat at Pen-y-groes in a by-election two months later.[131] This general pattern of failure was repeated in the parish council elections. At Berriew the seats were divided between the Liberals and Conservatives, with no mention of any Workers' Union candidate either here or at Llanbryn-mair. At Llanglydwen, Capt. D.G. Protheroe was returned unopposed on Whitland RDC, where seven of the ten seats were monopolized by farmers.[132] Power still tended to reside with a locally established oligarchy of farmers, and hardly any other parish council in Wales could emulate Mathry[133] or Llantwit Major (under the chairmanship of James Kennett)[134] with their Labour majority.

Prior to the establishment of a divisional Labour Party in Caernarfonshire in 1919, organization had been observed to be ineffective and hardly capable of achieving electoral success.[135] R.T. Jones had contested the county seat on a labour and nationalist platform in 1918 rather than as official Labour Party candidate.[136] Any future progress would have to take the triple alliance of quarrymen, railwaymen and farm labourers as its starting point. Of the three, only the railway unions had the support of the majority of their own work-force; the agricultural workers, despite the campaign of unionization, were recognized to be weak allies. To carry this unity into effect the labour movement would need a good organizer with ample financial backing. If they did not have the man in 1918, they did in 1922. The appointment of David Thomas as Labour Party organizer in Caernarfonshire in April 1922[137] enabled him to use his discarded organizational skills to mastermind R.T. Jones's victory.[138] This crowned a career that combined the qualities of a visionary with the stamina of a crusader in the field. He was, pre-eminently, the architect of the labour and trade union movement as it developed in north Wales. A few months later he took up a teaching post in Bangor and, although still active within Labour Party circles, it was here that another chapter opened in 1929 when he began his better-known connection with the Workers' Educational Association.

That David Thomas's name appeared on the short list of candidates to fight the constituency of Merioneth in 1922 was another indication of his high standing.[139] In the event, J. Jones Roberts, a London barrister, gave Labour a high poll (41.7 per cent) at the first attempt. Moreover, along with Robert Richards, David Thomas had also been considered by the Pembrokeshire Labour Party.[140] Having dismissed overtures from the NFU inviting farm workers to join them and the Landowners' Society in running an 'agriculturalist' as candidate,[141] the NUAW in the county pressed for a Labour candidate with farming connections.[142] As it claimed over 3,000 members and was affiliated to the Labour Party, the union's wishes had to be respected. So much so, that W.J. Jenkins, a former ILP activist who farmed at Wallaston, was selected with D.S. Jones as his election agent.[143] During the course of the campaign old hands were at work cultivating the rural vote. Despite fears that Jenkins's wartime pacifist stand might cause offence to ex-servicemen, there was an increase of 2,000 on Labour's 1918 result. When he stood again in 1923, John Davies, D.T. Lewis and Evan Anthony issued a special appeal to the agricultural workers to remain firm in their support,[144] although the farm workers' union by now was 'little more than a name'.[145]

After switching from Liberal to Labour, and losing Denbigh in 1918, E.T. John was in the hunt for a parliamentary seat. Turning down Pembrokeshire and Anglesey, he came to the view that Brecon and Radnor offered a better chance.[146] Labour was well established in the industrialized southern fringe and, thanks to the NUR, NUAW and the Workers' Union, the rural workers were also swelling its ranks. On gaining the nomination[147] he began to woo the constituency early in 1921. His supporters were acutely aware of the importance of the agricultural vote and how crucial it was to 'capture the agricultural labourer'.[148] Although agricultural decontrol had weakened trade union organization, E.T. John hoped to capitalize on the mood of antagonism aroused by successive wage reductions.[149] Due to T.J. Stokoe's influence in Hay, and a rousing tour of the constituency by the Revd J.H. Jenkins, Cilrhedyn, there were signs of a breakthrough in the remote outlying areas. Amongst the rural workers of Presteigne, Knighton and Old Radnor they found 'unexpectedly heavy support'. Yet, there was concern that the thrust of socialist propaganda in the rural areas was being blunted by poor organization and the opposition of the farmers' union aided by a hostile local press.[150] Socialism, warned the *Brecon and Radnor Express*, meant 'wholesale seizure of private possessions'.[151] When the Conservatives decided not to run (but to support the Liberal candidate) Labour's fate was sealed; all the same, E.T. John notched up 9,850 votes, which represented almost a third of the total poll. A three-cornered fight in 1924 offered a better prospect of success but, although the aggregate vote increased slightly, the task of politicizing the rural workers, now almost bereft of trade unionism, proved too difficult.[152]

In Anglesey, Sir Owen Thomas's political complexion continued to intrigue his constituents, with the argument over Undeb Gweithwyr Môn's apparent sell-out to the Workers' Union as a sideshow. E.T. John (who resided at Llanidan) shared Brynfab's view that Sir Owen Thomas's resignation from the Labour Party was an 'act of utter disloyalty'.[153] Because the Workers' Union branches were now affiliated to the Labour Party, E.T. John was 'approached repeatedly'[154] to contest the seat as the official Labour candidate. For a moment it seemed that the split in the Labour camp — between the Anglesey Workers' Union and the Holyhead Trades and Labour Council — would play into Liberal hands, especially as Sir R.J. Thomas had announced his intention of vacating the Wrexham seat to fight Anglesey at the next election. When E.T. John opted for Brecon and Radnor, the Anglesey Workers' Union was forced to swallow its principles and, at a meeting of the Joint Political Committee, they once more agreed that Sir Owen Thomas should stand as an Independent candidate with official Labour support.[155] Again, it was a choice dictated by circumstances, Sir Owen Thomas being willing to finance his own campaign. But Brynfab and a minority left-wing element felt that the arrangement consigned them to a political wilderness.[156]

In a further challenge Brynfab revived the controversy over Undeb Gweithwyr Môn's affiliation to the Workers' Union. He demanded to know what had happened to the union fund of £300 earmarked towards Labour Party organization in Anglesey and in further correspondence with the Registrar of Friendly Societies he ascertained that Undeb Gweithwyr Môn was still registered as a trade union.[157] As well as embarrassing the leadership of the Anglesey Workers' Union, Brynfab capitalized on this reply to regenerate interest in the formation of an official Labour Party organization.[158] But when he invited union officials and branch representatives to Llangefni in February 1922[159] in the name of the 'Anglesey Labour Party', only five turned up.[160] Whatever his political deficiencies, Sir Owen Thomas still retained a charismatic hold over the majority of labour leaders in the county. Left in almost complete isolation, Brynfab made the final dramatic gesture. On the eve of the general election he announced that he would be supporting Sir R.J. Thomas.[161] In the light of Sir Owen Thomas's 'betrayal' and in the absence of a Labour Party candidate, the workers of Anglesey were urged to follow his example. But he failed to sway opinion; such was the scale of Sir Owen Thomas's personal popularity that his total number of votes and his overall majority were both up on 1918.

Sir Owen Thomas's death a few months later put the labour movement to the test. Politically, it gave the Anglesey Workers' Union an opportunity to reassert itself although they had lost the services of the Revd Richard Morris, who had earlier left his post as full-time organizer to resume his calling as a minister of religion.[162] This time, the Anglesey Workers' Union would only give its backing to a candidate prepared to take the Labour ticket and at a meeting of the Joint Political Committee their influence prevailed.[163] E.T. John accepted the invitation to contest the by-election in April 1923 as a Labour Party candidate. The presence of a Tory seemed to increase his chances although, as he rightly recognized, the Welsh Nonconformist Radical farmer in Anglesey could be as conservative as his anglicized counterpart in Radnor.[164] Even so, it was to traditional Liberalism that Anglesey reverted and with a vote that outweighed the Labour and Conservative total combined. As a wealthy ship-owner, Sir R.J. Thomas's largesse in Holyhead had paid off;[165] industrial workers voted *en masse* against Labour.[166] In stark contrast, the agricultural labourers stood four-square behind E.T. John and loyal to the tenets originally propounded by Undeb Gweithwyr Môn.[167] At their Mecca in Aberffraw, Labour savoured a 'magnificent' political meeting.[168] Out of the ashes of defeat a divisional party organization arose to become, for the first time, officially affiliated to the Labour Party.[169] All the erstwhile Undeb Gweithwyr Môn leaders including Brynfab were present at that special conference at Llangefni, guided by T.C. Morris, the Labour Party organizer in Wales since March 1919.[170] As it happened, again within a month of the by-election, the executive committee of the Anglesey Workers' Union took the final decision to annul Undeb Gweithwyr Môn's registration as a trade union, thus closing a significant chapter in the rural labour movement.[171]

For the Anglesey Labour Party it was to be an inauspicious start. On the eve of the 1923 general election E.T. John withdrew because of ill health. Considerable pressure was then put on William Edwards, a recent convert to Labour.[172] Boasting an association with the labour movement that dated back to ap Ffarmwr and the genesis of Undeb Gweithwyr Môn, he had finally resigned from the Liberal Party in disgust at the way the Anglesey NFU was ganging up against the farm workers.[173] When he declined to stand, Sir R.J. Thomas enjoyed a walk-over. For the 1924 election Labour secured the candidature of another pioneering figure, Cyril O. Jones, now prominent within Labour Party circles in Wrexham. From his political platform he called for a restoration of the Agricultural Wages Board and the public ownership of land.[174] Despite his former connection with Holyhead he only raised the Labour tally by 1,212 votes; this time the Tories had stood down to help Sir R. J. Thomas 'kill Socialism in Anglesey for ever'.[175]

Much as it would have liked, the newly formed Carmarthen Divisional Labour Party did not feel sufficiently confident to put forward a candidate in the election of 1922. It contested the seat in 1923 as a 'propaganda effort'[176] with their candidate, Rolly Williams of Bala, providing a special appeal to his fellow railwaymen as well as to the farm labourers.[177] For the by-election in August the following year it selected the Revd E.T. Owen, Llangeler, the son of a farm worker, and first president of the constituency party. Owen increased the Labour vote by 1,200 and gained second place over the Tory. The year 1923 saw at last the formation of a county Labour Party in Montgomeryshire, partly conceived as a force to counter reactionary farmers.[178] In the majority on the county council, self-interested farmers had embarked on a cost-cutting programme which involved reducing the wages of roadmen to the level of farm workers in order to quell discontent among the latter. But here again a general election was called before the party had time to establish itself outside the urban centres. In this respect, the Machynlleth branch was especially anxious to increase propaganda in the rural districts.[179] When Labour presented its historic challenge in 1924 it did so with an indifferent candidate and suffered a crushing defeat. Organizational difficulties in the rural districts were also cited as the reason for Labour's failure to contest Monmouth before 1924.[180] The constituency organization had ceased to function soon after its formation and this forced the Revd Gordon Lang to withdraw his candidature in 1922.[181] On the instigation of T.C. Morris, an intensive propaganda exercise was undertaken in the rural areas during the summer of 1924 to 'educate' the agricultural labourers.[182] By enlisting the support of the Monmouthshire Federation of Trades and Labour Councils the party was able to run a candidate in 1924, but Luke Bateman of Bristol[183] trailed way behind the sitting Tory member.

The Labour Party's success in Wales in the general election of December 1923 had presaged the formation of the first Labour Government the following year. Robert Richards, an MP sponsored by the Workers' Union and its representative on the Agricultural Wages Board, became Under-Secretary for India, and Rhys J. Davies, MP for Westhoughton, who began life as a farm worker in Carmarthenshire, became Under-Secretary at the Home Office. Following a luckless performance by the Labour Government, the Conservatives were swept back to power in October 1924. The real casualties of the election, however, were the Liberals, now down to forty MPs. Losing three Welsh seats to the Conservatives — Brecon and Radnor, Flint and Pembrokeshire — they managed to hold on to their other rural strongholds in Wales and even regained Wrexham and the University of Wales seat, which the Christian Pacifist (cum Labour) George M.Ll. Davies had unexpectedly won the previous year. In the industrial south, Labour remained invincible. Yet, in an industrial constituency like Pontypridd the party made every effort to nurse the agricultural sector by holding an annual Labour Day in the Vale. Thanks especially to James Kennett, Llantwit Major had become a recognized Labour bastion.[184]

Any hope of a return to power would rest on Labour's performance in the rural areas, and in this respect the ten chiefly agricultural constituencies in Wales[185] were therefore crucial to the future prospects of the party. One of the reasons put forward to explain R.T. Jones's defeat at Caernarfon in 1923 had been the difficulties Labour faced in the rural districts.[186] The Merioneth Labour Party's complaint of 'very poor' organization also contained a familiar ring.[187] Everything turned on the ability to organize and mobilize resources. E.T. John's candidature in the Anglesey by-election was turned to advantage and, as a result of a meeting of prominent Labour leaders at Llangefni on 6 April 1923, party organization in north Wales generally also received a new lease of life.[188] The former North Wales Trades and Labour Council had become a victim of the war and so the groundwork was laid for a new body. Unity and mutual assistance to struggling divisional Labour parties in widely scattered rural areas became the necessary precondition for electoral success. With Caradog Jones and David Thomas as joint conveners, a conference was held at Rhyl in June, when the North Wales Labour Federation came into being.[189] Along with county Labour parties and various unions, the NUAW, Workers' Union and TGWU sent official delegates.[190] However, the Federation had little time to set up machinery for propaganda and organization prior to the 1923 election. Only after some difficulty was a divisional Labour Party formed in Denbighshire,[191] but without the strength of trade union support in the rural districts it lacked the resources to put up a candidate.[192] Even though T.C. Morris was also hard at work co-ordinating the party's efforts in Wales,[193] Labour's share of the vote over the period of three general elections fell steadily in Brecon and Radnor, Caernarfon, Merioneth and Pembroke. Montgomery and Monmouth, contested for the first time in 1924, produced dismal results, and, as in Denbigh (uncontested since 1918), no candidate stood in Cardiganshire despite the legacy of farm labourers' trade unionism in the county. All told, the Labour Party in Wales was a long way off from converting the mass of rural workers.

One thing was certain, the Labour Party could not count on attracting much support from the Nonconformist hierarchy. Very few ministers were bold enough to draw a parallel between the evils of bondage as depicted in Old Testament history and the industrial oppression which gave rise to the modern class struggle in the way the Revd D.D. Walters spoke from political platforms; or to claim, like the Revds J.A. Davies and J.T. Pritchard, that only Labour Party policy properly reflected Christian ideals.[194] When the Revd E.T. Owen declared during the Carmarthen by-election of 1924 that socialism meant putting Christian principles into practice he also criticized his fellow Nonconformist ministers for their reticence.[195] Actually to give up the ministry to serve the working class, as did the Revd Richard Morris, was a unique gesture, but in doing so he laid himself open to some very harsh criticism.[196] E.T. John's strictures on the Calvinistic Methodist body in Anglesey came near the truth when he accused them of ignoring the 'dire social squalor' by identifying with a 'very ruthless economic system'.[197] The hardship that followed decontrol of agriculture would seem the moment for religious leaders to show active compassion and speak out against social evils, but all the while they appeared indifferent to the people's suffering. A series of parliamentary elections provided that opportunity, but as E.T. John found in Anglesey, 'intense conservatism' of the supposedly Radical Nonconformists actually obstructed the march of Labour.[198] Only a small band of Welsh Nonconformist ministers had the courage to take a principled stand. Otherwise, John was dependent on a handful of clergymen like the Revds J.H. Jenkins, J.A. Rees and Benjamin Thomas, who broke with the Anglican-Tory image to espouse left-wing views. This interest by clergymen in social matters was evidently welcomed; indeed the fame of Revd J.H. Jenkins, Cilrhedyn, in Labour Party and trade union circles could be equated with that of the hymnologist William Williams, Pantycelyn, in religion.[199] The accepted notion that the Labour Party owed more to Methodism than Marx might be true in some other setting, but it is an unchallengeable fact that the rural labour movement in Wales had little cause to feel indebted.

One of the few redeeming features of the first Labour Government of 1924 was the ending of the *laissez-faire* situation in agriculture. The Government set out to restore the Agricultural Wages Board along with the local wage-fixing machinery and the principle of a minimum wage. Because of the government's minority position in the Commons, however, Noel Buxton, Minister of Agriculture, was forced to compromise and agree to Tory demands which diluted many of the original proposals. Modifications in the powers of the central Wages Board and the deletion of a 30*s*. minimum wage meant that the Agricultural Wages (Regulation) Bill was severely emasculated when it reached the statute book. Nevertheless, the farm workers' unions preferred to see a bill with no wage figure than have no bill at all. Almost as predictable as Labour's initiative were the objections raised by opponents. Worried farmers complained that the industry would be unable to meet increased costs, and a succession of NFU county committees voiced strong condemnation.[200] The chairman of the Glamorgan NFU detected sinister implications: here was a political ploy to introduce 'professional socialist agitators' into the rural areas to preach class warfare and secure the workers' vote behind Labour's bid to nationalize the land.[201] A defiant member of the Farmers' Union in Montgomeryshire vowed he would rather face prison than submit to 'interference' between himself and his servants.[202]

In accordance with the 1924 Act, eight district wages committees were set up in Wales.[203] Representing the workers on the committees was a familiar blend of organizers and labour activists. Among the NUAW nominations were D.T. Lewis, R.L. Jones, J. Kennett, Rolly Williams, A. Howells, T. Llew Williams and Robert Thomas; on behalf of the Workers' Union sat William Williams, Thomas Rowlands, E.T. Roberts, S. Box and William Harris. For the workers the new order brought its benefits, with almost immediate wage increases in the majority of districts. Once again there was a patchwork of local agreements but with much greater variation this time. By February 1925 the minimum rates in Welsh counties ranged between 30*s*. and 32*s* with Glamorgan out in a class of its own.[204] Settlement here had resulted in the phenomenal award of 37*s*.6*d*. (for 51 hours in winter and 54 hours in summer), compared with 32*s*. in Monmouth. Including Sunday overtime this came to 45*s*.5*d*., one of the highest rates in the kingdom, and it was gained without issuing any kind of threat!

Glamorgan's achievement proved all the more remarkable when compared with Norfolk, which had one of the lowest rates. Norfolk had long been regarded as an NUAW showpiece, but the best even its most experienced negotiators could secure was 29*s*. for 50 hours. And this was for 10,000 union members as opposed to some 10 paid-up members left in Glamorgan![205] Little wonder that employers were near apoplexy and talking depressingly of the end of agriculture in the Vale.[206] Nevertheless, in spite of over a hundred protests from various individuals and farming bodies,[207] the scale of wages in Glamorgan was officially ratified. Credit for this feat went to the men's representatives: J.E. Edmunds, J. Maynard, A. Pearson, M. Phillips, J. Kennett and B. Vaughan. Kennett aside,[208] all had been drafted from outside agriculture, being nominated by the Labour Party or a trades council affiliate. What they lacked in knowledge of farming was made up in trade union experience. As he later recounted,[209] Morgan Phillips's basic ignorance of agricultural conditions made him propose a minimum of 48*s*. which, as an SWMF official, he knew to be the miner's current rate. When the employers offered 28*s*., the independent members then decided to split the difference. Perhaps this simplistic explanation is as difficult to accept as it was for delegates at the NUAW Biennial Conference to acknowledge a wage success so at odds with the density of union membership.[210] Though they may be described as 'Welsh amateur negotiators'[211] in this context, the representatives proved to be in Arthur Pearson's words a 'fairly capable, efficient bunch'.[212] More to the point, whilst Glamorgan retained its position at the top of the wages league, four of these representatives later reached a higher plane within the Labour Party: Billy Vaughan (who remained leader of the workers' side on the Glamorgan Wages Committee) in connection with the Aberafan Constituency Labour Party, J.E. Edmunds and Arthur Pearson as MPs, and Morgan Phillips as General Secretary of the Labour Party.

Direct state intervention on behalf of the farm labourers in the matter of wages once more thrust the importance of trade unionism to the forefront. It was argued that the workers' representatives on the district wages committees would be better placed to secure improvements if they were seen to speak for a united and organized work-force. Experience following the Corn Production Act had shown how statutory collective bargaining boosted recruitment to unprecedented levels. At the 1924 Trades Union Congress, George Edwards of the NUAW initiated steps which he hoped would lay down the basis of a revived organization.[213] It was proposed that a rural campaign be instituted to secure a legal minimum wage and a guaranteed week of forty-eight hours. To assist the farm workers, spokesmen from the railwaymen's unions, their traditional allies, successfully moved that £1,000 be donated towards a rural campaign fund.[214] Like roadworkers, the railwaymen were perennially afraid that their wages might be dragged down to the level of the agricultural labourers' wages.[215]

In preparation for the organizing campaign a special bipartisan committee representing NUAW and the Workers' Union was formed. Talks with the Labour Party in February 1925 raised the possibility of undertaking a joint rural campaign, but in the end it was decided to concentrate on the purely industrial issues rather than complicate matters by infusing a political message.[216] Ten counties were selected, counties where morale had suffered badly since 1921, yet which it was thought had some potential. To avoid any unhealthy competition between the two unions involved, separate spheres of influence were marked out, with the solitary Welsh county, Anglesey, assigned to the Workers' Union. The plan of campaign involved village meetings, mass demonstrations, district conferences and the distribution of propaganda material. Local trades councils were expected to lend assistance and provide speakers to accompany TUC leaders and MPs. It was hoped that this initiative would lead to the resuscitation of moribund branches as well as encourage the establishment of new ones.

Trade unionism in Anglesey had suffered from the same atrophy that had sapped the parent body. At least twenty branches were closed in 1923, the year the Anglesey Workers' Union lost the services of the Revd Richard Morris. Although the separate insurance section of Undeb Gweithwyr Môn held its own in very difficult times,[217] farm workers had turned their backs on the collective ideal in ever-increasing numbers. The effort put in by William Williams, the district organizer, in recovering wages and winning cases of wrongful dismissal — even against the Marquess of Anglesey[218] — seemed to pass without appreciation. Once the TUC's agricultural workers' campaign got under way, a Workers' Union conference was held at Llannerch-y-medd in May 1925 attended by R.T. Jones and Will John MP.[219] A similar gathering at Llangefni in June underlined the union's determination to stir the land workers of the county.[220] Thomas Rowlands regretted that the majority were outside the union and he proposed the appointment of special emissaries to visit each district. The Workers' Union organization in Anglesey was revamped and, at an open-air meeting, Rhys J. Davies MP and David Thomas emphasized the advantages of solidarity.

While the overall success of the TUC initiative is not easily calculated in terms of enrolments,[221] its impact in Anglesey was largely negative. Two Workers' Union branches were revived, but another two disappeared between annual reports. All the same, the TUC displayed sufficient optimism to launch a follow-up campaign in 1926, more extensive in scope.[222] Boosted by further financial aid, the main co-ordinating committee negotiated a new demarcation agreement: the NUAW was allocated Flint (south), Merioneth, Cardigan, Glamorgan and Monmouth while the Workers' Union operated in Anglesey, Denbigh, Flint (north), Montgomery, Brecon and Radnor. In Caernarfon, Pembroke and Carmarthen each union was allowed to hold one demonstration.

Fresh organizing efforts by the NUAW in Wales were seriously handicapped from the start. Union organization was scuttled when its Welsh organizers were dismissed and since then membership had diminished into insignificance with an almost irreversible momentum of its own. A request from the Nefyn branch for a Welsh-speaking organizer,[223] like a subsequent plea from D.T. Lewis in Pembrokeshire, could not be countenanced because the situation in Wales was so 'disappointing'.[224] For the most part, success meant reviving a branch or two. When the NUAW organizer in Shropshire was able to turn his attention to north-east Wales he reopened the branches at Bettisfield and Chirk in 1924.[225] From time to time head-office officials came to Wales to show the flag, but such visits were confined principally to Monmouth, Glamorgan and Pembroke. E.J. Pay, a member of the executive committee, undertook a tour of five counties in May 1925 to address various branches.[226] Seven farm workers joined the union following his meeting at Chepstow; on the other hand he found Pembrokeshire labourers under the thumbs of their employers and 'very cowed' in disposition. Otherwise, it was left to local activists to try and rope in new members. W. Coles, the Portskewett branch secretary, enrolled eleven new members after canvassing the district in his spare time following Pay's visit.[227]

The best capacity for voluntary enterprise was shown by D.T. Lewis, who utilized his holidays from schoolteaching to undertake 'heroic work' on behalf of the union in north Pembrokeshire.[228] Due to his single-minded commitment the Mathry branch flourished through thick and thin; politically, too, Mathry stayed solidly

Labour. Early in 1925 Lewis took advantage of the opportunity presented by the new district wages committee to rekindle interest in trade unionism.[229] As part of a vigorous recruiting campaign he proposed to address a series of meetings.[230] It seems unlikely that his ambitious programme was fulfilled to any marked degree, nevertheless NUAW branches at St Nicholas (previously one of the strongest in Pembrokeshire) and Letterston were reopened and a record number of new members enrolled generally.[231] In the mean time, this burst of enthusiasm was mirrored by similar developments in the south of the county, only here the motive power was provided by the Workers' Union. With full-time divisional organizers in Matt Giles and W.J. Wardle, the Workers' Union launched an agricultural campaign in January from its well-established base at Pembroke Dock. Addressed by A.J. Collis, the branch secretary, Giles and Wardle, some promising meetings were held at Houghton, Lamphey, Manorbier, Angle, Pembroke, Redberth, St Florence, Amroth and Stepaside.[232] By the end of May practically the whole area south of the eastern Cleddau river had been organized, adding over 300 members to the agricultural section.[233] Plans were then laid to wage a similar campaign north of the river starting at Rosemarket.

Rivalry and competition between the NUAW and the Workers' Union was often a feature of recruiting drives in spite of the steps taken to avoid overlapping. But as the NUAW weakened its hold in Wales, others were ready to cater for the rural worker. Joint branch meetings with the TGWU in Brongest, Cardiganshire,[234] for instance, encouraged the TGWU to cast an eager eye towards the farm labourers.[235] In the absence of the NUAW, the Workers' Union tried to step in at Monmouth and Glamorgan by offering information concerning the 1924 Act.[236] The eventual collapse of the NUAW in north Wales enabled William Williams to push the Workers' Union case. If any local branch was dormant he appealed to the workers to write directly to him.[237] Concentrating on south Caernarfonshire in 1924–5 he addressed meetings at Chwilog, Rhydyclafdy, Sarn, Tydweiliog, Llannor and Mynytho[238] as part of a propaganda campaign to parallel that in Anglesey and Pembroke. Rather than be left in isolation, members of the Nefyn NUAW branch decided to transfer to the Workers' Union, much to the displeasure of head office.[239] Complaints of poaching by the Workers' Union were nothing new,[240] and on occasion the TUC was asked to arbitrate in inter-union disputes. It also explains why the unions were anxious to draw up well-defined regions of influence prior to the 1926 rural campaign.

The NUAW in 1926, then, was far from able to create an impression in Wales. A series of meetings had been recommended for Monmouth, Glamorgan and Pembroke in January,[241] but difficulties, mainly financial, caused delays and eventual postponement.[242] In April it was decided to write to the secretaries of the divisional Labour parties in those counties to ascertain the cost of running a propaganda campaign.[243] Labour officials in the Monmouth division were particularly keen to expand party organization and increase membership in the outlying rural districts and, early in 1925, a campaign to propagate socialism had indeed opened at Chepstow under the leadership of A.W. Pittman.[244] However, there is little evidence of a response from this quarter in 1926. Eventually a county conference was held in Monmouthshire in July and some canvassing work carried out by James Kennett in the Vale of Glamorgan.[245] All that happened in Pembrokeshire was the publication of a series of hard-hitting articles in the local press written by D.T. Lewis to expose the deplorable conditions endured by agricultural workers.[246] A proposal to send a member of the executive committee to the county foundered because they failed to get any response to their communications.[247] Only in the most superficial sense, therefore, could the NUAW be said to have campaigned in Wales.

The same appears true of the Workers' Union. As part of the TUC rural campaign, an open-air meeting was held at Gwalchmai with Robert Richards, William Williams and Thomas Rowlands, appealing for support from the agricultural labourers.[248] Over in Llŷn and Eifionydd, meanwhile, William Williams had continued to win converts.[249] But all the while branches were closing. The Kidwelly (agricultural) branch had closed in 1925. More branches lapsed in Anglesey, so that of the 46 Undeb Gweithwyr Môn branches affiliated in 1919, only 18 remained by 1926. The agricultural section in Pembrokeshire ran into difficulties when a number of Workers' Union activists, including A.J. Collis, were transferred from Pembroke Dock following the closure of the shipyard.[250] By now, the number of Workers' Union branches in rural Wales had fallen to 29.[251] When a final assessment of the 1925–6 TUC campaigns was called for, the NUAW and Workers' Union calculated that 5,000 and 1,000 new members had been added to their respective unions.[252] To justifiable doubts surrounding these claims[253] can be added the certainty of overall failure in Wales.

Perhaps the one bright spot for the NUAW was the Vale of Glamorgan, thanks to P.J. Smith, a Somerset man who had settled in the county to take up the job of railway signalman.[254] Through the NUR he became a delegate to the divisional Labour Party thus beginning a long political association which eventually, in the 1960s, gave him the leadership of the all-powerful Labour group on Glamorgan County Council. Moving to Llantwit Major in 1923, he had immediately put the labour movement on the map by forming a branch of both the NUR and the Labour Party. Three years later, P.J. Smith began to organize the agricultural workers of the Vale more for humanitarian reasons than anything else. Having started his working life as a farm boy, he felt a natural empathy with the men in their plight. Consequently, the NUAW branch at Llantwit Major was re-established, and the one at St Athan given a new lease of life. P.J. Smith then served as secretary of the two branches for a number of years as well as one of the workers' representatives on the district wages committee. Public service on behalf of the working class in a variety of spheres enhanced his standing in the area, and in 1934 he became the first Labour candidate to win a rural seat on Glamorgan County Council.[255] In defeating George Lougher, the farmers' leader, he captured the Cowbridge division which James Kennett had abortively challenged in 1919.[256]

To mark its twenty-one years in existence the NUAW proposed to launch a 'celebration campaign' in 1927 — to coincide with the Labour Party's agricultural campaign. Under Labour Party auspices demonstrations were held at Bangor, Carmarthen and Monmouth, to be followed by another series at the end of the year.[257] Prior to the proceedings at Monmouth, the Rolls Hall resounded to the sound of the 'Red Flag' for the first time in its history.[258] At Carmarthen a resolution in favour of land nationalization was passed and delegates heard W.J. Wardle allege that fifty per cent of west-Wales farmers were not paying the legal minimum wage.[259] Having eclipsed the NUAW in these particular districts, the Workers' Union inevitably reaped the publicity. Following the appointment of William Edwards as Labour Party organizer for Caernarfonshire,[260] the Workers' Union seized on the opportunity to extend their influence further in the county. During 1927–8 William Edwards and William Williams were working hand in glove, helped by former NUAW activists,

Richard Griffith and Morris Hughes.[261] By creating a going concern, William Williams was thus able to retain his position as district organizer. Dogged by financial troubles, the Workers' Union would otherwise have been forced to dismiss officials in those rural areas unable to pay their way.[262]

It was a former Workers' Union official in Dyfed, H.N. Hunt, who received the chance to regain some ground for the NUAW in south Wales in 1927. Following his role in the strike at the Mond Nickel Works at Clydach in 1917, he had served as district organizer between 1918 and 1921. Currently unemployed, Hunt entered an arrangement with R.B. Walker whereby he would work as temporary organizer on a retainer of 5*s*.6*d*. per week to top up his outdoor relief.[263] After some four months, however, it was decided to wind up his campaign in view of the expenses incurred.[264] Little resulted from Hunt's efforts; even the branch at Clydach which closed officially the following year had never really functioned. When the TUC was held at Swansea in September 1928, W. Holmes, who replaced R.B. Walker as general secretary of NUAW, took advantage of the opportunity to hold meetings at Llantwit Major and St Athan.[265] That summer, arrangements were made with the Monmouthshire Federation of Trades Councils and divisional Labour parties in the county to organize the rural districts.[266] But after an open-air meeting at Chepstow, when A.V. Cook, the divisional Labour Party secretary, offered to act as branch secretary if a branch could be formed, only one man came forward to seek membership! Early in 1929, Cook was being proposed by the Monmouthshire Federation of Trades Councils as a possible part-time organizer for the NUAW in the county, but a final decision had to be put off until after the general election.[267]

W.T. Fielding, who took charge of the surviving NUAW branches in the border counties, had to battle hard to hold together what little membership existed. That he suffered a nervous breakdown at one stage was hardly surprising. He attended a variety of committee meetings in the name of the union but with membership at 'rock bottom'[268] there was little substance to his authority. Throughout this time the idea of Wales as an entity (NUAW district no. 9), with a designated organizer, remained unfulfilled. But given the general circumstances little could be done to arrest the decline. From 1926, the year of the general strike — in which the agricultural labourers played no part — the NUAW was locked in a deadly downturn. Within two years (1926–8) the number of branches had been sliced from 28 to 14. By 1929 there were only 12 branches, each with a handful of members, strung over eight Welsh counties, fewer than in 1917. Of those left, Aber, Llanuwchllyn, Llanilar, Vale of Towi, Llantwit Major, St Athan, Little Haven, Mathry and Monmouth were kept alive through the efforts of individuals like Robert Thomas, T. Llew Williams, R.L. Jones, Henry Jones, P.J. Smith, Tom Evans,[269] D.T. Lewis (followed by A.J. John) and R. Ingram.[270]

The Workers' Union faced the same relentless decline and one of the organizers to suffer its consequences was Sidney Box. In economic terms he had become a liability. With membership down to fifteen branches in his district, their total weekly income of £6.6*s*. was not enough to meet his salary and provide benefits for members, and so he received notice to quit in February 1928.[271] Not one to go quietly, Box indulged in an unfraternal struggle with the union's executive, accusing them of whittling away the 110 branches he had personally founded since 1912.[272] As a final retaliation he promptly set up a new breakaway organization called The Counties Agricultural and General Workers' Union. By then, the losses in membership had brought the Workers' Union itself to the brink of disaster with former strongholds in Lancashire and Cheshire almost entirely extinguished. The union's agricultural membership was reduced to 5,000, the number in north Wales being put at 330.[273] Amalgamation with the TGWU in 1929 offered the best chance. Within the TGWU an agricultural workers' section was subsequently formed and William Williams retained as the north Wales organizer based in Port Dinorwic. Among the few farm workers' branches to outlive the devastation were Aberffraw and Cerrigydrudion, due to the loyalty of officials like David Lloyd and E.T. Roberts.

In many ways this marked the end of an era. Government legislation, economic depression and unemployment had all combined to defeat the farm workers' cause. A withdrawal into apathy finally broke their spirit and destroyed any interest they may have had in trade unionism. Perhaps the rural workers were never cut out to be successful rebels. In reality, the full impact of the various changes proved overwhelming to the ordinary farm-hand. Few had the capacity to withstand the external mechanisms which demanded acquiescence and, without the individual commitment, a mass demonstration of organized class solidarity could not possibly succeed. All this can be seen as the falling apart of an ideal; a movement which at one time promised so much had failed to live up to its expectations. Retreat on a wide scale was the inevitable outcome. After only a brief entry into the mainstream of the labour movement, farm workers' trade unionism slipped into an insignificant backwater. Above and beyond this, there were other important repercussions, both economic and political. As a work-force they would lack the industrial muscle to raise wage levels and safeguard living standards. Then, their weakness as a political force made it even more difficult for the Labour Party to achieve electoral success in the agricultural constituencies.

Average wage rates were to remain fairly constant at around 31*s*. for the second half of the decade.[274] But at every stage the farmers pressed for reductions. Wherever there was a fall in wages or increase in hours, union organizers made a point of emphasizing that the men were mostly outside the labour movement. Counties like Brecon, Radnor, Merioneth and Montgomery usually figured in this category.[275] But where fear of unemployment reigned there could be no resistance. In west Wales in 1925 farm-hands had requested permits to work under the minimum rate rather than walk the streets.[276] At a time of falling prices farmers were desperate to have the whip hand. NFU branches in Monmouth considered refusing to pay the minimum wage and cease recognition of the Agricultural Wages Board, such was the depth of opposition.[277] With their rate still pegged above the average, employers on the Glamorgan Wages Committee fought tooth and nail to bring it down to the level of other Welsh counties. They resented having to bargain with 'professional agitators' who knew nothing of agriculture and openly criticized the independent members when they sided with the workers' representatives.[278]

Large-scale housing problems that caused such wretchedness and disease in the urban slums often overshadowed a worse situation in the rural areas.[279] Here, ugly pockets of poverty remained. At the beginning of the decade, two-thirds of the cottages in the agricultural districts of Wales were considered to be unfit.[280] Delegates to the Welsh Calvinistic Methodist General Assembly in 1924 heard the standard of rural housing condemned by a spokesman from the Ministry of Health.[281] Only a few weeks earlier an attempt to shun chapel officials who profited from renting out insanitary dwelling houses or who declined to pay fair wages to employees was quashed by the west Merioneth monthly meeting.[282] D.T. Lewis was equally scathing in his condemnation of tied cottages in Cardigan and Pembroke; they were 'a disgrace to a Christian land'.[283] Visitors to the countryside in summer, reminded James Kennett, knew nothing of the misery within the houses of rural labourers.[284] Falling wages meant that the workers could do little to alleviate bad living conditions; low rents on the other hand were no inducement to owners to make improvements. Important legislative progress during the post-war years still failed to tackle the problem and this left many houses in rural districts totally unsuitable for human habitation. Wales's foremost housing reformer, Edgar Chappell, summed up housing conditions in the agricultural districts of west Wales as 'appalling — the worst in the country'.[285] Local authorities were at first slow to realize the value of the Rural Workers' Housing Act of 1926,[286] but by 1930 at least Anglesey and Pembroke County Councils had sanctioned a number of improvement schemes.[287]

The Labour Party's Achillean vulnerability in the agricultural constituencies was well evident; it 'always remained weak in any country area lacking an organized trade union base'.[288] The only rural area to return a Labour member without fail was north Norfolk, Noel Buxton's seat. Speaking from his experience in Montgomeryshire, the Revd T.D. James despaired at the farm workers' reluctance to grasp the political opportunity: 'Rhai araf yw y llafurwyr amaethyddol yn dod i weled ar ba ochr i'r dafell y mae'r ymenyn.'[289] If the party was to take office again, independent of the Liberals and Tories, it had to make substantial inroads into the rural areas. Hence the debate which led to the political initiative taken at the 1926 Labour Party conference.[290] It was pointed out that the party had not been able to fight some eighty seats at previous general elections because it often lacked organization. Under the direction of Noel Buxton and George Dallas (of the Workers' Union) an extensive agricultural campaign took Labour's message to all corners of rural Britain. The three conferences held in Wales before August 1927 were followed by another nine by April 1928,[291] when Labour's policy of state control was explained to farmers and farm workers.[292] When evaluating the campaign in 1927, R.B. Walker had emphasized the 'absolute necessity of advocating trade union organization as a basis for ultimate political success'.[293] However, there were few signs of this happening in Wales. Although the whole operation was deemed to have been worthwhile in 1928, within a year its true value was to be put to the test.

Following the general election of 1929, Labour became the largest party in the Commons, yet once again it lacked an overall majority. The party's advance in the industrial constituencies was in marked contrast to its performance in the rural divisions. Labour won only five new seats, two of which were in Wales. Predominantly rural, the Carmarthen and Brecon and Radnor constituencies also contained a crucial industrial element with solid Labour traditions. Success in Carmarthen was based largely on support in the Aman and Gwendraeth mining valleys; similarly the industrial districts stretching from Ystradgynlais to Brynmawr facilitated Labour's unexpected gain in Brecon and Radnor.[294] The capture of Carmarthen was already anticipated. At a by-election in 1928 over 9,000 votes had been slashed off the Liberal majority. Labour's candidate, Daniel Hopkin, a barrister, was the son of a Llantwit Major agricultural labourer who had himself worked on a farm in the Vale as a young boy. In tune with Labour's 'politics of moderation',[295] Hopkin skilfully eschewed all mention of nationalization in his speeches and election address. Significantly enough, during the whole campaign Labour candidates trod warily to side-step the party's newly enunciated policy on agriculture based on the public ownership of land.[296] Although it is claimed that only Robert Richards, who regained the semi-rural Wrexham constituency, ventured to commend the nationalization of land,[297] W.J. Jenkins in Pembroke was equally keen to do so in his political statements.[298]

Even a dilution of socialism was profitless if Labour's local organization remained second-rate. The party's failure to make headway in the agricultural constituencies, and particularly to recapture seats in Gwynedd, could, as *Y Dinesydd Cymreig* commented,[299] be attributed to deficiencies in this respect. Since 1926 the North Wales Labour Federation had fallen into abeyance.[300] Inability yet again to put forward candidates in Denbigh and Cardigan was a further reminder of the party's innate weakness in rural Wales. Apart from Carmarthen and Brecon and Radnor, Labour's percentage of the vote continued to drop further, enabling both the Liberals and Conservatives to hold on to their rural strongholds. Immediate post-war expectations never fulfilled their early promise; as in the agricultural constituencies of East Anglia, Labour's electoral challenge in rural Wales failed to materialize. Following the collapse of both the NUAW and Workers' Union the task of guaranteeing the vote of the rural labourers through a process of political integration was made immeasurably more difficult. Quite certainly, they were 'in no position to lead a Labour assault on the countryside'.[301] But to consider this as a realistic prospect raises questions which are indeed hard to answer definitively. To what extent could a few activists forge the working-class loyalty of the mass of farm labourers? Had the labourers the political potential to act as the torch-bearers of socialism? Would the Labour Party, with its utopian doctrine of land nationalization, have fared much better operating from a strong rural base underpinned by farm workers' unions? By 1929, at any rate, such questions proved academic. The rural revolt of the labouring class had experienced defeat on a scale that divested the movement of any immediate influence or, it would seem, lasting historical significance.

CHAPTER VII

TOWARDS THE FINAL RECOVERY, 1930–1950

BRITAIN fell into a yet deeper economic depression between 1929 and 1932 when trade and production slumped.[1] The number registered as unemployed now reached three million. Out of the economic catastrophe arose a political crisis which saw the formation of a National Government. But subsequent failure to produce an effective policy meant that little was done to arrest some of the underlying economic trends or solve their attendant social problems. Unemployment remained at a high level (above 1.5 million) up to the outbreak of the Second World War. The hardship was unevenly spread, and those areas dependent on the older basic industries remained under the cloud of depression throughout the thirties. By 1932 the percentage without work in Wales reached 36.5; in some of the mining valley blackspots it even touched 70 per cent. Weakened by recession, unemployment and loss of income, the trade union movement continued to decline as total membership dropped to 4.3 million by 1933, almost as low as it had been in 1915. Overall, the cumulative results of poverty and its suffocating gloom had a subduing effect on the workless. There was little labour unrest and expressions of serious discontent were surprisingly few.

Since 1921 agriculture, too, had experienced a prolonged period of depression that reached a new trough in 1931–3. The agriculture price index now tumbled almost to its pre-war level.[2] When prices had fallen rapidly in 1921–2 many farmers were at least cushioned by their spectacular wartime profits; this time the effects were ruinous.[3] One inevitable result was the accelerating drift from the land. Agricultural wages and working conditions held little incentive for the worker, whilst economic pressures forced farmers to cut down on capital costs by shedding labour. Quite often, a farmer might not be much better off than his men. Between 1929 and 1939 agricultural workers were leaving the industry at a rate of 10,000 each year.[4] Concern for the fate of agriculture compelled successive National Governments to follow a policy of direct intervention once more. Increased state aid and protection led to an improvement in the general prices of agricultural produce, whilst subsidies and guarantees turned the farmers into a privileged group.[5] Legislation setting up marketing boards to help and encourage the producers of milk and potatoes was particularly successful; it gave farmers a secure market and stable prices.

Welsh farming was to suffer an internal crisis more acute than in any other period in modern times.[6] From 1924–5 most farmers had seen a reduction in capital and a progressive decline in their standard of living. The continuing depression not only brought a fundamental change in the pattern of farming but also in the structure of the agrarian population. It was an age of rapid transition. Farmers adapted to the depression with a drastic move from arable to pastoral farming, and, with the concentration on rearing sheep and cattle, the area under cultivation was reduced to that of the 1860s. With the establishment of the Milk Marketing Board in 1933 the economic tide turned and by 1939 at least 50 per cent of Welsh farms had gone over to milk production.[7] The basic unit of Welsh farming was still the family farm. In 1939, 69.3 per cent of Welsh holdings were under 50 acres, 88.3 per cent under 100 acres.[8] The size of the farms and the trend towards stock-rearing and milk production offered less and less scope for employment. During the thirties farmers came to rely on fewer hired workers and more on the immediate family. Large-scale mechanization had yet to make an impact. In its social context, the stagnation in agriculture and the decline in the demand for labour substantially increased the extent of rural depopulation. Most counties witnessed a considerable exodus of farm labourers so that between 1929 and 1939 the number of male regular workers over 21, not including casual labour, shrank from 29,429 to 21,151,[9] a fall of 28 per cent.

With the worst of the slump over by the middle of the decade, trade unionism began to regain lost ground. By 1939 total membership had climbed back to 6.3 million. The two large general unions, the National Union of General and Municipal Workers and the Transport and General Workers' Union, swiftly reinforced their ranks. Between 1933 and 1939 NUGMW membership rose from 241,000 to 467,318. Under Bevin, the TGWU grew to be the largest single union in Britain.[10] When it took over the Workers' Union in 1929, membership stood at 422,836; within a decade it had reached 694,474. To hold such a massive conglomerate together the TGWU set its membership into national trade groups. Thus, when the

Scottish Farm Servants' Union was absorbed in 1932 some 4,000 farm workers were added to the general workers' group, part of which became the agricultural workers' section. Moreover, the TGWU divided Britain into autonomous territorial regions, with south Wales as Area No. 4 and north Wales as Area No. 13.

Area No. 13 had been formed following the amalgamation of the NWQU in 1923.[11] Along with a variety of general workers, including the remnants of the Workers' Union, its membership came to over 12,000 in 1930.[12] Ravaged by unemployment, north Wales presented a 'most depressing picture' when Huw T. Edwards was appointed TGWU district organizer in 1932.[13] Coming from farming stock, Edwards had turned his back on the land to become a quarryman. But it was his experiences as a miner in south Wales during the Tonypandy strike which turned him into a pugnacious champion of the labour movement. His first priority as TGWU organizer was to consolidate the existing membership before attempting to establish new branches. Certainly one of the things which made his task easier was the network of sub-offices manned by full-time officials.[14] Moreover, the composite character of TGWU rural branches helped to weld the membership together. Branches with county council roadmen, forestry workers and farm labourers were more likely to survive and flourish than a branch composed merely of a scattering of agricultural workers. In this respect, the TGWU had an inbuilt advantage over the NUAW, whose organizers in Wales worked from home.

Operating from the Port Dinorwic sub-office, William Williams assumed responsibility for the TGWU's agricultural membership in north Wales. At first, this meant nursing the few Workers' Union branches that had survived. As a result of subsequent propaganda campaigns Williams gradually built up the membership. In October 1930, H.H. Lawrie MP visited Aberffraw and made a strong appeal to the farm workers to stay loyal to the union.[15] During a special campaign in Anglesey and Caernarfonshire in the autumn of 1932 some 30 meetings were arranged.[16] Six new branches were opened and over 350 new members recruited, yet it was admitted that the results had not fulfilled expectations.[17] Another campaign in the winter of 1934–5, again mainly in Anglesey and Caernarfonshire, added 112 members.[18] Taking advantage of the new unemployment insurance scheme for agricultural workers, William Williams held a series of meetings in 1936 to explain the new act.[19] From the mid-thirties onwards, W.J. Wardle, the district secretary for Swansea and west Wales, embarked on similar recruiting drives in mid-Wales. He successfully enrolled a number of agricultural and forestry workers in Cardiganshire,[20] and when 10,000 farm workers in Dyfed won a 2*s*. rise in 1937 the TGWU claimed full credit for the increase.[21]

Each gain was hard won. Breaking into new territory at a time of depression and severe unemployment proved exceedingly difficult. For any lasting success the district organizer had to place his faith in the local branch secretary and hope for the sort of commitment shown by a dedicated trio in Anglesey. During the forty years he served as branch secretary in the Cerrigceinwen district, John Jones walked something like 200 miles each quarter to collect the union fees.[22] An ordinary farm labourer and veteran of the days of Undeb Gweithwyr Môn, William Williams was awarded the BEM in 1948 in recognition of his service as Llannerch-y-medd branch secretary.[23] O.R. Hughes, another farm worker, collected contributions from members of the Aberffraw branch for a period of fifty years.[24] Against all expectations, the union maintained a gradual momentum of expansion in the six north-Wales counties during the thirties so that by 1939 it claimed 200 branches and 30,000 members.[25] Along with East Anglia, Area No. 13 came to be considered a prime TGWU sphere of influence in the organization of farm workers.[26] All the same, it was the roadmen and forestry workers who provided the main backbone, particularly in Merioneth and Montgomery.[27]

What was true of the TGWU and other major unions was also in greater measure true of the NUAW. Only in this case the depression almost led to the dissolution of the union. Dwarfed both in size and importance, and with fewer resources, it had been far less equipped to weather the storm. A membership of 23,000 in 1930 only began to show improvement by 1938, when it rose to 33,000. Having reached a plateau of some 1,000 branches in 1930 the annual total remained at this level for most of the decade. Considering that well over 500,000 agricultural workers remained outside any organization,[28] rural trade unionism could well be dismissed as an episode of no permanent significance. Left with only a toehold in Wales there was a danger that the NUAW might even be written out of existence. When the branches at Mathry, Little Haven, Aber, Sennybridge and Talgarth disappeared by 1932, it was down to 7 branches in 5 counties. At its nadir in 1933 it counted 5 branches, with Pembrokeshire and Caernarfonshire left totally unrepresented. Throughout the thirties it was only the surviving branches at Llanilar, Vale of Towi, Llanuwchllyn, Llantwit Major, St Athan, St Fagans, Caer-went and Monmouth which kept the union's hopes alive.

Most of Wales, at least in name, was still administered from the union's London office. Except, that is, for the counties of Denbigh, Flint, Brecon, Radnor and Monmouth, which remained under the eye of W.T. Fielding. Aged sixty-five in 1932, Fielding found it heavy-going; he had too much work and too large an area to cover. He served on eight district wages committees, including five in Wales! Though he tried to arrange propaganda meetings in Monmouthshire in 1933 he met with little success.[29] Two years later it was noted that the membership within his district had continued to decline.[30] When Fielding officially retired in 1937 (he went on to serve the union on a voluntary basis up to 1951),[31] the NUAW might well have regarded the position in Wales as a lost cause.

One of the union's most conspicuous failures was experienced in Brecon and Radnor in 1934. Jointly with the local constituency Labour Party it planned an ambitious recruiting drive for the months of June and July mainly in the form of open-air meetings in markets and fairs.[32] The purpose of the campaign was to increase both party and trade union membership and explain Labour's agricultural policy. Politically, the Labour Party was out to reverse the tide of events. For in the general election of 1931 the party had suffered catastrophic defeat. All the Labour seats in Norfolk were lost. Reduced to sixteen seats in Wales, Labour fell back upon its solid bastion in the mining valleys of the south whilst the Conservatives regained Brecon and Radnor, and Carmarthen and Wrexham fell to the Liberals. Although the party fought Cardiganshire for the first time, and held its own in five other agricultural constituencies, it did not contest Anglesey, Denbigh, Montgomery or Pembroke. To regain some of the lost ground, therefore, Labour had to embark on new initiatives in partnership with the increasingly influential trade unions. Following the success of an experimental agricultural campaign in East Anglia in 1933, in association with the TGWU and NUAW, plans were prepared to cover a further 30 rural constituencies, including Brecon and Radnor.[33]

This special campaign opened with a conference in Builth Wells.[34] Over the next few weeks the loudspeaker van carried Labour's message to forty-four different localities, with Dr L. Haden-Guest, the parliamentary candidate, Tudor Watkins, Labour Party secretary and organizer, and W.T. Fielding as the principal speakers.[35] In his final report, Tudor Watkins expressed satisfaction at the way things had gone.[36] But whereas Labour could boast many new party members, not a single farm worker was enrolled into the NUAW![37] For trade unionism, the whole exercise proved a total flop. Thus, when A.D. Watkins, vice-chairman of the constituency Labour Party, offered to serve as a full or part-time union organizer in the district he could hardly have hoped to receive a favourable reply.[38] Unemployed and victimized, Watkins soon left the area for London.[39] Failure to unionize agricultural workers in the rural divisions was once again brought to the attention of delegates at the next annual Labour conference, this time by Haden-Guest.[40] Speaking from his experiences in Brecon and Radnor, he felt that the party would never score a political victory unless farm labourers and other rural workers were drawn into trade union organization.

Concern for the plight of the agricultural labourer in both counties continued to engage the attention of the divisional Labour Party. One particularly appalling case of underpayment provided a timely illustration of their desperate straits. A Knighton labourer with four people to feed and clothe worked a sixty-hour week for the sum of 20*s*.[41] Repeated efforts to get the NUAW to take up its organizational responsibilities in Brecon and Radnor proved ineffective; neither did the TGWU or NUGMW provide a better example.[42] Regardless of the difficulties, the Labour Party again stepped in where the big unions feared to tread. Under the slogan 'Victory for Socialism', it undertook an intensive rural campaign during July 1935 directed by Tudor Watkins.[43] Forty-five meetings were scheduled and 8,000 hand bills and 200 posters distributed.[44] But once again every hope was to be frustrated; workers on the land had apparently no wish to unite. The constituency still remained without a single trade union branch for the farm labourers. To mark its disgust the Labour Party sent strongly worded letters to the head office of both TGWU and NUGMW complaining of the inactivity of their district officers.[45]

Labour's recovery in the subsequent general election of November 1935 was reflected in the Welsh results, when it took 45 per cent of the votes and won eighteen seats. The party's share of the poll went up in the nine agricultural constituencies it contested, Montgomeryshire being the exception. Carmarthenshire was regained; so too was Wrexham for Robert Richards. Already the makings of a radical realignment in the rural heartlands could be detected as traditional Liberalism lost ground but, on the whole, there is no evidence of the rural working class playing any overt part. Right up until the war there was nothing but concern for Labour's continued weakness in the rural divisions, caused by lack of trade union organization and insufficient funds.[46] Agricultural workers were still isolated, intimidated, exploited and underpaid. Fear of losing their job and their tied cottage precluded many from taking an open interest in trade unionism; low wages meant they could not contribute to party funds. Yet, Labour persisted with the difficult problem of organizing the rural divisions and conveying the political message. A further propaganda campaign was undertaken in 1936 (although not in any of the Welsh constituencies) and again during 1938 when Anglesey, Denbigh, Wrexham, Pembrokeshire, Brecon and Radnor were included in an intensive campaign to enlighten the rural voters.[47] But in the Welsh countryside, at least, the necessary trade union strength was hardly present to provide even the nucleus of a political organization. Others would have to underwrite any electoral success. Even in Brecon and Radnor, which Labour retook in a by-election in August 1939,[48] there were no NUAW branches prior to 1944. During the period of Tudor Watkins's connection with the movement not a single branch of the agricultural workers' union became affiliated to the divisional Labour Party.[49]

Neither, according to Cliff Prothero, was any special effort made by the South Wales Regional Council of Labour to recruit members into the NUAW.[50] Founded by the Labour Party in 1937 its main function had been to co-ordinate political and industrial activity.[51] Within two years total membership from the various labour affiliations reached 212,700, but with none of the fraternal concern and practical assistance handed out to the farm workers' union as in the 1917–20 period, the NUAW was being left to work out its own salvation.

Taking these things into account it was hardly surprising that little was done to improve the material welfare of the farm workers and their families during the inter-war years. The eclipse of trade unionism and the Labour Party's inability to break into the structure of rural politics at local level continued to have its bearing on the lot of the working class. For most of the time nothing seemed able to protect the farm labourer from further suffering and neglect. Even tangible evils such as poor housing and disease were hardly mitigated.

Because of the general economic situation there could be no question of reversing the fall in wages. By 1931 minimum wage levels in Wales ranged from 30*s*. in Merioneth and Montgomery to 35*s*. in Glamorgan.[52] Moves by farmers' representatives on the district wages committees to trim these down again led to further decreases. Even after wages had been reduced to the miserable sum of 27*s*. in Merioneth and Montgomery in 1933, employers still sought another reduction of 3*s*.[53] At the same time wage rates in Glamorgan fell back to 33*s*.6*d*. In a protest against their inadequate wage, a large number of Llŷn farm workers staged a lightning strike at the Pwllheli hiring fair in May 1933.[54] Comparisons were made with the rates paid to county council roadmen (then receiving 46*s*. a week), and indeed it was a matter of general complaint among farmers that labourers were leaving the land in their hundreds to seek alternative employment on various public works schemes. Low wages and poor housing were stated to be the reasons why the number of farm workers in Carmarthenshire had fallen by 25 per cent between 1931 and 1936.[55] Manpower was also at a premium in Pembrokeshire, where farm labourers decreased in number from 4,100 in 1931 to 2,700 by 1939.[56] The problem became so serious that there were moves to arrange a joint conference of farmers and labourers to find a solution.[57] Such a departure was welcomed by R.L. Jones because it gave him an opportunity to organize workers in the county. However, his initial enthusiasm was soon doused by NUAW's negative response.[58]

A gradual restoration of wage levels during the second half of the decade meant modest increases in most Welsh districts during 1937, bringing the average weekly wage to 31*s*.7½*d*.[59] Yet, only two districts operated a working week of 48 hours. Cases of deliberate underpayment were again reported to be prevalent,[60] while employers continued to resist most requests for improved working conditions. NFU representatives in Glamorgan in 1936 were congratulated for deflecting a wage increase after a three-hour 'ding dong battle' with the workers' delegates on the district wages committee.[61] At the Pwllheli hiring fair in November 1938 scores of farm labourers returned home rather than engage at the terms on offer.[62] By this time, wages in Merioneth and Montgomery had reached 31*s*.6*d*., with Glamorgan rates up to 36*s*. Also in 1938, farm workers were awarded a week's statutory holiday with pay.

Very little had been done to ameliorate the housing conditions of agricultural workers. Cottages in rural areas were still being described as damp, overcrowded, insanitary and dilapidated. In spite of the revelatory reports of local Medical Officers of Health over a number of years, they remained unfit for occupation. Progress under the Rural Workers' Housing Act — whose powers were extended by amending acts up to 1945 — was disgracefully slow because local authorities failed to take full advantage of its provisions.[63] Even as late as 1934 Glamorgan had hardly taken notice of the act.[64] Not a single council house was built in Llŷn and no application was made under the act.[65] In the rural districts of Cardiganshire the response proved equally disappointing. Up until March 1938 only 1,466 applications for financial assistance had been sanctioned for the whole of Wales, 484 of which were submitted by Pembroke County Council.[66] Although that council did more to improve rural housing than any other Welsh county council, many farm workers still lived in cottages 'not fit for pigs to live in'.[67] Not surprisingly, the tuberculosis mortality rate in the Welsh rural counties exceeded that of England: Caernarfon, Merioneth, Anglesey, Cardigan, Pembroke, Glamorgan and Carmarthen occupied the top seven places in England and Wales.[68] Such housing and sanitary conditions were a disgrace to the Welsh countryside and a slur on the inactive local authorities and rate-conscious class that controlled them. Members of the rural district councils, in particular, did 'not seem to be communally minded: they are accustomed to fending for themselves, and they are slow to vote money towards the improvement of conditions'.[69] Regardless of the difficulties, their record compared unfavourably with most English counties.[70]

As things stood in the late 1930s, the NUAW was obliged to disregard Wales; the sharp swing from high expectation to dismal retreat had wiped out any prospect of rebuilding the union for a time. An official visit to Monmouth and Caer-went by W. Holmes in February 1939 was a rare incursion.[71] The opportunity to present a cheque for £300 to a member of the Caer-went branch as compensation for an accident brought home the material benefits of union membership, but the lesson went largely unheeded. Only one new member was enrolled in Monmouth and four at Caer-went.[72] At this time, the appearance of any new branch rested in great measure upon external factors, more especially the way it built up membership in other locations of rural employment. Already the Forestry Commission was busy developing afforestation and timber production. After a long recruiting drive by J.W. Smith, Fielding's successor, the union established its first forestry branch in Wales at Llangollen in 1940.[73] Within two years its membership of 169 represented almost 70 per cent of the forestry workers in the district.[74] Another important impetus to trade unionism was given by the Land Settlement Schemes; in a real way they provided the start to the 'great revival' in the west.[75]

To alleviate the economic and social distress in the worst unemployment blackspots, the National Government passed the Special Areas (Development and Improvement) Act in 1934. Somewhat half-heartedly, an effort was made to tackle these problems by attracting new industries into the worst-hit regions, among them the coal-mining areas of Glamorgan and Monmouth.[76] One aspect of this policy was the experiment by which groups of unemployed industrial workers were encouraged to settle on the land on co-operative farms and smallholdings. Under the chairmanship of Capt. Geoffrey Crawshay, the district commissioner for the South Wales Special Area, the Welsh Land Settlement Society Ltd. was constituted in March 1936. In the years 1936–9 land was acquired and five co-operative farms then opened under its direction: at Boverton (Trebefered), Glamorgan; Sealand Manor, Flintshire; Rosemarket, Pembrokeshire; Court House, Llanfair Disgoed, Monmouth and Fferm Goch, Llangan, Glamorgan.[77] Selected unemployed miners were then recruited to the farms, and after initial training became co-operators in the production of market garden crops with a share of the profits in addition to their weekly agricultural wage. Eventually, a total of 233 families were resettled by 1939. As ex-colliers, drawn from the various mining valleys, they were to a man red-hot trade unionists, pre-cast in the SWMF mould. Transferred to this new environment they turned out to be equally instinctive supporters of the NUAW and, in the case of Sealand, also the TGWU.

Soon after the first settlers arrived at Boverton, P.J. Smith was at their doorstep to organize a branch in 1937. Smith then acted as secretary until one of the members could be trained.[78] The branch at Sealand (1939) contained a militant element from Maerdy, the 'little Moscow' of the Rhondda, and when some of the drivers joined the TGWU, the settlement split into two conflicting factions.[79] After some bitter exchanges, and counter-accusations of poaching, the NUAW held sway. (In the same year the TUC's 'Bridlington Agreement' outlawed poaching by a rival organization when one union had the majority of workers in any establishment.) For the die-hard socialists, communists and ex-SWMF members who came to Fferm Goch it was a 'natural thing' that they should organize themselves.[80] Boverton branch officials and P.J. Smith were then sent to inaugurate the Fferm Goch branch formally in March 1940.[81] As trade unionists they knew when to take a stand on a point of principle. Not that there was anything comparable to the great strike of 1919; but when ordered to pick carrots without their gloves in the hard winter of 1941 they took industrial action.[82] After three days James Lunnon intervened to negotiate a satisfactory settlement to the dispute. At the two other settlements the situation was similar. Co-operators at Court House Farm were instrumental in revitalizing the neighbouring Caer-went branch;[83] two former SWMF activists, K. Harrison and F.L. Ward, became founder members of the Rose-market branch.[84] With a closed shop in each of the five branches, 'comrades' in the Welsh Land Settlements could well be counted 'keen supporters' of the NUAW.[85]

The Second World War saw a repeat of the upward trend in agriculture of the previous war. Suddenly, British farming received the kind of stimulus only associated with a major crisis and, as a key industry, it once again entered a period of prosperity. Dependent on overseas imports for as much as 70 per cent of its food requirements,[86] Britain faced the prospect of serious food shortages following German attacks on merchant shipping. Drawing on the experience of 1914–18, the government took similar steps to maximize home production: farmers who ploughed up grassland to grow crops were paid subsidies and given guaranteed prices for their produce. To implement the programme a greater supply of labour had to be secured and, as before, this increased the bargaining power of the farm workers. In addition, it meant utilizing an extra force of casual labour, which included the Women's Land Army, and accelerating the mechanization of farming operations. To prevent experienced farm workers from moving to better-paid construction jobs it became necessary to raise wages substantially; in 1939 these were calculated to be less than half the rates paid to unskilled workers in other occupations.[87] Farm workers' unions were already pressing for a uniform national minimum wage as opposed to local minimum wages. Consequently, in April 1940, following discussions with both sides of the industry, the Agricultural Wages (Regulation)

Amendment Act came into force, allowing the Agricultural Wages Board to set a national minimum. Fixed at 48*s*. in June, the basic weekly rate for ordinary workers was subsequently raised in stages to 70*s*. by March 1945. For the duration it did not mean, however, any appreciable reduction in the number of hours worked. But with wages doubling in the years 1939–45 it might have seemed to a cynical land worker that only war could secure him a just reward.

During the course of the war farming in Britain was transformed; it emerged more prosperous than it had been since the 'Great Depression' of 1873–96. Unlike during the First World War there were no sharp price rises or opportunities for blatant profiteering, although it went without saying that farmers did far better than their workers.[88] Indeed, the workers' pay still remained below the level of industrial wages. After a long interval, the war also radically transformed the farm workers' unions. As happened in the post-1917 period, higher wage rates gave rural trade unionism a tremendous fillip. Even before 1939, increasing membership had enabled the NUAW to appear more like a national organization in England than at any time since 1922.[89] Great strides in wartime recruitment brought the total number of branches up from 1,244 in 1939 to 2,750 by 1945, and membership from 36,000 to 100,000 strong.[90] Another 31,000 belonged to the agricultural section of the TGWU.[91] This meant that trade unionism was back at the centre of affairs.

At first, Wales remained adrift. In January 1941 the NUAW executive noted that no special meetings had been arranged for its isolated branches in south Wales for some time.[92] Yet, a number of enquiries were received and new branches opened in the Welsh Land Settlements. After James Lunnon addressed meetings in the Vale of Glamorgan in November, Billy Vaughan was pressing for an immediate follow-up campaign.[93] Cowbridge branch was re-established, and with a further campaign in the Vale in 1942,[94] local members were sufficiently confident to propose the appointment of a paid organizer for the area.[95] Meanwhile, R.L. Jones made similar efforts to regenerate interest in Cardiganshire. As a seasoned campaigner, who had kept the Llanilar branch going throughout the thirties, be was eager to pave the way for a revival. Upon gaining permission to place advertisements in the local press, and a guarantee that his own out-of-pocket expenses would be met, R.L. Jones embarked upon a recruiting drive in March 1942.[96] A promising start at Synod Inn enabled him to persuade James Lunnon to accompany him on a campaign tour in June.[97] A string of public meetings,[98] however, bore little fruit, but at least Jones convinced the NUAW of the importance of printing some propaganda leaflets in Welsh.[99] A similar effort to get organization going again in Pembrokeshire, spearheaded by Lunnon, met with total failure.[100] But with Billy Vaughan suggesting that Fielding be sent to organize Wales, and R.L. Jones pleading for a Welsh organizer at the union's biennial conference, the matter of organization in Wales was considered by the executive committee in January 1943. In spite of the clamour of local individuals, the executive still felt that the overall position did not as yet justify the engagement of a full-time official.[101]

It did not take long for the position in south Wales to improve. And more than any other factor it was the presence of a strong individual personality which accounted for this. In Eddy Jones, the Monmouthshire rural workers found a worthy champion in the tradition of William Harris. Born in Nantyglo Eddy Jones began his interest in the trade union movement during the years of depression. After periods of work as a miner, railway clerk, quarryman and farm labourer, he attended Coleg Harlech before settling at Skenfrith. From the start, he was intent on building up trade unionism and the Labour Party locally. He possessed all the necessary attributes to provide this leadership: strength, vigour, purpose, embellished with a persuasive style of oratory. As a county council roadman he became secretary of the NUGMW Monmouth branch in 1936, the same year he helped found the Monmouth Trades Council. And it was through his membership of the NUGMW that he first came into contact with his mentor, Sidney Box. Reduced to 106 members by 1935, Box's rebel organization, the Counties Agricultural and General Workers' Union, had merged with the NUGMW, leaving Box as Hereford area organizer.[102] Recalling this pioneering period, when the NUGMW made rapid strides in south Wales, Eddy Jones warmly acknowledged his personal debt to Sidney Box.[103] Having been privileged to spend time in his company, he had drawn on Box's 'vast courage, experience, knowledge and humour' to strengthen his own resolve to pursue the working-class struggle.

It was to be expected that Eddy Jones, as a disciple of Box, would at some stage turn his attention to the farm workers. At the close of 1941 he provided the dynamic behind the formation of an NUAW branch at Goodrich, Herefordshire.[104] From a band of four, membership soon grew to forty, with William Thomas as secretary. By April 1942 the union felt confident enough to hold its first inter-county conference of agricultural workers at Monmouth.[105] Naturally, Eddy Jones was keen to extend the area of activity and so he persuaded H.T. Pritchard, a stockman who had joined the Goodrich branch, to assist him to start a new branch in Pritchard's home village of Newcastle, Monmouthshire.[106] In a few months this branch flourished beyond expectation, with offshoots in Welsh Newton, Llanrothal and Broad Oak. By the end of the year membership in the Monmouth area was approaching 200 in spite of attempts by farmers to intimidate workers to stop them joining the union.[107] As Eddy Jones shrewdly supplied the *Monmouthshire Beacon* with regular reports,[108] favourable press coverage greatly helped to sustain the gradual ground-swell of interest.

In William Thomas, Eddy Jones had a very able lieutenant. More responsibility followed when he succeeded Jones as secretary of the Monmouth Trades Council. When W. Holmes and other NUAW leaders visited the county to lead a recruiting campaign in the summer of 1942, William Thomas undertook all the arrangements.[109] A second inter-county conference at Monmouth in May 1943 gave him another opportunity to show his mettle.[110] Collaterally, he was instrumental in opening new branches in Herefordshire and Monmouthshire.[111] Indeed, with all this renewed interest in trade unionism the secretary of the Abergavenny Trades and Labour Council also ran an advertising campaign urging agricultural workers to join the NUAW.[112] Enough had been achieved by now to convince the executive of the union that the necessary groundwork had been laid for a more interventionist role. Exactly twenty years after the dismissal of the last Welsh organizers, William Thomas commenced his duties as full-time NUAW district organizer for Hereford, Monmouth and Glamorgan in August 1943.[113] From this moment he began to recruit in earnest and with the most impressive results.

Utilizing the *Monmouthshire Beacon* to run a regular notice — headed 'Is there a branch of the NUAW in your district?'[114] — William Thomas pursued an energetic campaign to unionize rural workers in the three counties and beyond. A succession of meetings resulted in the establishment of branches as far afield as Barry and Bridgend in Glamorgan and Glasbury in Radnor.[115] Dozens of new converts were won, including members of the Women's Land Army. Within a year of his appointment he was celebrating the opening of the fifty-second branch in his district.[116] Once more, farm workers were taking to heart the concept of trade union solidarity. For the first time in many years they were being given the opportunity to discuss related issues and express their views publicly. They showed that it was not merely wage rises and improved working conditions which captured their interest, but matters concerning the welfare of the rural community in general.[117] Housing conditions aroused a good deal of comment, particularly the scandal of tied cottages and the lack of basic amenities. Schools and the quality of education for working-class children, improved transport facilities, indeed every aspect of social and cultural life in the rural areas entered the debate. Farm workers proved that they too were concerned with the direction of post-war reconstruction. As H.T. Pritchard commented, they were sick of being 'the industrial outcasts' for whom it was thought anything would do.[118]

Familiar problems were encountered, especially the antagonism of employers and the reluctance of farm workers to serve as branch officials lest they be blacklisted. Because they often proved more enthusiastic than the men, William Thomas had good reason to praise the contribution of the land girls. As the Women's Land Army consisted of gangs of workers who had been drafted into the countryside, the women were housed in special camps provided by the county War Agricultural Executive Committees (WAECs). In fact, an NUAW branch might sometimes be based in a WLA hostel or WAEC camp. In order to strengthen the network of NUAW branches county committees were formed: the Monmouthshire County Committee, for instance, was set up in November 1944 with Eddy Jones as its chairman.[119] Again, individual branches were encouraged to affiliate with their local trades and labour council.[120] By May 1945 the number of branches in William Thomas's district (which now included Radnor) had reached almost 100, with new members joining at a rate of 150 a month.[121] Since 1942 the number of branches in Monmouthshire alone had grown from 2 to 30.[122] In every way, Thomas had led a remarkable revival, and for the first time the NUAW organization in his district, representing a total of 2,000 members, became affiliated to the South Wales Regional Council of Labour in 1945.[123]

The accelerating rate of growth during the war years had brought the number of NUAW branches in 1945 to a total that surpassed the previous peak reached in 1919, with the difference that this time the numerical base, both in terms of branches and membership, was held and strengthened during the next two decades. Union funds were in a healthier state, and with greater status accorded to trade unionism in wartime, NUAW prestige and influence was never greater.[124] A time of rising expectations gave the union a grander perspective to its policy of expansion and in June 1944 the executive committee invited applications for posts of district organizers.[125] Thus, between 1938 and 1947 the number of organizers was increased from 16 to 38.[126] This readiness to build on the union's growth explains the decision to appoint a second organizer in south Wales in September 1944.[127] Once again, they found the right man for the job in D.J. Jenkins.

In D.J. Jenkins's case, a wide experience of agriculture was matched by a fiery inner conviction.[128] He had begun his working life as a farm labourer in Carmarthenshire before enlisting for war service. Upon demobilization he left for North America where he spent eight years as farm manager. Returning in 1937, he settled in Gloucestershire, again to work on various farms. Because of the part he played in opening four new union branches he was already well-known to the NUAW leadership prior to his appointment.[129] After spending a preparatory period with William Thomas, Jenkins returned to his native county to operate from his house in Pumsaint, Llanwrda, and was paid £6 a week. As a district, Glamorgan, Carmarthen, Pembroke and Cardigan presented a formidable challenge as it had in John Davies's and D.S. Jones's day, but this time it was at least the age of the car and telephone. Well to the left politically (and subscribing to the Communist *Daily Worker*), Jenkins had all the attributes of a committed activist. The fearless manner in which he championed trade unionism and socialism could hardly conceal his disdain for the landowner, the wealthy farmer and the rural 'establishment'. As a prominent member of the Carmarthenshire constituency Labour Party, he became equally dedicated to awakening the interest of the rural worker in class politics.

In the process of renewal, trade union success was usually registered in the number of branches founded. Taking a leaf from William Thomas's book, Jenkins opened up with an advertising campaign in the *Carmarthen Journal* directed towards farm, forestry, garden and nursery workers, including the Women's Land Army.[130] The Vale of Towi branch had been the sole surviving NUAW branch in Carmarthenshire in the years 1931–42. Soon the number of branches began to increase again, and within the year there were thirteen branches in the county. In Pembrokeshire the branch at

Rosemarket offered a base from which to reach other workers, and in this task D.J. Jenkins had the full-blooded assistance of F.L. Ward. Together they toured the county by car. Few public meetings were held;[131] their usual tactic was to approach the farm worker face to face, either by sneaking on to the farm or waiting until he finished work.[132] In the initial period there was fierce opposition from employers, especially those who underpaid their men. F.L. Ward recollected how they would find the tyres of their car let down outside the gates of a farm! Another close associate, Gwilym Evans, Llansawel, summed up the attitude of farmers as one of 'contempt'.[133]

No ally was more experienced or more valued than R.L. Jones, who gave assistance in Cardiganshire. A special campaign was arranged for the county and, along with William Thomas and some top NUAW officials, D.J. Jenkins addressed at least sixteen public meetings in the period 7–11 May 1945.[134] With lively speeches outlining the history of the union and the importance of unity, it seemed almost a repeat of T.E. Nicholas's inspirational crusade of 1917–18. However, this time the results were not as good. Only three new branches materialized, but eventually seven more would be added to the three that existed in the county prior to 1945.

Alongside the NUAW, the TGWU also sought every opportunity to swell its agricultural section. Farm workers were urged to join in 1939–40 in order to strengthen the union's arm in wage negotiations, and there was mention of a campaign to take in all the north Wales counties.[135] Early in 1943 the TGWU allocated a substantial sum for a special campaign. One result was the good progress reported by W.J. Wardle in west Wales, with farm workers joining the Llandovery, Cross Hands and Pencader branches.[136] Following the retirement of William Williams in 1939, Owen Edwards, a former NWQU official, took charge of the Bangor district. As wartime conditions boosted the cause, his declared intention was to establish branches from Aberdaron to the Conwy Valley.[137] Up to the summer of 1944 some 4,000 farm workers belonged to the union in north Wales. Attempts were also made to enrol farm workers in the Wrexham and Holt area, but without any noticeable results.[138]

As these advances were only limited in scope, there was little chance to harness the resurgence of rural trade unionism in time to play any vital part in the general election of 1945 and Labour's overwhelming victory. In Wales, the swing to the Labour Party was decisive: it won 58.5 per cent of the vote and 25 seats. Although in relative decline, the

Liberal Party tally of 7 seats included a gain from Labour at Carmarthen. Otherwise, it lost Caernarfon and only narrowly held off the Labour challenge in Merioneth, Pembroke and Anglesey. In six of the agricultural constituencies the Labour Party polled over 46 per cent of the votes cast. These included the Monmouth division, heart of the NUAW stronghold in Wales. As a reflection of its increasing confidence, the union's county committee had recommended branches to nominate Eddy Jones as parliamentary candidate, and again prior to the by-election that shortly followed.[139] On neither occasion was he selected; furthermore, William Thomas, who acted as party sub-agent, complained that Labour organization during the general election was extremely poor with the rural areas being 'forgotten entirely'.[140]

One of the most obvious effects of the current revival in trade unionism was the increasing level of local activity. Both William Thomas and D.J. Jenkins worked hard to build on their initial success. Thomas urged branch secretaries to draw up a winter programme of social evenings to nurture a strong *esprit de corps*.[141] Mass meetings, county conferences and demonstrations were held to put on a display of strength and press for further improvements. The demand for higher wages became an effective rallying cry. At a conference in Aberaeron in December 1945 members backed the union claim for a £4.10*s*. minimum wage and 48-hour week.[142] Farm workers in Monmouthshire were reported to be taking a firm stand on the matter, but whereas the threat of a strike was being made in other parts of Britain, the Gwent men decided against such action.[143] All this time the number of NUAW branches was multiplying: figures for 1946 showed that Monmouth had 28, Carmarthen 28, Glamorgan 23, Cardiganshire 11, Pembroke 11 and Radnor 3. The overall picture in south Wales was one of remarkable growth and optimism. In less than a year, D.J. Jenkins had set up 38 branches in a district that extended from Cardiff across to Aberystwyth.[144] Viewed from head office this was quite an achievement. They conceded that it would have been too much to expect a movement equal to that of Norfolk or Lincolnshire because of the comparative number of Welsh farm workers.[145] Even so, by 1949, D.J. Jenkins was claiming that 85 per cent of the men in Carmarthenshire had joined the union.[146] Be that as it may, he also found it hard over the years to maintain the loyalty of members. Consequently, the NUAW leaned heavily on its forestry branches — like Abergorlech and Cil-y-cwm — where it was easier to collect subscriptions and find men willing to act as local secretaries.

All that remained to complete the structure was for the NUAW to appoint an organizer for north Wales. Up to 1946, J.W. Smith had responsibility for Montgomery and Denbigh, with oversight for Caernarfon and Merioneth. But as Smith rarely visited north Wales the area was very poorly organized.[147] No NUAW branches were listed for Anglesey, Caernarfon or Montgomery, and Llanuwchllyn, the only branch in Merioneth, finally folded in 1942. The union presence in Denbighshire consisted of the forestry branch in Llangollen and a short-lived Women's Land Army hostel at Rhuthun. According to a later source, the NUAW had only fourteen members throughout north Wales prior to 1947.[148] However, because of a growing concern, stimulated by strong competition from the TGWU and NUGMW, the union paid more attention to correspondence from Gwilym Davies, a TGWU member in Merioneth, who suggested the possibility of organizing the county.[149] Although it was accepted that a full-time officer in north Wales would not pay his way for years, the NUAW, in conjunction with the Labour Party and TUC regional officials, went ahead and appointed Gwilym Davies as district organizer.[150] Once he had transferred his membership to the NUAW, he was given the five counties of Anglesey, Caernarfon, Denbigh, Merioneth and Montgomery, commencing duties on 1 August 1947.

What distinguished Gwilym Davies, like his counterparts in south Wales, was his working-class background and unswerving loyalty to the trade union movement.[151] His experiences as a collier in the Rhondda and as a slate quarryman in his native Blaenau Ffestiniog helped mould a strong character. For two years after the war he worked on a farm near Bala, during which time he became conscious of conditions in agriculture. For an NUAW organizer, enrolling members in the mountainous regions of Gwynedd remained the difficult task it had proved for R.G. Roberts. Eschewing public meetings, Davies relied on personal canvassing, and with no help from other labour organizations he thus built up the union single-handed.[152] Often he would return home to Blaenau Ffestiniog in the early hours of the morning disheartened at not having won any new members. On his missions the two great fears that he habitually encountered were fear of the employer and fear of losing a tied cottage. Nevertheless, in his own quiet, friendly way Gwilym Davies was to make considerable progress as district organizer. Though troubled by all the familiar obstacles encountered by each NUAW organizer, he was not without assets, and not least among them was the help given by individual members in the localities.[153]

Denbighshire was the best example of this help. On his inaugural visit to Denbigh in February 1948 he found a loyal branch secretary in E. Lloyd Roberts, a local farm worker. As membership grew from 5 to 70 in a matter of months, the union could well claim that Vale of Clwyd farm workers were 'awakened after a long sleep'.[154] Gwilym Davies's aim was to establish an NUAW branch in each village under the direction of a Vale of Clwyd district committee. On the first anniversary of the Denbigh branch there were 11 more branches in the district;[155] by 1950 the number had grown to 15 with a total membership of over 600 agricultural and forestry workers.[156] Beyond this, some, like the Wrexham branch, were affiliating with the local trades council;[157] others, like Llanfair Dyffryn Clwyd, were affiliating with the Labour Party.[158] When the Abergele branch was opened in March 1949 it brought the north Wales total up to 55. So also began Owen Alun Hughes's lifelong association with the union. Starting as secretary of the Abergele branch, he became secretary of the Vale of Clwyd District Committee and later chairman of the North Wales Counties Committee. Because of his union work he was threatened with eviction from his tied cottage in 1951; after a prolonged dispute with his employer he secured employment as a forestry worker and moved to a council house, whereupon he continued to serve the NUAW.[159]

In aiming to establish small village branches, which looked impressive enough listed together in the NUAW Annual Reports, Gwilym Davies set up a process that proved, in the long run, to be self-destructive. At the outset most branches flourished; they were regularly visited and Gwilym Davies took care to nurse them along. But he had charge of an extensive district which entailed his attendance on countless committees in the name of the union. To add to this, he undertook a great deal of public work as magistrate and councillor. Meanwhile, farming itself was undergoing great changes. With increased mechanization, and men leaving for better-paid jobs in local factories, the decline in the number of farm workers made his task considerably more difficult. E. Lloyd Roberts left to work in Courtaulds (spinners), Flint, although he continued to serve as secretary to a handful of NUAW branches in Denbigh and Flintshire. Against this background, many of the smaller north Wales branches began to deteriorate and eventually close. But as the position stood in 1949, Anglesey had 4 NUAW branches, Caernarfon 13, Denbigh 25, Flintshire 18,[160] Merioneth 7 and Montgomery 17. In south Wales Monmouth listed 16 branches,[161] Carmarthen 31, Glamorgan 32, Pembroke 19, Cardigan 13, Brecon 6 and Radnor 3.

The Labour Party's electoral triumph in 1945 had opened a new era in British society. Once in power it embarked immediately on a formidable policy of economic and social reconstruction. Highest priority went to economic recovery and the nationalization of basic industries. It also launched a substantial programme of social reform aimed at completing the Welfare State. At the centre of the new system were the National Insurance Act and National Health Service Act of 1946. To meet another desperate situation, the Labour Government laid plans for more public housing. Taken all together, the reforming and curative processes of the measures received the support of the trade union movement, through which a sense of optimism was mediated to all sections of the working class. In K.O. Morgan's words, the Attlee Government's social achievements in public health and housing 'brought the British labour movement to the zenith of its achievement as a political instrument for humanitarian reform'.[162]

The provision of adequate housing had remained as urgent as ever. In connection with the Agricultural (Miscellaneous Provisions) Act in 1943, an ill-conceived programme to build 3,000 wartime cottages for farm workers had been announced.[163] Under the scheme, the Welsh counties would be allocated 316 houses between them.[164] Rural district councils were to build and administer the cottages but, because of the high costs involved, there was considerable opposition. At a meeting of the Aberystwyth RDC they were dubbed 'white elephant cottages'.[165] Without the necessary goodwill, and without sufficient funding, the work of providing improved housing on any large scale could not be carried through. Given the unhelpful attitude of local authorities only sixty-six houses had been completed by June 1944.[166] Neither was much done to improve the amenities of rural life during the war years. As Minister of Health and Housing, Aneurin Bevan finally concentrated resources on council housing for the working classes, and under the government's new housing priority scheme Pembroke RDC became the first council to receive approval for 180 new houses for farm workers.[167] Improvements on a large scale, however, would of necessity have a long-term aspect, whereas the evils of the tied-cottage system were similarly destined to drag on. Not until the administration of James Callaghan did a Labour government fulfil a long-standing pledge and abolish tied cottages. To the delight of the farm workers' unions the Rent Agriculture Act of 1976 very largely achieved what organized labour had tried for more than seventy years to eliminate.

Under the National Health Service Act the state supplied a comprehensive range of free medical treatment. The National Insurance Act, which came into operation at the same time in July 1948, provided a single unified scheme of social security with a range of benefits. Friendly Societies lost the position they had previously held.[168] One of the societies to suffer in this way was the Undeb Gweithwyr Môn Approved Society. A product of the *gwerin* of Anglesey, and still proudly rooted in the ordinary Welsh-speaking working class,[169] it had struggled over the years to provide sickness, disablement and maternity benefits. From 771 members in 1913, the society had slowly expanded and maintained a small membership of some 2,000 during the early thirties. In 1935 it counted 1,794 members and assets amounting to £4,500.[170] But with 36 per cent of the insured population in Anglesey unemployed,[171] it proved difficult to raise contributions and so the benefits paid out hardly matched those of the large insurance companies. Even so, the Undeb Gweithwyr Môn Approved Society continued to hold membership levels through difficult times up to the introduction of the National Health Service.[172] Appropriately enough, at its last recorded meeting, when the new National Insurance Act became the subject of fervent discussion, the primary concern of officials was for their membership in Anglesey.[173] Not only did this signify the end of a long-established organization, but also the loss of a name replete with unique associations and linked directly to ap Ffarmwr and the first rural revolt in Wales.

In the mean time, events during the thirties had also sapped the Anglesey district of the TGWU of much strength. The great days were over, and how far they had gone beyond recall was clear in the aftermath of the 1945 election. During his campaign, Cledwyn Hughes, the Labour candidate, toured the rural villages in a vain attempt to rekindle the fire of trade union solidarity.[174] Most of the erstwhile Undeb Gweithwyr Môn branches were moribund and, with few exceptions, the local leaders either old or dead. Having lifted the Labour vote to within sight of victory, the Anglesey Labour Party and the district committee of the TGWU undertook a dual effort to revive interest. Time and again between 1947 and 1949, John Jones of Cerrigceinwen and Owen Edwards issued impassioned pleas to the farm workers of Anglesey to join in the same numbers as they had during the years 1918–22.[175] Now that the TGWU had 64,000 members in north Wales there could be no excuse. As a high point to its recruiting drive, the union organized a one-day school for Anglesey rural workers at Llangefni on 12 June 1948.[176] On the platform, reliving experiences of some thirty-four years earlier, were two of the foremost veteran campaigners, David Thomas and William Williams. Recalling a previous gathering in May 1914 when he had accompanied Cyril O. Jones, David Thomas appealed to the farm workers not to turn their backs on the trade union movement. To the same end, William Williams evoked the memorable names of ap Ffarmwr, Thomas Rowlands and Lewis Thomas. But their message fell on stony ground. Few farm labourers were even present that day. Gone was the feeling of solidarity, and throughout John Jones's subsequent reports his sense of frustration at their apathy and indifference ran like a bitter refrain.[177] The dispiriting effects of high unemployment had taken their toll. Cledwyn Hughes, upon his election as MP in 1951, realized that his task was not so much to recruit farm workers for political purposes as secure jobs for those labourers who lacked employment.[178] In such difficult circumstances no one could suppose that the possibilities glimpsed in 1918–22 might be revived.

Conversely, much more was being done for the farm workers in general. Since the war they had come to enjoy a greater measure of security and, with successive wage increases, they were relatively better off. As an industry, agriculture was being particularly favoured. To ensure that it did not revert to its depressed pre-war state, the Labour Government's Agriculture Act of 1947 gave farmers extended security and generous subsidies. If the policy of land nationalization had been shelved,[179] the lessons of the 1920s were not forgotten. Guaranteed prices for a wide range of products, fixed by an annual agricultural review, raised average farm incomes to six times their pre-war peak in 1949–50.[180] Also made permanent, and consolidated by the Agricultural Wages Act of 1948, was the transfer to the Agricultural Wages Board of all the major functions of wage fixing conferred on county wages committees. Improvements in wages and conditions had already taken place in 1946 when the minimum rate was set at £4 and a uniform week of forty-eight hours introduced, irrespective of season. Unlike the situation which followed the repeal of the Corn Production Act in 1921, when there had been a drastic fall in wages, the farm worker was at least guaranteed a better deal. The importance of wages as a recruiting factor is well illustrated as NUAW membership reached an all-time peak of 141,000 in 1948.[181] In terms of branches founded, these were years of great success. For the first time in its history the union had a branch in each of the thirteen Welsh counties. Anglesey and Montgomeryshire were finally added to NUAW lists, Gwilym Davies having done well to establish 17 branches in Montgomeryshire by 1949.[182] From 142 branches in 1947 the Welsh total reached 204 within two years, and a record 212 branches by 1950, way above the previous peak of 160 achieved in 1920.

Britain's trade unions had never been so powerful. Their part in the war effort raised their status and for the first time there developed a real partnership between the unions and the government. Workers joined in record numbers so that total trade union membership shot up to 9.3 million by 1950. For the majority of industrial workers, joining a trade union was now a matter of course. However reluctantly, farmers, like other employers, became reconciled to the concept of trade unionism, while the farm workers who sought membership considered it more a natural right than an expression of discontent as it had been during the Great War. Perhaps the absence of a rebellious aspect to trade unionism goes some way towards explaining the lack of publicity given to the farm workers' union. Unlike in the earlier period, little excitement was generated, few public meetings were held, and consequently (with the notable exception of Monmouthshire) NUAW activity in Wales was accorded very little press coverage.

What was true of the trade unions was also true of the Labour Party. With improved organization the party continued its advance. In 1947 the South Wales Regional Council of Labour gave way to the new Welsh Regional Council of Labour, with an affiliated membership of 350,000. Labour gained Pembroke in the general election of 1950, then Anglesey and Merioneth in 1951, bringing the total to twenty-seven seats. But it was the industrial developments within the agricultural constituencies which helped tip the balance; the farm workers played no part as an occupational group, and despite Labour's beneficence the farmers did not translate their appreciation into electoral votes.[183]

Another wage rise for farm workers in 1950 brought the minimum to £5 a week, yet they still failed to catch up with earnings in other industries. And it was this unbridged gap between industrial and agricultural wages which largely undermined the morale of the work-force.[184] As it happened, the fall of the second Labour Government of 1951 also marked the beginning of a steady but irreversible decline in NUAW membership. When Bryn Davies succeeded D.J. Jenkins as south Wales organizer in 1956, he noted that his area had the smallest membership in England and Wales.[185] NUAW membership in the whole of Wales by 1960 is estimated to have been 2,728, that is 10 per cent of the agricultural work-force and a mere 2.2 per cent of the total union membership (which stood at 123,330).[186] Similarly, the 191 branches represented 5 per cent of the total of 3,770.[187] During the decade 1960–70, when the number of regular full-time workers continued to decline,[188] the total of branches plunged from 191 to 127, and by all accounts it was within the progressively declining agricultural work-force that membership lapsed. Each passing decade had seen more and more members recruited from outside agriculture; very often county council roadmen, forestry workers, horticulturists and poultry-packing workers helped to keep a branch in existence.[189] The adoption of the title National Union of Agricultural and Allied Workers (NUAAW) in 1968 was a belated recognition of this extension into other occupations.

Also in 1968 Wales was to receive an overdue tribute when the NUAAW biennial conference came to Aberystwyth, the first time it had been held outside England. Attended by Harold Wilson, the Prime Minister, it provided an opportunity to salute R.L. Jones's life-long contribution as the 'father of the union in Wales'.[190] The previous year had seen Llanilar branch celebrate its golden jubilee, and R.L. Jones continued to act as local secretary for altogether fifty-seven years. Indeed, Llanilar remained the oldest-established NUAAW branch in Wales, which, together with the Vale of Towi branch, straddled the two great periods in the union's history. But the strength of the past had become a memory. Both

NUAAW and the agricultural group within the TGWU were rapidly losing members amongst a diminishing work-force, with the result that rural Wales was once again reverting into a trade union wasteland. By 1971 only five members were left in the Llanilar branch.[191] Wesley Jones, the last member of the Vale of Towi branch, retired in 1980. Aberffraw TGWU branch, with associations going back to Undeb Gweithwyr Môn and ap Ffarmwr, also saw its membership tail off from 250 (in 1941) to 7 by 1980.[192] When O.R. Hughes retired as secretary in 1978 the branch lost its one remaining farm worker. After a splendid tradition in the history of rural radicalism, Anglesey had reached the end of an era with the same poignant finality that marked the close of a distinct farm workers' movement elsewhere in Wales.

CONCLUSION

THE history of the farm workers' trade unions is one of defeat. In the context of rural Wales this was the revolt that failed. While three distinct periods of activity can be distinguished, there were few enduring achievements and they have hardly featured in studies of the Welsh labour movement. Yet, both in character and impact, the first two instances of agricultural labour unrest embrace some of the classic features of class struggle. As the social division between the middle-class farmers and their workers grew, the conflict of interest became more pronounced. For a brief moment in the early 1890s ap Ffarmwr's crusade to improve working conditions seized the imagination of farm labourers in Anglesey. An attempt was made to challenge the authority of employers by taking collective action and for the first time in Wales the concept of rural trade unionism was being mooted. Although ap Ffarmwr has received due recognition his character has not been adequately portrayed or the impact of his mission fully appreciated. But the Anglesey Agricultural Labourers' Union proved to be an idea ahead of its time. Things turned out better in the case of the tenant farmers. Ultimate success for the farmers in *their* struggles coincided with the beginning of a period of relative prosperity in Welsh agriculture at the turn of the century, and this effectively meant the demise of the Land Question as a major political issue. In contrast, the social life and working conditions of the farm labourers saw little improvement; neither was any great concern shown for their fate.

The failure of the first 'revolt of the field' in Wales did not mean the end of an ideal. Ap Ffarmwr bequeathed a vision that was eventually realized in Anglesey. The tradition of rural radicalism he founded proved sufficiently strong to result in the establishment of a unique local union, Undeb Gweithwyr Môn. Before long, other leaders, notably David Thomas, had come forward with similar aspirations. By 1914 the crucial groundwork was being prepared as the organized labour movement gradually extended its reach into the remote rural regions to end social isolation and raise working-class consciousness. Branches of various trade unions, particularly the NUR, were instrumental in initiating change and opening the way to the forces of liberation. At the same time, in England, the farm workers' own union was making substantial progress, but before it could penetrate into rural Wales the right contacts and conditions had to be established.

The watershed was the Great War. It took the unique social and economic changes precipitated by war for the agricultural working class to see the relevance of trade unionism. Whereas hardship on its own seemed insufficient to spur the rural labourers into mass action, the selfish and unjust attitude of employers now led to an astonishing outburst of rural protest and class hostility. Pre-existing resentments and social divisions were exposed. Pent-up feelings which had long lingered beneath the surface exploded as the farmer showed himself to be the match of the landlord in greed and heartlessness. So much hypocrisy was revealed as to make Caradoc Evans's infamous stories of life in west Wales seem guilty not so much of malice as of understating his case.[1] (Significantly enough, his most biting satirical works appeared during the years 1915–19.) This represented the 'new, sudden and intolerable outrage' that proved 'peculiarly offensive',[2] and which fuelled the major revolt of 1917–20.

War became the catalyst which enabled a core of experienced labour activists, most conspicuously railwaymen and miners' officials, successfully to exploit the seething discontent. Following vigorous campaigns by both the NALRWU and Workers' Union a trade union network covered the countryside, attracting scores of converts on an unprecedented scale. Whilst rural Wales finally shed its parochial, isolationist character, the working class was being absorbed into the wider British labour movement. For the first time the hegemony of the farmers came under threat in each of the thirteen counties. Farm workers gained not only material improvements as a result of the Corn Production Act of 1917 but also their dignity and self-respect. Between 1917 and 1920 the labourers' unions enjoyed days of power. Indeed, it may be said that this was the one short interlude in history when farm workers exercised some form of influence over their lives. It was the only real occasion when they seemed able to act like a mass movement rather than as individuals. That they even took strike action to secure justice in the manner of railwaymen and miners was proof of their maturity as workers. The striking farm worker of 1919 presented an image that would have seemed unthinkable only a few years earlier.

In the agricultural constituencies the initial progress of the rural labourers' movement also offered wider possibilities. The men's new-found class consciousness was being translated into a political awareness with the Labour Party as the key beneficiary. Ironically, the farming class which had overturned the rule of the land-owning gentry in the nineteenth century to create a Liberal, middle-class rural establishment was itself facing a radicalized challenge from below by a class which had espoused a separate political creed. As its greatest success it could claim the return of Sir Owen Thomas as MP for Anglesey in 1918. Modest gains in various local elections across Wales underlined the labourers' capacity for independent political action. All of this added further significance to the class solidarity engendered by the farm workers' revolt. But with the untimely collapse of rural trade unionism the Labour Party was deprived of a potential working-class base at its formative stage. The rise of Labour as a rural force was halted. In spite of every effort, it failed to reactivate interest in the countryside during the 1930s, and the traditional Liberal ascendancy remained generally unshaken. The Labour Party's gradual incursion into the political landscape of rural Wales after 1945 owed its success to other factors.

The onset of economic depression and unemployment had taken its toll. The men lost heart and everywhere union branches disintegrated. Unlike the well-publicized contests fought by tenant farmers, the labourers' class struggle had failed.

The farmers' success in removing the injustices of landlordism can be seen as one of the foremost achievements of Nonconformist radicalism. Together, the middle-class tenantry and Nonconformist hierarchy had displayed the political power of rural dissent, underlined by their control of local government after 1889. But this version of 'liberation theology' was never carried across the threshold of the stable loft or tied cottage. Organized religion made no attempt to initiate any movement against the oppression of the farm labourers, and on no occasion did it protest publicly and positively at the distressing social conditions their families had to suffer. Most probably, there was no wish to offend the farmers who formed the mainstay of increasingly worldly-comfortable congregations. Only a handful of Nonconformist ministers stood up for the working class. Those ministers who ventured to express their Christianity as a vehicle for social change showed rare moral leadership; to align with the underdog in the community took special courage. Nothing is more striking than the way the Revd Richard Morris chose to identify himself with the farm workers' struggle when he left the ministry to become organizing secretary of Undeb Gweithwyr Môn, or how George M. Ll. Davies epitomized in a single example the spirit of reconciliation. It was ironic, in a society which had enthusiastically vilified the Church of England, that it was individual Anglican clergymen like the Revds J.H. Jenkins, T.D. James and Gwilym Rees who showed the most genuine compassion for the rural workers. By championing the interests of the working class they broke with the political tradition that associated the parson with the Tory country squire.

The local leadership that formed the backbone of rural trade unionism came mainly from outside the ranks of farm workers. Poor education, a natural reticence, and a fear of intimidation precluded all but the most determined labourer. As can be seen from the biographical index, this leadership embraced a range of occupations, but more especially schoolteachers, railwaymen, craftsmen and postmen who came into direct contact with the farm workers and their families. A great many were Nonconformist deacons and lay preachers. Regardless of the official attitude of their denomination most held on to their deep Christian convictions. Quite often, inspiration stemmed from a socialist vision of a just society: Thomas Rowlands and D.W. Jones (ap Rhydwen) were disaffected Liberals turned Labour, D.T. Lewis and the Revd T.D. James had been erstwhile Tories. Other rural activists, significantly enough, had at some stage come into contact with aggressive trade unionism whilst working in the slate quarries or the south Wales coalfield. During the course of their mission in the countryside all were to face indifference on the one hand and opposition on the other. Moreover, as failure eventually robbed the farm workers' movement of its historical significance, it also obscured the names of those who had sacrificed time and family in pursuit of the cause. Pioneering figures like William Harris, D.S. Jones, W.J. Jones (Brynfab), David Rees, R.G. Roberts and William Williams remain unremembered. Even the names of ap Ffarmwr and David Thomas have never shed the same lustre as Gwilym Hiraethog, S.R., Thomas Gee or T.E. Ellis.

Perhaps it could be taken for granted that the revolt of the farm workers would never succeed. Perhaps it is remarkable that it should have happened at all. Ultimately, the labour unions had little chance of carving out a base in the countryside against such a powerful employer. In the long run, they could never hope to rival the NFU in terms of status, wealth and influence. Because of the fragmented nature of agriculture the men's unions lacked the tight organization of the miner and factory worker. Isolated in small groups on scattered farms they were without the essential ingredient for unity. Fear of dismissal, eviction and unemployment were the subtle mechanisms of acquiescence. To this day the farm worker is seen as 'the deferential worker' *par excellence*.[3] By the same token, their feeling of powerlessness has also subjected them to a degree of employer control unheard of in other industries. And, in general, the farmers were the worst of employers. In times of hardship one could understand their attitude, but even in times of prosperity they were equally hard-fisted and uncharitable. Around the period of the Great War, when the farmers' plenty gave the labour unions their opportunity, each improvement was resolutely opposed and every pay rise only grudgingly conceded.

The farm workers' unions in Wales were reduced almost to vanishing point during the 1930s. It took the special circumstances of another war to revitalize them. By 1950, the total number of NUAW branches far exceeded that of 1919. But in spite of the encouraging recovery, the unions were sadly ineffective; farm workers did not benefit from the 'golden years' of post-war British agriculture and once more decline set in. Another drift from the land, accentuated by mechanization, helped to reduce the agricultural work-force. Apart from the external difficulties, a second generation of trade union organizers had to reckon with the same self-destructive apathy that had brought so much despair before. Over the years the negative response of the farm workers contributed to the slow but inevitable demise of the NUAAW. By the end of the 1970s the union's 85,000 members represented less than 35 per cent of the total work-force.[4] In Wales, only a very small percentage of the 12,000 farm workers belonged to the union. Financially weak and with a declining membership it bowed to the inevitable. After seventy-five years, the history of the NUAAW as an independent farm workers' union finally ended in 1982 when members voted to merge with the TGWU.[5]

Even today the bitter legacy of defeat can be clearly seen. Farm workers are still paid poverty wages. Because of their weak bargaining power, they remain in the 1980s close to the bottom of the wages league. And while their pay continues to fall short of the average earnings of manual industrial workers there is always the wide gap between generously subsidized farm incomes and the derisory legal minimum wage. Throughout this time the Agricultural Wages Board has consistently failed to achieve a reasonable standard of living for the workers, with the result that many live below the recognized poverty line. The proportion of farm workers dependent on the Family Income Supplement has doubled since 1980.[6] Even Britain's entry into the European Economic Community and the adoption of the Common Agricultural Policy has not meant a new deal for the farm workers despite increased productivity and rising farm profits.[7] Too often nowadays the harsh reality of rural life is distorted by the false idyllic images perpetuated by folk museums and arcadian novels. The idealization of the countryside has, in turn, further clouded the historical memory of the 'revolt of the field' in Wales. Yet, for the vast majority of ordinary farm labourers these events did not involve any great ideological issue; it was but a simple concern that they be given a just reward for a fair day's work. What the failure of the collectivist struggles over the last century unquestionably meant, however, was that they would continue to receive miserable wages, to work excessive hours, to suffer poverty and deprivation, and to make do with the inadequate social amenities their class and community have all too long endured.

APPENDICES

APPENDIX 1

National Agricultural Labourers' and Rural Workers' Union (subsequently NUAW/NUAAW) Branches

County / *Year*	Ang.	Brecs.	Caerns.	Cards.	Carms.	Denbs.	Flints.	Glam.	Mer.	Mon.	Monts.	Pembs.	Rads.	*Totals*
1913						1								1
1914		1					1			1			1	4
1915		1												1
1916														0
1917			2	1		1			2	6		7		19
1918		2	16	14	5	7	3	10	6	16		19	1	99
1919		4	20	23	13	13	8	13	6	15		31	12	158
1920		5	20	18	15	12	9	15	7	14	5	29	11	160
1921		4	18	14	12	11	8	13	8	15	1	28	8	140
1922		3	12	9	6	6	2	7	1	11		19	6	82
1923			6	1	3	3		3	1	7		11	2	37
1924			3	3	2	1	1	2	1	5		4	1	23
1925			2	3	2	1	1	3	1	6		7	1	27
1926			1	2	2	1	1	4	1	7		8	1	28
1927		2	1	1	1		1	3	1	3		2	1	16
1928		1	1	1	1			3	1	3		2	1	14
1929		1	1	1	1			3	1	2		2		12
1930		2	1	1	1			2	1	2		1		11
1931			1		1			2	1	2				7
1932				1	1			2	1	2				7
1933					1			1	1	2				5
1934				1	1			3	1	2				8
1935					1			3	1	2				7
1936				1	1			2	1	2				7
1937				1	1			3	1	2				8
1938				1	1			3	1	2				8
1939				1	1		1	3	1	2				9
1940				1	1	2	1	4	1	2				12
1941				1	1	2	1	5	1	2	1			14
1942				3	1	2	1	6	1	4	1			19
1943				3	3	2	1	6		9		1		25
1944				3	2	3	2	11		24		1	3	49
1945				10	13	2	2	21		23		8	3	82
1946				11	28	1	4	23		28	1	11	3	110
1947	2	4	6	9	33	4	4	22	8	25	2	19	4	142
1948	3	8	15	12	32	24	14	27	7	19	6	18	4	189
1949	4	6	13	13	31	25	18	32	7	16	17	19	3	204
1950	2	4	15	14	37	26	20	29	4	15	22	19	5	212
1955	3	5	21	7	31	27	29	23	7	16	19	11	4	203
1960	4	5	19	7	29	28	21	19	13	13	18	11	4	191
1965	2	5	16	10	25	20	19	20	13	12	16	12	4	174
1970	2	7	13	7	22	11	15	15	12	5	9	9		127

APPENDIX 2

Workers' Union Branches (including former NFDWU and Undeb Gweithwyr Môn Branches)[a]

County	Ang.	Brecs.	Caerns.	Cards.	Carms.	Denbs.	Flints.	Glam.	Mer.	Mon.	Monts.	Pembs.	Rads.	*Totals*
Year														
1916				1									2	3
1918		1	1	2		19	10	2	6		13		1	55
1919	46	2	4	3		17	10	1	9	2	17	1	2	114
1920	42	5	4	2	1	14	10	1	9	7	14	4	3	116
1921	43	4	4	1	1	12	8	1	6	4	9	4	2	99
1922	42	2	2	1		6	2	1	2		3	1	2	64
1923	20	2	1	1		2	1	2	2		1	2	2	36
1924	21	1	1	1		2	1	2	1		1		2	33
1925	20	1	4	1	1	1	1	1	1		1	3	2	37
1926	18	1	3	1			1		1		1	1	2	29

[a]Reports for 1917, 1927–8 are not available

NOTES

Introduction

1. K.O. Morgan, *Rebirth of a Nation: Wales 1880–1980* (Oxford and Cardiff, 1981), p.170.
2. Alun Howkins, *Poor Labouring Men: Rural Radicalism in Norfolk 1870–1923* (London, 1985), ch.2.
3. Sam Kushner, *Long Road to Delano* (New York, 1976).

Chapter I

1. See D. Parry-Jones, *Welsh Country Upbringing* (London, 1948), p.85; E. Tegla Davies, *Gyda'r Blynyddoedd* (Lerpwl, 1952), p.10, 154; also the conclusions of Michael Birtwistle, 'Pobol y Tai Bach': some aspects of the agricultural labouring classes of Cardiganshire in the second half of the nineteenth century.' (Unpublished MA thesis, Aberystwyth, 1982), pp.130–2.
2. For an extended background study of the social and economic position of the agricultural labourer, see David W. Howell, *Land and People in Nineteenth-Century Wales* (London, 1978), ch.6.
3. D.J.V. Jones, *Before Rebecca* (London, 1973), p.64.
4. Ibid., pp.58–9.
5. Howell, *Land and People*, pp.107–8.
6. David Williams, *The Rebecca Riots* (Cardiff, 1955), p.75.
7. Ibid., p.243.
8. Ibid., p.262.
9. Ibid., p.291.
10. Howell, *Land and People*, p.109.
11. D.J.V. Jones, 'Crime, Protest and Community in Nineteenth Century Wales', *Llafur*, 1, No.3 (May 1974), p.10.
12. The growth of political radicalism in rural Wales is summarized by K.O. Morgan in *Wales in British Politics 1868–1922* (Cardiff, 3rd edn., 1980), pp.13–22.
13. E. Morgan Humphreys (ed.), *Gwilym Hiraethog: Llythyrau 'Rhen Ffarmwr* (Caerdydd, 1939), p.vii.
14. Parch W. Rees, *Llythurau 'Rhen Ffarmwr* (Liverpool, 1878), pp.39–40, Llythur XIV (c.1847–8).
15. See T. Eirug Davies, 'Cyfraniad Dr William Rees (Gwilym Hiraethog) i Fywyd a Llên ei gyfnod' (unpublished MA thesis, Bangor, 1931), pp.225–8.
16. Iorwerth C. Peate (ed.), *Cilhaul ac Ysgrifau Eraill Samuel Roberts, Llanbrynmair* (Caerdydd, 1951), p.29.
17. *Gweithiau Samuel Roberts* (Dolgellau, 1856), 'Landlords and Stewards and Tenants', p.53.
18. See David Williams, 'Rural Wales in the Nineteenth Century' in *Wales Through the Ages*, Vol.II (Llandybïe, 1960), p.151.

19. Morgan, *Wales in British Politics*, p.13.
20. W.T. Kevill Davies, *The Condition of the Agricultural Labourer* (Ludlow, 1854), p.10.
21. Ibid., p.13.
22. Quoted in Raymond Williams, *The Country and the City* (London, 1975 edn.), p.136.
23. Lewis William Lewis ('Llew Llwyfo'), *Huw Huws neu y Llafurwr Cymreig* (Caergybi, 1860).
24. See Kevill Davies, *The Agricultural Labourer*, p.11, also Ifan Gruffydd, *Y Gŵr o Baradwys* (Dinbych, 1963), pp.81–4; Guto Roberts (ed.) *Wel dyma fo . . . Charles Williams* (Penygroes, 1983), pp.60–2.
25. Aled Eames, *Shipmaster* (Denbigh, 1980), p.15, quoting the words of Captain Robert Thomas, Llandwrog, who recalled the Bontnewydd hiring fair.
26. Howell, *Land and People*, p.110.
27. *Commission on the Employment of Children, Young Persons and Women in Agriculture*. Third Report of the Commissioners, 1870 (C 70), p.6.
28. A.W. Ashby and I.L. Evans, *The Agriculture of Wales and Monmouthshire* (Cardiff, 1944), p.74.
29. J.P.D. Dunbabin, 'The Incidence and Organization of Agricultural Trades Unionism in the 1870s', *The Agricultural History Review*, Vol.16 (1968), pp.123–4.
30. Howell, *Land and People*, pp.93–4.
31. Reg Groves, *Sharpen the Sickle!* (London, 1949), pp.32–4.
32. Pamela Horn, *Joseph Arch* (Kineton, 1971), ch.4.
33. *Commission on the Employment of Children, Young Persons, and Women in Agriculture*, 1870, pp.12–13.
34. Ibid., Appendix, Part II to the Third Report, p.130. Evidence of David Jenkins, agricultural labourer.
35. See David A. Pretty, *Two Centuries of Anglesey Schools, 1700–1902* (Llangefni, 1977), pp.201–7.
36. See Howell, *Land and People*, pp.94, 98–9.
37. A farmer's ability to pay a fair day's wage naturally depended on his circumstances. See Hugh Evans, *The Gorse Glen* (Liverpool, 1948), pp.23–5 for a description of the 'farmers' hard lot' and a defence of their parsimonious reputation.
38. J.P.D. Dunbabin, 'The Welsh Tithe War' in *Rural Discontent in Nineteenth-Century Britain* (London, 1974).
39. T. Gwynn Jones, *Cofiant Thomas Gee* (Dinbych, 1913), ch.23.
40. *Inquiry as to Disturbances Connected with the Levying of Tithe Rentcharge in Wales*, 1887 (C 5195), Minutes of Evidence qus., 1082, 2524.
41. *South Wales Daily News*, 7 July 1887.
42. *Baner ac Amserau Cymru*, 31 Mawrth, 7 Ebrill 1886 (editorials). Although an Association at Nant Conwy incorporated 'Labourers' in its title, its aims were directed to the needs of the farmers.
43. Peris Jones-Evans, 'Evan Pan Jones — Land Reformer', *Welsh History Review*, 4, No.2 (December 1968), p.152.
44. *Y Celt*, 5,12 Chwefror, 12 Mawrth 1886. In vain, he urged the agricultural labourers to attend the conference at Rhyl in April so as to broaden the base of the Land League.
45. *Inquiry as to Disturbances Connected with the Levying of Tithe Rentcharge in Wales*, op. cit., qus. 3957, 3962, 3965.
46. *Baner ac Amserau Cymru*, 5 Mehefin 1886.
47. *Western Mail*, 29 October 1886.
48. *Y Celt*, 5 Tachwedd 1886.
49. See, for example, *Y Celt*, 19 Tachwedd 1886; 14 Ionawr, 30 Rhagfyr 1887.
50. Jones-Evans, 'Evan Pan Jones', pp.153–6. To this end he founded *Cwrs y Byd* in 1891.
51. 'Bleeding the common people'. Elwyn L. Jones, *Gwaedu Gwerin* (Dinbych, 1983).

52. *Baner ac Amserau Cymru*, 6 Tachwedd 1886 (letter from 'Un yn Teimlo').
53. Ibid., 17 Tachwedd 1886.
54. Ibid., 20 Tachwedd, 1 Rhagfyr 1886 (letters from H. Roberts).
55. Ibid., 1 Rhagfyr 1886 (editorial note).
56. 'Colofn y Gweithwyr' struggled on to February 1887. It attracted few letters, and relied mainly on brief syndicated reports of labour movements and strikes in England.
57. For a reassessment of Gee's political philosophy and a realistic counterbalance to T. Gwynn Jones's hagiography, see Emyr Price, *Ail-gloriannu Thomas Gee* (Pamffledi Rhoslas I, 1977), esp. p.7.
58. The idea was aired in *Baner ac Amserau Cymru*, 1 Mehefin, 20 Gorffennaf, 21 Medi 1887. Gee also urged the farmers to include farm labourers in their societies.
59. W.R.P. George, *The Making of Lloyd George* (London, 1976), pp.163–4. Letter from D. Lloyd George to Howel Gee, 7 November 1887.
60. Emyr Price, 'Newyddiadur Cyntaf David Lloyd George', *The Journal of the Welsh Bibliographical Society*, XI (1975–6), pp.210–11.
61. N. Masterman, *The Forerunner* (Llandybïe, 1972), pp.94–101.
62. 'Adfyfr' (T.J. Hughes), *Landlordism in Wales* (Cardiff, 1887).
63. Ibid., pp.43–5.
64. *Baner ac Amserau Cymru*, 21, 28 Rhagfyr 1887 (editorials). Lloyd George supported meetings of the League at Pwllheli and Porthmadog, see ibid., 26, 30 Mai 1888. See also Emyr Price, 'Lloyd George a "Rhyfel y Degwm" yn Llŷn ac Eifionydd 1886–8', *Caernarvonshire Historical Society Transactions*, 39, 1978, pp.164–8.
65. *Y Celt*, 30 Rhagfyr 1887.
66. *Baner ac Amserau Cymru*, 28 Ionawr 1888.
67. Ibid., 23, 30 Tachwedd, 28 Rhagfyr 1887 (letters from 'Cilanwr').
68. *Cambria Daily Leader*, 14 February 1888.
69. R.E. Prothero, *The Anti-Tithe Agitation in Wales* (London, 1889), pp.3–4.
70. See *Western Mail*, 18 February 1888 (editorial) and E. Pan Jones's comments in *Y Celt*, 21 Chwefror 1890.
71. *Baner ac Amserau Cymru*, 1 Mehefin (Gohebydd Llanbedr), 15 Mehefin 1889 (letter from 'Jones y Gweithiwr').
72. *Y Werin*, 27 Mehefin 1891 (letter from John Jones).

Chapter II

1. L.J. Williams, 'The New Unionism in South Wales, 1889–92', *Welsh History Review*, 1, No. 4 (1963) P.W. Donovan, 'A History of Unskilled Labour Unions in South Wales 1889–1914', (unpublished M.Phil. thesis, London, 1969).
2. *South Wales Daily News*, 8 October 1890 (letter from 'Hodge'), 11 October 1890 (letter from 'A.T.').
3. Ibid., 9 July 1890. Interview with Ben Tillett and Tom Mann.
4. Quoted in Williams, 'New Unionism', p.417.
5. P.L.R. Horn, 'Agricultural labourers' trade unionism in four midland counties, 1860–1900', (unpublished Ph.D. thesis, Leicester, 1968), pp.280–8.
6. J.P.D. Dunbabin, *Rural Discontent in Nineteenth-Century Britain* (London, 1974), ch.4.
7. Felicity Carlton, 'The Kent and Sussex Labourers' Union 1872–95' in A. Charlesworth (ed.), *An Atlas of Rural Protest in Britain 1548–1900* (London 1983), pp.173–7.
8. TUC *Annual Report*, 1890, pp.27–8; also *South Wales Daily News*, 8 September 1890.
9. *Y Cymro*, 11 Medi 1890 (editorial).

10. For an account of his career see also R. Maldwyn Thomas and Cyril Parry, 'John Owen Jones, "Ap Ffarmwr" 1861–1899', *Transactions of the Anglesey Antiquarian Society* (1967), pp.72–108.
11. *Y Genedl Gymreig*, 3, 10, 17, 28 Chwefror 1886.
12. Ibid., 24 Hydref, 19 Rhagfyr 1883; 27 Chwefror, 16 Ebrill, 7 Mai 1884.
13. Ibid., 29 Gorffennaf, 5, 12, 26 Awst, 16 Medi 1885.
14. *North Wales Observer and Express*, 11, 25 October, 8, 15 November 1889.
15. *Y Werin*, 2 Tachwedd 1889.
16. Ibid., 23, 30 Tachwedd, 7, 14, 21 Rhagfyr 1889 ('Gweision Ffarmwrs').
17. Ibid., 4 Ionawr 1890 (letter from 'Llafurwr').
18. Ibid., 11 Ionawr 1890.
19. *Royal Commission on Labour. The Agricultural Labourer*. Vol.II, Wales, 1893–4. Report by D. Lleufer Thomas on the Poor Law Union of Anglesey (31 December 1892), p.128.
20. Ibid., p.130.
21. *Y Werin*, 1,8 Chwefror 1890 (editorials).
22. Ibid., 8, 15, 22 Chwefror, 1, 8 Mawrth 1890. *The North Wales Observer and Express*, 11 April 1890, noted how 'letters from labourers, not too elegantly written' poured into the office.
23. *Y Werin*, 8 Mawrth 1890. The local Board school overflowed with farm labourers.
24. Ibid., 15 Mawrth 1890.
25. Ibid., 22 Mawrth 1890.
26. Ibid., 29 Mawrth 1890 (letter from Owen Thomas).
27. Ibid., 29 Mawrth 1890 (letter from David Rees).
28. *North Wales Observer and Express*, 11 April 1890; *Y Werin*, 12 Ebrill 1890.
29. *Y Werin*, 12 Ebrill 1890 (editorial).
30. Ibid., 12 Ebrill 1890 (letter from ap Ffarmwr).
31. Ibid., 1 Mawrth 1890.
32. Ibid., 22, 29 Mawrth, 5, 12, 19, 26 Ebrill 1890; *Yr Herald Cymraeg*, 29 Ebrill 1890.
33. *Royal Commission on Labour*, 1893–4, op. cit., Report by D. Lleufer Thomas on the Poor Law Union of Pwllheli (6 February 1893), pp.146–7.
34. *Y Werin*, 29 Mawrth 1890.
35. Ibid., 12 Ebrill 1890; Emyr Price, 'Lloyd George's pre-parliamentary political career' (unpublished M.A. thesis, Bangor, 1974), p.234.
36. *Cambrian News*, 4 April 1890.
37. Ibid., 25 April, 2 May 1890; *Royal Commission on Labour*, 1893–4, op. cit., Report by D. Lleufer Thomas on the Poor Law Union of Dolgellau (27 October 1892), p.104.
38. *Royal Commission on Labour*, 1893–4, op. cit, Report by D. Lleufer Thomas on the Poor Law Union of Ruthin (30 November 1892), p.113.
39. Ibid., p.118.
40. *Y Werin*, 19 Ebrill 1890.
41. Ibid., 19 Ebrill 1890 (editorial).
42. Ibid., 3, 10 Mai; *Yr Herald Cymraeg*, 6, 13 Mai; *Y Genedl Gymreig*, 30 Ebrill, 14 Mai 1890.
43. *Y Werin*, 10 Mai 1890.
44. *Yr Herald Cymraeg*, 20 Mai 1890.
45. *Y Werin*, 31 Mai 1890 (letter from 'Moses').
46. Ibid., 26 Ebrill 1890 (letter from ap Ffarmwr).
47. Ibid., 26 Ebrill 1890 (letters from Thomas Williams and 'Clorianwr').
48. *Holyhead Mail and Anglesey Herald*, 21 August 1890.
49. *Y Werin*, 3 Mai 1890 (letter from ap Ffarmwr).
50. *Gwalia*, 23 Ebrill 1890 (letter from R.R. Roberts).
51. *Y Werin*, 10 Mai 1890 (letter from ap Ffarmwr).

52. Ibid., 10 Mai 1890.
53. Ibid., 17, 24, 31 Mai, 7 Mehefin 1890 ('Cwestiwn yr Undeb').
54. Ibid., 21 Mehefin 1890 (letter from ap Ffarmwr).
55. Ibid., 12 Gorffennaf, 9 Awst 1890.
56. Ibid., 19 Gorffennaf, 23 Awst 1890 (letters from ap Ffarmwr).
57. Ibid., 6 Medi, 4 Hydref, 1890.
58. Ibid., 27 Medi 1890.
59. *South Wales Daily News*, 23 June 1890.
60. *Y Celt*, 25 Ebrill 1890.
61. *Y Llan*, 3 Ebrill 1890 (editorial).
62. *Y Goleuad*, 20 Tachwedd 1890 (editorial).
63. *Y Cymro*, 11 Medi 1890.
64. Ibid., 2 Hydref 1890.
65. For the background, see David A. Pretty, *Anglesey Schools*, pp.190–203.
66. *Y Werin*, 20, 27 Medi 1890.
67. Ibid., 11 Hydref 1890.
68. *North Wales Chronicle*, 18 October 1890.
69. *Y Werin*, 18, 25 Hydref 1890 (letters from 'Gweithiwr' and 'Hen Weithiwr').
70. Ibid., 23 Awst, 11 Hydref 1890 (letters from ap Ffarmwr and R.H. Thomas).
71. See 'A Scribe, A Pharisee and a Lawyer', *The Welsh Pulpit* (London, 1894), p.143. 'A Scribe' bears the unmistakable imprint of ap Ffarmwr.
72. *Y Werin*, 28 Mehefin 1890.
73. 'A Scribe, A Pharisee and a Lawyer', op. cit., p.143.
74. *Y Werin*, 26 Ebrill 1890 (letter from ap Ffarmwr).
75. David Thomas, *Diolch am Gael Byw* (Lerpwl, 1968), p.44.
76. *Y Werin*, 7 Mawrth 1891 (letter from ap Ffarmwr).
77. Ibid., 14, 21, 28 Mawrth, 4 Ebrill 1891.
78. *Baner ac Amserau Cymru*, 15 Ebrill 1891.
79. *Y Werin*, 25 Ebrill 1891.
80. Ibid., 11 Ebrill 1891.
81. *Holyhead Mail and Anglesey Herald*, 6 May 1891; *Y Werin*, 9 Mai 1891.
82. University College of North Wales, Bangor MSS, Papurau R.H. Thomas, Pentraeth, 1586, c.49. (ap Ffarmwr i R.H. Thomas, 2 Mehefin 1891).
83. *Y Werin*, 26 Medi 1891.
84. Ibid., 11, 25 Ebrill, 2 Mai 1891.
85. Ibid., 2 Mai 1891.
86. *Royal Commission on Labour*, 1893–4, op. cit. Report by D. Lleufer Thomas on the Poor Law Union of Pwllheli, p.151.
87. *Y Werin*, 18 Ebrill 1891.
88. *Royal Commission on Labour*, 1893–4, op. cit. Report by Roger C. Richards on the Monmouth Union (26 October 1892), p.69.
89. Ibid., Report by D. Lleufer Thomas on the Bridgend and Cowbridge Union (27 May 1892), p.48.
90. Ibid., Report by C. Chapman on the Builth Union (n.d.), pp.166, 172; ibid., Report by D. Lleufer Thomas on the Poor Law Union of Llanfyllin (27 September 1892), p.87.
91. See Pamela Horn, *The Tithe War in Pembrokeshire* (Fishguard, 1982).
92. H.A. Clegg, A. Fox, A.F. Thompson, *A History of British Trade Unions since 1889*, Vol. 1 (Oxford, 1964), pp.65–6, 79.
93. An obscure figure, Hazell was writing on behalf of the Pembroke Dock Labourers' Union in the early 1890s. *South Wales Daily News*, 20, 26 March 1890.
94. *Pembroke Dock and Pembroke Gazette*, 9 July 1891.

95. *Haverfordwest and Milford Haven Telegraph*, 20 May, 3 June 1891 (letters from Robert Hazell).

96. *Pembrokeshire Times*, 2 July 1891 (letter from 'A friend of the labourer'), 9 July 1891 (letter from 'Beryl' — but obviously Hazell in that he answers the charges laid against him).

97. Ibid., 4 June 1891.

98. *Haverfordwest and Milford Haven Telegraph*, 24 June 1891.

99. *Pembroke Dock and Pembroke Gazette*, 9 July 1891.

100. *Pembrokeshire Times*, 9 June 1892. The entrance fee was 1*s*. and the weekly subscription 2*d*.

101. *Royal Commission on Labour*, 1893–4, op. cit., Report by D. Lleufer Thomas on the Narberth Union (5 August 1892), pp.65, 69; also *Pembrokeshire Times*, 9 June 1892.

102. He led strikes of Pembroke Corporation labourers and Hook colliers in September 1891.

103. Clegg *et al., British Trade Unions*, p.83.

104. *Haverfordwest and Milford Haven Telegraph*, 2 March 1892.

105. *Y Werin*, 27 Mehefin 1891 (letter from John Jones).

106. R. Merfyn Jones, *The North Wales Quarrymen 1874–1922* (Cardiff, 1982), p.117.

107. *Royal Commission on Labour*, 1893–4, op. cit., 134–5.

108. Ibid., Summary Report by D. Lleufer Thomas (28 February 1893), pp.30–1.

109. Ibid., Report by D. Lleufer Thomas on the Narberth Union, p.71; *Haverfordwest and Milford Haven Telegraph*, 18 May 1892.

110. *Royal Commission on Labour*, 1893–4, op. cit., Summary Report, p.30.

111. *Y Clorianydd*, 2 Mehefin 1892.

112. Ibid., 9 Mehefin 1892.

113. *Y Werin*, 11 Mehefin 1892 (editorial).

114. *Y Genedl Gymreig*, 15 Mehefin 1892 (editorial).

115. *Y Werin*, 22 Hydref 1892 (letter from 'Cymro').

116. *Royal Commission on Labour*, 1893–4, op. cit., p.127.

117. Ibid., p.139 (Appendix C).

118. *Y Werin*, 12 Tachwedd 1892.

119. *Y Geninen*, Gorffennaf 1892, Ionawr 1893 ('Y Tir a'r Genedl').

120. American author of *Progress and Poverty*. George's second tour of England (1884) coincided with the start of ap Ffarmwr's journalistic career in London.

121. *Y Geninen*, 1893, p.111. What ap Ffarmwr offered was a synthesis of existing socialist propaganda in the Welsh language.

122. *Y Werin*, 18 Chwefror 1893.

123. *Holyhead Mail and Anglesey Herald*, 8, 22 December 1892.

124. Ibid., 12 January 1893.

125. *Y Werin*, 18 Chwefror 1893.

126. Ibid., 4, 11, 18, 25 Mawrth 1893.

127. Ibid., 15 Ebrill 1893 (letter from ap Ffarmwr).

128. *Y Genedl Gymreig*, 16 Mai 1893.

129. UCNW Bangor MSS, Papurau R.H. Thomas, Pentraeth, 1586, c.50–55. Letters with background details.

130. *Y Werin*, 27 Mai 1893 (letter from ap Ffarmwr).

131. Ibid., 20 Mai 1893.

132. Ibid., 17 Mehefin, 1, 22 Gorffennaf 1893 (letters from Owen Hughes).

133. Ibid., 9 Medi, 17 Tachwedd 1893 (letters from ap Ffarmwr.)

134. *Royal Commission on Labour*, 1893–4, op. cit., Summary Report, pp.33–4.

135. *Royal Commission on Land in Wales and Monmouthshire*, Vol.5 (1896), Report, p.928.

136. Ibid., p.609.
137. Ibid., Vol.3 (1895) Evidence, pp.505–10.
138. *Y Celt*, 18 Mawrth, 29 Ebrill 1892.
139. Under the pen name 'Deio'r Gwas', e.g. *Cwrs y Byd* Ebrill 1893; Chwefror, Medi 1894.
140. *Cwrs y Byd*, Ebrill 1892, Awst 1893.
141. *Y Celt*, 12 Ionawr 1894 (letter from 'Gweithiwr Caled').
142. *Royal Commission on Land in Wales and Monmouthshire*, Vol.2 (1894), Evidence, pp.148–53, 213–16.
143. Ibid., Vol.2 (1894), p.151, q.20,903.
144. Ibid., Vol.2 (1894), p.153, q.20,939.
145. *Y Genedl Gymreig*, 8 Mai 1894.
146. *Y Werin*, 12 Mai 1894 (letter from ap Ffarmwr).
147. See Groves, *Sharpen the Sickle*, p.87–8.
148. D. Lleufer Thomas, 'The Agricultural Labourer in Wales.' *Report of the Proceedings of the Eighth Poor Law Conference for the South Wales and Monmouthshire District, Swansea, 6 and 7 May 1897*, p.132.
149. 'A Scribe, A Pharisee and a Lawyer', pp.117–56, 'The Pulpit and Life'.
150. Ibid., p.117.
151. Cyril Parry, *The Radical Tradition in Welsh Politics* (Hull, 1970), p.13.
152. Horn, *Joseph Arch*, p.159; Groves, *Sharpen the Sickle*, p.89. As a loyal Liberal MP, Arch kept aloof from the Socialists.
153. *Y Geninen*, Ionawr 1893, p.35.
154. Conversely, Pan Jones did little to publicize ap Ffarmwr's mission and his death went unrecorded in the labour monthly *Cwrs y Byd.*
155. *Y Clorianydd*, 8, 15, 22 Chwefror 1894.
156. *Y Werin*, 20, 27 Hydref 1894.
157. *Y Clorianydd*, 13 Rhagfyr 1894.
158. Ibid., 14 Mawrth 1895.
159. Ibid., 3, 17, 24 Chwefror, 3 Mawrth 1898.
160. Ibid., 19 Mai 1898.
161. *North Wales Chronicle*, 21 October 1899.
162. David Thomas, *Diolch am Gael Byw*, p.44.

Chapter III

1. *South Wales Daily News*, 15 January 1912.
2. Cyril Parry, 'The Independent Labour Party and Gwynedd Politics 1900–20'. *Welsh History Review*, 4, No.1 (June 1968), 53.
3. Morgan, *Wales in British Politics*, pp.240–55.
4. Jones, *North Wales Quarrymen*, pp.315–21. The NWQU did not affiliate until 1920.
5. R. Page Arnot, *South Wales Miners* (London, 1967), pp.374–5.
6. Donovan, 'Unskilled labour unions' (unpub. thesis), p.178.
7. Workers' Union, *Record*, May 1914, p.7.
8. R. Hyman, *The Workers' Union* (Oxford, 1971), pp.45–8.
9. Workers' Union, *Record*, June 1916, p.9.
10. Dock, Wharf, Riverside and General Labourers' Union *Annual Report*, 1914, p.83.
11. Workers' Union, *Annual Report*, 1913. Modern Records Centre, University of Warwick Library, MSS 51 (Workers' Union) Working Papers for Dr R. Hyman's study.

12. National Union of Railwaymen, *Annual Report*, 1912, pp.99–101.
13. Donovan, 'Unskilled labour unions' (unpub. thesis), p.197.
14. *Y Dinesydd Cymreig*, 7 Ionawr 1914.
15. *Montgomery County Times*, 2 March, 24 August 1918.
16. A. Clinton, 'Trades Councils from the beginning of the 20th century to the Second World War' (unpublished Ph.D. thesis, London, 1973), Appendix 2.
17. Morgan, *Rebirth of a Nation*, pp.142–5.
18. M.J. Daunton, *Coal Metropolis, Cardiff 1870–1914* (Leicester, 1977), p.178.
19. *South Wales Daily News*, 9 November 1914.
20. The title of F.E. Green's book (London, 1913).
21. *Carmarthen Weekly Reporter*, 1 March 1912. After holding a meeting the men decided to go back to work.
22. M. Madden, 'The National Union of Agricultural Workers 1906–1956 (A study in the development of the policies of leadership)' (unpublished B.Litt. thesis, Oxford, 1956), pp.1–8.
23. Alun Howkins, *Poor Labouring Men: Rural Radicalism in Norfolk 1872–1923* (London, 1985), pp.103–13.
24. Groves, *Sharpen the Sickle*, p.127.
25. *Y Clorianydd*, 18 Hydref 1900.
26. Ibid., 10 Ebrill 1902.
27. Ibid., 6 Tachwedd 1902 (letter from 'Gweithiwr').
28. Ibid., 7, 14, 21, 28 Mai 1903.
29. Ibid., 15 Chwefror 1906 (letter from Thomas Rowlands).
30. Ibid., 28 Mawrth 1907.
31. Ibid., 1 Awst 1907 (letter from 'ap Dafydd').
32. Ibid., 18 Gorffennaf, 22 Awst 1907 (letters from 'Gweithiwr o Fôn').
33. Ibid., 27 Awst 1908.
34. Ibid., 3 Medi 1908 (letter from 'ap Dafydd').
35. Ibid., 14 Ionawr, 11 Mawrth 1909 (letters from 'Iorwerth').
36. Ibid., 27 Mai 1909.
37. Huw T. Edwards, *It was my Privilege* (Denbigh, 1957), p.25.
38. *Y Wyntyll*, 26 Awst 1909 (letter from John Eames).
39. *Labour Leader*, 2 July 1909 (letter from 'W').
40. Ibid., 9 July 1909 (letter from Hugh Pritchard).
41. *Y Wyntyll*, 30 Medi 1909.
42. Ibid., 21, 28 Hydref 1909.
43. Ibid., 11 Tachwedd 1909.
44. Ibid., 13 Ionawr 1910.
45. PRO F.S. 11/133. Rules of Undeb Gweithwyr Môn.
46. *Y Clorianydd*, 18, 25 Ebrill 1912 ('Colofn Llafur').
47. *Y Wyntyll*, 16 Mai 1912 (letter from Cyril O. Jones).
48. *Y Dinesydd Cymreig*, 26 Mehefin 1912.
49. *Y Wyntyll*, 19 Medi, 14 Tachwedd 1912.
50. *Y Clorianydd*, 4, 11, 18 Gorffennaf 1912 ('Colofn Llafur').
51. Ibid., 18 Gorffennaf 1912; *Y Wyntyll*, 23 Gorffennaf 1912 (letters from 'Iorwerth').
52. *Y Clorianydd*, 1 Awst 1912 (letter from 'Iorwerth').
53. *Y Wyntyll*, 1 Awst 1912 (letter from 'ap Dafydd').
54. Ibid., 29 Awst 1912 (report by Hugh Pritchard).
55. *Y Clorianydd*, 19 Chwefror 1913 (letter from 'Iorwerth').
56. *Y Dinesydd Cymreig*, 7 Mai 1913; *Y Wyntyll*, 8 Mai 1913.
57. PRO F.S. 11/133. Annual Return, 14 October 1913. At the beginning of the year it had only 37 members on its books.

58. Thomas, *Diolch am Gael Byw*, pp.27, 38.
59. Ibid., p.39.
60. UCNW Bangor MSS, Papurau David Thomas, 19161. List of ILP members.
61. Ibid., 19181. The words of J. Watt, 1 October 1913.
62. NLW, David Thomas (Bangor) Collection, letter from E. Pan Jones, 29 Medi 1909.
63. *Labour Leader*, 7 July 1911.
64. e.g. *Y Dinesydd Cymreig*, 1 Hydref, 17 Rhagfyr 1913.
65. Thomas, *Diolch am Gael Byw*, p.44.
66. UCNW Bangor, Papurau David Thomas 18975.
67. Ibid., 19159. ILP notebook kept by David Thomas, (c.1910–13).
68. *Y Genedl Gymreig*, 21 Mai 1912.
69. *Glamorgan Gazette*, 5 April, 10 May 1912.
70. It was advertised nationally, e.g. *Baner ac Amserau Cymru*, 18 Medi 1912.
71. The file of the Society was destroyed under authority in 1963, but it is known that the Society had been transferred to the Prudential Approved Society in 1917.
72. *South Wales Daily News*, 11 October 1913.
73. *Y Genedl Gymreig*, 2 Gorffennaf, 6 Awst 1912.
74. H.V. Emy, 'The Land Campaign: Lloyd George as a social reformer 1909–14' in A.J.P. Taylor (ed.), *Lloyd George: Twelve Essays* (London, 1971).
75. *The Report of the Welsh Land Enquiry Committee* (London, 1914).
76. Ibid., p.224.
77. *Y Dinesydd Cymreig*, 15, 22 Mai, 24 Gorffennaf, 14 Awst, 18 Medi 1912.
78. Ibid., 20 Tachwedd 1912.
79. Ibid., 12 Mehefin 1912.
80. Ibid., 19 Chwefror 1913.
81. Ibid., 9 Gorffennaf 1913.
82. UCNW Bangor, Papurau David Thomas, 19184 (letter from Morris N. Jones, 11 September 1913).
83. Gwynedd Archives Service, Caernarfon (GAS), XNWQU 298. Minute Book of the Caernarfonshire Labour Council 1912–27.
84. Ibid., Meeting, 22 Chwefror 1913.
85. Ibid., Meeting, 19 Mai 1913.
86. UCNW Bangor, Papurau David Thomas, 19184 (letter from R.B. Walker, 8 August 1913).
87. Reading, Records of the NUAAW, Executive Committee Minutes B/1/3. 15 June 1912.
88. *Wrexham Advertiser*, 1 March 1913.
89. A. Mutch, 'Rural Society in Lancashire 1840–1914' (unpublished Ph.D. thesis, University of Manchester, 1980), ch.8.
90. *Wrexham Advertiser*, 28 June 1913; *Y Dinesydd Cymreig*, 30 Gorffennaf 1913.
91. *Holyhead Chronicle*, 7, 28 February, 25 April, 23, 30 May 1913.
92. Ibid., 11, 25 April 1913.
93. Ibid., 5, 19 September 1913. Six unions were affiliated.
94. Ibid., 18 July 1913.
95. Ibid., 9 January 1914.
96. UCNW Bangor, Papurau David Thomas 19186 (letter from Edward Pritchard, 2 Ebrill 1914).
97. *Y Dinesydd Cymreig*, 18 Mawrth 1914.
98. Ibid., 27 Mai 1914.
99. UCNW Bangor, Papurau David Thomas, 19184 (letter from W.B. Jones, 11 April 1913).

100. Interview with Philip Snowden Foulkes (son), 29 May 1980.
101. Also a stonemason named John Foulkes, see *Baner ac Amserau Cymru*, 12 Mai 1888, 25 Ebrill 1933.
102. NLW David Thomas (Bangor) Collection (letters from John Foulkes, Awst, 1, 23 Medi 1911).
103. UCNW Bangor, Papurau David Thomas 19184 (letter from John Foulkes, 14 Awst 1913); also *Y Dinesydd Cymreig*, 20 Awst 1913.
104. *Dyddiadur a Llawlyfr y Bedyddwyr*, 1938, pp.136–7.
105. UCNW Bangor, Papurau David Thomas 19184 (letter from R.B. Walker, 8 August 1913); also *Y Dinesydd Cymreig*, 2 Medi 1913.
106. UCNW Bangor, Papurau David Thomas 19184 (letter from J.E. Edwards, 8 Medi 1913).
107. Ibid., (letter from John Foulkes, 6 Hydref 1913).
108. Ibid., (letter from John Foulkes, 9 Ebrill 1914).
109. PRO F.S. 11/133, Annual Return, 15 August 1914.
110. UCNW Bangor, Papurau David Thomas, 19185 (letter from R.B. Walker, 24 July 1914).
111. D.P. Evans had arranged meetings at Bettws, Llaneilian and Abergele, see ibid. (letter from D.P. Evans, 16 June 1914).
112. Ibid., (letter from Edward Pritchard, 5 October 1914).
113. Ibid., (letters from R.B. Walker, 14, 23 October 1914).
114. Reading, Records of the NUAAW, Executive Committee Minutes, B/1/4, 31 October 1914.
115. Ibid., 9 January 1915.
116. *Holyhead Chronicle*, 20 March 1914.
117. UCNW Bangor MSS 19300, Minute Book of the North Wales Trades and Labour Council, Circular, June 1914.
118. *The Labourer*, February 1915.
119. Minute Book of the North Wales Trades and Labour Council, op. cit. Report of the Conference.
120. *Holyhead Chronicle*, 11 September 1914.
121. Minute Book of the Caernarfonshire Labour Council 1912–27, op. cit., November 1914.
122. *Y Wyntyll*, 11 Chwefror 1915.
123. UCNW Bangor, Papurau David Thomas 19189 (letters from R.B. Walker, 18 February, 17 March 1915).
124. Ibid., (letter from Ivor H. Thomas, 14 April 1915). Why the union had consulted the secretary of the Mid Glamorgan Federation of the ILP is not clear.
125. Ibid., (letter from R.B. Walker, 28 April 1915).
126. Ibid., (letter from J. Fred Jones, 21 June 1915).
127. PRO F.S. 11/133. Annual Return, 26 June 1916.
128. UCNW Bangor. Papurau David Thomas 19189 (letter from R.B. Walker, 21 September 1915).
129. Ibid., (letter from R.B. Walker, 21 September 1915).
130. Reading, Records of the NUAAW, Executive Committee Minutes, B/1/4, 28 August 1915.
131. *South Wales Daily News*, 18 January, 13 March, 15 October 1913 (editorials).
132. Ibid., 24 July, 4 September 1913 (editorials).
133. *Haverfordwest and Milford Haven Telegraph*, 21 May 1913 (letter from 'Agricola').
134. *The Labourer*, October 1915.
135. Reading, Records of the NUAAW, Executive Committee Minutes, B/1/4, 30 May 1914.

136. S. Box, *The Good Old Days: Then and Now* (published by the author, 1955), p.2.
137. S. Box, *The Workers' Union in Herefordshire* (1925), p.3.
138. *Hereford Times*, 1 August 1914.
139. Ibid., 25 July 1914.
140. Workers' Union, *Annual Report*, 1915, p.23.
141. Workers' Union *Record*, September 1915, p.10.
142. Ibid., January 1916, p.6; March 1916, p.11.
143. UCNW Bangor, Papurau David Thomas MSS. 19885. 'An Economic and Social Survey of North Wales 1914–22' written by David Thomas, pp.182–4.
144. A. Marwick, *The Deluge: British Society and the First World War* (London, 1965) gives this theme the classic treatment.
145. Note the comments of A.D. Hall, *A Pilgrimage of British Farming 1910–12* (London, 1913), p.339.
146. *Wages and Conditions of Employment in Agriculture*, (1919) Cmd 24, Vol.1 (Wales), p.181.
147. Ashby and Evans, *Agriculture of Wales*, pp.74–5.
148. *Wages and Conditions of Employment in Agriculture*, (1919), op. cit., p.182.
149. Ibid., p.182.
150. Ibid., pp.190, 415.
151. Ibid., pp.398–9, 419, 431, 436–7.
152. Ibid., p.492.
153. Ibid., pp.456, 458, 476, 495.
154. Ibid., p.199.
155. Ibid., p.494.
156. Ibid., p.419.
157. Ibid., p.200.
158. *The Report of the Welsh Land Enquiry Committee*, op. cit., p.194.
159. *Wages and Conditions of Employment in Agriculture*, 1919, op. cit., p.191.
160. A.D. Hall, *A Pilgrimage of British Farming* (London 1913), p.338.
161. *The Report of the Welsh Land Enquiry Committee*, op. cit., p.216.
162. Ibid., p.211.
163. *Wages and Conditions of Employment in Agriculture*, 1919, op. cit., p.493.
164. *South Wales Daily News*, 5 March 1915.
165. *Holyhead Chronicle*, 30 June 1916.
166. *Denbighshire Free Press*, 29 July 1916.
167. G. Sherington, *English Education, Social Change and War 1911–20* (Manchester, 1981), p.49.
168. Board of Education, *School Attendance and Employment in Agriculture. Summary of Returns supplied by County Local Education Authorities of Children excused from School for Employment in Agriculture on 31 May 1916* (Cd 8302), viz. 503 boys, 92 girls.
169. *Holyhead Chronicle*, 23 April 1915.
170. *Wages and Conditions of Employment in Agriculture*, 1919, op. cit., p.468.
171. *Carmarthen Journal*, 3 March 1916.
172. *Wages and Conditions of Employment in Agriculture*, 1919, op. cit., pp. 188–9.
173. Ibid., pp.452–3.
174. Ibid., p.468.
175. Ibid., pp.408, 417, 429.
176. *Haverfordwest and Milford Haven Telegraph*, 3 March 1915.
177. Ibid., 10 March 1915 (editorial).
178. A.L. Bowley, *Prices and Wages in the United Kingdom, 1914–20* (Oxford, 1921), p.70.

179. *Report of the Committee appointed by the Agricultural Wages Board to enquire into the Financial Results of the Occupation of Agricultural Land and the Cost of Living of Rural Workers*, 1919 [Cmd 76], para. 128.
180. *Welsh Gazette*, 21 January 1915.
181. *Holyhead Chronicle*, 6 October 1916.
182. *North Wales Weekly News*, 13, 20 January 1916.
183. *County Echo*, 11 February 1916.
184. *Report of the Committee . . . Cost of Living of Rural Workers*, 1919, op. cit., para. 93.
185. Ashby and Evans, *Agriculture of Wales*, pp.15–16.
186. *Report of the Committee . . . Cost of Living of Rural Workers*, 1919, op. cit., para. 184, 192.
187. *Cambrian News*, 9 June 1916.
188. *Cardigan and Tivyside Advertiser*, 9 March 1917.
189. *Report of the Commission of Inquiry into Industrial Unrest*, No. 7 District — Wales and Monmouthshire, 1917 (Cd 8668), p.24.
190. *The Welshman*, 14 December 1917; *Carmarthen Journal*, 11 January 1918 (letter from 'A Voice from the Queue'); *County Echo*, 8 February 1917 ('Llythyr Jack y Gwas').
191. *Wages and Conditions of Employment in Agriculture*, 1919, op. cit., p.420.
192. *Welsh Gazette*, 15 February 1917.
193. Morgan, *Rebirth of a Nation*, p.164.
194. *Welsh Gazette*, 30 March 1916.
195. *Haverfordwest and Milford Haven Telegraph*, 25 October 1916.
196. *Pembroke County Guardian*, 16, 30 March 1917.
197. John Davies, 'The End of the Great Estates and the Rise of Freehold Farming in Wales', *Welsh History Review*, Vol. 7, December 1974, No. 2, p.192.
198. See A.D. Rees, *Life in a Welsh Countryside* (Cardiff, 1950), pp.142–3; D. Jenkins, 'Aberporth, a study of a coastal village in south Cardiganshire' in E. Davies and A.D. Rees, *Welsh Rural Communities* (Cardiff, 1960), pp.12–23; D. Jenkins, *The Agricultural Community in South-West Wales* (Cardiff, 1971), pp.166–71.
199. *Wages and Conditions of Employment in Agriculture*, 1919, op. cit., pp.202, 432.
200. *Welsh Gazette*, 24 May 1917 (editorial).
201. *Wages and Conditions of Employment in Agriculture*, 1919, op. cit., p.200.
202. Ibid., p.465.
203. *Social Problems in Wales* (Swansea, 1913?) Section III.
204. *Y Goleuad*, 24 Awst 1917; *Yr Herald Cymraeg*, 28 Awst 1917.
205. *Baner ac Amserau Cymru*, 20 Hydref 1917 (letter from 'Iago').
206. *Y Goleuad*, 12 Tachwedd 1913.
207. Ibid., 3 Rhagfyr 1913. This argument spilled over into the columns of the *South Wales Daily News*, 9, 13, 16, 19, 20 December 1913.
208. *Wages and Conditions of Employment in Agriculture*, 1919, op. cit., p.200.
209. Ibid., pp.419, 437, 443, 495–6.
210. Ibid., pp.182, 200.
211. Workers' Union, *Record*, July 1918.
212. Groves, *Sharpen the Sickle*, p.144.
213. TUC *Annual Report*, 1917, pp.373–4.
214. H. Pelling, *A History of British Trade Unionism* (London, 1963), p.262.
215. NUR, *Annual Report*, 1917, pp.19–21.
216. NLW, Edgar Chappell Papers (uncatalogued), evidence from the Workers' Union, 29 June 1917; letter from William Pugh, 23 June 1917; evidence from the NUGW, June 1917.
217. NALU, *Annual Report*, 1915.

218. NUGW, *Quarterly Report*, September–December 1917.
219. *Cardiganshire and Tivyside Advertiser*, 8 October 1915.
220. Ibid., 19 October 1917.
221. Ibid., 29 September 1917.
222. Ibid., 27 October, 3 November 1916.
223. Ibid., 24 November 1916.
224. *Welsh Gazette*, 26 July 1917.
225. F. McKenna, *The Railway Workers 1840–1970* (London, 1980), p.27.
226. Box, *Good Old Days*, p.3.
227. *The Land Worker*, July 1915, July 1916, April, July 1917; *Railway Review*, July, August 1917.
228. UCNW Bangor, Papurau David Thomas 19191 (letter from W.T. Bason, 1 May 1918); *Y Seren*, 29 Medi 1917 (letter from John Jones); *Yr Wythnos a'r Eryr*, 3 Hydref 1917 (letter from W.T. Bason).
229. *County Echo*, 9 August 1917.
230. *Pembroke County Guardian*, 14 July, 27 October 1916.
231. Peter Stead, 'Working Class Leadership in South Wales, 1900–1920', *Welsh History Review*, Vol. 6, June 1973, No. 3, 348.
232. *Wages and Conditions of Employment in Agriculture*, 1919, pp.425, 493.
233. *South Wales Daily News*, 9 November 1914, 15 February 1915, 14 June 1916.
234. Ibid., 4 December 1916.
235. UCNW Bangor, Papurau David Thomas 19187 (letters from William Harris, 28 June, 28 October, 2 December 1916).
236. *South Wales Weekly Argus*, 3 February 1917.
237. Ibid., 6, 13, 20 January 1917.
238. *Monmouthshire Beacon*, 11, 25 May 1917.
239. *Monmouthshire Weekly Post*, 9 June 1917.
240. UCNW Bangor, Papurau David Thomas, 19189 (circular) 'The Land Question in Monmouthshire. Organisation of the Agricultural Workers'.
241. Ibid., (letter from William Harris, 22 June 1917).
242. *Hansard*, 5th Series, Vol. XC, 23 February 1917; Vol. XCII, 5 April 1917.
243. Viz. E.T. John, R. McKenna, J. Williams. 19 voted against.
244. Although a separate Wages Board for Wales was being advocated (see *Welsh Outlook*, Vol. IV, No. 42, June 1917 [letter from Edgar L. Chappell]), no Welsh MP proposed an amendment to this effect.
245. *Wages and Conditions of Employment in Agriculture*, 1919, op. cit., pp. 190, 201.
246. Ibid., pp.409, 432.
247. See Cyril Parry, *The Radical Tradition in Welsh Politics*, op. cit., p.76.

Chapter IV

1. *South Wales Daily News*, 1 October 1917.
2. Reading, Records of the NUAAW, Executive Committee Minutes, B/1/4, 6 October, 1 December 1917.
3. *Merthyr Pioneer*, 20 October 1917.
4. *Monmouthshire Weekly Post*, 30 June 1917.
5. *South Wales Argus*, 31 July 1917.
6. *South Wales Weekly Argus*, 18 August 1917.
7. Ibid., 28 July 1917.
8. E.g. ibid., 28 July 1917; *South Wales Argus*, 15, 17 September 1917.

9. NLW, Edgar Chappell Papers (uncatalogued), Edgar Chappell to Geoffrey Drage, 16 February 1918.
10. E.g. *South Wales Argus*, 31 July 1917.
11. *South Wales Weekly Argus*, 15 September 1917.
12. NLW, Edgar Chappell Papers. Agricultural Wages Board 1918, Investigators' Diary 1, Monmouth: entry 1 February 1918.
13. *Monmouthshire Weekly Post*, 6 October, 24 November 1917.
14. *Wages and Conditions in Agriculture*, 1919, op. cit. p.477.
15. *Monmouthshire Evening Post*, 26 November, 31 December 1917.
16. *Pembrokeshire Herald*, 15 June 1917.
17. *Pembroke County Guardian*, 31 August 1917.
18. Ibid., 14 September 1917.
19. *Pembrokeshire Herald*, 21 September 1917 (letter from E.P. Harries).
20. *County Echo*, 20 September 1917.
21. *Pembroke County Guardian*, 24 March 1916.
22. *County Echo*, 9 August 1917.
23. For his personal testament note the speeches delivered at Goodwick and Letterston, ibid., 18 October 1917, 1 July 1920.
24. Ibid., 11 October 1917.
25. Ibid., 4, 25 October 1917.
26. *The Labourer*, October 1917.
27. *Pembrokeshire Herald*, 19 October 1917.
28. *County Echo*, 20 May 1920. D.T. Lewis was also the author of the weekly column, 'Labour Notes'.
29. *Pembrokeshire Herald*, 16 November 1917.
30. *Pembrokeshire County Guardian*, 23 November 1917.
31. Ibid., 26 October 1917; *County Echo*, 27 December 1917.
32. *Cardiganshire and Tivyside Advertiser*, 22 September, 13 October, 24 November 1916, 16 February 1917.
33. *Welsh Gazette*, 2 August–27 September 1917.
34. Ibid., 4 October 1917 (letter from 'Gweithiwr').
35. Ibid., 11 October 1917 (letter from T.E. Nicholas).
36. UCNW Bangor MSS. Papurau T.E. Nicholas 23359. Darn o Hunangofiant II, tt.3–4.
37. Ibid., III, p.1.
38. Cf. 'Paham y mae'r Werin yn Dlawd', *Y Geninen*, 1912, tt.156–7.
39. *Welsh Gazette*, 8 November 1917.
40. Ibid., 22, 29 November, 6 December 1917.
41. *Wages and Conditions of Employment in Agriculture*, 1919, op. cit., p.409.
42. *Brecon County Times*, 25 October 1917.
43. Cf. *Hereford Times*, 7 April 1928 (letter from S. Box).
44. Letter from F.W. Stokoe (brother) to the author, June 1980.
45. *Brecon County Times*, 6 December 1917.
46. *Merthyr Pioneer*, 8 December 1917.
47. *Y Dinesydd Cymreig*, 15 Awst 1917.
48. *Y Dinesydd Cymreig*, 1 Awst 1917; *Wrexham and District Trades and Labour Council Year Book*, 1918, p.36. With David Thomas as secretary it had 64 members.
49. Clwyd Record Office. DD/DM/344/1. Minutes of the General and Executive Committee of Wrexham Trades Council and Divisional Labour Party, 25 September 1917.
50. Minute Book of the Caernarfonshire Labour Council 1912–27, op. cit., 20 Hydref 1917.
51. *Y Clorianydd*, 23 Mai 1917.

52. PRO F.S. 11/ 133, Annual Returns 1916, 1917. Viz. Aberffraw, Bodffordd, Gwalchmai.
53. *Y Clorianydd*, 23 Mai 1917.
54. Ibid., 4, 11, 25 Gorffennaf, 1 Awst, 19 Medi 1917.
55. Personal information supplied by his son, Hugh Meredydd Jones, Llanfairpwll.
56. Notebook kept by Brynfab (in the possession of Hugh Meredydd Jones).
57. *Y Clorianydd*, 17 Hydref 1917.
58. *Y Wyntyll*, 25 Hydref 1917.
59. *Y Clorianydd*, 24 Hydref 1917.
60. 'Cofnodion Cangen Llanidan o Undeb Gweithwyr Môn', 27 Hydref 1917 (in the possession of Hugh Meredydd Jones).
61. *Y Wyntyll*, 1 Tachwedd 1917 (letter from 'Sylwedydd').
62. Ibid., 8 Tachwedd 1917 (letter from 'Iorwerth').
63. *Y Clorianydd*, 14 Tachwedd 1917.
64. *Y Wyntyll*, 15 Tachwedd 1917.
65. *Holyhead Chronicle*, 23 November 1917.
66. *Y Wyntyll*, 6 Rhagfyr 1917.
67. *Yr Herald Cymraeg*, 8, 16 Hydref 1917.
68. Ibid., 23 Hydref 1917.
69. Ibid., 30 Hydref 1917.
70. *Caernarvon and Denbigh Herald*, 2 November 1917.
71. Ibid., 9 November 1917.
72. Ibid., 16 November 1917. A report in *Yr Herald Cymraeg*, 13 Tachwedd 1917, claimed 1,200 members.
73. More than likely it was O. Ellis Jones who ran the column 'Byd Llafur' in *Yr Herald Cymraeg*, where the labourers' awakening received great attention.
74. *North Wales Pioneer*, 18 October, 1 November 1917.
75. *North Wales Weekly News*, 1 November 1917 (letter from 'Gwas').
76. Interview with Evan Weyman, Henryd, April 1980.
77. *North Wales Pioneer*, 8 November 1917.
78. *North Wales Weekly News*, 22 November 1917.
79. *Y Dinesydd Cymreig*, 28 Tachwedd 1917 (letter from 'Undebwr').
80. GAS, Caernarfon, Records of the North Wales Quarrymen's Union, XNWQU, 5, Union Minute Book 1912–21, 24 Tachwedd 1917.
81. *Y Genedl Gymreig*, 11 Rhagfyr 1917; *Y Dinesydd Cymreig*, 12 Rhagfyr 1917.
82. Personal details supplied by his son, Herbert J. Bason, Pontypridd, January 1980.
83. Personal details supplied by his son, Ivor G. Williams, Shrewsbury, December 1979.
84. *Yr Wythnos a'r Eryr*, 19 Medi 1917.
85. Ibid., 31 Hydref 1917.
86. *Y Seren*, 27 Hydref 1917 (notice).
87. *Yr Wythnos a'r Eryr*, 21 Tachwedd 1917.
88. Ibid., 28 Tachwedd 1917.
89. *Y Seren*, 8 Rhagfyr 1917.
90. *South Wales Daily News*, 11 October 1917.
91. *Montgomeryshire Express*, 9 October 1917.
92. *Wages and Conditions of Employment in Agriculture*, 1919, op. cit., pp.480, 485.
93. *Montgomery County Times*, 20 October 1917.
94. Enquiries by the author in the area proved fruitless.
95. *Montgomery County Times*, 29 December 1917.
96. *Montgomeryshire Express*, 1 January 1918 (letter from 'Looker On').
97. *Montgomery County Times*, 29 December 1917.

98. *Montgomeryshire Express*, 20, 27 November 1917.
99. I.e. cowmen, carters, bailiffs, stockmen, shepherds etc.
100. Viz. Anglesey and Caernarfon, Denbigh and Flint, Merioneth and Montgomery, Brecon and Radnor, Glamorgan and Monmouth, Pembroke, Cardigan and Carmarthen.
101. *Llandudno Advertiser*, 9 February 1918.
102. Madden, 'National Union of Agricultural Workers', p.299, Appendix C.
103. R. Hyman, *The Workers' Union*, op. cit., p.101.
104. TUC *Annual Report* 1918, pp.102–5.
105. NALRWU *Annual Report*, 1917, viz. Henryd, Llandudno Junction, Llanilar, Wrexham, Bala, Llanuwchllyn, Caer-went, Castleton, Catsash, Magor, Shirenewton, St Arvans, Castlemartin, Creswell, Croes-goch, Mathry, Merrion, Solva, St Nicholas.
106. Reading, Records of the NUAAW, Executive Committee Minutes, B/1/4, 15 December 1917, 5 January 1918.
107. NLW, Edgar Chappell Papers (D. Rees to Edgar Chappell, 25 January 1918).
108. *South Wales Daily News*, 25 January 1918.
109. *Glamorgan Gazette*, 1 February 1918.
110. *Merthyr Pioneer*, 16 February 1918.
111. *South Wales Daily News*, 18 February 1918.
112. *Cardiff Times and South Wales Weekly News*, 2 March 1918.
113. Enquiries on behalf of the Agricultural Wages Board, NLW, Edgar Chappell Papers (Edgar Chappell to G. Drage, Director of Investigations, 20 March 1918).
114. Ibid., Investigator's Diary III, 25 February 1918. Kennett probably gave the statements quoted in *Wages and Conditions of Employment in Agriculture*, 1919, op. cit., pp.452–3. (Quoted above, p.67.)
115. A bundle of letters relating to Kennett's case (February–March 1918) is to be found in the Edgar Chappell Papers. Chappell thought Kennett's evidence reliable but that he was something of a 'big romancer'. Other causes allegedly lay behind his sacking. David Rees felt the matter should be brought to court, yet nothing came of this.
116. *Monmouthshire Weekly Post*, 23 February 1918.
117. *South Wales Weekly Argus*, 30 March 1918.
118. Ibid., 15 June 1918.
119. *Pembroke County Guardian*, 14 March 1918.
120. NLW, Edgar Chappell Papers, Investigator's Diary VI, 13 April 1918.
121. *Pembroke County Guardian*, 22 March, 19 April 1918 (letter from 'A member of the Farmers' Union').
122. *Haverfordwest and Milford Haven Telegraph*, 6, 27 March 1918.
123. *Hansard*, 5th Series, Vol. 104, 21 March 1918, col.1198–9. No papers dealing with the case have survived.
124. Letter from Idwal Lloyd, Fishguard (son of John Lloyd) to the author, October 1980.
125. NLW, Edgar Chappell Papers (Evan James to Edgar Chappell, 21 January 1918).
126. *Wages and Conditions of Employment in Agriculture*, 1919, op. cit., p.420; NALU *Annual Report*, 1919, listed branches at Llangybi (44 members), and Ystwyth and Teifi (300 members).
127. *Dockers' Record*, February 1918; *Cardigan and Tivyside Advertiser*, 12 July 1918.
128. *Cardigan and Tivyside Advertiser*, 15 March 1918 (letter from 'Dafydd Iago').
129. Ibid., 29 March 1918.
130. NLW, Edgar Chappell Papers (T.E. Nicholas to Edgar Chappell, n.d. / March 1918?).

131. Ibid., (T.E. Nicholas to Edgar Chappell, n.d. / April 1918?)

132. *Welsh Gazette*, 28 March 1918. Remarks made at a meeting of the Cardiganshire Farmers' Union.

133. *Cardigan and Tivyside Advertiser*, 24 May 1918.

134. Ibid., 5, 12 July 1918; also NLW, Papers of the Revd D.J. Roberts, Cardigan (uncatalogued) which include Papurau y Parch D.D. Walters and the text of this lecture.

135. *Cardigan and Tivyside Advertiser*, 19 April 1918.

136. *Welshman*, 22 February 1918.

137. Interview with John Sharp, Llangynog (son), December 1979.

138. *Welshman*, 8 March 1918.

139. *Carmarthen Journal*, 29 March 1918; *Welshman*, 17 May 1918.

140. *Welshman*, 19 July 1918.

141. *South Wales Weekly Argus*, 22 December 1917.

142. *Brecon and Radnor Express*, 3 January 1918.

143. *Hereford Times*, 4 May 1918.

144. *Herefordshire Voice of Labour*, No. 1, May 1918.

145. *Brecon and Radnor Express*, 31 January 1918.

146. Ibid., 21 February 1918.

147. Ibid., 16 May 1918.

148. *North Wales Times*, 16 February 1918.

149. Ibid., 23 February 1918.

150. Ibid., 11 May 1918.

151. *Baner ac Amserau Cymru*, 9, 20 Mehefin, 6 Gorffennaf 1918.

152. Minutes of the General and Executive Committee of Wrexham Trades Council and Divisional Labour Party, op. cit., 9 April 1918.

153. *North Wales Pioneer*, 11 April 1918. W. Washington Owen had helped to set up the Aber branch in February, when 63 joined. *Yr Herald Cymraeg*, 19 Chwefror 1918.

154. Information supplied by Mrs Thomas, St Asaph (daughter), October 1979.

155. E.g. *Baner ac Amserau Cymru*, 7 Chwefror 1914.

156. *Flintshire Observer*, 10 January 1918 (letter from D.W. Jones).

157. *Baner ac Amserau Cymru*, 12 Ionawr 1918 (letter from D.W. Jones). The union published at least one pamphlet in Welsh, cf. UCNW Bangor, Papurau David Thomas, 19291.

158. *Flintshire Observer*, 7, 21 February, 14 March 1918.

159. Ibid., 4 April 1918.

160. Ibid., 25 April 1918.

161. Ibid., 9 May 1918.

162. *Yr Adsain*, 5 Mawrth 1918 (advertisement).

163. *Y Genedl Gymreig*, 22 Ionawr 1918.

164. *Yr Wythnos a'r Eryr*, 30 Ionawr 1918.

165. *Y Rhedegydd*, 15 Mehefin 1918 (advertisement).

166. *North Wales Weekly News*, 31 January 1918.

167. *Montgomeryshire Express*, 22 January 1918 (letter from 'An Agricultural Workman').

168. Ibid., 22 January 1918. 40 joined the union.

169. *Montgomery County Times*, 26 January 1918.

170. Ibid., 26 January 1918 (editorial).

171. *Baner ac Amserau Cymru*, 2 Chwefror 1918; *Montgomeryshire Express*, 12, 19 February 1918.

172. Letter from Iorwerth C. Peate (son) to the author, November 1979.

173. *Wages and Conditions of Employment in Agriculture*, 1919, op. cit., p.481.

174. *Montgomery County Times*, 2 March 1918.
175. Ibid., 27 April 1918, viz. Towyn, Llanegryn, Bryn-crug and Abergynolwyn.
176. *Yr Herald Cymraeg*, 8 Ionawr 1918.
177. The entrance fee was 6*d*. and the weekly contribution 3*d*.
178. Notes of the recollections of William Long, Brynsiencyn on 'The Start of the Labour Party in Anglesey' supplied by Emily Long (daughter), August 1979.
179. *Y Wyntyll*, 10 January 1918.
180. *Y Clorianydd*, 20 Chwefror 1918.
181. *Y Wyntyll*, 30 Ionawr 1918 (article by Brynfab).
182. *Y Clorianydd*, 22 Mai 1918; *Y Wyntyll*, 23 Mai 1918.
183. *Y Wyntyll*, 30 Mai 1918.
184. Cf. *Welsh Outlook*, February 1918, p.38.
185. *Y Dinesydd Cymreig*, 15 Mai 1918.
186. Ibid., 6 Mawrth 1918.
187. UCNW Bangor, Papurau David Thomas, 19258 (J.E. Thomas to David Thomas, 8 March 1918).
188. Ibid., 19258 (J.E. Thomas to David Thomas, n.d. / late March).
189. R.G. Roberts had left the manganese quarry at Rhiw to restart at Tal-y-sarn slate quarry.
190. UCNW Bangor, Papurau David Thomas, 19258 (J.E. Thomas to David Thomas, 1 May 1918); *Y Dinesydd Cymreig*, 1 Mai 1918.
191. *Y Dinesydd Cymreig*, 29 Mai 1918.
192. Letter from Caradog Jones to the author, October 1978, and subsequent interview.
193. *Y Dinesydd Cymreig*, 19 Mehefin, 10 Gorffennaf 1918. By now the paper carried a special column — 'Colofn y Gweithwyr Amaethyddol' — written by R.G. Roberts.
194. Ibid., 11 Rhagfyr 1918 (editorial).
195. Reading, Records of the NUAAW, Executive Committee Minutes, B/1/4, 6 July 1918.
196. A widower since 1914, he was left with eight young children. Letter from R. Glyn Roberts, Pen-y-groes (son) to the author, December 1977.
197. *Y Dinesydd Cymreig*, 31 Gorffennaf 1918.
198. Reading, Records of the NUAAW, Executive Committee Minutes, B/1/4, 10 August 1918.
199. *John Davies* (Gregynog Press, printed privately, n.d. 1938?).
200. Reading, Records of the NUAAW, Executive Committee Minutes, B/1/4, 10 August 1918.
201. Viz. Bangor-on-Dee, Bettisfield and Hanmer. Cf. *The Labourer*, January 1916 which reported on Lunnon's earlier (but abortive) drive into Flintshire.
202. *Y Dinesydd Cymreig*, 4, 11, 18 Medi 1918.
203. Ibid., 28 Awst 1918.
204. Ibid., 28 Awst 1918.
205. NALRWU *Annual Report*, 1918.
206. *North Wales Weekly News*, 10 October 1918.
207. *Y Dinesydd Cymreig*, 10 Gorffennaf 1918.
208. *Y Seren*, 12 Hydref 1918.
209. *Carmarthen Journal*, 3 May, 14 June 1918.
210. *Pembroke County Guardian*, 6 December 1918; *County Echo*, 3 April 1919. The NFU had 1,600 members.
211. Computed from the accounts of local meetings reported in the *Welsh Gazette* and *Cardigan and Tivyside Advertiser*, November 1917–October 1918.
212. *Welsh Gazette*, 21 November 1918; *Merthyr Pioneer*, 7 December 1918.

213. *Merthyr Pioneer*, 7 December 1918.
214. *Brecon and Radnor Express*, 8 August 1918.
215. *Monmouthshire Weekly Post*, 10 August 1918.
216. *Herald of Wales*, 19 October 1918.
217. *South Wales Daily Post*, 26 November 1918.
218. NLW, Edgar Chappell Papers (G.F. Godsell to E. Chappell, 20 February 1918).
219. NALRWU *Annual Report*, 1918.
220. *Welsh Gazette*, 21 November 1918.
221. *Denbighshire Free Press*, 29 June 1918 (letter from 'Land Worker').
222. Interview with Mrs P. Matthews, Caerphilly (daughter), January 1980.
223. *Brecon and Radnor Express*, 29 December 1921.
224. UCNW Bangor, Papurau David Thomas, 19193 (David Rees to David Thomas, 2 November 1918).
225. Workers' Union, *Record*, July 1918.
226. *Flintshire Observer*, 9,30 May 1918; *North Wales Weekly News*, 1 August, 28 November 1918.
227. *North Wales Pioneer*, 25 July 1918. O.E. Jones was also an active member of the NUT.
228. Ibid., 22 May 1919.
229. *Flintshire Observer*, 8 August 1918.
230. *Montgomeryshire County Times*, 25 May, 5 October 1918; Workers' Union, *Record*, August 1918.
231. *Y Wyntyll*, 18 Gorffennaf 1918; PRO F.S. 11 / 133 (letter from J. Fred Jones, 23 October 1918).
232. Cf. *Holyhead Chronicle*, 23 August 1918; *Y Wyntyll*, 5 Rhagfyr 1918.
233. *Y Wyntyll*, 11 Gorffennaf 1918; also Diary and Papers of the Revd William Morris. Notes of a lecture, 4 December 1967, with heading 'Helyntion Gweision a Ffermwyr' (by courtesy of his daughter, Mrs G. Roberts, Caernarfon).
234. Viz. Merioneth and Montgomery, Brecon and Radnor (30*s*.); Pembroke, Carmarthen and Cardigan (31*s*.); Anglesey and Caernarfon (31*s*. 6*d*.): Denbigh and Flint (35*s*.).
235. *South Wales Daily Post*, 28 April 1918.
236. Meetings were held in private behind closed doors and the only information came through a bland press release.
237. *Western Mail*, 25 July 1918.
238. *South Wales Daily News*, 13 August 1918 (editorial).
239. *Flintshire Observer*, 4, 11 April 1918.
240. Ibid., 12 September 1918.
241. *Brecon and Radnor Express*, 8 August 1918.
242. *Welsh Gazette*, 21 November 1918.
243. *Brecon County Times*, 25 April 1918.
244. *Welsh Gazette*, 5 December 1918.
245. *Haverfordwest and Milford Haven Telegraph*, 20 November 1918. The farmer in question was said to be a chapel deacon.
246. Interviews with James Kennett (son) and Mrs Clark (daughter), Boverton, January 1978.
247. *The Land Worker*, December 1967, pp.10–11. Also miscellaneous autobiographies kept by Miss E. Jones, Llanilar (daughter) entitled 'Hunangofiant Hen Weithiwr Fferm' (1959) and 'Hunangofiant Hen Hewliwr' (1968).
248. Minutes of the General and Executive Committee of the Wrexham Trades Council and Divisional Labour Party, op. cit., 27 August, 17, 24 September 1918.

249. Ibid., 12 November 1918.
250. Ibid., 17 December 1918.
251. Ibid., 14 January 1919.
252. Interview with Evan Williams, Llaniestyn (son-in-law), August 1979.
253. Interview with G. Thomas (son), Aber, August 1980.
254. *Radnorshire Standard*, 12 October 1918.
255. *Western Mail*, 2 December 1918.
256. *Yr Herald Cymraeg*, 19 Tachwedd 1918; *Y Dinesydd Cymreig*, 20 Tachwedd 1918.
257. *County Echo*, 17 October 1918 (letter from John Davies).
258. *Western Mail*, 23 September 1918 (letter from John Davies).
259. *Cardigan and Tivyside Advertiser*, 22 November 1918.
260. *Welsh Gazette*, 12 September 1918.
261. NLW, David Thomas Collection (W.T. Bason to David Thomas, 2, 4 December 1918; Humphrey Ellis to David Thomas, n.d.).
262. *Welsh Gazette*, 31 October 1918.
263. *Y Wyntyll*, 4 Gorffennaf, 8 Awst 1918.
264. *Wages Board Gazette*, Vol. 1, No. 8. 30 November 1918, p.93.
265. *Y Wyntyll*, 25 Gorffennaf, 8 Awst 1918 (letters from George Jones).
266. Ibid., 18 Gorffennaf 1918.
267. *Y Clorianydd*, 9 Hydref 1918.
268. *Y Wyntyll*, 9 Ionawr 1919.
269. *North Wales Weekly News*, 12 September 1918.
270. *Flintshire Observer*, 29 August 1918.
271. Ibid., 12 September 1918.
272. Ibid., 9 January 1919.
273. *Monmouthshire Weekly Post*, 10 August 1918; *South Wales Weekly Argus*, 24 August 1918.
274. *Monmouthshire Weekly Post*, 21 September 1918.
275. NLW, David Thomas Collection (correspondence, 1 July 1918).
276. *Brecon and Radnor Express*, 16 May 1918.
277. Ibid., 21 November 1918.
278. *Monmouthshire Weekly Post*, 31 August 1918.
279. *South Wales Weekly Argus*, 14 December 1918.
280. *North Wales Weekly News*, 12 September 1918 (letter from R.H. Wynne).
281. Ibid., 10 October 1918 (letter from W. Washington Owen).
282. *Welsh Gazette*, 27 June 1918.
283. *Cardigan and Tivyside Advertiser*, 12, 26 July 1918.
284. *Cambrian News*, 9 August 1918.
285. *Welsh Gazette*, 21 November 1918.
286. *Cambrian News*, 29 November 1918.
287. Ibid., 27 December 1918; also Howard C. Jones, 'The Labour Party in Cardiganshire 1918–66', *Ceredigion*, IX, No. 2, 1982, pp.153–4.
288. Morgan, *Rebirth of a Nation*, pp. 180–1.
289. *Flintshire Observer*, 5 December 1918.
290. *Y Dinesydd Cymreig*, 11 Rhagfyr 1918.
291. *North Wales Guardian*, 6 December 1918.
292. *Pembroke County Guardian*, 18 January 1918.
293. Ibid., 22 November, 6, 13 December 1918.
294. *Y Dinesydd Cymreig*, 10 Gorffennaf 1918.
295. Ibid., 4 Rhagfyr 1918.
296. *Pembroke County Guardian*, 3 January 1919 ('Labour Notes').
297. *Y Wyntyll*, 19 Medi 1917 (article V, 'Rhaglen Llafur').

298. Cofnodion Cangen Llanidan o Undeb Gweithwyr Môn, op. cit., 23 Chwefror 1918.
299. *Holyhead Chronicle*, 17, 31 May 1918.
300. *Y Wyntyll*, 23 Mai 1918.
301. Ibid., 13 Mehefin 1918 (letter from Brynfab).
302. Ibid., 20 Mehefin, 18 Gorffennaf 1918.
303. W.J. Pretty and W. Long made contact through his brother, Hugh Thomas, Carrog. I have followed the version in W. Long's memoirs 'The Start of the Labour Party in Anglesey', op. cit.
304. *Y Wyntyll*, 28 Tachwedd 1918 (letter from Sir Owen Thomas).
305. *Holyhead Chronicle*, 13 December 1918.
306. *Y Wyntyll*, 28 Tachwedd 1918.
307. Ibid., 28 Tachwedd, 12 Rhagfyr 1918.
308. *Liverpool Daily Post*, 30 November 1918; *Holyhead Chronicle*, 29 November 1918.
309. *Y Wyntyll*, 12 Rhagfyr 1918. The Liberals had only 5 sub-agents.
310. *Holyhead Chronicle*, 3, 24 January 1919.
311. Howkins, *Poor Labouring Men*, p.126.

Chapter V

1. C. Wrigley (ed.), *The British Labour Movement in the Decade after the First World War* (Loughborough, 1979), pp.1–17.
2. Madden, 'National Union of Agricultural Workers', p.299, Appendix C.
3. Hyman, *The Workers' Union*, p.101.
4. *The Land Worker*, 15 May 1919.
5. See *Brecon County Times*, 30 January 1919; *Brecon and Radnor Express*, 27 February 1919.
6. *Radnorshire Standard*, 3 May 1919. Only 12, however, are listed in NUAW *Annual Report* for 1919.
7. *Monmouthshire Weekly Post*, 1 February 1919.
8. *Haverfordwest and Milford Haven Telegraph*, 2 July 1919.
9. *Carmarthen Journal*, 31 October 1919.
10. *County Echo*, 31 July 1919; *Pembroke County Guardian*, 1 August 1919.

11 *The Land Worker*, 15 July 1920.

12 *County Echo*, 22 January 1920.

13 Reading, Records of the NUAAW, B/111/1, Organizing and Political Sub-Committee Minutes, 11 December 1919.

14 *Welsh Gazette*, 10, 17 October 1918, 11 December 1919.

15 *The Land Worker*, 15 April 1920.

16 Interview with R. Glyn Roberts (son); also *Y Dinesydd Cymreig*, 28 Mai, 19 Tachwedd 1919.

17 *Y Dydd*, 12 Tachwedd 1920.

18 *Y Dinesydd Cymreig*, 13 Awst 1919.

19 Llyfr Cofnodion Canghennau Llŷn o Undeb y Gweithwyr Amaethyddol 1919–22 (in the possession of Mrs Nellie Jones, Morfa Nefyn).

20 Reading, Records of the NUAAW B/111/1, Organizing and Political Sub-Committee Minutes, 10–11 October 1919.

21 Ibid., B/1/5, Executive Committee Minutes, 24 October 1919.

22 NLW, David Thomas Collection ('Bob' to David Thomas, 2 August 1919).

23 Workers' Union, *Record*, February, April 1919; February 1920.

24 Minutes of the General and Executive Committee of the Wrexham Trades Council and Divisional Labour Party, op. cit., 26 August 1919.

25 Workers' Union, *Record*, October 1920.
26 *Montgomeryshire Express*, 8 July 1919.
27 Ibid., 9 December 1919 ('Labour Notes').
28 UCNW Bangor, Papurau David Thomas 19193 (David Thomas to Arthur Henderson, 30 July 1918).
29 Ibid. (David Thomas to R.T. Jones, 26 January 1919; R.T. Jones to David Thomas, 28 January 1919).
30 NLW, David Thomas Collection (William Williams to David Thomas, 17 August 1920; also H.H. Lawrie to David Thomas, 3 September 1920).
31 UCNW Bangor, Papurau David Thomas, 19165. Notebook.
32 NLW, David Thomas Collection, Circular Letter, 7 October 1920.
33 *Baner ac Amserau Cymru*, 22 Mai 1920. A few weeks later the paper allowed ap Rhydwen to embark on a new column, 'Colofn y Gweithiwr'.
34 *Abergavenny Chronicle*, 3, 24 October 1919.
35 *Monmouthshire Beacon*, 6 August 1920.
36 NLW, David Thomas Collection (H. Hunt to David Thomas, 12 April 1919).
37 *Pembroke County Guardian*, 10 September 1920.
38 *Haverfordwest and Milford Haven Telegraph*, 18 June 1919.
39 Ibid., 9 July 1919.
40 E.g. Aberdaron, Llangybi, Four Crosses, Ysbyty Ifan, Llanfihangel Glyn Myfyr.
41 PRO, F.S. 11/133. Annual Return, 16 August 1919. Viz. 2,578 men, 35 women.
42 Ibid. It had £427 in hand.
43 From press reports and the PRO, F.S./133 File of Correspondence — containing letters written mainly by W.J. Jones (Brynfab) and R. Morris between August 1919 and January 1920 — it is possible to reconstruct the run of events.
44 *Y Clorianydd*, 11 Mehefin 1919.
45 Reading, Records of the NUAAW, B/1/5, Executive Committee Minutes, 20 June 1919; B/111/1, Organizing and Political Sub-Committee Minutes, 8, 28 August 1919.
46 *Y Wyntyll*, 7 Awst 1919 (letter from Brynfab).
47 PRO, F.S. 11/133. (letter from R. Morris, 9 December 1919).
48 Ibid., (letters from W.J. Jones, 4, 21 November 1919).
49 *Y Wyntyll*, 4, 18 Medi 1919.
50 Workers' Union, *Annual Report*, 1919.
51 *Y Wyntyll*, 13 Mai 1920.
52 Ibid., 30 Hydref 1919 (letter from Brynfab).
53 Ibid., 27 Tachwedd 1919.
54 PRO, F.S. 11/133. The words of the Assistant Registrar in a Minute dated 27 January 1920.
55 *Y Wyntyll*, 8 Ionawr 1920.
56 *Y Clorianydd*, 7 Ebrill 1920.
57 *The Land Worker*, 15 July 1920.
58 Ibid., January 1921.
59 The author's estimate.
60 UCNW Bangor, Papurau David Thomas, 19885. 'An Economic and Social Survey of North Wales 1914–1922', p.133.
61 Ibid., 19200. Circular from the Workers' Union to Divisional and District Organizers, 16 November 1921.
62 Viz. 6,000 in the NUAW; 4,000 in the Workers' Union.
63 1921 Census figure, Ashby and Evans, op. cit., p.75.
64 *Pembroke County Guardian*, 16 May 1919.
65 *Brecon and Radnor Express*, 27 February 1919.
66 *County Echo*, 3 April 1919. Note also the reply from 'Will y Gwas', ibid., 10 April 1919.

67. *Monmouthshire Weekly Post*, 8 March 1919.
68. *Montgomeryshire Express*, 11, 18 March, 6 May, 29 July 1919.
69. GAS, Dolgellau, Z/M/791/2. Minute Book of the Merioneth NFU, 16 December 1919.
70. *Pembroke County Guardian*, 8 August 1919.
71. *Wages Board Gazette*, Vol. 1, No. 13, 18 February 1919, pp.152–3.
72. *Pembroke County Guardian*, 8 August 1919.
73. *Cardigan and Tivyside Advertiser*, 4 April 1919.
74. *Y Wyntyll*, 20 Mawrth, 10 Ebrill 1919.
75. Ibid., 1 Mai 1919.
76. Letter from Owen Jones, Newport, Gwent (son) to the author, September 1977.
77. Huw T. Edwards, op. cit., p.23.
78. *Y Dinesydd Cymreig*, 11 Mehefin 1919.
79. *Y Seren*, 12, 19 Ebrill, 17 Mai 1919.
80. *The Land Worker*, 15 May 1919.
81. *Y Genedl Gymreig*, 28 Hydref 1919.
82. *Caernarvon and Denbigh Herald*, 14 November 1919; *Cambrian News*, 16 January 1920.
83. *The Welshman*, 4 June 1920.
84. *Hansard*, 5th series, 1920, Vol. 130, 9 June 1920.
85. *Y Dinesydd Cymreig*, 21 Mai, 11 Mehefin, 19 Tachwedd 1919.
86. *Baner ac Amserau Cymru*, 14 Awst 1920.
87. Ifan Gruffydd, *Tân yn y Siambar* (Dinbych, 1966), p.65.
88. *Wages and Conditions of Employment in Agriculture*, 1919, op. cit., pp.193, 454.
89. *Wages Board Gazette*, Vol. 1, No. 30, 1 November 1919, pp.441–4.
90. *North Wales Observer and Express*, 25 October 1889.
91. Norman McCord, *Strikes* (Oxford, 1980), p.4.
92. Groves, *Sharpen the Sickle*, pp.139–45.
93. Mutch, 'Rural Society in Lancashire', ch.8.
94. NUAW, *Annual Report*, 1919, p.7.
95. *Western Mail*, 28 March 1919.
96. *Caernarvon and Denbigh Herald*, 24 October 1919.
97. *Western Mail*, 28 August 1919.
98. *Montgomery County Times*, 12 April 1919 (letter from J. Holmes).
99. K.G.J.C. Knowles, *Strikes — A Study in Industrial Conflict* (Oxford, 1952), p.219.
100. *Y Clorianydd*, 11 Mehefin 1919.
101. *North Wales Pioneer*, 24 July 1919.
102. *North Wales Weekly News*, 24 July 1919; *Y Dinesydd Cymreig*, 30 Gorffennaf 1919.
103. *North Wales Weekly News*, 31 July 1919.
104. Ibid., 7 August 1919.
105. *South Wales News*, 7 February 1919.
106. Ibid., 3 February 1919.
107. Ibid., 24 February 1919.
108. Ibid., 10 February, 3 March 1919.
109. *Monmouthshire Weekly Post*, 8 February 1919.
110. *Wages Board Gazette*, Vol. 1, No. 16, 1 April 1919.
111. *South Wales News*, 21 March 1919.
112. *Monmouthshire Weekly Post*, 19 April 1919.
113. Ibid., 3 May 1919.
114. *South Wales News*, 14 April 1919; *Glamorgan Gazette*, 6 June 1919.

115. *South Wales News*, 21 April 1919.
116. Ibid., 28 April, 1 May 1919.
117. Ibid., 25 April 1919.
118. *Monmouthshire Weekly Post*, 31 May 1919.
119. *South Wales News*, 29 May 1919.
120. *Cardiff Times*, 21 June 1919.
121. *South Wales News*, 23 June 1919.
122. *Western Mail*, 24 June 1919.
123. *Glamorgan Gazette*, 27 June 1919.
124. *South Wales News*, 1 July 1919.
125. Ibid., 8 July 1919.
126. Pontypridd Trades and Labour Council Minute Book, 4 July 1919.
127. *South Wales News*, 10 July 1919.
128. *Glamorgan Gazette*, 11 July 1919. The executive committee of NUAW had decided to take up the matter with the Board. Reading, Records of the NUAAW, B/1/5, Executive Committee Minutes, 20 June 1919.
129. *South Wales News*, 8, 10, 12 July 1919.
130. Ibid., 10 July 1919.
131. Ibid., 12 July 1919.
132. *Western Mail*, 25 June 1919.
133. *South Wales News*, 14 July 1919.
134. *Western Mail*, 14 July 1919.
135. Ibid., 17 July 1919.
136. *Monmouthshire Weekly Post*, 19 July 1919.
137. *South Wales News*, 18 July 1919.
138. *Wages Board Gazette*, Vol. 1, No. 30, 1 November 1919, p.442.
139. *South Wales News*, 29 July 1919.
140. Ibid., 16 August 1919.
141. Reading, Records of the NUAAW, B/1/5. Executive Committee Minutes, 25 July 1919.
142. *Western Mail*, 18 July 1919.
143. *Monmouthshire Weekly Post*, 26 July 1919.
144. Ibid., 25 October 1919.
145. *South Wales News*, 8 November 1919.
146. *The Land Worker*, December 1920, January 1921.
147. *Western Mail*, 18 May 1920.
148. *Glamorgan Gazette*, 20 August 1920.
149. Ashby and Evans, *Agriculture of Wales*, p.87.
150. NUAW, *Annual Report*, 1920, p.3.
151. Workers' Union, *Annual Report*, 1919, p.29; 1920, p.17.
152. *Y Clorianydd*, 27 Hydref 1920.
153. *Caernarvon and Denbigh Herald*, 24 October 1919.
154. *Brecon and Radnor Express*, 24 June 1920.
155. *County Echo*, 26 February 1920; *Pembroke County Guardian*, 27 February 1920.
156. *Pembroke County Guardian*, 17, 31 December 1920.
157. *Abergavenny Chronicle*, 7 May 1920.
158. Ibid., 28 May 1920.
159. *Pembroke County Guardian*, 4 June 1920.
160. Ibid., 30 July 1920.
161. *South Wales News*, 13 December 1919.
162. *Glamorgan Gazette*, 5 March 1920.
163. *South Wales News*, 16 February 1920.

164. *Monmouthshire Weekly Post*, 14 February 1920.
165. *South Wales News*, 27 February 1920.
166. Ibid., 29 March 1920.
167. Ibid., 19 April 1920.
168. Ibid., 20 April 1920.
169. Ibid., 26, 30 April 1920.
170. Ibid., 20 May 1920.
171. Ibid., 18 June 1920.
172. Ibid., 4 November 1920 (editorial).
173. Ibid., 15 November 1920.
174. *Flintshire Observer*, 24 June 1920.
175. *Y Wyntyll*, 5, 19 Chwefror 1920; *Y Clorianydd*, 22 Medi 1920.
176. *Welsh Gazette*, 4 November 1920.
177. *Cambrian News*, 17 September 1920.
178. *Welsh Gazette*, 4 November 1920. The words of T.W. Hughes, district organizer.
179. Christopher Howard, 'Expectations born to death: local Labour party expansion in the 1920s', in J. Winter (ed.), The *Working Class in Modern British History* (Cambridge, 1983), pp.69–70. Also Howkins, *Poor Labouring Men*, pp.126–9.
180. R. McKibbin, *The Evolution of the Labour Party 1910–1924* (Oxford, 1974), pp.150–1.
181. Ibid., pp.161–2.
182. *Labour Leader*, 7 July 1911 (letter from David Thomas).
183. McKibbin, *Labour Party*, pp.167–70, 174–5.
184. *Welsh Outlook*, October 1919.
185. UCNW Bangor, Papurau David Thomas 19300. North Wales Trades and Labour Council Minute Book, 25 Ionawr, 20 Rhagfyr 1919.
186. *Y Wyntyll*, 16 Ionawr 1919.
187. Ibid., 13 Chwefror 1919. The Holyhead Trades and Labour Council, representing 19 unions and 1,800 workers, put up 7 of the 22 candidates.
188. Ibid., 6 Mawrth 1919 (letter from H.C. Parry).
189. Ibid., 13 Mawrth 1919.
190. Ibid., 20 Mawrth 1919.
191. Ibid., 10 Ebrill 1919.
192. Ibid., 5 Chwefror, 4 Mawrth, 13 Mai 1920. The advertisement was issued by the 'Anglesey Election Committee of Sir Owen Thomas, Labour Member'.
193. *Y Dinesydd Cymreig*, 9 Ebrill 1919.
194. Ibid., 12 Tachwedd 1919.
195. *Chester Courant*, 8 October 1919.
196. *Flintshire Observer*, 13 March 1919.
197. Ibid., 10 April 1919.
198. *North Wales Times*, 29 March 1919.
199. *Y Seren*, 12 Ebrill 1919.
200. *Montgomery County Times*, 26 April 1919; *Y Rhedegydd*, 6 Rhagfyr 1919.
201. *Baner ac Amserau Cymru*, 24 Ionawr, 29 Mai 1920.
202. *Y Seren*, 31 Ionawr 1920.
203. *Montgomery County Times*, 15 March 1919. 4 Labour candidates were returned.
204. *Montgomeryshire Express*, 18 March 1919.
205. Ibid., 3 June 1919.
206. *Montgomery County Times*, 22 March, 12 April 1919.
207. Ibid., 29 November 1919, 10 January 1920.
208. *Montgomeryshire Express*, 22, 29 April 1919.
209. *Brecon and Radnor Express*, 6 February 1919.

210. Ibid., 6 March 1919.
211. *Welsh Gazette*, 13 March 1919.
212. *Cambrian News*, 24 September 1920.
213. *Welsh Gazette*, 11 November 1920.
214. *Pembroke County Guardian*, 28 March 1919.
215. Ibid., 7 March 1919 ('Labour Notes').
216. Ibid., 14 March 1919.
217. *County Echo*, 13 March 1919.
218. Ibid., 20 March, 10 April 1919.
219. *Pembroke County Guardian*, 14, 21 November 1919.
220. *County Echo*, 21 October 1920.
221. NLW, E.T. John Papers, 2628 (D.T. Lewis to E.T. John, 23 July 1920), 2641 (D.T. Lewis to E.T. John, 2 August 1920).
222. *South Wales Weekly Argus*, 22 February, 8 March 1919.
223. Ibid., 22 March, 12, 19 April 1919.
224. E.g. Caer-went, Chepstow, Trelech, Catbrook.
225. *South Wales Weekly Argus*, 20 December 1919.
226. *Monmouthshire Weekly Post*, 10 July 1920.
227. *Cardiff Times*, 1 March 1919.
228. *Glamorgan Gazette*, 28 March, 18 April 1919.
229. McKibbin, *Labour Party*, p.111; *Y Wyntyll*, 27 Chwefror 1919.
230. *Holyhead Chronicle*, 11 July, 1 August 1919.
231. *Y Wyntyll*, 7 Awst 1919.
232. *Holyhead Chronicle*, 22 October 1920.
233. *Y Wyntyll*, 28 Hydref 1920.
234. Ibid., 18 Tachwedd 1920.
235. Note the observations of ap Rhydwen in *Baner ac Amserau Cymru*, 5, 26 Mehefin 1920.
236. *South Wales News*, 18 October 1919; *Cardigan and Tivyside Advertiser*, 26 November 1919.
237. WEA, *Annual Report*, 1919–20, p.5, 11; 1921–2, p.23.
238. Ibid., 1922–3, p.30.
239. Ibid., 1919–20, p.4.
240. *Cambrian News*, 1 October 1920.
241. WEA, *Annual Report*, 1919–20, p.5.
242. *North Wales Chronicle*, 4 April 1919.
243. *County Echo*, 4 March 1920.
244. *Y Seren*, 7 Chwefror 1920.
245. *Glamorgan Gazette*, 5 March, 20 August, 22 October 1920.
246. *South Wales Weekly Argus*, 6 September 1919.
247. *The Land Worker*, 15 April 1920.
248. *County Echo*, 1 July 1920.
249. *Montgomeryshire Express*, 13 January 1920.
250. *Y Dinesydd Cymreig*, 5 Mai 1920. The words of Humphrey Evans, Llandwrog.
251. *County Echo*, 8 April 1920.
252. Reading, Records of the NUAW, B/111/1, Organizing and Political Sub-Committee Minutes, 12 March, 15 April 1920.
253. E.g. *Baner ac Amserau Cymru*, 24 Ebrill, 29 Mai 1920.
254. *Cardiff Times*, 27 December 1919.
255. See *Welsh Outlook*, March 1920, Thomas Rees, 'The Crisis of Welsh Nonconformity'.
256. Thomas, *Diolch am Gael Byw*, p.31; *Caernarvon and Denbigh Herald*, 28 November 1919.

257. E.H. Griffiths, *Heddychwr Mawr Cymru: George M.Ll. Davies*, Cyfrol 1 (Caernarfon, 1967), tt.64, 84–5.
258. George M.Ll. Davies, *Profiadau Pellach* (Dinbych, 1943), tt.16–19.

Chapter VI

1. Morgan, *Rebirth of a Nation*, ch. 8.
2. J. Stevenson, *British Society 1914–45* (London, 1984), p.271.
3. Pelling, *British Trade Unionism*, pp.262–3.
4. Edith H. Whetham, 'The Agricultural Act, 1920 and its Repeal — the Great Betrayal', *Agricultural History Review*, 22, 1974, Part 1.
5. *Hansard*, Vol. 144, 4 July 1921, col.84.
6. *South Wales News*, 5, 6, July 1921.
7. *Cambrian News*, 8 July 1921.
8. *Western Mail*, 5 July 1921.
9. Ministry of Agriculture and Fisheries, *Agricultural Statistics*, 1921, Vol. LVI, Part 1, p.87.
10. *Llanelly Mercury*, 3 March 1921.
11. *South Wales News*, 16, 20 June 1921.
12. Ibid., 15 June 1921.
13. *North Wales Pioneer*, 19 May 1921; *Caernarvon and Denbigh Herald*, 20 May 1921.
14. *South Wales News*, 29 July 1921.
15. Workers' Union, *Annual Report*, 1921, p.11.
16. Ibid., 1922, p.3.
17. Madden, 'National Union of Agricultural Workers', p.299, Appendix C.
18. Reading, Records of the NUAAW, B/11/2, Finance and General Purposes Sub-committee Minutes, 16 December 1920.
19. Ibid., B/1/5, Executive Committee Minutes, 18 August 1921.
20. Ibid., B/11/2, Finance and General Purposes Sub-Committee Minutes, 17 January 1921.
21. Ibid., B/111/1, Organizing and Political Sub-Committee Minutes, 18 January 1921.
22. Ibid., B/111/1, 18 January 1921.
23. Ibid., B/111/1, 5 May, 7 June 1921.
24. See *The Land Worker*, November 1921.
25. Reading, Records of the NUAW, B/111/1, Organizing and Political Sub-Committee Minutes, 17 February 1921.
26. Ibid., B/1/5, Executive Committee Minutes, 27 April 1921.
27. Ibid., B/1/5, 25 November 1921.
28. *The Land Worker*, January 1921.
29. Ibid., February, March 1921.
30. *South Wales News*, 3 September 1921.
31. *The Land Worker*, January 1921.
32. Ibid., July 1921.
33. *South Wales News*, 6 January 1921.
34. Ibid., 22 January 1921 (letter from James Kennett).
35. Ibid., 20 May 1921.
36. Ibid., 18 June 1921.
37. *Glamorgan Gazette*, 1 July 1921.
38. *South Wales News*, 29 July 1921.
39. Reading, Records of the NUAAW, B/1/5, Executive Committee Minutes, 15 December 1921; B/1/6, 25 January 1922.

40. Interview with Mrs P. Matthews, Caerphilly (daughter).
41. Reading, Records of the NUAAW, B/111/2, Organizing and Political Sub-Committee Minutes, 22 March 1922.
42. Ibid., B/1/6, Executive Committee Minutes, 27 July 1922.
43. Ibid., B/111/2, Organizing and Political Sub-Committee Minutes, 26 July 1922.
44. Ibid., B/1/6, Executive Committee Minutes, 8 August 1922.
45. *Y Dinesydd Cymreig*, 25 Mai 1921.
46. Ibid., 23 Mawrth 1921 ('Colofn y Gweithwyr Amaethyddol').
47. *Yr Herald Cymraeg*, 10 Mai 1921.
48. Ibid., 24 Mai 1921 (letter from 'L.R.').
49. GAS, Caernarfon (uncatalogued), Pwllheli Union Minute Book, 1 June 1921.
50. *Y Dinesydd Cymreig*, 21 Medi 1921.
51. Ibid., 19, 26 Hydref 1921; *Yr Herald Cymraeg*, 25 Hydref, 1, 22 Tachwedd 1921.
52. *Caernarvon and Denbigh Herald*, 23, 30 December 1921.
53. *Y Genedl Gymreig*, 9 Mai 1922.
54. Ibid., 16 Mai 1922; *Caernarvon and Denbigh Herald*, 19 May 1922.
55. *Caernarvon and Denbigh Herald*, 9 June 1922.
56. *Yr Herald Gymraeg*, 20 Mehefin 1922; *Caernarvon and Denbigh Herald*, 23 June 1922; *Y Genedl Gymreig*, 27 Mehefin 1922.
57. *Caernarvon and Denbigh Herald*, 30 June 1922.
58. *Y Genedl Gymreig*, 4 Gorffennaf 1922.
59. *Liverpool Daily Post*, 30 June 1922.
60. *The Land Worker*, August 1922.
61. *Y Dinesydd Cymreig*, 20 Medi 1922.
62. (Notice) 'Cyflog am y Tymor o'r 11 Tachwedd hyd Mai 13 1923' — issued by W. Williams and R.G. Roberts. (MSS in the possession of Mrs Nellie Jones, Morfa Nefyn.)
63. Reading, Records of the NUAAW, D/11/4, 'Saturday Half Holiday: Summary of Reports received from organizers, October 1922' (NUAW Publicity Pamphlet).
64. Llyfr Cofnodion Canghennau Llŷn o Undeb y Gweithwyr Amaethyddol 1919–1922, op. cit., Ionawr, 25 Chwefror 1922.
65. Reading, Records of the NUAAW, B/111/2, Organizing and Political Sub-Committee Minutes, 10 January 1923.
66. Ibid., 31 October 1923.
67. *The Land Worker*, August 1923.
68. E.g. *Baner ac Amserau Cymru*, 23 Gorffennaf 1921.
69. Ibid., 23 Mawrth 1922.
70. Ibid., 25 Mai 1922.
71. NLW, David Thomas Collection, drafts of letters, April, May 1921.
72. Ibid., letter, September 1921.
73. *Montgomeryshire Express*, 21 June 1921.
74. *Montgomery County Times*, 24 December 1921.
75. NLW, David Thomas Collection, letter, 25 November 1921.
76. Ibid., letter, 22 January 1922.
77. Ibid., letter, 25 November 1921.
78. Ibid., letters, 25 November, 30 December 1921.
79. Ibid., letter, 16 January 1922.
80. UCNW Bangor, Papurau David Thomas, 19200 (H.H. Lawrie to David Thomas, 14 March 1922).
81. Ibid., 19199 (P. Grudgings to David Thomas, 12 June 1922).
82. Ibid., 19200 (David Thomas to Charles Duncan, 30 March 1922).
83. TUC Library, Workers' Union, H.D. 6661, A1. File of Papers from S. Box. Letter from S. Box to the Executive Committee, 1928.

84. *The Welshman*, 18 July 1923; also *Welsh Gazette*, 4 October 1923.

85. Viz. Anglesey, Caernarfon, Denbigh and Flint, Merioneth and Montgomery, Cardigan, Pembroke, Carmarthen, Glamorgan, Monmouth, Brecon and Radnor.

86. *South Wales News*, 17 October 1921.

87. Ibid., 22 October 1921 (letter from David Rees).

88. *Western Mail*, 17 October 1921.

89. *South Wales News*, 14 November, 17 December 1921.

90. *Montgomery County Times*, 3 September 1921.

91. *Brecon and Radnor Express*, 24 November 1921.

92. *The Land Worker*, December 1921.

93. Ibid., October 1921.

94. *South Wales News*, 7 January 1922.

95. *Hansard*, 5th series, Vol. 159, 2 December 1922, col. 1237–8. Parliamentary question on the Monmouthshire Wages Deadlock submitted by G. Barker (Labour, Abertillery).

96. *South Wales Weekly Argus*, 28 October 1922.

97. *Hansard*, 5th series, Vol. 159, 7 December 1922, col. 2001–2.

98. Groves, *Sharpen the Sickle*, pp. 196–205; also Howkins, *Poor Labouring Men*, ch. 8.

99. *Welsh Gazette*, 17 January 1924.

100. *Y Dinesydd Cymreig*, 4 Mehefin 1924.

101. *Welsh Gazette*, 19 June 1924.

102. E.g. advertisements in *Carmarthen Journal*, 15 December 1922 and *North Wales Chronicle*, 23 May 1924.

103. *South Wales News*, 1 July 1924.

104. Interview with Caradog Jones, August 1979. One example cited was that of Richard Parry, Rhoshirwaun. Cf. *Y Dinesydd Cymreig*, 17 Ionawr 1923.

105. *Y Goleuad*, 2 Chwefror 1921.

106. Ibid., 27 Ebrill 1921.

107. Hugh Owen (gol.), *Hanes Methodistiaeth Calfinaidd Môn, 1880–1935* (Lerpwl, 1937), t.14.

108. R.R. Hughes, *Y Parchedig John Williams, D.D., Brynsiencyn* (Caernarfon, 1929), pp.244–5.

109. R. Tudur Jones, *Yr Undeb. Hanes Undeb yr Annibynwyr Cymraeg 1872–1972*, (Abertawe, 1975), t.209.

110. Carmarthenshire R.O., ACC 4414, L.C.L.P. I. Minutes of the Llanelli Trades and Labour Council, 7, 11, 18, 21 April 1923.

111. *County Echo*, 25 January 1923.

112. Ibid., 7 April 1921.

113. *Caernarvon and Denbigh Herald*, 24 February 1922.

114. *Y Goleuad*, 25 Hydref 1922.

115. Ibid., 22 Tachwedd 1922; also *Caernarvon and Denbigh Herald*, 10 November 1922.

116. Revds Morris Thomas, Penmorfa, and J.T. Pritchard, Chwilog.

117. *Yr Herald Cymraeg*, 23 Ionawr 1923.

118. Ibid., 30 Ionawr, 20 Chwefror 1923.

119. *Y Dinesydd Cymreig*, 7 Chwefror 1923 (letter from 'Gweithiwr').

120. Ibid., 14 Chwefror 1923 (letter from 'Gweithiwr Arall').

121. J.O. Francis, *Cross Currents* (Cardiff, 1923), shortly after translated into Welsh as *Gwyntoedd Croesion* by R. Silyn Roberts.

122. *Pembroke County Guardian*, 17 June 1921.

123. NLW, E.T. John Papers, 2628, D.T. Lewis to E.T. John, 23 July 1920.

124. *The Welshman*, 25 February 1921; *Cardigan and Tivyside Advertiser*, 11, 18 March 1921.

125. *Cardigan and Tivyside Advertiser*, 3 March 1922.
126. The performance by the Ddraig Goch Dramatic Company at the Pavilion, Caernarfon, Easter Monday 1923. *Caernarvon and Denbigh Herald*, 25 April 1924.
127. *Welsh Outlook*, December 1922.
128. *Y Wyntyll*, 9, 16 Mawrth 1922.
129. *Montgomeryshire Express*, 21 February 1922.
130. *South Wales Weekly Argus*, 25 February, 11 March 1922.
131. *Y Dinesydd Cymreig*, 31 Mai 1922.
132. *The Welshman*, 24 March 1922.
133. *County Echo*, 23 March 1922.
134. *South Wales News*, 9 July 1923.
135. NLW, E.T. John Papers, 2408, Beriah G. Evans to E.T. John, 12 November 1919.
136. See Parry, *Radical Tradition*, p.66.
137. *Y Dinesydd Cymreig*, 26 Ebrill 1922.
138. For details of his organizational work, see UCNW, Papurau David Thomas, 19201, 19202. Among his list of contacts were Owen Chambers, Robert Thomas and Richard Griffith.
139. *Caernarvon and Denbigh Herald*, 30 June 1922.
140. *Pembroke County Guardian*, 25 March 1921.
141. Ibid., 2 December 1921.
142. *County Echo*, 2 February 1922.
143. *Pembroke County Guardian*, 27 October–17 November 1922 for details of the campaign.
144. *County Echo*, 29 November 1923.
145. Ibid., 22 March 1923.
146. NLW, E.T. John Papers, 2709, Illtyd Morgan to Beriah G. Evans, 12 October 1920.
147. Ibid., 2768., D.S. Davies to E.T. John, 18 December 1920.
148. Ibid., 3080, Beriah G. Evans to E.T. John, 20 February 1922.
149. Ibid., 3082, E.T. John to Beriah G. Evans, 21 February 1922.
150. Ibid., 3699, E.T. John to Beriah G. Evans, 20 November 1922.
151. *Brecon and Radnor Express*, 2 November 1922.
152. NLW, E.T. John Papers, 4252, E.T. John to Idris Davies, 1 November 1924.
153. Ibid., 2722, E.T. John to Beriah G. Evans, 19 October 1920.
154. Ibid., 2964, E.T. John to R.E. Roberts, 8 September 1921. (Indeed, he was first approached after his defeat at Denbigh in 1918).
155. *Holyhead Chronicle*, 4 November 1921.
156. *Y Wyntyll*, 22 Rhagfyr 1921.
157. PRO F.S. 11/133, W.J. Jones to the Registrar, 1 February 1922 and reply, 7 February 1922.
158. *Y Wyntyll*, 19, 26 Ionawr 1922.
159. Ibid., 23 Chwefror 1922.
160. *Y Clorianydd*, 8 Tachwedd 1922 (letter from R. Morris).
161. *Y Wyntyll*, 2 Tachwedd 1922.
162. Ibid., 21 Rhagfyr 1922.
163. *Holyhead Chronicle*, 9 March 1923; *Y Wyntyll*, 15 Mawrth 1923.
164. NLW, E.T. John Papers, 3811, E.T. John to Revd J.H. Jenkins, 18 March 1923.
165. £150,000 according to his own calculation, see *Holyhead Chronicle*, 24 October 1924; also £500 to the NFU, ibid., 21 August 1925.
166. NLW, E.T. John Papers, 3875, E.T. John to Arthur Henderson, 11 April 1923.
167. Ibid., 3889, E.T. John to Charles Trevelyan, 12 April 1923.

168. Ibid., 3881, Revd B. Thomas to E.T. John, 11 April 1923.
169. *Report of the 24th Annual Conference of the Labour Party*, 1924, p.285.
170. *Y Wyntyll*, 17 Mai 1923.
171. PRO F.S. 11/133. Correspondence and Official Minutes, 2 February–1 August 1923.
172. *Y Wyntyll*, 22 Tachwedd 1923.
173. Ibid., 8 Chwefror 1923.
174. *Holyhead Chronicle*, 17 October 1924.
175. Ibid., 24 October 1924.
176. *Report of the 24th Annual Conference of the Labour Party*, 1924, p.17.
177. *The Welshman*, 7 December 1923.
178. *Montgomeryshire Express*, 12 June 1923; also 15 May 1923 ('Labour Notes').
179. Ibid., 17 June 1924.
180. *South Wales Weekly Argus*, 8 March, 12 April 1924.
181. Ibid., 28 October 1922.
182. *Free Press of Monmouthshire*, 6, 27 June, 11, 25 July 1924.
183. An NUR activist, Bateman had spent much time organizing farm workers in Somerset.
184. *South Wales News*, 9 July 1923.
185. I.e. county constituencies with more then 20 per cent of the employed male population engaged in agriculture: viz. Anglesey, Brecon and Radnor, Cardigan, Carmarthen, Caernarfon, Denbigh, Merioneth, Monmouth, Montgomery, Pembroke. M. Kinnear, *The British Voter. An Atlas and Survey since 1885* (London, 1981), p.119.
186. Minute Book of the Caernarvonshire Labour Council, 1912–27, op. cit., 29 Rhagfyr 1923.
187. *Caernarvon and Denbigh Herald*, 22 February 1924.
188. NLW, H.T. Edwards Collection, Minute Book of the North Wales Labour Federation, 1923–30.
189. *Caernarvon and Denbigh Herald*, 20 June 1923. President, Revd D. Gwynfryn Jones; vice president, E.T. John; secretary, Caradog Jones.
190. UCNW Bangor, Papurau David Thomas, 19203, Trefniadau Gogyfer â Chynhadleddau Llafur Gogledd Cymru.
191. *Denbighshire Free Press*, 10 November 1923.
192. Minute Book of the North Wales Labour Federation, op. cit., 15 Mawrth 1924.
193. Aided by the formation of a national council of the Welsh Labour Party, *South Wales News*, 12 June 1924.
194. *County Echo*, 7 April 1921; *Y Dinesydd Cymreig*, 22 Chwefror 1922.
195. *Carmarthen Journal*, 1 August 1924.
196. *Y Wyntyll*, 14 Mehefin 1923.
197. NLW, E.T. John Papers, 3896, E.T. John to the Revd T. Charles Williams, 14 April 1923.
198. Ibid., 3923, E.T. John to the Revd John Owen, 31 May 1923.
199. *Y Llan*, 30 Ionawr, 9 Hydref 1925.
200. E.g. *South Wales News*, 31 March, 2, 8 May, 2 June 1924.
201. *Glamorgan Gazette*, 9 May 1924 (letter from James James).
202. *Welsh Gazette*, 23 October 1924.
203. Excepting Glamorgan, Monmouth and Carmarthen the counties were coupled together as before.
204. *Hansard*, 5th Series, Vol. 180, 19 February 1925, Col.1314–8.
205. Madden, 'National Union of Agricultural Workers' , pp. 113–15.
206. *South Wales News*, 23 February, 5 March 1925.
207. Ibid., 23 March 1925.

208. Nothing is known of J. Maynard.
209. *The Land Worker*, June 1950.
210. Ibid., July 1926.
211. Madden, 'National Union of Agricultural Workers', p.114.
212. Interview with Arthur Pearson, Pontypridd, August 1979.
213. TUC *Annual Report*, 1924, pp.430–3.
214. Augmented by another £1,000 from affiliated unions.
215. Cf. the fears of T.W. Hughes, TGWU organizer, who spoke of the 'menace' presented to Carmarthen roadmen. *Carmarthen Journal*, 18 May, 29 June 1923.
216. TUC *Annual Report*, 1925, pp.240–1.
217. *Y Wyntyll*, 26 Gorffennaf 1923.
218. Workers' Union, *Record*, August 1923.
219. *Y Clorianydd*, 27 Mai 1925.
220. Ibid., 1 Gorffennaf 1925.
221. R. Hyman, 'The Workers' Union 1898–1929', Ph.D. thesis, Oxford, 1968, p.309.
222. TUC *Annual Report*, 1926, pp.167–70.
223. Reading, Records of the NUAAW, B/111/2, Organizing and Political Sub-Committee Minutes, 1 July 1924.
224. Ibid., 15 September 1925.
225. *The Land Worker*, June 1924.
226. Ibid., July 1925. Viz. Monmouth, Glamorgan, Pembroke, Cardigan and Caernarfon.
227. Ibid., August 1925. Portskewett branch had only been resuscitated a few weeks earlier. *South Wales Weekly Argus*, 28 February 1925.
228. *The Land Worker*, March 1925.
229. *County Echo*, 8 January 1925 (letter from 'A Member of the Wages Board' — i.e. D.T. Lewis); also *Pembroke County Guardian*, 9 January 1925.
230. *County Echo*, 22 January 1925.
231. Ibid., 29 January, 12 February 1925.
232. *Pembroke County Guardian*, 23 January, 13 March, 17, 24, 30 April, 1, 8 May 1925.
233. Ibid., 22 May 1925.
234. *Welsh Gazette*, 8, 15 February 1923.
235. Ibid., 4 October 1923.
236. *Abergavenny Chronicle*, 10 October 1924; *Glamorgan Gazette*, 17 October 1924.
237. *Y Dinesydd Cymreig*, 6 Awst 1924; *Baner ac Amserau Cymru*, 11 Rhagfyr 1924.
238. *Y Dinesydd Cymreig*, 10 Rhagfyr 1924, 8 Ebrill, 24 Mehefin, 28 Hydref, 25 Tachwedd, 2 Rhagfyr 1925.
239. Reading, Records of the NUAAW, B/111/2, Organizing and Political Sub-Committee Minutes, 28 July 1925; B/1/6, Executive Committee Minutes, 16 September 1925.
240. E.g. *South Wales News*, 8 December 1924.
241. Reading, Records of the NUAAW, B/111/3. Organizing and Political Sub-Committee Minutes, 5 January 1926.
242. Ibid., 9 March 1926.
243. Ibid., 13 April 1926.
244. *South Wales Weekly Argus*, 14 February 1925.
245. Reading, Records of the NUAAW, B/111/3, Organizing and Political Sub-Committee Minutes, 15 July 1926; *The Land Worker*, August 1926.
246. *County Echo*, 28 January, 4, 18 February, 25 March, 1, 29 April, 2, 16 September, 7 October 1926.

247. Reading, Records of the NUAAW, B/1/7, Executive Committee Minutes, 26 October 1926.

248. *Y Clorianydd*, 7 Gorffennaf 1926.

249. *Y Dinesydd Cymreig*, 10, 17 Chwefror 1926.

250. *Pembroke County Guardian*, 9 July 1926.

251. Author's estimate based on the Workers' Union *Annual Report*, 1926.

252. TUC *Annual Report*, 1927, pp.155–6.

253. Cf. Hyman, 'The Workers' Union', p.309.

254. This paragraph is based on interviews with P.J. Smith, Boverton, January 1978 and August 1979, also the biographical article in *Pontypridd Observer*, 26 December 1959.

255. In supporting his candidature the NUAW had granted £1 towards his election fund. Reading, Records of the NUAAW, B/1/8, Executive Committee Minutes, 19 January 1934.

256. Both men had unsuccessfully fought the RDC election in April 1928, *Glamorgan Gazette*, 6 April 1928.

257. *Report of the 27th Annual Conference of the Labour Party*, 1927, p.17.

258. *South Wales Weekly Argus*, 28 May 1927.

259. *Carmarthen Journal*, 17 June 1927.

260. *Y Dinesydd Cymreig*, 15 Rhagfyr 1926.

261. Ibid., 25 Mai 1927; 26 Medi 1928.

262. Hyman, 'The Workers' Union', p.310.

263. Reading, Records of the NUAAW B/111/3. Organizing and Political Sub-Committee Minutes, 27 June, 28 July, 11 October 1927. Hunt was expected to hold three meetings a week.

264. Ibid., 9 November 1927.

265. *The Land Worker*, September, October 1928.

266. Reading, Records of the NUAAW, B/111/3. Organizing and Political Sub-Committee Minutes, 17 July 1928.

267. Ibid., 17 January, 14 February, 14 March 1929.

268. *The Land Worker*, February 1930.

269. A rural postman who acted as branch secretary and who, at one time, served as district organizer of 9 NUAW branches. *Pembroke County Guardian*, 6 March 1925.

270. A postman who served the branch between 1920–56. *Monmouthshire Beacon*, 3 February 1956.

271. *Hereford Journal*, 31 March 1928 (letters from S. Box and A.E. Ellery).

272. TUC Library. Workers' Union, H.D. 6661 A1. Case of S. Box as presented to the executive committee of the Workers' Union, 1928.

273. Hyman, 'The Workers' Union', p.310.

274. Ministry of Agriculture and Fisheries, *Agricultural Statistics*, 1930. Pt. II, p.106.

275. *The Land Worker*, February 1927, May 1928.

276. *Welsh Gazette*, 2 April 1925.

277. *South Wales Weekly Argus*, 15, 29 October 1927.

278. *South Wales News*, 17 January, 14 February, 31 October 1927.

279. J. Stevenson, *Social Conditions in Britain between the Wars* (London, 1977), pp.32–3.

280. Edgar L. Chappell, *The Housing Problem in Wales* (Cardiff, 1920) p.23.

281. *Caernarvon and Denbigh Herald*, 20 June 1924.

282. *Y Goleuad*, 11 Mehefin 1924.

283. *County Echo*, 16 September 1926.

284. *South Wales News*, 1 December 1926 (letter from James Kennett).

285. Ibid., 27 June 1928.

286. It was the first act to give money in the form of improvement grants.

287. *The Welsh Housing and Development Association Year Book*, 1930, pp.132, 139.

288. Chris Cook, *The Age of Alignment* (London, 1975), p.108.

289. 'Farm workers are slow to see on which side their bread is buttered.' Bangor MSS 1219. Dinesydd Papers 147, T.D. James to Percy O. Jones, 20 Ionawr 1925.

290. *Report of the 26th Annual Conference of the Labour Party*, 1926, pp.250–1.

291. *Report of the 28th Annual Conference of the Labour Party*, 1928, p.21.

292. E.g. *Montgomeryshire Express*, 22 November 1927; *Brecon and Radnor Express*, 1 December 1927; *Denbighshire Free Press*, 11 February 1928.

293. *Report of the 27th Annual Conference of the Labour Party*, 1927, pp.178–80.

294. D.M. Harries 'Carmarthen Politics: The Struggle between Liberals and Labour 1918–60' (unpublished University of Wales MA Thesis, 1980) pp.73–4, 80; J. Graham Jones, 'Wales and the "New Socialism" 1926–1929'. *Welsh History Review*, Vol. XI, No. 2, December 1982, p.190.

295. Cook, *Age of Alignment*, p.207.

296. *Report of the 26th Annual Conference of the Labour Party*, 1926. Appendix XII.

297. J. Graham Jones, 'Wales and the New Socialism', p.188.

298. Cf. *Pembroke County Guardian*, 10, 24 May 1929.

299. *Y Dinesydd Cymreig*, 5 Mehefin 1929 (editorial).

300. Minute Book of the North Wales Labour Federation, op. cit. Only in October 1929 was an attempt made to revive this organization.

301. Christopher Howard, 'Expectations born to death: local Labour Party expansion in the 1920s', op. cit., p.70.

Chapter VII

1. The standard summary on the thirties remains J. Stevenson and C. Cook, *The Slump* (London, 1977).

2. Edith H. Whetham, *The Agrarian History of England and Wales* Vol. VIII, 1914–39 (Cambridge, 1978) p.231.

3. Ministry of Agriculture and Fisheries, *Agricultural Statistics*, 1931, p.91.

4. Whetham, *Agrarian History*, p.236.

5. S. Pollard, *The Development of the British Economy 1914–1967* (London, 1969), pp.138–43.

6. Ashby and Evans, *Agriculture of Wales*, p.16.

7. Ibid., p.168.

8. Anne Martin, 'Agriculture' in Brinley Thomas (ed.), *The Welsh Economy* (Cardiff, 1962), p.78.

9. Ashby and Evans, *Agriculture of Wales*, p.231.

10. G.D.H. Cole, *British Trade Unionism Today* (London, 1939), p.311.

11. TGWU *Annual Report*, 1923.

12. Ibid., 1930.

13. Edwards, *It was my Privilege*, p.35.

14. Viz. Caernarfon, Blaenau Ffestiniog, Port Dinorwic, Shotton and Wrexham (later Bangor, Dolgellau, Newtown, Wrexham, Flint, Shotton and Ellesmere Port).

15. *Holyhead Chronicle*, 10 October 1930.

16. TGWU *Record*, October, November 1932.

17. Ibid., December 1932.

18. Ibid., January 1935.

19. Ibid., February, June 1936.

20. Ibid., June, July 1936.

21. *County Echo*, 15 July 1937.
22. TGWU *Record*, June 1960.
23. *Holyhead and Anglesey Mail*, 18 June 1948.
24. *Herald Môn*, 25 Rhagfyr 1979.
25. *North Wales Pioneer*, 15 June 1939.
26. NUAW *Annual Report*, 1939. These were the designated TGWU strong points during discussions prior to possible amalgamation with the NUAW.
27. See Huw T. Edwards, *Tros y Tresi* (Dinbych, 1956), p.92–3.
28. Cole, *British Trade Unionism*, pp.526.
29. Reading, Records of the NUAAW, B/111/5, Organizing and Political Sub-Committee Minutes, 17 August, 21 September 1933.
30. Ibid., B/ 1/8. Executive Committee Minutes, 18 January 1935.
31. *Shrewsbury Chronicle*, 30 January 1953.
32. *Radnor Express*, 26 April 1934.
33. *Report of the 35th Annual Conference of the Labour Party*, 1935, p.25.
34. *Radnor Express*, 28 June 1934.
35. Ibid., 5, 12 July 1934.
36. Ibid., 2 August 1934. Also, NLW, Brecon and Radnor Divisional Labour Party Records. Executive Committee Minutes, 28 June 1934.
37. Reading, Records of the NUAAW, B/111/5. Organizing and Political Sub-Committee Minutes, 19 July 1934. On another occasion W. Holmes claimed they won 10 members. *Report of the 37th Annual Conference of the Labour Party*, 1937, pp.228–9.
38. Reading, Records of the NUAAW, B/111/5. Organizing and Political Sub-Committee Minutes, 20 September 1934.
39. Letter from Lord Tudor Watkins to the author, March 1979.
40. *Report of the 35th Annual Conference of the Labour Party*, 1935, pp.137–8.
41. NLW, Lord Watkins Papers. *Labour Campaigner*, No. 3, June, 1935, p.7.
42. Ibid., pp.6–7, 'Trade Unionism in Brecon and Radnor'.
43. *Radnor Express*, 11, 18, 25 July 1935. Among the speakers were Rhys J. Davies MP and W.T. Fielding.
44. NLW, Lord Watkins Papers. *Labour Campaigner*, No. 4., July 1935, pp. 8–10.
45. NLW Brecon and Radnor Divisional Labour Party Records, Executive Committee Minutes, 9 May 1936.
46. *Report of the 37th Annual Conference of the Labour Party*, 1937, pp.226–9; *Report of the 39th Annual Conference of the Labour Party*, 1939, pp.315–20.
47. *Report of the 39th Annual Conference of the Labour Party*, 1939, p.68.
48. The Labour victor, W.F. Jackson, was a fruit merchant and keen member of the NFU. For an explanation of this socialist success see *Brecon and Radnor Express and County Times*, 10 August 1939 (editorial).
49. Letter from Lord Tudor Watkins, op. cit.
50. Letter from Cliff Prothero to the author, April 1980.
51. Cliff Prothero, *Recount* (Ormskirk, 1982), p.53. Prothero became secretary of the South Wales Regional Council of Labour in 1943.
52. A.W. Ashby and J.H. Smith, 'Agricultural labour in Wales under statutory regulation of wages 1924–1937'. *The Welsh Journal of Agriculture*, Vol.XIV, 1938.
53. NUAW *Annual Report*, 1933, p.4.
54. *North Wales Chronicle*, 19 May 1933.
55. *Carmarthen Journal*, 21 January 1938.
56. See *Pembroke County and West Wales Guardian*, 14 December 1945.
57. *Pembroke County Guardian*, 28 May 1937.
58. Reading, Records of the NUAAW, B/111/6. Organizing and Political Sub-Committee Minutes, 15 July 1937.
59. A.W. Ashby and J.H. Smith, op. cit., p.6.

60. Ibid., pp.19–20.
61. *Glamorgan Gazette*, 17 January 1936.
62. *Holyhead Chronicle*, 18 November 1938.
63. *Welsh Housing and Development Association Year Book*, 1931, p.35.
64. Ibid., 1934, p.25.
65. *Report of the Committee of Inquiry into the Anti-Tuberculosis Service in Wales and Monmouthshire* (HMSO, 1939), p.154.
66. Ibid., p.132.
67. *Pembroke County Guardian*, 28 May 1937.
68. *Report of the Committee of Inquiry into the Anti-Tuberculosis Service in Wales and Monmouthshire*, op. cit., p.24.
69. Ibid., p.140.
70. *Rural Housing: Third Report of the Rural Housing Sub-Committee of the Central Housing Advisory Committee* (HMSO, 1944), p.52.
71. *Monmouthshire Beacon*, 3 March 1939; *South Wales Weekly Argus*, 4 March 1939.
72. Reading, Records of the NUAAW, B/111/6, Organizing and Political Sub-Committee Minutes, 16 March 1939.
73. *The Land Worker*, December 1941.
74. Ibid., January 1943.
75. Ibid., December 1943.
76. Morgan, *Rebirth of a Nation* pp. 224–7.
77. *First Report of the Commission for the Special Areas*, 1935 (Cmd 4957), p.45; *Third Report*, 1936 (Cmd 5303), pp.108–12; *Fourth Report*, 1937 (Cmd 5595), p.152; *Fifth Report*, 1938 (Cmd 5896), pp.75–7, 120.
78. Interviews with P.J. Smith, August 1979 and M. Jackson, Boverton, August 1979.
79. Interview with Fred Evans, Sealand, April 1980; also Reading, Records of the NUAAW, B/111/6, Organizing and Political Sub-Committee Minutes, 18 May, 24 August 1939.
80. Interview with G.H. Davies, Llangan, May 1979.
81. Reading, Records of the NUAAW, B/11/6, Organizing and Political Sub-Committee Minutes, 11, 14 March 1940.
82. NUAW *Annual Report*, 1941, p.14.
83. Interview with Herbert Jones, Llanfair Disgoed, October 1979.
84. Interviews with K. Harrison and F.L. Ward, Rosemarket, August 1979.
85. *The Land Worker*, December 1943.
86. K.A.H. Murray, *Agriculture* (London, 1955), p.38.
87. Ibid., p.83.
88. Ibid., pp.352–3.
89. Madden, 'National Union of Agricultural Workers', p.179.
90. Ibid., p.299. Appendix C.
91. TGWU *Annual Report*, 1946.
92. Reading, Records of the NUAAW, B/1/10. Executive Committee Minutes, 17 January 1941.
93. Ibid., B/111/7. Organizing and Political Sub-Committee Minutes, 20 November, 10 December 1941.
94. *Glamorgan Gazette*, 13 February 1942 (advertisement).
95. Reading, Records of the NUAAW, B/1/10 Executive Committee Minutes, 18 September, 16 October 1942.
96. *Welsh Gazette*, 12 March 1942 (advertisement), 26 March 1942.
97. *Cambrian News*, 29 May, 5 June 1942 (advertisements).
98. Ibid., 12, 19 June 1942.

99. Reading, Records of the NUAAW, B/111/7. Organizing and Political Sub-Committee Minutes, 18 June, 16 July 1942.

100. Ibid., 16 April, 21 May 1942.

101. Ibid., B/1/10, Executive Committee Minutes, 15 January 1943.

102. NUGMW *Annual Report*, 1935.

103. TUC Library, Workers' Union, HD 6661 A1, Sidney Box Papers. Letter from Eddy Jones to Sidney Box, 5 December 1954 following the publication of Box's autobiography, *The Good Old Days*.

104. *Monmouthshire Beacon*, 10 October, 5 December 1941.

105. Ibid., 10 April 1942.

106. Interview with H.T. Pritchard, Newport, December 1979; also *Monmouthshire Beacon*, 1 May 1942.

107. Interview with H.T. Pritchard, op. cit.; also *Monmouthshire Beacon*, 28 August, 16 October 1942.

108. See *Monmouthshire Beacon*, 22 August 1969 (obituary account).

109. Ibid., 28 August, 11 September 1942.

110. Ibid., 21 May 1943.

111. Ibid., 9 July 1943.

112. *Abergavenny Chronicle*, 16–30 July 1943.

113. *Monmouthshire Beacon*, 6 August 1943.

114. Ibid., September 1943–6.

115. Ibid., 24 December 1943, 31 March 1944.

116. Ibid., 4 August 1944.

117. Ibid., 5, 26 March 1943; *South Wales Weekly Argus*, 27 March, 3 April 1943.

118. *Monmouthshire Beacon*, 30 April 1943.

119. Ibid., 3 November 1944.

120. *South Wales Weekly Argus*, 5 May 1945.

121. *Monmouthshire Beacon*, 4 May 1945.

122. *The Land Worker*, May 1945.

123. *South Wales Regional Council of Labour Report*, 1945, p.3.

124. NUAW *Annual Report*, 1944, p.6.

125. *The Land Worker*, June 1944.

126. Groves, *Sharpen the Sickle*, p.236.

127. Reading, Records of the NUAAW, B/1/11, Executive Committee Minutes, 22 September 1944.

128. Personal details supplied by Ieuan Jenkins, Liverpool (brother), in a letter to the author, January 1981, also Mrs H.A. Jenkins, Aberdare (wife), in an interview, February 1981.

129. *The Land Worker*, July 1944.

130. *Carmarthen Journal*, 16 February–18 May 1945.

131. For a rare example, see *Pembroke County and West Wales Guardian*, 22 February 1946. Meeting at Trefgarn Owen, where attendance was said to be small.

132. Interview with F.L. Ward, op. cit.

133. Letter from Gwilym Evans, Llansawel, to the author, February 1981.

134. *Cardigan and Tivyside Advertiser*, 4 May 1945 (advertisement); *Cambrian News*, 4 May 1945 (advertisement).

135. *Y Clorianydd*, 1 Tachwedd 1939–7 Chwefror 1940 (advertisement).

136. TGWU *Record*, 1943, p.211.

137. *Yr Herald Cymraeg*, 25 Gorffennaf 1944.

138. Letter from K. Wolfenden, Wrexham (chairman of the Wrexham Trades and Labour Council, 1934–45) to the author, April 1980.

139. *South Wales Weekly Argus*, 4 November 1944; *Monmouthshire Beacon*, 24 August 1945.

140. *Monmouthshire Beacon*, 31 August 1945.
141. *South Wales Weekly Argus*, 3 August 1946.
142. *Cambrian News*, 14 December 1945.
143. *South Wales Weekly Argus*, 9, 23 March 1946.
144. *Carmarthen Journal*, 31 August 1945.
145. The remarks of the NUAW president, E.G. Gooch. *The Welshman*, 23 May 1947; *The Land Worker*, June 1947.
146. *The Welshman*, 18 March 1949.
147. Reading, Records of the NUAAW, B/1/12. Organizing and Political Sub-Committee Minutes, 24 January 1947.
148. *The Land Worker*, October 1971.
149. Reading, Records of the NUAAW, B/1/12. Organizing and Political Sub-Committee Minutes, 1 November, 20 December 1946, 24 January 1947.
150. Ibid., 21 February, 11, 20 June 1947.
151. Personal information supplied by Mrs G. Davies, Blaenau Ffestiniog (wife), April 1980, also *Llafar Bro*, Rhif 43, Mai 1979.
152. Headland House, London. NUAW Executive Committee and Sub-Committee Minutes, 28–9 April 1948.
153. E.g. Gwyn Lloyd, Llanrwst; Dafydd Jones, Aber-erch; Isaac Thomas, Mochdre.
154. *North Wales Times*, 19 June 1948. The author is also indebted to E. Lloyd Roberts, Denbigh, for a detailed letter, 26 September 1979.
155. *North Wales Times*, 12 March 1949.
156. Ibid., 18 March 1950.
157. Minutes of the Wrexham Trades Council and Divisional Labour Party, op. cit., 17 April 1950.
158. *North Wales Times*, 10 September 1949.
159. Letter from Owen Alun Hughes, Abergele, to the author, October 1979.
160. Gwilym Davies took charge of the Welsh-speaking portion of Flintshire in September 1948.
161. Monmouthshire branches had begun to decline prior to the dismissal of William Thomas in February 1949 (he was discovered to have misappropriated union funds).
162. K.O. Morgan, *Labour in Power 1945–1951* (Oxford, 1984), p.503.
163. Marian Bowley, *Housing and the State 1919–1944* (London, 1945), pp.243–4.
164. See *Western Mail*, 5 February 1943, for the number in each Welsh county.
165. *Welsh Gazette*, 1 July 1943.
166. *Hansard*, 5th Series, Vol.400, 8 June 1944, Col.1512.
167. *Pembroke County and West Wales Guardian*, 7 November 1947.
168. Morgan, *Labour in Power*, p.171.
169. See *Y Clorianydd*, 4 Ionawr 1933 (advertisement).
170. Ibid., 7 Hydref 1936.
171. Farm workers formed the bulk of the unemployed. See *Holyhead Chronicle*, 3 February 1939.
172. Letter from J.O. Jones, Menai Bridge (secretary of Undeb Gweithwyr Môn Approved Society 1936–45) to the author, May 1980.
173. *Herald Môn*, 19 Mawrth 1946.
174. Interview with Lord Cledwyn of Penrhos, Bae Trearddur, April 1980.
175. *Herald Môn*, 14 Ionawr, 21 Hydref 1947: 20 Ionawr,13 Ebrill, 6 Gorffennaf, 12 Hydref 1948.
176. Ibid., 22 Mehefin 1948.
177. Ibid., 11 Ionawr, 5 Ebrill, 12 Gorffennaf 1949.
178. Interview with Lord Cledwyn of Penrhos, op. cit.

179. Morgan, *Labour in Power*, p.95.

180. Pollard, *British Economy*, p.384.

181. Madden, 'National Union of Agricultural Workers', p.297, Appendix B. Mills, 'National Union of Agricultural Workers', p.357, Appendix 3, puts the figure at 136,839.

182. A press advertising campaign was sanctioned in March 1948. Headland House, London, NUAW Executive Committee and Sub-Committee Minutes, 18 March 1948. Otherwise, local newspapers contain little information. For one recorded meeting (at Forden) see *Montgomeryshire Express*, 4 June 1949.

183. Morgan, *Labour in Power*, pp.305–6.

184. Madden, 'National Union of Agricultural Workers', p.278.

185. *The Land Worker*, December 1967.

186. Mills, 'National Union of Agricultural Workers', p.366, Appendix 6.

187. Ibid., p.389, Appendix 17.

188. Viz. 27,182 (1960); 14,981 (1970).

189. The Vale of Towi branch is a case in point. Of the 11 new members who joined 1940–62, 8 were forestry workers. Interview with Wesley Jones, Y Gelli Aur, September 1979.

190. *The Land Worker*, December 1967; May, June 1968.

191. UCW Aberystwyth, Department of Political Science Research Project. Transcript of an interview with R.L. Jones (1971) in the possession of Miss E. Jones, Llanilar.

192. Interview with Emyr Hughes, Aberffraw, August 1980. (Emyr Hughes succeeded his father, O.R. Hughes, as branch secretary.)

Conclusion

1. Though Caradoc Evans saw himself as a rebel against middle-class, Nonconformist tyranny, his books have little political content. T.L. Williams, *Caradoc Evans* (Cardiff, 1970), pp.97–8; also John Harris, *'Fury Never Leaves Us'. A Miscellany of Caradoc Evans* (Bridgend, 1985).

2. See J. Barrington Moore Jr., *Injustice: The Social Bases of Obedience and Revolt* (London, 1978), p.321, also pp.469–72.

3. Howard Newby, *The Deferential Worker* (London, 1977).

4. R. Taylor, *The Fifth Estate* (London, 1980), p.404.

5. Incorporated into the TGWU Agricultural and Allied Workers' Trade Group, total membership was down to 70,000 by 1985.

6. R. Danziger and S. Winyard, *Poor Farmworkers, Rich Farms* (Low Pay Unit Pamphlet No. 39, March 1986).

7. S. Winyard, 'Poor Harvest, Farm Workers and the Common Market', *Low Pay Report*, November 1980.

BIOGRAPHICAL INDEX

Evan Anthony (d. 1971)

Fishguard. Schoolteacher. Baptist deacon. Presided at first meeting of Goodwick and Fishguard Trades and Labour Council. Labour Party activist. Parish, urban district and county councillor. President of Fishguard NUT.

W.T. Bason (d. 1974)

Bala. Railwayman. English Presbyterian lay preacher. Member of the GWR executive of the NUR. Prime mover in the foundation of Bala and District Trades and Labour Council and Merioneth Labour Party. Member of Bala UDC. JP.

John Blayney (d. 1918)

Machynlleth. Signalman. Churchman. Pioneer trade unionist. Secretary of the Machynlleth NUR branch.

Edwin Davies (d. 1936)

Llanglydwen. Farm labourer. Trade union and Labour Party activist in Carmarthenshire. Contested Llanglydwen RDC by-election in 1921. Served on district wages committee.

Gwilym Davies (d. 1979)

Blaenau Ffestiniog. NUAAW organizer in north Wales 1947–79. Calvinistic Methodist deacon. Labour member of Blaenau Ffestiniog RDC and Merioneth County Council. JP. Served on several public bodies. Awarded MBE for services to the Labour Party in 1965.

George M. Ll. Davies (d. 1949)

Bank manager. Secretary of the Welsh Housing Trust. Leading member of the Fellowship of Reconciliation. MP for the University of Wales 1923–4 (as Christian Pacifist who took the Labour whip). Calvinistic Methodist minister.

Henry Davies (d. 1974)

Llanrwst. Farm labourer/gardener. Calvinistic Methodist deacon. NUAW local activist. Served on district wages committee.

John Davies (d. 1937)

Llangeitho. NUAW organizer in west Wales 1918–19. Calvinistic Methodist. ILP and socialist pioneer. Secretary of the Welsh district of the WEA.

Huw T. Edwards (d. 1970).

Penmaenmawr. Labour Party and trade union activist. Secretary of the North Wales Labour Federation. District secretary (1932), then regional secretary of the TGWU 1940–53. Served on numerous public bodies.

William Edwards (d. 1950)
Hologwyn, Llanddaniel-fab. Farmer. Lecturer in agriculture. Secretary of the Anglesey Farmers' Society in early 1890s. Supporter of ap Ffarmwr. Chairman of the Anglesey Liberal Association. Member of the NFU. County councillor 1910. Joined Labour Party in 1923. Labour Party organizer in Caernarfonshire 1926. Labour parliamentary candidate in Anglesey 1929.

Humphrey Ellis (d. 1942)
Bala. Shopkeeper. Independent. Active with Bala and District Trades and Labour Council and Merioneth Labour Party. Secretary of the Bala NUAW branch.

Henry Evans (d. 1972)
Goodwick. Farm labourer. Baptist deacon. Trade union pioneer in north Pembrokeshire. Served on district wages committee. Member of Goodwick Parish Council. JP.

Thomas Evans (d. 1949)
Little Haven. Postman. Independent deacon. Socialist and trade union pioneer in north Pembrokeshire. District secretary for nine NUAW branches. Served on district wages committee. Also active with the Union of Post Office Workers.

John Foulkes (Eithinfab) (d. 1962)
Llannefydd. Stonemason. Baptist deacon. Trade union and Labour Party local activist. Served on district wages committee.

Richard Griffith (d. 1971)
Madryn. Drover at Madryn Castle Farm School 1914–39. Calvinistic Methodist. Pioneer in the organization of agricultural workers in Llŷn. Labour Party activist.

E.P. Harries (d. 1963)
Pembroke Dock. Shipwright. District secretary of the Shipconstructors and Shipwrights' Association. Secretary of Pembroke Dock Trades Council 1913–17, and Pembrokeshire Labour Party 1916–20. JP. Alderman. Served on the district wages committee. Election agent. Left Pembrokeshire in 1925 to become full-time trade union official.

William Harris (d. 1925)
Pontllan-fraith. Miners' political organizer. Baptist. Member of the SWMF and Labour Party executive. Chairman of Abertillery UDC and member of Monmouthshire County Council. Secretary of the South Wales Labour Federation.

Revd J.H. Howard (d. 1947)
Colwyn Bay. Calvinistic Methodist minister. Well-known 'socialist minister' and pacifist. Staunch supporter of trade unionism and the Labour Party. Labour parliamentary candidate in Merioneth in 1931. Author of *Jesus the Agitator*, *Cristionogaeth a Chymdeithas*, etc.

Arthur Howells (d. 1950)
Llanfaches. Shepherd. Secretary of the Caer-went NUAW branch. Served on the district wages committee.

John Hughes (d. 1927)
Aberffraw. Farm labourer. Former collier. Calvinistic Methodist. Contested county council election as Labour candidate in 1895. Lifelong

spokesman for the rural working class from the days of ap Ffarmwr to Undeb Gweithwyr Môn.

O.R. Hughes (d. 1982)
Aberffraw. Farm labourer. Wesleyan Methodist. Joined Aberffraw TGWU branch in 1928. Treasurer, and later secretary, for fifty years.

H.N. Hunt (d.?)
Clydach. Member of the Clydach Strike Committee, 1917. Workers' Union organizer 1918–21. Employed as NUAW temporary organizer in 1927.

Richard Ingram (d. 1956)
Rockfield. Postman. Secretary of the Monmouth NUAW branch 1920–56.

David James (Dafydd Iago) (d. 1924)
Glynarthen. General labourer. Former collier. Local NUAW activist. Served on the district wages committee.

J. Gwendraeth James (d. 1954)
Blaen-porth. Schoolmaster. Churchman. Labour Party supporter. Member of Cardigan RDC and Board of Guardians. Served on district wages committee.

Revd T.D. James (Iago Erfyl) (d. 1927)
Rector of Llanerfyl, Montgomeryshire 1901–27. Poet and littérateur. Active Conservative Party supporter turned socialist. Member of Llanfyllin RDC and Board of Guardians. Represented the Labour Party on Montgomeryshire County Council.

D.J. Jenkins (d. 1968)
Pumsaint. NUAAW organizer in south Wales 1944–56. Left-wing socialist. Prominent member of the Carmarthenshire Labour Party who served on various public committees connected with agriculture.

Revd J.H. Jenkins (d. 1933)
Rector of Cilrhedyn, Pembrokeshire 1911–33. A courageous and uncompromising socialist. Prominent platform speaker on behalf of the Labour Party, well-known to coal-miners, dockers and rural workers alike.

W.H. John (d.1941)
Solva. Printer and journalist. Independent deacon. Pioneer of the Labour movement in Pembrokeshire. Chairman of the Solva NUAW branch. County councillor 1919.

Caradog Jones (d. 1979)
Mynytho. Schoolteacher. Independent. Principal founder of the farm labourers' movement in Llŷn. Secretary of the North Wales Labour Federation. Later WEA organizer. County councillor. Awarded BEM in 1977.

Cyril O. Jones (d. 1969)
Holyhead; Wrexham. Solicitor. Calvinistic Methodist. Secretary of the Anglesey Liberal Association. Active supporter of Undeb Gweithwyr Môn. Joined Labour Party in 1916. Moved to Wrexham 1919. Solicitor to NWMA and TGWU. Labour parliamentary candidate in Anglesey, 1924 and Flint, 1929, 1935.

David Jones (d. 1907)
Llwyngwyn, Henllan, Llandysul. Shoemaker. Former labourer. Independent deacon. Local public figure. Cousin to Dr Pan Jones.

Revd D. Gwynfryn Jones (d. 1954)
Flint. Wesleyan minister. Former collier. Liberal, who turned in 1914 to become one of the Labour Party pioneers in Flintshire. County councillor. JP. President of the North Wales Labour Federation. Labour parliamentary candidate in Flintshire 1922 and 1924.

D.S. Jones (d. 1968)
Penllwyn, Capel Bangor. Calvinistic Methodist. NUAW organizer in west Wales 1919–22 and the whole of Wales 1922–3. Labour Party activist. Moved to London in 1929.

D.W. Jones (ap Rhydwen) (d. 1932)
Whitford. Timber feller. Baptist turned Churchman. Organizer for the National Farm and Dairy Workers' Union, later Workers' Union, 1918–22. Liberal turned socialist who wrote on labour matters in *Baner ac Amserau Cymru.*

Revd E.B. Jones (d. 1940)
Independent minister at Gwalchmai 1911–35. Lifelong Liberal, and county councillor. Promoter of Undeb Gweithwyr Môn.

Eddy Jones (d. 1969)
Skenfrith. Roadman. Former collier, railway clerk, quarryman and farm labourer. Baptist lay preacher. Prominent trade union and Labour Party activist in Monmouthshire. Founder of the Monmouth Trades Council. Secretary of the Monmouth Federation of Trades and Labour Councils 1939–69. Labour parliamentary candidate in Leominster, 1950, 1951. Served on the district wages committee.

Henry Jones (d. 1959)
Golden Grove. Ploughman on the Cawdor estate. Calvinistic Methodist. Pioneer of rural trade unionism in Carmarthenshire. Secretary of the Vale of Towi NUAW branch 1919–58. Awarded BEM in 1949.

J.O. Jones (ap Ffarmwr) (d. 1899)
Dwyran. Schoolteacher and journalist. Originator of the farm labourers' movement in Anglesey.

R.L. Jones (d. 1976)
Llanilar. Farm labourer, roadworker. Calvinistic Methodist deacon. Founder member of the Llanilar NUAW branch. Branch secretary 1917–74. Served on the district wages committee for some fifty years. Founder member of the Cardiganshire Labour Party and later its president. Became a JP in 1929 — the first working man to become a magistrate in the county. Represented the NUAW on various public committees.

William Jones (d. 1936)
Llanfair-yng-Nghornwy. Farm labourer. Calvinistic Methodist deacon. Socialist and Undeb Gweithwyr Môn activist.

W.J. Jones (Brynfab) (d. 1940)
Brynsiencyn. Shopkeeper. Former quarryman. Revivified Undeb Gweithwyr Môn in 1917–18. Member of Dwyran RDC and Board of Guardians. JP. County councillor 1922–40. Prominent socialist.

James Kennett (d. 1961)
Llantwit Major. Hay-cutter. Prominent NUAW activist. Served on district wages committee. Member of Llantwit Major Parish Council.

C.H. Lawrence (d. ?)
Haverfordwest. Railway linesman. Calvinistic Methodist deacon and lay preacher. Chairman of local NUR branch. Served as secretary and president of Pembroke Labour Party.

D.T. Lewis (d. 1966)
Mathry. Schoolteacher. Churchman. One-time executive member of the Pembrokeshire Conservative Association turned Labour in 1918. Secretary and later chairman of the Mathry NUAW branch. Secretary of the Pembrokeshire Labour Party 1920. Election agent. Parish councillor. Author of 'Labour Notes' in *County Echo*. Served on district wages committee. Moved to Dinas 1930.

David Lloyd (d. 1937)
Aberffraw. Stonemason. Former collier. Calvinistic Methodist. Contested county council election as Labour candidate in 1913. Served as chairman of Aberffraw branch of Undeb Gweithwyr Môn.

John Lloyd (d. 1927)
Mathry. Farm labourer. Baptist deacon. NUAW and Labour Party activist. Parish councillor.

William Lloyd (d. ?)
Mathry. Farm labourer. Prominent NUAW activist in north Pembrokeshire. Served on the conciliation committee. Because of persecution forced to seek work at Blaengarw colliery.

Revd Richard Morris (d. 1961)
Independent minister at Llannerch-y-medd 1905–19. Former collier and steel worker. Agent to Sir Owen Thomas in 1918 election. Gave up the ministry to become full-time secretary of the Anglesey Workers' Union 1919–23.

Revd T.E. Nicholas ('Niclas y Glais') (d. 1971)
Independent minister at Llangybi and Llanddewi Brefi 1914–18. Outstanding poet and political author on social questions. Pioneer of ILP and trade union movement. Contested Aberdare as a Socialist and Pacifist in 1918 election. Organized farm workers and lead-miners in Cardiganshire and Pembrokeshire. Moved to Aberystwyth 1920. Joined the Communist Party.

Revd E.T. Owen (d. 1956)
Independent minister at Llangeler 1910–25. Former collier. Assisted in the formation of the Carmarthenshire Labour Party. Twice stood as parliamentary candidate in Carmarthen in 1924.

Revd W. Washington Owen (d. 1969)
Llandudno Junction. Baptist minister and railwayman. Secretary of Llandudno Junction NUAW branch and voluntary organizer of farm labourers in north Caernarfonshire.

G.H. Peate (d. 1938)
Llanbryn-mair. Builder. Independent deacon. Supporter of rural trade unionism. Member of Llanbryn-mair Parish Council.

John Picton (d. 1921)
Carew. Quarryman and farm labourer. Wesleyan Methodist. Promoter of the NUAW and Labour Party in south Pembrokeshire. Served on the district wages committee. Member of the Board of Guardians and Pembroke RDC.

Contested county council election in 1919. JP. Vice-president of the Pembrokeshire Labour Party.

A.W. Pittman (d. ?)

Portskewett. Signalman. Active NUR member who played a leading role in organizing Monmouthshire farm workers. Member of the Board of Guardians, Chepstow RDC and Monmouthshire County Council.

W.J. Pretty (d. 1928)

Llanfairpwll. Painter. Churchman. Served as president of Undeb Gweithwyr Môn, and active with the Anglesey Labour Party.

Edward Pritchard (Iorwerth) (d. 1921)

Gwalchmai. Builder. Independent. Pioneer of the Labour movement in Anglesey. Active in ap Ffarmwr's day and one of the leaders of Undeb Gweithwyr Môn.

Hugh Pritchard (d. 1961)

Llangefni. Inspector of Weights and Measures. One-time Editor of *Y Wyntyll.* Secretary of the Anglesey Liberal Association 1904–9. Turned Labour 1918. Llangefni UD councillor. Promoter of Undeb Gweithwyr Môn and later Undeb Gweithwyr Môn Approved Society.

Revd J.T. Pritchard (d. 1928)

Calvinistic Methodist minister in Aberdaron and Chwilog. Labour Party supporter.

David Rees (d. 1952)

Aberafan. Crane driver and Friendly Society official. ILP and Labour Party activist. NUAW organizer in Wales (later south-east Wales) 1918–22. Member of Aberafan Town Council 1903–29. Mayor. Glamorgan County Councillor.

Revd Gwilym Rees (d. 1939)

Rector of Llanbryn-mair 1911–25. Local supporter of farm workers' trade unionism. Served on the Board of Guardians, Llanbryn-mair Parish Council and Montgomeryshire County Council.

Urias Richards (d. 1948)

Cilgerran. Merchant. Independent deacon. Staunch Labour supporter. Member of Cardigan Board of Guardians, St Dogmaels RDC and Pembrokeshire County Council.

E.T. Roberts (d. 1945)

Cerrigydrudion. Miller. Wesleyan Methodist. Secretary to Cerrigydrudion Workers' Union (later TGWU) branch 1920–40. Served on district wages committee and county agricultural committee.

R.G. Roberts (d. 1926)

Pen-y-groes, Caernarfonshire. Quarryman. Calvinistic Methodist. President of NWQU 1914–15. Active in formation of the Caernarfonshire Labour Council and Labour Party. NUAW organizer in north Wales 1918–23. Member of the Board of Guardians, district council and county council.

Daniel Rowlands (d. 1920)

Penmynydd. Farm labourer; roadworker. Local Undeb Gweithwyr Môn activist.

Thomas Rowlands (d. 1935)

Gwalchmai. Gelder. Baptist deacon. Local Liberal official who pioneered the labour movement in Anglesey. Prominent with Undeb Gweithwyr Môn and the Labour Party. Member of the Board of Guardians. Parish and county councillor, 1929.

John Sharp (d. 1957)

Pendine. Smallholder. Former collier. Local trade union activist.

P.J. Smith (d. 1982)

Llantwit Major. Railway signalman. Churchman. Archetypal socialist politician. NUR activist who established NUAW and Labour Party branches in the Vale of Glamorgan. First Labour candidate to win a rural seat on Glamorgan County Council in 1934, he emerged as leader of the all-powerful Labour group in 1960 and effectively Glamorgan's political boss.

T.J. Stokoe (d. ?)

Hay-on-Wye. Businessman. Churchman. Member of Hay UDC. Liberal turned socialist. Active on behalf of the labour movement in Brecon and Radnor. Member of the Breconshire County Council.

David Thomas (d. 1967)

Tal-y-sarn. Schoolteacher. Wesleyan Methodist. Principal pioneer of the labour movement in north Wales. Began his socialist mission with the ILP and Fabian Society. Author of *Y Werin a'i Theyrnas* (1910). Trade union activist on behalf of numerous organizations. Prime mover in establishment of Caernarfonshire Labour Council in 1912 and North Wales Trades and Labour Council 1915. Workers' Union organizer in mid-Wales 1920–2. Served on district wages committee. Election agent to R.T. Jones 1922. Member of Gwyrfai RDC. Moved to Bangor 1922. In latter years associated with WEA movement. Editor of *Lleufer*.

H.J. Thomas (Huw Tudur) (d. 1954)

Trefriw. Lead-miner. Calvinistic Methodist. Trade union and Labour Party activist in the Vale of Conwy.

J.E. Thomas (d. 1941)

Pen-y-groes, Caernarfonshire. Schoolmaster. Former quarryman and collier. NUT activist. With David Thomas and R.G. Roberts he pioneered trade unionism and the Labour Party in Caernarfonshire. Secretary of the Caernarfonshire Labour Council and treasurer of the North Wales Trades and Labour Council.

J.W. Thomas (d. 1946)

Sarn Bach, Abersoch. Schoolteacher; district relieving officer. Independent. Prominent Labour Party activist. Member of the Board of Guardians.

Lewis Thomas (d. 1921)

Llangristiolus. Farm labourer; postman. Calvinistic Methodist. ILP, Undeb Gweithwyr Môn and Labour Party pioneer. Elected Labour county councillor in 1919.

Sir Owen Thomas (d. 1923)

Brynddu, Llanfechell. Agriculturalist and soldier. Independent. High Sheriff for Anglesey. President of the Anglesey Liberal Association 1894. County councillor 1889. Contested Oswestry as Liberal candidate in 1895. Knighted 1917. Elected Independent Labour MP for Anglesey 1918, re-elected as Independent MP in 1922.

Robert Thomas (d. 1967)

Aber, Caernarfonshire. Farm worker. Trade union activist in north

Caernarfonshire. Served on the district wages committee.

R.H. Thomas (d. 1934)

Pentraeth. Tailor. Calvinistic Methodist. Antiquarian and littérateur. Supporter of ap Ffarmwr.

W.H. (Billy) Vaughan (d. 1959)

Port Talbot. Railway guard. Independent. ILP and Labour Party activist. General secretary of the Aberafan Constituency Labour Party. Member of the Port Talbot Borough Council. Mayor. Leader of the workers' side on the district wages committee 1924–59. Awarded NUAW gold medal for his services in 1941. Succeeded Capt. Geoffrey Crawshay as chairman of the Welsh Land Settlement Society Ltd. in 1954.

Revd D.D. Walters (Gwallter Ddu) (d. 1934)

Independent minister at Newcastle Emlyn, 1890–1926. Poet and littérateur. Lecturer and writer on social topics. Labour Party supporter. Member of the Carmarthenshire County Council.

W.J. Wardle (d. 1946)

Swansea. West Wales district secretary of the Workers' Union (TGWU) 1920–46. Served on the district wages committee.

E.J. Williams (d. 1945)

Wrexham. Checkweigher. Calvinistic Methodist. Prominent trade union and Labour Party activist in east Denbighshire. Member of NWMA. Secretary of the Wrexham Trades and Labour Council and Divisional Labour Party. Member of Wrexham Borough Council and Denbighshire County Council. Election agent to Robert Richards. NUAW organizer in north-east Wales 1919–21. Served on the district wages committee.

Hugh Williams (d. 1903)

Rhyd Dafydd, Rhos-y-bol. Tenant farmer and butter dealer. Calvinistic Methodist. Liberal. Prominent in ap Ffarmwr's crusade.

Rowland (Rolly) Williams (d. 1969)

Bala. Engine driver. Calvinistic Methodist lay preacher. Trade union and Labour Party pioneer in Bala and Merionethshire. NUR official. Member of Bala RDC. JP. Labour parliamentary candidate in West Derby 1922, Carmarthen 1923, Wolverhampton East 1929.

T. Llew Williams (d. 1956)

Llanuwchllyn. Farm labourer. Independent deacon. Secretary of Llanuwchllyn NUAW branch. Served on the district wages committee.

William Williams (d. 1955)

Port Dinorwic. Tailor. Worker's Union (TGWU) organizer in north Wales 1918–39. Independent deacon. Important trade union and Labour Party pioneer in Gwynedd. Served on the district wages committee. JP. MBE 1955.

William Williams (d. 1957)

Llannerch-y-medd. Farm labourer. Calvinistic Methodist. Awarded BEM in 1948 for services rendered as secretary of Llannerch-y-medd TGWU branch.

BIBLIOGRAPHY

A. Manuscript sources
B. Official papers
C. Reports
D. Newspapers and periodicals
E. Interviews
F. Works of reference
G. Secondary works
H. Articles
I. Unpublished theses

A. **Manuscript Sources**

Museum of English Rural Life, University of Reading:
Records of the National Union of Agricultural and Allied Workers.

Headland House, 308 Gray's Inn Road, London:
Records and Reports of the National Union of Agricultural and Allied Workers.

Trade Union Congress Library, London:
Workers' Union H.D. 6661, A1, Sidney Box Papers.

British Library of Political and Economic Science, London:
Coll. E.B. CVI. 43, National Labour Federation Reports, 1887, 1889.

Public Record Office:
Records of the Registrar of Friendly Societies, F.S. 11/133, Undeb Gweithwyr Môn file.

Modern Records Centre, University of Warwick Library, Coventry:
MSS 51, Working Papers for Dr Richard Hyman's study of the Workers' Union.
MSS 126, Transport and General Workers' Union Records.

National Library of Wales, Aberystwyth:
Brecon and Radnor Labour Party Records.
Edgar L. Chappell Papers.
H.T. Edwards Collection.
Carl Hanson Collection.

E.P. Harries Papers.
E.T. John Papers.
Papurau y Parch. D.J. Roberts, Aberteifi.
David Thomas (Bangor) Collection.
Lord Watkins Papers.
University College of North Wales, Bangor:
Dinesydd Papers.
Papurau T.E. Nicholas.
Papurau David Thomas (Bangor).
Papurau R.H. Thomas, Pentraeth.
Gwynedd Archives Service, Llangefni:
Papers of the Calvinistic Methodists in Anglesey.
Records of the Anglesey County Council.
Gwynedd Archives Service, Caernarfon:
Minutes of the Caernarfonshire Labour Council, 1912–27.
Pwllheli Union Minute Book, 1917–22.
Records of the North Wales Quarrymen's Union.
Dyfed Archives Service, Carmarthen:
ACC. 4414 L.C.L.P., Documents of the Llanelli Divisional Labour Party.
Clwyd Record Office, Rhuthun:
DD/DM/344. Records of the Wrexham Trades Council and Divisional Labour Party.
Gwynedd Archives Service, Dolgellau:
Minute Book of the Merioneth NFU.
Pontypridd Central Library:
Pontypridd Trades and Labour Council Minute Books.
Wrexham Maelor Area Library, Wrexham:
Wrexham and District Trades and Labour Council Year Book, 1918.
Manuscript Sources in Private Possession:
Llyfr Cofnodion Cangen Undeb y Gweithwyr, Aberffraw, 1919–30 (in the possession of Mr Emyr Hughes, Aberffraw).
Llyfr Cofnodion Canghennau Llŷn o Undeb y Gweithwyr Amaethyddol 1919–22 (in the possession of Mrs N. Jones, Morfa Nefyn).
Papurau J. Foulkes (Eithinfab) (in the possession of Mr P.S. Foulkes, Llanrwst).
Papurau R.L. Jones (in the possession of Miss E. Jones, Llanilar).
Papurau W.J. Jones (Brynfab) (in the possession of Mr Hugh Meredydd Jones, Llanfairpwll).
Papurau y Parch. William Morris (in the possession of Mrs G. Roberts, Caernarfon).

B. **Official Papers**

Hansard, *Parliamentary Debates.*

Commission on the Employment of Children, Young Persons and Women in Agriculture, Third Report, 1870 (C 70).

Report of an Inquiry as to the Disturbances connected with the Levying of Tithe Rent Charge in Wales, 1887 (C 5195).

Royal Commission on Labour, The Agricultural Labourer, 1893, Vol. II (C 6894).

Royal Commission on Land in Wales and Monmouthshire, Evidence, Report and Appendices, 1894–6 (C 7439, 7661, 7757, 8221, 8222, 8242).

School Attendance and Employment in Agriculture. Summary of Returns supplied by County Local Education Authorities of Children excused from School for Employment in Agriculture on 31 May 1916 (Cd 8302).

Committee appointed by the Board of Trade to Investigate the Principal Causes which have led to the Increase in the Prices of Commodities. Interim Report on Meat, Milk and Bacon, 1916 (Cd 8358).

Report of the Commission appointed to Inquire into Industrial Unrest, No. 7 Division: Report of the Commissioners for Wales, including Monmouthshire, 1917 (Cd 8668).

Agricultural Wages Board, *Wages Board Gazette*, 15 August 1918–29 September 1921.

Wages and Conditions of Employment in Agriculture, 1919. Vol. I, General Report (Cmd 24); Vol. II, Report of Investigators (Cmd 25).

Report of the Committee appointed by the Agricultural Wages Board to Inquire into the Financial Results of the Occupation of Agricultural Land and the Cost of Living of Rural Workers, 1919 (Cmd 76).

Ministry of Agriculture and Fisheries: *Agricultural Statistics*, 1921–36 (H.M.S.O.)

Report of the Inter-Departmental Committee on Agricultural Tied Cottages, 1931–2 (Cmd 4148).

First Report of the Commission for the Special Areas, 1935 (Cmd 4957).

Second Report of the Commission for the Special Areas, February 1936 (Cmd 5090).

Third Report of the Commission for the Special Areas, November 1936 (Cmd 5303).

Fourth Report of the Commission for the Special Areas, 1937 (Cmd 5595).

Fifth Report of the Commission for the Special Areas, 1938 (Cmd 5896).

Report of the Committee of Inquiry into the Anti-Tuberculosis Service in Wales and Monmouthshire (H.M.S.O., 1939).
Rural Housing: Third Report of the Rural Housing Sub-Committee of the Central Housing Advisory Committee (H.M.S.O., 1944).
Report of Proceedings under the Agricultural Wages Acts for the Period 1 October 1937–30 September 1950 (H.M.S.O. 1952).
Co-operative Farms and Smallholdings with Centralised services in Wales (H.M.S.O. 1952).
George S. Bain, *Trade Union Growth and Recognition*. Royal Commission on Trade Unions and Employers' Associations. Research Paper 6 (H.M.S.O. 1967).

C. **Reports**

(i) *Annual Reports of the following organizations*:

Dock, Wharf, Riverside and General Labourers' Union.
Labour Party.
National Amalgamated Labourers' Union.
National Labour Federation.
National Union of Agricultural and Allied Workers.
National Union of Gasworkers and General Labourers/National Union of General Workers/General and Municipal Workers' Union.
National Union of Railwaymen.
South Wales Regional Council of Labour.
Trades Union Congress.
Transport and General Workers' Union.
Welsh Housing and Development Association.
Workers' Educational Association.
Workers' Union.

(ii) *Miscellaneous*:

Report of the Proceedings of the Eighth Poor Law Conference for the South Wales and Monmouthshire District, Swansea, 6 and 7 May 1897.
Report of the Welsh Land Enquiry Committee (London, 1914).
Steve Winyard, 'Poor Harvest, Farm Workers and the Common Market', *Low Pay Report*, November 1980.

D. **Newspapers and Periodicals**

(i) *Newspapers*:

Welsh:

Abergavenny Chronicle

Yr Adsain
Baner ac Amserau Cymru
Brecon County Times
Brecon and Radnor Express
Cambria Daily Leader
Cambrian News
Cardiff Times
Cardigan and Tivyside Advertiser
Carmarthen Journal
Carmarthen Weekly Reporter
Caernarvon and Denbigh Herald
Caernarvon Observer
Y Clorianydd
County Echo
County Herald
Y Cymro
Denbighshire Free Press
Y Dinesydd Cymreig
Y Dydd
Flintshire Observer
Free Press of Monmouthshire
Y Genedl Gymreig
Glamorgan Gazette
Gwalia
Haverfordwest and Milford Haven Telegraph (*Pembrokeshire Telegraph*)
Herald of Wales
Yr Herald Cymraeg
Herald Môn
Holyhead and Anglesey Herald
Holyhead and Anglesey Mail
Holyhead Chronicle
Llais Llafur (Labour Voice)
Llandudno Advertiser
Llanelly Mercury
Llangollen Advertiser
Merthyr Pioneer
Monmouthshire Beacon
Monmouthshire Evening Post
Monmouthshire Weekly Post
Montgomeryshire Express
Montgomery County Times
North Wales Chronicle
North Wales Guardian

North Wales Observer and Express
North Wales Pioneer
North Wales Times
North Wales Weekly News
Pembroke County Guardian (Pembroke County and West Wales Guardian)
Pembroke Dock and Pembroke Gazette
Pembrokeshire Herald
Pembrokeshire Times
Radnor Express
Radnorshire Standard
Y Rhedegydd
Y Seren
South Wales Argus
South Wales Daily News (South Wales News)
South Wales Daily Post
South Wales Gazette
South Wales Weekly Argus
South Wales Weekly Post
Tenby Observer
The Welshman
Y Werin
Western Mail
Western Telegraph
Wrexham Advertiser
Y Wyntyll
Yr Wythnos a'r Eryr
English:
Chester Chronicle
Chester Courant
The Clarion
Hereford Journal
Hereford Times
The Labourer
Labour Leader
The Land Worker
Liverpool Daily Post
Railway Review
(Workers' Union) *Record*
Shrewsbury Chronicle

(ii) *Periodicals*:
Y Celt
Cwrs y Byd

Y Geninen
Y Goleuad
Herefordshire Voice of Labour
Y Llan
Lleufer
Welsh Outlook

E. **Interviews**:
(Notes of interviews held by the author)
Mrs Clarke, Boverton
Lord Cledwyn of Penrhos, Trearddur Bay
Enoch Davies, Llandrillo-yn-Edeirnion
G.H. Davies, Llangan
Mrs Gwilym Davies, Blaenau Ffestiniog
S.R. Eames, Tair Onnen
Idwal Edwards, Y Bontnewydd
Fred Evans, Sealand Manor
Mrs Rose Edwards, Pontyclun
P.S. Foulkes, Llanrwst
Mrs Goode, Penhow
Kenneth Harrison, Rosemarket
Emyr Hughes, Aberffraw
Morris Hughes, Edern
O.R. Hughes, Aberffraw
Robert Hughes, Llangefni
Maurice Jackson, Boverton
Mrs H.A. Jenkins, Aberdare
Bert Jones, Llanfair Disgoed
Caradog Jones, Mynytho
Miss E. Jones, Llanilar
Hugh Meredydd Jones, Llanfairpwll
J. Daniel Jones, Valley
Revd Owen Jones, Llangwnnadl
Wesley Jones, Golden Grove
Mrs P. Matthews, Caerphilly
Tom Owen, Llanrwst
Arthur Pearson, Pontypridd
Hubert Pritchard, Newport
R.G. Roberts, Pen-y-groes
J. Sharp, Llangynog
P.J. Smith, Boverton
G. Thomas, Aber
F.L. Ward, Rosemarket

Evan Weyman, Henryd
Evan Williams, Llaniestyn
Correspondence to the author is acknowledged in the endnotes.

F. **Works of Reference**

Charlesworth, A., *An Atlas of Rural Protest in Britain 1548–1900* (London 1983).

Dictionary of Welsh Biography down to 1940 (London, 1959), with supplement *Y Bywgraffiadur Cymreig 1941–1950* (Llundain, 1970).

Eaton, J., and C. Gill, *The Trade Union Directory* (London, 1981).

The Herald Book of Labour Members (London, 1923).

James, Arnold J., and John E. Thomas, *Wales at Westminster: A History of the Parliamentary Representation of Wales 1800–1979* (Llandysul, 1981).

Jones, Beti, *Etholiadau Seneddol yng Nghymru 1900–1975* (Talybont, 1977).

Kinnear, M., *The British Voter. An Atlas and Survey since 1885* (London, 1981).

Rees, D. Ben (gol.), *Pymtheg o Wŷr Llên yr Ugeinfed Ganrif* (Lerpwl, 1972).

Cymry Adnabyddus 1951–1972 (Lerpwl 1978).

Who's Who in Wales (1st ed. 1920; 2nd ed. 1933; 3rd ed. 1937).

G. **Secondary Works**

'Adfyfr' (T.J. Hughes), *Landlordism in Wales* (Cardiff, 1887).

Aldcroft, Derek H., *The Inter-War Economy: Britain 1919–1939* (London 1970).

Arnot, R. Page, *South Wales Miners* (London, 1967).

Ashby, A.W., and I.L. Evans, *The Agriculture of Wales and Monmouthshire* (Cardiff, 1944).

Awbery, S., *Labour's Early Struggles in Swansea* (Swansea, 1949).

Bagwell, P.S., *The Railwaymen* (London, 1963).

Berry, Fred, *Housing: the Great British Failure* (London, 1974).

Bowley, A. W., *Prices and Wages in the United Kingdom 1914–20* (Oxford, 1921).

Bowley, Marian, *Housing and the State, 1919–1944* (London, 1945).

Box, S., *The Workers' Union in Herefordshire* (1925).

The Good Old Days: Then and Now (published by the author, 1954).

Brennan, T., E.W. Cooney and H. Pollins, *Social Change in South-West Wales* (London, 1954).

Brown, Marie, and Steve Winyard, *Low Pay on the Farm* (Low Pay Pamphlet No. 3, 1975).
Butt, J., and I.F. Clarke, *The Victorians and Social Protest* (Newton Abbot, 1973).
Chappell, Edgar L., *The Housing Problem in Wales* (Cardiff, 1920).
Clegg, H.A., A. Fox and A.F. Thompson, *A History of British Trade Unionism since 1889*, Vol. I (Oxford, 1964).
Clegg, H.A., *General Union in a Changing Society. A Short History of the National Union of General and Municipal Workers, 1889–1964* (Oxford, 1964).
Clinton, Alan, *The Trade Union Rank and File. Trades Councils in Britain 1900–40* (Manchester, 1977).
Cole, G.D.H., *British Trade Unionism Today* (London, 1939).
Collins, William, *Records of Organized Labour in the City of Hereford* (Hereford 1920).
Cook, Chris, *The Age of Alignment* (London, 1975).
Daunton, M.J., *Coal Metropolis: Cardiff 1870–1914* (Leicester, 1977).
Davies, Elwyn, and A.D. Rees (eds.), *Welsh Rural Communities* (Cardiff, 1960).
Davies, E. Tegla, *Gyda'r Blynyddoedd* (Lerpwl, 1952).
Davies, G. M. Ll., *Profiadau Pellach* (Dinbych, 1943).
Pererindod Heddwch (Dinbych, 1945).
Davies, W.T. Kelville, *The Condition of the Agricultural Labourer* (Ludlow, 1854).
Dunbabin, J.P.D., *Rural Discontent in Nineteenth-Century Britain* (London, 1974).
Eames, Aled, *Shipmaster* (Denbigh, 1980).
Edwards, George, *From Crow Scaring to Westminster* (London, 1922).
Edwards, H.T., *Tros y Tresi* (Dinbych, 1956).
It was My Privilege (Denbigh, 1957).
Hewn from the Rock (Cardiff, 1967).
Emmett, Isabel, *A North Wales Village* (London, 1964).
Evans, H.T., *The Gorse Glen* (Liverpool, 1948).
Francis, H., and D. Smith, *The Fed. A History of the South Wales Miners in the Twentieth Century* (London, 1980).
Francis, J.O., *Cross Currents* (Cardiff, 1923).
Frow, R. and E., and M. Katanka, *Strikes — A Documentary History* (London, 1971).
Fussell, G.E., *From Tolpuddle to TUC. A Century of Farm Labourers' Politics* (London, 1948).
George, W.R.P., *The Making of Lloyd George* (London, 1976).
Green, F.E., *The Tyranny of the Countryside* (London, 1913).

A History of the English Agricultural Labourer, 1870—1920 (London, 1920).
Griffiths, E.H., *Heddychwr Mawr Cymru: George M. Ll. Davies*, 2 vols. (Cardiff, 1967–8).
Groves, R., *Sharpen the Sickle: The History of the Farm Workers' Union* (London, 1949).
Gruffydd, Ifan, *Y Gŵr o Baradwys* (Dinbych, 1963).
Tân Yn y Siambar (Dinbych, 1966).
Guttsman, W.L., *The British Political Elite* (London, 1968).
Gweithiau Samuel Roberts (Dolgellau, 1856).
Hall, A.D., *A Pilgrimage of British Farming* (London, 1913).
Harris, John, *'Fury Never Leaves Us'. A Miscellany of Caradoc Evans* (Bridgend, 1985).
Hasbach, W., *A History of the English Agricultural Labourer* (London, 1908).
Hobsbawm, E.J., *Labouring Men* (London, 1964).
Holton, B., *British Syndicalism 1900–1914* (London, 1976).
Horn, Pamela, *Joseph Arch* (Kineton, 1971).
Labouring Life in the Victorian Countryside (Dublin, 1976).
The Tithe War in Pembrokeshire (Fishguard, 1982).
Howell, David W., *Land and People in Nineteenth-Century Wales* (London, 1978).
Howells, Roscoe, *Farming in Wales* (Llandysul, 1965).
Howkins, Alun, *Poor Labouring Men: Rural Radicalism in Norfolk 1872–1923* (London, 1985).
Hughes, R.R., *Y Parchedig John Williams D.D., Brynsiencyn* (Caernarfon, 1929).
Humphreys, E. Morgan (gol.), *Gwilym Hiraethog: Llythyrau 'Rhen Ffarmwr* (Caerdydd, 1939).
Hyman, Richard, *The Workers' Union* (Oxford, 1971).
Jenkins, D., *The Agricultural Community in South-West Wales* (Cardiff, 1971).
Jenkins, J. Geraint, *The Welsh Woollen Industry* (Cardiff, 1969).
Life and Tradition in Rural Wales (London, 1976).
John Davies (Gregynog, 1938).
Jones, D.J.V., *Before Rebecca* (London, 1973).
Jones, E. Pan, *Oes Gofion* (Bala, 1911).
Jones, I. Gwynedd (ed.), *Gwilym Davies 1879–1955* (Llandysul, 1972).
Jones, R. Merfyn, *The North Wales Quarrymen 1874–1922* (Cardiff, 1981).
Jones, R. Tudur, *Yr Undeb. Hanes Undeb yr Annibynwyr Cymraeg 1872–1972* (Abertawe, 1975).
Jones, T. Gwynn, *Cofiant Thomas Gee* (Dinbych, 1913).

Kingsford, P.W., *Victorian Railwaymen* (London, 1970).
Knowles, K.G.J.C., *Strikes — A Study in Industrial Conflict* (Oxford, 1952).
Kynaston, David, *King Labour* (London, 1976).
Lewis, Lewis William, ('Llew Llwyfo'), *Huw Huws, neu y Llafurwr Cymreig* (Caergybi, 1860).
Lovell, John, *British Trade Unions 1875—1933* (London, 1977).
Madgwick, P.J., N. Griffiths and V. Walker, *The Politics of Rural Wales. A Study of Cardiganshire* (London, 1973).
Marwick, A., *The Deluge* (London, 1965).
British Society Since 1945 (London, 1982).
Masterman, N., *The Forerunner* (Llandybïe 1972).
Maynard, Joan (ed.), *A Hundred Years of Farmworkers' Struggle* (Nottingham, 1974).
McCord, Norman, *Strikes* (Oxford, 1980).
McKenna, F., *The Railway Workers 1840–1970* (London, 1980).
McKibbin, R., *The Evolution of the Labour Party 1910–1924* (Oxford, 1974).
Milward, Alan S., *The Economic Effects of the Two World Wars on Britain* (London, 1972).
Mingay, G.E., *Rural Life in Victorian England* (London, 1976).
Moore Jr., J. Barrington, *Injustice: The Social Bases of Obedience and Revolt* (London, 1978).
Morgan, K.O, *Wales in British Politics 1868–1922* (Cardiff, 1980).
Rebirth of a Nation: Wales 1880–1980 (Oxford and Cardiff, 1981).
Labour in Power 1945–1951 (Oxford, 1984).
Morris, William, *Atgof a Phrofiad* (Caernarfon, 1961).
(gol.), *Atgofion Dau Gymro* (Caernarfon, 1968).
Murray, K.A.H., *Agriculture* (London, 1955).
Newby, Howard, *The Deferential Worker* (London, 1977).
Green and Pleasant Land: Social Change in Rural England (London, 1979).
Orwin, Christabel S., and Edith H. Whetham, *History of British Agriculture 1846–1914* (London, 1971).
Owen, Hugh (gol.), *Hanes Methodistiaeth Calfinaidd Môn 1880–1935* (Liverpool, 1937).
Parry, Cyril, *The Radical Tradition in Welsh Politics* (Hull, 1970).
Parry-Jones, D., *Welsh Country Upbringing* (London, 1948).
Peate, Iorwerth C. (gol.), *Cilhaul ac Ysgrifau Eraill Samuel Roberts, Llanbrynmair* (Caerdydd, 1951).
Rhwng Dau Fyd (Dinbych, 1976).
Pelling, Henry, *A History of British Trade Unionism* (London, 1963).

Popular Politics and Society in Later Victorian Britain (London, 1968).

Pollard, S., *The Development of the British Economy 1914–1967* (London, 1969).

Pretty, David A., *Two Centuries of Anglesey Schools 1700–1902* (Llangefni, 1977).

Price, Emyr, *Ailgloriannu Thomas Gee* (Pamphledi Rhoslas I, 1977).

Prothero, Cliff, *Recount* (Ormskirk, 1982).

Prothero, R.E., *The Anti-Tithe Agitation in Wales* (London, 1889).

Rae, J., *Conscience and Politics* (London, 1970).

Rees, A.D., *Life in a Welsh Countryside* (Cardiff, 1950).

Roderick, A.J. (ed.), *Wales Through the Ages*, Vol. II (Llandybïe, 1960).

Russell, Rex C., *The Revolt of the Field in Lincolnshire* (Lincoln, 1956).

Samuel, R. (ed.), *Village Life and Labour* (London, 1975).

Selley, Ernest, *Village Trade Unions in Two Centuries* (London, 1919).

Sherington, G., *English Education, Social Change and the War 1911–20* (Manchester, 1981).

Simon, B., *Education and the Labour Movement 1870–1920* (London, 1965).

Social Problems in Wales. Lectures on Aspects of the Social Problem, more particularly in Rural Wales, given at the Third Annual Session of the Welsh School of Social Science (Swansea, 1913).

Stevenson, J., and C. Cook, *The Slump* (London, 1977).

Stevenson, J., *Social Conditions in Britain between the Wars* (London, 1977).

British Society 1914–45 (London, 1984).

Smith, David (ed.), *A People and a Proletariat* (London, 1980).

Wales! Wales? (London, 1984).

Smith, J. Beverley *et al.*, *James Griffiths and his Times* (Cardiff, 1978).

Taylor, A.J.P. (ed.), *Lloyd George: Twelve Essays* (London, 1971).

Taylor, Robert, *The Fifth Estate* (London, 1980).

Thomas, Brinley (ed.), *The Welsh Economy* (Cardiff, 1962).

Thomas, David, *Y Werin a'i Theyrnas* (Caernarfon, 1910).

Diolch am Gael Byw (Lerpwl, 1968).

Thomas, D. Lleufer, *Labour Unions in Wales. Their Early Struggle for Existence* (Swansea, 1901).

Tillyard, F., and F.N. Ball, *Unemployment Insurance in Great Britain 1911–48* (London, 1949).

Whetham, Edith H., *The Agrarian History of England and Wales*, Vol. VIII, 1914–39 (Cambridge, 1978).

Williams, David, *The Rebecca Riots* (Cardiff, 1955).

Williams, J. Roose, *T.E. Nicholas. Proffwyd Sosialaeth a Bardd Gwrthryfel* (Bangor, 1971).

Williams, Raymond, *The Country and the City* (London, 1973).

Williams, T.L., *Caradoc Evans* (Cardiff, 1970).

Winter, J. (ed.), *The Working Class in Modern British History* (Cambridge, 1983).

Wrigley, Chris, *David Lloyd George and the British Labour Movement* (London, 1976).

A History of British Industrial Relations 1875–1914 (Brighton, 1982).

Wrigley, Chris (ed.), *The British Labour Movement in the Decade after the First World War* (Loughborough, 1979).

H. **Articles**

Ashby, A.W., 'The agricultural depression in Wales', *Welsh Outlook*, XVI (November 1929).

Ashby, A.W., and J.H. Smith, 'Agricultural labour in Wales under Statutory Regulation of Wages 1924–1937', *The Welsh Journal of Agriculture*, XIV (1938).

Bowers, J.K., 'British agricultural policy since the Second World War', *The Agricultural History Review*, 33 (1985).

Cook, C.P., 'Wales and the General Election of 1923', *Welsh History Review*, 4, No. 4 (December 1969).

Davies, J., 'The end of the great estates and the rise of freehold farming in Wales', *Welsh History Review*, 7, No. 2 (December 1974).

Dewey, P.E., 'Agricultural labour supply in England and Wales during the First World War', *Economic History Review*, 2nd ser., XXVIII, No. 1 (1975).

Dewey, P.E., 'Government provision of farm labour in England and Wales', *Agricultural History Review*, 27, 2 (1979).

Duffy, A.E.P., 'New Unionism in Britain, 1889–1890: a reappraisal', *Economic History Review*, 2nd ser., XIV (1961).

Dunbabin, J.P.D., 'The "Revolt of the Field": the agricultural labourers' movement in the 1870s', *Past and Present*, 26 (1963).

'Labourers and farmers in the late nineteenth century — some changes', *Bulletin of the Society for the Study of Labour*, XI (1965).

'The incidence and organisation of agricultural trades unionism in the 1870s', *Agricultural History Review*, 16 (1968).

Hobsbawm, E.J., 'General labour unions in Britain, 1889–1914', *Economic History Review*, 2nd ser., I (1948–9).

Horn, Pamela, 'Agricultural trades unionism in Oxfordshire 1872–81', *Oxfordshire Records Society*, XLVIII (1974).

'The Warwickshire Agricultural and General Workers' Union 1893–97', *Midland History*, I, No. 4 (1975).

Howell, David W., 'The agricultural labourer in nineteenth-century Wales', *Welsh History Review*, 6, No. 3 (June 1973).

Jones, D.J.V., 'Crime, protest and community in nineteenth-century Wales, *Llafur*, 1, No. 3 (May 1974).

Jones, H.C., 'The Labour Party in Cardiganshire 1918–66', *Ceredigion*, IX, 2 (1982).

Jones, J. Graham, 'Wales and the "New Socialism" 1926–1929', *Welsh History Review*, XI, No. 2 (December 1982).

'Montgomeryshire Politics: Lloyd George, David Davies and the Green Book', *Montgomeryshire Collections*, 72 (1984).

Jones-Evans, Peris, 'Evan Pan Jones — land reformer', *Welsh History Review*, 4, No. 2 (December 1968).

Jones, R. Merfyn, 'A trade union in nineteenth-century Gwynedd. The North Wales Quarrymen's Union, 1874–1900', *Trans. Caernarvonshire Historical Society*, 35 (1974).

Morgan, Kenneth O., 'Cardiganshire Politics: the Liberal ascendancy 1885–1923', *Ceredigion*, V, No. 4 (1967).

'Labour's early struggles in south Wales: some new evidence 1900–1908', *Nat. Lib. of Wales Journal*, XVII (1971–2).

'The New Liberalism and the challenge of Labour: The Welsh experience 1885–1929', *Welsh History Review*, 6, No. 3 (June 1973).

Parry, Cyril, 'Fabianism and Gwynedd politics, 1890–1918', *Trans. Caernarvonshire Historical Society*, 29 (1968).

'The Independent Labour Party and Gwynedd politics 1900–1920', *Welsh History Review*, 4, No. 1 (June 1968).

'Gwynedd Politics, 1900–1920: the rise of a Labour Party', *Welsh History Review*, 6, No. 3 (June 1973).

Price, Emyr, 'Newyddiadur cyntaf David Lloyd George', *The Journal of the Welsh Bibliographical Society*, XI (1975–6).

'Lloyd George a "Rhyfel y Degwm" yn Llŷn ac Eifionydd 1886–8', *Trans. Caernarvonshire Historical Society*, 39 (1978).

Rowlands, Eryl W., 'Yr Etholiad Gyffredinol ym Môn, 1918', *Trans. Anglesey Antiquarian Society*, (1976–7).

'Agweddau Gwleidyddol ym Môn, 1885–95', *Trans. Anglesey Antiquarian Society* (1983).

Stead, Peter, 'Working class leadership in south Wales, 1900–1920', *Welsh History Review*, 6, No. 3 (June 1973).

Thomas, R. Maldwyn, and Cyril Parry, 'John Owen Jones, "Ap Ffarmwr", 1861–1899', *Trans. Anglesey Antiquarian Society* (1967).

Whetham, Edith H., 'The Agricultural Act, 1920 and its Repeal — the "Great Betrayal"', *Agricultural History Review*, 22, (1974).

Williams, L.J., 'The New Unionism in south Wales, 1889–92', *Welsh History Review*, 1, No. 4 (1963).

I. **Unpublished theses**

Bainbridge, A., 'The agricultural community in Carmarthenshire, *c.* 1876–1896', MA, Swansea, 1975.

Birtwistle, M., 'Pobol y tai bach: some aspects of the agricultural labouring classes of Cardiganshire in the second half of the nineteenth century', MA, Aberystwyth, 1982.

Clinton, A., 'Trades councils from the beginning of the twentieth century to the Second World War', Ph.D., London, 1973.

Cunningham, M.M., 'Y gymdeithas amaethyddol yn Nyffryn Clwyd 1880–1900', MA, Bangor, 1977.

Davies, T.E., 'Cyfraniad Dr William Rees (Gwilym Hiraethog) i fywyd a llên ei gyfnod', MA, Bangor, 1931.

Donovan, P.W., 'A history of unskilled labour unions in south Wales, 1889–1914', M.Phil., London, 1969.

Gupta, P.S., 'The history of the Amalgamated Society of Railway Servants 1871–1913', D. Phil., Oxford, 1960.

Horn, P.L.R., 'Agricultural labourers' trades unions in four Midland counties (1860–1900)', Ph.D., Leicester, 1968.

Harries, D.M., 'Carmarthen politics: the struggle between the Liberals and Labour, 1918–60', MA, Swansea, 1980.

Howell, D.W., 'Welsh agriculture 1815–1914', Ph.D., London, 1970.

Hyman, R., 'The Workers' Union 1898–1929', Ph.D., Oxford, 1968.

Jones, J.G., 'The General Election of 1929 in Wales', MA, Aberystwyth, 1980.

Leng, P.J., 'The Dock, Wharf, Riverside and General Labourers' Union in South Wales and Bristol, 1889–1922', MA, Kent, 1973.

Madden, M., 'The National Union of Agricultural Workers, 1906–1956', B.Litt., Oxford, 1956.

Michael, P.F., 'Tenant farming in Merioneth, 1850–1925', MA, Swansea, 1978.

Mills, F.D., 'The National Union of Agricultural Workers', Ph.D., Reading, 1965.

Mutch, A.F., 'Rural Society in Lancashire, 1840–1914', Ph.D., Manchester, 1980.

Price, R.E., 'Lloyd George's pre-parliamentary political career', MA, Bangor, 1974.

INDEX

WYE VALLEY RAILWAY STORY

VOL. 1: 1855–1995

By Eric T. Rawlins

Published by

MELROSE BOOKS

An Imprint of Melrose Press Limited
St Thomas Place, Ely
Cambridgeshire
CB7 4GG, UK
www.melrosebooks.com

FIRST EDITION

Cover designed by Serena M. Robinson

Photographs not attributed are by the author and are included by courtesy of Wild Swan Publications, Didcot.

ISBN 978-1-906561-06-2

Printed and bound in Great Britain by:
CPI Antony Rowe, Chippenham, Wiltshire

Contents

WYE VALLEY RAILWAY
FEASIBILITY STUDY

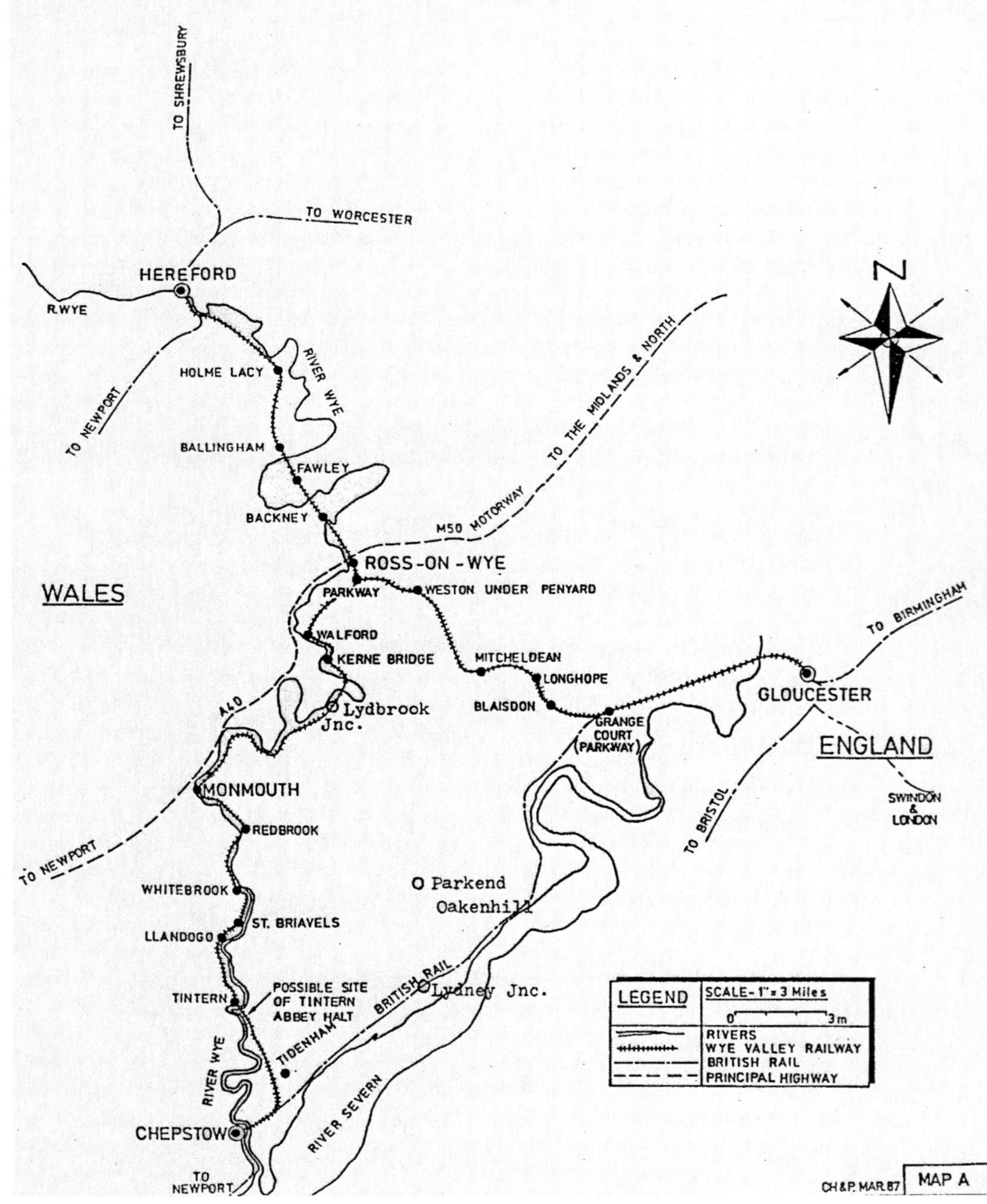

CHAPTER 1

The Brunel Heritage 1855 – 1965

The line-of-route commonly described in 1995 as the Wye Valley Railway has two distinct arms. Primarily, the 30 miles of railway which linked the cathedral cities of Hereford and Gloucester via Ross-on-Wye and secondly, the 27 miles Ross–Monmouth–Chepstow line, which has the more spectacular river and valley setting, the entire line from Chepstow to Hereford following the River Wye and constituting an Area of Outstanding Natural Beauty. Currently, InterCity trains from Paddington to Hereford are routed via Newport (Gwent), whereas Paddington–*Gloucester*–Hereford would be *60* miles less!

The Gloucester to Hereford route has an impeccable, and possibly unique, industrial heritage background, as the line was personally surveyed and engineered by the great Isambard Kingdom Brunel in 1851. He chose the newly associated contractors Peto, Brassey and Betts, almost equally eminent in their field. Indeed, the colossal earthworks raised between Ross and Hereford stand as a tribute to the men and horses which created them, leaving us a view of the countryside equalled only by that from a helicopter!

Quite amazingly, for a line requiring river crossings at Backney, Strangford and Ballingham, with tunnels at Fawley, Ballingham and Dinedor, the works were completed in just *four* years and the railway was opened for traffic in June 1855. An added distinction for this section is that it was chosen to trial the first part of the Great Western Railway to be converted from the broad gauge of 7ft 0¼ins to the present standard gauge of 4ft 8½ins between the rails. The changeover of the 21 miles 36 chains of line between Rotherwas Junction and Grange Court Junction was accomplished between 14th and 20th August 1869, 300 men pioneering the techniques which would be applied throughout the entire GWR system by May 1892.

South-west of Ross the line proceeds from pastoral to attractively wooded countryside, largely unseen by those travelling the dual carriageway to Monmouth. The railway crossed the Wye at Kerne Bridge and Lydbrook with a 634-yard tunnel at Lydbrook and ran for 434 yards beneath the famous Symonds Yat rock. The route between Ross and Monmouth May Hill, the town station, was engineered by Liddell and Richards but built by another famous contractor, Joseph Firbank. This line was opened on 1st August 1873 to the 'narrow' 4ft 8½ins gauge.

From Monmouth down to Chepstow, the Wye Valley Railway ran through an increasingly deep and spectacular gorge – almost completely invisible from the road. This section was built by London firms, engineered by Yockney and Son of Westminster with Reed Brothers as contractors. The Monmouth to Wyesham line opened in 1861, completed to the 4ft 8½ins gauge in 1876.

The useful service the railway provided broke the virtually medieval isolation of the area where low pay and limited opportunities for all but landowners, farmers and professional persons prevailed. Heavy passenger and freight traffic occurred during both World Wars (1914–1918 and 1939–1945) when the steam railways carried enormous loads without the need for rubber and petrol obtained at great human cost in lost shipping. In the 1930s the Government provided Guaranteed Loans to the railway companies to finance modernisation and employment. At Ross the bay platform was extended to serve the Monmouth line and a new brick signal box replaced two wooden cabins at either end of the station. In 1937 the tourism-orientated decision was taken to promote Ross as 'Ross-on-Wye' and the town was designated as the 'Gateway to the Wye'. Posters advertising this with a commendable painting could be seen on city station boards and most effectively 'sold' the story of an unspoilt market town to the commuters in the smoke and grime of Paddington Station and the London suburbs.

After the end of World War II the Labour Government took power, but I, as well as hundreds of other RAF aircraft tradesmen, was not demobbed until 1947, when I joined the Office of the Superintendent of the Line, Great Western Railway. Soon it became very apparent that both the extreme shortages of materials and, indeed, exhaustion of the human capacity to continue to pull out all the stops of wartime operation were impacting upon the railways. It was very much easier for transport which did not have the burden of maintaining the 'way', the bridges and signalling, plus the high capital costs of locomotives and rolling stock. Hence road transport flourished almost as an explosion to meet the needs of those now free to travel without defying the exhortation "Is your journey *really* necessary?" Indeed, as many as 1000 road coaches would leave Victoria Coach Station at holiday weekends, while many of our Paddington trains to similar places were lightly loaded in 1950.

I left Paddington in 1950 but continued to keep in touch with the GWR via my uncle, Bert Everall, and his wife Maud, both of whom had worked as passenger guards on the Ross–Monmouth line. It is not easy to encapsulate the war effort of the railways all over the country, but the following extract from a letter from Mrs B.L. Morris includes a tribute to her husband on his retirement as stationmaster at Ross:

> The following extract [is] from a letter, dated the 11th October 1946, sent to my late husband, on the eve of his retirement, by the then Divisional Superintendent of Gloucester, R.H.B. Nicholls Esq. I quote, 'You have many years of railway service to look back upon, but I feel that none could have been quite so valuable or as exacting as those of the most recent of the two world wars. In those years the staff position was critical in the extreme at a time when traffics were breaking all records and you will know that this Division was subjected to very great strain, possibly more so than most other Divisions. Your own station, Ross,

> was amongst those most affected by the presence, in the neighbourhood, of large numbers of service personnel with all that that entails.'

The post-World War II years were exceedingly difficult in recovery terms, but an article in *Trains Illustrated* in 1953 rather captures the flavour of a working day at Monmouth Troy and connecting services. The account, by Marcus Newman, is reproduced below:

> Any enthusiast depressed by the continued spate of British branch line closures should pay a visit to the two-platform station at Monmouth Troy. At this focal point of three branches, from Chepstow, Ross-on-Wye and Pontypool Road, there are admittedly long periods of drowsy inactivity every day, but this is because throughout most of the day the services on the three branches are scheduled to connect with each other at Monmouth Troy. Three times a day the station hums with sudden life as all three little trains bustle in, one after the other.
>
> The first invasion of Monmouth Troy begins at breakfast time with the emergence from the short tunnel at the west end of the station of the 8.31 a.m. arrival from Pontypool Road (two tracks lead into the tunnel, incidentally, but one is a siding; the westbound platform line is connected to the single branch running line, which runs into the eastbound platform by a crossover inside the tunnel). This train, which was being worked by a diesel railcar No. 30 in May last, then makes an unadvertised run out to Monmouth May Hill and back, regaining Monmouth Troy at 8.34 a.m. At 8.43 a.m. the Chepstow railcar (No. 21) halts at the westbound platform, and at 8.53 a.m. the Ross-on-Wye train pulls up behind it. Their passengers unloaded, the trains are then

re-platformed; at 9 a.m. the Chepstow and Pontypool Road trains set off simultaneously in opposite directions, and the Ross-on-Wye train is signalled away at 9.36 a.m.

At the next re-shuffle, between 11 a.m. and 1 p.m., the Chepstow train is the first to arrive and depart, the one from Pontypool Road the last to come in and the second to disappear. The afternoon concourse is similar to that at 9 a.m. The Pontypool Road train is again the first arrival, at 3.12 p.m., but after the Ross-on-Wye train has pulled in at 3.31 p.m. the former is extended at 3.35 p.m. to Monmouth May Hill on the Ross line. It returns from May Hill at 3.45 p.m., on its way back to Pontypool Road, whereafter the Ross train is away again at 3.51 p.m. and the Chepstow train follows four minutes later. This is the last tri-partite meeting of the day, for although the Chepstow and Ross-on-Wye trains meet again twice at Monmouth Troy around 6 p.m. and 8.15 p.m. (the second meeting is restricted to the summer timetables), the Pontypool Road train makes but one more visit, in lonely state, around 7 p.m. In addition to the passenger trains there are three morning freight services to Monmouth Troy, the 8.15 a.m. from Chepstow, arriving at 10.45 a.m. and departing for Severn Tunnel Junction at 12.20 p.m., the 12.05 p.m., (s.x.) from Ross-on-Wye, arriving at 1.40 p.m. and departing at 2.45 p.m., and the 8.50 a.m. from Pontypool Road, arriving at 11.10 a.m. and departing at 5 p.m. (1.15 p.m., S.O.). No train serves Monmouth Troy on Sundays.

The earliest history of the railways to Monmouth was discussed in articles on Coleford in September and November 1952, in issues of *Trains Illustrated*. The 18½-mile run through Raglan to Pontypool Road is mostly over the erstwhile Coleford, Monmouth, Usk and Pontypool Railway there mentioned; this

> line was leased by the West Midland Railway in 1861 and absorbed in 1887 by the GWR (which had amalgamated with the WMR in 1863). The Ross and Monmouth Railway was opened to Monmouth (May Hill) in 1873 and extended for ¾ mile to Monmouth (Troy) in the following year; it was always worked by the GWR but was normally independent until 1922. This 13-mile branch diverges eastwards beyond Monmouth (Troy), crossing the Wye on a steel girder bridge to reach Monmouth (May Hill). It traces a picturesque path up the Wye Valley, offering a view of Goodrich Castle near Kerne Bridge Station. At Lydbrook Junction it is joined by a branch from the former Severn and Wye Joint Railway; this branch was closed to passenger traffic in 1929 and to all traffic in late 1952. There are also two trains each way (one on Saturdays) between Ross and Lydbrook Junction only, and one midday return working in summer between Ross-on-Wye and Symonds Yat. Finally, the Wye Valley Railway from Monmouth to Chepstow was opened in 1876 and absorbed in 1905 by the GWR – a paper recognition, in fact, for the GWR had long operated its trains. It makes a sweeping southward curve out of Monmouth (Troy), crossing the Wye on a fine single-span steel bridge that is approached by a series of masonry arches. Running close to the ruins of Tintern Abbey, this 14½-mile branch follows the Wye downstream as far as Tidenham Tunnel, beyond which it joins the Gloucester–South Wales main line at Wye Valley Junction and uses Brunel's bridge across the river to reach Chepstow.

Indeed, Bert Everall worked up to his retirement in 1959 when the future for the railway was becoming doubtful. The Transport Users Consultative Committee machine was rolling and, after a public inquiry in Monmouth on 25th September 1958, it was announced that from October 1958 to October 1961 the track and facilities for Ross–Monmouth–Chepstow would remain in situ. I contacted the local authorities and individuals and we sought to obtain a diesel railbus service, which would use tax free fuel oil, whereas the road buses paid 2s 6d per gallon in tax. I wrote to Ross and Whitchurch Rural Council and Monmouth Rural Council putting some twenty points for consideration. Ross supported my views but one S.W. Jones of the Monmouth Public Health Committee (!) recommended no action and said, "I think it would be a waste of time to pursue the matter further." It was decided to leave the matter 'in abeyance'.

The final passenger train was chartered by the Stephenson Locomotive Society and ran through the snow of 4th January 1959. A souvenir booklet was issued and at Symonds Yat Station, alongside the Royal Hotel, Mr Tom Wainright brought out two bottles of champagne to be shared with the crew and others. The stationmaster, Mr Ernest Bartlett, was presented with an engraved mantel clock by hotelier Mr D. Elliott on behalf of local residents. This event was in the nature of a thank you to the GWR staff facilitating both passenger and stores traffic, especially when the roads were impassable over the years.

By January 1962 the Ross Branch of the National Farmers Union discussed rumours about closure and this resulted in a front-page report in the *Ross Gazette* headed 'Inquiry into Economy of Ross Railway Line'. In effect, their concern was with the failure to try diesel railbuses and the fact that 'all the sugar beet was being transported by road and British Railways had done nothing to encourage them to stay with the railway'. The fault here was, apparently, due to the fixing of rates remotely, either from Divisional Headquarters or even the Commercial Department at Paddington. Whatever the background, the result was that the stationmasters had no authority to negotiate locally and a road monopoly for both passengers and freight was on its way.

Remotely, from suburban London, I was inspired to write to the *Gazette* in order to try and shake up some action at Ross. This is reproduced below:

BLIND TO OUR HERITAGE

On the way to work this morning in suburban Surrey I was involved in traffic chaos after a heavy lorry accident and turned to my *Ross Gazette*, thinking of the comparative peace of your district. But what a picture of transport confusion you paint! The collapse of the new motorway virtually breaking down communication between Ross and Monmouth, the frightful incident of the lorry juggernauts fighting it out on Whitchurch Hill, the suffering Easter motorist going round and round the town, and the ripping up of the landscaped railway track through the 'most beautiful parts of the Wye Valley'. How is it that we accept a rationalised system of electricity and gas supply but are so stubborn and short-sighted when movement in this over-crowded island is concerned? Much more heavy goods transport could be put on the railways and the profits ploughed back into keeping such lines as the Ross–Monmouth route open. You have an extensive ready-made car park all along the wide approach of the Ross Station yard, from which visitors could stroll into town or ride down to Monmouth by rail in relaxed comfort; especially *Saturdays* and *Sundays*. (I can almost hear British Railways screaming that there has *never* been a service on Sundays – but in these times of weekend leisure and car-borne monotony, what an opportunity.)

The prospect of motorists mass sightseeing from the motorways will benefit only the car manufacturers and the undertakers. Real communications in the area are slipping back to the horse-buggy era; is it sensible that workers on the land should sacrifice their standard of living to cover the capital cost of individual transport? The domestic pressures created simply translate into depopulation and depression, and the concrete wilderness of motorways stamp a pattern of sameness that will destroy the character of our few beautiful areas completely.

Must this generation go down as one blind to its heritage and content to push its children into a fume-filled suburban sprawl around the biggest centres of population? And how long will the enormous revenue from overseas visitors be attracted to a picture we are so effectively destroying?

Yours faithfully,
E. T. Rawlins

I took the matter up with Mr L.J. Lickorish, then General Manager of the British Travel and Holidays Association, in 1962, and he pursued matters with BTC. Certainly, the British Transport statistics to the TUCC were open to challenge, i.e. the Chepstow–Monmouth section being actually 'worked by a 20-year-old diesel railcar' was costed as a 'steam' working! From my local contacts it was not possible to reconcile the staff levels, including permanent way workers, claimed by BTC with actual numbers. The best part of the permanent way was suddenly completely renewed and it is possible that this was a cost booster. A revised timetable, offering a 45 mph average speed using modern railbuses, was proposed but ignored. The BTC statistics were believed to relate to a Monday (!), possibly as a way of avoiding including the revenue from the 'block' freight trains of Tuesdays and Thursdays!

Just about the same time, Dorothy O'Neill, a curate's wife living in Weston Grove, Ross, wrote a simple story which reflects the *social* loss the absence of a rural railway means to a community. How many elderly people whose only contact with other humanity was the wave from the engine footplate? How many were saved after collapsing indoors and the railwaymen had reported lack of activity around the house?

Mrs O'Neill's letter appeared in the *Guardian* headlined 'Wave of Regret':

"A train, a train!" they shout in delight, and race down the path to the bottom of our garden where the branch line snakes its steely way. I look up from my work at the kitchen sink, thankful for at least a few minutes I shall be free from demands for water, biscuits, and comfort for scratches or toilet. Four-year-old goes first, talking incessantly to herself in the third person. "She runs down the path with flying feet," I hear her say. Behind her stumbles her younger sister, a marionette with knickers perpetually at half-mast. The train shudders out of the station just up the line and excitement reaches fever pitch. "Wave – wave," I hear them scream to each other. Hands shoot up and wave ecstatically as the train passes. Then with shining eyes and radiant smiles they shout back, "He waved – the driver waved!" The train curves out of sight but the thrills are not over yet. "Wait for the signal," says Big Girl. "Wait for the signal," echoes Half-mast. There is a satisfied sigh as the signal returns to horizontal. Two gardens away another toddler (Graham Edwards) has also been watching and waving. My imagination marches down the line, in and out of suburban gardens where small fry are successively enjoying the playtime drama of the trains. At kitchen sinks other mothers are enjoying a brief hiatus in the daily ordeal by children.

But, alas, our branch line has been axed, and soon will be closed. Who will wave then? Who can possibly take the place of that genial company of drivers, firemen and guards who are never too busy, Monday morningish or superior to wave to the children posted on fences along the line? For wave they do. If they do so while muttering terrible oaths into the firebox, we know nothing of it. The faces they turn on us are benign and patient. We like them.

My proposals costing steam trains against diesel railbuses showed an annual saving of £47,112 per year. But the BTC response in July 1962 added that a number of bridges 'between Chepstow and Monmouth would require repairs amounting to some £50,000'; I do not know whether or not this was mentioned at the TUCC. However, as the consulting engineer and myself were to find from the GWR Bridge Book (in 1987), it was Tintern and Kerne bridges which were in urgent need of renewal. But the die was cast and the last Chepstow–Monmouth–Ross train ran on 3rd January 1959. The Hereford–Ross–Gloucester passenger service was withdrawn on 31st October 1964, although the freight service Lydbrook–Ross–Gloucester continued to operate until 30th October 1965.

I was still living in Thornton Heath in 1965, and it would be 20 years before I could move to Ross-on-Wye.

CHAPTER 2

The Local Fightback

The year 1965 saw a resurgence of local activity, led by the indefatigable member of the Railway Invigoration Society, driver H.H. Williams. His letter in the *Ross Gazette* of 20th May 1965 reflects the overall problems, which new diesel cars would have solved on the passenger front and local rates flexibility the freight situation. His letter is reproduced below:

RAILWAY FREIGHT SERVICE

With reference to the Ross–Gloucester–Lydbrook freight service, I appeal to all employers of labour to patronise it. I am in correspondence with a member of the British Railways Board and he has informed me that no decision has yet been taken with regards to the closure of this service. As you are aware, sir, it was lack of patronage that was responsible for the closure of the Hereford–Gloucester passenger service. I sincerely hope this will not happen to this freight service, and it is now the responsibility of employers of labour and trades people to save the town of Ross from isolation from any form of rail transport.

Can anyone visualise Ross in the year 1970 with only the remembrance of railway transport?

Harold H. Williams, Hildersley, Ross-on-Wye.

On 6th September 1965 the Rev. S.E. Pulford of Linton, Ross-on-Wye, weighed in on the only ground allowed for public protest: that of 'hardship' – a condition as difficult to prove in law as 'negligence':

ROSS–GLOUCESTER RAILWAY

The closure of this line is a definite 'hardship' to many, and will become increasingly so with the rapid expansion of Ross-on-Wye. Bus drivers seem to reserve to themselves the right to start when they like, irrespective of schedule, and connections with the trains at Gloucester are uncertain owing to increasing road congestion. Car to Gloucester is attended by risk owing to having to part with one's car for the day – or longer – in unattended car parks.

Can there possibly be any valid refusal of BR to run a diesel coach on this line? This ought to be studied before the rails are ruthlessly ripped up. I would be glad to support any effort to secure this boom.

(Rev.) S.E. Pulford, The Rectory, Linton

However, the public inquiry had apparently happened at Monmouth in 1958! To my knowledge, no further opportunity to protest would be given other than to a TUCC, at which arguments against 'official' figures were exceedingly difficult to mount. The historical facts of the situation that the area was faced with are well summed up in the letter I wrote to the *Ross Gazette* on 9th September 1965 and that of Mr E. Stroud the following week:

ROSS TO GLOUCESTER RAILWAY

Four years ago, in defence of the Ross–Monmouth line, I was denigrated by certain council officials as being a 'railway fan'. You have now had some small experience of what it is like to be without a railway to Gloucester and, perhaps, are in a more susceptible frame of mind. However, this is your *last chance* to take action before Ross is condemned and confirmed as a one-bus town. Fortunately, the Railways Board has handed you the final opportunity to take positive steps.

(1) At the Transport Users Consultative Committee the Western Region undertook to arrange that bus services would provide adequate connections for the London trains at Gloucester. Since that time 90 per cent of the London trains have been diverted from Central to Eastgate, 15-20 minutes' walk from the bus station! The condition of hardship to prevent closures as allowed by the 1962 Transport Act has now occurred.

(2) The immediate need is for all authorities and industry to telegraph the Minister of Transport to (i) reconvene the TUCC on the grounds that the Railways Board has changed the situation unilaterally and (ii) to stop the Railways Board taking any closure, contractual etc., action meanwhile. Wake up the local MPs requesting urgent support and action.

(3) Insist that Lord Hinton (appointed to report to the Minister of Transport in England) attends the TUCC and makes an objective report personally to the Minister.

(4) At the TUCC all local residents who have suffered hardship between Gloucester Bus Station and Eastgate should insist upon giving evidence. Include the Red and White instructions to conductors not to wait more than five minutes for delayed railway passengers.

(5) At the TUCC press for a large single diesel unit for Ross–Gloucester services, conveying passengers,

parcels and Royal Mail. There is every opportunity for profitable operation with Board of Trade minimum operational requirements. Emphasise that Ross now has only one collection per day compared with six clearances each way when the railway ran. Local industry to provide details of deterioration of service and insist upon giving evidence at TUCC.

(6) Urge that the Railways Board act responsibly and 'hold' the connecting railcar service to Ross when mainline trains are delayed. Emphasise that for 20 years the railway made no attempt to encourage traffic by good, fast connections, [and] that stock up to 30 years old was regularly employed etc.; [emphasise the] failure to make this effort, [and the] inadequate reserves against civil work etc. At the TUCC accept only itemised £ figures agreed by independent consultants.

(7) Ross is an expanding residential centre of people who cannot all find work locally; by 1975 fast means of commuting between Ross and Gloucester will be essential. Local authorities have a plain duty to link extra housing provision with improved transport facilities. The slow bus on the switchback hairpin road is no substitute for the speed and freedom from congestion possible by rail.

(8) The motorcar is no answer to the problem; remember, when nervous strain and advancing years combine, one is forced back to public transport and without the railway this means the bus, if you can climb the steps and stand the 'ride'. Your taxi fare to your local Eastgate Station will be £3 5s, plus the cost of living increases.

(9) Remember: Railway Day Return fare to Hereford was 3s 4d.

By bus	3s 6d
NOW by bus	4s 9d (plus 38%)

Just consider for a moment what you are leaving in Ross for your children – if they have not already flown to a more accessible area – a town dependent very largely upon (i) the holiday trade and (ii) residential expansion. A fast commuting link and direct access to the main network of modern rail services are absolute musts if there is to be a future for Ross.

This is my last letter to you and your last chance to help yourselves.

E.T. Rawlins, Thornton Heath, Surrey

ROSS TO GLOUCESTER RAILWAY

I refer to the letter in your issue of 9th inst. and submit the challenge therein must be taken up. When the rail passenger service was closed it was definitely promised that an improved bus service with implied rail connection would be substituted in replacement. This now appears to be have been a complete falsehood.

The rail service has gone; the bus service is utterly inadequate and getting worse. Even the alternative of private car is often rendered useless by the hopeless traffic jams in Gloucester. Recently it took three hours to get by bus to Gloucester on a Saturday morning. Lesser but very serious delays are common and make nonsense of any timetables. This is only to get to the bus station after which one has to carry one's luggage a quarter of a mile or more to the railway station to

> get a train to London. For old people this is nearly impossible.
>
> In plain facts, Ross is very nearly cut off from the metropolis. Is this 'progress'?
>
> When the inevitable oil shortage – or the next big freeze – arrives, Ross may well be without essential supplies.
>
> I suggest that in view of the increasing congestion on the roads we want more public transport service – not less. Surely a regular rail service with light diesel coaches providing rail connections with the main line would be a paying proposition. I submit that rail traffic should be encouraged (for a change) by fixing fares cheaper than the road services, which latter could well be increased. Do you consider that the Urban District Council could take further action or would the best approach now be through our active local Member of Parliament?
>
> Lastly, I would ask – is Ross on the map or off it?
>
> E. Stroud, Eastfield Road, Ross

On 30th September 1965 I was responding to a letter by Mrs B.L. Morris, the widow of the stationmaster at Ross from 1934. She had remarked upon the dangerous times in which we lived and the possibility of a World War III. My commentary makes interesting reading:

> A major indication of Government unwillingness to face all possibilities was the decision to abruptly abandon steam haulage for diesel. The correct decision would have been the slow phasing out of steam (so many modern engines have been scrapped) and the minimum use of diesel with the main effort to *electrification*, the power being supplied by the CEGB generating stations, which have *three* fuel sources. As

> matters stand, a sudden oil shortage, through political or even minor military action, would stop the country.

My letter closed with a reference that I was again coming to Ross for a meeting at the Chase Hotel, which was the last stand of the Chamber of Commerce and many local people against the closure, the occasion at which I helped draft a telegram to Tom Fraser, then Transport Minister, as a last resort to the effect that the tracks should not be removed and the new technology (i.e. railbuses) be tried. This meeting was well recorded in the reproduced front page of the *Gazette*; the telegram to the Minister was formally proposed, seconded and carried unanimously:

TRANSPORT MINISTER URGED TO KEEP RAILWAY OPEN

All facilities at Ross Station due to end on November 1st

PUBLIC MEETING CALLS FOR DIESEL PASSENGER SERVICE

> A few hours after British Rail announced on Monday that the goods trains between Ross and Gloucester and Lydbrook would be withdrawn on November 1st, a telegram was sent from a public meeting at Ross to the Minister of Transport, Mr Tom Fraser, urging that the line should be kept open and that a diesel passenger service should be instituted. The withdrawal of the once-daily goods train, which has run since passenger services were ended 11 months ago, will mean that Ross and Lydbrook railway stations will close for public business on November 1st. A staff of seven at Ross and two at Lydbrook, besides the engineering gangs, are affected by the closure. Mr R.H. Underhill, the stationmaster, said the parcels

service and all other facilities at the station would cease. Those needing parcels or any other goods collected for delivery by railway would make arrangements with the Gloucester depot for collection by the road vehicle.

The public meeting had been previously called by Ross Hoteliers and Caterers Association and Ross Chamber of Commerce and was held at the Chase Hotel on Monday evening. Ross Urban Council and representatives of other public organisations among the attendance of 40 gave their support to the following telegram to Mr Fraser:

'Most immediate. Personal for Mr Fraser, Minister of Transport. Public meeting in Ross-on-Wye requests new hearing by reconstituted Transport Users Consultative Committee before closure of Ross–Gloucester line, due on November 1st. Bus connections with London trains most unsatisfactory due to congested roads since passenger traffic ceased. In the event of hard winter, as 1963, coal and fuel position would be acute within days. Meeting convinced that diesel service for both passenger and goods, well managed and competitive, would pay.'

At a meeting in the afternoon, the Hoteliers and Caterers Association had sent the following telegram to Lord Geddes, President of the British Travel Association:

'Request urgent approach to Minister of Transport to withhold consent to close Ross to Gloucester railway until operated trial period with good London connections. Abandonment of this line completely severs overseas visitors' access to Wye Valley. Please act against this positive threat to tourism revenue.'

HARDSHIP INCREASE
Change of Station

Opening the public meeting, Mr O. Goodwin, President of the Chamber of Commerce, said it was a matter vital to Ross. Hardly any article used by businesses in the town was not carried by the railway at some time. Mr E.T. Rawlins, of Thornton Heath, Surrey, addressed the meeting and said they would be justified in calling for another meeting of the Transport Users Consultative Committee because British Rail had altered the situation by changing the departure station for London trains from Gloucester. "We are at the eleventh hour, if not the twelfth hour. We may only just get there in time," Mr Rawlins said. If they were successful in getting the Consultative Committee reconvened they would have to look into various aspects of hardship; difficulties of walking with luggage from the bus station at Gloucester to Eastgate station; parcels and mail difficulties; luggage in advance getting lost; manufacturers' difficulties with freight on a larger scale; the difficulties of farmers and the hotel and catering interests. The council thinking ahead to the development of the town would feel the loss of the railway. If the Consultative Committee were to be reconvened he (ETR) suggested that signed statements be taken at the Market Hall. The railway would be needed more and more as the motorcar becomes less and less useful.

10–1 AGAINST
Time for Reappraisal

The Beeching plan had closed 170 lines and only 17 had been saved by local pressure. The odds were 10–1 against them but the time had now arrived for a reappraisal of the situation, Mr Rawlins said. Miss C. Crampton remarked that she had attended the two meetings of the Consultative Committees when the future of the line was discussed and she thought that enough cases of hardship had then been put forward to convince anyone. With congested roads, it often took three hours to reach Gloucester, Miss Crampton added. Mr S.G. Little said Ross Urban Council had fought the closure all the way and they were still firmly behind anything that could be done to stop the complete closure. Mr H.T. Allen said Ross and Whitchurch Rural Council had done everything they could to keep the line open and were still willing to do so. He spoke of the problems of women with cases and pushchairs using the buses and said they should push for a diesel car, which would not be all that expensive.

TUCC BLAMED
Made up Mind Before Evidence

Mr A.H.C. Sykes, Secretary to the Wyedean Tourist Board, said a great deal of the blame lay with the Consultative Committee. When the Wye Valley line was to be closed he had attended their meeting at Monmouth and he had gained the impression that they had made up their minds before hearing the evidence. Any other country with scenery comparable with the Wye Valley would have *built* a line for tourists, but here a ready-made line had been closed! He had received a similar impression at the meeting of the committee which considered the Hereford–Ross–Gloucester railway and said that unless they had an impartial committee they could get nowhere. Mr L. Drayson-Russill, vice-chairman of the Rural Council, said he had no mandate and was there with a watching

> brief. In the greater part of the rural district the railway had already been taken up. He thought it would be flogging a dead horse to reconvene the Consultative Committee. His council always kept a watchful eye on the bus companies' proposals for route timings and fares to see that the people in the district had a fair deal. The general feeling was that the alternative arrangements were *totally inadequate*. "My council would support any worthwhile protest to improve the bus services and the freight and postal services in the rural district," Mr Russell said. Mr R.J. Childs, vice-president of the Chamber, said that 90–95 % of the goods delivered by rail used to arrive intact. Now 90–95% were damaged! That had been happening for months and no notice was taken of the complaints. "Diesels could be made to pay, but the workmen of today on the railway do not have the old pride there used to be in the Great Western," Mr Childs said.
>
> Mr T.W. Lane said they had been told they would get a better goods service, but it had deteriorated. He had 19 pieces of correspondence regarding a damaged article, but the only reply he could get was, "It is receiving our best attention." That had been going on for 2½ months. The proposal to send the telegram to the Minister was proposed by Mr Little and was seconded by Mr Drayson-Russill and carried unanimously.

I believe this reporting to represent very fairly contemporary feelings that Ross and district had been sold down the river by the powers that be; the foundations of the 1995 'Rural Area in Decline' had been well and truly laid.

CHAPTER 3

The Inevitable Hiatus

Another 20 years would pass before we as a family could move to Ross and resume the fight for restoration of the railway, a matter sadly beyond the capacity of local people and at a time when even the most active preservation bodies were at the pioneering stage. In the meantime, I had escaped from increasing frustration (seen it all, done it all, got the T-shirt, as we say in 1996!) from Central Electricity Board Headquarters alongside St Paul's Cathedral. I moved to the London Borough of Southwark as the town clerk's personnel officer and employment law specialist. We kept in touch with Ross by visits to Chasedale Hotel, and it was after one such visit that I sent to Geoff Lancashire, the proprietor and keen supporter of the renewal, a considerable paper of eleven pages in September 1978.

This comprised an introduction, proposed board of management, line-of-route, funding, primary capital works, locomotives and rolling stock and WVR in operation; this was particularly in respect of the Ross–Monmouth–Chepstow Railway. Geoff Lancashire planned to discuss this paper with a 'distinguished neighbour', but as he mentioned, the fact that I did not then live locally was a factor almost impossible to bridge. This work became known as a feasibility study and by May 1979 had reached the Wyedean Tourist Board.

My commentary to the Board was prophetic in the following respect: the 'Wye Valley is an increasingly attractive tourist area which is likely to desperately need a "diffusing" agent – this function the railway would perform.' Perhaps also this was virtually the *last* of the 'Valley' lines in Britain which had not been reinstated by effective local action. In due course, this study reached Martin Morris, son of the Ross stationmaster and now chief reporter of the *Ross Gazette*. He did what I described as a 'good, straightforward write-up' in the paper but doubted whether sufficient support would be aroused. Better than I, he knew just how disparate were local interests when it came to common-good proposals. I supplied Martin with a picture of the general Ross Station layout, number 133 in my negative collection; this duly appeared in his book of Ross-on-Wye. Again, we holidayed at Chasedale in July 1979 and I discussed the railway with anyone expressing interest; so, with the newspaper article the WVR remained a live issue.

The next three years were unrewarding from the railway renewal point of view. My work with Southwark was increasingly onerous and, sadly, the generation at Ross that knew, worked and travelled on the railway were slipping away. Maud (Everall) sent me the *Ross Gazette* weekly, and it was rather miserable reading. However, by 1982 the Tyne and Wear Metro had been inaugurated and although an urban north-east coast location, much of the modern developments were transferable in principle to the Wye Valley. Certainly, I revised my 1978 paper and the introduction for 1982 reads: 'The priorities can now be reversed. The aim can be restoration of rail services to meet a work-a-day local and tourism need for fast, all-weather travel in the area.' Such a modern system of signalling and electric railcars instead of steam would reduce, on Southern Railway experience, the overall costs by 50%. The new WVR would be a less labour-intensive system with radio signalling and continuous communication between 'control' and the driving cab, offering greater safety even for a single-line operation. Confident operation to time, even in the prevailing white fog of the area and darkness, would be facilitated. With welded track joints, operation would be virtually silent with no disturbance to nearby residents or animal and bird life. Indeed, British Rail environmental officers had found that the railway corridors make ideal conservation areas, free from human interference.

It would seem relevant to include this 1982 2nd edition of my Wye Valley Railway paper in order that posterity may decide how this would guide the scheme's later development. The following examines a wider range of alternative routes extending from Ross and in the context of constructing a completely modern system consequent upon the technology since developed for the Tyne and Wear Metro rapid transit system:

INTRODUCTION

The first edition of this appraisal was completed in 1978 and so pre-dated the inauguration of one of the most significant modern developments in rail transit in Britain. The Wye Valley is not the same as the urban northeast coast, but the research, development and manufacture of the now operational hardware is no less relevant. The Tyne and Wear Metro experience opens up the practicability of an entirely NEW operational philosophy other than the concept of running occasional 'preserved' steam trains almost entirely by voluntary labour.

The priorities can now be reversed. The aim can be the restoration of rail services to meet work-a-day local and tourist needs for fast, all-weather travel in the area. Such a modern system removes much of the labour-intensive work of the past, particularly in terms of preparation and operation. But there will certainly be some new paid jobs on the WVR and substantially more opportunities will arise simply from the presence of the line and the traffic stimulated by such up-to-date and efficient facilities.

METRO TECHNOLOGY

The concept was the greatest single British transport project when research and construction began in 1974. The management studied transit systems worldwide; Ross can benefit from all that costly knowledge and application of up-to-date technology, which has since been manufactured, tried and tested. No less than 90 fast, brand new two-car articulated coaches for one-man operation have been built in the Midlands by Metro-Cammell. Trains normally signal themselves and drivers are in radio contact with control. Herefordshire residents will readily understand the significance of the harsh North Sea coast environment in which the Metro operates. Thus, the conditions of dense fog, ice and snow, which make the roads of this area highly dangerous, will be overcome by the all-weather capability of the WVR railcars. Due to the use of modern track and suspension, the railcars will operate virtually silently, with no disturbance to nearby residents or animal life.

FUNDING

Practical consideration has to be given to the raising of Treasury funds and private venture capital and to have in mind that the European Regional Development/Social Funds may well grant 40% of the sum required. In this connection there are a variety of factors such authorities consider, e.g. the primary aim – in this case being restoration of direct access to and from Ross and District to the BR network. The importance of this relates to the need to improve mobility for employment in an area where 14% are without work and, by providing an alternative to road access, reducing the rising impact of tourist damage to the Forest of Dean environment in particular.

There is no parallel example of financing such a modern railway facility in Britain today; the Ross WVR project would be unique and an outstanding attraction in its own right. Think of it as a MINI-Metro and also as a system to operate in a recognised area of 'outstanding natural beauty' and the following examples become clearly relevant.

KIELDER DAM

In the North Country, in the area of Tynedale District and Northumberland County Council, much co-operative effort surrounded the Kielder dam project. Authorities included the Forestry Commission, English Tourist Board, Countryside Commission, Sports Council, Nature Conservancy Council and the Council for Rural Industries. Two-thirds of the capital cost came from the National Loans Fund Department of the Treasury and the European Investment Bank at favourable interest rates. The remaining third came as a grant from the European Community's Regional Development Fund. Further grants of £8 million came from other interested parties.

TYNE AND WEAR METRO

This began in 1979 with a European Social Fund grant of almost £3 million, being 40% of staff training costs. British Government support was 70% of the capital involved, concurrent with the Act of Parliament. The final part of the system (1983 built) is aided by a 30% European Regional Development Fund towards civil engineering, stations and general equipment of the lines.

TOURISM

International tourism in 1979 reduced Britain's balance of trade deficit by almost one third. Therefore, even in slump conditions, tourism is virtually a 'boom' industry. In 1981, British people holidaying in this country contributed a massive £4,660 million to the home industry. But in 1981 there were four million FEWER holidays of four days or more than in 1980. Just consider how many MORE might come to Ross in the autumn, at Christmas, Easter and spring if a civilised train journey from London or Plymouth or anywhere replaced the chore of driving each way! And this applies equally to the ever-expanding market of catering for out-of-town conferences, business courses etc.

The United States of America is the richest country in the world but in 1981 less than 1% of that country's population was attracted to Britain. It surely follows that tourism is virtually important to any area which has the potential to attract visitors, PLUS the foresight to protect the environment from being swamped by the overwhelming number of cars – destroying the very peace they so earnestly seek. The tourism case should, of course, be included in the planning brief, the Act (if found necessary) and in the financial support case made to the Treasury.

BOARD OF MANAGEMENT

The Wye Valley Railway would need a full range of professional skills to steer the project from planning through to operation. It is anticipated that this would be an area in which local, newly retired professional people would be prepared to give some time, the appointment of a full-time general manager and some staff being necessary in due course. It is difficult to imagine a more satisfying project in which to have a personal role – laced with something of the trials, tribulations and ultimate success experienced by our Victorian forebears.

It would be hoped that representatives in public life would indicate general supportive interest – MPs, district and county councillors – recognising that the WVR opens up a wide variety of exciting opportunities for the exceedingly COMMON GOOD of the entire neighbourhood.

ROUTES

Since 1964 the town of Ross has suffered, both practically and psychologically, the LOSS of the all-weather, highly civilised form of transport which good railway communication represents. Indeed, for those without cars, or who are too young or too old to drive or are unemployed, Ross is ISOLATED to a degree which would have been INCONCEIVABLE 40 years ago!

Reinstatement of the railway has, therefore, to serve TWO equally vital needs: that of the indigenous POPULATION (before all who can, do leave) and to cater for the vastly expanding numbers of TOURISTS, who must be accommodated but carefully guided and contained to avoid excessive pressure on the environment.

Within the triangle of rail-less communication, local opinion would be tested to consider the priorities of route reinstatement, the outcome of which would identify the task upon which all effort must initially concentrate. It is suggested that the following be rated in order of preference, bearing in mind that both bureaucratic and practical considerations are involved and that the prime essential is to get a 'limb' underway:

(i) Ross–Gloucester; with direct passenger access
(ii) Ross–Hereford; to and from BR (WR)
(iii) Ross–Monmouth; later to Chepstow and BR (WR).

Deciding priorities/routes may be assisted by aerial photography from Aerofilms, Borehamwood, Herts, with half a million negatives, and for new photography from the Committee for Aerial Photography, University of Cambridge. Since the line would be electrified (overhead system), the city of Hereford may well wish to be associated with the provision of current. It should also be borne in mind that the BR (WR) line between Hereford and Worcester (for Birmingham and London) is under constant threat of closure by BR. The possibility that the Hereford–

Worcester line could be reinvigorated by electrification and, indeed, have a through service to and from Ross is worthy of consideration.

REINSTATEMENT

There are a number of alternatives in terms of choice of route and it has to be kept in mind that new, but smaller, station and halt sites may now be required. Similarly, some diversions from the original line of Mr Brunel's survey may be inevitable but usefully so, for example to serve the new housing and factory developments. The most basic point to make is that it is immaterial that track and top ballast has gone; it is the continued existence of most of the underlying formation and way leave which makes reinstatement a practicable proposition. Included in the still-remaining civil works will be the tunnels cut through the rock, bridge piers and abutments.

All previous iron and steel work would have HAD to have been replaced by now and this renewal task applies particularly to the bridges, where required. At least one Midlands firm will supply bridge components made to measure for site assembly. We should remember that one of the oldest regiments of army engineers is stationed at Monmouth and might well wish to be associated with the professional and general work of reconstruction. Much clearance work will be necessary along the line-of-route and it would be hoped that the Ross Steam Engine Society would assist, say, working towards a barrel of beer at half-mile intervals – some great days out for the traction engines.

Experience of recent years shows Government willingness to pay the wages of as much labour as can be properly supervised upon projects offering good work knowledge. Platform restoration is a good example, whereby the efforts of two bricklayers upon the front elevation can be supplemented by others moving and filling rubble etc. to complete. The new track would comprise steel Vignoles rail (to BR standards) laid upon reinforced concrete sleepers in stone ballast; this will result in far less maintenance work than was necessary in former times.

BUILDINGS

Basically, the headquarters of the Wye Valley Railway would be at Ross, likely contained in a single industrial building of the type already familiar on the newly developed estates in the district. Such a building would provide secure office and station facilities and covered accommodation for all the stock, perhaps three twin sets of Metro pattern railcars. (NB. It is possible that by the time these are required, Tyne and Wear Metro might sell three sets to WVR, which would be renovated and repaired appropriately.)

The headquarters building would be the control centre, both for management and the electricity feeder installation plus the radio-controlled signalling/communications system. Again, as with reinstatement, most of the work would be undertaken with Manpower Services Commission labour, under professional and tradesmen's guidance. Hopefully, such young people would be more attractive to local employers as well as some becoming permanent employees of the WVR. Platform buildings on intermediate stations would be as basic and vandal proof as possible; constructed in conjunction with local needs and, for example, incorporating the ideas of interested parties, such as the Forestry Commission.

STEAM OPERATION

Today there is such public demand for steam trains operating in beauty spots that it must be a cast iron

> certainty that the Wye Valley would never have lost its railway had the proposal to close it happened NOW! It is, therefore, very desirable that the local preservation society of steam trains, the Dean Forest Railway Society at Norchard, be invited to participate in this regeneration of the WVR. It is, however, very likely that we should require them to pay the insurance premium against fire risk to farms etc. Subject to mutual arrangements at the time, it can be envisaged that 'specials' of both Dean Forest origin and elsewhere might run from time to time upon the WVR lines. Indeed, it could be that most summer season Sunday operation might be by steam (the overhead electricity supply having been switched off at Ross by the electrical engineer with full safety inter-locks). In these circumstances it is NOT anticipated that the Wye Valley Railway would become an operator/owner of any steam locomotives or contemporary rolling stock.

Since this 1982 paper, time has moved on, but many of the points made still hold good as I look back from 1996! By September 1982 the *Gazette* carried a report by Sir Henry Marking, Chairman of the British Tourist Authority, indicating the enormous potential for active areas to share the £3,850 million spent by overseas visitors in Britain. Even so, the 11.5 million visitors represented a drop of 8% on the previous year. Britons spent £4,660 million travelling in Britain, of which £3,075 million was on holidays. A simple challenge really: the country and seaside resorts that make the effort could better their share of the market. No effort of sufficient significance existed in this area and in the Forest the only growth appeared to be in the advertisement volume representing dealing in second-hand cars!

On the 16th September 1982 the South Herefordshire District Council published 'the long-awaited draft District Plan' to the 1991 horizon. It proposed a pedestrian and cycle way along the old railway line from Walford Road to Hildersley, saying that the route was owned by the Hereford and Worcester County Council and previously identified as a possible north–south bypass, the most significant sentence being: 'Escalating fuel costs and diminishing public transport services could deter many residents from finding work outside the town [Ross] in the future, thus aggravating unemployment problems.' Clearly, the problem had been identified but the will to seek renewal of the railway was lacking; this would encourage individuals to hire purchase vehicles and lead to the congestion, parking and pollution problems just around the corner.

On 23rd September 1982 I sent two copies of my revised Wye Valley Railway paper to Hugh Leigh, then secretary to the Wydean Tourist Board, Ross. He had mentioned he saw Ross–Gloucester as a priority for renewal. I said that it was "URGENT to inject into councillors' and planners' minds the need to preserve the wayleave line of possible routes." I rejected the *Ross Gazette* commentary by Wyecider of 16th September 1982, implying that renewing bridge/civil works was of overriding significance in the light of civil engineering progress in the late 20th century! No doubt Hugh Leigh discussed the matter with Doug Woodman, Wyedean Tourist Board Chairman. I offered more copies as required.

In 1983 the mayor of Ross, Councillor M. Littlefield, sought the Prime Minister's (Mrs Thatcher's) help to make the district a Special Development Area (SDA), but this was rejected on the grounds that 14% unemployment was not sufficiently high!

A Bristol University seminar of July 1983 invited elected members (i.e. councillors) to listen to proposals to amend European regulations and for a Transport Infrastructure Fund towards developing a Community Transport Policy. Did anyone locally attend?

But a development announced by the Department of Transport notice in the *Ross Gazette* of 1st September 1983 was the most important of the year. In effect, the local councillors had been persuaded to agree a so-called relief road linking the A40

Hildersley roundabout with the Newport–Worcester trunk road. The local people gathered that unless a deal was accepted immediately they would have to pay for it through local council taxation, whereas national income tax would fund it if quickly agreed. So, with *no* discernible research it was 'agreed', much to the, later, considerable criticism by the Audit Commission when it seemed surcharging of the councillors concerned could take place. The cost for the 1,445 metres (about one mile) was said to be £1 million and, of course, it cuts through the Ross–Gloucester railway line-of-route, immediately to the east of the listed Brunel engine shed. Indeed, the road is so close to the shed that it would be difficult to contrive a greater insult to a piece of industrial heritage, the frontage of which displays the original broad gauge stone arch, later reduced to suit the new standard gauge. Only Philistines or the crassly ignorant would have permitted this, for the new road should have been lowered both to effect a simple bridging for the railway and to reduce the impact of the road so close to the shed.

Sensibly, an underbridge was built into the Newport–Worcester dual carriageway where the Ross–Hereford rail line-of-route passes to the north near Hildersley. The basic excuse for the 'relief road' was to keep heavy lorries out of Ross from the Gloucester direction; this it has singularly failed to do, whereas a simple 7-ton load restriction, as applied at Windsor, advised by notices placed well away from Ross on the A40 toward Gloucester would have succeeded.

Looking back six months to 23rd March 1983, I had written to Colin Shepherd MP regarding Ross unemployment, the lack of a town museum and the proposed reinstatement of the Wye Valley Railway. He promised to "make some enquiries" and to "get in touch again", but I heard nothing more.

I continued to subscribe to the Railway Development Society, which on 6th June 1983 received a letter from Margaret Thatcher, Prime Minister, saying that: 'We want to see productive investment in the railway system and we are committed in principle to electrification. Re-opening railway lines on an experimental basis is a matter for consideration by British Railways normally in consultation with the local councils concerned.' She defended 'something like £1000 million a year in various subsidies from the Exchequer.' The inclusion of so many weasel words, e.g. 'productive', 'in principle' – 'subsidies' for railways rather than 'investment' had roads been the subject – avoided anything actually beneficial to the railways and such places as the Wye Valley and Herefordshire.

On 24th November 1983 the *Gazette* published in considerable detail the proposals of a Department of Transport consultant, John Grimshaw, for a Wye Valley Cycleway. This would be from Hereford to Ross, via Walford and Kerne Bridge to Lydbrook and hence to Chepstow by an unspecified route. Cycleways over Herefordshire bridges were costed at £65,150, stating: 'The railway route is treated as the main choice.'

It was difficult for me to see this as anything other than tinkering at the basic public transport problem in the area. Cycling is a minority interest and a nonsense as a practical alternative for all age groups, in all weathers, in darkness etc. Most basically, whether considering potential local or tourism use, no attempt seems to have been made to estimate whether any economic benefit would be returned over the capital costs. I was sceptical about whether any capable engineering assessment had been made of the proposals when reading that Stowfield viaduct (Lydbrook) was considered to be 'intact'. Our WVR engineering feasibility report of 1987 would indicate that considerable replacement of upper girders at Lydbrook would be essential. Although the costs of railway bridge girders between Ross and Hereford could well be higher than a cycle/pedestrian-only bridge, the necessary safety precautions necessary to allow unsupervised public access in these remote places would be substantial. Use by motorcyclists and even horse riders was a distinct possibility. In terms of a matter receiving serious consideration by the Department of Transport, one could only see provision being made as an out-rigging from railway bridging, which provided a majority user facility plus some overview of public access alongside.

CHAPTER 4

The Last London Year

A Hereford and Worcester County Council study was examined by Ross Town Council in January 1984, which included a typical developers' proposal that 'railway land' should be disposed of permanently. The town council strongly opposed this view, saying: 'Although certain bridges have been demolished this land remains as a strategically important potential route for a future relief road.' This can be seen as an example of the Tory dominated Hereford and Worcester County Council, whose statutory remit specifically included strategic planning and *transportation*, evading its responsibilities for covert motives.

In March the results of the 1981 census were published, showing that the Ross Urban District numbers had increased by 12% to 7,160 over the 1971 figure of 6,405. The biggest fall in population occurred at Holme Lacy, from 479 to 336; a village with a further education college, a WVR station but no trains. Goodrich dropped by 9% to 464, a location once served by the WVR Kerne Bridge station, which today would also include the Youth Centre. Also, in March 1984, the South Herefordshire District Council confirmed the view that the railway land should not be disposed of piecemeal and suggested 'use as a footpath to the industrial area'. A vague but helpful decision.

Glorious sunshine throughout the Easter holiday 1984 'brought visitors flocking to Ross and other spots in the Wye Valley', so recorded the *Gazette*. A shopkeeper noted up to 30 people in his shop, but they all left without buying a single item! How well this fitted my concept of the 'marginal' motorist – just able to pay for the hire purchase, petrol, insurance etc., but left with minimal spending power!

Symonds Yat was the usual tourist pressure point and Special Constables were drafted into the area to deal with traffic jams. On the balance sheet, who won? The indigenous population or the visitors? Perhaps, like Waterloo, a very close-run thing as to whether there was economic benefit to the Wye Valley.

The *Ross Gazette* of 17th May 1984 front-paged a very back-handed item, apparently contributed by Michael Draper, then combining the role of Financial Director and General Manager of the Severn Valley Railway. It related how the design of Ross Station would rise again as the Kidderminster terminal of the SVR. I, who had supplied 34 half-plate photographs of the station, free of charge, to the likewise volunteer architect Bob Marrows of Lydney, was not even mentioned. I presumed that Bob had my drawings of Ross Station also, which were published in the *Model Railway Constructor* in 1963. Despite some written protests from myself, neither Bob nor myself are recorded at Kidderminster, which has a plate attributing all to the jobbing architect and builder. Bob and I worked up the Kidderminster exterior and interior details, disabled access, security of booking office etc.; he did all the drawings so those who received all the credit did very little in comparison. Setting this down (even in 1996) puts the record right to some extent.

In June 1984 I had a letter published in the *Gazette* proposing an Action Seminar with Ross Community Enterprises, of whom Howard Ellis, of Blake Avenue, was a director. This was the first attempt to draw together well-meaning people other than councillors, and was known as 'ROSCOE'. The location was the Chase Hotel, by courtesy of Geoff Lancashire, and the date was 20th July 1984. Ron Smith of the Railway Development Society, Midlands, could not supply anyone to give the Society's views. I have no record of the outcome, which I suppose was somewhat inevitable since I could only attend for a single day. Despite his dedication to many matters, including the Ross Museum and the weather station, Howard became increasingly dissatisfied with the area and a couple of years later left to move up north near his daughter, where there was a frequent bus service *and* an operating railway station!

That summer the Hereford and Worcester County Surveyor

was saying how once the 'relief road' was open, the 7.5 tonne limit on lorries in Ross would be applied and it would be a 'wonderful day'. Needless to record, by 1996 this still has not happened and it would be interesting to know by whom or how this was quashed. About this time I discovered that a shooting range had been constructed on the line-of-route in a cutting at Greytree. This had a building erected, which was opened by Colin Shepherd, the Conservative MP, this being an example of how the district and town council views could be got around in a piecemeal fashion.

In October 1984 the county council published a Highways and Transportation Report. Since 1980 the number of road vehicles had risen by 11% to the record level of 264,000. In 1983 there were 3,437 casualties and 74 killed on the roads, at an estimated cost to the community of £25 million! (In 1987 the cost of renewing the entire WVR would be calculated at £20 million!) The increased road use was said to conflict with the environment, create noise, intimidation, smell, congestion and risk to person and property in many of the older towns. Truly, the chickens so casually left to breed had come home to roost.

In December 1984 Parliament announced that the loss of 'Rural Development Area No. 8' status would be replaced by the classification 'Intermediate Assisted Area'. There would be no automatic grants but the area would be eligible for selective assistance and EEC aid. Tourism and hotels' etc. needs were excluded. Cinderford was added to Ross, the two towns being regarded as one (!) for 'travel to work' purposes. No explanation was offered for this geographical nonsense but it appeared that Paul Marland MP and Colin Shepherd MP had so persuaded the Minister.

In Ross, 533 men and 261 women spent Christmas 1984 out of work.

The New Year, 1985, was to be a critical one for the family, in the summer of which Mary, Susan and myself, having obtained early retirement, would leave Thornton Heath. Serena in Bristol helped us in the search for accommodation at Ross and this concluded with the purchase of our current home in Merrivale in July.

Maud Everall had kept up the supply of *Ross Gazette*s and the 10th January edition revealed that the county council was being recommended to rescind the decision to dispose of the railway line-of-route between Tudorville and Hildersley. Some parts of the line had been released on temporary licence and it was thought unlikely, by keeping the route as a footpath, to cost more than £500 per year. It was noted that the line was NOT part of the projected Hereford–Bristol (!) Cycleway project.

By mid February the winter had really taken hold, with snow and ice continually blocking the Ross to Monmouth dual carriageway. The diesel in the buses froze; three vehicles were frozen on 11th February and the country roads had drifts up to five feet deep. By March, fog caused a considerable number of accidents and mile-long queues. Following recriminations, the Hereford and Worcester County Council said that £300,000 had been spent in the Ross area on clearance, £200,000 over budget. Over the Welsh border the Glamorgan County Councils, working with BR Cardiff Valley's services manager, were establishing parkways and a new station (at Cathays) and had achieved in one year the traffic levels projected for five! By lowering fares they had increased the overall revenue for 1985 by 14%. What a difference county council members *could* make to an area – the WVR would have to suffer Gloucestershire, Gwent and Herefordshire and Worcestershire County Councils acting like a very slowly animated British Railways symbol – pulling in different directions or sitting on the fence.

In Europe the Commission pointed at the advantages of 'integrated transport systems and effective energy policies'. In Britain there was NO Government enthusiasm for either. Tourism figures for 1984 were published, with Tintern Abbey rated the fifth most popular venue with 95,000 visitors! The implications for the static, non-operational station *should* have been obvious.

Uniquely, on 21st November 1985, *The Times* carried a full-page advertisement headline: 'A Pay-as-you-enter bus is no help when you're getting on.' It pointed out that even if you had a bus service, the vehicles were a struggle for women with babies/ buggies, the pregnant, the disabled, the old, and that the loading times were four times as long, the stops were longer and there were overriding fare losses – and there were more ex-conductors on the dole. Not to mention, I thought, the pitching and rolling of the old double-deckers as they swing into the stopping places on the country roads. By comparison, the railway gives a first-class ride, but this is denied to those served only by third-class buses in a monopoly situation.

On 20th November 1985 my latest letter was acknowledged by Colin Shepherd MP, but nothing happened: par for the course. An approach to the 'Railway' MP, Robert Adley, allowed by the Tory whips, likewise proved useless, he responding with the usual statement that he could not be involved in matters involving other Members' constituencies. This completed the catch-22 circle of Conservative determination to have no transport policy.

On 21st November 1985 a unique event happened at the Chase Hotel, Ross, when the chairmen (all male, of course!) of the then Tory dominated Hereford and Worcester County Council responded to general Herefordshire disgruntlement by actually appearing in the town. It was a less than harmonious occasion, for these chairmen of committees were quite unused to having their actions questioned when at County Hall, Worcester. Ross is at the extremity of their 'empire' and conveniently ignored. Although a new boy in the area, when it became apparent that the audience was quite overawed by the occasion, I stood up and asked how the council would react to renewing the WVR for local and tourism use. I said that through the grants of the Manpower Services Commission it could be possible to provide electric railcars.

The chairman of the Strategic Planning and Transportation Committee appeared shocked at receiving such a direct, positive question and replied that the "need for this would have to be closely investigated before they could proceed further." How it could be so examined before "proceeding further" remained obscure, but the matter was front page in the *Gazette* of 21st November 1985. This occasion would, however, be the beginning of a process I was to lead for the next decade!

CHAPTER 5

The Paperchase Begins

The year 1986 began with a dismal review by Councillor John Sewell, Gloucester County Council, of the few enquiries for economic development in the Forest of Dean and the lack of 'strategic' finance to put into the infrastructure. I asked the Gwent, Gloucester and Hereford and Worcester County Councils to produce a planners' feasibility study of the WVR route in each county, the aim being to then prepare a presentation to the European Economic Community for about 40% capital, to British Government agencies for c.40% and to offer 20% equity, i.e. privately held shares.

I wrote to the head offices of the high street banks, enclosing a copy of a supportive letter from Sir James Scott-Hopkins MEP, on 3rd February 1986. The *Ross Gazette* carried a front-page story regarding a move to close the night casualty service at the cottage hospital. Dr R.J. Cooke remarked that: "Inevitably, many of the patients would require ambulance transport to Hereford involving a return journey of 30 miles at a cost of about £60 per journey." The rail alternative of smooth, swift travel had been lost. By 6th February 1986, in the snow, the 4 p.m. bus from Hereford did not leave until 4.40 p.m. and did not reach Ross until 8 p.m.! Yes indeed, the anticipated 'hardship' had arrived, but those who had taken the decision to close the line were NOT affected.

At the AGM of wardens of the Wye Valley AoONB, Mr T.E. Wilcox, Chairman of the Joint Advisory Council, felt they were only scratching at problems and that without the voluntary wardens "the system for looking after the Valley would collapse." I thought he had, probably quite unwittingly, uncovered the hidden agenda of the JAC, i.e. to give the appearance of doing something but withholding sufficient funds/manpower. This does much to explain how the lack of ongoing management would inevitably lead to exploitation, the later to be discovered 'degradation' and the unwillingness to offend local landowners by supporting the return of the best means of transportation to wider work opportunities and facilitating the tourism trade. The South Herefordshire District Council's planning officer, John Loynes, deplored the 18% unemployment in Ross and lamented that becoming an Intermediate Area had failed to draw any sizeable employer to the area. He saw it as a retirement area to the detriment of working-age people.

By early March 1986 we had letters back from Lloyds, Barclays and the Midland Banks, regretting that there was no one available to help WVR. At Monmouth the district council sought to persuade British Rail not to demolish the Troy viaduct as the preservation notice was not to be renewed. This viaduct was not part of our renewal plans, as we sought to serve a station only in the Mayhill 'town' area and did not intend to run down to Usk and Pontypool Road. But having created about keeping the viaduct, the district council, in the person of Councillor John Parker, leader of the majority Tory group, aligned himself with a landowner element and declared the renewal "a non-runner". This evoked a strong response from me in the *Forest of Dean and Wye Valley Review* of 21st February 1986, led in by a flyer – 'Wye Rail Plan is on course' – on the front page. Inside, accompanied by a rather unfortunate photograph of me subtitled 'A great tourism spin-off', was a useful piece of public relations which would make plain that this project would not be put down by biased commentary:

RAILWAY PLAN IS A RUNNER, SAYS ERIC

The man behind plans to re-activate the Wye Valley Railway told the *Review* this week, "The project is still very much on course." Mr Eric Rawlins, of Ross-on-Wye, hit back at Councillor John Parker, leader of the majority Tory group on Monmouth District

> Council, who has described the scheme as 'a non-runner'. The council decided to take no action on a letter from Mr Rawlins after several members raised fears that he would be looking for financial support from ratepayers. Mr Rawlins flatly denied that the railway would be doing so – indeed, he claimed, the boot would soon be on the other foot. He explained: "Just as soon as the new Monmouth Town Station is bringing in the paying visitors, so will the district council be demanding rates from the railway.
>
> "I fought against the closure of the lines at the time and have very likely spent as many years studying the nitty-gritty as the council has spent [in minutes] in reaching such generalist conclusions. Happily, it is still not a sin to work full time, even without attendance allowances, on a project beyond the imagination and competence of most."
>
> Mr Rawlins revealed the contents of a letter which he had written to Councillor Parker in which he stressed that in no way had the practical and financial difficulties been overlooked. He added, "These difficulties are inevitable when faced with a renewal of primary facilities in an area of 25 years of random developments. However, the Wye Valley Railway proposals are for exceptionally modern transport which is safe, all-weather and provides great tourism spin-off in work opportunities."

John Kendrick, assistant secretary to the Forest of Dean District Council, was most supportive and considerable help was given to attendance by Serena (Rawlins) and me at a seminar and exhibition at Bell's Hotel, Coleford, on 16th April 1986. The key theme was 'Marketing Tourism' and we met nothing but enthusiasm and common purpose. We met Mrs Bobbie Heavens of the Association for the Promotion of Herefordshire, and she became a long-term supporter, working to influence those we hardly knew existed! We also met Clive George of the Regional Enterprise Unit, Department of Employment at Bristol, a vital contact to whom I will refer later.

We were seeking the appointment of liaison officers to WVR as contacts with the councils, and it seemed that Neville Nelder of the Surveyor's Department, Gloucester County Council, would be the first. I recognised that this could be a two-edged situation because it would depend upon good faith and maintaining the common good rather than, say, creating a barrier between WVR and councillors who might be covertly against the reinstatement of the railway. At the suggestion of Bobbie Heavens, I sent the editor of the *Hereford Times* a question and answer format of some 1,300 words to give the city readers some knowledge of the project; in vain, I looked for acknowledgement or publication.

A talk which I gave, supported by Serena, to Monmouth Town Council on 3rd March 1986 attracted the attention of Bill Price, then editor of the *Forest of Dean and Wye Valley Review*. We wrote an article of 1,380 words and supplied the print of the auto-engine No. 1455 and trailer approaching Kerne Bridge, also the distant view of the same area with the camping coach. A print of Symonds Yat read: 'The idyllic outlook for passengers near Symonds Yat station; note how well the railway blends with the scenery'. Indeed, only a trail of steam betrays the presence of the inconspicuous service to local people and tourists. This article made the centre pages of the 25th April 1986 edition and was very well received.

Within a week the Gloucestershire and Gwent County Councils were deploring a crisis of bus provision in the area and an operator was quoted as saying that if he needed £1,000 a week to run a service but was only getting £400, it would be up to the council to find the extra £600. The public, needless to say, had no details of these costings, but the use of old, second-hand vehicles prevailed and there was no mention of tourism revenue. In May I supplied a railway photograph at the request of a farmer and offered to give a talk to any NFU meeting; this was not taken up and to date (1996) I have never been asked to address this body or the closely aligned Country Landowners Association, although some members of wider audiences belong to these bodies.

By mid May I became aware that publication of my article for the *Hereford Times* had been blocked, apparently awaiting a feasibility report. It turned out that the editor did not think reinstatement was possible, but this seemed an extraordinary excuse for refusing a really newsworthy story about such a major project for the county. Bobbie Heavens indicated that it may be necessary to 'sponsor' it by paying for it – as with motor advertising articles. I decided to bear in mind that this was probably pressure of vested interests being applied to counter the good reception of the *Review* article.

Interest in the Monmouth area was high and on 8th April 1986 we talked to the Monmouth Action Committee, on the 27th to the Civic Society and on 25th May we had a stand alongside the river at Monmouth regatta. On 16th April I gave a well-received talk, under a banner provided by the Forest of Dean District Council, at Bell's Hotel, Coleford.

It was on 3rd May 1986 that a most significant letter arrived – from Richard Eagle, then of Treworgan Common, Llandenny. He had read the *Review* article and was keen to help; I replied, mentioning that Cass Hayward, Consulting Civil Engineers of Chepstow, had offered a feasibility study 'close to my timescale of two weeks and for a fee estimate of around £1,500 plus VAT'. Our correspondence began and Richard recommended we devise a printed letterhead. We soon identified a number of factors, including the difficulty local people have with the 24-hour clock and the 'status' basis to car use that stopped some walking even sufficient distance to keep their legs working! I mentioned the possibility of a knight of the realm becoming chairman, this being a reason to delay letterhead design. By June 1986 Richard was advocating starting the renewal from the Chepstow end, with Fairfield Mabey nearby as bridge engineers and the nearby quarry a famous BR source of ballast. Unfortunately, we had not the finance to proceed and although Gwent County Council had expressed willingness to 'co-operate with a comprehensive study of the whole', we heard nothing more of this proposition. When in touch with Mrs E.M. Lewis, owner of the Paddocks Hotel, Symonds Yat West (and chairman of the Ross-on-Wye and District Hoteliers and Caterers Association) we discussed the colour film of the WVR known to have been commissioned in about 1958. This proved a difficult matter to pursue, and even in 1996 it remains elusive.

To counter the difficulty of publicity in Hereford, I put some notes in the *Ross Gazette* to the effect that a 20-minute talk, with maps etc., was available to any organisation in or around Ross or Hereford. In June also, Mrs Lewis was front page in the *Review*, complaining of the ineffectiveness of the South Herefordshire District Council regarding tourism – citing the closure of five hotels and guesthouses in 18 months. She asked for a meeting with the council with the object of reversing the present downward trend in what should be one of the most beneficial industries in the area. I already had found that the general local attitude, especially in the small minds of some councillors, was that tourism was not really of prime importance; factory work was much more important! Tourism employed over one million people in Britain, and visitors were attracted to the ready-made asset of the Area of Outstanding Natural Beauty but would only continue to come if the district was not spoilt by the detritus found around industry and old vehicle dealing etc.

In the same paper, of 6th June 1986, the Forest of Dean District Council supported in principle the reconstruction of the Wye Valley Railway between Chepstow and Ross-on-Wye, but no money or staff would be devoted to the project! This indication of support was welcome, given that a district council did not have 'transportation' as a statutory responsibility.

On 12th June a Ross resident, Mr Keith Wally, was amazed to find that the "last bus service from Ross to Monmouth is 2 p.m.!" He highlighted the difficulties of commuting and shopping, stating that: "the bus companies have priced themselves out of a market which is crying out for a service. A reduction in fares would bring more business." Such a truism which is the foundation of the enormously successful Indian railways and which had begun to pay dividends when the Greater London Council ran London Transport, but does involve *real marketing* effort. It is much easier to rely on county council subsidies – through which the uninformed public has to pay *twice*, once in fares, secondly in council tax precepts.

The chairman of Gloucestershire County Council, the Liberal Eric Radley, expressed his dismay at the Transport Act, saying that it would reduce bus services in rural areas. Public transport was a lifeline for many people, and without it either villages would die or become extremely isolated. I had been in touch with Eric Radley since December 1985, and from February 1986 when the county was spending £750,000 per annum on bus subsidies the correspondence was intensive and as detailed as I could be in advance of any professional studies. By 26th March 1986 John Cordwell, the chairman of the Planning and Transportation Committee, took over. I responded to his requests for even more information to prove feasibility in advance of the council, even assisting with research finance! On 5th April I set out 14 paragraphs of detail to the extent then possible – ending with the offer to 'hand over the WVR files' to anyone of greater competence than myself. The main outcome was the allocation of Neville Nelder as 'contact' officer with the council, and on 7th May 1986 I advised them of the approach of Cass Hayward and Partners to do the engineering feasibility study.

A teacher, David Adams of Monmouth School, wrote for some information for 6th-form projects, mentioning the need for a railway at Monmouth for tourism and that pupils had used the trains daily in the past. On June 22nd, and again on 13th July 1986, we had a stand at the Bulmer Railway Centre, Hereford; this was an outside occasion with considerable numbers attending. I was also able to answer a few questions regarding the locomotives, with 'King George V', 'Clan Line' and 'Princess Elizabeth' then being on view.

On 10th July 1986 I had a letter in the *Gazette* responding to both the Red and White bus manager and a Mrs Davidson of

Birmingham, the latter deprecating the lack of rail connection and travel through the AoONB. I was then hopeful that physical work on the renewal could begin within a year – had WVR been over the border in Glamorganshire, no doubt this could have been so! On 14th July I spoke at the Ross Rotary Lunch and indicated that the renewal did depend upon the feasibility study proving successful and so countering the 'technical' doubts of those unacquainted with Victorian, let alone modern, civil engineering capacity.

On the broad front, Gwent County Council confirmed their co-operation for a comprehensive study and appointed liaison officers. The leader, Councillor Lloyd Turnbull, wrote saying the council was considering a proposal to re-open the Chepstow to Tintern section. He was not prepared to allocate any funding to the feasibility for the entire WVR; the Catch-22 was that until the study was done, the council would not even support it in principle!

With Hereford and Worcester County Council, the renewal project was in the hands of V.E. Jones, then county surveyor and bridgemaster. He, naturally, was familiar with all the physical problems. I responded in detail on 10th December 1985 and wrote to the chairman of the council on 27th February 1986. Getting no response, I wrote to the chairman of the Planning and Transportation Committee on 9th April 1986, saying: 'I am fed up with defending the apparent lack of action of Hereford and Worcester County Council in respect of the WVR reinstatement proposals. I have to tell you that there is increasing opinion that anything for Worcestershire "happens" but anything for Herefordshire is "blocked"'. No response. I wrote on 4th December 1986 to County Councillor Ray Smith, with no outcome.

On the parliamentary front, I wrote to Sir John Stradling-Thomas, MP for Monmouth, also to Roy Hughes, MP for Newport East, putting them in the picture. The Railway Development Society, Re-openings Committee, submitted the Wye Valley renewal to the Department of Transport, which was examining the 'Development of Scenic Rail Routes as Tourist Attractions for Foreign Visitors'. Tourism locally was described as 'quiet'.

I then met Frank Dallard, aged 85 years and one-time relief foreman at Ross engine shed. He hadn't had a holiday for 16 years and regretted the loss of the railway day trips to London, which would depart Ross at 7.23 a.m., travel via Gloucester and arrive in Paddington by 10 a.m. The return was at 6.35 p.m. and reached Ross at 10 p.m. The fare he mentioned was 13s, but that may have been in the 1930s! He would, in 1986, require wheelchair provision, which the new WVR railcars would accommodate. Alas, we were too late for Mr Dallard, but one in three residents are now over 60 years of age and wheelchair access is undoubtedly necessary to raise horizons – so that holidays and days out to special events may be practicable.

Mr P. Tolley of Brampton Road, Ross, wrote deprecating the growth of residential building and the town, which was 'now almost encircled by industrial units and is in great danger of becoming a duplicate of Milton Keynes or Telford'. I agreed, but the approach to Ross on the dual carriageway from Worcester looks much more like Slough awaiting the bombs which Sir John Betjeman saw as the desired fate for such hideous development. Surely the potential visitor will merely put his foot down to get past the excrescences rather than turn off and seek accommodation.

A petition, containing 863 signatures, protested about bus cuts, which had stopped the last bus from Hereford used by evening students and the early afternoon last bus to Monmouth etc. The growth of cars was overwhelming the Ross car parks, surprise, surprise. On 31st August 1986 the WVR stand attended the Mayor's Garden Party at the Chase Hotel, Ross; a most enjoyable occasion.

However, by early September I was sufficiently exasperated with the Hereford and Worcester County Council's failure to respond, feeling that this amounted to maladministration, that I was considering involving the ombudsman. A council spokeswoman said in the *Western Daily Press*, 'We are looking into the matter'.

Meanwhile, Richard Eagle saw great public relations advantage in naming the WVR railcars, suggesting 'Electric Executive', 'Electric Endeavour', 'Ivanhoe', 'Star of Midnight' etc. Since there are said to be a million railway enthusiasts in Britain, the collecting of such 'namers' would certainly be a stimulus both to the 'buffs' and family travellers.

Richard enclosed some drawings for a unique style of station name boards and fencing. This brought me to consider the concept of the 20 or so halts being adopted by the local community and parish councils. A volunteer called the 'halt warden' seemed appropriate to keep an eye on all matters, including telephoning the WVR headquarters at Ross in emergencies. We would need to train such people, particularly in operational safety, and encourage a general interest, including floral arrangements etc. By mid September 1986 Richard had produced livery designs for the railcars – a malachite green, chrome and white with yellow high-visibility ends. He also designed an attractive halt building; I mentioned visualising a Ross Central Station at Fiveways – a high-level miniature Worcester Foregate Street.

We decided that electrification would need to align, technically, with the intentions of British Rail for the area, i.e. a 25kV overhead system. Richard forwarded another set of designs, this time for the uniformed staff, male and female, uniquely different from those prevailing on British Rail. Serena, Susan and Mary were much impressed – the waistcoated Pullman style being seen as very practical, bearing in mind they had served refreshments in the Great Western Society's Ocean Mail saloons!

The 25th September 1986 saw a meeting at Ross where I spoke to the tripartite Ross, Monmouth and Chepstow Action Committee. On the hoteliers and caterers front, Paul Rynehart of the Chase Hotel, Ross, tabled information from me to a meeting at Ironbridge with the Heart of England Tourist Board on 5th September. I asked that there be liaison with the Wales Tourist Board, as the WVR is one-third in Wales. On 6th October 1986 I wrote fully to Malcolm Connor, Heart of England Tourist Board, giving details of finance, viability subject to the renewal as a whole, marketing as the key to success and consultancy for engineering feasibility etc. My letter concluded: 'We are only 14 years off the end of the century and permanent means to visit the Wye Valley from Hereford and Chepstow in a non-destructive manner while simultaneously improving the transport infrastructure must be a prize well worth the effort'. Unfortunately, the Heart of England Tourist Board declared that the English Tourist Board had 'no funds to assist consultancy work'. They referred us to the Department of the Environment regarding European Regional Development Funding. Another paperchase, for ERDF cash depends upon the British Government's support.

By October Richard and I were considering the general philosophy of multi-skilled staff for the line and the passenger accommodation. He felt there should be no 'muzak' in the railcars, but that to stop smoking entirely might prove too severe. 'Customer satisfaction must always be kept in mind.'

An autumn advertisement by the Wales Tourist Board showed the railways in Wales but merely had the A40 road through the Wye Valley; most uninteresting – but indicative of the potential for extending the tourism season by railways unaffected by the white fog and darkness which shortens the golden days. On the 23rd October 1986 a row hit the headlines when Roger Gates of ABT Products attempted to expand across the Chase Meadows at the rear of Alton Industrial Estate. He had a strip licence from Hereford and Worcester County Council and claimed to have spent £25,000 destroying the railway embankment and levelling the ground for storage. Colin Shepherd MP was said to have made 'representations', but it was not clear what he was advocating. In the event, ABT moved to the Ashburton site, north of the original Ross Station.

At the end of October, Wyedean Tourist Board sought more financial support from the South Herefordshire District Council. Mr Burgess, secretary of the board, gave some interesting and important statistics. In 1985 there were 663,000 day trips to the area, 2,100,000 overnight stays, with an income in the district council area of £20,750,000; 3,000 jobs were associated with tourism. He emphasised that tourism should be supported as an INDUSTRY; even in 1996 some are unable to grasp this elementary fact.

A proposal by the Hereford and Worcester County Council engineer and planning officer that the Hildersley–Walford Road railway route to be sold off was deferred. Councillors Ray Smith and Mrs E.M. Saunders found the proposal absolutely ridiculous. A classic situation, whereby a Worcester-based officer was prepared to ignore the statutory transportation responsibilities of a county council in an area sufficiently remote to be conveniently set aside. Will we ever know what motives were behind such a proposition and which county councillors approved it?

Mr J.G. Stroud of Osbaston, Monmouth, wrote to me on 31st October 1986, enclosing a copy of his letter to *Rail Wales* asking: 'Why is the Railways Board so subservient to the Road Lobby?' To that I would add the 'Oil Lobby'. My reply included: 'There is little doubt that many people/organisations are scared witless by the scale of this project, despite it being close in mileage/technology to the Swiss private railways. Further, it is easy to ignore the 30-55% who have no private car. I spent 30 minutes driving to Gloucester on Thursday, queued 20 minutes to get into a car park; the WVR schedule is 26 minutes to central Gloucester with six stops.'

The dark days of November were cheered by full details of Richard Eagle's WVR uniform proposals, including material colour, which he saw as charcoal grey with Staybrite buttons with logo, the top cap badge showing the company coat of arms and the wearer's designation/job. The styles covered guard/collector, driver, buffet staff and stationmaster. Would that we could get some made up and put on show at public relations occasions. I first met Richard in person in Ross at the appropriately named Eagle public house, identifying myself earlier by saying, "I am silver-haired, gold alloy specs, look about 55 on a good day." It was an auspicious occasion.

On 1st November 1986 I wrote to the Department of the Environment, Bristol, seeking help towards funding a feasibility study. Although handled by an understanding civil servant, Richard Dew, there was a Catch-22 situation in that a most complex tender procedure had to precede such a survey, linked with the Derelict Land Grant etc., for which funds were said to be 'very limited'. He outlined Euro Grants, ESF for training and ERDF for capital, but these did NOT cover feasibility studies. In conclusion he referred us to Clive George, the officer in the Department of Employment, Bristol, with 'special responsibility within the South West for encouraging and promoting tourism projects which are likely to create new jobs.'

I wrote, on 2nd December, to Mr George, and although he promised to look into the matter he was not then optimistic. I mentioned to the Department of Environment that from 1st December onwards, Ross people found it impossible to park in Gloucester and that no improvement was expected until after the January sales! Indeed, the more people who became car-borne, the worse the situation would become.

Early in December I wrote to Councillor Ray Smith, deprecating the lack of attention to tourism, and a working party was set up to examine why only £7,700 (!) per annum out of a budget of £290 million was spent on tourism, with not even one officer dealing with the tourist trade. It was decided to prepare a 'tourism action plan for Hereford–Worcester' as an urgent priority. Needless to say, I was *not* given the opportunity to take any part!

An interesting summary – Wye Valley Railway, projection of fares income as a % of capital applied – was condensed into a single sheet and dated December 1986, reproduced below:

WYE VALLEY RAILWAY:
Projection of fares, passenger use as % of capital applied

Mileages:	BR	WVR
Glos–Ross–Hfd	8.51	21.37
Ross–Mon		12.31
Mon–Chep	3.23	11.46
TOTAL	11.74	45.14

Assuming that BR/WVR share revenue 50/50 over the 11.74 miles = 5.87 at a full rate single journey. Therefore, 45.14 miles + 5.87 = 51.01 for a single journey throughout at full rate, and return journey mileage = 102.02.

The BR fare in 1986 was approximately 4p per mile, and for the return journey £4.08p.

VISITORS:

(NB. For simplicity, one return journey is taken as 100 miles for £4.)

Statistics from Wyedean Tourist Board: 2,100,000 overnight stays in the area in 1985.

Department of Environment requirement to show at least 50% of over-night stays would use railway (letter of 28.11.86, para. 10) – to be publicised/packaged accordingly.

Calculation: if 50% take full railway route and return, then 1,050,000 x £4 = £4,200,000 per annum.

Example: If 50% take HALF the railway route and return, 1,050,000 x 2 = £2,100,000.

If 25% take the FULL railway route and return, 525,000 x £4 = £2,100,000.

POPULATION:

In the Wye Valley area the population is 337,087. Possibly, 33% have no access to a car. Therefore, of 111,238 without a car, assume that 50% (55,619) will use rail occasionally.

Example 1: If 55,619 make a return journey of HALF the route 26 times per annum, 55,619 x £2 x 26 = £2,892,188 per annum.

Example 2: If 1 in 10 of the population make a return journey of HALF the route once a fortnight, 33,708 x £2 x 26 = £1,752,816 per annum.

NB. Above EXCLUDES other sources of revenue income, such as:

1. School children
2. Commuting adults
3. Buffet service
4. Ambulance facility
5. Carriage of mail
6. Carriage of parcels
7. Special steam trains
8. Weddings; anniversaries; race meetings; Chepstow and Hereford specials
9. Publications
10. BR trains; Hereford–Gloucester Severn Tunnel diversions (number, weight = £s)
11. BR ballast trains from Tintern Quarries (number, mileage on WVR, weight = £s)
12. Use of railway by non overnight-staying day visitors.

REVENUE EXPENDITURE:

Operating/working expenses
Salaries and wages
Diesel oil for shunters
Consumables: oil, paint etc.
Electricity for railcars
Motor of Transport maintenance
Civil engineering
Maintenance: (i) rolling stock; (ii) permanent way; (iii) buildings; (iv) workshops
Depreciation of buildings/equipment
Radio/tele. controls
Administration
Officers' salaries
Bank charges
Rent, rates, insurance
Lighting and heating

Postage/telephone
Printing/stationery
Professional fees
Publicity
Contingencies
Auditors' fee
Office repairs
Car allowances
Leasing
Depreciation

Assuming that wages and salaries comprise 60-70% of revenue expenditure, it is possible to make an approximate calculation of the whole, for example:

25 staff at £7,800 p.a. = £195,000, 60% of total expenditure (100% = £325,000 p.a.).

35 staff at £7.800 p.a. = £273,000, 70% of total expenditure (100% = £390,000 p.a.).

CAPITAL:
Showing revenue income as a % of capital expenditure, for example:

£20,000,000 capital
+ Visitors income £4,200,000
+ Population income £2,892,188
Giving a total of £7,092,188 = 35% gross.

£40,000,000 capital with the same revenue income of £7,092,188 = 18% gross.

Taking a less successful level of revenue income from the above range:

£20,000,000 capital
+ Visitors income £2,100,000
+ Population income £1,752,816
Giving a total of £3,852,816 = 19% gross.

£40,000,000 capital with the same revenue income of £3,852,816 = 9.6% gross.

NB. BR East Coast electrification 'expected to show 7% return on investment'.

No allowance for company taxation in foregoing.

Even paying interest on part of the capital, assuming the balance to be by grant, a healthy situation appears using the Wyedean Tourist Board's visitor statistics, which were almost certainly gathered from the hoteliers and caterers and so had considerable reliability.

All in all, 1986, the first full year of the project to renew the Wye Valley Railway, had well rewarded the hard endeavours of Serena (then still a Rawlins), Richard Eagle and me.

CHAPTER 6

Civil Engineering Feasibility

The year 1987 began with the Hereford and Worcester County Council engineer and planning officer (a curious combination of functions!) again advocating sale of the Tudorville–Hildersley trackbed. This was opposed by Ray Smith, county councillor, whereas Roger Gates of ABT Products pressed to be allowed to expand up the Chase Meadows across the railway route. Councillor Smith was most persuasively able to cause the Strategic Planning and Transportation Committee to 'defer' the issue. The mayor and, it was said, four out of five district councillors also opposed development into the fields behind the line. Councillor Smith saw that anyone owning the line would be in possession of 'an enormously valuable ransom strip'. No one mentioned that the Secretary of State for Transport, Rt Hon. Paul Channon (1986), had given an undertaking that attempts to hold up rail schemes by ransom strips would not be acceptable.

Richard Eagle kept up his supply of practical ideas for the WVR: reflective paint for station name boards, number series for railcars and support locomotives (diesel), naming locomotives and the formation of a supporters' association. The latter idea I could, and did, immediately adopt and the orange file of names and addresses followed wherever I spoke to the public.

Then, out of the blue, opportunity arrived! Clive George, of the Department of Employment and Tourism, Bristol, telephoned me on 22nd January 1987 to say that he had just had the OK from London that they would fund the £1,800 for Cass Hayward and Partners to do the engineering feasibility study. I gave the good news to John Kendrick, assistant secretary, Forest of Dean District Council, and he responded, "Go, GO!" I considered that this might be an indication of Government commitment and could attract capital funding from mainland Europe. I already had an estimate of the cost of the work from Alan Hayward, as long ago as April 1986, and this enabled me to give the word to proceed on 24th January 1987. I outlined in paragraphs 1–10 what I felt we should cover, visually and in calculations; in particular, the Heart of England Tourist Board had asked for capital costs and it is of interest to include the 'guestimate' I gave in that letter:

	Miles	£(thousands)
Rails, sleepers and ballast (mileage inc. some double etc.)	48	4,800
Earthworks and bridging	48	4,800
Electricification, lightweight (inc. 9 miles BRWR)	57	1,710
Buildings, halts, platforms (drawings completed)		2,000
Land wayleave purchase @£62,500 per mile, 6 yards wide	48	3,000
Second-hand railcars, workshop equipment, 2 diesel engines, control and communications etc.		3,600
TOTAL		19,910

I mentioned that Serena had been engaged with me for WVR speaking occasions throughout the previous year and wished to come with me to the Chepstow offices on Monday 2nd February 1987. At that meeting I agreed to write to the Midlands Electricity Board regarding the power supplies and also to Mr Mabey of Fairfield Mabey, Bridge Builders, Chepstow. The meeting was fully minuted and is quite a model for a civil engineering consultancy. It was agreed that Steve Matthews, MSc, DIC, MICE, MiStructE, would do the legwork of the survey and I would accompany him, site visits to commence on Monday

16th February, together with the county liaison officers, if available. Welsh Water was also contacted regarding the river crossings.

Meanwhile, the Local Boundary Commission was inviting representations upon the future of Hereford and Worcester County Council. I explained that whereas Gloucester County Council was properly receiving communications and had appointed a liaison officer, Hereford and Worcester had not replied to my letters of 27th February 1986 and 9th April 1986, and I had written again on 24th January 1987. I submitted that this was a ridiculous state of non-administration as contrasted with Gwent and Gloucester County Councils. I also pointed out the short-term expedient of filling the WVR Strangford cutting with waste, describing the then current situation: 'The tip is the usual wind-blown, vermin-ridden, smelly heap with a life of only two more years'. This is an Area of Outstanding Natural Beauty and already the 'effluent is said to be draining towards the River Wye and that WVR may well require indemnity from the council' etc. I was keeping an eye on the mainland European doctrine that the polluter pays.

On the wider front, Richard Eagle and I looked for a motto for the company. I favoured 'The future today', which – subject to Latin scholarship check – might read *Futurus hodie*. A down to earth, red-circled sign, equal to the compulsory road signals, which read: "WARNING: ELECTRIC RAILWAY. KEEP OFF THE TRACK", was under consideration; we would check what British Rail was using on overhead electrified lines, possibly a reverse lightning flash in yellow could be incorporated.

Our press release, appearing on 21st January 1987, announced that the work on the engineering feasibility study would begin the following week, and be done by Cass Hayward and Partners of Chepstow, funded by the Department of Employment and Tourism. After a blizzard where 'frost was so severe that salt could not clear the snow from the roads', with drifts up to 20 feet and a 'piercing, bitter wind', the task looked daunting! The week of on-site walking with Stephen Matthews of Cass Hayward was exceedingly hard work, using the roads to pick up the line-of-route and then walking the track where closer than distant viewing was necessary. Tunnel interiors were generally good with five rows of engineering blue bricks at the crown. Some wet spots were caused by blocked drains. At Walford we saw that an S-curve would be necessary to avoid the 400kV tower, which the MEB engineers, however, offered to move!

We examined the bridges at Lydbrook and Redbrook where new RSJs on the upper works would be necessary. At Tintern and Kerne we saw the abutments still in place from which the new crossing girders would be supported; designs for these bridges would be included as Appendix A to the report. In the vicinity of Ross and Monmouth we saw the need for alternative routing and these would be proposed in the report at Maps B and C. At Fiveways, Ross, we noted the suitability of the location as a high-level town station; the report would contain a preliminary design by Richard Eagle.

At Strangford tip we photographed the enormous mess the Hereford and Worcester County Council had allocated for the South Herefordshire District Council to use. This was examined and several alternatives mooted, including transfer by rail via Rotherwas Junction to a properly sealed clay pit site – some 2,000 tons per train – or to go over the top with a steel mesh grill as used for airfield reinforcement in the Falklands.

Towards Hereford the amazing height of embankments created by men and horses only, under the direction of Brunel's contractors, were wonderful to behold. The industrial heritage was explained by the fine condition of the piers for the Fawley and Backney viaducts, which Steve and I agreed were simply awaiting replacement of the missing steel spans – which would have required renewal anyhow.

We photographed the location of Grange Court Junction, where the WVR would join the Regional Rail/GWR route, 7½ miles from Gloucester City. This would, later, be seen as a parkway for Forest of Dean commuters by the county council. Despite our attempted contact, none of the county councils' 'liaison' officers appeared on the route – perhaps the weather was too discouraging. It was, however, ideal from the engineering point of view to see the river high and fast moving.

Steve and I visited Swindon British Rail and were very well received on 31st March 1987. We spent a full day working through the massive GWR Bridge Register (about 5 feet by 2 feet in size!), during which I noted the chainage (miles/chains of bridge from Paddington), location, span (feet and inches whether on square or skew) and with comments as to condition etc. It was then that we realised why the bridges at Kerne and Tintern over the Wye had been dismantled immediately the railway closed! The Tintern notes said: 'cracking 1947'; the main girder was wrought iron. The full details were included as Appendix B to the report and are an important basis for all that needs to be done. By agreement with Cass Hayward, I was responsible for getting the electrification considerations and estimates for the report. This was arranged very quickly during February 1987 by the MEB, Ted Holmes BSc, ChEng, FIEE, Principal Engineer, System Planning. Steve Mullens, Mike Eades and other colleagues met with me in Hereford on the 27th. We had been pressed by the Department of Employment to get the job done within the financial year and the 'stops' were really pulled out. By 5th March we had 'broad brush' figures from the MEB, which included consideration for South Wales EB supply at Chepstow.

My sincere thanks were expressed and whether the response had been partially due to me being an old CEGB Research Headquarters man I don't quite know; in any event, it was the community which would benefit from the information so readily provided. There was considerable pressure to reinstate the line initially between Chepstow and Tintern Abbey halt, Gwent County Council having earlier costings obtained from British Rail to up-rate Wye Valley junction for use by passenger trains. I had estimated the cost as £½ million, but it was by no means clear how such finance would be obtained. I asked the Departments of Employment and Tourism, Trade, Environment and Transport, the Welsh Office, Wales Tourist Board and the

Forestry and Development Commissions to consider sharing the cost.

Down at Llandenny, Richard Eagle had been out photographing much of the area, including Chepstow, and was looking at trenching units, which it seemed BR was making surplus. If only we had the cash to take advantage of the opportunity! He had heard about but missed seeing the HTV news item on 17th February 1987, which included scenes at Tintern and a map of the line. Apparently, I appeared in the shoot for this, but I was unable to secure a copy. However, I got in touch with *Treasure Hunt*, a production shot in Switzerland featuring railcars powered by an overhead electricity supply. In due course we obtained an official copy for showing whenever possible to dispel ignorance and show the close similarity between the scenery in the Lower Wye Valley and Switzerland.

Chairman Mabey of the Chepstow Bridge Builders offered to do whatever work we required at COST price. On 9th February 1987 Ross Town Council said that they believed the WVR could bring hundreds of thousands of visitors, passing a resolution of support for the railway renewal; I enquired whether they could give any practical help, e.g. legal time. There was no response to this matter.

My letter to Richard at the time indicates my working 9 a.m. to 9 p.m. on railway aspects, and as I write (in 1995) it is confirmed by the amount of papers already involved by early 1987, which I now seek to summarise for posterity!

Early in February 1987 I wrote to Major Peter Oliver, HM Inspecting Officer, Department of Transport, London, upon the advice of the DoT/Environment at Bristol. I forwarded our running set of papers and was pleased to accept his invitation to visit Marsham Street on 11th February. This was a very happy occasion because we talked the same language and ranged over the then considerably inflexible British Rail policies; however, he suggested that I write to Sydney Newey, General Manager, Regional Rail, Swindon, especially regarding the pressure of the overhead electrification.

We discussed maximum speed, axle loading, the legal situation etc. A thoroughly satisfactory meeting of minds and knowledge – contrasting sharply with the capacity of some local people and their 'leaders'. Richard Eagle checked out the Berne gauge as height 14ft 0½ins and width 10ft 4ins. If this were applied to WVR, having the Hereford–Ross–Gloucester section, as originally, to the Brunel broad gauge would be most convenient. We also worked out the various ways of laying the track through the tunnels and lowering the level, if necessary, for the overhead electrification. A friend of Richard's, Peter Jones, then teaching in Saudi Arabia, expressed his interest in producing a timetable for the line – this we happily accepted! I had advised the unions, NUR, ASLEF and the Transport Salaried Staffs' Association, and received particular good wishes from the latter, of which I had been a member 40 years ago!

Also, in February, the South Herefordshire District Council's chief executive, Derek Cole, gave a real lead when he urged members to talk to Hereford City Councillors and seek a "strategic master plan" for tourism. This meant linking Hereford City, Ross and the Wye Valley as a whole, and was supported by Ray Smith, county and district councillor. I felt his message was beginning to get through with his conclusion that: "The enormous employment potential of an expanded tourist industry in the area has not been fully realised." The editor of the Symonds Yat Official Guide for 1987 asked for a half-page entry for the WVR and I included: 'Whenever guides are talking on Yat Rock, someone visiting is sure to say, "Whatever happened to the railway which gave us marvellous views of the riverside we simply cannot see from the roads?"' I continued: 'the railcars would have all-weather capability, so effectively extending the season. No car will be necessary to enjoy a holiday; leaving London by rail just after 9 a.m., the visitor will travel via Gloucester and reach Symonds Yat Station in good time for one o'clock lunch. Thereafter, a Golden WVR Travel Card (included with an accommodation package) will give free travel to two cities, three towns and all the historic sites and countryside events in between'.

A good summary of all that was missing in terms of economic benefit to all, I felt!

Yet another happening in February was the lack of electrification of the Western Region lines, a matter raised by Royston Hughes MP in the *News and Weekly Argus*, Newport. I responded, including the following: 'Passenger travel will be by all-weather railcars, effectively extending the season for hotels, management centres etc., and the use of electrification [on the WVR] could well lead to the Western Region beginning an electrification programme to stimulate traffic. The railway will be today's equivalent of "getting on your bike," both to seek out job opportunities further away from home and still have the means to travel to work daily without having to buy a car and make it uneconomic to do so!'

On 10th February 1987 the Local Government Boundary Commission responded to my representation and said I might wish to ensure both SH District and the Hereford and Worcester County Council were aware of my feelings! There was no real doubt of that. Meanwhile, the current owners of the Royal Hotel, Symonds Yat, were reacting quite contrarily to the views of those who had had visitors brought by the railway and much lamented the closure of the line. Indeed, it had also so many times proved a lifeline to get people and supplies through the awful roads in the depth of winter! The new owners were apparently unaware that there was, and again would be, no problem in car-borne visitors arriving via the level crossing between the new halt and the tunnel. The owners of a cottage which had been expanded into the Forest View Hotel, with part of an over-wide drive spread out towards the railway, were also antagonistic. I responded, also in the *Ross Gazette* of 19th February 1987, expressing my surprise and hoping that these hoteliers would give the matter deeper thought, particularly about visitors arriving by rail for winter breaks. I pointed out that by rail from London, visitors could be sitting down for lunch at the Royal Hotel by 1 p.m. I also quoted a leading Ross hotelier who said he would "give his eye teeth to be in the position of the Yat Royal if and when the new rail line comes through."

I added the obvious, that in an area when bed occupancy hardly ever exceeded 50%, 'the railway will open up the dead season for the hotels'. Currently, hotels and guesthouses were closing up and down the Valley, but I had in mind that when the Wye Valley Railway was constituted as a company, we would have the ability to carry on such associated businesses as would further the business; this would certainly include hotels, as had so many of the old railway companies. I also had in mind the estimated one million railway enthusiasts in the country, many of whom would welcome the opportunity to stay alongside such a unique country railway!

On 19th February (was there ever such a busy month!) I wrote to Sydney Newey, general manager of Western Region. This was a useful interchange of information, the most significant point he made being that: 'on the mainline we would expect to use only a system which fully met current British Rail standards, that is 25kV'. This was, of course, within our expectations, as the overhead system to this pressure, excluding the Southern Region, had been decided by Parliament as long ago as 1959. The fact that the Government had resisted paying for the Western to be so modernised is another story.

Serena (Rawlins) wrote a quite brilliant letter, which appeared in the *Ross Gazette* of 26th February 1987; it is reproduced here in full:

WYE VALLEY RAILWAY: SYMONDS YAT

I was surprised to read the attack on the reinstatement proposals for the line, particularly as the hoteliers in question have had no contact with my father. The situation is that this opposition is based on a misunderstanding of the facts, which are as follows:

(i) The Royal Hotel had always enjoyed the advantage of both rail and road access; the latter would be maintained by a level crossing protected in the manner considered appropriate by HM Inspector of New and Altered Railways.

(ii) The restored railway line would be single track at Symonds Yat upon a double track formation; this will allow space for the alignment to avoid the septic tanks and access to same.

(iii) The six-yard wide trackbed required from the tunnel portal will not destroy but be alongside the drive access to the new Forest View Hotel.

(iv) The civil engineers undertaking the feasibility study are already consulting with the water authorities; I have no doubt that such matters are receiving proper attention.

(v) All work necessary will be executed to the highest statutory engineering and landscaping standards.

The purpose of the railway is to serve everyone in one way or another – not to kill trade but to promote it. Without doubt, Ross and the surrounding areas will see far more visitors in the future and if these do not choke the place with cars, it cannot do anything but increase business for the local traders – including hoteliers.

One other major factor is that travelling around the Wye Valley will be easier and provide transport for non car-owning people, giving much needed freedom and more importantly to give unemployed people the opportunity to look to Gloucester and Hereford for work. After months of unemployment, both my sister and I secured work in Gloucester and are totally dependent on our non-company vehicles to enable us to get to work. It would be marvellous to be able to travel in the railcars to work, a view I am sure other commuters will share.

The Wye Valley Railway will, where possible, and I stress where possible, run close to the original line and hopefully all problems will be solved by negotiation. But there are 48 route miles of railway and it would be a miracle if there were no places where other uses or part-uses of the line have arisen. As with all major provisions for the public benefit involving continuous services, matters of wayleave arise. In the case of the Wye Valley Railway, no one has written to my father objecting to the passage of the railway across their land. Where this is necessary, a proper valuation will be made and settled by cash payment or shares in the railway. Quite positively, requests for stopping places both new and on the original sites have already been made.

Providing the feasibility report indicates that it is sensible to proceed, letters will be written to over 100 organisations next month, including parish councils, giving more details and inviting response. The Wye Valley Railway is something absolutely unique in this country, bringing a blend of modern technology into a rural Area of Outstanding Natural Beauty and offering a non-destructive means of visitor access.

I hope that the foregoing puts the record straight and that matters will stay on the right lines in the future.

Yours sincerely,
Serena M. Rawlins

This month I found the address of John Grimshaw of the Railway Path Project Charity, Bristol. I had been advised by Rod Brain, a planner with Gwent County Council, that the scheme for cycleways was already experiencing wayleave difficulties with landowners. I was able to advise him that John Kendrick, assistant secretary, Forest of Dean County Council, and myself had discussed the matter and we felt that the statute which originally authorised the railway might still hold good. We found some common ground with respect to the renewal of the rail bridges, for which provision to walk/cycle across might be made at the time of renewal. Although John Grimshaw expressed 'delight with the thought that you may be re-opening this railway', he was unable to 'prepare meaningful details at this time'.

Monmouth District Council welcomed the Countryside Commission's policy paper 'Enjoying the Countryside', which showed that 84% of the population visited the countryside and that on any summer Sunday, 18 million people were likely to be out and about in rural areas! An officers' report to the council emphasised how, with even more leisure time towards the year 2000, there would be great opportunities to supplement the rural economy through tourism. Here, indeed, was some breakthrough, for if the steam railway had ever run on Sundays, it might still be operating and countering both over-motoring and marginal economic returns for local businesses.

This report caused me to attempt a summary of the known attractions served by the WVR: excluding Gloucester and Hereford cities, the three towns of Ross, Monmouth and Chepstow had some five attractions each easily accessible from the town stations, and in between there is Yat Rock, Tintern Abbey, Goodrich Castle, Wye Valley Open Farm, two PGL Adventure centres and Hill Court, as well as the regular carnivals, fetes, garden parties, horticultural, agricultural and sporting shows and regattas. Also reachable by short bus links are Hereford and Chepstow races and the Monmouth agricultural show etc., all currently choked up by cars coming from all directions. By offering so many destinations on a regular basis, setting down and picking up from perhaps three places per day, the railway would effectively 'manage' the problems by dispersion, whereas cars concentrate on the only destination known to the driver!

The latest from Richard Eagle was his scheme for painting of freight, permanent way and engineering vehicles; this reflects his hands-on experience in preservation and he is especially safety conscious. On 26th March 1987 the *Ross Gazette* carried a notice regarding an application by Mr. R. Mann, of nearby Stockholm Place hamlet, to install a septic tank prior to development of the Mitcheldean Road Station site. I sought to establish whether the building of some 14 houses could be accommodated without destroying the embankment and road overbridge layout etc., so that a halt could be installed. Accordingly, I also carried out a house-to-house survey (in June 1987), which resulted in an overwhelming 'Yes' to the prospect of having the railway back with a halt on the old station site. This was hardly surprising since the residents were mostly retired and complained that the bus on the A40 road stopped too far away for them to walk and that their road (the B4224) was dangerous and without footpaths. They complained that the one bus per WEEK, which went directly to and from Stockholm Place on Ross market day, imposed a strict regime of a two-hour stay and return. This for people who might need medical attention plus want to do shopping and visit the hairdresser etc., seemed to me like nothing more than the minimum necessary to keep such isolated folk alive – rather than transport facilitating a decent rural life in 1987! Small wonder that in Britain one in five of the population are said to have mental health problems, for while electricity, gas, water and telephone are seen as necessary for normal everyday life, plainly the ability to move about with reasonable flexibility is *not*!

I received the initial timetable for the WVR from Peter Jones and was able to show Stockholm Place residents that 15 railcars were scheduled Monday to Saturday, either in the Gloucester or Hereford direction. However, the application became a residential development by June 1987, and on 4th July I submitted a representation to the planning authorities requesting adjustment to accommodate the railway halt on the northern extremity of the site. By September, Lea residents and local farmer,

Mr Geoff Savidge, added their protests to the development, but the planning committee chairman, Vincent Preece, said, "We should not blight a piece of land just because something [i.e. WVR] might take place years into the future." This despite the fact that the development was *contrary* to the district council's structure plan! Plainly, also, there was no reference to the fact that a district council has no responsibilities for transportation, but can, if it feels so inclined, allow piecemeal development on a strategic route pending the Department of the Environment's PPG 12/13 firm guidance. Needless to say, I did not know when this planning committee met; neither were the Stockholm Place householders willing to appear as witnesses!

On 10th September 1987 I wrote to the Department of the Environment, Bristol, pointing out that the *county* council should have been involved and that I wished the Secretary of State to consider the WVR position (having by then a successful feasibility study available), and also that the site was *outside* the structure plan. On 5th November 1987 the D of E wrote saying that the Secretary of State (Ridley) had decided not to intervene – pushing the matter back to the district council. On 15th December the District Planning Committee, *against* the advice of the planning officer, granted 'outline' permission. I responded by seeking protection of the route and provision for a halt. By 29th September 1988 an application to build 14 houses was made and my representation was published in the *Ross Gazette* of 8th December 1988. Nevertheless, the district council authorised the planning officer to 'determine' the application, subject to provision of a public sewer.

I have related these events in some detail since they highlight two nonsenses of the D of E planning machinery before the firm guidance of PPG 12/13 to protect the line-of-route of established railway projects:

(i) District council members could give away piecemeal sections of railway line-of-route to facilitate *private* developments, even against the broad *public* interest, even ignoring its own structure plans designed to protect 'green belts' and prevent speculative housing in isolated places without adequate public transport.

(ii) County councils *with* responsibility for 'transportation' in an area could either be ignored or turn a blind eye to vested interest developments, even when national railway land had been bought cheaply with *no* planning rights.

Back to March 1987. When the National Railway Museum had a display of posters, the *Ross Gazette* featured the famous 1935 Yat Rock painting by Frank Newbould. The brief of such artists was to draw attention to holiday resorts on the GWR, and Paddington and the suburban stations 'sold' Ross and district most effectively, but the 'Golden Age' came to an end with the outbreak of war in 1939. This was a lesson the new WVR will never forget: simply putting new lines down is not good enough; only constant, lively marketing will attract sufficient day and overnight visitors to effectively subsidise daily travel and local commuting etc. throughout the year.

I then heard from Lance Humphries, an industrial engineer interested in the renewal from the Chepstow end; he had started the interest of Gwent County Council and had hoped to involve Norchard (i.e. Dean Forest Railway) in the Wye Valley line. Richard Eagle completed the large one inch to the mile map, which was to accompany us to most public occasions. We considered the advantage of having the catenary posts coated in olive drab (shades of the US Army!) plasticised, and I believed that the steel bridge spans could be similarly treated.

On 13th April 1987 I received a preliminary draft of the engineering feasibility report, up to Section 8. We had a further interchange of details and on 1st May Alan Hayward forwarded a special copy of the final report, which included colour prints; this also went to the Department of Employment/ Tourism, Bristol. It was, indeed, a tour de force: 70 pages of carefully researched work based upon the Western Region records and the expertise of consultant civil engineers worthy to be following in the footsteps of Brunel – some 140 years earlier. My master copy included 16 colour photographs depicting important places, from the engineering point of view, en route, plus Richard's drawing of the high-level Ross Town Station at Fiveways and sections through the permanent way; Alan Hayward contributed drawings for new river crossings at both Kerne and Tintern Bridges, the Chepstow–Tintern section, alternatives for Wyesham (Monmouth), the exit of the Monmouth line out of Ross and a frontispiece showing the railcars in operation near Brockweir.

It is interesting to record the construction costs at early 1987 prices, and (as I write in 1996) to note how foolish it is to delay a thoroughly worthwhile project with the inevitable rise in costs:

		£(thousands)
(i)	Land acquisition	620
(ii)	Trackbed clearing and reinstatement	450
(iii)	Clearing of cuttings and embankment reforming	1,400
(iv)	Bridgework and viaducts	2,300
(v)	Various additional works	400
(vi)	Tunnels (minor works)	85
(vii)	Track contractor laid to secondary line specification	7,800
(viii)	Halts	285
(ix)	Stations	560
(x)	Level crossings	210
(xi)	Electrification power supply	2,300
(xii)	Electrification catenary etc.	1,714
(xiii)	Rolling stock, depot, communications etc.	3,000
TOTAL		21,124

Most satisfactorily, the report concluded that it *was* technically feasible to reinstate the Wye Valley Railway between the cities of Hereford, Gloucester and the towns of Ross-on-Wye, Monmouth and Chepstow:

> The greater part of the route appears, with some repair work and the removal of obstructions, to be suitable. Certain features and obstructions have been identified as requiring further investigation, and tentative solutions proposed for consideration. Interim use of diesel traction is suggested during reinstatement of each portion of the line. A pilot scheme of reinstatement between Chepstow and a temporary halt at the south end of Tintern tunnel is proposed.

It would be an understatement if I did not declare my delight at the contents and conclusions of the report. All the cold and bitter wind of the February survey was forgotten in a comfortable glow of what had been achieved. I would not say I was surprised at the conclusions, for the entire line had been built with Victorian technology of the highest quality and engineers of equal excellence – 140 years on there surely would be expertise to overcome any problems. I ordered 34 extra copies, at a cost of £472, and prepared a list of recipients; distribution took place generally on 7th May 1987. All applicable county, district, city and town councils, the Welsh Office and Wales Tourist Board were included, as were the Government departments of Environment, Transport and Trade, Wyedean and Heart of England Tourist Boards and Mr Mabey of Fairfield Mabey, Chepstow, the Forestry Commission and Railway Unions, Western Region BR and the Bank of England 3i capital source. Also the public libraries in the area were invited to take a copy for their reference sections up and down the line. Press notices were issued to the *Ross Gazette* and *Forest of Dean and Wye Valley Review* and these were syndicated to the *Western Daily Press* etc.

In all, 36 copies of the engineering feasibility report were distributed during early May 1987. About one in three of the recipients paid the £17 requested, which was merely a print cost. It was generally well received, with an undistinguished exception that for rude arrogance was unique and inexplicable in view of the partial renewal which the council in question apparently supported. This is the full text of the reply from one L.R. Turnbull, then Gwent County Council leader:

> Enclosed is the copy of the report by Cass Hayward and Partners. It is not my intention to forward you a cheque for £17.00.

Perhaps he and some of his officers were so out of their depth in railway and civil engineering matters that no other reaction could be expected, or was some hidden, covert influence at work? A letter was individually typed to each recipient, and a copy of that to the English Tourist Board is reproduced here:

> **WYE VALLEY RAILWAY: FEASIBILITY REPORT**
>
> I hope that you may be aware, through the various press references over the past 18 months, of the proposals to reinstate the lines Gloucester–Ross–Hereford and Ross–Monmouth–Chepstow. My tourist area contacts have been with Wyedean TB and with Mr Malcolm Connor, Heart of England TB, who, perhaps, has kept you, advised. I am now pleased to enclose a copy of the feasibility report just completed. Although funded by the Department of Employment, I have to finance the reproductions and to make a charge of £17, which I trust, is acceptable. Please make cheque payable to the undersigned.
>
> Subject to certain reservations, the report is favourable and you will see that the recommended

start point is Chepstow BR to a new halt at Tintern Abbey. The Abbey records 95,000 visitors annually and the new halt would be about 10 minutes' pleasant walk from the Abbey/car park. The initial operation would be joint with BR, the Western Region providing a diesel multiple unit. Running would be at weekends and holidays with a return trip of 10 miles' attractive travel.

British Rail earlier quoted Gwent County Council in the sum of £350,000 for works to upgrade the existing Wye Valley Junction line to Tintern Quarry to passenger standards. From the quarry to a new Tintern Abbey Halt only one and three-quarter miles of extra single track is needed, the new halt, trackbed preparation and track laying being within the capabilities of an MSC scheme. Further, Mr Mabey, chairman of Fairfields Steel Erectors of Chepstow, has undertaken to do any works required by the Wye Valley Railway at cost price.

Overall, I estimate the total cost of this five miles upgrading/renewal to passenger standards to be half a million pounds. Reinstatement of this section should effectively underwrite success of the Share Issue for WVR in entirety and be a useful indication of firm intent for the application to the EEC. I have discussed this matter with the Western Region management and, if finance is forthcoming, it could just be possible to open Tintern Abbey to Chepstow for the school summer holidays THIS YEAR. The target revenue, at £1.70 for adults, 80p for children, is £1,000 per day of joint BR operation. Both ASLEF and NUR are in the picture.

The next step is a meeting with Mr Clive George, Dept. of Employment, at Forest of Dean DC offices. Hopefully, the Depts of Trade, Tourism and Transport/ Environment will be represented. The Welsh Office,

Wales TB, the Development and Forestry Commissions, Monmouth DC and Gwent and Gloucester County Councils also have the report. The likely constitution of the railway is as a charitable trust, as suggested by the Department of the Environment. I have said that I do expect the parties concerned to take a cumulative interest in meeting the half-million pounds required to get the Welsh end of the WVR open and earning revenue.

As you will note, Cass Hayward estimates the overall capital needed as £21.2 million, and that the second stage of renewal is the Ross–Gloucester BR arm. Both Ross and Grange Court Junction will have 'parkway' facilities, designed to persuade car owners commuting or travelling via Gloucester to park this side of the Severn. Such renewal should come 'on-stream' in line with Gloucester Docks leisure development – for mutual tourist benefit.

Attached is a draft financial projection for the WVR as a charitable trust; the company should then be eligible for 50% capital grant from EECRDF, plus training aid from the Social Fund. I hope that British Government agencies/local government may find two-thirds of the remaining 50%, the last third being raised form BES venture capital.

I trust that you will find the report and other information of interest to your board; a supportive response would be valuable in every way.

Yours sincerely,
Eric T. Rawlins

Looking back, from 1996 and the word processing computer keyboard, the load such letters put on my mind and fingers, not to mention the postage, was considerable! Paul Dicken, Regional Liaison Manager for ETB, responded on behalf of the chairman, saying, 'We were very interested to read of your proposals to reinstate the Wye Valley Railway. We are very supportive of the plan as interest in private railways is increasing all the time and your proposal would add significantly to the visitors' experience of the area.' He suggested that I continued to work with Allen Armstrong of the Heart of England Tourist Board.

Meanwhile, Clive George, our liaison officer with the Department of Employment, was orchestrating a meeting at the Forest of Dean District Council offices on 24th June 1987. My contribution made plain that *only* if the half-million pounds required was made available in partnership could the 'starter' section Chepstow to Tintern Abbey Halt be commenced. I spoke for 35 minutes and most councils and tourist Boards etc. were represented at officer level. An important contribution was that from Rod Brain, our liaison officer with Gwent County Council, who introduced us to Bill Jenkyn-Jones of Touche Ross, who said that I had already greatly exceeded what any one person could achieve and that a management team was an urgent need. (No one present could have anticipated that in 1996 this need had not been met!) Bill J-J was sure Touche Ross could produce a financial feasibility study as a priority need. Clive George agreed, indicating that the Chepstow–Tintern section could not be financially viable *unless* it led automatically to the complete renewal; I could not agree more. Next would be market research and a business plan, probably also from Touche Ross. Clive asked that the county and district councils be requested to share with his department the cost of engaging Touche Ross – the work of which could be used in the applications for EEC and British funding.

It was noted that last year's (1986) cost of fatal and injury accidents on the roads in Gloucestershire was published as £26½ million! This put in sharp perspective the entire cost of renewing the Wye Valley Railway at £21 million as an exceedingly good bargain for the community.

More relaxed but equally valuable in its own way was the occasion of the Goodrich Fete on 20th June 1987, where maps and plans for WVR were displayed and well received.

The Touche Ross financial study was expected to cost £5,175 (including VAT) and I asked the county councils for £794 each and the districts £667. It will be noticed that this development spelt the end to seeking £1½ million for the Chepstow to Tintern section and the inevitable lack of viability, control, stock safety and maintenance facility etc., problems which had to be avoided even at the risk of substantial delay to the project as a whole. The *Ross Gazette* of 30th July 1987 carried a front-page banner – 'Financial Study of Wye Railway' – and a very full outline of the situation written by myself; it was also carried by the *Western Daily Press* the next day and, on 7th August, by the *Forest of Dean Review*.

A letter in the *Ross Gazette* of 6th August 1987 was a plea for better transport from Mrs M.J. York of Pontshill; she complained that the county subsidised the bus service, which ran *only* on the Thursday market day and which could run over half an hour late – on July 30th it was an hour adrift – this on a timetable allowing only just over two hours in Ross for visiting the library, medical appointments and shopping etc. 'We wait in rising anger and fading expectation,' she wrote. Someone moaned about the WVR seeking Japanese capital – as though there were British finance houses queuing up to invest in the infrastructure!

The fact is that several years would be involved seeking the alleged tranche of Far East capital just waiting to be invested in Britain, but *only* as a way into Europe for the products allegedly of British origin! This game is still being played in 1996! It was not until 1994 that the Japanese Government indicated that it expected Britain to invest its *own* money in its *own* infrastructure! I gave some explanation of the funding problems in the *Gazette* of 8th August 1987. In Monmouth the unemployment rate rose by 3% – above that 'for the whole of Wales'.

On July 18th we had a stand at the Bishopswood Fete, attended by Serena Rawlins and Richard Eagle; the one-man-railway-buff image was beginning to fade. The 1st August saw us with a tent and stand at Ross Carnival, meeting the people and getting more and more supporters' names on record. On 18th August 1987

I had agreed to speak at a lunch meeting of the Forest of Dean Rotary, held at Speech House. This began in the usual sceptical fashion, but after questions were fully answered it was well received. The speaker who extended the vote of thanks was highly prophetical and/or knowledgeable, for after saying he had originally thought this could be another amateur proposal, he now understood the depth of research behind it. His final observation, which shook me at the time, was his considered opinion that the reinstatement would take ten years! For every possible reason, I hoped that this would not be so, particularly as the national economy *appeared* to be on a rising curve of prosperity; sadly the bonuses of North Sea oil and the pressures from the roads/car lobby would squander these resources to burst the bubble by the time our business plan was ready in 1990!

This occasion led me to consider the need for a public meeting in Ross to put into context the history of the scheme, i.e. that we had simply picked up the WVR renewal baton from the engineer who had begun earlier work on the project; that the consulting engineers had approached us to do the technical feasibility study; and that the current pursuit of the financial organisational and funding options was because a supporter had introduced Touche Ross to the project. Because I had been in correspondence with Councillor Ray Smith before we had moved to Ross, I decided to put the idea of an open meeting to him, suggesting the 26th August 1987, and asking him as an independent person, who was well respected, if he would be willing to chair the meeting.

He responded in the affirmative and Paul Rynehart, then the owner of the Chase Hotel, very public-spiritedly gave us the hotel's facilities on that date. The occasion was divided into two sessions: the first from 2.30 p.m. featured a display of Richard Eagle's drawings and some photographs, and there was a scattering of chairs for informal chats and for those not wanting a formal meeting situation. Hardly had I arrived at 1.55 p.m. than a managing director from a firm leasing a building on the Ashburton Estate (the site of Ross Station) arrived asking where the parkway would go. In a few minutes he was happy it would not affect him, but I was immediately faced with a simmering female whose husband had already talked to me at the carnival. They lived in Corinium Way, a new development where a deep railway cutting would be re-excavated and which separated the council estate from private housing. Their objection was that they would have to 'draw the curtains' at night. I explained that due to the current Walford Bridge being widened and now being a non-arched crossing, the WVR lines would be deeply recessed to give sufficient overhead clearance.

The owner or agent for one and three-quarter miles of scrubland ten yards wide immediately to the north of Monmouth pumping station between the river and lane next sought audience. This was the original trackbed and he said, "Over my dead body would I let the railway back." "Well," said I, "exactly what is your objection?" He said, "It's the vandals; they would throw paper out of the carriage windows." This seemed a thin reason to die for, so I responded, "The railcars will be double-glazed, air-conditioned, with fixed windows." He calmed down and went away.

About 50 people attended during the afternoon and were overwhelmingly supportive of the renewal. The Chase staff kindly set up the TV to show the Anneka Rice and Swiss Railway videos. We staged a more formal presentation in the evening when the senior partner (next to Alan) of Cass Hayward, Steve Matthews, who had worked on the engineering feasibility study, joined me, with Ray Smith in the chair. I spoke for about 20 minutes and all went well until a gang of apparent landowners entered en masse from the bar, still carrying their glasses of Dutch courage! Some claimed we must have trespassed on their land to have undertaken the feasibility study, and did we realise what fencing would cost etc.? The chairman prevented a 'leader' from putting a resolution to the meeting that all should be abandoned.

Next day, Steve Matthews said that Alan Hayward told him it had been good experience for him to see how tempers must be kept in such situations! I contemplated how, in the 1850s, one can imagine the great-grandparents of these landowners making a similar attempt to prevent a railway which could give hitherto unknown opportunities to the poor devils who worked their land.

My letter relating all this to Richard Eagle concluded that the above reaction had merely strengthened my resolve as far as matters could be within my power. We had the good news that the DTI would be considering us for two-thirds of the Touche Ross fee for the organisational and funding options report. Meanwhile, I wrote on 27th August 1987, thanking Ray Smith for his control of the boozy opposition so used to having their own way in this area for generations. Reaction to the meeting appeared in the *Ross Gazette* of 3rd September 1987 from three erudite scribes, namely H.J. Ellis, Derek Glover and Serena Rawlins. Mr Ellis made the point that further reports, even from public funds, would be 'a relatively small sum to ensure that which might be a great opportunity is not missed'. Mr Glover pointed out that the afternoon session had seen many supportive of the scheme, as had happened when I had spoken at other meetings in the area; the emotions of the evening session had indicated the almost inevitable 'conflict between public good and private interest'. He felt that the 'business world' might be prepared to resource such efficient transport, enhancing tourist facilities. Serena's letter gave a close insight into what had been two years' exceedingly hard, wide-ranging work, largely by me but with considerable help from Paul Rynehart, Doug Woodman, Richard Eagle and the family. It is reproduced below to give a flavour of the occasion:

> The Editor
> *Ross Gazette*
>
> I am writing with regard to the public meeting held at the Chase Hotel on Wednesday 26th August in connection with the proposed reinstatement of the Wye Valley Railway. I was incensed at the blinkered attitude of certain individuals who did all but call

my father a liar and trespasser. It seems that people are not prepared to listen to what they are being told but prefer to jump to conclusions. It is so very easy to criticise rather than to try to understand the many benefits that this project could bring to the people of Ross and surrounding areas. It was obvious to see that the people who were opposed to the reinstatement would be the ones who would not take advantage of the railway, simply because they travel everywhere by car. They are very privileged to be able to do this and seem to forget that not everyone can afford to run a car. Families who do are trapped when the breadwinner takes the car to work. Why should these people be penalised?

There is high unemployment in the area and the introduction of a reliable transport service will enable people to travel to the larger towns, giving a better opportunity of gaining employment. Why should people be forced to work for below average salaries simply because they can't get to the larger towns that could offer more? At least they would have the choice. It would appear that the privileged few would be happy to deny this.

The argument was raised that people would not use the railway and that the buses are running at way below capacity. Maybe they are, but it is because people have become used to NOT having the facility that the railway would provide. Someone even had the audacity to suggest that my father had not done his homework with regard to costings and proposed usage. For almost two years, letters and reports have been written to various bodies, all of which my father has produced virtually unaided, and I will not stand by and allow rash statements to be made by people who have no understanding of the complexity of such a project. It was pointed out that it is simple to 'get figures'; surely, relevant figures are more important.

That is why a professional financial feasibility study is being undertaken. If it is proven not to be feasible, then the project will simply not go ahead.

If this is the case, then at least my father can say that he tried to introduce something that would have been of benefit to the community, instead of being one of the many who are happy to sit back and criticise two years' hard work.

Yours faithfully,
Serena M. Rawlins

A front-page *Gazette* write-up gave much space to the farmers' views, but the three letters had restored the balance. I feel that the element of resentment was not so much for the scheme but an innate reaction to an 'outsider' daring to put forward a public-good scheme rather than let the landowning establishment know what is best for the area, regardless of the unemployment and general decline all around. My letter of 3rd September 1987, correcting a couple of reported errors, was not published and may reflect covert representation:

The Editor
Ross Gazette

May I be permitted to correct a couple of errors which appeared in your otherwise factual report of the public meeting, which, doubtless, were due to mishearing in the lively atmosphere! Firstly, the expected value of overseas tourists to this country this year is £6 billion; in perspective, equal to the entire gold output of the South African mines per year. The other figure was given as my pre-Touche Ross International estimates of the proportion of tourism income compared with local use. The figures should read: 57% tourism; 43% local use for commuting, shopping, leisure etc.

I was pleased to note that Wyecider sees the renewal as incredible value for money today. It is true I estimated the overall cost as £20 million in 1986, but by May this year we had the definitive consultant's report quoting capital costs of £21.2 million. Details may be read in the reports in both Ross and Hereford libraries; for particular purposes, further breakdown is available, for example details of the electrification costing has been requested and supplied to Hereford and Worcester County Council.

I join with Wyecider in looking forward to a time when the railway would ease the 'harassment both in driving and parking'. Lord Hume on BBC Radio on 10th July 1987 said that 'age research' has calculated that in 13 years' time over one million British people will be over 80 years of age. How many of that age will be able to drive cars, even if they can afford to do so? Increasingly, they must rely on taxis for short journeys and need the facilities of rail travel for longer distances.

Anyone using their eyes in Ross today can see that it will be a relatively short time before it is necessary to limit Gloucester Road car parking to Registered Disabled Persons only during normal shopping hours; and it will be the same in other towns in similar situations. Fit persons will get the exercise they need to help them to remain so by carrying their shopping to the most distant car-parking places because more nearest-to-shops places will also have to be allocated to the disabled. It follows that properly sited railway and bus stops will soon be no more distant than average car parking for the majority.

Frankly, every extra house built on infill land created by the 'relief' road etc., plus the latest batch of over-scale industrial buildings, increase the town congestion problem automatically. I support Mr Geoff Gartside, who at Rotary summed up the dreadful distortions to which Ross is being subjected currently. The Wye Valley railcars will offer some comfort to those who, like Wyecider, would 'love to abandon the roads'. Where properties are within a few minutes' walk of the projected railway out of town halts, then the value of such homes will *increase*, as well as giving families the principal advantage of access to the towns and cities without contributing to growing congestion.

May I publicly thank Mr Ray Smith for his admirable and neutral chairing of the meeting, additionally expressing my appreciation to Mr Paul Rynehart, Chase Hotel, for his public-spirited hospitality for the meetings, including free refreshments for all attending the afternoon session.

Yours faithfully,
Eric T. Rawlins

On 1st September 1987 I received our *only* written enquiry from a local solicitor to date about the line of the railway route on behalf of a property purchaser in the Symonds Yat area. I replied fully immediately and David J. Barry responded, saying, 'I am most grateful to you for the information contained in your letter. I have passed this to my clients for their information'. This was a properly exercised enquiry, but it became apparent that some new arrivals to this area had failed to ask any questions. Some may have thought, as mentioned in Celia Glover's 1994 edition of the *Ross and Monmouth Railway*, that purchasers would be protected from the incidence of new roads, restored railways, flood plains, transmission lines etc. if they bought in 'good faith'. As any solicitor would tell them, the land or property is bought caveat emptor – let the buyer beware. Inevitably, a speculator may choose to buy on or near the railway route in the hope of obtaining a 'ransom strip', for which she or he would seek a sky-high price from the rail constructor. However, the Department of Transport has already made plain that this form of public exploitation will not be accepted.

Of course, the railway land was sold merely as unused track-bed – no planning permission was involved either to convert to a garden or much less to build upon.

Another ploy is to spend money recklessly, changing premises into something other than as originally bought and then claiming a vast sum in compensation. The legal test applied in such cases is straightforward: if the railway or road project and line-of-route were known when such expenditure was incurred, then the developer carried the obvious risk. In the case of Owen v Dept of Transport, High Court, 3rd November 1995, the plaintiff knew of a bypass planned within 100 yards of the house.

Since January 1986 I was prepared to answer any questions upon the line-of-route, and from May 1987 the engineering feasibility report with maps could be consulted through the public libraries' reference sections. At the time of writing (June 1996) we know of those few who have left the area because they did not wish to use the railway and, conversely, of others who have moved to this relatively isolated area in anticipation of the return of rail travel for their own convenience and also for the clients it will bring to accommodation owners.

Back to August 1987. When a telephone call was received from a most agitated lady living at Sellack, a village north of Ross, saying that she and her neighbours were much concerned by the sudden destruction of a large arch which goes under the railway by the bridge piers at Backney, I immediately contacted Phil Hart, the local county councillor, asking him what was going on. The caller said it was rumoured that the council was going to blow up the stone bridge piers – which to our knowledge it did not own! Cllr Hart said he knew nothing of either the destruction of the arch or the threatened blowing up of the piers! It was too late to stop the arch destruction – which probably happened legally or otherwise in order to sell the stone. This is just an example of how difficult it is over a decade to keep under control the continuity of a public-good line-of-route fifty miles long.

My thank you letter to Paul Rynehart for the hospitality of the Chase brought his response that the 'opposition will prove to be greater than originally anticipated and attitudes have changed considerably by those who originally opposed the closure of the lines'. So be it. The congestion, pollution, even the doctor who eventually stops them driving, are all waiting in the wings.

In September the matter of a funding contribution to the financial study was played out in the local papers, including the *Hereford Times'* leader remarking, 'The line would run through some magnificent scenery and could not fail to be a tourist attraction – a factor on which Herefordshire will increasingly have to rely'.

However, Cllr Ray Smith felt there was 'no way' the entire route could be opened because of the rubbish tip etc., and the county council voted against granting the tiny contribution of £794 towards the financial study.

Such ignorance of reconstruction capability (what would Brunel have said, even with the limited capability of his day!) no doubt appeased the invisible obstructive landowners, but it was a convenient peg on which the ignorant or those with vested interests could hang their hats. Cllrs David Hyde and Derek Davies, of Hereford City Council, and colleagues thought otherwise, accusing the county council (who had the statutory responsibility for transport) of displaying their ignorance about the needs of South West Herefordshire. The city agreed to contribute £700; the committee chairman, David Short, commended the potential for "a great tourist attraction and [giving] us a better link with Gloucester." From the Forest of Dean and Monmouth District Councils came entirely unfounded doubts that the outcome was so uncertain as to be unworthy of a contribution of £676 each! The usual doubts had been covered by the engineering feasibility report; it was plain that minds had been made up before the facts had been considered; will those behind such an ill-considered decision ever explain their actions?

Bill Price, then editor of the *Forest of Dean and Wye Valley Review*, was concerned that I had a fair press. The article published in the 26th September 1987 edition is reproduced below. It is justly critical of the way 'officers' had advised councillors, and of the slur implied upon our consulting engineers:

> The Editor
> *Forest of Dean and Wye Valley Review*
>
> I was appalled to read the way officers of both Forest of Dean and Monmouth District Councils have apparently misrepresented the facts of renewal progress to the councillors. In such circumstances I must correct the situation as reported and then give a factual update:
>
> (i) The request from me that the councils consider contributing a small amount (£667, not as officers quoted) to the financial study by Touche Ross International was at the direct instigation of the Department of Employment (NOT Environment) and put in the precise terms that Department required. Plainly, it is a moral commitment which is needed, that the councils simply acknowledge the common-good benefits the railway will bring and be within, rather than without, those constructively working to achieve this purpose.
>
> (ii) The status of the Technical Consultant's Report is not that it 'has already been commissioned' but that it has been published by Cass Hayward and Partners, Chepstow, and been in the hands of council officers since May 1987. Granted that planners are not civil engineers, it requires only

> the ability to read to observe that ALL the problems of the line-of-route have been assessed and accounted for in the report, which recommends reinstatement in modern terms. If the advising officers could not grasp the technical details then they had a duty to communicate with Cass Hayward and seek explanations BEFORE attempting to brief councillors.

Indeed, if the facts of what has happened are as reported, then the officers have cast a slur upon the competence of eminent consultants (to British Rail and London Docklands as well as to WVR) and have misled councillors in an inexcusable manner in a matter of prime importance for the future prosperity of the region. In view of the situation, it may be some comfort to readers to know that district councils have not statutory responsibility for the overall 'strategic planning' of transport. However, I call upon the respective chief executives to take the necessary disciplinary action to ensure that such a debacle, extremely close to gross misconduct in nature, does not again take place. It is the officers whose competence is in question, NOT that of those who advise and progress the Wye Valley Railway.

Let us now look at the matters which officers might have been expected to bring to councillors' attention, and ask why it costs tourists so much to stay in our area that some may never return. The statistics provide the answer for the average hotel bedspace occupancy; ONLY in September and October do they exceed 50%! This is a measure of how much the Wye Valley Railway could contribute by direct connections with British Rail to tap the market for more visitors spread throughout the year. English Tourist Board records 26 million one- to three-night stays annually; this is why the WVR tourism income is provisionally assessed as 57% of the total revenue, and so will effectively subsidise local travel throughout the year.

Opportunity is the name of the game for all who support and would ride the Wye Valley Railway. Easy travel to work by all-weather railcars running directly between Chepstow, Monmouth and Ross to Gloucester (and also to Hereford) will increase the chances for the average person to get and retain a better-paid job. There will also be direct trains between Hereford and Gloucester via Ross in accordance with the express wishes of Hereford City Council. I have personally been saddened by the number of over-50s people who are willing to work but are apparently not wanted locally; restoration of rail transport facilitates a wider job search and more distant travel to work becomes practicable.

Throughout the summer I have attended, by request, fetes and other public occasions where nine out of ten local people were enthusiastic for the return of the railway in modern guise. Some insisted that I register their wish to invest in the line and have priority in share purchase. Please write to me if you wish your name to be added to the register. Interest has now spread into Wales, Merseyside, the Midlands, Home Counties and London.

I have promised the local people that every town and parish council and women's organisation up and down the route of the railway would be consulted in order to obtain their views of location of stopping places and details of timetables etc., matters to which local management centrally based at Ross can give ready response.

The updated position is that the fifth largest UK financial consultants, Touche Ross International,

London, have offered to undertake market research, construct a business plan showing investment return for the five years after renewal in 1991, and examine sources of capital funding (at home and abroad) for the WVR. All being well, this report should be available about Christmas with the share prospectus following in the New Year.

What councils who refuse the tiny financial contribution to the financial study put at stake is that they could put themselves apart from those fully consulted about the development of the railway. Perhaps some councillors will read for themselves the technical report and readers of the *Review* will, together, persuade some councils to extract themselves from what is indeed a most unfortunate 'own goal' situation.

Eric T. Rawlins

I am reluctant to go to the press unless attacked by ignorant or reckless opinions, but unfortunately it was necessary to do so when the reported views of Cllr Ray Smith appeared in the public domain. Everyone is entitled to their own opinion, but the very purpose of professional advisers, whether medical, legal, and engineering or whatever, is that they put their reputation at risk; that is why their objective opinion is so valuable and should not be lightly rejected for political or similar subjective reasons. Accordingly, I reproduce below my letter of 1st October 1987, which appeared in the *Ross Gazette*, so that readers today may judge for themselves the situation:

The Editor
Ross Gazette

I feel I must comment upon the reported opinion of Councillor Ray Smith, who, after commending the proposal to renew the railway Chepstow–Monmouth–Ross, then gave his reason for not supporting the important Gloucester–Ross–Hereford section.

As most readers are aware, professional opinion has already been obtained upon the practicalities of renewal and by eminent civil engineering consultants. Specifically, the crossing of the Strangford tip cutting, although a deplorable despoliation in an Area of Outstanding Natural Beauty, can be solved.

The technical report, available to all councillors through their clerks and to members of the public at Ross and Hereford public libraries, indicates at page 33, paragraph 8.3.2. (iii) Strangford Cutting just two of a range of engineering techniques available to reinstate the track.

In the matter of the Ross–Gloucester line, this is the first major section of renewal recommended by the consultants; see page 42, paragraph 10.6 (ii) in the report. Again, all the difficulties are known and capable of solution, both in engineering and socially equitable terms, to bring the benefits of rail communication to all en route.

On August 8th 1987 I received an extensive questionnaire from the county engineer, Hereford and Worcester County Council. I responded with a detailed breakdown of electrification, halts, stations, central depot etc., costs plus information upon financial consultancy, share issue, company constitution and the 57% tourism revenue basis.

Whether or not this six-page response has been put before the Public Transport Committee, it is plainly only one of a number of committees who have equal responsibility in a council, for example tourism, strategic planning, policy and finance and full council, to reflect the importance and breadth of benefits the WVR will bring.

Basically, the £794 of the county's contribution is insignificant, but Councillor George Hyde has the vision to see the essence of the matter is that an opportunity to have future input into the Wye Valley Railway, in every way, is the stake before the councils currently.

Eric T. Rawlins

The Hereford and Worcester County Council, after uncertainty, refused the £794 requested – another nail in the coffin of this multi-million pound spending, but anti-Herefordshire, authority.

Battle continued on the front page of the *Forest of Dean and Wye Valley Review* because either the officers of the Forest of Dean and Monmouth District Councils had misled councillors by ignoring the engineering report *or* pressure had been exerted on the members for which the officers were lined up to take the blame! My response, front page on 9th October 1987, appears below:

Officers accused by £30m campaigner.
Councils 'misled' over rail plan.

Officers of the Forest of Dean and Monmouth District Councils were this week accused of misrepresenting the facts over the proposed Wye Valley Railway. The accusation came from the man behind the project – Mr Eric Rawlins of Ross-on-Wye – who claimed that the officers had cast a slur on the competence of eminent consultants. Mr Rawlins added: 'They have misled councillors in an inexcusable manner of prime importance for the future prosperity of the region. I call upon the respective chief executives to take the necessary disciplinary action to ensure that such a debacle – extremely close to gross misconduct – does not take place again'. Mr Rawlins has in recent months been trying to build up support for the proposed railway – which is likely to cost in excess of £30 million [editorial price adjustment from £20 m!] – and he asked the two councils to contribute towards a financial study. But the officers, who told their respective local authorities that they had considered the plan in detail, argued that it was not practical and that no financial contribution should be made.

Mr Rawlins hit back: 'Opportunity is the name of the game for all who support and would ride the Wye Valley Railway. Easy travel to work by all-weather railcars running directly between Chepstow, Monmouth, Ross to Gloucester – and also to Hereford – will increase the chances for the average person to get and retain a better-paid job. I have been saddened by the number of people over 50 who are willing to work but who are apparently not wanted locally – restoration of rail transport facilitates wider job search and more distant travel to work becomes practicable.'

Mr Rawlins said he had attended many functions explaining the scheme and nine out of ten local people were enthusiastic – some had registered their wish to invest in the line and have priority in share purchase. He explained: 'The updated position is that financial consultants, Touche Ross International of London, have offered to undertake market research, construct a business plan and examine sources of capital funding at home and abroad. All being well, this report should be available about Christmas with the share prospectus following in the New Year. What councils who refuse the tiny financial contribution to the financial study put at stake is that they could put themselves apart from those fully consulted about the development of the railway. Perhaps some

> councillors will read for themselves the technical report and readers of the *Review* will persuade some councillors to extract themselves from what is, indeed, a most unfortunate home goal situation.'

This front-page story seemed to put the record straight, but I regretted the need. Meanwhile, on the positive and national Government level, Clive George of the Department of Employment and Tourism had been in touch with the Department for Trade and Industry. The outcome was a visit from Mr Best-Dunkley, a senior consultant for the DTI, via support for marketing at the University of Warwick. The purpose was to assess the WVR's eligibility for the Enterprise Initiative, which as this was then an Assisted Area would pay two-thirds of the cost of between five and 15 days' consultancy. I felt that Mr Best-Dunkley was considerably impressed with the renewal scheme and with the progress made. He was able to understand and appreciate the significance of the engineering feasibility report; the application of such intelligence was in sharp contrast with some local persons. He seemed surprised that no knight of the realm had come forward to front the project!

Locally, the road congestion in Ross raised the matter of converting the section of the railway line-of-route from Walford Road (near Tudorville) to Hildersley as a 'south-eastern' bypass. Basically, it seemed superfluous to me, as anyone actually wanting to bypass rather than park in Ross could turn off at Walford, through to Merrivale Lane, into Alton Street and so gain the A40 Gloucester road clear of the town. Nevertheless, on behalf of WVR I sketched out an arrangement of road-alongside-rail for this section, as is common on the European mainland. However, it soon became apparent that no developer would provide such a road without housing on the Chase feeding into it! This would, at a stroke, destroy any notion of a bypass, as the road would simply be so linked into the housing as to make a nonsense of the term; it would merely be a service road to hundreds (!) of new houses on the AoONB green belt!

During an incredibly busy month, September 1987, I also met Department of Transport consultants regarding an A40 improvement scheme; this would involve demolishing two houses at Weston-under-Penyard, so was less than popular. Where bridging by road and rail would be involved it seemed sensible for the crossing to proceed with side-by-side road/rail to reduce costs. This proposal would rumble on, but the seed for reinstating the railway instead had been sown.

I had tried to reach the apparently mythical Joint Committee for the Area of Outstanding Natural Beauty; a sort of public/private/voluntary gathering of persons rumoured to be 'against' everything happening in the Lower Wye Valley, and with office support from the Gwent County Council. I wrote to Richard Eagle, recording my efforts to contact this legendary body; my efforts to contact them and to offer to speak etc. were always ignored. I felt that this body was being manipulated by the backwoodsmen landowners with vested interests in keeping communications to and from the Valley to the minimum. Musing was interrupted by a phone call from Touche Ross's London office; the DTI had agreed to fund two-thirds of their fee! This left £1,600 to find, which I felt the councils would find between them. It was possible that the Department of Employment and Tourism would be willing to help further, but there was a sort of unwritten rule that only one Government department can assist per assignment.

The contact with the English Tourist Board, in May, had been most encouraging and I felt sure that support would be forthcoming eventually. In October the Hereford and Worcester County Council's Strategic Planning and Transportation Committee overthrew the Planning Services Subcommittee, which was trying to break the WVR line-of-route by selling off the Tudorville–Hildersley trackbed. At last the county's action was matching its legal statutory responsibility for strategic planning and transport.

October also saw a supportive letter from Howard Ellis in the *Forest of Dean Review*, who laughed at the reaction of the Monmouth District Council officers, saying, 'Of course the WVR project involves new or renewed bridges and work on tunnels.

So did the original line!' A strong 'by the way' in the *Ross Gazette* exclaimed: 'Only Hereford City Council has had the courage and foresight to pay a contribution to the costs of the financial study. It seems that too many in positions of authority are dismissing the project out of hand. A radical departure and far-reaching solutions are called for to avoid problems ahead. A lightweight, high-technology rail service should be seriously considered.'

The South Herefordshire District Council, with no statutory responsibility for transport, handed the WVR request to the Amenities Committee. The planning officer, John Loynes, recommended the grant, as did Councillors Bernard Butler and Michael Goodson. Opposition came from a Jamie Bott and Bill Chinn, the latter saying that the WVR was 'pie in the sky'. Councillors Eunice Saunders, Edward Vines, Ron Levy and Ray Smith joined the 'antis', whose combined ignorance was sufficient to lose the vote. But Councillor Butler had the most powerful last words: 'Nothing is impossible. This is a terrific challenge. We should support it to the hilt. How did this railway get built in the first place? The problems initially were far greater than they are today. Civil engineering is far easier now.' Well said, was my reaction. How nice to hear a reasoned response from an intelligent representative of the people.

But the battle lines had been drawn against the overall public good; politicians, as ever, would waver back and forth in accordance with short-termism and their own limited perspectives. My response in the *Gazette* of 29th October 1987 sums up the situation rather well:

The Editor
Ross Gazette

THAT PIE IN THE SKY

I read with profound regret that the South Herefordshire district councillors had ignored the advice of their officers and turned down the Department of Employment's request that they share the cost of the financial study to complement the satisfactory technical report upon the Wye Valley Railway.

Plainly, the councillors acknowledge the desirability of the WVR since they liken it to pie in the sky! Happily, the civil engineering and line-of-route matters are not for councillors to solve; they have been recorded, assessed and planned to be dealt with by professionals. My only regret is that it has taken councils so long to decide whether or not to respond to this test of simple resolution; I shall soon know how matters stand overall. No doubt constituents represented by the negative or vacillating councillors will react appropriately in due course. The WVR will later consult all town and parish councils in detailed matters, so individuals should not feel disfranchised by how their more remote representatives have voted currently.

Who, knowing me, would expect I should hazard progression of this crucial and widely beneficial project by leaving matters entirely to the caprices of district and county councillors? Indeed, to allow any vested interest elements to have their way simply because some councillors are out of their depth technically and in imaginative capacity would simply be letting the grass-roots majority down. Accordingly, I have other irons in the fire, which will be disclosed at the appropriate time.

Meanwhile, Wycider's words of wisdom cause me to relate that others have the vision some locals lack, for every post brings letters regarding investment in the WVR from all parts of the country and I am compiling a register of these inquiries. Obviously, I should prefer as much local control and interest as possible, and if any local businesses or residents together wish to contribute to the £667 the district council refused

I should be very pleased. The Touche Ross International London office will handle the financial study, including market research, capital finance sources and a business plan projecting a balance sheet from the 1991 date of opening five years ahead.

Councillors unfortunate enough not to have served in the Royal Air Force should at least understand the motto *Per ardua ad astra* (Through difficulties to the stars); this 'pie' is much nearer than that. I close with the words of Richard Eagle, designer of the stations, coat of arms, uniforms etc. for the Wye Valley Railway, who writes: 'When a banquet is held to celebrate the re-opening of the WVR, should those who attend to eat their words be offered gravy or custard?'

Eric T. Rawlins

At the close of 1987, the previous year's visitor figures were becoming available: 79,031 to Tintern Abbey; 63,670 to Chepstow Castle. In Gwent, 22,915 were now on the dole (16.8%); 2,645 were registered as unemployed in the Forest of Dean. How helpful to the general economy would be the WVR, extending the season of visitors into late autumn, Christmas and a pre-Easter start-up when the area was so dead.

How typical of the lack of the Gloucester–Hereford line that football supporters returning from London were carried an extra 60 miles via Newport! Enough to make any superintendent of the old Great Western Railway turn in his grave!

Early in November we had a visit from a civil engineer from Wimpey's Major Projects; how refreshing to close the year in the company of someone who talks the same language!

CHAPTER 7

International Consultants' Reports 1988 – 1989

The year began by considering a range of name and number plate designs by Richard Eagle; we felt a chrome finish preferable to brass, as it would not tarnish. On the broad front, we were waiting to hear whether the English Tourist Board would contribute to the Touche Ross consultancy fee of £5,175. We had £500 from the Department of Employment and Tourism, £700 from Hereford City Council and £3,450 from the DTI. The dithering of the district and county councils meant that although the Government departments were keen for a 'more formal structure' for the WVR, it was apparent the county councils here had no stomach for such a positive role, as has been demonstrated by the Glamorgan Councils in rail renewal. In my 'spare' time I constructed a 4ft 6in x 3ft 6in map of the Wye Valley Railway for use at meetings, to the scale of 1½ inches to the mile.

The *Forest of Dean and Wye Valley Review* noted 2,756 persons out of work in the Monmouth Parliamentary constituency, 950 being women. The New Year would surely be unhappy for many; it hurt both Richard Eagle and me that we would not immediately offer work reconstructing the railway. Early in February 1988 we heard from Rod Brain, planner with Gwent County Council, about Lance Humphries who had produced a report called 'Lower Wye Valley Tourist Rail Link'. I wrote to Lance, then working in Saudi Arabia, to keep him advised throughout the summer as to how the proposal for a Chepstow–Tintern link would unravel. He sent me a fine set of GWR Wye Valley track formations, which are even now in our files (1996)!

On 10th February 1988 I gave a talk to the Ross Civic Society, which was duly reported in the *Gazette* and which gives the flavour of such occasions:

> With facts and figure at his fingertips, his relentless belief in his vision, in spite of the many set-backs, he gained the respect of his audience, even from those sceptics who thought the whole thing a mere quixotic tilting at windmills. Without slides or any other visible aids he gave those present plenty to think about and discussion after his short introduction was as lively as any generated by Civic Society speakers – yet even while he talks more railway land is being made ready for building operations. The massive cost, bound to rise spectacularly should the scheme go ahead, will not deter Mr Rawlins, whose complete dedication to the task will not be in the least shaken by such inconveniences.

I noted 60 people present; I spoke for 20 minutes and answered questions for one hour 40 minutes! At this time (1996) I cannot recall what railway land was being made ready for building operations; perhaps it simply failed to happen. Richard Eagle forwarded a drawing of a Class 20 diesel locomotive which we had in mind for engineering and general back-up work, including emergency towing of the railcars; it was beautifully coloured in green, yellow, black and chrome, adding most usefully to the range of items for WVR display occasions.

At the very last minute we heard about a Herefordshire Tourism and Leisure Fair at the Holmer Road Leisure Centre on 23rd March 1988. By agreement with the chief executive of the city council, we were fitted in with our stand. This was a midweek occasion and Mary attended and quite enjoyed the general atmosphere; we met mainly local people, hoteliers etc., who *all* welcomed the prospect of the return of the railway. Showing the flag at Hereford was important, for it would always be difficult to keep even such a major project in the eyes of the public over a 50-mile geographical spread. We were advised, by David Phillips of Queenswood Country Park, to forward details of the WVR to Miss Elaine Barnett of the Country Wardens organisation; this I did, but cannot recall any outcome.

Unfortunately, there was no likelihood of the half-million pounds appearing from the county councils in time for renewing the Chepstow–Tintern section for the summer of 1988. The practical matters of safety, control, storage and employment etc. were always outside my personal evaluation of what should happen. The entire renewal was the Department of Employment and Tourism's condition for funding last year's engineering study and it was, of course, my view that only the whole would comprise a viable short-haul line. That being so, the next stage would be the Touche Ross financial appraisal.

A notice in the *Ross Gazette* called a public meeting regarding 'Pedestrianisation and South Eastern Relief Road' at the John Kyrle High School on 19th April 1988. This was a distinctly unsatisfactory occasion, probably due to the alcoholic stimulation given to the platform party. When I got a chance to speak, I explained that *if* there were justification, a Tudorville to Hildersley road could be accommodated alongside the reinstated railway – in a fashion common on the European mainland. However, I pointed out that a road secured in return for a housing development on the Chase slopes would have to serve that huge estate and would therefore become another 'Merrivale Lane' rather than a bypass! The audience were almost entirely elderly; where, I wondered, were the young mothers of Tudorville who would derive much more benefit from a railway halt there, which would save them pushing their children all the way into town.

Meanwhile, Heart of England Tourist Board, in the form of Dr Allen Armstrong, had put our application to the Board and the £525 needed was granted on 2nd April 1988. It was agreed that there should be a meeting at Ross to commission Touche Ross in the presence of town, city, district, county and Government department representatives – as would attend! This situation gives some idea of the immense load of 'paper', communications etc. which I was handling almost on my own, and reminds me of the MEB meeting on the electrification, where it was said I needed a team of 20 staff to maintain the rate of progress to date.

The chosen day for the Touche Ross meeting was 21st April 1988 at the Chase Hotel. In the morning we had a private meeting with Dr Tony Fletcher and Miss Heather Adams of Touche Ross; in outline we saw the consultancy examine the history and background of the WVR, make some organisational suggestions, assess the human resources requirements, list possible sources of finance and propose a future strategy. I had prepared a considerable amount of detail, especially regarding management and staffing. Heather stayed overnight at the Chase and went through the pile of drafting I had already compiled. Susan Rawlins (later Mrs John Gartside) took the minutes of the afternoon meeting, which was fully reported in the press. Doug Woodman, president of Wyedean Tourist Board, took the chair. Councillor Mary Dew proposed that we contact the MEP Sir James Scott-Hopkins regarding assistance from Europe. Mr David Baxter, representing Hereford City Council, noted our discussions with Western Region BR and saw the need for ongoing contact. Mrs Jenny Joyce, from the Department of Employment and Tourism, asked me for the numbers we would employ during construction and permanently in operation. I drew attention also to the spin-off jobs in refurbishing underused hotels, tourist attractions and shops etc., which would share the prosperity the railway would bring.

Mike Walter, public transport co-ordinator for Hereford and Worcester County Council, advised that their subcommittee considered the sections Kerne Bridge, Symonds Yat down to Tintern to be 'feasible'. John Loynes, planner, South Herefordshire District Council, expressed reservations about a Ross Station at Fiveways and the headquarters at the Ashburton Estate. There was comment that some people in the very large area which the railway would serve still did not realise where it would run.

I explained that an ongoing series of talks was given up and down the line and also that a display in the new Cantilupe Road Library, Ross, was likely shortly.

Doug Woodman thanked all present and we showed the Anneka Rice Swiss railcar video. Doug said that he was "quite amazed" as to how inconspicuous was the overhead electrification, being almost invisible from any distance. The press report concluded with anticipation that the Touche Ross report would be completed by the end of June 1988.

On 22nd April I attended a press session at Lydbrook viaduct, where Rob Judge was photographer. From the correspondence received it would seem that the WVR project was now known from Bristol in the east to Newport in the west – as newspapers syndicated the story. On 26th April 1988 the Defence Minister announced the New European Fighter aircraft, the EFA. In response to an opposition MP, he said the cost would *not* be revealed to the British taxpayer, but it was released on the European mainland as being £36 million each! This put the cost of the entire WVR renewal at £21 million in perspective and was mentioned by me at meetings.

I had written to Miss Elizabeth Teiser, our very able head of the library, indicating that as a total of £6,975 of public money had been put into the WVR reinstatement work, I thought the new library and information centre in Cantilupe Road was the right place to hold an exhibition. She agreed and we set up a considerable display during the week 17th to 21st May 1988. This occasion went well – in the usual quite exhausting manner – and overwhelmingly, the views of the public were supportive of the renewal. Quite a number of people had only recently moved to the area and had been accustomed to decent, frequent transport systems; I wondered how many would remain enamoured with Ross as it existed today.

Also in May occurred the opening of an enlarged station at Kerne Bridge (for Goodrich Castle, as the guard would shout!), which was to be used by the Gloucestershire Association of Boys Clubs. It was good to see it raised from near dereliction;

I did not see the going of the GWR bogie coach which was used until it became 'unfit' through lack of maintenance by the Gloucestershire County Council; I only hope it moved into the hands of those capable of restoring it properly.

The tourism figures for 1987 were coming out at an all-time high of 15.6 million from overseas – worth over £18 *billion* to this country; this just showed the potential for economic improvement where, as the report 'Tourism '88' put it, there was 'investment, imagination, diversification and new ways of attracting visitors such as installing all-weather facilities'. Why did they not say the Wye Valley with its railway as an obvious example just waiting to happen!

John Loynes, planning officer with South Herefordshire District Council, expressed concern in the *Hereford Times* about the lack of success of this 'Rural Development Area'; he recommended the appointment of an RDA project officer.

Monday 13th June 1988 was an important day for the WVR, for we met someone actually competent to assess the project from a professional standpoint. The visitor was Mr Maurice Davies, Fellow of the Institute of Civil Engineers, on behalf of George Wimpey International. He also had discussions with Touche Ross in Bristol and examined our 'critical path' A3 sheet, which outlined the initial legal process and the alternatives identified for the civil works. He had told Touche Ross that he considered the reinstatement would take 'two good summer seasons', and this seemed good sense in 1988 – for with only picks and shovels, men and horses, Brunel's contractors took four years for the 30 miles Gloucester–Ross–Hereford way back in 1851! Towards the close of our most congenial discussion, Mr Davies asked whether I was a member of the Permanent Way Institution. I said, "No, but I get by!" and had more trouble with bureaucrats and other ignorant persons! By 1988 I had spent some 50 years in general study of railways, including three years at GWR Headquarters, so could discuss 'trailing crossovers' etc. with the best. It was hoped that Wimpey would join with us and that Maurice would take a seat on the WVR board; however, the bubble that was the peak of the Thatcher boom years was dangerously close to bursting, taking with it even the most eminent civil engineering contractors.

Talks continued with Tony Heaford, Partner, and Colin John of Touche Ross, and the outline of the organisational and funding options report was beginning to emerge, although the original thoughts of a June completion became too optimistic. I had contacted Sir James Scott-Hopkins MEP (as Ccllr Mary Dew had suggested) and he proposed a meeting later in the summer when he would return from Europe. This was then a target date to draw together those outside my immediate family but from whom support had already been given and who could form a pro-forma board of directors for WVR. This would include Richard Eagle, Doug Woodman and Paul Rynehart. A strongly supportive letter was received from the owners of Hill Court, Walford, a garden centre and showground open all year round, and for whom a halt within walking distance would be valuable.

In June 1988 ABT Products (Mr Anthony Beach-Thomas) again sought to expand across the railway at Alton/Chase; this would later be resolved by re-allocation to Ashburton on a site to the north of the original Ross passenger station. The national battle continued to be ignored; 1,100 killed on the roads, 15,000 seriously injured in the first three months of 1988 – the price of getting from A to B.

On 2nd August I responded to John Banham, Director General of the Confederation of British Industries (CBI), who had said, 'There is no shortage of money – what there is a shortage of is a vehicle which enables that private money be put to use for the public good'. His reply regretted they could be of no help, referring us to the clearing/merchant banks – quite incapable of making long/medium-term investments.

Doug Woodman, who lived at Goodrich, asked for a WVR stand at their show on 18th June 1988. This was a most pleasant occasion and Mary and myself set up in some shade from the hot sun. It was, however, marred by an incident in that it was to be the only occasion from 1986 to 1996 when I would be actually physically threatened to abandon the project! Mary had taken cups back to the school and I began dismantling the stand for loading into our Triumph Dolomite. Suddenly, a rough-looking fellow lurched out of the beer tent and leered at me. "We don't want the railway back here," he said, waving an arm in a gesture both threatening and embracing the general countryside. "Oh," say I, catching on rather rapidly, "I should have thought you would have been glad to get to Gloucester, Hereford etc. so easily..." I cannot recall any reply and concluded that the briefing which had paid for his beer all afternoon had not covered any logical argument. I don't know to whom he reported back and with no one else around could not find out his employer; very much in the tradition of Victorian landowners and of how attempts would have been made to frighten off surveyors by their grandfathers!

That summer I wrote to the British Coal Corporation regarding possible movement of coal from Parkend to Lydney – from which the WVR via our Wye Valley Junction could facilitate traffic to Hereford, Crewe etc. This brought the incredible reply that: 'The connection to the north is of no benefit to British Coal because the movement of trains will be *into* South Wales'. The world turned upside down – but also indicated such stupidity as to imply that trains would only be capable of proceeding loaded in *one* direction!

The 6th August 1988 found us down by the Wye at Ross Carnival – eight hours in the sun at 110 degrees Fahrenheit! In September the Touche Ross 'Organisational and Funding Options Report' arrived, and included in its recommendations was the proposal that we formed a public limited company in conjunction with a consultative committee of tourist boards and councils. We should take advice from a Parliamentary Agent and seek a business planning overview under the DTI initiative. Assuming the overview indicated that the project was viable, we should seek to form a consortium to reinstate the line. The various fund sources were indicated.

As I related to Richard Eagle, it had been hoped that this report would have included a business plan, but the terms of reference had to be agreed with the DTI and were more limited. Nevertheless, from such a cautious accountants' viewpoint as Touche Ross International, we were certainly not discouraged. It must also be remembered that we were breaking new ground in so many respects – a modern electric railway in a rural area – in a place where tourism *properly* marketed could subsidise pollution-free day-to-day travel for all.

By 21st September 1988 we were distributing the report to the subscribers plus twenty others, including Doug Woodman, Richard Eagle and Paul Rynehart. I invited them, together with Betty Gartside, to join Serena as directors. This would give some cohesion to our efforts and let it be known locally that an organisation rather than just myself would represent a corporate image to take the project further for the public good.

Others had not been idle and one R. Henderson, who had bought the Forest View Cottage at Symonds Yat tunnel entrance, applied to add two additional bedrooms. I determined that the eventual Memorandum of Association for the WVR would include the purchasing of any hotel that might come on the market should the owners not see the advantages of railway service, including the visits many of the one million or so railway 'buffs' might be keen to make to a new line. Note the obvious legal point of a person pressing on regardless of the by then very well known project to reinstate the railway. It is interesting to note the 'Backward Glance' item in the *Ross Gazette* of 29th September1988, which recalled the views of Mrs M.B. Elliott when owner of the Royal Hotel, Symonds Yat. She said in 1958: 'It is not just a branch line, it is a special and beautiful line, but nothing has been done to make it popular'. She feared that following the withdrawal of the midday Symonds Yat service, the next step would be the closure of the Hereford–Ross–Gloucester line.

On the 22nd September 1988 an excellent article by Jeremy Taylor appeared in the *Gloucester Citizen* on the £25 million plan to re-open the Wye Valley Railway. This carried Cass Hayward's map and a picture of an electric multiple unit; the hopeful up and running date was 1993. The capital sum advanced to

£25 million included the views of the DTI's assessor, in particular to allow for survey etc. fees, legal fees, Parliamentary process and any water/electricity diversions not covered by Cass Hayward. Richard Eagle and I were particularly aware that success of the WVR, after reconstruction, would depend on the most effective and ongoing publicity. It is worth reproducing the text of a wall poster we showed at the Ross Library, which provoked much good will and thoughtful comment:

WHERE ARE YOU NOW?

Filling in your pools coupon
Going to brief counsel
Telling grockles you're a shareholder
['grockle' is the local term for a visitor/tourist]
Learning your lines in *Pygmalion*
Writing your talk for the Women's Institute
Having another cup of coffee
Looking at those quantities again
Wondering whether London has changed
On the way from Ross to Rome via the Tunnel
(pie in the sky to locals!)
Reading the newspaper you never had time for
Admiring the scenery you never knew existed
Watching the kingfisher do it better than you
Learning German to improve your business prospects
Calculating accurately the annual cost of running a car
Actually TALKING to people again
Like ways of heating homes – WE now have a choice of transport
There's time to read the latest P.D. James mystery
How quiet and fast – no traffic jams – no parking problems on arrival
So relaxing – I often nod off to sleep
Are we HERE ALREADY!?

TRAVELLING IN STYLE – ON THE WYE VALLEY RAILWAY

In September the BBC challenged the Government's figures for disabled persons, saying that 14% were so affected. The Office of Population was now saying the totals were 6.2 million, of which four million were 'old' – 70% being pensioners. As with the 'preserved' railways, we would provide some accommodation in the railcars for the disabled. At Ross the Merton House holiday facility had disabled folk staying throughout the year and the WVR would try to arrange trips on a regular basis to the other towns and countryside attractions.

The Ross and District Hoteliers and Caterers Association met at the Chase in October to celebrate 40 years of effort. Mr Ray Thomas, the secretary in 1948, recalled how at that time "posters advertising Ross and the Wye Valley were to be seen on railway stations as far away as Penzance." On-going advertisements, then as now, renamed 'marketing', is critical to selling *anything*. Richard Eagle and I evolved the idea of 'halt wardens' – local persons who would be trained to supervise the local stopping place – perhaps with WVR armbands and with travel concessions on the line. On 6th October 1988 the then Ross Mayor, Drewe Lacey, asked to see the Touche Ross report and phoned back for more information. On 4th October we drew together in what was to be a preliminary board meeting. Doug Woodman was appointed deputy chairman to head the board until we met with Sir James Scott-Hopkins MEP. Embryo board members would be Drewe Lacey, Richard Eagle, Betty Gartside, Paul Rynehart and me. The idea of Touche Ross to move the WVR directly to become a public limited company was easier said than done, since under the Companies Act 1985, a minimum share capital of £50,000 must be declared, of which £12,500, 25%, must be paid up. It was agreed we would each put up £500 initially.

On 19th October 1988 the University of Warwick, which had helped with the DTI's 'Marketing Initiative', asked us to complete a questionnaire on the effectiveness of the scheme. We responded fully and believe this was mutually beneficial throughout the life of this project. The *Daily Telegraph* on 27th October contained an unhappy report after two years of bus deregulation. The consumer group Bus Watch found the vehicles to be dirtier, shabbier, less comfortable and less reliable. About half ran late due to congestion; overall, 'The number of people using buses has dropped'. New operators were buying old buses 'for £1,000 compared with around £70,000 for a new one'. In effect, a third-class service which people avoided using if possible – much to the joy of the car manufacturers and to the exasperation of the environmentalists.

In November, British Rail placed its first order for commuter trains fitted with telephones; a useful development for passengers, but I think the LMS and LNER had such a feature pre-World War II!

Out of the blue, the Audit Commission caught up with the amount of national taxpayers' money which had been hurriedly spent on the so-called Ross relief road at Hildersley. Surprise, surprise, the road was carrying 'far less' traffic than was originally envisaged – by whoever. I wondered who did the original estimates. Certainly, I could recall no consultancy prior to what became a road costing about £1 million. It was thought to have been 'nodded' through by councillors who were persuaded that national tax rather than local tax would fund it. Would they be surcharged for reckless behaviour, I wondered? The hideous insult to the Brunel engine shed is there for all to see, the wretched road having been cut to pass by as closely as possible without causing the collapse of the structure; as it is, a more inappropriate setting for a broad gauge building would be hard to imagine.

In November 1988 the matter of the colour film of the line taken c.1959 for the Chamber of Commerce, Ross, arose again. Mr Jack Coombes had contact with the widow of the photographer, Mr Ward, who rumour said held the Chamber's master 8mm film with magnetic sound track. Jack Coombes telephoned back to me saying that I was to make an announcement from Mrs Ward to the effect that the film would *never* be made available to the people of Ross. I said that I heard what he said, but would not be making such an announcement. If the facts were that the Chamber had commissioned and paid for the film which Mr Ward had been allowed to retain and 'show' as required, then the widow had no title to it. Would such a curious situation ever be resolved before the 8mm film deteriorated beyond recall?

December 14th 1988 saw a good front page in the *South Wales Argus* entitled 'Wye Valley £25m railtrack plan'. At Christmas came news of a scheme to link Ledbury and Newent with trams by the Leadon Valley Electric Railway Association. One of the principals talked to me, and after a car breakdown due to overheating one day, I found myself in a Ledbury garage with a single-decker tram around the back! Some house building had, inevitably, taken place, where the builder had taken advantage of the sound railway base, but I wished them good luck over their eight-mile route. Perhaps it will yet come into being, but in 1996 nothing more has been heard.

Paul Marland, Forest of Dean MP who lives in the Cotswolds, advised me that he had received anti-rail letters from constituents; I sent him a four-page letter suggesting he might copy it to Colin Shepherd and John Stradling Thomas. One had no quarrel with MPs seeking to ensure that their few constituents affected by either road or rail schemes got fair play; however, actual opposition before appreciating the overall advantages to an area could frustrate all improvements, e.g. the removal of 1960s' hideous flats, the Beeching cuts, which were to be implemented *without* an assessment of the consequences etc.

West Mercia police published a report for the first quarter of 1988; the number of accidents was up, mainly due to speeding. Over 1,250 people had been involved, who suffered fatalities to minor injuries, and the 'cost to the community was estimated as more than £13.4 million'. I made this over £10,000 per occurrence – the *un*necessary price of getting from A to B – without any measurement of the human suffering behind the figures.

The DTI Birmingham, handling our request for financial assistance for the business plan, had their assessors' report, which stated: 'it is apparent that the Wye Valley Railway has considerable potential'. But it had to await us forming a company, after which they would 'approve the full Business Planning consultancy'.

Quite a satisfactory close to 1988!

The New Year, 1989, saw a report by the Heart of England Tourist Board entitled 'A Tourism Action Programme', which was generally critical of Ross and Symonds Yat, including the commentary: 'Ross was heavily dependent on its ability to live up to people's expectations, but unfortunately there were too many ways in which it was disappointing as a place to visit, for there was little of interest.'. Nevertheless, the *potential* was clearly there, for South Herefordshire took £10.8 million from 700,000 accommodation nights, which supported 2,500 jobs. An industry indeed! And to my mind a great deal better than low-paid factory or industrial bird and animal production for an Area of Outstanding Natural Beauty. The month also saw the appointment of Coopers and Lybrand and Lazards to advise Paul Channon, Transport Secretary, upon the denationalisation of British Railways. Would this facilitate the WVR, especially in the matter of 'joint' running into current BR stations? I thought that it might well break the monopoly's worst features.

The *South Wales Argus* carried a splendid article by Mike Buckingham, 'Putting the Wye Valley back on the right lines', with a map of the 'The Revived Line' and two good photographs of me at Lydbrook Viaduct and at the mouth of the tunnel. Keith Shawcross, Ross solicitor, had recommended a Bristol solicitor to form the company. I opposed this and, from the solicitors' regional directory, found Flint Hands of Gloucester, who were relatively local and listed as specialising in 'business affairs'. They had already worked for Drewe Lacey. A meeting was arranged for 3rd February 1989 in Gloucester with Drewe and myself attending. I had already drafted our Memorandum of Association etc., and Flint Hands promptly said I should be the company secretary! Let that be a warning to anyone who studies law as a matter of personal interest! Not my idea of an 'action' role, but no real alternative, and one which virtually incorporated a day-to-day executive responsibility for years to come.

On 3rd February an article also appeared in the *Forest of Dean Review*, claiming the line would cause disruption at Longhope; it spoke of 'dual overhead power cables' and bringing 'noise and litter and danger to people and animals'. I wondered whether the toffee-paper man from Monmouth was behind this, but it turned out that one David Burren of Velthouse Lane, Longhope was the instigator. I agreed to attend an open meeting at Longhope on 16th February 1989. John Gartside and Susan took me and photographed the scene after I had given the presentation, and we had to listen to a long and tedious prolongation by Mr Burren instead of the expected questions from parishioners. He was determined to gather as many 'anti-WVR' names as possible, and I was telephoned next day by a villager saying that she was outraged by Burren's attitude and had herself collected 62 names in support of the WVR! It was, of course, the usual case that the 'silent majority' had either stayed away or felt unable to take part in an atmosphere where sweet reason would not be allowed to prevail. I thanked the lady but begged her not to put herself in any difficulties with the long-term inhabitants who, unlike Mr Burren, were resident when the railway ran and appreciated the service. It was plain that the WVR would restore what had been lost; Mr Burren was a typical commuter who used the village as a dormitory; once he missed his train from Gloucester a few times due to road congestion, we could expect his views to change.

Our second pre-board meeting took place on 22nd February 1989, when we decided to form a private limited company as appropriate to our financial limitations. Compared with Longhope, a much more reasoned occasion took place on 23rd February, when I addressed the Ross Conservative Association. The letter of thanks said it all: 'On behalf of the Ross Conservative Association, many thanks for your most interesting and informative talk upon your efforts to bring back railway communication to this area. Our members were very impressed with your detailed information and you gathered much support for your ideas.'. This was reflected in the *Ross Gazette*, which noted: 'Much work has already gone into studies which showed that the type of electric traction envisaged would be quiet and unobtrusive. Tourism will thereby benefit as well as commuters and long distance travellers.' In reading this very fair and accurate account and reaction I wondered why Mr Burren, apparently, had not sought any expert advice before buying a property with a railway trackbed at the bottom of the garden – caveat emptor: let the buyer beware

A good letter, from Rosemary Verity of Linton, appeared in the *Gazette* of 2nd March 1989. She pointed out that the adverse reaction was from those whose land would be affected and 'not from people representing wider interests'. Further, and regarding the parallel A40 road, that 'constructing roads causes enormous upheaval, requires more land and when completed, causes rain and air pollution. An electric railway does not'.

In London the Institute of Transport heard Professor Bill Bradshaw, Salford University, advocating a transport fund *separate* from the Department of Transport and that: 'Treasury rules inhibiting the use of private capital in transport projects should be revised or abolished'. We would soon find that our approaches to Japanese and British venture capitalists were being inhibited one way or another, plus the long-term nature of returns on transport infrastructure (whether road *or* rail!) and an all-round reluctance to lend without a substantial Government contribution. After all, public-good work by its very nature *deserves* national support, as affected everywhere but in Great Britain!

A *Times* article of 8th March 1989, dealing with the route of the high-speed trains linking London with the Channel Tunnel, found that property prices were likely to rise by 10 to 20%. House agents believed that the number of people whose properties would *benefit* in value would be *far greater* than those who found their properties blighted.

I applied for a stall at the Tourism and Leisure Fair, Hereford, on 22nd March 1989. This was a 12-hour stint, which was 'completely exhausting' for Richard Eagle and ourselves. Serena's employer, Proticol Design Associates of Gloucester, supplied fine quality typeset posters at a special price. We met, among many others, Mrs Price of Dinedor, who was pleased about the convenience of the railcars bringing her horse riding clients out of Hereford but lamented that her loose boxes might have to be moved. Richard Eagle undertook to design a new set for her and did so! Never can it be said the WVR is uncaring of the community!

The third preliminary board meeting happened on 14th April 1989, in the Town Council Chamber, Ross, when we considered the matter that the Welsh Development Agency might fund the Bill to authorise the line – 'enabling it to be got in to Parliament by November 1989'. The formation of the company was underway by Flint Hands – this would cost £500. Betty Gartside very kindly arranged the use of her home as the company's registered office. The magazine *Business Direction*, published in Gwent in April, contained an article by me, with map, a photograph of an EMU (electric multiple unit) and of us at the Hereford show. In response to a notice in the *Ross Gazette* regarding the Hereford and Worcester Structure Plan, we contacted the organising Government offices at Fiveways Tower, Birmingham. The reply on 15th May 1989, by Mrs S.M. Todd, is worth recording: 'The matter you raise, although of very obvious importance to the community, is not related to any of the strategic matters which will be discussed at the Examination in Public'. The 'likely programme' of so-called strategic matters was 95% housing! The message was plain: although the county council had statutory responsibility for transportation, it was *not* going to discuss the matter in public, especially in an 'inquiry' setting! Perhaps not a direct hit on the Worcester County Hall, but what we might have said in another setting. A very near miss, that almost certainly had some unheard repercussions.

On 24th April 1989 I gave a well-received talk to a good audience of Church Wives at Walford. Deryck Lewis wrote an intelligent article on the project for *Rail* magazine, June edition. He said: '£25 million is a lot of money to raise in a starting-from-scratch venture that echoes the pioneering days of the railway era. An electrified rural route in Western Region territory is in itself unique, and would be a magnet to the railway fraternity'. Mr Lewis also indicated the possibilities of steam excursions, by the Dean Forest Railway, on bank holiday weekends. Indeed, he saw the spending power of railway enthusiasts as a particular segment of the necessary marketing campaign.

On 21st June Doug Woodman and I went along to the Dean Forest Railway, and I invested £10 in their Pannier Tank No. 9681 to keep it going! Hereford and Worcester CC referred the Harrogate Ripon Northallerton Railway project to us, which, interestingly, was certainly an admission that they well knew of the WVR project. The Harrogate people were getting the same erratic responses from local authorities as ourselves; the concept of any real 'partnership' in 1989 was so 'new' and had yet to be 'invented' by the establishment!

I noted the cost of removing refuse from a cutting; such a common problem with railway reinstatement, for local authorities up an down the country were quick to find a short-term answer to rubbish disposal by dumping it in railway cuttings and hoping that they would retire before the problems came home to roost! The removal costs were quoted as £1 per cubic metre in 1989; I trust Hereford and Worcester CC will arrange for their budget to accommodate this when we require the clearance.

On 1st July 1989 we had the fourth board meeting, but Doug Woodman could not attend, being, sadly, in the Nuffield Hospital. As the secretary, I was asked to write to Balfour Beatty, Richard Branson, Fairclough, Mabey Holdings, Alfred McAlpine, Robert McAlpine, Metro-Cammell, Monk, NEI/Mitsibushi, Peter de Savary, Tarmac, Westinghouse/AEG and Wimpey, seeking funding assistance for the Bill to authorise the line. We were still awaiting responses from Hereford and Worcester and Gloucester County Councils.

Down the line at Tintern, Gwent CC made much of the seven and a quarter inch gauge short steam railway – giving me the chance to respond in the *Forest of Dean Review* to the effect that the numbers presented of 'over 100,000 visitors per annum' indicated the scope for the full-size operation to serve an idyllically located and typical Victorian GWR station. This is simply industrial heritage of the highest quality for the area, and yet ignored by the planners and council members. What is the value of a station without a railway service?

The Railway Development Society, under the headline 'Wye not?', carried an article by Julian Langston and a photograph looking along the bridge at Lydbrook; in the *Sunday Times* of 2nd July 1989 there appeared what we believe to be the first mention of the WVR scheme in a national paper.

In August, Ray Smith, writing in the *Ross Gazette*, made plain his opposition to any so-called bypass on the rail trackbed from Hildersley to Walford Road; he wrote: 'If Mrs Clayton means, by a ring-road, a new southern relief road, then I can assure her that none of the proposals will incorporate that concept. I remain implacably opposed to a southern relief road because it would remove the last remaining restraint to massive speculative development in the southern half of the town – thus creating more problems than it would solve'. Well said, I felt; the renewal of the railway would put a steel ring around both the industrial and housing developments that already are enough, if anything, if the character of Ross is to be conserved for future generations.

The 4th August 1989 saw quite an occasion at the Lost Street Museum, Ross, where the Rev. David Tipper addressed an 'open' meeting upon the old GWR and I described the plans for reinstatement. Very enjoyable for all, if tiring – particularly as a full day with the WVR stand at the Ross Carnival followed the next day.

I gave an interview to the *Gloucester Citizen* early in September, and this was used as a basis for a piece in the *Forest of Dean Review* on the 8th, the main point being that the formation of the company was proceeding and, indeed, at the fifth board meeting, on 16th September 1989, the Articles and Memorandum of Association were signed. Most sadly, we had to accept the resignation of Doug Woodman on medical advice. We decided to keep the position of chairman vacant but agreed that Drewe Lacey would be deputy chairman, and that Betty Gartside, Paul Rynehard, Richard Eagle and I, as company secretary, would comprise our first board of directors. It struck me that to be able to form a private limited company, with minimal resources, in two years nine months was no mean achievement. Whether or not Sir John Scott-Hopkins would join the board was uncertain, since we did not know how much or to what degree his joining depended on the finance 'being sorted out'. All five members agreed to invest the sum of £500 in ordinary shares of £1 each. Serena Rawlins (as she then was) acted as minute secretary, since I was finding it exceedingly difficult both to guide the proceedings as well as note decisions etc. Encouraging responses were boarded from Balfour Beatty, Peter de Savary, Tarmac and Wimpey, but there was no instant finance.

However, the key matter, as far as the Department of Trade was concerned, was that the WRV project was no longer dependent upon me continuing to function, but would be carried forward by a board of directors with limited liability. Shades of the Duke of Plaza Toro in the *Gondoliers*! Boris Johnson, journalist, wrote from Brussels of the urgency of the Euro mainland railways to standardise upon the technical standards of the new electrified lines. He further commented that: '60,000 people are killed on European roads each year'. My mind switched back to World War II, where over the six years 1939–45, RAF Bomber Command lost 55,500 aircrew. How can the crazy disregard for lives in exchange for the alleged 'freedom/convenience' of driving be brought home to the politicians of 1989? Boris Johnson related the Swedish situation whereby the state covers the railway infrastructure costs; the germ of Railtrack for Britain was so born.

On 4th October 1989 Tony Shadforth, Senior Enterprise Counsellor for the DTI, advised me that it seemed a two-thirds' grant would be payable to Touche Ross for carrying out a business planning review. He asked that we keep the three MPs advised of the latest developments – likewise the unresponsive venture capitalists. The grant was confirmed on 12th October.

At Drewe Lacey's suggestion, I met Tim Masters of the Design Works, Ross, who worked up the WVR totem into a very attractive, spray-shaded, GWR button-style symbol for use on our new letter heading. Drewe had indications of interest from Mr R.W. Michaelson, who ran an electronics business in Malvern and who wished to become a director. We went into print with 2,000 copies of the letterhead, but then Mr Michaelson, with his business in difficulties, had to withdraw his application. This, together with the reluctance of the construction companies/venture capitalists to make any commitment to WVR, rang warning bells as to the duration of the Thatcher 'boom' years.

The Transport Users Consultative Committee for Western England had produced a 'pump priming' report to encourage local authorities to support private rail schemes. The chairman, Sir Robert Wall, wrote to us saying, 'I found your letter of very great interest because I was brought up just outside Ross-on-Wye and in my youth spent many happy hours travelling between Hereford, Ross and Gloucester on the one hand and down to Monmouth on the other. I was at school in Monmouth for seven years. It would be a tremendous achievement to pull off the reconstruction of the Wye Valley Railway.' Both Sir Robert and his secretary, D.I. Nalder, endeavoured to engage the interest of the Gloucester and Hereford and Worcester County Councils, but we were not invited to any meetings and indeed, as I write in 1996, are quite unaware of the outcomes!

Paul Rynehart pursued a number of contacts from Wimpey to Sun Valley, Queens Moat Hotels' chairman to various MEPs. Hopes, indeed, were high in the autumn of 1989! The Midland Metro light-rail transit scheme between Birmingham Snow Hill and Wolverhampton had its Parliamentary Bill receive the Royal Assent on 16th November. I received an invitation from The Friends of Hereford Record Office to give a talk on Friday

24th November, which they entitled 'The Wye Valley Railway'. This was well publicised by The Friends and well attended by an intelligent audience with wider than usual mindsets! The prospect of a restored WVR was well received and, despite a frosty night, some 35 people attended.

Yet another meeting about pedestrianisation took place in Ross in November, with side-pressure from Mr Austin Wallace for measures "to protect the town centre". Ccllr Ray Smith was quick to drop on this, since the aim of Wallace was to get a so-called 'relief road' from Tudorville to Hildersley; Smith said that it "would lead to 1000 houses being built in that part of the town" and "it will make Ross so different than what it is and the day that by-pass is built I am going to look for somewhere else to live." How sensible, I reacted. A road serving 1000 houses with two people plus two children in each, all car-borne, would completely destroy any 'relief road' function! Since the traffic pouring into Ross via Edde Cross Street is largely seeking all-day business parking in the town centre, it is patently obvious it would *not* be diverted via Hildersley on to the Gloucester road.

The second board meeting after the formal formation of the company took place at Inpro House on Friday 1st December 1989. We were all pleased to see Doug Woodman present, but he was far from well. However, he took the chair and a group photograph included Drewe Lacey, Mrs Betty Gartside, Richard Eagle and me. This was published in the *Ross Gazette* on the 7th December, together with a press release setting out our aim to have a Local Private Bill put to Parliament 1990/1, route acquisition/reconstruction in 1991/3 and partial operation by 1994. I gave telephone interviews to the Gloucester *Citizen* and the *Western Daily Press*. Most exciting was a video film for ITV News, in which I took part on and around the Lydbrook Viaduct.

Our writing to Sir James Scott-Hopkins and other possible investors would await delivery of our letterheads. Karen Williams, tourism officer, South Herefordshire District Council, advised that a tourism sub-committee resolution of support for the WVR would "not be conveyed in writing"! This was a sign of the covert anti-rail element which we knew existed – the landowning 'tail' which for centuries has 'wagged the dogs' in Herefordshire, Gloucestershire and Monmouthshire. Would the public ever find out how vested interests always triumph? The real public-good measures would be set aside, denied, hidden etc.

We were glad to see that Mrs Bobbie Heaven's Association for the Promotion of Herefordshire was to receive a modest annual grant of £1,000. She was an enthusiastic supporter of the railway renewal, having genuine public-interest reasons, and speaking whenever she had the opportunity – no doubt to the extreme annoyance of certain factions. On the 15th December 1989 I sent a 500-word article with map to the *Financial Weekly*, published in the City of London. This was not acknowledged and I suspect got lost in the usual pre-Christmas festivities!

A great local railway enthusiast and cameraman, Jack Coombes, helped out with stills for the ITV film, despite being struck down with flu. I reproduce his letter, published in the *Ross Gazette* of 21st December, for this gives some idea of the impact of the WVR scheme in an area where so little for the general public good had ever happened!

> The Editor
> *Ross Gazette*
>
> Sir,
> In these days and age, anyone who answers a call to the front door hardly knows what to expect. On Tuesday morning the following true event happened to my wife, who answered the bell in the normal way and upon opening the door found Mr Eric Rawlins (of WVR fame) and a TV camera crew. Mr Rawlins asked if he could see a selection of railway photographs, to which my wife agreed.
>
> I could do nothing in the matter because I was in bed with a temperature of 101, having fallen victim to the present flu epidemic.

Upon presentation of a selection of albums containing railway photographs, the team carefully selected a number of prints, and when the cameras were set up in the square in front of my house the team promptly started to photograph them. The whole procedure took about one hour to complete, the albums being returned with grateful thanks and a request to watch ITV Channel 3 Southern that evening 12th December 1989.

For my pleasure, a small TV was set up in my bedroom and in the second part of the programme Mr Rawlins and his associates were interviewed on TV, followed by a selection of photographs of Kerne Bridge and Lydbrook, which I had not seen before. With reference to my own copious selection of prints, nine of my own prints relating to Ross Station in its heyday were seen on the TV news programme.

J. C. Coombes

Quite a pleasant close to another busy year upon the Wye Valley Railway project!

CHAPTER 8

1990 Business Planning Report

The New Year 1990 began with the third board meeting, on 12th January, at Inpro House, attended by Doug Woodman, Richard Eagle, Drewe Lacey, Paul Rynehart, Robert Michaelson and me; apologies were received from Betty Gartside. Two considerable bills had to be met: £1,050 from Design Works for the letterheads and an account from Flint Hands, solicitors, Gloucester, whom I, wearing my company secretary's hat, had beaten down from £851 to £562 for forming the company. We had an oral contract for 'approximately £500' for the work, so a minor tussle was justified! We rejected a letter from the Welsh Development Agency, which considered investment in the WVR to be 'not appropriate'. I believe the activities of what this agency *had* considered 'appropriate' would shortly fall under close scrutiny.

It was agreed that four of the directors would meet with Touche Ross on the 16th January 1990, regarding the business planning consultancy. Sir James Scott-Hopkins agreed to chair the WVR board. Drewe Lacey had written letters, of 13th December 1989, to 42 venture capitalists, but the indications were that there was very little 'venturing' by these largely City-based organisations, clearly stuck in the mould of looking for 'instant' returns upon gold-plated collateral! Where, indeed, were the entrepreneurs of Brunel's day?

Colin Shepherd MP asked that we "continue to keep him informed from time to time". I had kept Paul Marland MP fully briefed since 1st December 1988, updated in December 1989, and he was invited to view our Ross Library exhibition in March. On the wider transport front, the sale of National Bus raised £323 million for the Government and released a spate of very cheaply acquired companies, with asset stripping by sales of central bus stations to superstores and allowing Stagecoach and other predators to go on a buying spree which included the local Red and White operation. Public reaction was not publicised, but usage fell and was reflected in the average return on capital of just 2.6%.

Meanwhile, on the WVR, we contacted a further 50 venture capitalists, of which four did indicate some interest. Our immediate aim was to fund the Act of Parliament, which would have to be started by June to catch the next session; the cost would be £100,000 approximately. We were this year already committed to pay Touche Ross £2,012 – the balance not funded by the DTI's 3i Enterprise Support. The above figures show just how inadequate was Government support for infrastructure renewal schemes, which surely deserved no fewer resources than the road schemes which were merely encouraging more traffic, more congestion and more pollution.

Nick Howard, of Touche Ross, came to see me on 22nd February 1990, and we went through the passenger seat mileages etc. March saw the WVR stand, with supporting material by Richard Eagle, in use at two venues, firstly at the Herefordshire Tourism and Leisure Fair at the Holmer Road centre. This cost £20 and involved our presence from 9 a.m. to 8 p.m.; a stimulating but exhausting occasion, but good to meet with some of the Hereford City councillors who had given financial support for the earlier Touche Ross organisational and funding options. The press release announcing the Hereford Fair also referred to the exhibition we would stage during National Railway Week at the Library and Information Centre, Ross. A separate release, on 14th March 1990, is an excellent summary of where the WVR project stood at the time and is reproduced here:

WYE VALLEY RAILWAY: EXHIBITION

The end of March is National Rail Week and the opportunity is taken by the directors of this local enterprise to renew the Wye Valley Railway to hold a progress exhibition in the Library and Information Centre, Cantilupe Road, Ross-on-Wye. The exhibition, which also sets the project in the context of reducing pollution and road congestion, begins on Tuesday 27th until Saturday 31st March, both dates inclusive. Admission is free and open at usual library hours.

The occasion is a response to widespread interest to be kept advised of progress on this £25m capital project, which began with an engineering feasibility report by consulting engineers Cass Hayward and Partners in 1987. The Touche Ross International report of 1988 covered organisational and funding options, the recommendations of which are in process and include a business planning review under the auspices of 3i Enterprise Support Ltd and is grant aided by the Department of Trade and Industry.

The company is interesting venture capital sources and also seeking a grant under the Industrial Development Act, 1982, for funding the Local Private Bill necessary as an Act to give statutory authority for the line in session 1990/1, with line-of-route acquisition and reconstruction to follow 1991/3. Partial operation, coinciding with the opening of the Channel Tunnel rail link to the European mainland, is expected 1993/4.

The project is to link, with electric railcars to British Railways standards, Hereford–Ross–Gloucester and Ross–Monmouth–Chepstow, giving across the platform access to the National Rail network both for tourism and all year round local use.

ROSS AND MONMOUTH!
Back on the map for the 21st century!

It is also a matter of historical record to reproduce the letter I wrote to Martin Morris, chief reporter of the *Ross Gazette*, on 31st March 1990. To this letter is stuck the five-bar gate attendance record for the library week, 27th–31st March, which Richard Eagle and myself maintained. Of the 416 attending, 17 (spread over the five days) represented the opposition to the renewal, which is 4%. What Government wouldn't marvel at 96% support for anything it proposed!

> Martin Morris Esq
>
> After a most exhausting (but exhilarating!) week's exhibition at Ross Library, I now respond to your request for attendance details. I am somewhat concerned in certain respects. Richard Eagle and I recorded 416 visitors, and we were overwhelmed on occasions and unable to mark the paper, so I think this is certainly under the total figure. Of these, 131 completed a sheet as new supporters of the renewal. Persons who told us of their individual opposition to the reinstatement totalled 17 for the week. Some, even those who feel strongly about what they see as private disturbance, now appear much more aware of the pollution, congestion and oil limitation on the horizon for road movements. Most knew of the countrywide developments for tram/railcars now proceeding and were particularly interested to read the exhibition display referring to the Cheltenham–Gloucester, Ledbury, Newent, Gloucester and the huge Bristol/Avon County in process of obtaining Parliamentary authority. Expressed opinion by residents up and down the Wye Valley has clearly moved on from the insular perceptions of four years ago.

Entirely unsolicited comments were written by visitors, being general expressions of goodwill: 'greatly needed; long overdue; hope the Minister of Transport takes note; investment details please; excellent access for hostel; travel to London frequently; should help us and tourists; look forward to it' etc. As company secretary, I acknowledge this response with satisfaction and similar sentiments expressed last week at the Hereford Tourism Fair by the Leader of the City Council. But I must point at the incredible burden this places upon a small private company to carry out a *major* task which is plainly for the OVERALL PUBLIC good.

The most frequent question was, "Why do the local authorities continue to allow piecemeal developments on the railway line-of-route?" I said they must ask this of their district or borough councillors who make the planning decisions *despite* the fact that the statutory responsibility for strategic planning, major projects, traffic and transport infrastructure rests squarely upon the *county* councils for Gwent, Gloucester and Hereford/Worcester.

During the exhibition I accepted three further engagements to talk about the WVR reinstatement: at Ross, Monmouth and Hereford. I invite the county councils to acknowledge the public expectation of a better means of transport by putting up a corporate spokesperson on each occasion to explain what actions of positive support may be expected for the future.

At the annual general meeting of the company on 30th March 1990, Sir James Scott-Hopkins MEP was unanimously elected as chairman.

Eric T. Rawlins

Whenever practical, and this was not usually so at evening talks, I kept the pink file of potential private investors and supporters available. It was a matter of some surprise to record the 131 new supporters during the library week; Paul Marland MP did not appear. Was his head just too firmly in the sand? A report by the Chartered Institute of Transport and the Department of Transport related to charging for car use in the cities. The secretary, Cecil Parkinson, said: "The theoretical case for road pricing is irrefutable." It seemed that London was likely to be the first; would the cities of Gloucester and Hereford develop alternatives to car use in time?

On the short horizon was our first annual general meeting, for which, as secretary, I was lumbered with all the hated 'administration', for which I am ill-suited and already swamped by day-by-day strategic/tactical matters! The date was fixed as Friday 30th March at the library. This venue was chosen as it was being 'insisted' upon in some quarters that *any* member of the public could attend! As company secretary, I was entirely against this; only founder subscribers and directors would be admitted. Directors were invited to put forward such items as they thought applicable to an AGM and I drew up a brief agenda. Unfortunately, both Paul Rynehart and Robert Michaelson were facing business pressures which needed their attention and would take both away from the Ross locality. With regret we accepted their resignations. Richard Eagle, Betty Gartside and myself offered ourselves for re-election, as did Doug Woodman by proxy. Drewe Lacey proposed the election of Sir James Scott-Hopkins as chairman, seconded by the secretary. Sir James expressed his goodwill and intention to do what he could to facilitate the aims of the company; he asked that we contact Tim Smith MP and asked for a list of interested venture capitalists.

Behind the scenes, Bob Michaelson had triggered the interest of Trafalgar House and this would be pursued when the business plan became available. Sir James indicated that: "assistance for the director acting also as company secretary must receive priority". I could not agree more – even in 1990 – but knew there was no cash spare to fund such help. We resolved that Thorne and Co., Chartered Accountants, Ross, would be our auditors, and I was grateful for the personal attention Peter Metcalfe gave to the embryo WVR organisation.

On 5th April 1990 the *Ross Gazette* carried the full report I had provided, via Martin Morris, upon the library week. This provoked a rather snide piece emanating from a 500-acre landowner, one Major Patrick Waller of Hadnock Court in the lower Wye Valley. He was obviously incensed that the WVR Company was able to attract Government finance, but failed to indicate to what extent his farm benefited from the same source. He made a great deal of the figure of '500,000' passengers, implying these would be *additional* to the existing tourism numbers, the facts being that this was the estimated *car-borne* numbers we would seek to divert to rail. The piece was spiced with emotive statements and the 'danger' of the 25kV overhead, heedless of the fact that Parliament in 1959 had laid down the standards! He even sought names and addresses to petition against the non-existent Bill! I considered this all to be a bit rich from a serving magistrate charged with applying common-good rather than vested-interest principles in this area.

At the end of the month Touche Ross forwarded a draft of their Business Planning Report. The conclusions and recommendations indicated an 'in excess of £34 million investment of high risk due to [its] innovative nature'. The need for high seat occupancy was basic and recommended that fares be 'increased in excess of inflation'. 'Should the present assumptions on passenger numbers prove accurate, the proposed business has the potential of becoming a successful operation with a healthy cash flow.' The 'unique characteristics of the business can be exploited' and 'a detailed market survey should be undertaken at the earliest opportunity'. An experienced project manager should be recruited to 'front and co-ordinate the project'. The most critical change was the Touche Ross adjustment of the later 1987 capital cost of £25.694m; to this 20% was added for contingencies, £5.14m, plus 20% for inflation to January 1990, £6.168m, making a total of

£37.002m. The most significant matter of how to obtain this £37 million was seen as £8m equity (shares), £24m loans (at 15% interest) and £5m in various grants (i.e. from Government). The latter sum of £5m was very low due to the fact that neither Touche Ross nor ourselves then knew of Circular 3/89 (actually produced in November 1989 but given very restricted circulation, e.g. to county councils expert at sitting on information). When this circular was read in conjunction with Section 56 of the Transport Act, 1968, it was evident that up to 50% capital grant was available via the Department of Transport.

Ignorance of this potential extra 45% capital grant, rather than a greater loan against interest repayments, meant that the profit and loss figures in the Business Plan (pages 25/6) did not move into profit until Year 5 (over half a million pounds) and Year 6 (£1.5 million) pre tax. Despite this unfortunate omission, the Business Plan could be summed-up as an endorsement of the practical nature of the scheme to operate a high-quality, all-year-round service, subsidised by tourism/leisure revenue income of approximately 60%, and to operate at a profit. The correspondence between Nicholas Howard, Touche Ross, and me indicates just how great was the amount of work necessary to produce such a unique report in a difficult and much specialised area.

In April 1990 we obtained a safety film from the Swiss Federal Railways, where, of course, overhead electrification is standard. April 14th also saw an excellent letter from Mr W. Bayliss of Bromsash, reacting to the Major Waller piece; it is comprehensive and worthy of reproducing:

> The Editor
> *Ross Gazette*
>
> **RAIL LINK DESIRABLE**
>
> I was most disappointed to read the comments of Major P. Waller with reference to the proposed Wye Valley Railway. This scheme is most desirable as a

public service and requires all the encouragement it can get so that we can bring South Herefordshire into the 21st century.

For economy and 'pollution-free' transport and to service the majority of the public, the scheme must proceed forthwith. Although the scheme may require some support in the initial stages, landowners should remember that farmers are being paid subsidies to produce surplus food, so why not divert some of this money to projects such as the Wye Valley Railway, which is of benefit to all?

The motorcar is pricing itself beyond the means of many (particularly the less well-off) and therefore a rail link to the local cities and further afield would be a tremendous asset. It would also bring relief to road congestion and could easily develop into an economic means of commuter transport. With regard to the point made referring to 'trains running through gardens', this would have little impact since the type of locomotion is quiet and environmentally acceptable.

As to houses which have been built on the railway line-of-route, the blame lies entirely on the planning committee involved for giving permission, and therefore compensation would be forthcoming to the householders concerned.

Self-interests must not be allowed to destroy this project and a much more publicly spirited approach should be made.

W. Bayliss

The Automobile Association came up with figures indicating that the average motorist spent £1,240 on his car per year; this would, indeed, provide 12,400 miles of family travel on the WVR, even at a premium rate of 10p per mile! Major Waller had been busy writing letters again, this time to the *Monmouthshire Beacon*;

this drew an effective response from a Mr D.F. Stroud of Osbaston, Monmouth, which is reproduced from the 20th April 1990 edition:

> The Editor
> *Monmouthshire Beacon*
>
> With reference to Patrick Waller's letter in last week's *Beacon*, probably a number of people first saw the scheme displayed at Monmouth Regatta some years ago and since then have read accounts of progress made from time to time. If the promoters have indeed managed to lay their hands on a fair amount of tax-payers' money, then it must be because the nature of the scheme qualifies for such, and engineering schemes generally are harder to attract grants or funds than some others.
>
> As far as the operating voltage is concerned, this is general throughout the British Rail overhead network. Many have regretted the Beeching/Marples reign, probably none more than Monmouth, the last town to be connected to the mainline system and among the first to lose this useful link. Personally, I believe all those concerned with the scheme deserve as much encouragement as they can get in their efforts to divert tourist and other traffic from the roads, the intensity of which otherwise can only increase with time.
>
> D. F. Stroud

Meanwhile, bus transport in the Forest of Dean area had sunk to a very low level, with the *Forest of Dean Review* complaining about the 'mass reduction in the available services' and the fact that 'many communities are now cut off completely'. 'No one wants to be a driver,' said Mr Bill Neen of Stagecoach/Red and White. 'We do not know the answer,' exclaimed the *Review* editorial.

Looking for a moment into the future, by August 1995 *The Times* would be quoting statistics that bus fares had risen by 17% and passenger numbers had fallen by 27% – leaving revenue 10% lower. Even with ancient, many-handed vehicles up to 18 years old, the industry was not only unpopular with passengers but also with drivers who, since 1986, had seen their 'real pay fall by an average of 12%'. Small wonder that the clever-devil planners' (on car allowances!) ideas that buses could easily replace trains even when they create a monopoly had proved to be a delusion.

Back to 1990. I gave a talk to PROBUS (the Professional and Business people of Ross) on 23rd April; this went well. But on 27th Drewe Lacey received a most welcome invitation from Gregory Lowden for him and me to give a presentation to Trafalgar House, Berkeley Square, London on 1st May 1990. I contrived a breakdown, totalling £185,000, which covered the cost of a Local Private Act of Parliament, firming up the route by Cass Hayward, compiling a register of line-of-route landowners and an environmental statement. Drewe drove us to London and we circled Berkely Square some four times before finding a space to park. We met Gregory in the Trafalgar House boardroom, all plush upholstery, crystal chandeliers and the necessary hardware to show the ITV News video. All went really well, but there was apprehension in the air regarding how long the Thatcher bubble of prosperity was going to last. Drewe had another engagement in town and I returned to Gloucester by InterCity – a most relaxing close to a most hectic day.

On 12th June 1990 Drewe Lacey wrote to me to the effect that he had had further discussions with Gregory Lowden and had put him in touch with Nick Howard of Touche Ross. We had a problem of a letter addressed to me which had not been passed on by Inpro House from the Rural Development Commission, where we experienced a most involved process with £25k at stake. This was to be part of an entirely fruitless correspondence with one Roger Grimley, who represented the RDC at Malvern.

On 10th May I was asked to give an 'open' talk at the Hereford Railway Club; the audience included several actual or retired railwaymen and it was good to find understanding of the technical matters. The 18th May saw me speaking at another 'open' meeting, this time to the Monmouth Association; the appearance of a tiny proportion of disgruntled people from outside the town was a nuisance to Keith Kissack, the able chairman. I also met Mr Hopton of the Country Landowners Association; he seemed a constructive person within his brief.

The fourth board meeting, chaired by Sir John Scott-Hopkins, took place at Inpro House on 25th May 1990. There was a packed agenda of 19 items in various stages of balls-in-the-air, and it was resolved that Drewe Lacey, who held the stock of business plans, would send copies to interested venture capitalists.

On the Euro mainland stage, the 10th May newsletter announced 'aid for rural regions' as a five-year plan 1989–1993 in what would be applied to 'Rural Areas in Decline' – the Objective 5b assistance. But it would be *years* before any cash materialised anywhere in the Ross area.

Also, in the busy month of May, I noted that Mr R. Henderson, the builder who had converted the Forest View Cottage at Symonds Yat, was continuing to expand its size, this time for 'new living quarters'. This was quite close to the tunnel exit, near the Royal Hotel, and the development was watched with interest. Undoubtedly, it was the sort of place which would be most attractive to rail buffs wishing to photograph trains at the new Symonds Yat halt on the site of the old GWR station. Coincidentally, the Forestry Commission announced the largest scheme in Great Britain up at the top of the Yat rock, where over 400,000 visitors per year arrive, mostly by car. Such new car parking areas were destroying the ambience of the beautiful place I had known before the War; to pay for this sacrifice to the car, the charges for parking were raised from 20p to £1! Indeed, the peaceful days of arrival by train and walking up the shaded woodland path to the Yat rock had been forgotten – and would remain so until we got the WVR back!

Major Waller managed to get a distorted version of the happenings at the Monmouth Association meeting into the

Gloucester Citizen on 23rd May. A lady reporter, Jo Walmsley, quoted my reaction and referred to my confidence in the plan and that a million visitors per year would surely subsidise commuting and winter travel. I pointed out that Major Waller only held a small percentage of the land which was the original railway trackbed, and also that we had the backing of many landowners who respected the overall common good of the project. Major Waller said he planned to "stop the railway any way he could". In a repeat version in the *Ross Gazette*, he referred to 'demolition of homes, the felling of hundreds of mature trees etc.' He made no reference to the destruction of homes which Monmouth people told me Waller's father had caused by persuading the Secretary of Transport of the day to have the Ross to Monmouth dual carriageway diverted, at great engineering cost to the public purse, higher up the valley side, away from land he then owned.

But I already knew from experience in my own family in Worcestershire, where as yeomen farmers our land was foreclosed against loans granted in desperate times by the landowner. We had been warned that the backwoodsmen element would fight dirtily, covertly and as viciously as possible. Against this background I learned, with some apprehension, that the first business plan had been released to a private person on the grounds that he was considering being a founder shareholder in the company.

On 26th June 1990 came a letter from Sharpe Pritchard, Parliamentary Agents, Westminster, advising us that Sir Geoffrey Howe had announced in the House of Commons that the Private Bill route for authorising railways would 'in future be authorised by order'. 'This,' he said, 'will provide a more appropriate way of dealing with infrastructure projects in the modern age while protecting the interests of all those involved.' A consultation process was set in motion and the outcome would, eventually, become the Transport and Works Act, 1992. This new mechanism took the immediate pressure off the company to (i) fund and (ii) follow the old Local Bill process. Major Waller, yet again, went into print, misinterpreting the reasons for Sir Geoffrey Howe's changes, which were plainly to *facilitate* new rail in accordance with Government policy! Again, a very sensible letter from a Mr G. Rogers, dated 14th June 1990, put Major Waller back in his box; it is reproduced herewith:

> The Editor
> *Ross Gazette*
>
> I suppose it was inevitable once it was found that the Wye Valley Railway had a reasonable chance of becoming reality that the latter-day Luddites and other misguided and misinformed opponents would arise to try and throw a spanner in the works. That this time has now arrived has become clear from recent correspondence in the *Ross Gazette*. I am unable to understand the objections of these people. After all, there was a railway here before for many years and everybody accepted it. In fact, there were many objections, and rightly so, to its ultimate closure. Why should its proposed replacement not be welcomed as the reinstatement of an efficient and necessary means of transport in the area, which should never have been removed in the first place?
>
> I could understand the objections had a motorway been proposed, with the attendant continual noise, pollution, considerable loss of land, and environmental damage, but an electric railway is quite another matter. Nowhere near the amount of land would be required and it would create no pollution or environmental damage. Also, even if operated reasonably intensively, which at limited notice might result, it would be only spasmodic and entirely with acceptance levels. In fact, Major Waller's emotive comment (*Ross Gazette* May 24th) that 'those living nearby would have no peace and quiet' is entirely devoid of truth.
>
> In view of the present poor public transport in this area, this new railway is a necessity and would

> prove a great asset to the community. It would be a pity if the objections of a few individuals and councils should hinder its construction. As far as I am concerned, the sooner it is built the better.
>
> G. Rogers

A Mrs E. Burren of Longhope supported her husband against the railway because they had bought a piece of railway land 'in good faith' to extend their garden. I spoke to her on the telephone and wrote to her, pointing out the experience of a Ross lady who clearly enjoyed the presence of the rural railway. The Burrens, being outsiders in local parlance, as it had been put to me by other Longhope folk, had bought cheap national railway land with no planning permission for *any* other use, but, of course, purchased caveat emptor – let the buyer beware. The letter of 20th June 1990 is reproduced herewith:

> Mrs E. Burren
> Longhope
>
> Further to our telephone conversation, which I hope was as helpful to you as it was to me in discussing not only our immediate points of view but also seeing that in the perspective of maintaining the best possible environment despite the pressures of newcomers, congestion, pollution etc., we have more in common than otherwise.
>
> As we talked I was reminded of an article (copy attached), which appeared in the *Guardian* in 1959 and, I think, helped to save the railway for some years until technical bridge problems sealed its fate. I recall the local feeling up and down the line that Mrs O'Neill spoke for many and was certainly an inspiration to me that such a facility was worthy of reinstatement in modern form.

Mrs O'Neill tells in an extremely practical way that a local railway means so much more to the community, even when at the bottom of the garden, than being the quickest way from A to B. Indeed, it represents contact for many otherwise lonely people – especially in the dark days of winter – and I believe that lives have been saved by a driver missing the usual wave from a cottage window. This is no less valid today when so many breadwinners from this recognised area of low pay have to travel to work in order to pay the mortgage. No doubt Mrs O'Neill's children are all grown up, but with my equal opportunities attitude, do wonder whether her girls are among those who have approached me for a job on the line in due course!

In transport terms, time has moved full circle since the closure of the line; an infrastructure entirely dependent on the car/bus becomes more destructive than constructive (per Lake District) and in places like the Wye Valley AoONB and the Forest of Dean, the villages develop as dormitories/retirement areas for the towns. Problems of visits to hospitals in distant towns and lack of capability to drive etc. are already significant.

In the matter of visitors, the Forestry Commission say there are 700,000 per annum in that area alone – with 400,000 converging on Yat Rock. Only a railway can more widely disperse visitors to the less well-known attractions and have the capacity to meet the inevitable growth in numbers while providing a service for local residents, independent of road congestion. I feel, therefore, that a railway is not so much an intrusion but an integral part of rural life, perhaps even more beneficial today than in the past.

Eric T. Rawlins

By June 1990 the personal pressures on me were exceedingly great and after 38 public occasions, I sought a break from the series of covertly 'weighted' occasions, which were being organised in such a way as to make my continued appearances untenable. Hence, it was when such a meeting was called on 2nd July, for Weston under Penyard, that Drewe Lacey, for the first and last time, attended instead of me. Major Waller, many miles from his own territory, put in an appearance and the meeting was chaired by Richard Evans for the parish council. Drewe reported back to Sir James Scott-Hopkins and myself. Waller was allowed to repeat all his usual wild statements; Drewe put our case but was allowed only ten minutes to answer questions! Drewe stayed for 40 minutes "with a reasonable amount of applause much motivated by my courage in attending"; his notes pointed out our need for more financial support and market research to underwrite the feasibility of the project. However, when the *Ross Gazette* reported on 5th July 1990, it became plain to me that Major Patrick Waller JP had simply gone too far when he quoted the break-even point for the number of WVR passengers required per year. This information was *only* available from *one* source: the business plan – at least one copy of which I believed was in the hands of the opposition. This situation would be borne in mind. I was back again 'in harness' on the 10th July 1990, when I attended the Walford Parish Council 'open meeting'. No notes were taken and views were freely expressed, both for and against the renewal; at least there was no war dance by Major Waller or Mr Burren.

Back in mid June, involving Paul Marland MP, a meeting was arranged at Lydney in his constituency. Sir James Scott-Hopkins would attend also for WVR Ltd, and the occasion took place at 3.30 p.m., Friday 13th July 1990. For the record, it is necessary to reproduce my letter to Mr Marland of 14th June, as this spells out the restrictions upon the business plan and which he acknowledged on 19th June:

Paul Marland Esq. MP
House of Commons

Thank you for your letter of 12th June 1990 in which you confirm the above arrangements. I hope that Sir James and I will be present. I will bring the wall map we usually show, on 38 occasions since 1986, together with a copy of the engineering feasibility report available through the libraries' reference service since May 1987. The Touche Ross report 'Organisational and Funding Options' of September 1988 will also be to hand.

The Business Planning Report of April 1990 is a document restricted by contract to those approved by Touche Ross; such consideration by venture capitalists is now in process. Its status is, therefore, of absolute commercial confidentiality currently, and it is critical to this company that detail is not released at this meeting to a person who has publicly declared his intention to 'stop this railway any way he could'. I have today suggested to Sir James that if you have some specific matters in this area to raise that we do so privately outside the meeting.

A further area where no depth of detail can be given is that of the level of compensation for line-of-route bought back. This is because although we monitor British Rail/Dept of Transport policy in this area – including Kent – we are concerned to create no precedents and give no promises which may simply not be compatible to the general practice for railway developments at a later date.

I trust that fate will allow us to meet on this occasion!

Eric T. Rawlins

Present on the 13th July was Paul Marland alone of the MPs; he said he had invited Sir John Stradling-Thomas and Colin Shepherd, but they did not appear. The opposition group comprised Major Waller, Mr Burren, Mr J. Silver and Mr P. Clarke, the latter three apparently from the Longhope area. Sir James sat at one side of a long table; Marland and Co. at one end and I alongside our large-scale map and a set of the earlier consultancy reports. I began by setting out the overall project but felt I was dealing with closed minds, disinterested in the common-good purpose which might in any way clash with their individual interests. The matter of the Parliamentary Bill came up and Marland said he would "block it". Sir James shook his head and said, "No, you cannot." Mr Burren rose to his feet clutching what I guessed was a copy of the business plan!

Despite my warning in my letter to Marland, the 'gang' were clearly going to ignore it. Striking a pose, Burren began to read out some parts of the report. "Just a minute," says I, "you would appear to be reading from a *restricted* document – the business plan – which is currently absolutely confidential in nature, as I have explained to Mr Marland. If you have a copy it must have been acquired by deception, which I remind you is a criminal offence under Section 15 of the Theft Act, 1968." Mr Burren ceased to speak and sat down; Waller, Silver and Clarke looked as though they wished the floor would open up under them.

Paul Marland got to his feet and started to read from a prepared statement, saying he was also representing Stradling-Thomas and Colin Shepherd. I interrupted and said I would wait to hear their own views from their own lips. Marland became increasingly obnoxious and after about ten minutes I decided I had heard enough. I stood up, thumped the table and said, "I have heard enough from you; it is *your* job to support your Government's policy on the renewal of railways and it is plain you do not understand that Empowerment Orders are being brought in to stop the long-winded nonsense of the Victorian railway Private Bills. This company respects your role to assist any of your constituents who feel unfairly treated in matters of compensation, but even that is subject to Government guidance. We expect you MPs *and* the county councils to strongly support the work of this small, private company. If you have nothing constructive to offer then I suggest we draw this meeting to a close." Silver and Clarke slipped away; I intercepted Marland at the door, shook him by the hand and said, "I was pleased to meet you and feel the meeting has cleared the air." As I dismantled and rolled up the map, Mr Burren sidled across and asked what he should do with the business plan. I said he should send it straight away to Tony Heaford, the Touche Ross partner at Bristol.

This meeting was supposed to be 'private', but this did not prevent Waller providing his version to the press. However, Mary (my long-suffering wife) was waiting in the car at Lydney some 30 yards from the meeting place – she said she heard me shouting and guessed that something in the nature of a rout of the opposition was in progress! It later came out that Paul Marland would have been a great deal better off had he invested in the WVR rather than being involved in one of Lloyds syndicates, which 'performed most poorly'; rumour had it that he faced an immediate bill of £150,000 for 1990, with a total up to half a million pounds. Would anyone in future trust his judgement, let alone 'leadership', in such an enterprise as the renewal of the Wye Valley Railway?

The *Western Mail* carried a fine, constructive article with a remarkably clear map on 26th July 1990, written by David Vickerman, their environmental correspondent. The *Daily Telegraph* seemed to listen to Major Waller and it carried a one-sided piece and a tale of woe about the *one* house at Weston under Penyard built on the site of the railway halt which served that parish. Its name, 'Beechings', says it all, reflecting the exploitation of a piece of cheap railway land and gambling on obtaining planning permission; the local residents were not amused. The *Telegraph* featured Major Waller sitting on the trackbed which skirts his 500-acre farm; he seemed quite unaware of the reaction I heard from those who saw it: didn't the Major understand how Mr and Mrs Average would feel as they guessed their own house and garden might fit 10,000 times into the Major's holding! Some more twisted and exaggerated comment emerged in the Chepstow Press, and I scotched the general nonsense with a letter dated 4th August 1990:

> WVR Limited
>
> The Editor
> *Chepstow News*
>
> May we take this opportunity to give your readers the facts upon this project, which bear little relationship to the 'figment of imagination' rubbish published in your edition of 2nd August 1990. I have spoken to Mr Marland but never referred to this proposal as a railway buff's dream. The project is in fact a soundly researched matter, using consultants of the same calibre as would British Rail if they were reinstating the lines, and is as follows:
>
> ENGINEERING FEASIBILITY: By Cass Hayward and Partners, Chepstow (consultants also to British Rail), funded by Dept of Employment and Tourism.
>
> ORGANISATION AND FUNDING OPTIONS: By Touche Ross International. Funded by Depts of Employment and Tourism, Trade and Industry, English Tourist Board and Hereford City Council.
>
> BUSINESS PLANNING REPORT: By Touche Ross International, managed by 3i Enterprise Support Ltd, funded by Dept of Trade and Industry and WVR Ltd.
>
> British venture capitalists are now considering the business plan and the Government is now making available capital grants to part-fund private sector

rail initiatives, also accepting the costs/benefits principle hitherto reserved to justify new roads.

A Local Private Bill is the correct legal procedure to obtain overall authority for a standard railway operation currently and the WVR would be worked by electric railcars necessary to provide across-the-platform access to the national network at Chepstow, Hereford and Gloucester. However, the Government has decided to alter the authorising procedure for railways and it is expected that the necessary legislation will be effected towards the end of this year.

We see this project essentially as a dual-purpose facility: a renewal of the transportation infrastructure both for local day-to-day use and also for tourism. Growing population is increasing the pollution and congestion situation on the roads, particularly between the Forest, Ross and Gloucester. Reports of the area emphasise the need to distribute tourists throughout the Area of Outstanding Natural Beauty, so spreading the economic benefits and reducing the pressure upon such places as Tintern and Symonds Yat.

If this proposal is successful it will guarantee the survival of the Wye Valley as we know it now into the new century. Doing nothing will ensure its piecemeal destruction; we are certain your readers are able to make up their own minds as to the benefits the railway will bring.

Eric T. Rawlins
Company Secretary

Most sadly, I was advised by Betty Gartside of the death of Doug Woodman, which had occurred on 13th July while I was battling with Paul Marland and Co. I attended a packed memorial service at Goodrich Church for Doug; he was a typical ex-RAF type;

we spoke the same language, and only his love for golf I did not share! He is still missed as I write now in 1996.

On 17th August 1990 the supportive Monmouth Town Council asked that we firm up the route in the Wyesham area. I advised them that as long ago as 1988 it was suggested that Gwent CC commission Cass Hayward to do the necessary work. I had to point out that we were now in a "recession situation nationally", with exceedingly high interest rates particularly hitting the civil engineering industry as well as all the implications of the Gulf crisis. However, I concluded that it was "surely not asking too much for a county council to put up a little finance if your members (i.e. town councillors) feel there is a specific need". Needless to say, Gwent CC, despite its statutory responsibility for transportation, looked the other way.

A leader in the *Forest of Dean Review* of 17th August 1990 tried to pour oil upon the way feelings were being fanned into overheating with respect to the railway. Nevertheless, they doubted whether the finance could be raised and said: 'if the railway is ever built we will eat our hats in public'. I look forward to that day!

On Thursday 2nd August 1990 BBC TV Wales made a film with myself at Tintern Station, with a crowd of visitors lining the platform and pretending to be waiting for the train. They also filmed our model railcar with the 'overhead' wiring, demonstrating just how inconspicuous this was against the normal riverside background. Although the Gwent CC spends some money keeping the station in reasonable order, it remains a half-and-half display, with two items of immobile coaching stock. Inevitably, both children and adults are disappointed to see that no trains run in such a superb setting – yet another failure for the Wye Valley AoONB Joint Advisory Committee, the body that loves to sit on its hands.

Trafalgar House was annoyed that Touche Ross had not provided cash flows and net present value as a means of measuring the worth of capital investment. Gregory Lowden of Trafalgar was most helpful and Touche Ross had indicated we might give them a first refusal option on the scheme in exchange for £10,000 to pay for the market research and the cost benefit analysis, the latter a Department of Transport requirement. An interesting proposal was made in August to set up holiday railway coaches on the Monmouth Troy Viaduct. Mr Stephen Weeks seemed confident of applying for £80,000 from the British Rail Property Board and the Railway Heritage Trust for the purpose. He was confident that the carriages, on one side of the dual trackbed, would be adequate for access, but I really could not see how such a viaduct could be 'secure and safe for children'. This viaduct originally served the route to Usk and Pontypool Road, so would be of no interest to WVR.

On 24th August 1990 the *Monmouthshire Beacon* published a letter from Mrs Valerie Adams of Wyesham, which put into perspective the jumping-up-and-down consternation which Major Waller generated every time he opened his mouth:

> The Editor
> *Monmouthshire Beacon*
>
> I was surprised to read that Councillor David Hill has told the Town Council that Wyesham people are worried about plans for the new Wye Valley Railway. My husband, son, daughter-in-law, parents and myself live in Wyesham and have heard very little of this enterprise.
>
> Councillor Hill could be right, but many of us would also welcome an environmentally friendly railway system to the town. We have dreadful bus connections to the major cities and this move must be welcomed at a time when rural transport as a whole is under decline. A large number of people still do not have their own transport for one reason or another, so this proposed railway could meet a great general need.
>
> Monmouth is not a town any longer just for the retired; it is a home of many young families and young people. To make the town more accessible will

> mean greater opportunities in terms of growth and development, perhaps leading to increased employment and prosperity. It will help young people to have a future in the town and surrounding areas.
>
> We need to know a lot more about this scheme before we can make a rational judgement. Is it fair to all to dismiss it out of hand at this early stage?

A very fair letter, but by this time I had given no less that 40 public talks, including five in Monmouth, one to the Association on 18th May 1990!

In the *Forest of Dean Review* the normally garrulous 'Sally Sunshine' piece deplored the attitude of Paul Marland MP regarding statutory authority for the line, i.e. for him to 'be on the committee and not let it through'. However, this referred to the Bill we would not now pursue since it was the old process. 'What,' said Sally, 'sort of democracy is that? Since when did Mr Marland appoint committees and how can he speak on behalf of this particular one which will not sit for months yet, if ever at all?'

On 10th September 1990 I addressed the Hereford Electric Society; this went well, as far as I can recall, being somewhat punch-drunk from so busy a year. A piece of vague nonsense from anonymous Gloucester CC officers appeared in the *Forest of Dean Review* and I batted back on 21st September 1990, as below:

> Wye Valley Railway Limited
> Ross-on-Wye
>
> The Editor
> *Forest of Dean Review*
>
> How interesting to hear Gloucestershire County Council officers concluding that the Wye Valley Railway project is 'beset with funding difficulties' and that the WVAoNB working party are complaining they have no feasibility analysis, business plan

or environmental statement. Since the WVJAC do not communicate with WVR Ltd, it is not possible to comment upon the basis of their conclusions.

However, the Engineering Feasibility Report recommending the renewal has been available through the library service since May 1987. The 1990 Business Plan is a commercially confidential report, restricted by contract to specific parties and under consideration by certain British venture capitalists. The Environmental Statement is a specialist independent consultancy matter, which, together with additional work by the engineering consultants, is planned for the future.

Obviously, if the WVJAC or any county council is concerned to have such work undertaken earlier, then WVR Ltd will be pleased to apply such funds as they supply. County councils have a role only in improving the transportation infrastructure, not in opposing those who are working to the same public benefit end. This company particularly resents *Review* editorial commentary that we have too few resources. We should have thought the record of successful research over the past four and a half years indicates that the basic requirement is brains before finance. *Every* enterprise of this magnitude needs to attract *outside* capital; no business starts with £37 million in the bank.

Some of your eagle-eyed readers might have noticed a tiny, one-inch-column announcement in the *Daily Telegraph* that Gloucestershire CC has launched its plans for the £165 million light railway link between Gloucester and Cheltenham. Compared with WVR Ltd, that council has ample resources both of staff and finance, but it too is 'seeking private backers for the 15-mile route'. A most relevant question is why with good roads between the two towns, plus

British Railways operating, is this project so necessary? Between Ross and Monmouth catchment area, transit to Gloucester is entirely by roads converging upon Over and entering the city in ever-increasing congestion.

What might we on the 'poor' side of the Severn expect of Paul Marland MP for 25% of the WVR line? Will he again threaten to go against his Government's policy of support for new rail by seeking to prevent statutory authority for the Gloucester–Cheltenham project? We hope the *Review* will be assiduous in seeking details of Gloucester County Council's feasibility and business planning studies; no doubt readers will be most interested to observe how much is made public. As a resident of Ross said yesterday to me, "I bet you're not getting any objections now for an electrified railway – everyone's talking about the £5 gallon of petrol by Christmas!" A sound observation from a representative of the silent majority, I feel.

Eric T. Rawlins
Company Secretary

On 17th October I drove to attend the Whitchurch and Symonds Yat Residents Association at their local hall; there were some 50 persons present who asked most intelligent questions. Sir James Scott-Hopkins was stated to be calling for an early public inquiry on the scheme and saying the scheme should be shelved unless £37 million could be raised by "next April". But by November 1990 the economy had virtually ground to a standstill; it was plain that *all* new rail schemes would be held up and that construction companies, although willing to work, would also be seriously strapped for funds. The WVR scheme was more advanced than most; we would ride out the storm that was affecting some 40 projects. The National Economic Development Office surveyed and found that 'hopes of funding by private enterprise are fading as recession bites'. Sir James' views needed to be considered in the light of the fact that, as an MEP, he could well be seeing how infrastructure railways were being rebuilt at a rapid rate even in the poorest places of the European mainland and was simply too optimistic that venture and Government resources in Britain were just awaiting to be tapped by a good railway scheme.

The autumn was extraordinarily busy, with Serena Rawlins marrying Haydn on 27th October. Then Mrs Maud Everall, war-time GWR guard on the Ross–Monmouth auto-train and my aunt, became ill and died peacefully on 4th November 1990. There were four deaths in the family within 12 months, with much of the subsequent matters resting with me.

We were contacted by Pieda, consultants for environmental assessments, market analyses and cost benefit appraisals, and also TerraQuest for map management, land references, notices to treat/enter and acquisition support etc. Both firms had familiarised themselves with the WVR scheme, but we were unable to fund these essential stages as yet. On the South Herefordshire District Council a request was received to protect the original route of the former Herefordshire and Gloucestershire canal. Planning officer, John Loynes, told the committee that restored sections of the 34-mile canal would act as a major tourist attraction.

The committee 'gave the protection sought'. Despite the Department of the Environment's planning guidance giving equal weighting to line-of-route protection for canals and railways, this was plainly not happening at SHDC. In fact, the WVR had to fight for every separate piecemeal development proposed on the line, whereas the canal scheme had 'blanket' protection. Was it that the restored railway would reduce the commuting car traffic, which no canal could handle and reduce the pollution, congestion, accidents and pressure for even more car parking? The matter would have to wait until the 9th January 1996, when I would represent the company at the public inquiry into the SHDC Local Plan.

The public occasions for 1990 concluded with two weeks

in the Ross Library and Information Centre – from 4th to 15th December. We put on a wide-ranging display showing the Avon scheme and various other light-rail development plans. It was well received and plainly the return of the railway would be welcomed by the vast majority of local people. What political party would not give its eye teeth for such a level of support?

CHAPTER 9

The Obfuscation Years: 1991 – 1992

As usual, the correspondence between Richard Eagle and me continued and by the New Year he had found a reference to a Gwent County Council report by their engineer and surveyor. It turned out that this 'in-depth study' had *excluded* the Wye Valley! It had investigated the feasibility of re-opening the Western Valley line. Mr Owen (the engineer) said: 're-opening the line to passenger traffic was viable, although the cost to the County Council could not be justified'. This curiously contradictory conclusion was what we expected from the mix of officers and members of the Gwent CC Department of Dirty Tricks!

Alun Hughes, chief executive, South Herefordshire District Council, wrote to the company, advising people that the council had been advised that *we* were compulsorily purchasing the land belonging to the individual to whom the letter was addressed. The letter said that the council would keep such persons advised and recommended that they seek legal advice. The specimen we received had been created by photocopying old council headed notepaper, top and bottom, with typed words in between and signed by a pretend 'Chief Administrator'. The addressee was in Cinderford and referred only to the 'Hereford–Ross Railway Line'. Alun Hughes asked if we could help.

I checked the four 'opposers' of the renewal held in our files, but could not match the typeface; I suggested a disclaimer in the local press, but do not think this was done. Nothing more was heard about this, but it was a warning that almost anything, however stupid, could be expected from even a tiny number of people whose stability might be in doubt.

The RDS (Railway Development Society) published a timely warning for developers not to under-engineer new schemes.

If trams were to be put in initially, the track and structure should be suitable for conversion to full rail standards. 'Such schemes should also be closely integrated with existing BR operations in the area and not seen in isolation. There should be plenty of interchange stations and, if possible, through ticketing.' This was, indeed, an endorsement of the strategy we were pursuing for WVR. Internationally, Los Angeles had calculated its car pollution as costing £14 billion per year in health damage; in Switzerland the Zurich tram system was doing well with a maximum of six minutes' passenger waiting time!

In the *Forest of Dean Review* of 22nd February 1991 WVR somehow became front-page news under a white on black banner headline: 'War boosts rail plan'. There was reference to the Gulf War and the 'fragility of the West's dependence on oil for transportation. We can prove that our new railway, with its overhead power, will provide quick, safe and comfortable travel for millions of tourists and locals – without any pollution. We expect to see our electrified rail up and running during this decade. It was possible that the scheme would not now require a special Parliamentary Bill, but could go ahead after a "massive" [insertion by *Revie*w] public inquiry. When trains begin to run, some people will kick themselves that they didn't try to get it started earlier.' Quite a good effort – rather spoilt by use of the worst photograph of me in circulation!

On 8th March 1991 we held the fifth board meeting of the company, because we had not met since May 1990, and we decided to 'open' it to our Founder Members. The attendance listed: Sir James Scott-Hopkins, Drewe Lacey, Malcolm Clivery, Dr Brian Smith, Dr Roderick Brown and Michael Pavlimby; Betty Gartside and Richard Eagle sent apologies. We formally recorded our appreciation of the role of Doug Woodman up to his death on 13th July 1990. I was asked to pursue with the Rural Development Commission, Malvern, funding for a cost benefit analysis, required by the Department of Transport as we pursued a 50% capital grant under Circular 3/89 to the S56 Transport Act, 1968.

The nationwide slump had now hit Trafalgar House and they suggested we seek further funding from the DTI or elsewhere; the failure of the economy was now so widespread. Drewe Lacey reported a negative response from venture capitalists; the City was reeling and we were hardly surprised. The so-called Investors in Industry, 3i Birmingham, were unsatisfactory towards us, being only interested in management buy-outs of existing operations.

Mrs Joan Woodman retained Doug's shares in the company and proposed that Malcolm Clivery, a civil works plant engineer, be elected a director. Most sadly, Sir James, at 70 years of age, announced his intention to resign from the board due to pressure on his time and the Euro travel etc. I wrote expressing our corporate regret, but putting forward, at Dr Brian Smith's request, a proposal for Sir James to remain as informal adviser to the company. He responded: "Of course, I shall be happy to act in that capacity."

The local talk of the day was the proposal for trams to link Gloucester and Cheltenham. Mr R. Taplin, an officer of Gloucestershire County Council, described the scheme at a Railway Development Society meeting on 23rd March 1991.

On 29th March 1991 a most peculiar leader appeared in the *Forest of Dean Review*. From the style of it – 'a dream conjured out of no realistic assessment by Eric Rawlins' – it seemed simply a letter from Major Waller which the editor had promoted to the leader column! It concluded: 'if he [meaning me] persists in pushing it, he will be in serious danger of becoming a figure of fun'. If this was so, thought I, it would be a difficult task to wrest Major Waller from that position, which his arrogance combined with ignorance had already made his own.

On the Euro front, we had the Commission proposing that the rail infrastructure should be managed separately from services. This was the birth pang of what has become Railtrack in Britain. In a letter to Richard Eagle I reported that our list of supporters now contained 524 names and addresses. On 24th April 1991 we took the WVR display material to Hereford for the Tourism and Leisure Fair. The departure of Mrs Thatcher from the post of Prime Minister brought the usual crop of revelations, including the fact that her economic adviser, Sir Alan Walters, had failed in an attempt to get the Government to embark on a Beeching-style cut-back of the railway, regardless of the consequences, in the early 1980s. In mid May Major Waller and I had an exchange of letters in the *Ross Gazette*; an attempt to discredit me rather than the common-good purpose of the WVR company:

The Editor
Ross Gazette

Your report in your May 9th edition is disturbing. Sir James Scott-Hopkins gave an assurance last summer at a meeting with Paul Marland MP that if the money for the Parliamentary Bill was not available by Easter 1991, the whole project would be abandoned.

In his recent letter to me, telling me that he was resigning, he says 'the company still has no money'. This is good news, but still does not remove the blight that has been placed on properties along the line-of-route. The owners of these properties have indulged Mr Rawlins in his hobby for long enough. They have suffered financially, and the issue has even formed a major part of the election address of a recently elected Monmouth councillor.

Would it be too much to ask that Mr Drewe Lacey, the vice-chairman of the company, should do the honourable thing and announce the abandonment of the project, and that Mr Rawlins should confine his activities to his attic train set?

Patrick Waller

The Editor
Ross Gazette

Mr Waller holds the public position of chairman of the Ross Magistrates; I am, therefore, surprised that such a person has descended to what amounts to an attempt to discredit me as an individual. If this renewal was in British Rail's hands, would he engage in personal attacks on the chief executive and what he may or may not keep in his attic? Although I have no doubt that a fine model railway could be installed in the attics of Hadnock Court, I'm afraid *my* attic is too small even to stand upright in, let alone for a model railway layout!

I don't know what Mr Waller is referring to when he mentions some councillor at Monmouth apparently opposing the renewal; someone, somewhere will always oppose improvements. Perhaps the upturning of the Tory status quo in Monmouth indicates that *most* residents are *not* happy with its isolation and road congestion. The Wye Valley Railway Company will continue to follow the correct procedures towards the reinstatement of the railway and the Government requirement for the cost benefit analysis takes priority over the Bill process, about which the Government has not made up its mind.

Any undertaking Sir James Scott-Hopkins might have given to Mr Paul Marland about the Bill cost has been overtaken by the need for the cost benefit analysis, which the Government now sees applicable to rail instead of roads only as previously the case. It may be overlooked by Mr Waller that since we met Paul Marland there has been the Gulf War and a severe recession, which has caused most schemes requiring substantial capital to be deferred. Meanwhile, we proceed to add to the research stages.

In August and September 1990 the company had correspondence with Monmouth Town Council regarding the firming up of the line-of-route in the Monmouth area; we explained that this would be undertaken by our consulting engineers, who drew up the original Engineering Feasibility Report, in accordance with whatever authorisation procedure preliminaries the Government institutes. In the meantime, if Gwent County Council wishes to fund particular matters we would effect this immediately; the company had NO RESPONSE to this initiative.

The benefits of this renewal with electrical rail-cars to reduce pollution, enable access to the Wye Valley in a non-destructive way and bring economic and social benefits to hundreds of local people seems something Mr Waller can NO LONGER PUBLICLY ATTACK – so he is reduced to implying I am just a railway enthusiast. But the record over the past five years demonstrates my competence to manage this project and to do so without personal invective.

Eric T. Rawlins

The second annual general meeting of the company was held at Inpro House, Ross on 24th May 1991. Present were Dr R. Brown, Drewe Lacey, Richard Eagle, Malcolm Clivery and me. The usual process was followed and it was noted that the Euro Commission had changed its mind and would allow the UK Government to make grants under S 7/8 of the Industrial Development Act, 1982. As secretary, I was asked to seek £10,000 from Trafalgar House as working capital, but which would give them a first call option for corporate action per Touche Ross's advice. Our press release reflected 'the continued recession and the Gulf War, which, together, had created an almost sterile climate for substantial investments such as the Wye Valley Railway rein-statement requires'. The release referred also to the House of

Lords Committee of December 1990, which required a cost benefit analysis for all railway infrastructure investment and which we hoped could be completed by the time the Government had reformed the old Private Bill procedure for rail authorisation. At the AGM the board commended my work since 1986, and concluded that had this complex public service work been undertaken by a multi-discipline team, the bill would have reached at least half a million pounds to date. This press release was printed in full in the *Ross Gazette* and attracted no opposition.

On the Eurotunnel front, it was announced that drivers would be expected to maintain trains and look after passengers etc.! ASLEF jumped up and down, claiming that drivers were an 'elite', but Eurotunnel pointed out the need to avoid boredom. This was close to the philosophy of the WVR as a short-haul operation. London Transport, meanwhile, were assessing the implications of the new Croydon Tramway, for which they found 80% of the residents on the 18-mile route had signified their approval. In Ross, the Monmouth line, between Tudorville House, was cleaned up and named as Betzdorf walk – a town-twinning move. The WVR would need to recreate the cutting at this point in order to pass under the Walford Road, but the halt nearby might be called Betzdorf *if* that is what the local people agreed.

On 29th May 1991 I wrote a letter to *The Times*, but am unsure whether or not it was actually published. However, I will reproduce it now because the contents, if applied, could have guided the approaching privatisation of British Rail:

> The Editor
> *The Times*
>
> **From the mouth of an old iron horse**
>
> As one of the few who once worked in the rolling stock department of the last superintendent of the line, Great Western Railway, in 1947, I bridge the gap

by being also an executive director of a company which today seeks to be part of Mr Rifkind's railway renaissance. The GWR working timetable of that time is seven inches (175 millimetres) thick, which is some indication of what is involved in a properly integrated railway where the express passenger trains (InterCity today) directly connect to the feeder lines which serve the rural perimeters, tourist attractions etc. It would, of course, be quite impracticable to run trains owned by outsiders other than upon the 'paths' laid down by the operating company. Note that this does not prevent a government owning the tracks and civil works, ensuring that development is maintained year by year as it does with the roads.

Forget integration with bus services; buses will attempt some degree of co-operation with associated coach services, but not otherwise, as the past 80 years have shown. It follows that InterCity services must provide connections, both outward and return, with the feeder lines, and this can *only* be effected if both are under the same management. The biggest mistake of nationalisation of the railways in 1948 was that it was so huge a combination that only regarding it as an 'army' was the inevitable conclusion. The attempt to run it by this means simply destroyed the last vestiges of individuality and company loyalty, which had just survived the 2nd World War, by imposing standardisation by certain 'old company' officers upon their previous competitors.

It was the 1923 grouping which created the Big Four, GWR, LMSR, LNER and SR. Whether by accident or design, these divisions represented four workable units in geographical and personnel terms; there are distinct limits to what could then or now be actually MANAGED, rather than be allowed to bump along just somehow. Remember how Wales was largely absorbed by the GWR, Scotland by the LMS and LNER, all three companies running into London, and by 1993 have this connection via the Tunnel to mainland Europe. No attempt should be made to separate Welsh or Scottish regions, which would only wither away.

The administrative model for the railways has already been proved by local government re-organisations in London, where small boroughs were combined; for example, the 'rich' end of South London – Mrs Thatcher's Dulwich – was joined to 'poor' Bermondsey to form the London Borough of Southwark. In railway terms, this means that profitable InterCity should be integrated on the Big Four grouping principle with regional feeder lines much more intensively marketed than at present within the appropriate group. This is the balanced and *only* way to run operations which will actually benefit the customer, whether freight or passenger.

The Wye Valley Railway Company seeks to renew 48 miles of line linking Hereford–Ross–Gloucester and Ross–Monmouth–Chepstow with modern British Rail compatible electric railcars with cross-platform access to the National network at Gloucester, Hereford and Chepstow. Since 1986, engineering feasibility, organisational and financial options and business plan reports have been produced. In accordance with the Government's requirements under Section 56 of the Transport Act, 1968, the Department of Transport's Circular 3/89 and the House of Lords Committee of December 1990, we are now seeking funding for the cost benefit analysis which is to be applied to all railway infrastructure investment.

Sadly, a major construction company, which had approached us as a potential consortium member, recently had to withdraw due to the recession.

> It is now quite essential that the Government does provide up to 50% capital under S56 Transport Act, 1968, so that Mr Rifkind's attention may bear fruit by a mixture of public and private capital ploughed into neglected infrastructure which can alone absorb mainland Europeans and local car users by their thousands across the country. By ensuring that new railways are electrified from the start, the Government has a double-barrelled weapon which provides both a high quality alternative to road use and reduces pollution at the same time.
>
> Eric T. Rawlins
> Company Secretary

I wonder even now whether or not this letter got through to Cabinet level, as I believe Mr Major liked the Big Four option but would be overruled by a voracious Cabinet.

A letter from Richard Eagle spoke encouragingly of the prospects of a halt down the Lower Wye Valley, at Lady Park and Biblins, with siding space for timber. An organisation called Gloucester Railway Limited caused us some work and diversion since it was proposing that WVR ran via Newent into Gloucester! We turned all this down, unless the Department of Transport could be persuaded to fund a feasibility study, initially, which I knew could cost £400 per day plus VAT.

I had to deal with another approach by Monmouth Town Council in June 1991, owing to agitation by certain Wyesham residents. I referred them to an attempt in 1988 to get Gwent County Council, so adept at examining transport issues *elsewhere* in the county, to fund our consulting engineers to firm up this section of the route. We quoted the Transport Secretary, Malcolm Rifkind, saying, 'most transport decisions are difficult and each one is bound to displease one section of the community or another.'. I added, 'We seek to serve the general public good no less than do your members'. There was no response.

But nemesis, in the form of David Hunt, Welsh Secretary, was nearby and the *Daily Telegraph* recorded 'the break up of the great rural monoliths', including Gwent County Council; never was such a fate more deserved, but it would take five years to execute the sentence! In the talk I gave at Ross Carnival on 2nd August 1991, actually held in the Larruperz Centre, some 40 people were present and it's worth recording the flavour of the time. John Prescott, then Labour's Transport spokesperson, said Mr Rifkind's Tory rail proposals were 'a massive conversion, greater than that of St Paul on the road to Damascus'. I made the point that Mr Parkinson's attitude represented the final fling of the 'roads only' mentality; Mr Channon had applied some new thinking, which hopefully Mr Rifkind may develop before he too gets shuffled around the Cabinet lest he begin to understand what he is doing! I mentioned the great advantage to professional people using the WVR in that someone who charges himself out at £60 per hour and who drives himself loses the half-hour's average time he might usefully use writing and reading on the train.

Preceding my talk was that of the Rev. David Tipper, who also showed some slides of the Ross railways in operation. David, in another life, had been a fireman on the GWR, so with me as an ex-Great Western rolling stock man we represented a knowledgeable duo. The chairman of the Ross Conservatives treated me to an English ale, which went down exceedingly well! In the *Daily Telegraph* David Watkinson, BR's director of employee relationships, was extolling the benefits of their 22 lady train drivers. He saw them increasing to 50 in the near future, with their 'cool heads, manual dexterity, lower absenteeism and more flexible attitudes becoming the heart of a new corps of professional, salaried drivers free of old headaches such as overtime wrangles'. He forbore to mention the perpetual thorn in his flesh – the ASLEF Union. How closely his basic philosophy underpins our views on the WVR, but we see the flexibility embracing other 'star-rated' functions beneficial both to the company and the staff.

In August/September 1991 the South Herefordshire District Council Planning Area Subcommittee (East), at Ray Smith's request, hid behind closed doors from press and public. This was to consider what to do about a foolish idea to allow the Salvation Army Housing Association to build on the old Cawdor Market Site, Ross, which was a concrete skim over a waste dump. This was an area regularly flooded and so the National Rivers Authority refused consent. The matter was solved secretly by allowing the project to be set back into and onto the line of the railway route Ross to Hereford. I photographed the outcome of the building, which proceeded in part-flooded conditions. This is an example where, despite the theoretical openness, authorities continue to operate behind the backs of press and public. The members concerned deserve the maximum possible condemnation, especially when the chickens come home to roost.

The bad news on the London front was of a change of personnel at Trafalgar House and a response reflecting the 'current economic climate', due to which they could not invest in WVR at that time. So the Thatcher bubble for us and so many burst. I had a telephone call from the DTI saying that they were unable to help with the cost benefit analysis, despite my personal guarantee for £3,000 being the WVR share of the consultancy. The Department regretted that the Government had stopped funding feasibility work. I wrote advising Richard Eagle of the situation, adding that this stop on funding was 'presumably on the grounds it could lead to more jobs!' An absolute reversal of the policy of the Government in the 1930s had been applied to counter that slump!

I responded to two students, one at Longhope, the other at Coleford, doing A-level projects on the WVR renewal; nice to note teachers and young people were so aware. Meanwhile, we would seek to survive in an era where businesses were going bankrupt at 50 per day – we should concentrate on staying 'in the black'.

On 7th October 1991 the *Daily Telegraph* carried more detail of the Stephen Weekes/Monmouth Trust idea to put a static train on the Monmouth Troy Viaduct for holiday lets. It was estimated to cost £150,000, including 'cottages', i.e. carriages, 'in the livery of the old Wye Valley Railway Company'. The latter probably meant GWR colours. In an application to the Monmouth District Council, Mr Weekes ingeniously claimed that: 'It is not a change of use because the viaducts were built to carry trains'. We were not contacted at all and the matter apparently 'died', most likely of lack of finance and, as earlier mentioned, the practical difficulties connected with child safety, emergency access, evacuation etc.

On 9th October Malcolm Rifkind, Transport Secretary, said, ahead of privatisation, that BR should respond positively to private sector traffic proposals to allow private operators to use their own locomotives *and* crews. He said: "we must remove any unnecessary legal restrictions or antiquated rules." At long last the BR/trade union implacable autocracies were being addressed. On 24th October 1991 the *Ross Gazette* published a letter from me setting out the costs to the community of death on the local roads compared with the costs of renewing the WVR. This put the boot into the Hereford and Worcester County Council for setting aside its statutory responsibility for transport development etc. Inevitably, an obnoxious response appeared from Mr Waller, which is reproduced now with my letter in order that his lack of objective argument may be plain:

> The Editor
> *Ross Gazette*
>
> I am sure your readers were both saddened and exasperated to note that there were 4,078 deaths and injuries on the county roads last year. These tragedies being calculated to have cost the community £74.2 million in just one year!
>
> This project, to renew with electric railcars 48 miles of line through three county council areas, would cost HALF that amount at £37 million (1990 Touche Ross Business Plan) and would be permanently

advantageous. Each death on the roads costs the community £670,000, and if the new railway service only prevented ten deaths per year, then £6.7 million would be saved; or, over six years, £40.2 million compared with the new rail cost of £37 million.

How minimal, in the light of Hereford and Worcester County Council's statutory responsibility to improve the infrastructure, are the minor road improvements, which in no way address the terrible price road travel today exacts. In Britain we already have TWICE the traffic density of West Germany; THREE times that of France – do our politicians and transport 'experts' suffer from the same condition?

Had the County Council subscribed to our Business Plan they would know that for bus equivalent fares and 60% tourism revenue we can not only meet all interest charges on capital but also operate local services all the year round at a substantial profit. Despite recession, this project for the overall benefit of the community continues, but the very obvious cost benefit of the railway has to be quantified in the application for 50% capital grant under S56 Transport Act, 1968. As with all Government hurdles, we are required to employ consultants to compile a cost benefit analysis and there is just time for the County Council to catch the train this time by offering an appropriate contribution and buy into some objective research.

Perhaps your readers will wish to ensure that the Herefordshire infrastructure needs now and for the new century are not neglected.

Eric T. Rawlins
Company Secretary

The Editor
Ross Gazette

TOY TRAINS

Mr Rawlins in his letter last week asked people to put pressure on the County Council to fund his company's cost benefit analysis. Let us hope that the County Council will follow Gwent's example and give a firm 'no' to this impertinent demand. His company should pay for this work from its own resources. It is hard to reconcile this apparent poverty with his optimistic remarks about cost and profitability. Those interested would do well to count how many shares have been sold and who the chairman of the company is.

This divisive and destructive scheme has already been vigorously rejected by those on the line-of--route. As I have said previously, it is high time Mr Rawlins went back to the toy trains in his attic.

Patrick Waller

Unfortunately, the saga of the Ross Cattle Market housing scheme was raised again and the WVR letter to the South Herefordshire District Council of 25th October 1991 describes the situation:

The Planning Officer
South Herefordshire District Council

911314PF Salvation Army Housing Association

We thank you for the notice of the above application. We note the essence of this revision of 91067PF is that the original application had FAILED to take into account common knowledge that the site has always been liable to flooding and a reputed rubbish tip. No doubt members will wish to know whether or not it has been fully surveyed to ascertain the flood, settlement, methane etc. risks.

Now that the National River Authority has indicated an official flood-line, we are faced with an Application proposing the ENTIRE DESTRUCTION of the railway embankment and Cawdor Arch per drawing 6985/SK2. Even this drastic solution could only be possible by cutting a cliff into the hillside, extending substantially BELOW the track level on the embankment and directly under the site of yet another building scheme upon the allotments!

The sketch (not reproduced here) indicates (by a side elevation) that it is difficult to imagine a less desirable location in which to live – even without wading through winter floodwater. Members will wish to know that the Government may instruct British Rail NOT to sell off lines piecemeal, which other enterprises can re-open for off-road transit.

There is NO ALTERNATIVE WHATSOEVER for the railway renewal between Ross and Hereford to bypass this embankment and the elevation to the station at Fiveways. We cannot guarantee to form the consortium to reinstate the railway by any specific date, but despite the recession are actively pursuing the matter. What certainly can be foreseen, however, is that if the embankment is 'removed' and buildings erected thereon then they, in turn, will be 'removed' by compulsory purchase if necessary and the embankment restored as it is today. If it were not so serious it would be laughable to see so much of the site devoted to parking the disadvantaged residents' cars. Where are the JOBS to support this level of affluence? Provision of the railway would ensure residents could travel to work to Hereford, Gloucester, Monmouth etc. without incurring capital expenditure/HP debt.

As I write we have yet another incident of hideous deaths on the local roads; provision of modern rail means a cost benefit of high quality, SAFE transport into the new century. That is the pay-off for safeguarding the line-of-route today.

Eric T. Rawlins
Company Secretary

On 14th November 1991 the *Ross Gazette* reported how the matter had been 'pushed through'. The problem had been overcome by moving the scheme *across* the WVR line-of-route! Mrs Eunice Saunders and Edward Vines, councillors, agreed on the grounds that the site was 'a disgrace and we are responsible for it'. Councillors Marilyn Teague and Betty Smith opposed it on traffic grounds. Phil Cutter made a sideways reference to the WVR by saying 'the application should go ahead because the housing would be of more help to the community than other schemes'. So once again, the district councillors with no responsibility for transport were able to look no further than the end of their noses.

On 7th November I had attended a Herefordshire Business Support Day at the Town Hall, Hereford. I circulated to the Rural Development Commission stand, but it appeared interested only in finance, marketing and buildings – a curiously limited outlook. The Enterprise Agency and, more productively, the Hereford and Worcester Training and Enterprise Council suggested the WVR's need for a project manager. How I agreed, but who would fund him or her?

That month I contacted no less than ten large Japanese companies, which their London Trade department thought might be interested in the WVR. We await the outcome. In *The Times* of 7th November 1991 there appeared a letter from David Gillan, the director of the Railway Industry Association. It was so appropriate to the situation as to warrant reproduction here:

Railway Industry Association

The Editor
The Times

No light at end of railway tunnel.

There is another important angle to the adverse effects of recession on the 'railway renaissance' (report, October 29). Failure to find a way out of the financing impasse could not only condemn passengers to many more years of travelling in old, dirty, overcrowded trains; it could also condemn a successful sector of the British manufacturing industry just at the point when the European market is about to open up to competition. British industry has a history of success in the railway markets of the world. Australia, Brazil, China, Hong Kong, India, Korea, Malaysia, Morocco, New Zealand, Singapore, Thailand and many other countries all benefit from British-made railway equipment. It is ironic, to say the least, that the Metro system in Hong Kong, which so impressed the Prime Minister during his recent visit, was almost down to the last nut and bolt made in Britain, whilst the London Underground system is falling apart for want of sufficient investment.

Two years ago the future for the British Industry looked very promising. Most sectors had good order books and the forward plans for British Rail and London Underground held out the prospect of substantial business for the foreseeable future. The reality has been totally different and the industry now stands on the brink of a major crisis. Virtually no new rolling stock orders have been placed in the last two years and only one tender, for night coaches for the Channel Tunnel, is being adjudicated. We simply do not know when the next orders will be placed. And

> yet the need for replacing existing rolling stock, signalling and trackwork is apparent to all, quite apart from the strong case for new investment to provide much-needed new capacity.
>
> From a national viewpoint the situation is incomprehensible. Customers want a better rail service but can't get it; British Rail and London Underground want to provide a better service but can't afford it; and British manufacturers who have the capacity to build new trains are having to shed skilled people. Across Europe, on the other hand, the national railways, backed by supportive governments, are investing in new railways for the next century. WE HAVE NO COHERENT INVESTMENT PROGRAMME. The emphasis is on how the railways are organised, how social support should be minimised and in what form the railways should be privatised.
>
> Meanwhile, optimism in the railway manufacturing industry as measured in my Association's quarterly trends survey is LOWER than any time since the exercise was started in 1987. This contrasts markedly with the other recent surveys from the Association of British Chambers of Commerce, the Institute of Directors and the CBI, all of whom see some light at the end of the tunnel. In the railway industry it is difficult to know where the tunnel even begins.
>
> David Gillan (Director)
> Railway Industry Association

I have added upper case lettering above since this appears to be the essence of the matter – to which might be added the Government's complete lack of foresight in transport in general and the roads which are leading us into a cul-de-sac of congestion, pollution and the awful medical consequences of the latter.

On 20th November 1991 I represented the company at our first public inquiry against an appeal to build nine bungalows too near our reverse curve to Monmouth out of Ross at Hildersley. The district council was against this building, but on the general grounds that the 900 (!) new houses allowed up to the year 2000 had already been agreed to the extent of 896 – leaving only four to go! Actually, from the builder's drawing, our renewal embankment would affect only three gardens. While I went to the toilet my drawing vanished! However, I was congratulated by a parish councillor for putting over our case "brilliantly". The eventual outcome of the inspector's view, a lady, was that she had examined the site and concluded that the bungalows would not actually prevent our embankment being re-erected – so our exit to Monmouth would be safeguarded. I was happy about this, but basically such an awkward site was not suitable for dwellings due to traffic and at the time that this is written (August 1996) no building has taken place.

Early in December the *Forest Weekly News* was lamenting the lack of Assisted Area status for the Monmouth travel-to-work area. Needless to record, the WVR was not asked to contribute to this belated plea by Monmouth Borough Council who moaned about job losses over the past *seven* years.

The year closed with the broadsheets urging Mr Rifkind to sort out BR's problems; the *Daily Telegraph* leader of 6th December 1991 concluded: 'But if this or any government can give Britain a privatised rail service that works, it will earn the devoted gratitude of millions of rail passengers. Japan and Sweden have shown the way – cutting fares, transforming labour relations and staff morale, improving punctuality and, consequently, increasing passenger traffic by as much as 40%. We wish Mr Rifkind luck. He will need it.'

The Times of December 18th carried an authoritative article: 'How to run a railway' by Simon Jenkins, British Rail board member 1979–1990. He pointed at the autocracy prevailing in BR, which led to the smothering of any individuality – from bacon sandwich removal to the removal of local livery distinctions.

Make-work schemes for accountants were cited and I record below my view of the way ahead, briefly summarised:

> Privatisation, in transport as in public utilities, offers the provinces the chance to fight back. A public offer for Great Western or East Anglian or the flourishing LMS route would evince local interest and pride outside London. Railways would be freed of the incubus of government. Like private railways in Japan and Sweden, they would see a surge of efficiency and market share as they ceased to be organisation led and became customer led – witness the airlines and coaches. British Rail should be divided into its geographical components and put on the market. Then John Major could really look Mrs Thatcher in the eye.

The Manchester tram scheme was announced as ready in January 1992, and a Loughborough to Derby rail link was approved by Malcolm Rifkind, the Transport Secretary. The latter would be a joint effort by the Leicestershire and Derbyshire County Council and called the Ivanhoe Line, indicating what can be done where the will exists and the advantages understood by members and officers. A stimulating leader in *The Times* of 16th January 1992 was headlined 'Chocolate and Cream' and saw the privatisation best effected by the old regional boundaries with the land and a legal obligation to supply rail services, most importantly saying that: 'John Major is reportedly in favour of a regional break up. He should have the courage to stand out against the corporatist and Treasury interests that are now enveloping him in Downing Street.' Unfortunately, the idiots in the Cabinet prevailed and Railtrack nonsense followed the Swedish Banverket pattern, whereby the Government owned and subsidised the track base as *it* felt necessary. Considering our intention to supply buffet food in the WVR railcars, I was interested to see how regional was British Rail's experience. The Home Counties favoured prawn sandwiches with gin and tonic; in the north, bacon butties and cans of bitter; on the Newcastle route, jam sandwiches with brown ale; in Scotland, chocolate biscuits with vodka; in the south-west, pasties with cider! This confirmed our views that the Wye Valley Railway should evolve buffet snacks to suit commuters' tastes, developing to suit day and longer-term visitors towards local raspberries and ice cream and a special whiskey from the Brecon distillery etc. I had written to the Panel for Historical Engineering Works of the Institution of Civil Engineers following the Director General's plea for a 'greater degree of Government support for public transport systems' in *The Times*. The reply indicated interest in the WVR renewal, regretted they had no funds to help, but that they 'do support your initiative and would be interested to hear further of your progress'. They would be pleased to advise regarding the historical structures en route; I hoped that Mr Brunel would approve.

On 28th January 1992 *The Times* carried an announcement that British Railways were selling 50 viaducts at £1 each plus a dowry of about £70,000 each to maintain them into perpetuity. Monmouth Troy was not included; perhaps this ploy would save some viaducts where rail renewal was in hand. Also on 28th January, Malcolm Clivery and I attended a big meeting organised by the Hereford and Worcester Training and Enterprise Council at the Chase Hotel, Ross. A considerable cross-section of business people attended and I met Alan Curless, the chief executive of the TEC. We had asked for a grant for a cost benefit analysis, but on 9th March 1992 Alan Curless wrote advising that the council preferred to support a formal market research survey. I replied on the 16th March, explaining that Drewe Lacey's business at Inpro House had collapsed in the depression and so the mail was late reaching the company. However, I mentioned that we had always regarded the need for the cost benefit analysis (a DTI requirement) and market research essential in a somewhat chicken and egg relationship. The TEC would pay 50% of the survey cost up to £3,750.

On 25th to 29th February 1992 we put together an exhibition at Ross Library, which displayed items from my Railways in Miniature Museum, including Ross Station etc., and also the Wye Valley Railway project. Thus the flag was kept flying on both counts! On 9th April the *Ross Gazette* published a very sensible letter from a Mr D.J. Walters of Valley, Anglesey, which is reproduced below:

> The Editor
> *Ross Gazette*
>
> **Railways as Walkways**
>
> I see from a recent *Ross Gazette* that another part of the Ross–Monmouth rail line is to be turned into a walkway. Closed in 1965 and lain derelict since then, why the sudden urge to destroy what is left? Could it be that a far-sighted group of people are investigating re-opening it? The rebuilding (if it happens) could open parts of the Wye Valley to view that can only be seen from the comfort of a train.
>
> One has only to look at the success of other preserved railways in the country, and importantly the extra revenue earned by the businesses on the routes (Keighly Worth Valley, North York Moors, Severn Valley) as examples. The objectors to the scheme remind one of the Victorians who opposed railway building in the 19th century, and later insisted that a man with a red flag should walk in front of cars 'for fear of frightening the horses'.
>
> A number of members of preservation societies are not, in the words of objectors, 'people who play with trains', but former serving railwaymen and people prepared to do something to provide an attraction for the people to come to the area to spend money in the local businesses.
>
> D.J. Walters

My response followed and includes a reference to the company being advised to seek a formal market survey:

WVR Limited
Ross-on-Wye

The Editor
Ross Gazette

Mr Walters, of Anglesey, who wrote in the *Gazette* on 9th April 1992, is clearly a person with the insight to examine a situation objectively and reach conclusions in the light of wide knowledge of how other places are enjoying their reinstated railways. It is already true that over-walking is almost as significant a problem as over-motoring in many areas of outstanding natural beauty; in fact, a report to Gwent County Council referred to damage sustained in the lower Wye Valley.

Provision of a railway does provide an environmentally attractive alternative, which does not deny other forms of movement and, with electric railcars, is both quiet and non-polluting. It also relieves the problem of congestion and the wasting of even more land for car parking. However, the company has no objections to the line-of-route being used for walking at present. What is much more serious, to the point of national stupidity, is the fact that although county councils have the overall responsibility for transport development, it is the DISTRICT/BOROUGH councils which have the power to give piecemeal planning permission upon cheap ex-railway, national asset land. Every so often the Government realises its folly and indicates that 'ransom strips' bought to frustrate reinstatement will not be allowed. Although constructing and operating a standard railway would have powers of compulsory purchase within the statute, such a situation is better avoided by county councils raising objections to piecemeal planning applications. Indeed, if the county councils are not there to provide long-term vision in such crucial matters, what is their purpose?

What is urgently required is for national and local government to get their acts together. It was a funding requirement of the Department of Employment and Tourism in 1987 that the engineering feasibility study should cover reinstatement of the entire route Chepstow–Monmouth–Ross, Hereford–Ross–Gloucester, linking two cities and three towns with three interchange points with British Rail. The Touche Ross Business Plan, after meeting interest at 15% on capital loans, indicates a seven-figure profit by year six, revenue being calculated as 60% from tourism. Certainly, our research also bears out Mr Walters' views as to people coming to the area to spend money and I quote a detailed review just completed by independent businessmen which acknowledges the 'prospective economic and social benefits' the railway will bring.

In a time of recession, what would a joint Government/private sector renewal mean in job terms? For two years about 150 jobs including bridge fabrication locally; thereafter, 50 permanent jobs and substantial business spin-off. Currently, we have been advised to update our traffic estimates by a formal market research survey. We have obtained a quotation for this consultancy and hope to put this in hand shortly. The Wye Valley Railway is the best-researched, best prospect for new rail for the new century. We hope Mr Walters and all our local supporters approve.

Eric T. Rawlins
Company Secretary

The *Ross Gazette* of 16th April 1992 carried the news that the Civic Society had, after 12 years' work, succeeded in having the monument to Wallace Hall re-erected in the town. In 1821 he had founded what is now the solicitors' firm Shawcross and Co., but he is particularly remembered for his work for charities and the Ross Dispensary, which later became the Ross Cottage Hospital. He also led the meeting in 1849, which was late in terms of general railway development in Britain, but his efforts led to the building and opening of the Gloucester, Ross and Hereford railway in 1855. He lived from 1799 until 1860 and was certainly the John Kyrle of his day.

On 1st May 1992 Richard Eagle advised me of his monitoring of the privately run, enthusiast-operated Severn Valley, Dean Forest and West Somerset railways. This was an ongoing contribution since 1986 by Richard, because in planning a renewal it is essential to know the strengths and weaknesses of contemporary short-haul lines – even lacking the WVR advantage of commuter use.

He had already arranged to visit the Swanage Railway (fare 65p per mile with steam!) but this clashed with our arranged third annual general meeting on 15th May. This was rather a subdued affair since Drewe Lacey had resigned his directorship and Inpro House was no longer available to us. Betty Gartside kindly let us use the registered office, and she, Dr R.J. Brown, Malcolm Clivery and I attended. Dr Brown proposed that Malcolm be elected chairman and this, together with Richard's vote by proxy, was unanimously approved.

I proposed our acceptance of the £3,750 grant by Hereford and Worcester TEC for the market research, and this was agreed. I was asked to pursue with Trafalgar House, Wimpey, Regional Rail, Mitsui, Mitsubishi and ITOH the matter of each taking a £1,000 stake in this research. We also agreed, by press release, to invite contributions from local authorities or other corporate bodies. Betty Gartside reported the progress towards making a Wye Valley Railway flag, to Richard's design, and which we might fly at the carnival in August. The press release was moderately optimistic of our progress.

Gloucester County Council were promoting a 'light railway system' between Cheltenham and Gloucester, for which £125,000 was required for a 'detailed survey' with a capital cost of £165 million! As previously noted by me, it seemed to be quite insane, since the full size railway already operated! Surely, some updating of rolling stock with greater frequency was all that was needed?

Comparatively locally, Dean Forest Railway was seeking planning permission to re-open Lydney Town Station to 'bring prosperity to the town and surrounding area'. Good luck to them, said I. In early June 1992 British Rail InterCity announced 16 'vulnerable services' and that the 'connections to Worcester and Hereford would have to be withdrawn'. Another detriment to Herefordshire's already distressed area.

The Treasury clampdown on public investment (which they mis-describe as spending) was the work of Michael Portillo; this infected the latest Transport Secretary, John MacGregor, who told councils that they "must seek cheaper ways of moving passengers around than tramways and light railways". No one in the Cabinet, one assumes, had the sense to see that the billions paid out in unemployment and associated benefits could be corrected if people were put back to work on all the new rail/tram projects only awaiting Government investment priming to proceed!

After a fatal accident, British Rail introduced drug and alcohol testing; it was clear that cannabis was being smoked by drivers and this could well put passengers at risk by a moment's inattention to signals etc. I, not unused to the smell in an inner London borough, had smelt cannabis being smoked in Ross, and the WVR would certainly be wary of this insidious problem. We were aware that an Empowerment Order under the Transport and Works Act, 1992 would make operations under the influence of drugs or alcohol a criminal offence.

Meanwhile, Industry Minister, Tim Sainsbury, was reviewing the Cinderford and Ross travel-to-work area, which had 'intermediate area status'. Yet another attempt by the Tory Government to avoid its contribution to match anything granted by the European

Commission. *The Times*, in its 15th July 1992 leader, saw a silver lining in the national rail situation, quoting Mr MacGregor's hint 'that Railtrack might be broken up at some later date. Since it holds the key industrial assets of land, tracks, signals, workshops and termini, its privatisation and geographical fragmentation is the only privatisation which has any meaning'. However, even in 1996, Railtrack remains in one awful lump!

This month saw the completion of a new display board for the WVR at the instigation of Geoff Gartside, my brother-in-law. The *Ross Gazette* published a photograph of this and a couple of tourists from Fife on 23rd June 1992. Richard Eagle and I exchanged views upon the new system of rail authorisation which would replace the old local Private Bill process. The exact route would depend upon whether the WVR renewal would be classed as being of 'national significance'. If so, it would go initially to the Secretary of State and then to a Parliamentary Committee. More likely, our route would be via a public inquiry, hopefully persuading the minister of the day to sign an Empowerment Order.

I put some more finance into the WVR by funding two £500 share purchases for my daughters, but we still needed some £4,000 to fund the market survey.

Herefordshire Friends of the Earth were blaming the rising number of asthma attacks in the county upon high levels of nitrogen dioxide pollution. The Friends were critical of the £20 billion national roads programme and urged Colin Shepherd MP to join with them in protesting to Mr MacGregor. It is not recorded how Colin Shepherd reacted, but the Department of Transport was renamed by many as the 'Department of Roads', reflecting the enormous numbers of civil servants employed solely on roads compared with the few confined to railway matters in Marsham Street only. On 1st August 1992 we showed the new display board at the Riverside Carnival stand, and it received general approval.

On 6th August 1992 one E.D. Cutcliffe of Hoarwithy wrote about the proposed return of navigation to the Wye and described it as 'impractical' as the 'bring-back-the railway lobby'.

This gave me an opportunity to respond with a letter mentioning the recognition the WVR was receiving, as demonstrated by the Hereford and Worcester TEC grant of 50% for updated market research, plus other matters as set out below in the *Ross Gazette* of 13th August 1992:

WVR LTD
Ross-on-Wye

The Editor
Ross Gazette

Mr E.D. Cutcliff writing in the *Ross Gazette* of August 6th is perfectly entitled to his views upon navigation of the River Wye, but when referring to the reinstatement of the railway is out of his depth. The research undertaken by this company since 1987 has confirmed that it is indeed 'practical' in engineering, legal and financial viability terms to renew the lines with electric railcars. In fact, the economic and social benefits the railway will bring have again been recognised this year, resulting in a 50% grant by Hereford and Worcester Training and Enterprise Council for an updated market research survey.

This is one of the largest rail-less areas in Britain and unemployment and business stagnation must be kick-started, as the Treasury did in the 1930s, to rebuild railways, as at Ross, putting people back into productive work. The WVR could lead the way by a training/working operation now to prepare the route where trackbed is owned by local authorities and other landowners willing to co-operate. Two teams, one male, one female, each of 15 people, would work clearing the line, removing and replanting saplings, shrubs etc. from actual trackbed to the line-side guidance of the Department of Transport's programme, each team having a graduate arboriculturist

> or civil engineer in charge, according to task. These people would become the nucleus of the permanent 50 multi-skilled WVR staff.
>
> Your readers are invited to stretch out a hand to raise their MPs and councillors off their backsides in order to press the Government to accelerate release of a 50% capital grant under S56 Transport Act, 1968 for the reinstatement within two years of the Wye Valley Railway.
>
> To paraphrase Mr Cutcliffe's observation, the only 'practical' cure for vastly increased population, tourism, congestion and pollution is a new electric railway serving Gwent, Gloucestershire and Herefordshire.
>
> Eric T. Rawlins
> Company Secretary

A letter in the *Sunday Telegraph* of 16th August 1992 brought home to me just what a burden a poor population, as in Herefordshire, has to face in order to travel by car on under-average wages! Cyril Myerscough writes:

> Most motorists claim that their running costs are a mere 11p a mile. But they do not take account of fixed costs, which, the AA admits, amount to an annual £2,510 for the average household. For someone who drives the national average of 8,900 miles a year, the total cost works out at 39p a mile.

The Times leader of 19th August 1992 sought to point the Treasury in the right direction, and I quote: 'But it should encourage one-off public investment programmes. This means that familiar list of recovery measures: constructing railways and repairing houses, hospitals and schools while the private sector is depressed and constructing contract prices are at rock-bottom ... That is the way both to hold the economy and control public spending at the same time.' Needless to record, the Treasury continued its devastating stranglehold and nothing happened.

The Forest of Dean's main source of employment today seemed to me to be based on the renovation, buying and selling of old motor cars. But the *Forest of Dean Review* of 21st August 1992 described it as the blackspot of Gloucestershire with unemployment at 8.8%, 2,783 people in all out of work. Councillor Betty Smith, a long-time supporter of the railway living in Tudorville (Ross, Walford outskirts where a WVR halt is planned) asked me to give her an outline of our latest problems and I wrote the following to her on 8th September 1992:

WVR Ltd.

Ross-on-Wye
Councillor Betty Smith

Line-of-Route: Ross–Hereford Section

Two matters have been brought to our notice which represent interference with the original railway track in an area which the reinstatement must closely follow:

(1) Salvation Army Housing Association:
Ross Cattle Market site.

No doubt you will recall that we made representations about this matter, specifically, after the National River Authority indicated an official flood line across the site. This caused the developers to press to set back the buildings outside the original boundary and proposing destruction of the existing railway embankment. Having persuaded Members to agree to this, as a matter crucial to implementing the scheme, the embankment has now been destroyed. However, it now appears that a further block of buildings is being erected directly upon the ex-rubbish dump and in the NRA floodplain! Obviously, the developers have doubled the build at the expense of the reinstated railway, which will have to buy back the right-of-way by compulsory purchase. Was this the members' intention?

(2) Homs Road, Ross–Hereford Section

After leaving the railway underpass beneath the dual carriageway, the line-of-route passes the edge of Hildersley bungalow development where a station 'halt' for residents has been asked for and is intended. It is understood that fencing has now appeared around this piece of land. If this has been acquired by the County Council, in line with their responsibilities for transport infrastructure, then this company is happy. If, on the other hand, it is further private speculation on national railway asset land then we are not amused and it is plainly against the public interest.

We feel that the return of the railway in 21st century form to restore proper communications, cut congestion, accidents and pollution is no longer a dream but a practical proposition. In a slump, as deep as in the 1930s, there is need for similar action and we quote a recent *Times* leader:

'But it should encourage one-off public investment programmes. This means that familiar list of recovery measures: constructing railways and repairing houses, hospitals and schools while the private sector is depressed and construction contract prices are at rock-bottom.'

Herefordshire has suffered so much in so many ways – we are surely entitled to, among the rest, fight for Government support and, as ever, this company is always willing to meet with members and explore closer collaboration, particularly as the role of town and district councils moves towards the county responsibilities – well exercised for Severn Valley Railway (50 paid jobs) and Worcestershire in general, but ignoring ourselves.

Eric T. Rawlins
Company Secretary

I feel that this letter demonstrates just how disorganised, fragmented and unplanned the South Herefordshire District Council administration is.

In October 1992 a very tentative report emerged from the Forest of Dean District Council, which mentioned 'the possibilities for the development of *existing* rail links'. Perhaps the headline in the *Forest of Dean Review* said it all: 'REVIEW MOTORING – Council's pledge on road transport'. Anything more inept and less forward thinking would be hard to imagine.

The *Daily Telegraph* published a neat juxtaposition of articles on the 28th October 1992, one headed 'Train makers fear empty order books within two years' and the other 'Bus firm told to get 1,800 MoTs'. The latter applied after MoT tests failed 108 West Midlands Travel vehicles and the entire fleet of 1,800 buses were to be inspected! Indeed, the Traffic Commissioner said that the Licence to Operate was not at risk. Yes, indeed, one might conclude that the Government's wild obsession to free the bus industry for enormous financial gain, but leaving the public with only third- or even fourth-class facilities, had arrived. But why shouldn't the common man, woman or child enjoy the comfort and safety of rail travel equivalent to a Minister's Jaguar? Letting the train makers go out of business or become completely owned by foreign companies would complete the actual but unsaid transport 'policy' of the Tory Government.

Referring to current correspondence with Richard Eagle, I now include an extract of a letter I wrote to him on 2nd October 1992:

> Your reports of the private railways are really unbelievably GOOD considering everything! Just shows that real enthusiasts like yourself are retaining interest and travelling on the lines whenever possible. Quite amazing quarter of a million on the old GCR. Severn Valley equally good; too crowded for comfort is excellent news!

On September 13th I wrote to Sir James Scott-Hopkins following a good piece by him in the *Review* of 11th September. He advocated more public transport use, reducing congestion of cars/pollution etc. Trafalgar House shares of 423p in 1989 were now down to 43p (!) and Wimpey lost £7 million in half a year in 1992. I told him the Government had killed any hope of private finance in infrastructure for this decade and said that the Government should re-introduce the 1930s' Government Guaranteed Loan Scheme for capital and revenue (rolling stock), which in conjunction with an S56 Capital Grant under the Transport Act, 1968 would enable us to proceed. Sir James' reply was friendly but not really adequate:

> If effort is rewarded, you should certainly rake in the money – but I know it is not as easy as that, particularly in these times.

Since it is his Government which has just wasted between £15 and £20 *billion* propping up the pound, which was then devalued by 13%, this was rich, as they say. Anyhow, I know he talks to Tory MPs and quite a few do want something done – even to save their shareholdings in Wimpey etc., one feels. I feel the pressure is on for the Government to actually put cash into rail infrastructure – it would be a good idea to get the motor industry into rolling stock building to get the cost down through something approaching mass production, since stock is needed all over the country.

I feel the foregoing to be quite a wide-ranging summing up of the British situation for infrastructure and railways in the autumn of 1992.

In November the DTI organised an open day at Clearwell Castle in the Forest of Dean, which would focus on the Assisted Area scheme, which still applied to Cinderford and Ross-on-Wye. However, my enquiry of the Bristol organiser quickly came to nothing as our 50% grant for the market research by Hereford and Worcester TEC counted as a Government Department already assisting.

Our last board meeting of the year, the sixth, took place at our registered office on 27th November 1992. Richard was otherwise committed but Malcolm Clivery, chairman, Mrs B. Gartside, Dr R. Brown, Mrs S. Robinson, Mrs S. Gartside and I attended. As usual, the lack of response from the Malvern office of the wretched Rural Development Commission was noted. Responses from Trafalgar House, Wimpey, JETRO (Japanese Trade Office) and British Rail South Wales and West seemed to 'reflect the depth of the recession'. As secretary, I was asked to pursue a cheaper consultant for the market survey than Touche Ross at £7,500, specifically to ask the views of the Severn Valley Railway management. Most importantly, Betty Gartside and Malcolm Clivery proposed the election of Mrs Serena Robinson to the board; she was duly elected. This reflected Serena's great help to me, for she looked in at my home most weekdays when I was struggling with the WVR's daily post. She gave her opinions from the feminine point of view and was anxious to help in what she saw not just as the secretary of a small company attempting a major scheme by any standard which justified a daily team effort by many more than represented by her elderly father! Susan Gartside, my other beautiful daughter, also put money into the company and was welcomed as a Founder Shareholder. Most critically, we had to resolve as quickly as possible the matter of finding the balance of the HAWTEC grant of £3,750 for market research, otherwise this would be withdrawn.

My first task was to renew my acquaintance with Michael Draper, general manager of Severn Valley Railway. Nearly ten years earlier I had contributed 34 photographs of Ross Station to Bob Marrows, the architect of the new Kidderminster Station terminus – so closely based upon Ross. Michael welcomed the contact and although feeling the Touche Ross quotation was "by no means unreasonable", drew our attention to Anthony Kenney-Herbert, a marketing and planning consultant who had recently worked for the revived Great Central Railway. I wrote to Anthony K-Herbert early in December and awaited his full response for the New Year. The press release for the meeting was carried in full by all local papers, although the headlines varied: 'Re-open lines call for county'; 'Group urge return of rail travel'; 'Railway company seeking Government backing'; and 'Market Survey could boost Wye Rail plan'. Perhaps these rather diverse word-bites are confusing, so the release is reproduced below:

WVR Limited

Hereford Journal
9th December 1992

In welcoming new members, Eric Rawlins, secretary, said that since the work for renewal of the lines had started in 1986, driving standards had deteriorated and congestion had increased. Even more urgent was the need of pollution free, safe transport, with cities such as Hereford and Gloucester becoming virtually no-drive areas for the average country motorist . In considering a market research survey, with financial assistance from Hereford and Worcester Training and Enterprise Council, the directors anticipate corroboration of the phenomenal population growth since the railway closed in 1965, and the mobility and ageing problems of outlying villages and the moving away of young people who might otherwise have stayed. The presence of a living railway removed the depressing isolation factor from lives in difficult times, putting people and places back on the map, making travel to work practicable without tying up capital or adding hire purchase burdens.

> Introduction of modern electric railcars would have the capacity to serve both local use and increased tourism, as the Channel Tunnel will soon generate, but without damage to the environment as the economy benefits. It was resolved that all local authorities, other organisations and individuals with an interest in better communications be invited to forward their views to the company secretary for putting before the market research consultants. The directors noted that the European Commission was pressing member states to develop new rail infrastructure as a primary policy which would also address the persistent economic and unemployment problems.
>
> The company will continue to urge the Government to accelerate access to 50% capital grants under the Transport Act, 1968, also to re-introduce the 1930s' guarantee loan scheme, as used to rebuild the railways in a period of similar recession.

The Times of 18th December 1992 carried a frightening piece by the motoring correspondent, Kevin Eason, who suffered serious injuries in a crash in which his wife was also injured. The first letter he opened afterwards was the bill from the Ambulance Service, and the tone of his article was much removed from the usual macho nonsense of his contemporaries writing both nationally and locally. I noted that the current DoT fatal road accident cost was now £658,000 per person for the 4,500 killed per year, equal to £2.9 *billion* per year. Happier, by far, was the news that Lionie Alderman, aged 21, had been appointed one of the youngest lady train drivers on Network South East. She had followed in the footsteps of her father and was an ideal example of the railway family tradition I wanted to see develop on the Wye Valley Railway!

On the 30th December 1992 the *Daily Telegraph* announced the conclusions of the Royal Commission on Environmental Pollution. Described as a 'stark analysis', the road traffic increase for rural roads was likely to be between 127 and 267%! Growth on this scale is 'likely to have a major and damaging effect on the countryside'. Increased traffic on minor roads was already 'making many rural villages dangerous and unpleasant places to visit'. That, we would say, applies also to what *were* unpolluted rural towns, such as Chepstow, Monmouth and Ross! The Royal Commission, the Government's statutory conservation adviser, 'calls for the full assessment of all transport options, including rail, before a road is chosen'. But will a Government so dependent on political funding from the oil and road lobbies *dare* to take such advice? Perhaps it needs the Cabinet members to suffer injury and pollution-caused disease in their families before the message sinks home – an unpleasant but so real theme with which to end the old year.

CHAPTER 10

Market Research and Five-Year Revenue Projection: 1993

The New Year began with the usual interchange of views in the *Forest of Dean Review*; these I will reproduce without comment except to wonder who is writing the leaders.

Enthusiasm is not enough

Oh dear, here we go again – Mr Eric Rawlins of Ross-on-Wye is back on his favourite hobby horse of a Wye Valley railway, a dead duck if ever there was one. For years Mr Rawlins has argued the case for the new railway and the *Review* has given him plenty of coverage while pointing out that in our view the project was a total non-starter. Nevertheless, Mr Rawlins aroused a good deal of opposition from people who believed it might all come about and that it would adversely affect their properties and communities, particularly when he started talking about European funds and backing from businessmen, a consortium and the rest. Then came the crunch. It was estimated that well in excess of £30 million would be needed and at the last time of asking, Mr Rawlins appeared to have raised little, if any, funds at all.

Those who had supported him got their feet from under the table and Mr Rawlins went quiet for a long time – now, however, he is back with talk of a new but rather obscure market research survey which is to be commissioned into the proposition. We are in no doubt that Mr Rawlins is genuine but we feel it is right

> to point out that all the available evidence suggests that his enthusiasm for railways – which we share – has got the better of his judgement on this occasion.

I responded in the edition of 29th January 1993 and the editor thoughtfully added the heading 'Safe Travel':

> WVR Ltd
>
> The Editor
> *Forest of Dean Review*
>
> I regret due to pressure of work my response to your recent leader as to my personal 'enthusiasm' and of going 'quiet' has been delayed. However, we issued press releases following our latest board meeting so that the duty of press and company to keep our potential customers up to date has been carried out to the best of our ability. Inevitably, in a situation where we now enter into the 33rd month of deep recession, progress of a capital-intensive public service enterprise requires more attention to the complex procedures involved, which are hardly headline news in nature. But we are in the forefront of the new generation of private railway companies and have advanced forward thinking with which the establishment, in the form of the Government's statutory advisers, now agree.
>
> The Countryside Commission sees traffic on rural roads growing between 127 and 267% and is 'gravely concerned' at the dangers involved, advocating reduction of car use by promotion of public transport. In submission to the Royal Commission of Environmental Pollution, English Nature, the Government's nature conservation adviser, recommends all transport options, including rail, to be considered before new roads are built.

A single road death is now costed by the Department of Transport at £750,000. The £37 million reinstated railway, with infrastructure lasting 100 years and 45 miles of route, might soon save 50 lives, and in this alone recoups the expenditure.

In terms of the cost benefit analysis required for S56 Government capital grants, the factors of relieving road congestion, reduced pollution, economic regeneration and a top quality ride for tourism and local use must all be addressed.

The 'enthusiasm' of me, as an officer of Wye Valley Railway Limited, is transitory, neither here nor there in the context of bringing safe, modern travel to the people of this community.

Eric T. Rawlins
Company Secretary

Mainstreamwise, the new Railway Inspectorate of the Health and Safety Executive were advertising for Principal Inspecting Officers at over £30,000 p.a. plus £5,000 relocation allowance! At 67+ years of age I was obviously ineligible, but as I write now (in January 1996) I have only just finished responding to their latest consultative document of Railway Safety Legislation. Surely an endorsement of the credibility with which this project is held by the knowledgeable!

On 19th January 1993 Anthony Kenney-Herbert sent his promised proposals for the market research survey. These eight pages were sufficient for me to see that although his grasp was less than we would have expected if taking a third consultancy with Touche Ross, the makings were there for a satisfactory project. His fee would be £500 less than Touche Ross and this would include the number crunching of the questionnaires by the Marketing Centre, Bournemouth. Another factor was that Touche Ross had themselves suggested that the market research be carried out with the 'help of an outside agency'.

I attended the Ross Initiative dinner at the Chase Hotel on 28th January – an invitation which enabled me to spread the WVR word. On the 29th I circulated some notes on Anthony K-H's proposals to our directors and also to Doctors Brown and Smith. We would aim for 500 completed questionnaires by the public with a draw for £100 vouchers to encourage completion and return. The quote of £7,000 including VAT was valid from 1st March 1993, with a mid-month start, aiming to complete by the end of August 1993.

Although to proceed would strain our resources, despite Serena Robinson making a further investment to place her next to me in share-holdings, we had only March in which to revive the HAWTEC £3,750 grant. All directors agreed we should go ahead, despite reservations concerning the load upon the secretary, the recession and the long haul ahead. Richard Eagle's reply analysed the situation step by step and concluded, 'Anthony Kenney-Herbert and the Marketing Centre are ideally suited to our purpose'. Malcolm Clivery applied consideration from his insight into the construction industry, which he summarised as 'very flat at the moment and bad debts have been incurred'. Nevertheless, as a personal victim of the slump, he gave his support.

On 3rd March 1993 Anthony K-H met with Serena and me at my home. We discussed many matters and agreed that we could work together and find ways forward through the new ground, as it were. We agreed payment of £7,000 including VAT in two stages and to a set time scale (were that the Channel Tunnel building contracts had been so soundly arranged!). We exchanged letters of confirmation on 3rd and 5th March 1993.

As we made progress, a matter typical of Worcester County Hall's remote stupidity had been lingering on since November 1992; it had been submitted to the district council for planning approval. It was proposed to put in a 'viewing platform' on the railway embankment at Backney with a ramp so 'that wheelchair users could enjoy the view'. A more incongruous proposal in an almost isolated and difficult area served only by tiny lanes could not be imagined! The parish council and I opposed it for the

WVR, since damage to the embankment was certain. I described it as a 'lightweight' proposal against the railway reinstatement project and in the press said: 'We have held out a continuous hand to the county council, but we have had no assurance that the vertical support to the viaduct would not be damaged by this development'. Our representation to the District Development Control of 12th November 1992 is reproduced below, because such matters need recording for posterity to examine; an extract follows:

> It appears not widely known that the county council is responsible for transport infrastructure and with the surge of road accidents, deaths, injury and vehicle destruction on the A49 and B4224 Ross–Hereford roads it is high time the county paid attention and subscribed to the rail renewal rather than tinker about with a sound engineering structure. Although we are well aware that the residents in the Backney area wish a halt to be available on the railway, we can imagine no such call for access for canoes at such a location. Tourists have great difficulty in finding their way in the narrow local lanes and utility vans with canoes, provision of toilets, parking land waste etc. is the sort of development already spoiling the Wye Valley and ought to be opposed, NOT proposed by local authorities. As we make plain, the primary responsibility of the county council (or district if later applicable) is to ensure the retention and preservation in good order of the railway line-of-route, because, despite the recession, sooner or later the modern renewal will take place. As this is written, the Chancellor is outlining his plans for private and public funding developments for infrastructure and it is upon such matters that Herefordshire needs the county council to apply its activities and NOT to the frivolity which this application represents. If the

existing railway structures are damaged or destroyed by this proposal we shall require the local authority at the time to make good the line-of-route at no cost to Wye Valley Railway Limited.

Despite district council opposition, it was plain that the £50,000 (!) involved had *already* been allocated by the anonymous members of the county council committee – so expert in redistributing the cash acquired from Herefordshire by precept tax! I had described this project as 'frivolous' in the legal sense, which was translated by the papers as 'lightweight'. One would have thought this was sufficient to get the situation in perspective, but the county engineer, to his everlasting shame, described their proposal as an 'exceptional opportunity'! What for, indeed, but to attempt damage to the railway line-of-route, *contrary* to the statutory responsibilities for which the county council exists!

It is hardly necessary to record that in February 1993 the wretched matter was pushed through by the council, putting yet another nail in its coffin, as the cause for a unitary Herefordshire was furthered by this latest example of Worcester knowing best how to waste other people's hard-earned money.

A brief return to sanity occurred when Haydn Robinson helped me to do the seemingly impossible task of joining the 81-inch wings on my Pathfinder model of the Mosquito BM XV1, a worthy task indeed to commemorate an age when the difficulties were all overcome and the bureaucrats were as nothing. As proposed by the WVR directors, I wrote as secretary to Michael Palin and Dennis Potter, without response.

Sir John Harvey-Jones doubted our passenger numbers prior to the market research, but added, 'I would be only too delighted to be proved wrong'. On March 11th Anthony K-Herbert forwarded a draft questionnaire designed to be used by 'potential regular commuters and the visitors'. Serena and I applied our considerable talents to the design and on 13th March sent back our views in ten paragraphs. I wrote to Woolworth's plc and arranged to purchase gift vouchers, ten to the value of

£10 each, which would all go to the winner of a draw. The questionnaires were headed 'Market Research – Help us to help you – please complete this questionnaire for your chance to win £100 of Woolworth's Gift Vouchers'.

At the end of the month I wrote to Michael Draper of Severn Valley Railway, thanking him for introducing Anthony Kenney-Herbert and telling him of the virtually unique situation here when the inspector at a public inquiry into the Hereford bypass actually rejected the Department of Roads (sorry, Transport) proposals! The 1992 tourists to Britain figures were now released, showing that the lower value of the pound had brought record numbers: 18.1 million spending £7.6 billion. But, as usual, UK residents went abroad in increasing numbers and the Treasury ended up £3.4 billion in the red – no doubt balanced by extra tax paid by the British who stayed at home! The fumbled handling of the route to the Channel Tunnel from London got another airing, with the Government under pressure from protest groups in one direction and Union Railways concerned about the jumping up and down of 'every local politician' and saying, 'What we cannot have is parish councils dictating whether something so important can go ahead'. We would endorse this sentiment; by the time such parochial folk realise the road pollution that their children are now suffering could be averted, many beneficial years of rail travel could be lost. Down south it appeared that the extraordinary diversion via Stratford to Kings Cross would be less damaging to Tory MPs' chances of re-election – so is likely to be favoured. A piece from the London office of the Country Landowners Association appeared in the local press, referring to the failure of the Railways Bill 'to indicate adequate safeguards for rail services to isolated communities'. Geoffrey Hopton, the Regional Secretary, added the usual 'constituency' type commentary, referring to fences and 'rabbits and other vermin which live on railway land'. However, it was a peg to justify a 4th March 1993 letter to the *Ross Gazette* which would also introduce the market research consultancy for WVR Ltd:

Wye Valley Railway Ltd

Ross-on-Wye

The Editor
Ross Gazette

RAILWAY PROGRESS

We would like to voice our approval of the Country Landowners Association, the *Ross Gazette* of February 25th, advocating the importance of railway communications to the quality of life in the countryside. How remarkably this was demonstrated in the same edition, but in personal terms, by the extracts from Effie Allen's diary when, in 1905, she enjoyed a then quite common day trip from London, Paddington Station, to Ross. She returned on the 8.10 p.m. train after spending the then vast sum of 5s on postcard views, and even on arriving back in London had the energy left to read her post!

Amazingly, nearly 90 years of 'progress' has left local people in their 20s who have never even been to London! Perhaps we should broaden their horizons by organising a trip to London and via the Channel Tunnel to Paris within the next 12 months.

Even more desperately needed in this area are jobs and we are pressing the Treasury to reintroduce the Guaranteed Loan Scheme, used in the 1930s to combat unemployment and modernise the railways. Renewal of the lines would employ 150–200 people for two years, 50 permanently, and this week we continue our efforts by commissioning consultants to undertake updating of studies by a market research survey throughout the next six months and the entire line-of-route.

Eric T. Rawlins
Company Secretary

The editor had changed my headline 'Rural Railways' to 'Railway Progress', which seemed very fair!

The next week brought a very erudite letter from Paul Eward of Ross, a member of the Transport Users Consultative Committee based at Bristol. He outlined many problems privatisation would bring and the questions he gets currently and complaints about delays in answering enquiries at Gloucester etc. I wondered how many local people are even more fed up with being *dis*connected from convenient local station access to the national network! Richard Eagle's indomitable rail travel on our behalf had reached the Isle of Wight, where he commented upon the frequent, every 20 minutes, Saturday service upon the electrified line Ryde Pier to Shanklin. Every half-hour seems quite adequate for Saturday and holiday weekend workings on the WVR, but it is very true that the public respond to high frequency services and the independence and convenience the passengers enjoy.

Alan Hayward, senior partner of Cass Hayward and Partners, our consulting engineers, asked for an update on our situation while forwarding a letter from Leslie Oppitz, the railway author.

In March 1993 the organisers of the Ross Unemployment Group asked for a talk on the WVR project. This took place at the Larraperz Centre on 19th March, and although I had met the public on over 50 occasions, it was unusually traumatic for me. This would not be facing the powerful rich, who for so long, some would say too long, had the lives of the ordinary working people in the district at their beck and call. These men were at their lowest ebb and slumped in the chairs before me; two were architects which the slump had thrown out of work. To introduce a major project with the potential for up to 200 jobs, with proper training leading to 40 multi-skilled and ten professional people, was most heart-rending in the circumstances. How I wished the casually powerful members of the district and county councils were present, and the MPs and the small element of selfish landowners and farmers whose voices intimidated and sought to run the countryside entirely for their own benefit. Given the financial backing, we could have employed all these unemployed folk on a six-month trial basis; some we would retain, others would seek pastures new, but as things were, it was tea and sympathy – which was the best I and the organisers could offer that day.

The abandonment of the DoT scheme to put a bypass from the east to west of Hereford came as a relief to the company, as it could prove difficult currently to insist upon bridging for the railway. I composed a comprehensive piece for the *Hereford Journal*, making a bid for the sum of £43 million, which was saved by this rejection, and requesting that it be allocated to WVR Ltd via a S56 Application in due course. I was conscious that we still had to complete a cost benefit analysis and an environmental statement for the Department of Transport or any public inquiry; the matters were covered fully in an article published on 7th April 1993:

VALLEY RAIL GROUP CALLS FOR BYPASS £43M ALLOCATION

A call for the £43 million from the abandoned Hereford bypass plan to be made available has come from the Wye Valley Railway. The group now wants to call an urgent meeting of local tourism and transport bodies to press for immediate action on the cash. In a statement this week the secretary, Mr Eric Rawlins, says that now is the time for local authorities to recognise abandonment of the Hereford bypass scheme as the first indication of the Department of Transport accepting its role as something more than an arm of the road traffic lobby.

But if the finance involved is not quickly allocated to an alternative vital infrastructure improvement, then it will surely be spent otherwise than to the benefit of Herefordshire. The travel need is to get from A to B comfortably, safely and in good time, he says. Ownership of a car, in many cases, is a great burden upon the family income and is not the most economical way of meeting the need. Too often a so-called bypass is later 'phased' into being part of a motorway with real destruction of the environment.

In general, they simply speed traffic flow between even more congested junctions at both ends! A recent study concludes that cars are paying about a third of the social and environmental costs they impose, by way of tax. London will be the first with electronic road pricing, but within about seven years it can be confidently predicted that such cities as Hereford and Gloucester will be forced to adopt the same traffic limiting measures. Road building alone is at best a temporary expedient, rapidly overwhelmed by the new traffic generated. The 1989 national road traffic forecasts predict that by 2025 the full capacity of towns will be reached and that traffic levels in the countryside could be between two and four times the existing situation!

But new railways are permanent and capable of great flexibility to cope with an increasing population and their all-year-round local needs and give tourists relaxed travel by Golden Railcards included in their accommodation packages. The group say that the capital cost of the Wye Valley Railway (including 20% contingencies) is £37million to connect with electric railcars Hereford–Ross–Gloucester and Ross–Monmouth–Chepstow. Given the £43 million diverted from the bypass scheme and applied with close contractual control we could, in conjunction with the parish councils, put in even more than the planned 19 stopping places between the main towns. If, and when, the Hereford bypass is constructed, the Wye Valley Railway would expect the Hereford and Worcester County Council to arrange a bridging upon the same conditions as applied to Bewdley bypass on the Severn Valley Railway.

> In December 1992 the Department of Transport declared its willingness to accept their (WVR Ltd) application for a grant under the Transport Act, 1968. Two consultants' reports since the engineering feasibility study will leave them with a cost benefit analysis and the environmental statement to compile. This could be rapidly achieved if working capital could be allocated now and the balance of the £43 million set aside as a grant or Guarantee Loan Scheme funding.
>
> With part-funding from the Hereford and Worcester Training and Enterprise Council, new market research for the Wye Valley Railway begins at Easter and will continue to the end of August this year. Dual purpose questionnaires, to cover both local use and tourism, will appear up and down the line-of-route and further afield as the consultant advises. Local authorities, tourist boards and others to whom tourism revenue is important may take a stake in this work and receive the report in September.
>
> Mr Rawlins says that it would seem that there is an immediate need for all parties with transport, environmental, tourism etc. interests to meet soon, perhaps under the auspices of Hereford City Council, who supported earlier Wye Valley Railway consultancy. The aim would be to put into immediate effect a bid for the £43 million to be applied to this rail infrastructure, the only tenable route to ensure permanent travel progress into the new century.

Sad, indeed almost incredible to relate, there was no response whatever from either local authorities or tourist boards! By such blindness one may well question whether or not there is any life left in the management of the county of Herefordshire!

Richard Eagle had sent me a copy of 'Trends in Transport in the Countryside' by the Countryside Commission. This was described as a 'national overview' which recommended local studies. I had already written to Dr Phil Goodwin, Director and Reader in Transport studies, Oxford University; he was willing to undertake a local study for the WVR which would incorporate an environmental statement, useful for a public inquiry or Parliamentary Committee, and almost a necessity should a grant become available from the European mainland. This study would, however, have to await further financial resources and unless something unexpected happened, would not be given priority over the cost benefit analysis.

Stagecoach, the predatory Scottish bus operator, was making its power felt on the East Midlands Motor Services, where 250 staff were required to accept a '£20 a week or 10% pay cut before the implementation of a profit-related scheme which offered the company tax advantages', so noted *The Times* 'City Diary' of 16th April 1993. On WVR we would wish to introduce PRP (profit related pay), but gradually and with less traumatic impact. Both TUC and CBI leaders saw advantages in principle and the Government issued some guidance in April. A horrifying report by the Council for the Protection of Rural England, 'Driven to Dig', said that if road plans were implemented by 2025 then *seven billion* tons of aggregate would be needed. This would occupy about 3.5 billion cubic metres – equivalent to the area of Oxfordshire excavated to a depth of more than a metre!

As we moved towards the 1993 AGM, I found out that the lack of interest by the Japanese banks was due to their Government instructions that investment in Britain would be confined to 'Anglo-Japanese' projects that would facilitate them breaking into Euro-mainland markets, e.g. cars, TVs, electronics etc. The Tory Government continued to offer subsidised sites for this purpose, but, of course, while the British did the work, the dividends went home to Japan. World War III would be won without guns.

The AGM was held at the registered office on 21st May 1993, attended by Dr R. Brown, Betty Gartside, Malcolm Clivery, Serena Robinson, Richard Eagle and myself. We noted, sadly, that Doug Woodman's widow Joan had passed on to join him with the Happy Spirits in the world beyond our comprehension.

We noted the need to raise £1,500 by further share issue to settle the cost of the market survey by September. The board approved that when it could be afforded we should commission the local study and environmental statement by Dr Phil Goodwin's Oxford Transport Studies Unit. It was noted that we had been consulted by Hereford and Worcester County Council upon a draft Symonds Yat Management Plan, published by the Council for the Wye Valley AoONB Joint Advisory Committee. The secretary provided his response for the company and pointed to the thread of almost invisible but invaluable railway trackbed largely in place. The directors approved the action taken and could see that if any 'management' of numbers/pressures was to be effected, then the WVR had an obvious role. We would take part in any meetings as always, but it seemed unlikely given the organised inertia. Serena and I showed the market research questionnaire, which was well received and all looked forward to examining the returned completions in the autumn. The AGM press release duly appeared in the *Ross Gazette*, headed 'Year of Progress for Railway Project', and also in the *Hereford Journal*, headlined 'Your views invited on railway line', but was apparently suppressed by anti-rail influences elsewhere to whom 'progress' was anathema. In fact, the *Forest of Dean Review* began to carry the 'Cycle tracks over railway and tram trackbeds' story in the Forest. This was seen by the Forest of Dean District Council as 'very large and costly' in concept and the economics seemed to be entirely ignored; the WVR trackbed, effectively on the edge of the Forest, did not lend itself to the idea of 'easily graded cycle routes laid out in circuits'. It was difficult to see the scheme as other than a novelty which would have limited appeal compared with the numbers likely to use either the Dean Forest Railway or Wye Valley Railway for visitors' enjoyment and spending.

In May the first pictures of the Channel Tunnel terminal, with five platforms at Waterloo, appeared; an absolute feast of glass and steel. It was of particular interest because Cass Hayward had been contracted to work on the design, which, iceberg-like, actually comprised four levels of operation! A pilot 'workfare' scheme began in Norfolk and the North Norfolk Railway enthusiasts gained some new employees, who were paid an extra £10 per week over their £44 unemployment benefit. Those interviewed had been out of work for two years, so at least they got out of the house, as they put it. The Tory backbencher, Ralph Howell, believed the rate of pay should be £100. It remains to be seen if men can be persuaded to work for £54 per week and it could be that the scheme needs better consideration. Obviously, more administration than we had plus cash for working capital would be necessary before WVR would find this useful. We had been promised a project manager by HAWTEC, but this failed to materialise.

Both Serena and I, but particularly Serena, had real reservations about the design of the questionnaire for the market research, and it is worth reproducing the letter we wrote to the consultant on 3rd May 1993:

> I have discussed the draft with a fellow director who is accustomed to training and dealing with the local population. In brief, we feel your questionnaire addresses an audience of AB/*Daily Telegraph* readers, whereas the area seems overwhelmingly C2/tabloid in nature. Had we been aiming at the professional/graduate level your questionnaire would be ideal, however we are aiming for response across the board. This view leads us inevitably to conclude that the response rates from a questionnaire in your original mode would be destined to disappoint us all. Accordingly, we have applied our feelings to a constructive re-hash of your draft, which we feel will be more effective …

Happily, this opinion was well received by the parties and it is included to guide others who employ consultants outside their normal geographical area and where the company must be prepared to work closely to ensure that the results are a good 'match' for local conditions and the tourism expected. The questionnaires were printed in green ink upon a cream base. By mid June 1993 the questionnaires were being circulated to distribution points up and down the line, to libraries, tourist information centres and to five travel agents.

Surprise, surprise to the company, the *Forest of Dean Review* apparently relented in not publishing our AGM press release, and on 11th June 1993 published a re-hash headed 'Autumn Report on Wye Rail Scheme', which appeared as though the secretary had given an interview; it is reproduced below:

> A market research survey has been launched into plans for reviving the old Wye Valley railway line using electric railcars. The survey, partly funded by Hereford and Worcester Training and Enterprise Council, is expected to be published this autumn, said Eric Rawlins, originator of the project, this week. In a report on the recent fourth annual meeting of the Ross-based Wye Valley Railway Ltd he said: "Response to the survey is invited from potential local users and tourists. It will guide the likely level of demand and operation over a five-year timescale. Local authorities, tourist boards and others with an interest in the economic and social betterment of the area are being invited to have a stake in the survey." Mr Rawlins said there had been "buoyant progress and recognition for the project, despite a further year of recession". The company's assets of engineering, organisation, funding and business planning reports," he said, "represented significant work accomplished in a relatively short timescale for a major project."
>
> Funding was now being sought for detailed studies in the Wye Valley by the Transport Studies Unit at Oxford University. Mr Rawlins said, "A railway on a reserved trackbed already in place is an

> invaluable heritage requiring comparatively little adaptation to facilitate access by railcars without congestion and pollution." The company is pressing for part of the £43 million savings on the abandonment of the South Hereford bypass to be set aside for funding the railway.

We felt the foregoing to be a useful and informative article, reaching some 35,000 people in the local area. On the national front, the AA costing of running a car had increased to almost *four times* the rate of inflation, and the price of running a 1.4-litre car had jumped to 46p per mile over 10,000 miles, i.e. £4,600 per annum. Perhaps such calculations should be included in the O-level children's examination papers so they would be aware of the costs of becoming car-borne in a low-wage economy.

Anthony Kenney-Herbert related, on 22nd July, that he had "spoken to a great many people in the WVR's catchment area over the last few weeks in connection with the railway. Nearly everyone is enthusiastic about the project and would like it to succeed, although I understand that some people close to the line are less keen." At the Ross base I received a stream of letters, the questionnaires all going directly to the Marketing Centre Bournemouth from the individuals responding. I replied to all the letters and also, later, to the questionnaires, after processing, which had been made virtually letters of support! It is appropriate to reproduce a letter here from the Methodist Guild Holidays, who have a hotel at St Briavels which we had not previously known about:

> ... Our hotel can accommodate over 60 guests and is open throughout the year. If the proposed line was open between Chepstow and Monmouth I am sure many of our guests would use it to get to either town. The degree of frequency is difficult to guess, as we do organise some trips or excursions for the guests, but not all choose to go on them, and although most

> come by car, some do come by train as far as Lydney. Would it be possible for those coming by train to use your proposed service, say from Gloucester? Is it proposed to have a halt near Bigsweir Bridge?

I was able to reply positively to Mrs P.M. Preston, director of the Guild, and assure her that we planned a halt at St Briavels. Hopefully, rail access to such places would relieve the road pressures as well as increasing the lettings through convenient all-weather travel across an extended season.

Anthony K-H's contact with Gloucester County Council, Jackie Harris, said they saw Ross–Gloucester as a primary commuter route and that we should be prepared to operate on a quarter-hour headway! Such a frequency could be at least part possible, from Grange Court Junction, where the regional rail trains to and from Lydney and beyond (i.e. Wales) would add to our half-hour headway, which I saw as our maximum practicable service. Richard Eagle and myself discussed the reliance of the enthusiast lines upon revenues other than fares. We anticipated that catering, rail/tourism publications and some children's souvenirs etc. could raise an additional 25% or even more above the ticket prices. This could be the key to keeping the finances in the black; an important factor in this business is that passengers pay-as-they-go or buy – there is not a threat of hire purchase losses etc.

Again, on 10th July 1993, we approached Roger Grimley of the Rural Development Commission, Malvern, for help with the market research consultancy. All we received was a useless response from him in August, even after he had received a supportive letter of 13th July from Gloucester County Council; we also had the support of Ccllr Martin Baines of the Transport Committee of Hereford and Worcester County Council! Sooner or later, the anti-WVR bias of the Malvern RDC would have to be examined, but I had no time to do so at this stage. Adding insult to injury, the new 'Ross Initiative' had been granted £48,000 by the RDC, with promises for up to £76,000 for the next two years!

However laudable the aims of the Initiative, there could be no doubt whatever about the research which backed the WVR and of its very plain and much longer commitment to the public good via the most advanced project in the county! How much we could do with a fraction of these five-figure sums.

As matters stood, I proposed to purchase £2,500 in shares in August to ensure that we met the bill for the market survey. On the questionnaire front, Anthony K-H kept in touch by telephone, relating his experiences as he circulated around the line-of-route. A Red and White bus manager said that tourism was only worth 10% over winter travel to them; I responded that the limited services and old vehicles deserved nothing better; it was the *potential* that concerned the WVR!

There was a rather particular problem emerging from Gloucester City, where the Tourist Information Centre admitted not encouraging tourists to cross the River Severn (to visit Ross or Dean Forest), as happened when the railway ran and the slogan 'Ross Gateway to the Wye Valley' was in use. Nowadays, tourists are being turned around at Gloucester and pointed in the direction of the Cotswolds, where the Forest of Dean MP Paul Marland happens to live. Such revelations were obviously matters our ongoing marketing of the WVR would address. Richard Eagle monitored the appearances of the questionnaires at his end of the line and confirmed that at Chepstow Tourism Information Centre they were in a 'prime position' impossible to miss.

Locally, we had a Wye Valley Railway stand on the riverside for Ross Carnival, 7th August 1993, where questionnaires were available. Clearly, local residents enjoyed the situation of actually being consulted individually on this very important project and a goodly number of visitors were pleased to participate. On the rather significant date to all of us (the date the Second World War began) I wrote a press release to the *Ross Gazette, Hereford Times, Hereford Journal, Monmouthshire Beacon, Gloucester Citizen,* the *Forest of Dean Review* and *Forest Weekly News*; the text is reproduced below:

Not since the Great Western Railway's famous 'Gateway to the Wye' promotion has this area seen anything approaching current efforts to recapture the lost image and achieve economic regeneration. Now, from north, south, east and west the WVR market research questionnaires are winging their way back to Bournemouth for analysis. The county councils and other corporate bodies have expressed their wish to study the results upon both daily traffic flows and tourism prospects. The WVR system of twin railcars resembles that already enjoyed in Lancashire with the Metrolink operation, having receipts substantially exceeding the best predictions! Certainly, to avoid tourism traffic excesses of such money-pots as the Cotswolds, an Area of Outstanding Natural Beauty in the shape of the Wye Valley needs to implement off-road access for the new century if the environment is not to be further degraded.

As with all real initiatives, there are no cast-iron guarantees of success in this work, and particularly where a leap of imagination is required, some were slow to grasp that as with the Wye Valley Railway, there is no sustainable alternative. But this year, face-to-face interviews and other research has indicated greater understanding of the advantages of a pollution and congestion-free form of transport, which with job spin-offs, a widened tourist season and fewer accidents will contribute to HM Treasury's requirement that the WVR should effect 'wider social benefits'.

The Wye Valley Railway Company thanks all readers who have already returned completed questionnaires post-paid to the Marketing Centre. The final print run has now been distributed to libraries and tourist centres etc. The last date for the return of the questionnaires is 15th September 1993, after which the draw for £100 of Woolworth's vouchers will take place.

Someone from the *Forest of Dean Review* interviewed me before publication of the above and it was published under the headline 'Rail 'rebirth' report out soon', added the cost of £7,000, the fact that the questionnaires would be independently analysed at Bournemouth and a mention of the Metroline tram scheme in Lancashire, where receipts substantially exceeded the 'best predictions'. I also spoke of the DoT road deaths' costings, now at £750,000 (!) per person, concluding that: 'We need off-road access for the new century if the Wye Valley environment is not to be further degraded'. Almost inevitably, such objective reporting spawned an inane response inaccurately claiming, despite the Hereford and Worcester TEC current funding, that the WVR 'appeared unable to raise a single penny from anywhere ...' This gem was included under the 'Sally Sunshine' heading, but could have been contributed by Major Waller, I felt. In the same issue of the *Review* appeared a more singular commentary by D.J. Budier of Caldicot – with a station on the Gloucester to Newport line. Why he suddenly felt obliged to write *against* the renewal of other people's railway was a point put to me by those who read his effort. In referring to 'a thick file of reports', of which he obviously had no actual knowledge, he implied our consultants were against the renewal! He further implied 'a level of gullibility in those who helped us with public funds that needs to be looked at'. He referred to the bus services which 'have to be subsidised' at fares 'not considered cheap by some'. While knocking the tourism potential, he then said that had the renewal been 'secured 20–25 years ago and restored as a steam railway, it would be a greater draw than Norchard'. His final words, reflecting a probable joint effort by him and Major Waller, concluded: 'It is high time this whole business was knocked on the head, once and for all'. I was later told that Mr Budier had interests in the Wye Valley itself, which he had chosen not to disclose when seeking to deny the area its reinstated inheritance.

The *Forest Weekly News* had a neat leader the next week: 'I think we all have our private dreams. Some of us would like to be very rich so that we would not have to work again. Others would like to play football or rugby for their favourite clubs; others would like to run in the Olympics. Eric Rawlins would like to see the old railway which used to run through the Wye Valley reinstated. However, unlike some of us, Eric has worked hard to try and turn his dream into reality. Cynics say it will never happen and that it would be too costly. I say, "Dream on, Eric, you never know what you can achieve if only you try".' How extremely pleasant and encouraging from someone with no fish to fry!

Throughout the summer of 1993, Serena Robinson and I worked on the draft submissions for the overall report and financial projections from Anthony K-H. Anthony had obtained a vast range of statistics from the Department of Transport, the tourist boards, the three county councils, bus operators and British Rail. The 1991 census looked at local day-to-day traffic flows, such information as was available on tourism and the potential for joint marketing/WVR publicity across the county borders, which had become the current parameters of quite uncoordinated activity which attempted to box visitors into county frames! The local bus and car use was quantified and Anthony provided a projection of revenue forecast over five years; this would update the 1990 Touche Ross business plan. A most critical change involved an alteration from a possible 5% Government grant of capital, as contained in the business plan, to the WVR's present work towards a 50% capital grant, now technically available under the Circular 3/89 (November 1989) to S56 Transport Act, 1968.

As earlier recorded, in April 1990, when the business plan was written, neither we nor Touche Ross knew of the DoT November 1989 Circular, which apparently had very limited actual circulation. This new report, upon two levels of sensitivity, showed that after deducting interest on the 50% capital obtained by debt (i.e. loans) in the third year of operation, a profit of £1.16 million was the 'most likely case'. If, however, most of the 'loan' capital could be funded by a 45% EEC Infrastructure Grant, then even better results would be applicable, and earlier.

On the front of the market research questionnaire, attendance at the WVR display on 7th August 1993 at Ross Carnival and the Model Show, Larraperz Centre on 5th September represented the drawing to a close of this part of the survey, which had been advertised as finishing on 15th September. Nineteen hundred proformas had been distributed and over 400 completed questionnaires were returned to Bournemouth. The computer indicated that the Ross to Hereford section would be most used for commuting, with Ross to Gloucester only just behind, followed by Chepstow to Monmouth. The key tourist lines would be Hereford to Ross and Ross to Monmouth; the weakness, as we suspected, was that the absent railway meant the Gloucester–Ross Tourism Trail of old had been affected by the TIC turning Gloucester City visitors back towards Cheltenham and the Cotswolds. The report had as frontispiece a hand-coloured electric railcar set, by Richard Eagle, which was not only a striking illustration but also demonstrated the simplicity and unobtrusive nature of the overhead power supply. Key factors that potential passengers wanted were a regular service, cheap fares and a good view for the tourists; one third of residents sought a half-hourly rather than hourly service.

In 1993 we saw advantage in charging more than the slower bus services on a one hour headway, but at the time of writing (January 1996), Ann Gloag (Stagecoach) has bought Red and White and fares fluctuate slightly around 10p per mile for return journeys, with buses up to 18 years old! Charging equivalent fares on WVR would suit us very well indeed and benefit the passengers, since lower mileage was often involved with a direct rail route, e.g. Ross to Hereford is 14 miles by road but 12 by rail.

The 1993 cost of running a small car was (on AA figures) 35p per mile; it was plain that with top-class marketing and services, the transfer of at least a worthwhile proportion of commuters from road to rail were a reasonable projection. In tourism terms, the maximum numbers coming to the WVR catchment area per year was calculated as 3.1 million in 1993; these figures *excluded* day visitors, which Anthony K-H saw as likely to be a key component for WVR. For example, the report mentioned that: 'The WVR could immeasurably improve a visit to Symonds Yat' – this being a problem with road access and identified, without solution (!), in the Symonds Yat Management Plan. As with any other product/service, it was not enough simply to put down the rails and expect the 'customers', in BR terms, to automatically flock to whatever was on offer; the vital factor between profit and loss is marketing and motivated staff, keen to meet the needs of the passengers.

Richard Eagle's commentary summed it all up: 'The report is very pleasing; the more I read the more pleasing it becomes.' When the questionnaires reached the secretary, after collation, I endeavoured to answer all who had kindly added some comments or made further enquiries; this would take my 'spare' time through to December 1993! One elderly person signed himself 'An ex-resident of Ross-on-Wye', but failed to give his address. A resident of Velthouse Lane, Longhope indicated that he would never, never, never, et seq., use the trains! I looked at his age range and wondered whether when he, like me, is over 70 and far from fit he will still relish driving that tortuous A40 to Gloucester.

I sent a copy of the market research and five-year revenue projection to our chairman, Malcolm Clivery, on 29th September 1993, when he was working in Yorkshire. I arranged to purchase a further £2,000 in WVR shares, which, perhaps, says it all about my reaction to the potential of the scheme at this time.

The next requirement was for a meeting of the board, and this was arranged for 22nd October 1993. Present were Mrs Serena Robinson, Richard Eagle and me. Betty Gartside sent her apologies and Malcolm Clivery was prevented from attending by a horrendous pile-up on the motorway between Yorkshire and Ross! At least our aim was to try to provide a safer means of transport.

However, Malcolm had earlier told me that he was 'greatly heartened' by the report and the new revenue projections. I was asked to convey the board's appreciation of his work to Anthony Kenny-Herbert and the Marketing Centre, Bournemouth; this

I did, together with the balance of his £7,000 fee, £3,500. The directors emphasised that the further use of consultants must be self-financing. The market research report contained much of wide-ranging value to the community as a whole; however, much in the revenue area was commercially confidential and so the report would be available only to corporate bodies with public responsibilities including transport, tourism, economic development, employment, AoONB environment, pollution, congestion and accident limitation etc. It was further resolved that such bodies be invited to make a research grant appropriate to their means, minimum 10% of the cost, i.e. £700, to receive a copy of the report and support continued consultancy needed by other bodies for a cost benefit analysis and the environmental statement.

A letter from Sir John Harvey-Jones was read to the board: 'I am delighted that you have made such good mileage and would like to wish you good luck for the future.' A total of 403 questionnaires were put into a draw and Mary (my long-suffering wife) drew No. 286 and Mr Christopher Toms of Shrewsbury received £100 in Woolworth vouchers. After the meeting I set about writing an outline of the research outcome, inviting requests for the full report on the terms the directors had decided. The addressees were: the County Councils of Gwent, Hereford and Worcester and Gloucester; the District Councils of South Herefordshire, Forest of Dean and Borough of Monmouth; the English, Wales and Heart of England Tourist Boards; the Government Departments of Environment, Transport and the Treasury; the Hereford City and Town Councils of Ross, Chepstow and Monmouth; Ross Initiative and the Rural Development Commission at Malvern; Richard Branson and Peter de Savary; and the Export/Import Bank of Japan. I also advised Sharpe Pritchard, Parliamentary agents, and Cass Hayward, our consulting engineers. In the event, nobody offered the £700 required, which was plainly exceedingly good value in an area which *should* have received close attention of every council representing the public at whatever level. The letters inviting this contribution were sent in early November 1993 and there was also a press release; it is thus true to say that in summary terms we announced the successful outcome of the work, which (1) saved any study of the small print and (2) could enable members of councils to deny ever have seen the actual report. The press release did not appear in the *Forest of Dean Review* and we could only speculate in this respect; the *Ross Gazette* led with 'A re-born Wye Valley Railway could be well-used and highly profitable, a major new study has claimed'. I feel it is worthwhile reproducing the article that was in the *Hereford Journal* of 10th November 1993 under the banner-headline 'PUBLIC VOTE FOR BETTER TRANSPORT NOT ROADS':

> The responses of local people and visitors have contributed to a unique study, drawing together for the first time experience of Department of Transport traffic flows, the tourist boards, Association for the Promotion of Herefordshire, the county councils of Gwent, Gloucester and Hereford and Worcester, and the bus and rail managements. A Wye Valley Railway board meeting on October 22nd received the report by Anthony Kenney-Herbert, Marketing and Planning Consultant, Weston-super-Mare and the Marketing Centre, Bournemouth.
>
> Nineteen hundred proformas were distributed and 403 completed questionnaires were entered into a draw for £100 Woolworth's gift vouchers. The lucky number was drawn by Mrs Mary Rawlins and the winner is Mr Christopher Toms of Shrewsbury, who visits this area at least five times a year. Essentially local research in nature, the WVR Report coincided with the enormous 8,000 responses to the *Daily Telegraph* national questionnaire showing that 83% want improved public transport, compared with only 17% supporting road spending. This is reflected in the WVR report, which finds good local demand for the service, both for regular commuting and leisure.
>
> Most local use indicated is for the Ross to

Hereford line, with Ross to Gloucester just behind. The Monmouth to Ross section would be the third busiest followed by Chepstow to Monmouth. The key tourist sections of the line are Hereford to Ross and Ross to Monmouth. The Gloucester to Ross and the west is seen in need of tourism development, since Gloucestershire concentrates upon the Cotswolds and Cheltenham.

The WVR aim of 50% capital grant under the Transport Act, 1968 is central to the study, which finds that the railway is likely to be profitable. The cost of interest would then be £3.25 million per annum, plus running costs, leaving a profit of £1.16 million in the third year of operation in the most likely scenario. If the second 50% of capital need is by Government Guaranteed Loan Scheme, interest might be waived due to the wider social benefits contributed by the railway.

Alternatively, if the EC would contribute a 45% infrastructure grant, the overall profit in the third year would rise to over £2 million. The report, which effectively updates with a five-year revenue projection the 1990 business plan, will be available to corporate bodies with responsibilities for economic development, tourism and transport, including road traffic and accidents, congestion, pollution and the environment of the Area of Outstanding Natural Beauty.

The directors accepted the report's recommendation that a cost benefit analysis be the next stage, required in connection with an application for capital grant.

In *The Times* of 26th October 1993 a very sensible article by Nicolas Faith clobbered the 'notorious anti-investment Treasury' and claimed that: 'Even so, the Government's fanatical determination to hive off the railways would not have mattered if it had taken the advice of everyone who knew anything about the subject and privatised BR in sensible chunks, either geographical (come back, the Great Western) or, as at present, organised in business sections, instead of chopping it up into little lumps'.

As I note, in January 1996 the whole set-up above the Railtrack base was unravelling into some 25 pieces – shades of pre-1923 grouping! In the *Daily Telegraph* of 28th October 1993 Richard Ehrman had heard that 60 new bodies would be involved, i.e. about 50% of the numbers of private railway companies existing in 1922! Advice to the latest (!) Transport Secretary, John McGregor, from Charles Clover and Toby Moore in the *Telegraph* of 8th November 1993 said: 'The Government should aim to make the least environmentally damaging and safest form of transport – rail – the cheapest'. *The Times*, joining the campaign on 15th November 1993, said: 'Food is, in fact, one excellent reason for opting for rail travel. A meal en route can save valuable time.' Too true: how much per mile does it cost an executive to waste his time doing the manual job of driving a car?

At least the Government was supporting the Sheffield Tram project, 29 kilometres and 25 sets of stock costing £240 million. It was hoped to redress the decline by 25% of bus use in the city – while car traffic was up by 20%. How would this slow, slow investment programme solve the nationwide problems against the motor manufacturers' endeavours to sell more and more cars? At the end of November 1993 we heard that Ann Gloag's Stagecoach empire had paid £9.25 million for the Red and White bus company in this area. What variety of old multi-hand vehicles would we see now in Herefordshire?

Writing in *The Times* on 17th December 1993, John Adams, reader in Geography at University College London, indicated that 95% of a car's life is stationary! He said that if Government estimates of car growth prove to be true, rising to 27 million, then this would require a motorway stretching from London to Edinburgh which has 257 lanes!

At Ross, unemployment meant that 11.5 people were chasing every job, so said the GMB Union. The simplistic but highly uneconomical scheme to convert rail track into routes for the small proportion of the public who buy today's very expensive bikes (costing the equivalent of a small second-hand car!) received another airing in the *Forest of Dean Review*. The bridging alone to link the Forest by cycle to routes comprising Gloucester to Bristol and Hereford was ludicrous as a stand-alone proposal. If a cycleway was suspended from a new railway bridge, then this might prove more economically sound, but who would pay to ride a bike across or, inevitably, apply sufficient supervision to prevent idiots riding into the river etc.?

I advised Richard Eagle that I had made a submission to Mike Cottell (ex-Institute of Civil Engineers' president), who was handling the proposals for the Hereford bypass. I said that WVR would expect a rail-over-road bridge on one of the proposed alignments and that the DoT/Highways Authority/county council should fund this, at least in part, as happened with the Severn Valley Railway and the Bewdley and Bridgnorth bypasses. This bypass matter seemed to be drifting into the usual state of abeyance as the tired old year of 1993 came to a close.

Viewing the East prospect of Ross station with the signal box which replaced two in 1937. Immediately behind the GWR spear fencing is the Monmouth Bay terminal facility.

Ross-on-Wye station, down-side main building, as in British Railway days – 1960.
Always a joy to step off Gloucester connection from Paddington into gas-lit refreshment room.

In British Railway days a corridor train comprises brake 1st/3rd composite, brake third and straight third, leaving Ross for Gloucester and the London connection. 1932 engine.

The halt at Weston-under-Penyard, two miles East of Ross, had the notice advertising day trips to London.
There is nothing comparable in the South Herefordshire area today.

Popular view of the Auto train approaching Kerne Bridge station (for Goodrich Castle) returning to Ross; Garry is fireman at cab window; author waiting to board in 1950.

Symonds Yat station in 1960; a destination for many visitors all the year round.
Indeed, in the Winter the nearby hotel was dependent on the trains for supplies when roads closed.

The Wye at Symond Yat with train to Ross approaching; Royal Hotel in background.
Modern equivalent being a 60 passenger, fuel cell/methane ex-landfill powered, railcar.

At the far end of the Auto-train route was Monmouth Troy station, with connections to Chepstow Pontypool.
Photograph showing considerable recovery after World War 2.

CHAPTER 11

Councils' Confusion Continues: 1994

The New Year began with the announcement in the broadsheets of the Great Central Railway £2.1 billion scheme to link Leicester, Rugby, Brackley (used by me in 1944 when stationed at RAF Silverstone!), High Wycombe, Beaconsfield, Gerrards Cross, Acton, Kensington Olympia, Croydon, Redhill and Ashford to the Channel Tunnel. The loading-gauge would be to Berne standards, enabling large lorries/containers to be conveyed quickly from the Midlands to mainland Europe; the same trucks would also carry express passenger trains. It was hoped that the Private Finance Initiative, headed by Sir Alastair Morton, would attract the necessary cash. As I write, in February 1996, both the (Great) Central and WVR have yet to see *any* output from the Treasury's PFI!

Two quite confusing messages were spelt out in the Forest of Dean. Firstly, George Irvine of Gloucestershire Economic Strategy was deploring the removal in November 1995 of Assisted Area Status – this against an almost 300% increase in unemployment in Gloucestershire since 1990, up from 8,000 to more than 20,000. I wondered how the car-owning statistics, just now unearthed from the 1991 Census, were standing up to people on benefit who were committed to both the capital costs of home and vehicle. I was trying to understand the responses we were getting from the authorities that had received our market research letter inviting their purchase of copies. Hereford and Worcester County Council had sent a 'very supportive and sympathetic' letter regarding not being 'able to assist with financing the market report'. I replied, indicating that our letter had not been understood – the report had *already* happened! Doesn't anybody actually read the written word today? At Forest of Dean

District Council the Planning and Leisure Services committee were against buying a copy – with no reason given. Monmouth Borough, signed by George Ashworth, wrote the usual deprecating response. Gwent CC quoted their irrelevant studies of the western valleys. Gloucester CC got confused about some non-existent work by Anthony Kenney-Herbert 'three years ago'! The South Herefordshire DC economic and development officer agreed £700 was a reasonable charge, but then apparently left the service without authorising the purchase. Reading this stuff through it is difficult to say anything good about the authorities upon which the local residents depend for long-term decisions on major matters clearly outside the experience of those in positions of responsibility.

In correspondence with Richard Eagle, I remarked on the splendid work of the Mid and South Glamorgan County Councils and the five renewed valley lines. This would be mentioned from now onwards to encourage the bureaucrats to get off their bottoms! On 25th January 1994 the *Daily Telegraph* carried news of the decided route for the London–Folkestone railway; it would go the long way round, crossing the Thames at Northfleet and via Rainham, Stratford and Islington to reach St Pancras! John MacGregor, Transport Secretary, claimed it would cost between £2 and £3 billion and demolish 'fewer than 40' houses; the latter seemed most optimistic, but indicated a Tory Government spokesperson very willing to play down the number of houses in non-Tory voting areas. Already the 'nimbys' were jumping up and down, but it had certain compensations. A Mr and Mrs Daly were able to buy a Tudor house in Boxley from British Rail 'at a much reduced price; we knew about the railway, but the house was so lovely and we could not possibly have bought it unless it was blighted'! Yes, there are always *two* sides to a story!

Nearer home, the Dean Forest Railway had some help from volunteers from the Government's new Community Action programme. The unemployed receive £10 per week over their benefit to help clear scrub from the trackside, with some relaying and vehicle maintenance. Would this scheme still exist when we needed it? The annual clearance work around the Chase line-of-route was probably already in this programme. The Director General of the Institution of Civil Engineers made a plea for integration and strategic vision in rail renewal 'that the nation so urgently requires'. Surprise, surprise, a 25th February 1994 leader in the *Forest of Dean Review* reported that 16% of the motorways have 'less than a year of life remaining', deprecating Marples' rush to build them and concluding: 'could we, please, take another look at the railways'. Saul on the road to Damascus?

On 11th February 1994 the latest (!) Transport Minister, Roger Freeman, gave the OK to a Light Railway Order for the Dean Forest Railway to run through to Lydney, with a replica of the 1920s' station. Over the water in Gloucester City, a talk was being given upon the car congestion etc. situation entitled 'Are we reaching breaking point?' I arranged to attend but the weather clamped down with ice and snow, so I had to apologise to the organiser, Helen Shorcross of BBC Radio, giving me the opportunity to explain that *had* the railway been operational I should have had no difficulty in attending! "Point taken," said she. The event, and the *Forest of Dean Review* leader's change of heart, enabled me to write the following, published on 4th March 1993. It was headed 'ALL CHANGE':

> Reading the *Review* editorial advocating taking another look at the railways was followed the same evening by viewing Michael Palin's BBC Two Transport 2000 programme, which vividly illustrated the broad problems of roads, pollution and congestion, offering a way forward with modern trams and electric railways.
>
> How stands our local record? Well, Gwent County Council and Monmouth Borough Council have a history of trying to avoid studying the reports of the WVR independent consultants, and the former's attempt to extrapolate 'western valley' conclusions upon the Wye Valley is irrelevant. In a complete

> contrast to these regressive attitudes is the example of South and Mid Glamorgan County Councils, where no less than four valley lines, headed by Treherbert, Aberdare, Merthyr and Rhymney, have been renovated by new trains with over 50 stations in operation, thanks to the commitment and investment by those county councils. Indeed, as a passenger remarked in Michael Palin's example on those lines, a journey which "took 45 minutes by car into Cardiff now takes ten minutes by train".
>
> Gloucester County Council is also progressive and in the Structure Plan advocates that 'opportunities should be taken to re-open stations in appropriate circumstances...where the problems of increasing congestion and pollution are causing concern'. The Second Review of the plan found that 'use of the private car and the resulting traffic congestion not only pollutes the environment but also wastes time, the costs of which are borne by both businesses and individuals'. The WVR park-and-ride at Ross (already in place) and Grange Court Parkway, clear of Gloucester's western congestion, are obvious solutions awaiting implementation.

In April 1993 we were consulted by Hereford and Worcester County Council upon the Symonds Yat Management Plan, which showed how the renewed railway would both serve local residents wishing to make cross-platform connections with the new Great Western Railway and accommodate an infinite number of tourists within a dispersing and managed environment. Indeed, it is perfectly plain that without the reinstated railway no effective 'management' is possible.

The problem in remote places is that no local authority employs railway specialists, so to whom at the Department of Transport at Bristol, Cardiff or Birmingham can local officers or members turn for expert advice? The answer is no one. Such civil servants who are railway specialists are confined to Marsham Street, Westminister. Nevertheless, both members and officers have a duty to become thoroughly aware of the economic advantages which railway development can bring to an area now classified by the European Union as of '5b' status, the shameful 'Rural Area in Decline'.

But the lids on the boiling pots in the kitchen cannot be sat upon indefinitely and if the cooks cannot cope, the way out is by early retirement before the chickens come home to roost. Perhaps the new generation of members and officers will have more females in influential places, since it is the women, children and elderly who suffer mostly from bad transport decisions. Not to mention the one in six children suffering from asthma and the at last acknowledged threat of leukaemia caused by benzene and soot particulates in the exhausts of diesel lorries, buses and cars.

The very successful WVR market research and updated five-year revenue projection undertaken in 1993 by independent consultants confirms the demand for local use, including commuting, with sound tourism benefits. This report, which quantified local bus and car use, traffic flows etc., was based upon all the latest statistics and recommended a cost benefit analysis as the next step towards capital grant allocation. This report was available now to all local authorities at 10% of the cost price. Reading this would dispel the ignorance and hearsay in some quarters where minds were made up without recourse to the evidence.

Regrettably, the Wye Valley Railway Company had no direct input into BBC Radio Gloucestershire's traffic programme 'Are we reaching breaking point?'. This was due to me deciding that the weather on the night the recording was made was simply too bad to hazard myself and my non-company car. As the producer echoed on accepting my apologies, the case for all-weather, reliable and safe rail transport had been made by the circumstances in which I found myself.

On Saturday 19th March 1994 there was a chance to meet prospective Liberal candidates, including Paul Keetch, so I attended to wave the flag. I had written to Babcock and Brown, said to be 'transport financiers', to explore the possibilities of them seeking capital on a commission basis. No response to date. Richard Eagle, full of praise for the Glamorgan rail renewals, had travelled from Bridgend to Maesteg; I must say I envy him living near Lydney and being on the direct line to Gloucester in the south and Cardiff to the west.

At Moreton Hall School in Shropshire, 12 A-level girls were acting as directors of a scheme to re-open Gobowen Station on the Birmingham, Shrewsbury and Chester line. They ran the otherwise unmanned booking office and a travel agency from the school. The station has operational toilets and a warm waiting room – so much better than waiting in the streets for buses. We would bear this useful introduction to the commercial world in mind, possibly for Monmouth Station, where a number of schools vied for educational experiences somewhat more advanced than newspaper rounds etc.

On the Severn Valley Railway a share offer of £750,000 was launched by Alun Rees, with the aim of buying land at Kidderminster, to pay back a bank loan of £350,000 and build the station restaurant within the lookalike Ross outline. At Perrygrove Farm on the outskirts of Coleford, Michael and Frances Crofts got planning permission for three-quarters of a mile narrow gauge railway as an attraction. Quite incredibly, neighbours objected to this project, which would create five new jobs in an area which included Puzzle Wood and Clearwell Caves. Why does the very word 'railways' attract paranoid reaction from those who so readily accept lorry, bus and car pollution, congestion and accidents etc.?

On 6th May 1994 the country witnessed on television the formal opening of the Channel Tunnel – pie in the sky to some local ignoramuses – heralding a new era of land transport between the countries which would be unaffected by the weather!

Next on the WVR horizon was the 1994 AGM, which we held at my home on Saturday 14th May. Present were Mrs Serena Robinson, Richard Eagle, Malcolm Clivery and me. We resolved to keep the market survey and five-year revenue projection restricted to those willing to pay 10% of the cost for a copy. We would now seek funding for the cost benefit analysis required by the Treasury and the Department of Transport; the likely cost would be £7,000.

It was not easy to be enthusiastic about the CBA, an idea originating from the House of Lords as a measure of justification for capital expenditure upon the national infrastructure in the eyes of politicians. Unfortunately, it would say nothing we did not know about the viability and need for the WVR renewal. We noted that the Symonds Yat Management Plan had been adopted as policy by the Wye Valley AoONB JAC, with the priority identified as 'reduction of seasonal traffic pressures and promoting alternative means of access'. This plausible purpose fitted the reinstated railway precisely, but to my knowledge, this quango had no funds and little stomach for doing anything actually effective.

There was some prospect of Rotherwas Station being opened for local passengers under the David Williams/Hereford 2000 scheme. At the Gloucester end, Grange Court was seen as a park-and-ride renewal by the county council, this location being seven and a half miles from Gloucester City and the junction between the WVR and the Regional Rail/GWR from Lydney etc. I reported to the board a Gwent CC consultancy, costing £20,000 (!), upon tourism in the Wye Valley, saying that I had written a 13-paragraph letter to Dr Richard Denham of Ledbury, who was responsible. I will refer to this matter again when the report materialised in December 1994.

It was agreed that there should be a transport exhibition at Ross in the autumn. I wrote the customary AGM press release, which appeared under a variety of headlines locally; *The Forester* chose 'Ross to Rome by Rail', the *Chepstow Press* 'Full Steam Ahead', the *Hereford Times* 'Rail Directors seek fast return' and the *Ross Gazette* as reproduced below:

Wye Valley Railway Limited
Ross-on-Wye

The Editor
Ross Gazette

PROSPECTS ARE GOOD FOR RAILWAY SCHEME

Prospects of the return of the Wye Valley Railway are good, the fifth annual meeting of Wye Valley Railway Ltd heard. Director, Mr. Richard Eagle, retired and offering to stand again, was duly re-elected. The directors noted the Department of Transport's interest in the market research completed last year, but that a cost benefit analysis is also required to enable consideration of an application for 50% capital grant to be given.

It was resolved that the market research report remain available to local authorities at 10% of the cost and that obtaining funding for the cost benefit analysis, addressing such matters as reduction of pollution, congestion and accidents, be the priority for 1994.

The company had been consulted upon the Symonds Yat Management Plan, now adopted by policy by the Wye Valley AoNB Joint Advisory Committee, and the value of a reinstated railway to effect the priority of 'reduction of seasonal traffic pressures and promoting alternative means of access' was apparent. With prospects of a Rotherwas Station being opened, under the Hereford '2000' scheme, and Grange Court as a park-and-ride station to reduce road traffic into Gloucester, the indications are plain that the importance of modern rail to local communities is being entirely revalued. Already Glamorgan County Councils have renovated, with new trains and facilities, no less than five 'Valley' lines, bringing over 60 stations into operation and reducing congested road journey times from 45 to ten minutes.

Unlike the Wye Valley lines, these services have little hope of subsidy from tourism revenue to support local travel, but nevertheless are well worthwhile.

The secretary recalled the furore caused some years ago by the newspaper heading 'Ross to Rome by Rail'. Today such travel is no longer mere prophecy and a director, as a founder member of the Channel Tunnel Association, is arranging for WVR colleagues to travel through the tunnel to visit the French railway centre in Lille this summer. In view of the satisfactory developments proceeding, the directors decided that a further public occasion, actually the 53rd since 1987, will be held in Ross in the autumn. Provisionally entitled 'Transport – Past, Present and Future', this would be a combined exhibition with the rural transport adviser, Hereford and Worcester Community Council, featuring models, photographs and plans etc. Overall, the directors have confidence in the progress made and believe the prospects for the Wye Valley Railway's return are good.

Richard Eagle had arranged a supply of pretend tickets for WVR to act as 10p souvenirs for enthusiasts and youngsters (around here so many had not even stepped upon a train!). These had been bought from the West Somerset Railway's printing department. I managed to make a wooden dispenser which would release one ticket at a time onto an aluminium tray – much as once used in the old railway booking offices. Five hundred cost us £43.85p, and we stepped up the price to 15p each.

On 21st May 1994 I attended a so-called Transport Forum at Ledbury. It was poorly organised by cyclists from Bromyard. Regional Rail, Midland Red and myself had just seven minutes each to speak against a background of the advocates of cycling and car sharing etc. It would be a kindness to say that it was not a waste of time, but I wrote to Hereford and Worcester CC planners, advocating something properly professional for South Herefordshire at Ross.

By far the most important contemporary matter was contained in a letter to us of 7th June 1994 from Mr S.G. Kinsella, the Director UK of Business Development for Balfour Beatty Limited. After explaining that their current situation made it inappropriate for them to 'stretch our interests any further at present', he said: 'We do, however, fully support the aims and objectives of your organisation and believe that the Wye Valley Railway is a practical and environmentally acceptable public transport measure.'

We could hardly ask for a more valuable professional endorsement of our work from engineers of greater competence than this international company. As I wrote to Richard Eagle, advising him of this view, he replied, 'Beatty's reply is a good smack in the face for moronic councils, RDC etc., which I shall use as necessary'.

Richard and I discussed the new rented Salvation Army Housing Association scheme near Fiveways, Ross, which now breached the WVR embankment to get it off the Wye flood plain. He commented that it would appear that both the householders and the WVR were victims of the planners/South Herefordshire District Council members who *certainly* knew what they were doing. I explained that I had done my best, but the final push into our embankment was both (i) determined and (ii) effected covertly. However, we would have to re-organise that section considerably because an island platform for Ross Station was an operational necessity to provide a double-track interchange so that passengers on a Monmouth–Hereford train, for example, could cross over and change if they wanted a Hereford–Ross–Gloucester service.

One of the last decisions of the next departing Transport Secretary, John MacGregor, was to give the go-ahead to 23 miles of renewal of the 2ft-gauge Welsh Highland Railway. This would be from Caenarvon to Porthmadog and built by Ffestiniog

Railway Holdings and *not* by a rival consortium compiled by Gwynedd County Council. It was hoped to bring 'much needed' employment to the area; I hope it will do so, but it seemed that the Government was only endorsing a public inquiry about granting a Light Railway Order; *no* Government finance was promised! The basic difference between the WVR and them is that 2ft-gauge steam is virtually impractical as a commuting operation today, and the LTO will have a 25 mph speed restriction. The WVR has the *two* strings of local use plus tourism and *three* connections with the national network!

During May 1994 I was telephoned by Bob Smyth, one-time deputy leader of Southwark Council, where our lives had crossed, but who was now a freelance journalist. He asked if I would provide background information for an article on me in the now less anti-rail *Forest of Dean Review*. I provided two closely typed A4 sheets, which Bob developed into a centre-page spread in the edition of 29th July 1994. The accompanying photograph was of me in serious mood to counter the previous too happy bloke on their files! It showed me in the study at home together with the predecessor of the railways I had just modelled – an 19th century mail coach which ran through Ross on the Milford Haven–London route. The article was headlined: 'Bob Smyth meets a railway visionary', which seemed to be 'subbed' by a more tabloid version reading: 'Eric's £40 million railway dream'. Reading this as I type, in February 1996, a similar sum has just been paid out in Lottery winnings – so the 'dream' has already come true for some! Bob's introduction included that 'while railways are recognised as being a good thing – non-polluting, safe and user-friendly – not a single former line has been reopened as a commercial service in England during the last 30 years'. This could, of course, be attributed to the power of the oil, car, lorry, bus and coach lobbies in Parliament; one day I hope the whole truth of these times will be told. It was a first-class article – almost a tribute to my efforts – and illustrated also by Cass Hayward's map. Excuse the ego trip if I reproduce it here:

The Ealing comedy *The Titfield Thunderbolt* has a cast of familiar stereotypes – petty bureaucrats, rough diamond with a heart of gold (usually played, as here, by Stanley Holloway) – and their favourite storyline of a community fighting the authorities (as in *Passport to Pimlico*). The story of a village battling to keep its train service, filmed in the 1950s, is one of many fictions testifying to the British love affair with its railways – *Thomas the Tank Engine, The Railway Children* and so on. David Shepherd's paintings of old locomotives hang in a million sitting rooms (next to his elephant pictures). Steam railway preservation societies such as the Norchard Centre flourish around Britain, attracting thousands of visitors on sunny summer afternoons. And opinion polls show that a majority of the population are against rail privatisation – railways being seen as part of the national heritage rather than just another business.

USER-FRIENDLY

The Beeching cuts closed down dozens of loss-making branch lines in the 1960s as car ownership grew and freight switched to lorries. Yet, while railways are recognised as being 'a good thing' – non-polluting, safe and user-friendly – not a single former line has re-opened as a commercial service in England during the last 30 years. This does not deter Ross-on-Wye's Eric Rawlins, now 68. While looking more like the official he once was rather than Stanley Holloway, he has spent the past ten years trying to reopen the Wye Valley Railway. To jump ahead of the story, the estimated cost of the project is nearly £40 million. This makes it highly unlikely it will ever come about – but his crusade is in the great tradition of other railway sagas.

Eric's first contact with the railway was in the 1930s. As a schoolboy visiting his uncle, a guard on the Ross–Monmouth line, he spent his holidays riding the auto-train.

MECHANIC

He worked as a mechanic on the Mosquito bombers of Pathfinder Squadron at the end of the war. On leaving the RAF he joined the Rolling Stock Department at Paddington Station. Later he joined the CEGB's Research Department as a statistician. "I had no great love of the GWR," he says. "I was getting married and wanted a job with better prospects." He maintained his link with the railways nevertheless. "When the Ross lines were threatened in the late 1950s, I attended protest meetings at the Chase Hotel," he recalls. "Local people were proposing modernisation of the service through [the] introduction of up-to-date railbus trains. I helped with the final telegram appealing to the Minister of Transport. It was to no avail. The last passenger train ran from Chepstow to Ross in 1959. The Hereford–Ross–Gloucester line, (still steam-hauled) continued up to 1964. The Lydbrook–Ross–Gloucester freight service survived until the following year."

LISTED

Bits of Ross station were preserved as listed buildings – notably the goods and engine sheds – amid what is now an industrial estate. Using drawings and photographs he made in 1960, the Severn Valley Railway was, more recently, able to build a station at Kidderminster based on the Ross design. Taking early retirement from his last job in a London Borough's legal department, he moved to Ross to be near one of his daughters. Since then he has concentrated on preparing plans for the reopening of 45 miles of track between Gloucester, Ross and Chepstow, with a spur between Ross and Hereford. (Gloucester–Ross–Hereford is actually the WVR's 'main line').

INTACT

The route is, he says, substantially intact. The Gloucester–Hereford line was designed and built by Brunel in 1855 as part of the GWR. It can be followed from where it diverges from the Chepstow–Gloucester line at Grange Court near Northwood Green. After Longhope, it passes Lea before turning north towards Ross via Weston under Penyard. The Ross–Chepstow line was constructed by the Wye Valley Railway in the 1870s, being added to the GWR network in 1905 when it encountered financial difficulties. From Ross it follows the left bank of the Wye to Monmouth before crossing to the right bank at Redbrook. At Tintern it crosses back to run past Tidenham Chase before diving under the tunnel taking it to the coastline at Tidenham and thence Chepstow Station. The Hereford line forms a track towards Backney, crossing the Wye three times before joining the Hereford–Newport line just short of the town. The line has human as well as engineering history, including the rags to riches story of Frederick Burrows. In Born at Bollow, near Westbury-on-Severn, he worked as a checker on the local railway before moving to work on the Ross line. Having been secretary of the local branch of the NUR, he became the union's national president during the last war. Admired by Churchill and Atlee alike, he was appointed Governor-General of Burma and knighted in 1946. On retiring to Herefordshire, when Burma achieved independence, he became High Sheriff to the county, chairman of the Ross magistrates and chairman of the Wye Valley Authority – dying in 1973.

No one doubts the spectacular beauty of the route and its tourist potential, but a railway needs paying passengers all the year round. In order to test the market and the engineering feasibility of restoring the line, Eric Rawlins commissioned various surveys. A 1987 study by the Chepstow-based civil engineers Cass Hayward and Partners was funded by the Department of Employment and Tourism. The giant accountancy and management consultants company Touche Ross undertook an organisational and funding study in 1988, financed from various sources including the Department of Trade and Industry.

CORRESPONDENCE

In 1989 the DTI required Eric to form a company, Wye Valley Railway Ltd, of which Eric is secretary. A room of his house is now an office surrounded by files of the voluminous correspondence he has generated over the years. A business plan was prepared by Touche Ross in 1990. A market research and revenue update, part-funded by the Hereford and Worcester Training and Enterprise Council, was issued last year. This year he is concentrating upon a cost benefit analysis and environmental assessment, to be carried out by Dr Phil Goodwin of Oxford University's transport unit. ("The Government never gives us any money, and we are operating a line which is already up and running," a Norchard centre enthusiast had earlier remarked a little sourly.) He is cheered by the interest shown by the Gloucester County Council in opening at some future date a station at Grange Court to fill the gap between Lydney and Gloucester Stations. His hopes for the project are based on the possibilities of attracting 50% of the £37 million as Government grant and 40% from the European Union, leaving £3.7 million to be raised commercially.

PROFIT

"In the third year, after deducting interest on capital and running costs, a profit of £1.6 million is the most likely case," he says. Decorating his office is a handsome model of the Ross Mail Coach. A keen modeller, Eric has built a 00-gauge reconstruction of the Ross Station layout, and in an upstairs room is a replica of the Wilton Castle steamer, which used to carry tourists down the Wye from the Ross riverside. Occupying most of the room is an enormous model of a Mark XV 1 Mosquito bomber – which actually flies. "It is so unusual that I have been asked not to risk an accident by putting it up in the air," Eric smiles. "My other big bug is the Ross heritage museum," he adds. "The old Market Hall has been empty since 1988, which is a scandal."

The Ealing comedy writers would have been proud of him.

Bob Smyth has encapsulated quite a slice of my life in the foregoing; perhaps my obituary might say I always did my best – whatever the odds!

A week earlier, on 22nd July 1994, was held the first Business Fair at the Chase Hotel, Ross. I was in two minds whether or not to attend with the new WVR display board, due to the cost of £75. This was, of course, peanuts to exhibitors seeking to sell computers or cars that day – we, obviously, had no way of securing such revenue. However, most generously, Henry Kaye and Patrick O'Reilly, the organisers, sponsored the WVR. Betty Gartside, Mary and I ran a double-sided island stand, not the easiest of exercises but rather clever in operation, since visitors missing us on the initial circuit of the stands walked past our second side later! I was especially pleased to meet Paul Scudamore, who owns one and a half miles of the trackbed immediately to the north of Ross en route to Hereford. He appeared to have none of the characteristics of Major Waller!

We turned down an appearance at Ross Carnival this year, as no tenting was available and it has proved a notorious venue for sudden high winds and rain squalls to develop during the day! In August 1994 Celia Glover of Ross had edited a little history of the Ross to Monmouth section of the WVR, as originally written by her 12-year-old son. I was asked to provide half a dozen photographs and the cover print is my shot of an autotrain at Kerne Bridge. Although the architecture of Ross Station provided the design for Kidderminster, I was not credited for the drawings and photographs which made this possible. The fact that the new WVR would have overhead electrification supports was mentioned as something intrusive for today; well, no one ever complained about the much larger diameter telegraph poles in more than 100 years of steam operation! The possibility of reinstatement of a 'small section' of the route was trailed despite the Department of Employment and Tourism's insistence that they would fund only a *full* reinstatement study by the engineering consultants. The mind boggles at the planning implications of putting in a rolling stock depot and control centre in the Monmouth–Symonds Yat area! Anything less viable in standard gauge and unconnected with the national system would be difficult to imagine. What, however, attracted some exasperation from me, fellow directors and the educated public was the commentary 'the appeasing of residents who bought properties in good faith and now discover they might have an EMU, or even Mallard, running along the line at the end of the garden'. The authority for building and operating the WVR would be by Public Inquiry/Empowerment Order under the Transport and Works Act, 1992; any 'appeasing' would be by negotiation in line with the Dept of Transport's current terms. Only in extremis would we invoke compulsory purchase. *All* land and property is bought caveat emptor – let the buyer beware; it is not a question of good faith but of professional enquiry. Since the engineering feasibility study has been in the public domain, i.e. the reference libraries, since May 1987, there is no need for any 'discovery'. If the buyers employed solicitors to do a search and this failed to reveal the established reinstatement scheme, then the remedy lies elsewhere. Every local authority, from parish to county councils, was also well aware of the WVR plans and we have the records to prove it. A good little book, one might sum up, but one which has pitfalls for anyone who is not a professional writer on railways and who seeks to include much of reminiscence and current developments. For a contrast in style and detail, I commend the Great Western Journal No. 2 of spring 1992 by William H. Smith, which also contains many of my photographs and covers additionally the Hereford–Ross–Gloucester line.

On 4th September 1994 I took the four-foot long models of the mail coach and the 'Wilton Castle' pleasure yacht to the Larraperz Centre, Ross, together with the new WVR display board and ticket machine; the latter was popular with the children, most of whom seemed never to have seen a real train! The Government's Family Expenditure Survey had appeared in August and showed that an 'average' family spent £43.20 on motoring, £2,236 per year! The highest earners spent £84 per week on motoring, £4,368 per year. For even the poorest, this amount would enable them to travel 500 miles a week by public transport, and most journeys to work would be less than ten miles per return day, i.e. 50 miles a week! What pay-as-you-travel by public transport (where it exists) saves is the hidden car cost of insurance, road tax, capital outlay, repayments of loans, maintenance, MOT, garaging and parking; all additional to fuel – the *only* cost the simplistic are encouraged to examine.

Earlier in the year I had met Madeleine Sumner, rural transport adviser of the Hereford and Worcester Community Council. She was sitting rather forlornly in the Ross Library with a display of bus timetables etc. She was disappointed about the amount of interest shown and I suggested a joint exhibition with WVR in the autumn, offering to arrange sufficient local publicity in the papers to make it worthwhile. She agreed and I put a trailer in the press early in October, which is reproduced below:

THE SHAPE OF TRANSPORT TO COME

An exhibition of transport past, present and future is to be held at Ross Library from Tuesday October 18th to Saturday October 22nd. The exhibition is being organised by Hereford and Worcester Community Council and the Wye Valley Railway Ltd. Getting around Herefordshire before the coming of the railways in 1855 depended on walking, horses, coaches, wagons and boats.

When King George IV was delayed passing through the town in September 1821, he threatened to take Ross off the mail route from London to Milford Haven unless the Old Gloucester Road were improved. The result was the causeway upon which the present Gloucester Road is built, and at the library will be a large scale model of an 1827 mail coach, with passengers riding both inside and outside and pulled by a team of four horses.

The old steam railways of this area, which took so many on their first day-excursions to London and the seaside, are remembered with affection by the elderly in the community who value what has been lost. When the trains were withdrawn in 1964 the bus monopoly was created for better or for worse. The exhibition will include posters outlining all road transport available today, the Community Transport Association work, schools and social services transport and rail services from Hereford.

Merely being by-passed by a dual carriageway has done little for the prosperity of Ross, with ever-greater residential development year after year. Now the detriment of lacking direct connections to the national rail network for business, commuting and the vital tourism function has been realised. Work by Wye Valley Railway Limited is now widely

> recognised to reinstate the lines, but the exhibition will show just how far behind Herefordshire is compared with no less than five 'Valley' lines completely renovated and operational in Wales this year. Additionally, the 'Swanline', Bridgend to Swansea, demonstrates a new service where rail was withdrawn, as with Ross in 1964, and restored with new track, signalling, stations and new railcars in 1994!
>
> Faced with further increases in the average cost of car ownership (the Government figure is £43 per week), higher capital prices, fuel, parking and road tolls to restrict predicted growth, the value of new developments in public transport cannot be overemphasised. Facilities of park and ride and bus connections from rural settlements to local stations and halts result in less pollution and congestion in towns and cities.

I feel that the foregoing was a useful piece of educational publicity for the cause, but for several days Sod's law applied at the library, despite the best efforts of Miss Elizabeth Tieser, Librarian in Charge, due to ongoing work to install new sliding doors. We used the side door and no doubt some turned away, assuming all was shut. We took a five-bar gate record and 165 people were noted; two were against the WVR, one being the 'Beeching' lady from Weston who expended her wrath against Madeleine! She coped with competence and did not mention it until I had a free moment from the usual enthusiastic members of the public. Twenty-nine new local people added their names to the WVR Supporters List and thirty-two to my heritage centre supporters – everyone much impressed by the mail coach but deprecating the entire lack of progress since the library had left the Market Hall vacant six years ago! The idea of an independent trust running the heritage centre rather than the local authority was thought most important. On the Wednesday of the week in the library a most curious coincidence arose: the *Gloucester Citizen* paper had sent a photographer and he was most interested in the mail coach. Suddenly, he jumped back when he read that they were all made by the London firm of Besant and Vidler of Millbank. His name? Dick Besant!

He took ten photographs and I would guess that some found their way into the family album. I think Madeleine enjoyed the occasion and began to realise just how well off some places are compared with Ross and district, her office at Great Malvern Station being almost instantly accessible to Hereford and Worcester and beyond. A press release summed up the occasion: 'Transport exhibits arouse much interest' it said in the *Ross Gazette*.

In *The Times* of 26th October 1994 an outline of computer games carried an illustration of a train-driving simulator, whereby a person was receiving an in-cab warning that his 'required speed of 100' was been exceeded by 20 mph. Clearly, an example of how relatively cheap technology would be to teach those whose duties including driving in the future. The last public engagement of 1994 was carried out by Director Richard Eagle, following an approach to me by the Lydney Ladies Group. Apart from one appearance, by Drewe Lacey at Weston-under-Penyard, I had been present at 63 occasions to date; Richard lived nearby in this case and I felt he would be more attuned to local interests. I sent him a copy of my latest version of 'the talk', telling him to just vary it as seemed right for the audience. Writing to the 'office' after the date, 24th October, he wrote happily that it went down so well and with his additions held their attention for an hour! The ladies actually donated £5 to WVR funds and Richard sold them ten souvenir tickets for £1.50 p. I don't know which of us was most pleased; the audience was the salt of the earth – little people who really count.

On 4th November 1994 we received a questionnaire from the Health and Safety Commission, Railway Industry Advisory Commission. Although they were aware we were not in operation as a 'Minor Railway Operator', we completed the proforma regarding workforce, our multi-skilling plans and medical examinations etc. This was apparently well received, for they would request wider views from us in 1995.

Richard asked whether I had sought to contact Stagecoach in the context of being a possible consortium member. I felt that contacting further big boys might be held over just at this time, but was answering a letter from GEC Alsthom Transportation Projects, which read: 'We are interested in the proposed reinstatement of the Wye Valley Railway with electric railcar sets and would be pleased to receive further information on this subject'. I responded with three pages of detail, but heard nothing more; possibly the uncertainty about Lord Weinstock had aborted any substantial commitments at that time. The Royal Commission on Transport had just reported in favour of rail, cutting car use and road building. It remains to be seen how much *this* Government can be persuaded to change course.

The Government office for the West Midlands appeared to hold at least one rail-oriented civil servant – what a change! Mr P.E. Langley of the Planning and Transport Division wrote saying that further advice would be available to us, which they 'can best do when the cost benefit analysis results are available'. He also said, 'The means by which heavy rail schemes can be progressed is currently reviewed by ministers. I will write to you again when a way forward has been decided'. We heard nothing further but would obviously pursue this later to get the DoT to set out what headings the CBA should address as soon as we could finance that consultancy – and find a company capable of doing it.

In *The Times* of 19th November 1994 appeared a notice for the Channel Tunnel Rail Link Public Bill; there would be a new St Pancras station under the existing one; so that was how the obvious problems would be solved! Dr Brian Mawhinney, whose turn it was to be Transport Secretary, announced his support for the Midland Metro and the £150 million Croydon scheme of trams; this was accompanied by a photograph of a fine Feltham Union Construction tramcar, so familiar to our family on the 16 and 18 route but now wrongly attributed to 'the turn of the century'.

The drawing of the Croydon tram of the future was shown on normal double-track standard railway permanent way – which I found difficult to place!

In mid December 1994 we received a copy of 'A Strategy for Sustainable Tourism in the Wye Valley AoONB' by the Tourism Company, Ledbury, as earlier mentioned. I discussed it briefly with the principal of that company, Dr Richard Denham, but the content was vague regarding 'keenness to promote more use of alternative transport'. A proposal to restore the former Chepstow to Hereford railway has evoked much interest, but practicability and viability is not proven. More limited restoration on the southern section might offer more potential.

These were most exasperating conclusions to me and close to stupid in content; the idea that short sections of railway could simply be dropped into such a situation was quite ludicrous; only the *entire* renewal connecting with the national network at Chepstow, Hereford and Gloucester had the necessary potential. Dr Denham admitted he had not thought to engage in any discussion with ourselves nor to seek an objective view on "practicality and viability" from our consulting engineers at Chepstow! I sensed some embarrassment in his talking to me and I felt he had been constrained from writing or researching (over nine months!) that which the hidden establishment that runs the JAC did not want to hear. Who will write the full story of this quango, I wonder? I wait with interest!

CHAPTER 12

Gleam of Light – 1995

As I look back to January 1995 it is early February 1996. The snow is four or five inches thick in Ross and cars cannot even get out of Blake Avenue onto the Merrivale Lane. The telephone line is down to Susan Gartside at Sellack, and Geoff Gartside has decided to walk into Ross from Brampton Abbots – the risk of using a car is too great. I wonder how many people on the 50-mile route of the WVR are looking in frustration at a trackbed along which a safe, easy means of travel even in these conditions had been denied to them.

Back in January 1995, Richard Eagle wrote to Paul Marland MP in the belief that his current support for Dean Forest Railway etc. indicated a re-think (following his Government's 'way to Demascus' volte-face) of his attitude towards railway travel. Needless to record, Richard received no reply. Malcolm Clivery, our chairman, and Richard did an exploratory drive between Mitcheldean Road and Hereford, but it was so wet that they were hardly able to leave the car. They had visited St Briavels, Ballingham and Fawley Stations, and the latter was occupied by people who gave them a good welcome and seemed interested in the prospect of becoming halt wardens in the future. We had an invitation to speak to the Forest of Dean Business Club at Coleford on 9th January 1995. I gave a provisional positive response provided they could provide transport from Ross. This was readily agreed to, as committee members lived here; both Serena and myself attended and the occasion went well despite an unheated venue!

At Parkend in the Forest of Dean, the landlord of the Rising Sun, Kevin Howell, proposed the re-opening of a mineral loop line and tried to have it included in the Forest's Structure Plan.

This was, of course, linked to further opencast coal mining proposals and to avoid all the lorry traffic otherwise involved. As I write I believe the wretched opencast mining scheme has died. However, if Mr Howell's scheme could link up with the DFR there must be the prospect of tourism, even some local use, without the coal traffic. In the *Daily Telegraph* of 1st February 1995 the soon-to-be-privatised GWR was shown as including the Worcester–Hereford line and South Wales, Cardiff, through to Fishguard and Milford Haven, the Wales lines being Regional Rail currently. This could be important to us once the GWR attained separation from British Rail.

Upon WVR matters, both Serena Robinson and I were already much involved making applications for the Millennium Commission's Lottery grants and European Union Objective 5b funding applicable to a 'Rural Area in Decline', which we are. We decided the other directors should meet on 1st April 1995 to see the complexity of this work and to add their views etc. They were surprised that the market research report had unearthed no day visitor statistics – so important, even critical to our marketing operation. However, Serena and I already had in mind doing such a survey in Ross later in the summer.

As company secretary, I had arranged with the Millennium Commission to attend an Application Workshop on 5th April in the Forte Post House Hotel, Cardiff; it was agreed that Serena and myself would represent the company. The Millennium application was for £18.5 million, being 50% of the WVR capital requirement, in accordance with the rules. The Objective 5b application was for £100,000 as working capital to cover funding staff, leasing office space at the registered office and the consultancies for the cost benefit analysis and the environmental statement. It was also agreed that Serena and myself would attend a 5b seminar, organised by the Hereford and Worcester County Council, at the Swan offices in Ross on 20th April. The chairman, Malcolm Clivery, and Richard Eagle expressed their appreciation of the load Serena and I were carrying for the project.

Another invitation to speak, dating from September last year, came up on 19th April; my dad's birthday, I recalled. This was with the Rotary Club of Monmouth at the Queen's Head Hotel, St James Street; their previous venue at the King's Head had been most regrettably closed, reflecting some of the lack of visitors, which the railway would help to redress. As Geoff Gartside was a member of Ross Rotary, I asked if he would be attending and if so could Serena and myself travel with him? "Yes," says he, and we were grateful for his warm car on a bitterly cold night; I didn't thaw through until wrapped around a hot toddy in the bar! It was a jolly occasion, preceded by dinner and with wives present. I always wonder why for the majority of the time these and other clubs prefer to be single sex, especially after two major wars when both sexes worked so closely together.

We had received leaflets advertising the second Ross Business Show on 28th July 1995 from Henry Kaye and, as secretary, felt I should ask (i) whether any sponsorship was available for the non-revenue earning exhibitors or, if not, (ii) whether we might appear 'on credit'. Henry said he would put the matter to the meeting; we were, by far, the largest scheme in the area with wide common-good business potential. Henry told us that the WVR's bank, Barclays, was actually the only one *not* to participate in the show last year! I was not surprised!

On 26th April 1995 we received a long letter from Eric Barbery, Railway Development Society, Stroud, commenting on the Kevin Howell proposals for restoration of the Forest Mineral Loop line. This I forwarded to Richard Eagle, as he is so much more knowledgeable in that area. His reply was an excellent analysis of the proposition and saw a renewal as a sensible part of the tourism investment subsequent to any coal removal. On Radio 4, Chris Ellis, of the embryo GWR, spoke of a *Daily Telegraph* and coffee as an incitement for regular travellers. I thought that this could well be implemented on the WVR to holders of quarterly season tickets. We saw great advantage in a clocks-back winter season for motorists, who do not like bad weather/darkness, and the ability to read a paper or do productive work instead of driving would be obvious.

Richard had just been on a week's Freedom of Wales Rover Ticket – £47 for unlimited travel including the Ffestiniog Railway, discounts on other narrow gauge lines and a flat rate for any buses of £1. He used only one bus link and found British Rail Enquiries without bus timetables; 'one hopes for the best' seemed to be the motto. I can only comment that in my lifetime, actual integration between rail and road has always been less than satisfactory to the passengers, who have little real influence in the ongoing battle for revenue.

The AGM of 20th May 1995 was inevitably a quiet affair following so quickly on the April meeting with Millennium and 5b applications content. Malcolm Clivery and I were re-elected as directors and the financial statement and directors' report were accepted. Due to Government changes in the reporting procedures for small companies, our auditors, Thorne's of Ross, resigned as such, but a partner would act as financial adviser as necessary. I handed out a brief to directors to assist with any press approaches should we be successful in our grant applications.

On 17th May 1995 David Williams of Optimum Property Services renewed a contact we had made in 1993 regarding the proposed Hereford bypass. His particular concern was the Hereford 2000 group's scheme to create Rotherwas Station for passengers and possibly freight. This would be our junction with Regional Rail before entering Hereford, the WVR route to Ross and Gloucester offering the fastest and most direct communication with that city, Bristol, Swindon and London etc. I expressed the willingness of our company to take part in any meetings with the 2000 group and the local authorities etc. David borrowed a copy of the engineering feasibility report and so gained a much better grasp of the practicalities than he was getting from hearsay and those who would over-emphasise the element of controversy, so inevitable when there is *any* change in an area where only the most powerful get their way. We would keep in touch.

June was cheered by a light-hearted appearance by Richard Eagle as the Slim Controller in top hat and morning dress when the Dean Forest Railway made history as the first steam train for 35 years pulled into Lydney Junction! The engine was auto-train locomotive No. 1466, on loan from the GWR Society, Didcot; it was way back in 1961 when the chairman of the GW Society, Graham Perry, a mere schoolboy (!), six other founders and I took my suggestion of having a whip-round at £5 a time to save that locomotive and its trailer coach for posterity.

In the same paper, the Rural Development Commission announced £850,000 for new transport projects! I had an ongoing but completely fruitless correspondence with the RDC Malvern office – dating from 1987! It was quite obvious that Roger Grimley, rural services officer, was, for reasons which have yet to be revealed, entirely against the renewal of the WVR. It is not the purpose of this book to weary the reader with the circular nature of the one-centimetre thick correspondence ('thick' is probably the right description for the lack of logic) from 1987 to 1995, but it would seem worthwhile reproducing our letter of 29th November 1994 to Tessa Turner, RDC Malvern, after which I referred the whole matter to the Rt Hon. Lord Shuttleworth, who sat atop this awful quango:

Wye Valley Railway Limited
Ross-on-Wye

Ms Tessa Turner Limited
Project Officer
Rural Development Commission
Malvern

29th November 1994

COST BENEFIT ANALYSIS FOR WYE VALLEY RAILWAY

Thank you for your letter of 23rd November 1994, received this morning. May we first correct the implications of your 'Feasibility' heading: the feasibility of the renewal was established by the engineering study of 1987 and the consequential consultancies of financial, organisational, business planning and marketing have all confirmed the viability of this project.

We respond, below, to the particular aspects which you raise:

COUNTY COUNCILS:

Whether or not the three county councils will say publicly at any one time whether or not they support this renewal is academic. It is a political judgement which has varied over the years, affected by deaths on the roads locally through to the Royal Commission on Environmental Pollution. Specifically, practical local matters are (for Hereford and Worcester CC) the degradation of Symonds Yat and management thereof, which the WVR would facilitate. With the Gloucester CC, the re-opening, in about two years' time, of Grange Court Station as a parkway alternative to cars entering the city; the viability of this depends upon a WVR junction operating in order to provide sufficient service frequency for commuters. Providing an off-road facility connecting Symonds Yat, Monmouth, Tintern and Chepstow is the subject of a Gwent CC consultancy not due until January 1995.

The facts are that the problems and policies planned by the counties DO inevitably involve reinstatement of the lines because there is no other SOLUTION to pollution, congestion, accidents, AoONB degradation and the economic revival of this 'Rural Area in Decline'. It is also unwise to regard the current views of Hereford and Worcester and Gwent County Councils as anything other than of passing interest, since their dissolution is very likely.

NEW BUILD ON LINE-OF-ROUTE:
Our consulting engineers, with whom we keep in touch, have all aspects of diversions, alternatives, growth of communities etc. in mind and can be commissioned at short notice to firm up these matters. We know of only one bungalow actually built on the site of Weston-under-Penyard Halt – much to the chagrin of the villagers registered as our supporters, who realise they have been left only with the dangerous road system. Where Nicholas Ridley overruled his inspector and the Local Plan to agree housing at Mitcheldean Road, we will still serve the community by a diversion. If the RDC wishes to ensure action from a factual base, we suggest they fund our consulting engineers to revise the feasibility study as at 1995. Mr Grimley might consider the full-page notice of the Channel Tunnel Rail Bill (*The Times* of 19.11.1994) to put into perspective how little disturbance the WVR renewal will incur. The WVR Ltd authority would be under the Transport and Works Act, 1992.

VIABILITY OF WYE VALLEY RAILWAY:
We do not know why Mr Grimley is seeking a higher standard of proof for the matter than that of the Commission's chairman, Lord Shuttleworth, who has said: 'The loss of essential services saps the vitality of local communities and causes particular problems for people who cannot easily get into town. Services play a major part in helping rural communities to thrive and prosper, in attracting investment and enabling people to live and work in the countryside. There is urgent need for ACTION to maintain and improve services. The challenge for POLICY MAKERS and SERVICE PROVIDERS is to find ways of providing essential services and facilities ...' Surely, since 1986 we have been doing precisely what Lord Shuttleworth requires.

We have received grant aid assistance from the Department of Employment and Tourism (twice), the Department of Trade and Industry (twice, after examination by their independent consultants), Hereford City Council, the English Tourist Board and (in 1993) from the Hereford and Worcester Training and Enterprise Council. Perhaps, most immediately relevant, you could write to the Government office of the West Midlands, P.E. Langley, Planning and Transport Division, to be assured that their current requirement from WVR Ltd is for the COST BENEFIT ANALYSIS.

Our 1993 consultancy, market research and five-year revenue projection proves, as nearly as anyone can 'prove' the future that the renewal is a viable project. This report is available at 10% cost price, i.e. £700. Further, BALFOUR BEATTY, writing on 7th June 1994, says they do 'fully support the aims and objectives of your organisation and believe that the WYE VALLEY RAILWAY is a PRACTICAL AND

ENVIRONMENTALLY ACCEPTABLE public transport measure'.

We consider that by all reasonable standards we have nothing more to prove, but have to ask why Malvern RDC is applying double standards in the matter of grants. What proof of viability has the Commission received in exchange for the £20,000 it has granted for cosmetic railway nostalgia at Fiveways, Ross? We have to bear the brunt, by association, for criticism of this expenditure, which can in no way improve the current infrastructure situation being but a slight and reminder of a common-good facility the town has lost.

You are welcome to copy this to whoever may be involved; we are certainly most concerned that the local RDC chairman and local commissioners appear not to have considered a matter we began in May this year.

Eric T. Rawlins
Secretary

Wye Valley Railway Ltd
Ross-on-Wye

The Rt. Hon. Lord Shuttleworth
Development Commission
London

13th January 1995

COST BENEFIT ANALYIS GRANT

It is a matter of considerable concern to this company that I have to write to you about the difficulty this substantial project for the benefit of this 'Rural Area in Decline' is suffering in the operation of the RDC office at Malvern. In summary, this project has in the years since 1987 produced four substantial research reports (two by Touche Ross International) and all supported by the DTI (twice), the Department of Employment and Tourism (twice), the English Tourist Board and the Hereford and Worcester Training and Enterprise Council. The reports examine engineering feasibility, organisation and funding, market research and the business plan.

Early last year matters were sufficiently advanced for the Department of Transport (London and Birmingham) to agree to consider an application for a 50% capital grant under S56 Transport Act, 1968. This would be subject to a satisfactory COST BENEFIT ANALYSIS. On 17th May 1994 we wrote to RDC Malvern for a response to our advice of availability of our market research and five-year revenue projection of 4th November 1993. An RDC letter of 15th June 1994 refers to 'difficulties', to which we replied; see copy letter of 18th June 1994. Mr R. Grimley RSO enjoys the facility of Regional Railways at Malvern, but seems to be biased against the WVR because some landowners might object to renewal in what is one of the most populated areas in the country without railways.

However, it is surely not the function of the RDC to take sides in a matter for which there is a statutory right to object at a public inquiry under the Transport and Works Act, 1992. Mr Grimley's office also seeks, by letter of 23rd November 1994, to require 'some sort of proof that the railway is a viable project'. This information is contained in our consultants' reports and referred to in our letter of 29th November 1994. Again, the viability of the railway is not an appropriate concern for RDC, since there is no indication that they will build/operate the line. The date of our formal application for 50%, i.e. £3,500, as a grant towards the cost benefit analysis was 7th July 1994. We have had no reply to our letter of 29th November 1994, but were amazed to see in the local press that Malvern RDC has given no less than £20,000 to a scheme to tidy up the site where Ross Station will be built, with old GWR seating and a display of old GWR photographs showing the local people what they have LOST! This looking backwards is the complete opposite of facilitating RURAL DEVELOPMENT today! However, in the public mind such expenditure is automatically associated with THIS Company – and we have already had oral criticism. Our application to RDC followed a record of carefully applied grants, subject to 'due diligence'; indeed, the DTI employed a different assessor on each occasion. Consequently, our application to RDC was made in good faith following what we noted as the Commission's 'priorities', expressed by your good self as: 'The loss of essential services saps the vitality of local communities and causes particular problems for people who cannot easily get into town. Services play a major part in helping rural communities to thrive and prosper, in attracting investment and enabling people to live and work in the countryside. There is urgent need for ACTION to maintain and IMPROVE services. The challenge for POLICY MAKERS and SERVICE PROVIDERS is to find ways of providing essential services and facilities.'

We fully affirm our commitment to this philosophy and the work since 1986 is evidence of actual progression. However, if the foregoing is the RDC 'National' POLICY, what on earth is operating at Malvern? Perhaps it is time for devolution, as with

Hereford and Worcester County Council, so that Herefordshire may have its own RDC office.

The purpose of this letter is that when the protests about the waste of money at Fiveways, Ross, become a press matter, you will personally be aware of the background. Had the small grant requested been made to the company we could have joined in the inevitable 'opening ceremony' as a step in the right direction. As matters stand, the treatment by Malvern RDC is an affront to our dedicated directors and the expectations of the travelling public.

Eric T. Rawlins
Secretary

A letter signed by Lord Shuttleworth on 1st February 1995 merely indicated the *existing* involvement of Tessa Turner; another five months was wasted and then a further useless letter appeared from a Mr R.A. Kessler, Area Manager, unknown to the WVR company, which is reproduced below:

WYE VALLEY RAILWAY: COST BENEFIT ANALYSIS RURAL DEVELOPMENT PROGRAMME HEREFORD AND WORCESTER 1995/6

Thank you for your application under the above scheme. While appreciating how strongly you feel about this proposal, I am afraid that approval cannot be given to a project which does not have the support of other local partners with whom the Commission works closely on a day to day basis. They have advised us of considerable doubts they have regarding the viability of such a scheme.

Indeed, the Commission has its own serious concerns as to the ultimate possibility of constructing such a line, and notes that at the time of application no other match funding for the study had been found. After careful consideration, I regret that the Commission is unable to fund this study in 1995/6.

The Commission has continued to correspond over a considerable period of time on this subject and while it is willing to give full consideration to fresh or significantly revised proposals, I am afraid that there is nothing of a substantive nature that I would wish to add to the comprehensive replies provided to you by my colleagues on several previous occasions.

R.A. Kessler
Area Manager – West Midlands

The correspondence closed with my letter of 29th July 1995 to Lord Shuttleworth:

Wye Valley Railway Ltd
Ross-on-Wye

Lord Shuttleworth
RDC London

Positive work for this scheme has left to one side another negative from the RDC stable; namely, a letter of 1st June 1995 from Malvern but bearing the signature of one R.A. Kessler, apparently an area manager. It came as a surprise to me that any 'area management' could (a) have neglected over ten years to meet with this company with a major infrastructure project and (b) could have allowed Malvern to develop an anti-rail attitude against Government policy. However, the content of Mr Kessler's diatribe indicates that, as with Mr Grimley, he has avoided reading our consultants' reports of engineering feasibility and financial viability. It should be noted that these factors are not doubted by the Millennium Commission.

The issue is quite simple: instead of granting our application for £3,500 towards a DoT-required cost benefit analysis for a genuine rural development, Malvern RDC has acted in a role appropriate only to English Heritage. Perhaps Messrs Kessler and Grimley should be transferred to EH, for they clearly operate outside the spirit of your policy speeches.

We have made substantial progress since 1986, when we invited the concept of 'partnership' by inviting liaison officers from all interested local authorities etc. You should know from Gloucester County Council's letter of 13th July 1993 to Mr Grimley that they SUPPORTED an RDC Grant for our CBA. As long ago as 30th May 1990, Councillor Martin Baines, Hereford and Worcester CC, wrote wishing WVR Ltd the 'GREATEST SUCCESS with the project and I will support it when the issue arises in Committee'. Indeed, this council is currently most supportive.

We note, from the local press, that an RDC manager, John Edwards, has £850,000 available and says, 'people just need good ideas about meeting rural transport needs to put in a bid from the fund' and 'public transport locally was a serious issue with three out of four rural parishes within Hereford and Worcester lacking a daily bus service and one third of rural households with a car. This limits access to services, jobs and training'. No contact address is given for Mr Edwards, but at the suggestion of a fellow director, we decided to delay this letter until we could meet with representatives of RDC on stand 27 at the Ross Business Show yesterday 28th July 1995. However, the stand appeared otherwise occupied with no RDC persons around; the opportunity to clear the air and perhaps meet with John Edwards had been lost.

However, we revert to the reason for our letter to you of 13th January 1995, referring to anticipated local reaction to the wasted 'matching funding' expenditure at Fiveways, Ross. This scheme of 'enhancement' contributes NOTHING towards the new town STATION 'development' necessary on this site required to bring the wide-ranging economic benefits which alone (because all else has FAILED) will REVIVE this 'Rural Area in Decline'. This is, indeed, a classic example where two wrong decisions do not make a right and the public junketing with district councillors who spend £20k of local taxes is now hitting the fan. We expect to have to issue a disclaimer in the press shortly because at the Business Show we met with universal APPROVAL for the renewal and cannot accept responsibility for what is seen as cosmetic irrelevance at Fiveways.

At least you will know we sought to avoid this situation. Should Mr John Edwards operate your national policies, independent of the current Malvern management, we should be pleased to meet with him and seek a way forward, given his address.

Above all, perhaps now is the time for YOU to decide for what the Rural Development Commission will be remembered when the Wye Valley Railway is re-opened. As a quango with a biased local bureaucracy which raised all manner of obfuscation OR a support of a visionary concept, tested by a decade of independent research and for which no practicable alternative for the Millennium and new century exists?

Eric T. Rawlins
Company Secretary

This biased response of Lord Shuttleworth is reproduced below and concludes the correspondence; it is dated 15th August 1995:

SHUTTLEWORTH
Chairman RDC

The Secretary
Wye Valley Railway Ltd

Thank you for your letter of 29th July 1995. The Commission does appreciate the strength of your support for this initiative. However, we cannot fund a project which does not have the support of the key local partners, and their concerns about the viability of your proposal are shared by the Commission. We are committed to helping new and innovative projects which clearly demonstrate they can tackle rural transport problems. Any scheme, however, must command the support of the local community, the public and private sector.

The Commission has made its views clear on this project on a number of occasions. You need to address the issues raised in Ray Kessler's letter to you of 1st June before we can take the possibility of Commission assistance any further. We await details of a fresh, or significantly revised, proposal which has the backing of key local partners before we are able to consider your application any further.

SHUTTLEWORTH

This circular tour of old ground is laughable after a decade of positive research for a major project plainly outside the understanding of the Commission's staff even in London; needless to say, neither Messrs Kessler or Edwards ever made contact in order that we might answer any *genuine* concerns they might have. But I had wasted enough of my life on this quango of little consequence if it weren't for its ability to splash about public taxes locally with no responsibility to follow their chairman's public words. Perhaps Lord Nolan will find time to examine the RDC, for which process I shall be most happy to give evidence.

Serena Robinson and I had completed a full application for the Millennium Commission and on 13th June 1995 we received a letter signed by Jennifer Page, chief executive. The crucial paragraph reads: 'Your application met our key criteria for millennium projects but was judged not to have as distinctive an impact as others we received, and it has not therefore been selected for further examination'. Note that WVR had, therefore, *not* been faulted due to 'unproven viability or failure to meet published criteria'.

It seemed we had left the tricky RDC quango only to fall foul of a different subjective view by another! I wrote back asking for further clarification, as we could imagine nothing more 'distinctive' for the overall benefit of this community than to have advanced off-road passenger travel, acceptable to tourists also, between two cities, three towns and the AoONB.

I wrote to Richard Eagle, taking a somewhat cynical view that *had* we already got 50% of our capital need in the bank then the Commission might have reacted differently; note that the Government game of insisting an enterprise supplies half the capital needed *ahead* of actual Government help even for an infrastructure project had been quietly adopted by the Lottery Commission. I suspect that the average punter had no idea whatever that the Commission would be applying every bureaucratic device in the book to avoid assisting a project which its Government-selected members had been told to avoid – these, we heard from the Lottery, were the exclusion of health, educational and railway projects.

I wrote to a dozen or so of the construction companies advising them of our Millennium application in the rather vain hope that the Prime Minister (John Major) and the Chancellor of the Exchequer (Kenneth Clarke) were right in claiming that after years of recession the economy was recovering. If there were any response from the construction side, I proposed to ask for sponsorship of a professional video that could be sent to grant sources in order to present a visual counter to the 'insufficiently distinctive' excuse for not assisting the WVR project. As Richard Eagle put it, "We have a toehold on the threshold of success; if the door opens we can step inside."

We now knew, in July 1995, that Ffestiniog's application for Millennium money had been successful to renew the Welsh Highland line. We considered that it was a good precedent that such a long-abandoned, narrow gauge tourism only line should be renewed. Richard considered that the Commission would have known that Welsh Development Agency etc. grants would also be triggered. Yes indeed, there were many advantages to being over the Wales border entirely; the WVR was only 33% into Monmouthshire and so slipped through full consideration, for we have had no success with the WDA.

Contact with Brian Knowles, Hereford and Worcester County Council, on the matter of a possible grant under the Single Regeneration Budget developed in June 1995. Basically, the need for this was caused by the Government removing the Hereford and Worcester Training and Enterprise Council's funds, which had part-paid for our market research report in 1993. These funds were put in the SRB budget, which, for this area, covered the Midlands Region – stretching from the Welsh border to the east coast north of the Wash! This huge area was administered, in theory, from Leicester, in practice by civil servants from the Government offices of the West Midland, Fiveways Tower, Edgbaston, Birmingham. This was complicated by the 'new' idea of 'partnerships' with local authorities – a concept which we of the WVR had sought to effect since 1986! On 2nd June 1995 Jeremy Snape, Hereford and Worcester County Council, forwarded an Outline Bid proforma to be submitted to GOWM Birmingham by 16th June 1995. We requested £100,000, being, as Brian Knowles described it, a 'mirror' application for the working capital requested under the Euro 5b scheme. Readers may find interesting a breakdown of this sum, which we put forward for consideration:

Rent and Local Business Tax for accommodation at registered office	£4,000
Furniture, filing cabinets, stationery, telephones, fax, copier, computing time, heating, electrics etc.	£3,000
Staff equal to two full-time persons covering normal office hours, including on-costs	£32,900
Work by our consulting engineers (Cass Hayward, Chepstow) to firm up line-of-route alternatives etc. of feasibility study	£3,100
Cost Benefit Assessment consultancy required by Dept. of Transport, HM Treasury and 5a Regulations	£7,500
Environmental Statement by Dr Phil Goodwin, Oxford University Transport Unit	£6,500
Line-of-route maps, land search ownership, legal input towards negotiations and conveyancing to WVR	£7,000
Instructing our Parliamentary Agent (Sharpe Pritchard, Westminster) for procedures concerning Public Inquiry, the Parliamentary Committee, if ruled applicable, and obtaining the Empowerment Order under the Transport and Works Act, 1992	£10,000
Negotiating agreements with construction/ rolling stock companies to form a consortium for WVR and conversion to plc to facilitate public participation in balance of capital requirements	£22,000
Contingencies	£4,000
TOTAL	£100,000

The company has considerable experience in applying 'due care and diligence' to contracted consultants and the necessary monitoring. Consequently, the

> processes outlined above must be advanced gradually because of the multitude of disciplines/techniques involved in business and financial strategy, civil engineering, economic development, statutes and law, environment, railway matters, public relations, and liaison with local administrations, government departments, GWR/Railtrack etc. Given the complexity of this large infrastructure project, using the parallel critical path technique we anticipate affecting the foregoing expenditure over two years.

We felt the foregoing to be a very economical allocation of £100,000 working capital and it certainly demonstrates a grasp of the project and the management already involved. We reminded Mr Snape and Ms Pam Barratt GOWM of the commendation we had received for HAWTEC, the predecessors of this SRB scheme, quoting Ms Gaynor Field, head of HAWTEC Economic Development: 'We do, however, think that the Wye Valley Railway is a wonderful project and hope you obtain regional/ national support to enable you to proceed.'

On 13th June 1995 I also wrote to John Nicholls, regional director, English Partnership at Leicester, giving the full background of the WVR research plus a map of the line. We heard that our £100,000 request was considered appropriate as a 'pilot ceiling', that the 'partnership' held £240 million (!) non-committed and that our old contacts at RDC Malvern, Alison McLean and Tessa Turner, were being moved to Hereford with changed responsibilities involving both Euro 5b and SRB. I heard that my bête noire at Malvern Rural Development Commission, Roger Grimley, was to retire.

In order to give the reader some idea of the complexity and problems of dealing with a rolling bureaucracy of local and national Government officers, I will reproduce a letter of 12th July 1995, signed by P.F. Williams, Single Regeneration Budget, Government Office for the West Midlands, and my response of 21st August 1995:

Govt Office for West Midlands
Birmingham

Wye Valley Railway Ltd
Ross-on-Wye

I refer to your letter of 7th June, submitting an outline bid for the reinstatement of the Wye Valley Railway. In the Government Office's current view, given the high standard of many of the 73 outline bids received and the limited resources available, it is unlikely that your bid would succeed, based on the information provided.

If you decide to develop your bid, please note that the closing dates for the final bids, as stated in the Bidding Guidance, is 18th September 1995, and that no further information relating to the bid can be accepted after that date.

P.F. Williams

Wye Valley Railway Ltd
Ross-on-Wye

Mr P.F. Williams
Govt Office for West Midlands

We refer to your letter of 12th July 1995, in which you imply that the standard of our outline bid is insufficiently high. While it is true that our resources preclude a glossy mind-blowing application, we do consider our letter to Ms P. Barrett and the submission Annex B were completed thoroughly, in the fullest detail, and that your word-processor response is unfitting.

Indeed, in fulfilling the CRITERIA of 'Principal Outputs' we seriously doubt whether ANY of the 'competitors' have schemes in any way a close rival.

Is this preliminary rejection based on ANY understanding of the difficulties faced by companies like WVR Ltd, who over a DECADE have attempted to carry out the GOVERNMENT'S commitment to rail renewal without road-equivalent resources?

If by 'developing' our bid you wish to consider even more of our research as supplied, not criticised for any reason of lacking viability or not meeting criteria by the Millennnium Commission, we can forward another 14 pages. However, we seek only £100,000 for necessary working capital from SRB and enclose herewith a breakdown which has been developed to the extent the real world permits.

Reinstatement of the Wye Valley Railway has become even more vital as pollution, congestion, accidents and degradation of the AoONB has increased. This is a 'RURAL AREA IN DECLINE' for the salvation of which NO OTHER alternative of significance exists. We trust that no less time will be given to fair and full consideration of this application, in September, than we have given to this submission to date.

Eric T. Rawlins
Secretary

Hearing nothing more in 1995, the record shows that we offered a meeting to explain any matters beyond the experience of the assessors in January 1996; needless to say, there was no further communication from the Government office.

An incredible non-event occurred in May 1995, when £40,000 was spent to tidy up the railway bridge piers at Fiveways, Ross. The Rural Development Commission's Malvern office, while denying WVR Ltd £3,500 for the cost benefit analysis, gave no less than £20,000 of tax payers' cash, the rest coming from local ratepayers via the district and county councils! I was asked by

John Loynes, apparently no longer in the SHDC's employ, to provide photographs from my GWR negatives. This I refused to do unless 'our failure to receive the £3,500 RDC grant is due to some administrative oversight'. In effect, the RDC obviously intended a personal slight to me, but simultaneously sought to take advantage of my photographic collection.

The grand 'opening' ceremony was an occasion for much over-the-top celebration by councillors, which was cut down to size by a letter, here reproduced, from an unimpressed ratepayer, Mrs M. Wiles, to the *Ross Gazette* of 13th July 1995:

ANGER AND DISGUST

> Sir,
>
> I write in anger and disgust at the blatant attitude taken by local council officials to myself and, I feel, the community as a whole. On the evening of Thursday June 28th I encountered various council officials drinking and patting themselves on the back (no doubt at tax payers' expense) on the completion of the Fiveways/railway area. I pointed out that one of the main captions had a spelling error, namely Hereford was missing an 'r' (Herefod), only to be rudely told, "It can't be changed now it's up!"
>
> Must all who visit Ross think we are all illiterate, even if some of the council/councillors are!
>
> M. Wiles
> Ross

At least Mrs Wiles and other tax payers reading this account can understand something more of this matter, but a small garden and rail display simply emphasises both to local residents and visitors just what an asset the town has lost! Looking backwards is no help at all to a district classified by Europe as a 'Rural Area in Decline' – while nearly everywhere else has co-operated in the renewal of its lines – but then the county councillors almost all live in Worcestershire and enjoy good rail services in all directions! The subject remains a nuisance to us when speaking to the public, who can hardly believe we have not been involved in this cosmetic stuff on the site where a new Ross Station is the practicable requirement for the new century!

The road accident statistics for 1994 now appeared, showing 'only' 3,650 actually killed last year; we wondered how the bodies are counted. Pulled from wrecks dead? Died within less than 24 hours of the crash? The Government's record for rigging the unemployment and other statistics were beyond a joke and the criteria were constantly shifted. Unfortunately, over 300,000 were injured and the sharpest increase was for children, which rose 6%, including an 8% rise in deaths and serious injuries. It is important to realise that exhaust pollution deaths were counted separately and amounted to around an *additional* 10,000. What are we leaving our grandchildren for the year 2000 and beyond if getting from A to B has such a wicked price tag, both in cash and human suffering?

A major Forest of Dean survey, part funded by the Rural Development Department, said that 'now was the time to act – sufficient energy has been expended in identifying the problem issues'. The factors identified included the immobility of those without cars, particularly elderly and the 16 to 25-year-olds without employment. I wondered (i) how much it cost to be told the obvious, and (ii) what actual *action* would follow. I decided not to hold my breath.

On 2nd June 1995 a *Forest of Dean Review* leader recorded its joy at the departure of the secretive Gwent County Council, 'because for the best part of ten years they have refused to supply us with any council documents'. Although Labour in flavour, we had also found this council useless and looked forward to the break up of both members and officers, particularly the latter.

On 8th June 1995 the *Ross Gazette* mentioned the 'restoration' of the GWR main goods shed at Ross; the SHDC planner, John Loynes, and Derek Cole, then chief executive, had told me that they had 'listed' it, but this apparently did not prevent the original slate tiles being replaced by modern concrete at some time. On 22nd June 1995 the same paper published a letter from Mr J. O'Donell of Hildersley, Ross, which is included below, because he is not the only person to come home to Ross and knows the area has lost the steel threads that used to connect us with the wider world. As this is written, in February 1996, all roads except the dual carriageway and in town are blocked with snow; I have been contacted by some residents whose minds are much concentrated by this, as they are effectively trapped in the country locations. I have suggested that they ask their local councillors to engage brains and support the renewal of the all-weather Wye Valley Railway, which got through so well to such places as the Royal Hotel at Symonds Yat in winters past. Mr O'Donell's letter appeared under the by-line 'TRAIN SPOTTER':

Hildersley
Ross-on-Wye

The Editor
Ross Gazette

My love for train spotting brought me to Ross as a boy, indeed I can remember standing on the platform in my anorak and scarf inhaling the train fumes and thinking this must be heaven. It was quite by chance my work brought me back to Ross all those years later and I was even able to buy a house in Hildersley which backs right on to the old railway line.

The anorak no longer fits, but I still have my train-spotting records, which I flick through while sitting in my garden and gaze up and down the empty track and hope one day we will see the trains clattering past again.

John O'Donell

Our response of 29th June 1995 was headlined by the editor: 'Bring back the railway'; the reference to the 'LNER A4 Mallard at the bottom of your garden' is a note of the detriment, as Celia Glover saw it in her *Ross and Monmouth Railway* booklet. However, at subsequent public occasions I was being pressed to ensure that steam excursions *did* feature that record-breaking engine! Knowing the nature of some of the folk around here, I wonder how many of the few so privileged would be making a charge to photograph such trains from their gardens!

Wye Valley Railway Ltd
Ross-on-Wye

The Editor
Ross Gazette

Mr John O'Donell's letter of June 22nd has caused the directors and me to divert briefly from our efforts, on 15 fronts, to obtain resources for the reinstatement.

Currently, the Millennium Commission, while giving immediate support to the narrow-gauge Ffestiniog tourism railway, has initially found the WVR to be 'not sufficiently distinctive'. On behalf of you all, we have responded 'From the point of benefit to the local community and tourism (scenery – mini Switzerland)', and we can imagine nothing more distinctive than the re-introduction of advanced passenger movement between two cities and three towns.

The renewal will enable the aims of the Symonds Yat Management Plan and the Strategy for Sustainable Tourism in the Wye Valley AoONB to be effected by access without further degradation. In addition to increasing the tourism revenue to a viable level, we have the advantage of connecting with the Hereford 2000 strategy and reinstatement of Grange Court Junction, as a parkway, to relieve Gloucester City commuting congestion, pollution and accidents.

Although it is our aim to co-operate with steam operators, on an occasional basis, we cannot guarantee the record-breaking Mallard at the bottom of your garden, although on the Hereford–Ross–Gloucester section and, therefore, within Mr O'Donell's view, this would be quite practicable. Down the line at Tintern we would hope to house a characteristic GWR auto-train (as now on the Dean Forest Railway) to operate summer season excursions to bring back the happy times when a trip by train alongside the river really made the day!

The electric railcars will be so quiet we feel Mr O'Donell will have to set his alarm to spot their passing – but that's progress! We hope to be present at the Ross Chamber of Trade and Industry's second Business Show at the Chase Hotel, July 28th. This will be our 59th public/special interest occasion since 1986 when the renewal project began; we look forward to meeting Mr O'Donell and our patient supporters.

Eric T. Rawlins
Company Secretary

We had no news of sponsorship for the Business Show at the Chase Hotel, so Mrs Robinson and I decided we would appear and circulate among the interested parties. The day duly dawned, promising blue skies and hot sunshine, as I toiled up through the Chase car park. Alongside, a figure alighted from his car and we passed the time of day; it was John Edwards, Chairman of South Herefordshire District Council. Would I, asked he, be kind enough to help him on with his chain of office? This I did, wearing my WVR director's tag, and he explained a speech was required of him upon such 'initiatives', about which we chatted in general. Serena Robinson joined me and we met with the Ross Initiative representatives, including Geoff Gartside and the high street bank ladies; a number of curiously non-local activities were also represented. I sought the Rural Development Commission's stand, determined to shake their representatives either by the hand or neck as seemed appropriate. However, it turned out they felt much safer at Malvern and no one actually appeared on their stand. Part of the covered area was tented and the temperature rocketed, surely into the upper nineties!

Mary Rawlins joined us for lunch in the Chase bar, recalling many happy holidays when to visit Ross was a relaxation – *not* having to drive a major project as today! Afterwards, I circulated further until the heat became too oppressive and we were glad not be tied to one location. A tractor disguised as a 'road train' operated in the Chase grounds; its trailers were well adapted to moving people and their luggage around at Butlins, but I saw no day-to-day use for it in Ross against a capital cost of around £80,000 plus staff and operating costs.

Back at the office we had a visit from Ken Kemp of Gloucester County Council's Transport Section. It seemed that Mike Taplin, of the same place and who had advocated to the Rural Development Commission, Malvern, that we be given support, had not told him a lot either about this scheme or their own aim to re-open Grange Court Station as a parkway. Serena considered him to be better advised when he left with a loaned copy of the market research survey, later returned marked 'Very interesting'. If only the WVR could attract half the positive action of the Glamorgan County Councils!

In order to plug a vital lack of statistics of the day visitor leisure situation in Ross and immediate area, Serena Robinson and I decided to carry out a survey over three days in August, during which the temperature never dropped below 90 degrees Fahrenheit! This exposure to the sun, continuing an exceptionally hot summer, almost certainly triggered a skin condition, possibly dating from Africa in 1946, and I would soon have to face a serious medical condition. The basis of the survey was a questionnaire drawn up in conjunction with Karen Williams, South Herefordshire District Council's tourism officer. In fact, we failed to get a response to one of her areas of interest because of the 100 interviewed no one had arrived by touring coach!

We found just under half (49%) were day visitors; they had simply got into their cars and driven – many from 100 miles away – mostly with no particular purpose in mind. None knew it was Ross Carnival weekend. All except three had arrived by car; on United States research we calculated that each round trip by car had put 2lbs of pollution into the air! About half would use the train if available, either to travel to the area via the national network or as a change from driving on arrival. We could not, of course, even guess at the numbers without cars, but who might visit should the WVR trains be in operation. We felt satisfied that this report, of August 1995, containing a range of pie diagrams, graphs etc. and 47 pages in length, shone new light on a neglected subject. When responding to how they had enjoyed the attractions of Ross, most had said, "*What* attractions?" The upper floor of the Market House, empty since the departure of the library in 1988, had proved the natural focal point, only to become a frustration at the locked doors. This survey would be a useful foundation on which to base the WVR day marketing and considered well worth the effort by the participating and other directors.

In the *Forest of Dean Review* of 4th August 1995 there appeared two railway-themed letters, from A. Reeve and Yvonne Dawson. Ms Dawson's excellent analysis included 'Millennium money could provide an extension to the rail system'; so true. These letters were connected with a Forest of Dean Regeneration Strategy so awful as to cause considerable dismay, as it was an advocation of even more road transport presences. My response coincided with a no-letters edition of the *Review* and so was published in *The Forester* of 25th August 1995:

Wye Valley Railway Ltd
Ross-on-Wye

The Editor
The Forester

REGENERATION STRATEGY

It seems to us that Mr and Mrs Sensible see more in the above report to favour the road and car lobbies than the primary concern to retain the fast disappearing character of the Forest. Although the government now recognises the advantages of non-polluting off-road transport, it is much slower in providing the essential transfer of funding.

The advent of the Millennium Commission's support for Landmark Schemes for the year 2000 exactly fits the Wye Valley electric railcar system and the company, as ever, is working exceedingly hard for assistance for this common-good project. Important, for some Forest car commuters, will be the renewal of Grange Court Junction as a parkway. This facility, some seven and one-half miles west of the city, is equal in distance to the Croydon area to London terminals. Reg Ward will know just how impossible all-road commuting to major work centres will become.

Our 59th 'public interest' occasion took place at the Ross Business Show in July. But readers may like to be reminded that between Gloucester and Hereford and the three towns on the line will be 20 parish halts serving small communities – essential if the Government's aim to reduce car use is to be effected.

However, despite our well-established relevance to the transport infrastructure, we have not been consulted or favoured with a copy of 'A Regeneration Strategy'. Even at this stage we would be pleased to make a constructive response to a problem which we have examined through ten years of work with independent consultants.

Perhaps Cllr Bruce Hogan should consult with his Glamorgan County Council colleagues, who, last year, were instrumental in the re-opening of FIVE 'Valley' railway lines.

Eric T. Rawlins
Company Secretary

Needless to say, no one from the Forest of Dean District Council, the Gloucester Rural Development Commission etc. deigned to respond to the company. We had another urgent problem in that the newly resurrected cycle industry was pressing to increase trade, as does the SMMT for the car manufacturers. In the Forest we had the Railways to Cycleways scheme being flogged by the Forestry Commission and the Forest of Dean District Council. But the parish councils, via John Marchant, chairman of West Dean, saw the need for consultation before changes were implemented with little regard for the opinions of local people. Certainly, as this is written in February 1996, I look out upon thick snow and wonder just what dividend the Foresters are getting out of the cycle tracks no one is using.

Serena Robinson and myself continued to fight for Millennium, 5b and SRB grants, but the weight of bureaucracy and paper was beginning to tell. Does the average punter realise what an industry of paper movers and committee members has been created to distribute their money with no understanding of local needs?

During September 1995 Michael Madeley, Railway Policy, Health and Safety Executive, forwarded a copy of the Draft Approved Code of Practice on the Hours of Work of Safety Critical Staff. We believe it is important to note the credibility which the WVR project enjoys at this level and our response of 11th September 1995 is reproduced below:

Wye Valley Railway Limited

Michael Madeley
Railway Policy
Health and Safety Executive

Thank you for the copy of the draft ACoP on the Hours of Work of Safety Critical Staff. We are pleased to note the developments since we responded to the questionnaire on 4th November 1994. Were it that the Government's facilities for PFI and the transfer of finance from road to rail were equally progressive.

As a prospective 'minor' railway, there are certain peculiarities with a line of 45 miles (plus 12 joint) compared with, say, one of 450 miles. In respect of drivers, but also other operating staff, there is a safety-orientated problem of BOREDOM/OVER-FAMILIARITY with the task. Today, there is no need for a long apprenticeship 'on the shovel'; indeed, with simulators also available, actual driving becomes a straightforward job, especially for operations never likely to exceed 80 mph.

With a 'new' railway (actually a renewal) the initial work will be line clearance, with separate male and female teams. These people will take some part in contractor laid pw, and so gain extremely valuable knowledge of the 'road', particularly (this being the Wye Valley) conditions of white fog, flooding, rock falls, trackbed slippage, heavy rain/snow, public and occupation crossings, bridges, 'sighting lines' etc.

Staff passing their probation period in this testing environment and retained become 'One-star' Permanent Way trained. From these (over and above pw needs in numbers) we select those wishing to train as drivers, guards/money collectors, buffet operators and maintenance (specialities). Power current and radio signalling will receive separate consideration when the electrical engineer is appointed. As staff pass trade training in extra areas, up to 5-star status and pay becomes applicable, in effect, a career situation from the employees' point of view and excellent flexibility, given reasonable notice, for staff interchanging. Hence, management can really respond to operational needs WITHOUT excessive overtime. Further, the multi-skilling will largely prevent the 'voluntary' overtime for standby and others purposes, which can soon become habitual/out of control. Personal safety is such an on-going factor on a railway, but the more staff know about the OTHER jobs the more they are able to sensibly ASSESS the risks, e.g. when crossing running lines etc.

Our managers will each have health and safety responsibilities in their individual disciplines and generally. We see no problem in working within the 'Group Standard' hour's limits of Para. 10. But we have reservations about the British Rail statistics of hour's worked/accidents/incidents. Are these, for example, hours PAID rather than hours actually in the CAB driving? Is travel time from home counted because it is paid? If there is no fall-off of human capability, then why isn't everyone working 100-hour weeks! The documentaries featuring zombie-like young doctors (who should be at the peak of physical fitness) indicate a less than satisfactory situation.

However, as you can see from the policy outline above, we seek to avoid the potential safety hazards by pre-design and training a new generation of railway persons rather than having to react to unfortunate occurrences.

We endorse the proposal to commission an HSE/ Railtrack project to examine the hours/fatigue scenario. It would be interesting to compare the private companies as and when available; meanwhile, we suggest that the consultancy should include statistics from the European mainland and the reviving railways of the United States.

Eric T. Rawlins
Company Secretary

Michael Madeley acknowledged this reply and added, 'Your interesting comments have been noted and copied to colleagues with particular responsibility for minor railway issues and for HSE Research'. It is satisfying to know that the WVR plans are so relevant to railway developments today; surely this completely counters nonsense criticism from the ignorant that we are mere railway 'buffs'.

On 7th October 1995 I met with David Hallam MEP and Chris Chappell, Hereford City and County Councillor, at a Labour Party meeting in Ross.

As secretary of the company, I was invited to forward two sheets of A4 explaining the WVR project to both. Chris wrote back saying he thought the WVR a very good idea and would talk to David Hallam 'to see how we could help with this project'. David Hallam wrote to the Government offices of the West Midland at Edgbaston on the 5b issue, resulting in a proposed meeting between Keven Griffiths, Head of the European Unit, and ourselves. As this is written, this meeting has yet to happen.

It came to my notice that our old hometown of Croydon was to have a new tramway system, New Addington to Wimbledon, and amazingly, Welsh Water was a member of the tendering consortium! I immediately wrote to them on 16th October 1995; readers will not be surprised to hear that not even an acknowledgement has been received for this local project's obvious need!

During September/October we corresponded with Morrison Construction Limited, an Edinburgh company now working from Derbyshire, and the Magor freight centre in Wales. We sought sufficient interest so as to be able to get the cost benefit analysis on its way, and a meeting was arranged for the New Year.

We were not amused by seeing yet another letter by Austin Wallace of Copse Cross Street, Ross, seeking to have the railway foundation from Tudorville to Hildersley converted to a road. He still seemed under the impression that such a road would not mean hundreds of houses right up to the Chase tree-line – so ruining the last bit of countryside and rural backdrop left on the Ross skyline – the hideous Brampton developments having destroyed that area right through to back gardens on the dual carriageway edge! As long ago as September 1987, we had shown drawings of rail alongside road in that area (Continental or modern tramway fashion), but always developers would only provide a road plus housing, which would create yet another Merrivale Lane to serve them. In no way could such a road be a bypass or be used by cars wishing to reach central Ross.

November 1995 saw the official opening of Holme Lacy House as a Warner Holidays' third country hotel. This represented an investment of £6.5 million and comprised 117 new bedrooms additional to 65 in the main house! A perceptive local supporter of the WVR renewal, Mrs Cutcliffe of Hoarwithy, drew our attention to the great convenience to that hotel of a re-opened Ballingham Station for visitors preferring the comfort of rail travel. This situation may be said to apply to almost every mile of the WVR route, where many hotels and guesthouses have closed due to lack of year-round viability. This particularly applied to winter visitor potential, where all-weather transport is missing and no one in their right mind drives for 'pleasure'!

On 29th November 1995 a comprehensive letter by Mr J.G. Davies appeared in the *Hereford Journal*. This, with my response, rather sums up the lack of a transport policy both locally and nationally. Mr Davies' piece was headlined 'No Mention of the Railways':

Westfaling Street
Hereford

The Editor
Hereford Journal

I have been asked by Hereford Trades Union Council to report on the Hereford City Council Economic Development Plan 1995/6. I was impressed by some of the initiatives proposed in the document, such as education and training, developing European links, access to funding and environmental issues.

The area I found ignored was transport. Other than a mention of the A49/A465 bypass, there was little mention of transport – no mention at all of rail.

We do at present have rail facilities in the city, although the freight yard is little used at this time. I understand rail freight services could return as the company running freight through Hereford, Transrail, have recently launched an enterprise to convey single-wagon loads, a business they are anxious to expand.

PASSENGERS.

The company could, under privatisation, be sold to an American company, who I am sure would wish to expand this single-load business. With regard to the passenger service, Hereford Trades Council has been in correspondence with our MP and the BR Office of Rail Regulators regarding the worsening of services on the Hereford–Birmingham (New Street) services. I feel that a rail link is an integral part of any city transport planning.

W.G. Davies

Our response carried an editorial heading and appeared on 13th December 1995:

Wye Valley Railway Ltd
Ross-on-Wye

The Editor
Hereford Journal

PLEA FOR RAILWAYS

When my directors read your 29th November headline, 'No mention of the railways', they thought it to be a criticism of the Budget! But perhaps our concern for the lack of development of the railways, rather than the grotesque pursuit of the wrong sort of privatisation, is at the root of the letter by Mr J.G. Davies. Readers with long memories will recall that Hereford City Council made an unsolicited investment in the first Touche Ross International Consultancy for WVR in 1988. Since that time we have had a positive mid-slump business plan and a successful market research and five-year revenue projection.

Our line-of-route provides for a direct service London–Gloucester–Ross–Hereford, saving 60 miles on the current detour via Newport. The WVR from Ross via Monmouth to Chepstow will provide a leisure/tourism attraction, as well as subsidising the day-to-day local use and countering, by a practicable off-road means of access, the AoONB 'degradation' of the Lower Wye Valley.

Currently, we are in touch with possible consortium members to construct and operate the lines. We have requested 50% of the £37 million capital requirement from the Millennium Commission; we were, initially, turned down on the grounds of being 'insufficiently distinctive', NOT for failing criteria or viability. This subjective view is being reappraised and we are also seeking £100,000 working capital via mirror applications to West Midlands 5b and the Single Regenerative Budget. The WVR 'star' career training scheme for Safety Critical Staff has been studied by the Health and Safety Executive's Railway Policy Group; it was copied to colleagues with particular responsibilities for minor railways and HSE research.

This company UNDERSTANDS the railway business and merits more active formal support.

The Government is now said to be supporting projects to 'develop the rail system from whenever they emerge'. We have worked exceedingly hard for ten years to reinstate our local railway heritage. But Sir George Young, Transport Secretary, is now backing a four-year-old £3 billion proposal to build the 180 miles Central Railway. Good luck to the Central scheme, but we would ask all those wishing the return of a modern Wye Valley Railway to join with us in persuading Sir George that there is great advantage also in our short-haul line to reduce congestion, pollution and accidents.

Faced with pressures to reduce car use and road building, an ALTERNATIVE needs to be in place. If it has spin-off benefits, such as the renovation of hotels, attractions etc., and can redress our shameful 'Rural Area in Decline' classification then so much the better.

Eric T. Rawlins
Company Secretary

On 1st December 1995 the Welsh Development Agency, always ready to pass the buck, advised us that Clive Hammersley had been appointed Assistant Director Implementation for the new

Monmouth Borough Council, replacing, apparently, the old Gwent County Council set-up. I wrote to him on 2nd December 1995, suggesting a meeting to put him in the picture and to have the Wye Valley Railway project properly absorbed into the 'economic development strategy for the new Monmouth Borough', which was one of his tasks. Almost needless to record, there was no response; no doubt the existing bureaucracy had swallowed him up to prevent objective consideration.

As earlier mentioned, it was not impossible that my cancer, diagnosed at the close of 1995, was a legacy of a tiny part I had played in the Labour Government's strategy of 1945 to increase the margarine ration by growing more ground (pea) nuts on the Gold Coast (Ghana) in West Africa. Having some time to await demobilisation from the RAF (demob. No. 57!), I was happy to go to Africa for an uncertain time with photoreconnaissance Lancasters. We wore bush hats only on occasions of urgent afternoon work on the aircraft; otherwise the 'forage' caps left the port side of our heads uncovered and this area became the site of my troubles in 1995. Having been spared for over 70 years, I have no regrets as I hope my autobiography shows.

But the WVR project has taken much of my theoretical 'retirement' since 1986, together with extraordinary daily support from my daughter/director Serena Robinson, and kept me in the study away from Mary, my wife, my other daughter, Susan Gartside, and Natalie, my granddaughter. With the agreement of the board of directors, Serena and I, company secretary, would now seek an injection of new daily management and greater finance for the company by a Transfer of Undertaking within a consortium. The year 1996 must concentrate upon facilitating this restructuring and, if this leads to less 'local' involvement in the new railway, then this book will surely have demonstrated the efforts of the past decade to do everything humanly possible to ensure a proper 'partnership' with authorities. Be it on the heads of those, whether as officers or members of authorities, who have procrastinated and failed to make objective assessment of the project for public-good infrastructure renewal for the new century. Such persons *should* have had the vision and will to undertake, without resort to hearsay, their statutory duties and responsibilities for strategic planning, major projects and transportation.

Mr J.G. Davies, whose letter is reproduced above, wrote again, and although this has crossed the line to the New Year, 3rd January 1996, readers may find it an inspiration with which to close Volume 1 of the WVR story –1855 to 1995:

Westfaling Street
Hereford

The Editor
Hereford Journal

WVR FILLS THE BILL

I was pleased to learn from the response to my letter of November 29th that the Wye Valley Railway is still in business. I first learned of this project from the late Rev. David Tipper, whose knowledge of and enthusiasm for this scheme left me in no doubt that this was a scheme that deserved to succeed. Perhaps WVR can take heart from the number of schemes now being agreed by the DoT.

The Midlands link between Birmingham and Wolverhampton – work has now started. Transrail, now back in single-wagon loads, have recently introduced a service to convey house coal by Rail Commuter Link, supported by the Highlands and Islands Enterprise. These are just a few of the many services now being offered by rail.

With the number of initiatives now being put forward by the Department of Environment on rural regeneration with emphasis on transport and tourism, I would suggest that the WVR scheme fits the bill on both accounts.

> I can only wish WVR well in their future negotiations and hopefully before I depart this planet I will be able to take a train ride through this beautiful countryside.
>
> J.G. Davies

Known for our knowledge of most of the relevant statistics, may I leave the reader with the following comparison and very neat perspective: the *entire* Wye Valley Railway up and running for £37 million; *1* Eurofighter for £40 million. Yes, we do need both, but you may judge the product value from a railway reducing disease caused by pollution, congestion and the enormous physical and financial burden of road accidents into the new century.

When all the lessons of Volume 1 have been understood, it will be a pleasure to read Volume 2 of the Wye Valley Story.

INDEX

WYE VALLEY RAILWAY STORY VOLUME 1: 1855 - 1995

NB Due to the repetition of the events etc., it is practical to give only one reference to each individual, organisation etc.

GOVERNMENT QUANGOS

HALT WARDENS 50

INDUSTRIAL HERITAGE

LOCAL AUTHORITIES

PERSONALITIES

PLACES

Hereford	1
Hildersley	97
Hoarwithy	185
Holme Lacy	290
Kerne Bridge	2
Kidderminster	245
Lady Park and Biblins	167
Lea	70
Ledbury	113
Longhope	169
Lydbrook	2
Lydney	184
Malvern	192
Mitcheldean Road/Stockholm Place	262
Monmouth	1
Monmouth May Hill	2
Monmouth Troy	4
Monmouth WVR	232
Newent	132
Newport (Mon.)	216
Paddington (London)	1
Parkend	256
Pontypool Road	4
Raglan	5
Redbrook	61
Ross-on-Wye	1
Ross 'Relief' Road	103
Rotherwas Junction	61
St Briavels	212
St Pancras	234
Sellack	87
Severn Tunnel Junction	5
Stockholm Place	70
Strangford Cutting	1
Symonds Yat	1
Tintern	11

PRIVATE ASSOCIATIONS AND SOCIETIES

PRIVATE AND PUBLIC COMPANIES

PUBLICATIONS

PUBLIC AND SPECIAL INTERESTS OCCASIONS 1985 to 1995

1985

Hereford and Worcester Council Chairmen, Chase Hotel, Ross, 19th November

1986

Monmouth Town Council, Shire Hall, 3rd March
Monmouth Action Committee, 8th April
Forest of Dean District Council, Bells Hotel, Coleford, 16th April
Monmouth Civic Society, 27th April
Monmouth Regatta, 25th May
Bulmers Railway Centre, Hereford, 22nd June and 13th July
Rotary Club, Ross, 14th July
Mayor's Garden Party, Chase Hotel, Ross, 31st August
Monmouth, Chepstow, Ross Tri-partite Action Committee, Monmouth, 15th September

1987

Goodrich Fete, 20th June
Forest of Dean DC and Dept Employment/MSC, Cinderford, 24th June
Bishopswood Fete, 18th July
Ross Carnival, Riverside, 1st August
Forest of Dean Rotary Club, 18th August
Public Meeting, Chase Hotel, Ross, 26th August

1988

Ross Civic Society, 10th February
Herefordshire Tourism and Leisure Fair, Hereford, 23rd March
South Eastern Relief Road Meeting, John Kyrle High School, 19th April
Consultative Meeting, Touche Ross, Chase Hotel, Ross, 21st April
Press session and photographs at Lydbrook Viaduct, 22nd April

Wye Valley Railway exhibition, Ross Library and Information Centre, 17th to 21st May
Wimpey Major Projects, Civil Engineering assessment, 13th June
Goodrich Fete and Show, 18th June
Ross Riverside Carnival, 6th August

1989

Longhope Village Hall, Open Meeting, 16th February
Conservative Club, Ross-on-Wye, 23rd February
Herefordshire Tourism and Leisure Fair, Hereford, 22nd March
Walford Church Wives, Village Hall, 24th April
Open Talks with Rev. David Tipper at Lost Street Museum, Ross, 4th August
Ross Riverside Carnival, 5th August
Friends of Hereford Record Office, Hereford, Open Meeting, 24th November
ITV News, 6.25 p.m., Company Secretary interviewed at Lydbrook, 12th December

1990

Herefordshire Tourism and Leisure Fair, Hereford, 21st March
Ross Library and Information Centre, WVR Display National Rail, 27th – 31st March
PROBUS (Professional and Business people), Ross, 23rd April
Hereford Railway Club, British Rail Centre, Open Meeting, 10th May
Monmouth Association, Public Open Meeting, 18th May
Weston-under-Penyard, Open Meeting, 2nd July
Walford Parish Council, Open Meeting, 10th July
Lydney, private meeting with Paul Marland MP and others, 13th July
BBC TV Wales at Tintern Station, with tourism visitors, 2nd August
Hereford Electric Society, 10th September

Whitchurch and Symonds Yat Residents Association, Whitchurch, 17th October
Wye Valley Railway exhibition, Ross Library, 4th – 15th December

1991

Herefordshire Tourism and Leisure Show, Hereford, 24th April
WVR talk and Rev. David Tipper, Larraperz Centre, Ross, 2nd August
Ross Riverside Carnival with WVR display stand, 3rd August
Herefordshire Business Support Day, Hereford Town Hall, 2nd November
Public Inquiry, Larraperz Centre, Ross, re Hildersley Dev. Proposals, 20th November

1992

Seminar with Hereford and Worcester TEC, Chase Hotel, Ross, 28th January
Joint Wye Valley Railway and 'RiM Museum' at Ross Library, 25th –29th February
Ross Show and Carnival with new WVR promotion display, 1st August

1993

Ross Initiative Dinner at Chase Hotel, Ross, ETR photograph in press 28th January
Unemployment Group at Larraperz Centre, Ross, 19th March
Ross Carnival, Riverside, with display boards for WVR, 7th August
WVR exhibition at the Model Show, Larraperz Centre, Ross, 5th September

1994

Meeting with councillors, including Paul Keetch, prospective Lib. MP, 19th March

Open Meeting, Transport Seminar at Ledbury, 21st May

First Business Fair, Chase Hotel, Ross, with Wye Valley Railway stands, 22nd July

Wye Valley Railway display at Model Show, Larraperz Centre, Ross, 4th September

Transport Exhibition, Joint with H and W Rural Tspt, Ross Library, 18th – 22nd October

Lydney Ladies Group; presentation by Richard Eagle, WVR director, 24th October

1995

Forest of Dean Business Club, Coleford, with Serena Robinson, director, 9th January

Monmouth Rotary Club, Queen's Head Hotel, Monmouth, 19th April

Second Business Show, Chase Hotel, Ross, with WVR stand, 28th July